Anonymous

List of Canadian Patents from the Beginning of the Patent Office,

June, 1824,

to the 31st of August, 1872

Anonymous

List of Canadian Patents from the Beginning of the Patent Office, June, 1824,
to the 31st of August, 1872

ISBN/EAN: 9783337222352

Printed in Europe, USA, Canada, Australia, Japan

Cover: Foto ©Suzi / pixelio.de

More available books at **www.hansebooks.com**

LIST

of

CANADIAN PATENTS,

FROM THE

BEGINNING OF THE PATENT OFFICE,

JUNE, 1824,

Patents in this List were granted for the periods and under the Acts stated.

————o————

1st SERIES.

Nos. 1 to 165 granted for 14 years.

Part in force in Lower Canada and part in Upper Canada under various acts.

Nos. 166 to 258 granted for 14 years.

In force in the Province of Canada, under the Act 7th Geo. IV, Cap. 25

Nos. 259 to 3,325 granted for 14 years.

In force in the Province of Canada, under the Acts 12th Vic., Cap. 24, and Con. Stat. Canada, Cap. 34.

2nd SERIES.

Nos. 1 to 1,644 granted for 5 years.

In force in the Dominion of Canada, under "The Patent Act of 1869,' 32nd-33rd Vic., Cap. 11.

LIST OF CANADIAN PATENTS.

FROM THE BEGINNING OF THE PATENT OFFICE, (JUNE, 1824.)

—o—

No. 1—CUSHING, (*Noah,*) of the city of Quebec, in the district of Quebec—for a WASHING and FULLING Machine. Quebec, dated 8th June, 1824.

No. 2—BARNARD, (*Isaac Jones,*) of the city of Quebec—for an Improved Machine for CUTTING NAILS. ·Quebec, dated 21st July, 1824.

No. 3—GEORGE, (*James,*) for an improvement in the construction of WOODEN RAIL-ROADS. Quebec, dated 13th December, 1824.

No. 4—DALKIN, (*Robert,*) of the city of Quebec—for an Improvement in the DRUM-CYLINDER, and Double Drum-Cylinder, used in the manufacture of Ropes, Cables, &c. Quebec, dated 30th November, 1825.

No. 5—JACOB, (*Justin,*) of the city of Montreal, for a LEVER ENGINE. Quebec, dated 31st October, 1826.

No. 6—LAURIER, (*Charles,*) of the parish of La Chenaye, in the district of Montreal, for a Machine or Instrument called LOCH TERRESTRE, for accurately ascertaining the number of Rotatory motions or revolutions of carriage-wheels, mill-stones, &c. Quebec, dated 31st October, 1826.

No. 7—CUSHING, (*Noah,*) of the parish of Lotbinière in the district of Quebec; and, WELTON, (*Ranson,*) of the city of Quebec—for a THRESHING and WINNOWING Machine. Quebec, dated 31st October, 1826.

No. 8—HOYLE, (*Robert,*) for an Improved Machine for DRESSING FLAX or HEMP. Quebec, dated 3rd October, 1829.

No. 9—SPENCE, (*William John,*) of the city of Montreal, for a Machine for DISTRIBUTING INK over Printing Types. Quebec, dated 19th December, 1829.

No. 10—SCHOOLCRAFT, (*Philip,*) of the seigniory of St. Armand, in the district of Montreal, for a Machine for Cutting Timber into SIDINGS, CLAP-BOARDS, SHINGLES, LATHS, &c., &c. Quebec, dated, 15th May, 1830.

No. 11—SCHOOLCRAFT, (*Philip,*) of the seigniory of St. Armand, in the district of Montreal, for a " New and Improved SPINNING MACHINE." Quebec, dated 26th June, 1830.

No. 12—HOYLE, (*Robert,*) of the seigniory of Lacolle, in the district of Montreal, for an " Improved HYDRAULIC STEAM ENGINE." Quebec, dated 25th June, 1830.

No. 13—ANDRES, (*Samuel,*) of Blairfindie, in the district of Montreal, for a " Machine for Manufacturing HAT BODIES." Quebec, dated 9th August, 1830.

No. 14—ANDRES, (*Samuel,*) of Blairfindie, in the district of Montreal, for a " Gauge or Instrument to ascertain the WEIGHT or TONNAGE of GOODS, Shipped on board Canal Boats, &c., &c. Quebec, dated 9th August, 1830.

No. 15—ANDRES, (*Samuel,*) of Blairfindie, in the district of Montreal, for an " Improved GRIST MILL." Quebec, dated 25th October, 1830.

No. 16—MANNING, (*John,*) of the Township of Hinchinbrooke, district of Montreal, for a " Machine for THRESHING GRAIN and HULLING CLOVER SEED." Quebec, dated 1st November, 1830.

No. 17—AUSTIN, (*Amos,*) of Bolton, in the district of Montreal, for a " Machine for THRESHING GRAIN." Quebec, dated 3rd January, 1831.

No. 18—ANDRES, (*Samuel,*) of Blairfindie, in the district of Montreal, for a " Machine for manufacturing CRACKERS and BISCUITS." Quebec, dated 3rd January, 1831.

No. 19—McCANNA, (*John,*) of the seigniory of St. Armand, district of Montreal, for an " Improved STRIKING CLOCK." Quebec, dated 1st March, 1831.

4

No. 20—SINGER, (*Frederick*,) of St. Philip, district of Montreal, for a " New and Improved THRESHING MACHINE." Quebec, dated 2nd March, 1831.

No. 21—ANDRES (*Samuel*,) and ANDRES, (*Stephen R.*,) of Blairfindie, district of Montreal, for a "TREAD WHEEL or ENDLESS CHAIN for Propelling various kinds of Machinery, with either Water or Horse Power, &c." Quebec, dated 14th March, 1831.

No. 22—BELANGER, (*Edouard*,) of River Ouelle, County of Kamouraska, district of Quebec, for a " New and useful Machine for THRESHING GRAIN." Quebec, dated 30th March, 1831.

No. 23—DAILY, (*Uriah*,) of Bolton, County of Stanstead, district of Montreal, for a " New and Useful GRIST MILL." Quebec, dated 7th April, 1831.

No. 24—DOUGLASS, (*John C.*,) of the city of Montreal, for a " New and Useful Improvement in the Construction of STEAM ENGINE BOILERS, called SAFETY STEAM BOILER." Quebec, dated 27th September, 1831.

No. 25—RATCLIFF, (*John*,) of Odelltown, in the district of Montreal, for a " New and Useful Invention and Composition for Preparing LAMPS and CHANDELIERS for producing Light similar to Gas." Quebec, dated 3rd October, 1831.

No. 26—RATCLIFF, (*John*,) of Odelltown, in the district of Montreal, for a " Machine for THRESHING all kinds of GRAIN and HAY SEED." Quebec, dated 3rd October, 1831.

No. 27—HENRY, (*Hugh*,) of St. Francois, district of Three Rivers, for an "Improvement in the LEVER POWER, so as to be applicable to the movement of all Machinery. Quebec, dated 19th November, 1831.

No. 28—DUCHAINE, (*Amable*,) of Ste. Marie de la Nouvelle Beauce, district of Quebec, for an "Improvement in the manner of Building or Constructing BRIDGES." Quebec, dated 30th November, 1831.

No. 29—MATHEWSON (*John*,) of the city of Montreal, for a " SOAP CUTTING MACHINE." Quebec, dated 27th December, 1831.

No. 30—MOLT, (*Theodore Frederick*,) of the city of Quebec, for a " CHRONATOMETER." Quebec, dated 6th April, 1832.

No. 31—FRENCH (*Edward Jewet*,) of Saint Armand, in the district of Montreal, for an "Improvement in the THRESHING MACHINES now in use." Quebec, dated 18th December, 1832.

No. 32—BAIRD, (*Nicol Hugh*,) of the city of Montreal, for a " New Mode of Constructing SUSPENSION WOODEN BRIDGES." Quebec, dated 29th April, 1833.

No. 33—LEGGO, (*William Augustus*,) of Quebec, for a " Machine for EXTRACTING STUMPS from New Lands." Quebec, dated 23th January, 1834.

No. 34—BETHUNE, (*Norman*,) city of Montreal, for an " Improvement in the Construction of STEAM VESSELS and other Water Craft." Quebec, dated 4th February, 1834.

No. 35—McKENZIE, (*James*,) of the city of Quebec, for a "Machine for RENDERING LINENS, WOOLLENS, COTTONS, &c., &c., Impervious to Water, by means of a Preparation of Indian Rubber." Quebec, dated 19th January, 1834.

No. 36—SPALDING, (*Joel*,) of Farnham, county of Shefford, for an "Improved CRIBBLE for Separating Indian Peas from Wheat." Quebec, dated 30th June, 1834.

No. 37—WARREN, (*Otis*,) of Stanstead, in the district of St. Francis, for a "New and Useful WEIGHING BALANCE." Quebec, dated 30th June, 1834.

No. 38—BETHUNE, (*Norman*,) of Montreal, for a " New and Useful Model for Building and Constructing STEAM VESSELS and other Descriptions of Water Craft." Quebec, dated 14th August, 1834.

No. 39—BADDELY, (*Frederick Henry*), Quebec, for a " New and Useful WATER CEMENT." Quebec, dated 9th October, 1834.

No. 40—WICKSTEED, (*Gustavus William*), of Quebec, for a " New method of Constructing SUSPENSION BRIDGES of Wood or Metal." Quebec, dated 31st October, 1835.

No. 41—BUTTERY, (*Sampson*,) of William Henry, district of Montreal, for a " New and Useful Discovery in the Process of FERMENTATION." Quebec, dated 4th November, 1835.

No. 42—HARRINGTON, (*Elisha William*,) of Foucault, district of Montreal, for a

"Composition of Matter distinguished by the name of LIME WATER." Quebec, dated 29th February, 1836.

No. 43—ANDRES, (Samuel,) and ANDRES, (Stephen R.,) of Chambly, district of Montreal, for a "New Discovery in the application of STEEL SPRINGS as a Propelling Power, with a moveable Iron Rim for the purpose of applying the Lever." Quebec, dated 2nd February, 1837.

No. 44—ANDRES, (Samuel,) and ANDRES, (Stephen R.,) of Chambly, district of Montreal, for a "MOVEABLE, FALLING or DRAW IRON and WOODEN BRIDGE, applicable to Rapids and other Streams." Quebec, dated 4th February, 1837.

No. 45—ANDRES, (Samuel,) and ANDRES, (Stephen R.,) of Chambly, district of Montreal, for a "FIRE-PROOF SAFE, as applicable to Vaults, Cells for Gaols, &c., constructed of Hydraulic Cement or Water Lime." Quebec, dated 1st April, 1837.

No. 46—VANNOVOUS, (John,) of Quebec, for a "New and Useful STOVE." Quebec, dated 7th November, 1837.

No. 47—JOHNSON, (William Pople.) of Riviere du Loup, district of Quebec, for a "Method of connecting STOVE PIPES and other Tubes of thin Metal." Quebec, dated 8th June, 1838.

No. 48—SISSON, (Zebediah,) of Quebec, for an "Improved PLANING and MATCHING MACHINE." Montreal, dated 13th June, 1839.

No. 49—McKENZIE, (James,) and BOWLES, (Thomas,) of Quebec, for a "New and Improved Method of GRINDING PLASTER of PARIS." Montreal, dated 7th August, 1839.

No. 50—NUNNS, (William,) of Sorel, district of Montreal, for "Certain New and Useful Improvements in the construction of STEAM ENGINES." Montreal, dated 4th December, 1839.

No. 51—McKENZIE, (James,) of Quebec, for a "New and Improved WINDLASS PROPELLER." Montreal, dated 13th March, 1840.

No. 52—NUNNS, (William,) of Sorel, district of Montreal, for a "New method of constructing STEAMBOATS and other Vessels propelled by Paddle-wheels." Montreal, dated 20th June, 1840.

No. 53—MORIN, (Moyse,) of Riv ere du Loup, district of Quebec, for a "NET or SEINE for the Capture of Porpoises." Quebec, dated 5th August, 1840.

No. 54—WALKER, (Nelson,) of Montreal, for an "Improvement upon SMITH'S PATENT ARCHIMEDIAN SCREW." Montreal, dated 24th March, 1841.

No. 55—WALKER, (Nelson,) of Montreal, for an "Improved method of Constructing the PROPELLERS by him discovered and invented, and for which he obtained a Patent, dated 24th March. Kingston, 18th January, 1842.

No. 56—FLEMING, (Peter,) of Montreal, for a "New and Improved PADDLE-WHEEL called the OSCULATORY PROPELLER." Kingston, dated 12th March, 1842.

No. 57—OGDEN, (Isaac Gouverneur,) town of Three Rivers, for "A method of Propelling VESSELS by means of Heated Air acting on the fluid in which they Float." Kingston, dated 27th June, 1842.

No. 58—ARMS, (William,) of Sherbrooke, district of St. Francis, for "A machine called a SMUT MACHINE for cleaning Grain." Kingston, 25th July, 1842.

No. 59—BELANGER, (Edouard,) River Ouelle, district of Quebec, for a "New and Useful MACHINE, hung with Nets, for fishing and taking Eels." Kingston, 25th August, 1842.

No. 60—ROSS, (David Alexander,) of Quebec, for "Certain new Improvements in the STOVES cast in Scotland, and Three Rivers, in Canada, commonly called CANADA BOX STOVES." Kingston, dated 31st August, 1842.

No. 61—TRIPP, (Harvey,) of the seigniory of Vaudreuil, for a "New and useful method of constructing WHEELS to be driven by Water." Kingston, 12th December, 1842.

No. 62—McDONALD, (Donald Alexander,) of Beauharnois, for a "DRILLING MACHINE for the purpose of boring and drilling holes, &c., in Rock, Canal Quarries, or for any other purpose." Kingston, dated 19th December, 1842.

No. 63—LAMB, (John,) of Montreal, for a "New and Improved WATER-WHEEL." Kingston, dated 3rd April, 1843.

No. 64—LEMOINE, (*Louis,*) of Quebec, for a "Machine for extinguishing Fires, to wit, a FIRE ENGINE." Kingston, dated 1st June, 1843.

No. 65—BROWN, (*John O.,*) of Montreal, for "New and Improved TRUSSES." Kingston, dated 7th July, 1843.

No. 66—GINGRAS, (*Edouard,*) of the city of Quebec, for a "New and useful method of constructing Springs for CARRIAGES." Kingston, dated 16th September, 1843.

No. 67—ADAMS, (*Austin,*) of the city of Montreal, for a "Machine for GRINDING CLAY." Kingston, dated 8th January, 1844.

No. 68—BIGELOW, (*Hiram,*) Coteau du Lac, district of Montreal, for a "New and improved REVOLVING DRYING KILN." Kingston, dated 9th January, 1844.

No. 69—HOLLAND, (*John M.,*) Sault au Recollect, district of Montreal, for a "SPIKE MACHINE." Kingston, dated 6th March, 1844.

No. 70—PROUDLOCK, (*Thomas,*) of the township of Wentworth, district of Montreal, for a "Method of pumping Ships and other Vessels, called the SEAMAN'S FRIEND." Montreal, dated 16th October, 1844.

No. 71—MILLIGAN, (*George,*) of Quebec, for a "New method of constructing PIANO FORTES." Montreal, dated 21st November, 1844.

No. 72—SMOLINSKI, (*Joseph,*) of the city of Quebec, for a "New cast iron cooking and caloriferous STOVE, and an alteration in the construction of the crockery or brick STOVE, BEING AN IMPROVEMENT ON THE STOVE INTRODUCED BY ONE JOHN VANNOVOUS." Montreal, dated 21st November, 1844.

No. 73—HOSKYNS, (*Chandos,*) of Montreal, for an "Improvement in the TRUSS for the alleviation and cure of Hernea." Montreal, dated 31st January, 1845.

No. 74—OUELLET, (*Jean F. C.,*) of Montreal, for a "New method of propelling VESSELS, CARRIAGES, &c., &c., by machinery, without the agency of fuel." Montreal, dated 26th March, 1845.

No. 75—NICHOLS, (*Elius,*) of the town of Sherbrooke, district of St. Francis, for a "New method of constructing WATER-WHEELS." Montreal, dated 4th April, 1845.

No. 76—GILBERT, (*Ebenezer E.,*) of Montreal, for a "New and useful method of constructing COUNTER-BALANCE Machines." Montreal, dated 21st May, 1845.

No. 77—BAIRD, (*Nicol Hugh,*) of Montreal, for a "New method of constructing PADDLE WHEELS of the description termed SWEEPING PADDLE-WHEELS, for propelling Steam and other Vessels." Montreal, dated 30th May, 1845.

No. 78—WARREN, (*Samuel R.,*) of Montreal, for a "Method of constructing HARMONIC ATTACHMENTS for Piano Fortes." Montreal, dated 9th July, 1845.

No. 79—WATTS, (*William,*) of Montreal, for a "Method of constructing Instruments for digging Potatoes, called POTATO DIGGERS." Montreal, dated 19th July, 1845.

No. 80—YOUNG, (*Albert,*) of the township of Stanstead, for a "New method of making RAKES for HAY and GRAIN." Montreal, dated 22nd August, 1845.

No. 81—McKAY, (*James,*) of the city of Montreal, for a "New and improved STEAM ENGINE." Montreal, dated 10th September, 1845.

No. 82—NADEAU, (*François,*) of the city of Quebec, for a "New and improved mode of constructing WINDOWS." Montreal, dated 18th September, 1845.

No. 83—HEBERT, (*Alexis,*) of Napierville, in the district of Montreal, for a "New and improved SAWING MACHINE." Montreal, dated 10th October, 1845.

No. 84—MORRIN, (*Moyse,*) of Riviere du Loup, in the district of Quebec, for "New and improved NETS for taking Seals and Porpoises." Montreal, dated 15th October, 1845.

No. 85—TIBBETS, (*Benjamin F.,*) of the city of Montreal, for a "New and improved STEAM ENGINE." Montreal, dated 10th November, 1845.

No. 86—BALL, (*Jasper,*) of the township of Stanstead, in the district of St. Francis, for a "New and improved CHURN." Montreal, dated 7th January, 1846.

No. 87—YOUNG, (*Albert,*) of the township of Stanstead, in the district of St. Francis, for a "New and useful HOUSE PUMP or FIRE ENGINE." Montreal, dated 26th February, 1846.

No. 88—TREPANIER, (*Augusta,*) of the city of Quebec, for a "New and useful Machine for WORKING STONE." Montreal, dated 4th March, 1846.

No. 89—RILEY, (*George,*) of the city of Montreal, for a "New and improved STILL for DIS-TILLING and RECTIFYING Spirituous Liquors." Montreal, dated 18th March, 1846.

No. 90—ROCKWELL, (*Horatio A.,*) of the township of Farnham, in the district of Montreal, for a "New and improved YOKE for OXEN. Montreal, dated 24th March, 1846.

No. 91—LEE, (*Jonas Philip,*) of the town of Sherbrooke, in the district of St. Francis, for a "New and useful improvement in the method of constructing KNITTING LOOMS." Montreal, dated 4th June, 1846.

No. 92—DUELL, (*Ephraim,*) of the parish of St. Armand West, in the district of Montreal, for a "New and improved CHURN." Montreal, dated 6th May, 1846.

No. 93—COLBY, (*Harrison,*) of the parish of Abbotsford, in the district of Montreal, for a "New and improved GAS GENERATOR." Montreal, dated 22nd June, 1846.

No. 94—CAMPBELL, (*James,*) of South Georgetown, in the district of Montreal, for a "TOWING MACHINE, for towing vessels up Rapids." Montreal, dated 22nd June, 1846.

No. 95—JOHNSON, (*Gordon Warren,*) of the city of Montreal, for a "New and improved HOISTING MACHINE." Montreal, dated 24th June, 1846.

No. 96—SHAW, (*Noah,*) of Montreal, for a "New method of constructing portable GRIST MILLS." Montreal, dated 3rd August, 1846.

No. 97—MIDGLEY, (*Charles,*) of Montreal, for a "New method of constructing PLANING MACHINES for planing Boards, Planks, &c. Montreal, dated 10th August, 1846.

No. 98—RUTTAN, (*Henry,*) of Montreal, for a "New method of constructing FURNACES, for heating houses and other buildings with hot air, called HOT AIR GENERATORS." Montreal, dated 23rd August, 1846.

No. 99—TAYLOR, (*Amos,*) of the township of Compton, district of St. Francis for a "Method of constructing COUPLING MACHINES for Railroad Cars, or SELF-DETACHERS." Montreal, dated 26th September, 1846.

No. 100—TAYLOR, (*Amos,*) of the township of Compton, district of St. Francis, for a "New and useful method of constructing BEE-HIVES." Montreal, dated 26th September, 1846.

No. 101—TAYLOR, (*Amos,*) of Compton, for a "SNOW EXCAVATOR, for removing the snow from the tracks of Railways." Montreal, dated 26th September, 1846.

No. 102—TAYLOR, (*Amos,*) of Compton, for a "Method of constructing a SPARK ARRESTER and EXTINGUISHER." Montreal, dated 26th September, 1846.

No. 103—MILLS, (*John,*) of Montreal, for a "Method of constructing HOT AIR FURNACES for generating, and the diffusion of Heat, in and about dwelling houses and other buildings." Montreal, dated 10th October, 1846.

No. 104—RILEY, (*George,*) of Montreal, for a "Method of constructing STILLS, for distilling and rectifying Spirituous Liquors." Montreal, dated 1st October, 1846.

No. 105—MILLS, (*Stephen,*) of Montreal, for a "New and useful improvement in the method of constructing WOODEN BRIDGES." Montreal, dated 28th November, 1846.

No. 106—PARADIS, (*Joseph,*) of Montreal, for a "New method of constructing RAKES for raking hay and grain, called the IMPROVED REVOLVING JOINT TOOTH SPRING LEVER HORSE RAKE." Montreal, dated 8th October, 1846.

No. 107—LEMIEUX, (*Louis,*) of the city of Quebec, for a "Machine for making WOODEN SHAVINGS suitable for the fabrication of Band-boxes for Hats, Matches, and cases of all descriptions." Montreal, dated 25th January, 1847.

No. 108—MASSEY, (*Jonathan B.,*) of the city of Montreal, for a "New and improved method of constructing CISTERNS." Montreal, dated 3rd April, 1847.

No. 109—DAVISON, (*Horace H.,*) of Montreal, for a "Useful method of constructing STEEL RINGS for fastening the Scythe to the Snath." Montreal, dated 14th April, 1847.

No. 110—DAVISON, (*Horace H.,*) of Montreal, for a "New method of compounding portable LAMP FLUID." Montreal, dated 15th Apr   1847.

No. 111—ARMSTRONG, (*William,*) of Montreal, for a "Method of constructing portable FIRE EXTINGUISHING MACHINES." Montreal, dated 3rd May, 1847.

No. 112—DAVISON, (*Horace H.,*) of Montreal, for a "New method of constructing double REVERTABLE FLUE STEAM GENERATORS and BOILERS." Montreal, dated 19th April, 1847.

No. 113—LEMOINE, (*Louis,*) of the city of Quebec, for an "Apparatus for raising all kinds of NETS, or other Instruments, used in taking Porpoises and other species of Fish." Montreal, dated 6th April, 1847.

No. 114—McMICKEN, (*Gilbert,*) of Montreal, for an "Improvement in the method of constructing an ELECTRO-MAGNETIC TELEGRAPH." Montreal, dated 29th June, 1847.

No. 115—DEAL, (*Peter,*) of Phillipsburgh), district of Montreal, for a "New method of compounding a Preparation for all kinds of OIL PAINTS, for House Painting, and other kinds, especially to be used with Lead Paint." Montreal, dated 7th August, 1847.

No. 116—DE ROTTERMUND, (*Edward Sylvester,*) of the parish of St. Cesaire, in the district of Montreal, for a "New and useful method of constructing FLOUR SIFTERS." Montreal, dated 26th August, 1847.

No. 117—DE ROTTERMUND, (*Edward Sylvester,*) parish of St. Cesaire, district of Montreal, for an "Improvement in the method of constructing GRIST MILLS." Montreal, dated 21st August, 1847.

No. 118—McGEE, (*James,*) of the city of Montreal, for a "New and useful method of ROTTING HEMP and FLAX by artificial means." Montreal, dated 6th August, 1847.

No. 119—ADAMS, (*Austin,*) of the city of Montreal, for "A REVOLVING BRICK RECEIVER." Montreal, dated 14th August, 1847.

No. 120—PROWSE, (*George Fabes,*) of the city of Montreal, for a "HOT AIR FURNACE." Montreal, dated 11th September, 1847.

No. 121—BRILL, (*Thomas,*) of the parish of Saint Armand, East, in the district of Montreal, for a "New and improved WATER WHEEL, called the SCREW RIGHT and LEFT REVERSED WATER WHEEL." Montreal, dated 3rd September, 1847.

No. 122—MUIR, (*William,*) of the city of Montreal, for a "New mode of constructing the BED PLATES of end working FIRE ENGINES, and in the method of placing the supply and delivery Valves of such Engines." Montreal, dated 27th October, 1847.

No. 123—DWYER, (*Michael,*) of the city of Montreal, for a "New method of constructing SHOWER BATHS." Montreal, dated 10th November, 1847.

No. 124—WALSH, (*William,*) of the city of Quebec, for a "New and improved HORSE COLLAR." Montreal, dated 8th January, 1848.

No. 125—BROWN, (*Thomas,*) of the township of Dunham, district of Montreal, for a "Method of constructing SMUT MILLS for cleaning Grain." Montreal, dated 16th March, 1848.

No. 126—BAILIE, (*James,*) village of Aylmer, district of Montreal, for an "Improvement in the construction of SAW GATES for Saw Mills." Montreal, dated 12th April, 1848.

No. 127—RITCHIE, (*John,*) of Etchemin, district of Quebec, for a "Method of constructing SAW MILLS for Slabbing Logs and Sawing Slabs." Montreal, dated 19th June, 1848.

No. 128—JONES, (*Edward T.,*) ot Carrillon, district of Montreal, for an "Improvement in the construction of FOUR-WHEELED CARRIAGES, to wit, a plan for facilitating the turning of the same in a short space." Montreal, dated 27th June, 1848.

No. 129—BYRON, (*Antipas M.,*) township of Compton, for a "Method of constructing HAY RAKES." Montreal, dated 19th June, 1848.

No. 130—RUTTAN, (*Henry,*) of the district of Montreal, for a "New mode, or art of Ventilating Buildings, called the CANADIAN VENTILATOR." Montreal, dated 25th July, 1848.

No. 131—WARREN, (*George P.,*) of the city of Montreal, for a "Useful method of constructing an Apparatus for taking off the Friction of the Axle of a BELL, and for making the Tongue of a Bell strike the top, when elevated." Montreal, dated 16th August, 1848.

No. 132—MIDGLEY, (*Charles,*) of the city of Montreal, for a "New and improved PADDLE WHEEL for Steam and Horse-boats, and for propelling Vessels." Montreal, dated 10th August, 1848.

No. 133—NEWMAN, (*Walter Perkins,*) of the village of Elora, in the Wellington district, Upper Canada, for "The HYDRO PNEUMATIC WATER WHEEL." Montreal, dated 12th September, 1848.

No. 134—PIERCE, (*Martin,*) of the township of Stanbridge, in the county of Missisquoi, for a "New and improved WASHING MACHINE, for washing clothes, &c." Montreal, dated 15th September, 1848.

No. 135—WELLS, (*Walter Holt,*) of the city of Montreal, for a "New and useful invention, called the AERIFORM or ATMOSPHERIC CHURN." Montreal, dated 13th November, 1848.

No. 136—BOWEN, (*Peleg,*) of the city of Montreal, for a new and useful "Coiled Spring Tooth revolving HORSE RAKE." Montreal, dated 14th November, 1848.

No. 137—LA GRANGE, (*Omie,*) of the parish of St. Armand, district of Montreal, for a "New and improved CARRIAGE and WAGGON WHEEL." Montreal, dated 6th November, 1848.

No. 138—BOSTWICK, (*John P.,*) of the township of Compton, district of St. Francis, for "An Office SLIDING CALENDAR." Montreal, dated 20th November, 1848.

No. 139—McQUILKIN, (*Patrick,*) and HENRY, (*Joseph,*) of the city of Quebec, for a "New and useful improvement in the machinery of a SHIP'S WINDLASS." Montreal, dated 20th January, 1849.

No. 140—ROCKWELL, (*Nirum W.,*) of Farnham, district of Montreal, for "A Limited HORSE SWING." Montreal, dated 5th February, 1849.

No. 141—SEVERANCE, (*Elias Jas.,*) township of Ascot, district of St. Francis, for "An Improvement in the method of constructing THRESHING MACHINES." Montreal, dated 6th March, 1849.

No. 142—BAIRD, (*Nicol Hugh,*) of Nepean, district of Bathurst, for a "Method of constructing BRIDGES on combined principles, called the SUSPENSION WOODEN BRIDGE." York, dated 14th July, 1831.

No. 143—CLEGHORNE, (*John W.,*) of Cobourg, district of Newcastle, for "A Machine for THRESHING GRAIN." York, dated 13th September, 1831.

No. 144—SISSON, (*Zebediah,*) of Cobourg, district of Newcastle, for a "Machine for PLANING AND GROVING FLOORING." York, dated 27th June, 1832.

No. 145—HATHAWAY, (*Jonathan G.,*) of the town of Hamilton, for "A Cooking Stove called the HOT AIR COOKING STOVE." York, dated 24th December, 1832.

No. 146—FOSTER, (*Ambrose,*) of Kingston, in the Midland District, for "An Improvement in the Steam Engine, called the RE-ACTING ENGINE." York, dated 21st November, 1833.

No. 147—SANDFORD, (*Nathan,*) of Prescott, in the district of Johnstown, for "A New and useful Improvement in the principle of building STEAM VESSELS." Toronto, dated 23rd May, 1834.

No. 148—CARPENTER, (*Alexander,*) of the town of Hamilton, district of Gore, for "A Revolving Flue, as applied to a COOKING APPARATUS, &c." Toronto, dated 17th February 1834.

No. 149—BURLINGHAM, (*Joseph,*) of the town of Hamilton, U. C., and BEWLEY, (*Thomas,*) of Laprairie, L. C., for "An Improved method of BUILDING SHIPS, BOATS, and other CRAFT, suitable for Navigation on Seas, Rivers, Lakes, and Canals, to be propelled with Steam or any other power." Toronto, dated 6th November, 1834.

No. 150—TALBOT, (*Edward Allen,*) township of London, for "A new method of Propelling Vessels and Carriages, designated by the name of TALBOT'S ATMOSPHERIC PROPELLING ENGINE." Toronto, dated 18th July, 1834.

No. 151—GRAHAM, (*Thomas,*) township of Thorold, district of Niagara, for "A new method of PROPELLING VESSELS Navigated by Steam, &c." Toronto, dated 25th March, 1835.

No. 152—RICH, (*Martin,*) and JACKSON, (*William M.,*) of the town of Kingston, for "A certain Apparatus to be attached to SAW MILLS." Toronto, dated 28th April, 1835.

No. 153—VAN NORMAN, (*Joseph,*) of Long Point, district of London, for "A new improvement on the COOKING STOVE." Toronto, dated 1st June, 1835.

No. 154—CAHILL, (*James,*) of the town of Hamilton, for a "COOKING STOVE upon a new and improved principle." Toronto, dated 1st June, 1835.

No. 155—JUDSON, (*Samuel,*) of the township of Burges, and JUDSON, (*Lyman,*) of the township of Yonge, both of the county of Leeds, for "A machine for Planing, Jointing, Grooving, Tonguing, Bevelling, Rebating, Beding, and otherwise preparing for immediate use Boards, Plank, and other description of TIMBERS." Toronto, dated 25th March, 1835.

No. 156—VAN NORMAN, (*Joseph,*) of Normandale, in the district of London, for "An improved method of producing CHARCOAL FROM WOOD." Toronto, dated 29th January, 1836.

No. 157—BROWN, (*Levi R.*) of the city of Toronto, for "A new improvement in the COOKING STOVE, and a new method of carrying off steam." Toronto, dated 15th April, 1836.

No. 158—WILSON, (*James Lorenzo,*) of the town of Hamilton, in the district of Gore, for "A new improvement in the COOKING STOVE." Toronto, dated 26th January, 1837.

No. 159—WHITE, (*William,*) of the township of Hamilton, in the Newcastle district, for "A new and useful Machine for removing SMUT FROM WHEAT." Toronto, dated 23rd February, 1837.

No. 160—SCRIMGER, (*Duncan,*) of the township of Dumfries, district of Gore, Upper Canada, for "A new method of applying a multiplying LEVER to the working gear of SAW MILLS." Toronto, dated 10th May, 1839.

No. 161—MACKELCAN, (*George Josiah,*) of Guelph, in the district of Gore, for "Certain Improvements in the STEAMBOAT PADDLE." Toronto, dated 8th February, 1840.

No. 162—HOWARD, (*John G.,*) of the city of Toronto, for "A new method of constructing TIMBER BRIDGES." Toronto, dated 24th February, 1840.

No. 163—THOMAS, (*John Morgan,*) and SMITH, (*Alexander,*) of the city of Toronto, for "A new improvement in the construction of PIANO FORTES, by means of which their durability is much prolonged, and the tone of the instrument preserved." Toronto, dated 23rd March, 1840.

No. 164—MACKELCAN, (*George Josiah,*) of Guelph, in the district of Gore, for "A further Improvement in the STEAMBOAT PADDLE." Toronto, dated 29th February, 1840.

No. 165—AINSLIE, (*James,*) of the village of Galt, in the district of Gore, for "Ainslie's CLAY SLATE and Ainslie's CLAY SLATE MACHINE." Toronto, dated 21st August, 1840.

No. 166—CHATTERTON, (*Richard Dover,*) of the town of Cobourg, in the district of Newcastle, for "An improved PADDLE WHEEL for propelling Steam or other vessels." Kingston, dated 22nd June, 1841.

No. 167—TRIPP, (*Harvey,*) of the township of Haldimand, in the Newcastle district, for an Improved Water Wheel called "THE SUBMERGED ANFRACTUOUS WATER WHEEL." Kingston, dated 1st September, 1841.

No. 168—ROGERS, (*George,*) of the township of Haldimand, in the Newcastle district, for an "Improved Water Wheel called the vertical percussion Re-action WATER WHEEL." Kingston, dated 3rd December, 1841.

No. 169—WALKER, (*Nelson,*) of the city of Montreal, for "An Improved Guard PROPELLER." Kingston, dated 15th January, 1842.

No. 170—TATE, (*Charles Maitland,*) of the town of Kingston, for "An improved method of giving Motion and efficacy to the PROPELLER in Steamboats and other vessels." Kingston, dated 13th January, 1842.

No. 171—TATE, (*Charles Maitland,*) of Kingston, for "An improved method of constructing CAMBS for the purpose of opening the cut-off, or other valves of Steam Engines." Kingston, dated 21st January, 1842.

No. 172—TATE—(*Charles Maitland,*) for "A new method of TANNING Hides or Skins." Kingston, dated 27th January, 1842.

No. 173—TATE, (*Charles Maitland,*) of Kingston, for "A new and improved method of extracting the Tannin from Bark." Kingston, dated 27th January, 1842.

No. 174—FLEMING, (*Peter,*) of the city of Montreal, for a "Paddle Wheel for propelling vessels by STEAM." Kingston, dated 7th March, 1842.

No. 175—BEACH, (*Mahlon,*) of the township of Oxford, for "A new and useful description of THRESHING MILLS." Kingston, dated 27th April, 1842.

No. 176—BAIRD, (*Nichol Hugh*,) town of Cobourg, for a "New and useful description of PADDLE WHEEL." Kingston, dated 12th January, 1842.

No. 177—DISSETT, (*Thomas*,) and SMITH, (*James*,) of Portsmouth Harbour, Kingston, for a "New and improved method of laying down MARINE RAILWAYS." Kingston, dated 16th May, 1842.

No. 178—HALLOWELL, (*William*,) of the town of Kingston, for "A new and useful description of "SHOWER BATH." Kingston, dated 16th July, 1842.

No 179—BAKER, (*Jacob*,) township of Vaughan, Home district, for "An improvement in the construction of PENSTOCKS and WATER WHEELS." Kingston, dated 20th September, 1842.

No. 180—LAMB, (*John*,) township of Hawkesbury, for "A new and useful description of WATER WHEEL." Kingston, dated 3rd October, 1842.

No 181—RILEY, (*George*,) of the town of Kingston, for "An improved method of BREWING Ale, Beer, Porter and other malt Liquors." Kingston, dated 6th July, 1842.

No. 182—HOUGH, (*Asa H.*,) of the town of Kingston, for an "Improvement upon a newly constructed SUCTION and FORCING PUMP." Kingston, dated 20th February, 1843.

No. 183—CREIGHTON, (*William*,) of the town of Niagara, for "An improvement in the ROTARY STEAM ENGINE, heretofore in use." Kingston, dated 31st March, 1843.

No. 184—BROWN, (*John O.*,) of the town of Kingston, in the Midland district, for "Certain Improved TRUSSES." Kingston, dated 5th July, 1843.

No. 185—LAMB, (*Peter R.*,) of the city of Toronto, for "An improved WASHING MACHINE." Kingston, dated 7th July, 1843.

No. 186—MONTGOMERY, (*John*,) of the township of Pittsburgh, Midland district, for "A Composition for preventing and extinguishing FIRES." Kingston, dated 9th August, 1843.

No. 187—OGDEN, (*Isaac Gouverneur*,) of Three Rivers, for "A Machine for PROPELLING vessels, or other floating bodies, by the action of heated air, gases, steam, or other expansive or explosive materials on the fluid in which they are intended to act." Kingston, dated 14th August, 1843.

No. 188—BIGELOW, (*Hiram*,) of the township of Tecumseth, in the district of Simcoe, for "A REVOLVING DRYING KILN, for the purpose of drying Wheat, or other Grain.' Kingston, dated 29th September, 1843.

No. 189—CARPENTER, (*Alexander*,) of Hamilton, district of Gore, for "A new mode of applying heat, in the process of Cooking with Stoves, by means of a horizontal and perpendicular RETURN FLUE." Kingston, dated 10th October, 1843.

No. 190—MECKELCAN, (*George J.*,) of Guelph, district of Wellington, for "A new construction of MANGLE for mangling Clothes." Kingston, dated 24th November, 1843.

No. 191—RILEY, (*George*,) of Toronto, for "A new mode of DISTILLING and RECTIFYING Spirituous Liquors." Kingston, dated 15th December, 1843.

No. 192—HUTT, (*Frederick*,) township of Stamford, for "A Machine called a SELF-PROPELLING GATE." Kingston, dated 27th January, 1844.

No. 193—McCALL, (*William*,) of Dumfries, district of Gore, for "A mode by which power, to be derived from the use of the wheel and screw, may be applied to any kind of MACHINERY." Kingston, dated 30th May, 1844.

No. 194—DISTIN, (*William Langmead*,) town of Hamilton, for "An improvement in the manufacture of COOKING STOVES." Montreal, dated 29th June, 1844.

No. 195—HEARLE, (*John*,) of Galt, in the district of Gore, for "An improved ENGINE PUMP, or FIRE ENGINE." Montreal, dated 29th June, 1844.

No. 196—ARMSTRONG, (*William*,) of the town of Niagara, for a "Portable FIRE EXTINGUISHING MACHINE." Montreal, dated 3rd September, 1844.

No. 197—GILBERT, (*Ebenezer E.*,) city of Montreal, for "A new method of constructing COUNTER BALANCE MACHINES, for raising and lowering casks or other weights." Montreal, dated 25th June, 1845.

No. 198—GRIFFITHS, (*John*,) city of Toronto, for "An improvement in the RIDING SADDLE. Montreal, dated 14th July, 1845.

12

No. 199—IVES, (*Lewis,*) of the town of Kingston, for " An improved Capstan for loading or unloading merchandize, or timber, from vessels, denominated " IVES' CONNECTED CAPSTAN." Montreal, dated 16th July, 1845.

No. 200—IVES, (*Lewis,*) of the town of Kingston, for " An improved method of loading and unloading timber vessels, denominated " IVES' improved method of LOADING and UNLOADING vessels." Montreal, dated 19th July, 1845.

No. 201—WATTS, (*William,*) of the town of Cornwall, for " An improved method of constructing instruments for digging potatoes, called POTATO DIGGERS." Montreal, dated 19th July, 1845.

No. 202—HARRIS, (*John,*) of Mount Pleasant, in the Gore district, for " A Revolving HORSE RAKE." Montreal, dated 4th August, 1845.

No. 203—MAITLAND, (*John,*) of the city of Toronto, for " A New principle of Distillation and Rectification, by means of a new STILL CONDENSER and RECTIFIER." Montreal, dated 12th August, 1845.

No. 204—YOUNG, (*Albert,*) township of Stanstead, district of St. Francis, for " A new and useful Machine, termed a " METALLIC COIL SPRING-TOOTH HOUSE RAKE, for raking hay and grain." Montreal, dated 16th August, 1845.

No. 205—CULL, (*James,*) and CULL, (*Charles,*) of Bath, Midland district, for " A new principle in the construction of a STILL for the distillation and rectifying of spirituous liquors, called a COMBINATION STILL." Montreal, dated 29th November, 1845.

No. 206—LLOYD, (*Jenkins,*) of Oshawa, in the 'Home district, for " A new and improved CAST IRON PLOUGH." Montreal, dated 17th January, 1846.

No. 207—YOUNG, (*Albert,*) of Stanstead, in the district of St. Francis, for " An Improved HOUSE PUMP or FIRE ENGINE." Montreal, dated 14th February, 1846.

No. 208—BURROWS, (*George Kirk,*) of Toronto, for " A new method of making Presses for the purpose of pressing clay, and other ductile substances, into any form, such as BRICKS, TILES, &c." Montreal, dated 27th February, 1846.

No. 209—McKINLAY, (*William,*) township of West Flamboro', district of Gore, for " An Improvement in Horse-threshing MACHINES." Montreal, dated 27th February, 1846.

No. 210—RUTTAN, (*Henry,*) of the town of Cobourg, for " A FURNACE by which Houses and other Buildings may be Heated by HOT AIR." Montreal, dated 2nd May, 1846.

No. 211—OATES, (*Richard Hawkins,*) of the city of Toronto, for " An Improved method of making MILL STONES, for the purpose of grinding grain, without heating the meal so much as with the ordinary Mill Stone." Montreal, dated 25th April, 1846.

No. 212—ELLIS, (*David Jacob,*) of the township of Southwold, in the London district, for "An Improved Machine for making BRICK." Montreal, dated 25th April, 1846.

No. 213—McLEAN, (*William,*) of the city of Toronto, for " A REVOLVING BATTERY." Montreal, dated 26th May, 1846.

No. 214—JONES, (*Samuel S.,*) of Hamilton, in the Gore district, for " An Improved COOKING STOVE." Montreal, dated 13th June, 1846.

No. 215—JOHNSON, (*Gordon Warren,*) of Williamstown, in the county of Glengarry, for " An Improved HOISTING MACHINE." Montreal, dated 26th June, 1846.

No. 216—MILLS, (*John,*) of the town of St. Catharines, in the Niagara district, for " An Improved method of Generating and Distributing HEATED AIR." Montreal dated 1st September, 1846.

No. 217—BARNES, (*William T.,*) of the town of Hamilton, in the district of Gore, for " An Improved description of TUBE IRON to be used in Blacksmith's Forges." Montreal, dated 21st October, 1846

No. 218—PARDEE, (*Joseph,*) of the town of Barrie, in the district of Simcoe, for " A Revolving Joint-tooth HORSE RAKE." Montreal, dated 24th December, 1846.

No. 219—LIVINGSTON, (*John,*) of Cavan, Newcastle district, for " A new description of WATER WHEEL." Montreal, dated 14th December, 1846.

No. 220—McLEAN, (*William,*) of Toronto, for a "STEAMBOAT REGULATOR." Montreal, dated 17th December, 1846.

13

No. 221—COLBY, (*Harrison*,) of Lancaster, in the Eastern district, for "A New Gas Generator." Montreal, dated 12th December, 1816.

No. 222—RUTTAN, (*Henry*,) of Cobourg, for "A Metal Heater for Houses, &c., and a Cooking range and Hot Air and Vapour Generator." Montreal, dated 12th December, 1816.

No. 223—McLAREN, (*John*,) township of Nelson, Gore district, for "An improved Stump Extractor." Montreal, dated 11th January, 1847.

No. 224—CLEAL, (*Daniel*,) city of Toronto, for "A new mode of setting Boilers and arranging the Flues and applying heat to the same, for Steam Engines." Montreal, dated 23rd January, 1847.

No. 225—RUTTAN, (*Henry*,) of Cobourg, in the district of Newcastle, for "An improved Cooking Range and Hot Air Vapour Generator." Montreal, dated 27th January, 1817.

No. 226—DAVISON, (*Horace H.*,) of the township of Sidney, in the district of Victoria, for "An improved Portable Lamp Fluid." Montreal, dated 10th April, 1817.

No. 227—DAVISON, (*Horace H.*,) of the township of Sidney, in the district of Victoria, for "An improved Heel Ring for fastening the Scythe to the Snath." Montreal, dated 10th April, 1847.

No. 228—DAVISON, (*Horace H.*,) of the township of Sidney, district of Victoria, for "An improved Double Revertable Flue Steam Generator and ... ... for Locomotives, Steamboats, and other purposes." Montreal, dated 10th April, 1847.

No. 229—GILLETT, (*Jason C.*,) of the township of Sandwich, in the Western district, for "An improved Machine for cutting Shingles, Staves, Veneers, &c." Montreal, dated 1st May, 1847.

No. 230—WESTMAN, (*Joseph*,) city of Toronto, for a "Machine usually known by the name of Bellows." Montreal, dated 9th May, 1847.

No. 231—McMICKEN, (*Gilbert*,) of Queenstown, district of Niagara, for "Certain Improvements in the application of the principle of the Electro Magnetic Telegraph, designated the Notifier and Connector or Transfer Magnet." Montreal, dated 8th June, 1847.

No. 232—FLEMING, (*Sandford A.*,) of the town of Peterborough, district of Colborne, for "A new method of propelling Locomotives." Montreal, dated 4th June, 1847.

No. 233—FRAER, (*Peter*,) of Dundas, Gore district, for "A new description of Machine for Churning." Montreal, dated 26th June, 1847.

No. 234—BEAUPRE, (*Peter R.*,) city of Kingston, for "Improvements in the manner of making, using, and working a lifting and floating Marine Dock." Montreal, dated 19th July, 1817.

No. 235—McGEE, (*James*,) city of Toronto, for "A new method or process for Rotting of hemp and flax by artificial means." Montreal, dated 11th August, 1847.

No. 237—BOWEN, (*Peleg*,) of the township of Clarke, in the district of Newcastle, for "A new Coiled Spring Tooth Revolving Horse Rake." Montreal, dated 13th December, 1847.

No. 238—BROWN, (*Thomas*,) of Dunham, in the district of Montreal, for "A new and useful machine or Smut Mill for cleaning grain." Montreal, dated 2nd March, 1848.

No. 239—BUTTER, (*John*,) of the city of Toronto, for "An improved machine for manufacturing Bricks." Montreal, dated 2nd May, 1848.

No. 240—PARTRIDGE, (*William*,) of the town of Windsor, in the Western district, for a "Ditching Machine." Montreal, dated 22nd April, 1848.

No. 241—McMICHAEL, (*John*,) township of Dumfries, Gore district, for "An improvement or addition to a Stump-Extracting Machine." Montreal, dated 26th May, 1848.

No. 242—HELM, (*John*,) of the town of Cobourg, for "Certain improvements in the construction of Mills for the manufacture of Lumber with Circular Saws." Montreal, dated 28th June, 1848.

No. 243—McQUEEN, (*Angus*,) of the township of Trafalgar, district of Gore, for "An Economical power or Hydraulic Force Pump Machine, for raising Buildings, Stumps, &c." Montreal, dated 24th June, 1848.

No. 244—RUTTAN, (*Henry*,) of Cobourg, for "The true Philosophical principles upon which Buildings may be Ventilated; and also of Machinery by which the Ventilating air may be Warmed. Montreal, dated 23rd June, 1848.

No. 245—JONES, (*Edward Thomas*,) of Carillon, district of Montreal, for "A plan for facilitating the turning of FOUR-WHEELED CARRIAGES in a short space." Montreal, dated 23rd June, 1848.

No. 246—LAMB, (*Peter R.*,) of the city of Toronto, for "An improved method of Manufacturing GLUE." Montreal, dated 26th June, 1848.

No. 247—COLTON, (*Reuben P.*,) of the town of Brockville, for "An improved Air-tight Box STOVE." Montreal, dated 1st August, 1848.

No. 248—COLTON, (*Reuben P.*,) of the town of Brockville, for an improvement on "Buck and Hathaway's Patent Cook Stove, called the CANADIAN HOT AIR STOVE." Montreal, dated 1st August, 1848.

No. 249—WHARTON, (*Nathan*,) of the town of Johnstown, in the district of Johnstown, for "A new process for Tempering and Hardening the teeth of saws used for MILLING and other purposes." Montreal, dated 1st August, 1848.

No. 250—NEWMAN, (*Walter Perkins*,) of the Village of Elora, in the Wellington district, for "A HYDRO-PNEUMATIC WATER WHEEL." Montreal, dated 5th September, 1848.

No. 251—STEWART, (*James*,) of the city of Hamilton, for "An Improved method of constructing HORSE POWERS to be applied to Threshing Machines and other description of Machinery." Montreal, dated 14th October, 1848.

No. 252—WELLS, (*Walter Holt*,) city of Toronto, for "A new and useful machine called the Æraform, or Atmospheric CHURN." Montreal, dated 17th November, 1848.

No. 253—MIDGLEY. (*Charles*,) city of Montreal, for "A new and useful PADDLE WHEEL for steam or horse boats, and for propelling vessels." Montreal, dated 27th January, 1849.

No. 254—SMITH, (*Ananias*,) of Simcoe, Talbot district, for "A new and useful AIR DISTRIBUTOR, or GRATE, for the purpose of burning saw-dust, tan, peat, turf, coal, or any other fine fuel, in stoves or any other chambers of combustion." Montreal, dated 30th January, 1849.

No. 255—HALE, (*James Webster*,) of Fitzroy Square, in the County of Middlesex, England, for "Improvements in Machinery for cleaning or freeing WOOL, and other fibrous materials of burrs and other extraneous substances." Dated Montreal, 2nd March, 1849.

Being an English Patent, bearing date 16th October, 1845, registered in Canada.

No. 256—BAIRD, (*John*,) city of Toronto, for "Improvements in the arrangement and construction of the STEAM ENGINE." Montreal, dated 5th May, 1849.

No. 257—SEVERANCE, (*Elias James*,) of the city of Montreal, for "An improvement in the manufacture of THRASHING and WINNOWING MACHINES." Montreal, dated 5th May, 1849.

No. 258—TATE, (*Charles Maitland*,) of the city of Montreal, for "An improved method of raising and lowering WEIGHTS." Montreal, dated 11th May, 1849.

No. 259—MIDGLEY, (*Charles*,) of the city of Montreal, for an "Improved HINGE." Montreal, dated 2nd August, 1849.

No. 260—MIDGLEY, (*Charles*,) of the city of Montreal, for an "Improved ACCOUCHEUR'S ASSISTANT." Montreal, dated 13th August, 1849.

No. 261—HIGLEY, (*Peter Row*,) of Oshawa, township of Whitby, in the Home district, for an "Improved CHURN, called the PROPELLER CHURN." Montreal, dated 30th August, 1849.

No. 262—MANDIGO, (*Daniel*,) of the parish of St. John's, in the district of Montreal, for "A Japan Varnish, called the CHEMICAL ELASTIC JAPAN VARNISH." Montreal, dated 31st August, 1849.

No. 263—TATE, (*Charles Maitland*,) of the city of Montreal, for "A new and improved method of Raising and Lowering WEIGHTS." Montreal, dated 3rd September, 1849.

No. 264—TREMAIN, (*Richard*,) township of Clark, Newcastle district, for "An improved STRAW CUTTER." Montreal, dated 24th September, 1849.

No. 265—WINGER, (*John*,) village of Berlin, district of Wellington, for "A Reaction PUMP." Montreal, dated 28th September, 1849.

No. 266—CULL, (*John Angell*,) city of Toronto, for "Improvements in the art of STARCH MAKING, whereby the process is greatly improved, and rendered more certain and effectual." Montreal, dated 24th September, 1849.

No. 267 –MIDGLEY, (*Charles,*) city of Montreal, for " A new and useful SAW MILL." Montreal, dated 13th August, 1849.

No. 268–GILMOUR, (*John,*) city of Quebec, for " A new method of constructing Capstans, called GILMOUR'S PATENT CAPSTAN." Toronto, dated 11th December, 1849.

No. 269–ARMS, (*William,*) town of Sherbrooke, for "The LION PLOUGH." Toronto, dated 28th December, 1849.

No. 270–MANDIGO, (*Daniel,*) of the town of St. John's, for " An improved Plough, called MANDIGO'S IMPROVED PLOUGH." Toronto, dated 30th January, 1850.

No. 271–MANDIGO, (*Daniel,*) of the town of St. John's, for an " Improved CARRIAGE SPRING." Toronto, dated 22nd January, 1850.

No. 272–NIXON, (*William,*) of the township of Grimsby, in the county of Lincoln, for " An improved SEED DRILLING MACHINE." Toronto, dated 28th February, 1850.

No. 273–SAMPSON, (*James Henry,*) of the township of Glanford, Upper Canada, for " A new and useful machine or apparatus for CUTTING MEN'S BOOTS, and determining with accuracy, the situation of the spring in centre upon which the foot moves." Toronto, dated 6th March, 1850.

No. 274–PENNEY, (*Thomas,*) of the city of Kingston, for " An improvement in the process of TANNING LEATHER." Toronto, dated 6th March, 1850.

No. 275–CARPENTER, (*Alexander,*) of the city of Hamilton, for " A portable and stationary SAFE for holding Ashes." Toronto, dated 13th March, 1850.

No. 276–WILSON, (*Francis Gore,*) of the township of Saltfleet, in the County of Wentworth, for "Important improvements in the FANNING MILL." Toronto, dated 13th March, 1850.

No. 277–CARTER, (*Isaac,*) of St. Johns, in the County of Lincoln, for a " HOT AIR COOKING and HEATING STOVE." Toronto, dated 13th March, 1850.

No. 278–CARTER, (*Isaac,*) of St. Johns, in the county of Lincoln, for " An improved Summer and Winter ventilating AIR STOVE." Toronto, dated 13th March, 1850.

No. 279–BONNELL, (*David P.,*) of the township of Sandwich, in the county of Essex, for " An improvement in the process of Grinding and manufacturing wheat and other grain into MEAL and FLOUR." Toronto, dated 13th March, 1850.

No. 280–WILBUR, (*Alfred,*) township of Ancaster, county of Wentworth, for "An improved Heater of WATER and other LIQUIDS." Toronto, dated 25th March, 1850.

No. 281--WILBUR, (*Alfred,*) township of Ancaster, county of Wentworth, for an "Improvement in COOKING STOVES." Toronto, dated 27th March, 1850.

No. 282–ST. ONGE, (*Norbert,*) parish of St. Leon, county of St. Maurice, for "A STUMP EXTRACTOR." Toronto, dated 22nd March, 1850.

No. 283–LLOYD, (*John C.,*) of the city of Toronto, for " An improved Obstetrical SUPPORTER." Toronto, dated 27th May, 1850.

No. 284–HOUCK, (*Louis,*) township of Markham, county of York, for " An improvement in FANNING MILLS." Toronto, dated 27th May, 1850.

No. 285–FLECK, (*Alexander,*) city of Montreal, for a " New and improved PLOUGH or SUBSOIL GRUBBER." Toronto, dated 25th May, 1850.

No. 286–BARNES, (*Jacob,*) of the village of Oakville, township of Trafalgar, county of Halton, for " An Apparatus serviceable as a blast regulator, applicable to SMITHS' FORGES." Toronto, dated 13th June, 1850.

No. 287–BENNET, (*Albert,*) township of Farnham, district of Montreal, for " An improved self-protecting BEE HIVE." Toronto, dated 12th June, 1850.

No. 288–TREHEARNE, (*James,*) city of Toronto, for "A new method of constructing Portable SAW MILLS for sawing timber." Toronto, dated 27th June, 1850.

No. 289–ARMSTRONG, (*James R.,*) city of Toronto, for a " New and improved COOKING STOVE." Toronto, dated 28th June, 1850.

No. 290–HOUCK, (*Lewis,*) village of Markham, county of York, for " A further improvement in FANNING MILLS." Toronto, dated 22nd July, 1850.

No. 291--SEAVER, (*William R.,*) of the city of Montreal, for an "Improved STAVE DRESSER." Toronto, dated 2nd April, 1850.

No. 292--SEAVER, (*William R.,*) of the city of Montreal, for an "Improved STAVE JOINTER." Toronto, dated 2nd April, 1850."

No. 293--COUNTER, (*John,*) of the city of Kingston, for "The manufacture of STOVES of a new pattern and principle." Toronto, dated 28th August, 1850.

No. 294--TROUT, (*Henry,*) of the city of Hamilton, for "An improvement in LOCOMOTIVES, and RAILS for Railroads, by means of which Locomotives can be propelled along inclined planes." Toronto, dated 7th October, 1850.

No. 295--MACLARAN, (*James,*) of the city of Quebec, for a "New and improved TILE for covering Houses and other buildings." Toronto, 5th October, 1850.

No. 296--KIDD, (*David,*) of the city of Montreal, for "A new and portable GRIST MILL." Toronto, dated 14th October, 1850.

No. 297--HULBERT, (*Samuel,*) of the town of Prescott, for "A useful improvement in the Agricultural PLOUGH." Toronto dated 17th October, 1850.

No. 298--TIFFANY, (*Oliver,*) of the city of Hamilton, for a "Certain improvement in the apparatus for WARMING houses and other inhabited apartments, green houses, grain, fruit, malt drying and other kilns, and for other uses." Toronto, dated 30th October, 1850.

No. 299--MIDGLEY, (*Charles,*) of the city of Montreal, for "A new and useful Machine called A SPARK KILLER and HEAT RETAINER." Toronto, dated 2nd November, 1850.

No. 300--SMITH, (*Ithamar P.,*) of the village of Dundas, in the county of Halton, for a "New and improved Combination of Machinery for a CUTTING BOX, for cutting Straw, Hay, or Stalks." Toronto, dated 7th December, 1850.

No. 301--HAMILTON, (*James,*) of the town of Peterborough, for "An improved PLOUGH.' Toronto, dated 13th December, 1850.

No. 302--LAMB, (*Daniel Mathias,*) of the city of Toronto, for "An improved Machine for making NUTS and WASHERS." Toronto, dated 28th December, 1850.

No. 303--DUPONT, (*Eusebe,*) town of St. John's, for "A new and Improved PUMP or Apparatus for lifting Water." Toronto, dated 17th December, 1850.

No. 304--GRIFFIN, (*William,*) of the township of Brantford, for "A CLOVER SEED GATHERER." Toronto, dated 9th January, 1851.

No. 305--McLEAN, (*Thomas Hewson,*) of the city of Quebec, for "An improved method of making HORSE SHOES." Toronto, dated 9th December, 1850.

No. 306--MEAD, (*George Hooper,*) of the city of Montreal, for "An improved method of constructing PIANO FORTES." Toronto, dated 8th January, 1851.

No. 307--PROWSE, (*George Fabes,*) of the city of Montreal, for the "The PROWSONIAN HOT AIR COOKING RANGE or FURNACE." Toronto, dated 8th January, 1851.

No. 308--WATSON, (*Joseph,*) of the township of Norwich, in the county of Oxford, for "An Improvement on PATENT BEDSTEADS for the Sick and Wounded." Toronto, dated 31st January, 1851.

No. 309--HEARLE, (*John,*) of the village of Galt, in the county of Halton, for "An improvement in ENGINE PUMPS and FIRE ENGINES." Toronto, dated 31st January, 1851.

No. 310--DARLING, (*John,*) of the township of Yarmouth, in the county of Middlesex, for "A new and useful composition to be used as a SOAP for the saving of labor in washing clothes." Toronto, dated 31st January, 1851.

No. 311--RUTTAN, (*Henry,*) of the town of Cobourg, for "A machine called a VENTILATING STOVE and the means by which the ventilating air may be made to circulate under a floor and between the joists." Toronto, 31st January, 1851 ....*Surrendered and a new patent issued*, 29th *November*, 1858.

No. 312--GRIFFIN, (*James Kent,*) of the village of Waterdown, in the county of Holton, for "Several important improvements in COOKING STOVES, and in the method of applying and using heat for cooking purposes." Toronto, 13th March, 1851.

No. 313--HOLTON, (*William,*) of the township of East Tilbury, in the county of Kent, for "A new kind of PLOUGH." Toronto, dated 15th March, 1851.

No. 311—CULL, (*John Angell,*) of the city of Toronto, for "Certain Machines called a HOUSER and a BRAN WASHER to be used in the manufacture of starch." Toronto, dated 17th March, 1851.

No. 315—CULL, (*John Angell,*) of the city of Toronto, for "Certain improvements in the method of making STARCH." Toronto, dated 17th March, 1851.

No. 316 KELLY, (*John,*) of the town of London, in the county of Middlesex, for "A new kind of SUSPENSION TRUSS to be applied in constructing bridges and roofs." Toronto, dated 22nd March, 1851.

No. 317—THOMSON, (*Archibald John,*) of the town of Woodstock, in the county of Oxford, for "A new and useful improvement upon the PLOUGH" Toronto, dated 24th March, 1851.

No. 318—HOLMES, (*William John,*) of the city of Montreal, for "A new and useful improvement in the meth .d of applying the HEAT generated in stoves or fire places for the purpose of warming apartments or houses." Toronto, dated 12th April, 1851.

No. 319—FOX, (*Thomas S.,*) of the city of Montreal, for "A Rabbeted revolving air and water tight JOINT." Toronto, dated 12th April, 1851.

No. 320—ARMSTRONG, (*James Rogers,*) of the city of Toronto, for "A new and improved Cooking Stove, to be called the GIANT COOKING STOVE." Toronto, dated 17th April, 1851.

No. 321—ROURKE, (*John,*) of the city of Montreal, for a "Self-acting Ribbed Warp KNITTING LOOM." Toronto, dated 1st May, 1851.

No. 322—MANDIGO, (*Daniel,*) of St. John's, in the district of Montreal, "A new and improved method of cutting Hay, Straw, Chaff, or other vegetable food for CATTLE." Toronto, dated 2nd May, 1851.

No. 323—SHATTUCK, (*Chester,*) of the township of Durham, for "A CROSS CUTTING MACHINE." Toronto, dated 21st May, 1851.

No. 324—McLEAN, (*Thomas Hewson,*) of the city of Quebec, for "A new shape of bar iron for HORSE SHOES." Toronto, dated 1st May, 1851.

No. 325 - McKENZIE, (*John Hare,*) of the township of Mariposa, in the county of Peterboro', for "A new mode of constructing a Cider MILL and PRESS." Toronto, dated 16th June, 1851.

No. 326 - JEWETT, (*Sherman S.,*) of the city of Toronto, for "An improved IRON STOVE for heating rooms, and other purposes." Toronto, dated 16th June, 1851.

No. 327—JENNEY, (*Edwin,*) of the township of Sandwich, in the county of Essex, for "A new and useful Machine for Cutting and Sawing STAVES with unprecedented rapidity and correctness." Toronto, dated 16th June, 1851.

No. 328—ROSWELL, (*Tompkins Merrill,*) of the township of Sandwich, in the county of Essex, for "A new and useful Machine for separating and cleaning WHEAT and other GRAIN." Toronto, dated 16th June, 1851.

No. 329—FULLER, (*Thomas J.,*) of the city of Toronto, for "A new and improved Cooking Stove to be called the SALAMANDER COOKING STOVE." Toronto, dated 18th June, 1851.

No. 330—LEMON, (*Charles,*) of the township of Augusta, in the county of Grenville, for "A new and improved Plough called a Double Iron Beam PLOUGH." Toronto, dated 25th June, 1851.

No. 331—LADD, (*Calvin Palmer,*) of the city of Montreal, for "An improved WEIGHING MACHINE." Toronto, dated 30th June, 1851.

No. 332—HAWLEY, (*George,*) of the township of Eaton, in the district of St. Francis, for "A SHINGLE MAKING MACHINE." Toronto, dated 4th July, 1851.

No. 333—MARKLE, (*Henry,*) of the township of Flamborough East, in the county of Halton, for "Certain improvements in the construction of Agricultural PLOUGHS." Toronto, dated 12th July, 1851.

No. 334—TREHEARNE, (*James,*) of Port Dover, in the township of Woodhouse, and county of Norfolk, for "A new method of running the Perpendicular SAW for sawing Timber." Toronto, dated 24th August, 1851.

No. 335—CARTER, (*Isaac,*) of the town of St. Catherines, in the county of Lincoln, for "A COOKING STOVE, the hot air from which is applied to heating purposes." Toronto, dated 21st August, 1851.

No. 336—COLTON, (*Reuben Powers,*) of Brockville, in the county of Leeds, for "A new and improved method of constructing Cooking Stoves, as exemplified in what he calls the Brockville Air Tight COOKING STOVE." Toronto, dated 8th September, 1851.

No. 337—FULLER, (*Benjamin,*) of the township of Townsend, in the county of Norfolk, for "A new and improved WHIRLPOOL WHEEL, or pressure water power." Quebec, dated 6th November, 1851.

No. 338—FULLER, (*Thomas J.,*) of the city of Toronto, for "The Excelsior Cylindrical THRESHER, also a new and useful Machine for driving the above, or for any other suitable purpose, called the Excelsior HORSE POWER." Quebec, dated 6th November, 1851.

No. 339—COLEMAN, (*William,*) of the City of Toronto, for "A Circular and Straight Moulding, Rabbetting, Ploughing and Architrave Machine." Quebec, dated 6th November, 1851.

No. 340—LAMB, (*Peter Rothwell,*) of the City of Toronto, for "A new and important Machine for the manufacture of LATHS." Quebec, dated 6th November, 1851.

No. 341—HIGLEY, (*Peter Row,*) of Oshawa, in the county of York, for "A new and improved Machine for cutting HAY or STRAW." Quebec, dated 6th November, 1851.

No. 342—MILLS, (*Thomas,*) of the City of Toronto, for "A new method of constructing CARRIAGES and other vehicles by which they are enabled to turn in much less space than formerly." Quebec, dated 25th November, 1851.

No. 343—MACLAREN, (*James,*) of the City of Quebec, for "An improved mode of making BRICKS and Architectural Ornaments." Quebec, dated 8th January, 1852.

No. 344—PAGNUELO, (*Joseph,*) of the City of Montreal, for "An improved FURNACE." Quebec, dated 8th January, 1852.

No. 345—JONES, (*Nevens,*) of the Village of Stewartstown, in the Township of Esquesing, in the County of Halton, for "A new and useful improvement in the construction of WAGGONS, combining the springs and coupling." Quebec, dated 19th January, 1852.

No. 346—ANDERSON, (*Alexander,*) of Markham, in the County of York, for "Certain Improvements to a Machine called a GRAIN SEPARATOR, for the purpose of cleaning grain and separating it from the straw and chaff." Quebec, dated 19th January, 1852.

No. 347—ANDERSON, (*James,*) of the Township of Blenheim, in the County of Oxford, for "A new and useful plan for building HOUSES." Quebec, dated 19th January, 1852.

No. 348—NICOL, (*Thomas,*) and NICOL, (*Prudent,*) of the Parish of St. Thomas, in the District of Quebec, for "An Improved THRESHING MILL." Quebec, dated 14th January, 1852.

No. 349—WILLARD, (*Asa,*) of the City of Montreal, for "A BUTTER MACHINE." Quebec, dated 23rd January, 1852.

No. 350—JONES, (*Justus Sherwood,*) of Brockville, in the County of Leeds, for "A new and improved method of constructing CARRIAGES." Quebec, dated 20th March, 1852.

No. 351—DAWSON, (*Charles,*) of the Town of Cobourg, in the County of Northumberland, for "Improvements in the manner of working MULEY SAWS and the machinery attached thereto." Quebec, dated 20th March, 1852.

No. 352—LEMON, (*Charles,*) of the Township of Augusta, in the County of Grenville, for "A new and improved method of constructing PLOUGHS." Quebec, dated 31st March, 1852.

No. 353—CUTTER, (*Samuel,*) of the City of Montreal, for "A new and improved Apparatus or LAMP for burning Benzole or HYDRO CARBONS." Quebec, dated 19th April, 1852.

No. 354—PERRY, (*William,*) of the city of Montreal, for "A Direct Action FIRE ENGINE." Quebec, dated 30th April, 1852.

No. 355—GREGORY, (*Thomas Currie,*) of the City of Hamilton, for "A Self-acting Apparatus for disconnecting the CARRIAGES of a Railway Train from the Tender, upon the Engine leaving the Rails." Quebec, dated 28th May, 1852.

No. 356—ROCKWELL, (*Horatio A.,*) of the Township of Farnham, in the District of Montreal, for "A new and useful Method of constructing YOKES for OXEN." Quebec, dated 8th May, 1852.

No. 357—MURDOCH, (*Peter,*) of the Township of Ancaster, in the County of Wentworth, for "An improvement in the composition and form of WHEELS for all kinds of Carriages." Quebec, dated 28th May, 1852.

No. 358—LEMOINE, (Louis,) of the City of Quebec, for "A new and useful improvement in the manufacture and construction of a STEAM GENERATING APPARATUS." Quebec, dated 9th June, 1852.

No. 359—GUMEAR, (Benjamin,) of the Town of London, in the County of Middlesex, for "A Churn called The RECIPROCATING CHURN." Quebec, dated 15th June, 1852.

No. 360—HAGER, (Lawrence,) of the Village of Palermo, in the Township of Trafalgar, in the County of Halton, for "A new and useful improvement in the SEED DRILL." Quebec, dated 30th June, 1852.

No. 361—KNAGGS, (William,) of the Township of Etobicoke, in the County of York, for "An increasing Twist and Curvilinear MOULD BOARD for Ploughs." Quebec, dated 30th June, 1852.

No. 362—LONGBOTTOM, (Abram,) of the City of Montreal, for "A new and improved mode of Purifying ILLUMINATING GAS." Quebec, dated 20th July, 1852.

No. 363—MIGHT, (Robert,) of the Township of Cavan, in the County of Durham, for "R. MIGHT's Portable Horizontal and Self-Acting SAWING MACHINE." Quebec, dated 10th August, 1852.

No. 364—ANDRES, (Samuel,) of Chambly, in the District of Montreal, for "A new and scientific mode of constructing FLUES or CHIMNIES." Quebec, dated 12th August, 1852.

No. 365—LESTER, (George William,) of the Township of Sidney, in the County of Hastings, for "A Smoothing Iron called The Improved Draft and Damper Box SMOOTHING IRON." Quebec, dated 24th August, 1852.

No. 366—ROURKE, (John,) of the City of Montreal, for "MILL STONE PICKERS." Quebec, dated 24th August, 1852.

No. 367—TRENHOLM, (Edward,) of the Township of Kingsey, in the County of Drummond, in the District of St. Francis, for "A Machine called TRENHOLM's ELEVATOR." Quebec, dated 26th August, 1852.

No. 368—FULLER, (Thomas J.,) of the City of Toronto, for "A new and useful Improvement in MULEY SAW MILLS." Quebec, dated 31st August, 1852.

No. 369—GRIFFIN, (James Kent,) of the Village of Waterdown, in the County of Wentworth, for "Several new and useful improvements on COOKING STOVES." Quebec, dated 7th September, 1852.

No. 370—LOSSING, (Richard,) of the Township of Norwich, in the County of Oxford, for "A WASHING and CHURNING MACHINE." Quebec, dated 31st August, 1852.

No. 371—HURLBERT, (Samuel,) of the Town of Prescott, in the County of Grenville, for "An Improvement on the PLOUGH, for which he has already obtained a Patent, dated 17th October, 1850. Quebec, 20th September, 1852.

No. 372—GIFFORD, (Alfred,) of the Township of Whitby, in the County of Ontario, for "A new and useful improvement on a Machine for CUTTING STRAW, patented by Richard Tromain, the 24th of September, 1849. Quebec, dated 20th September, 1852.

No. 373—SPERRY, (George March,) of the Parish of St. Joseph, of Chambly, in the District of Montreal, for "An improved method of constructing a CORN CRACKER." Quebec, dated 21st September, 1852.

No. 374—RUSSELL, (Samuel Irwin,) of Oshawa, in the Township of Whitby, for "A new and improved HARROW." Quebec, dated 8th October, 1852.

No. 375—ENNIS, (Edward Carroll,) of L'Islet, for "A Machine for making CARRIAGE WHEELS." Quebec, dated 30th September, 1852.

No. 376—BERNIER, (Henry,) of the Parish of Lotbinière, in the District of Quebec, for "A new and improved COOKING STOVE." Quebec, dated 5th October, 1852.

No. 377—PARADIS, (Joseph,) of the City of Montreal, for "A new and useful improvement in the method of constructing THRESHING MACHINES." Quebec, dated 15th October, 1852.

No. 378—GOSSELIN, (Charles,) of the Parish of St. Anne de la Pocatière, for "A new and useful improvement in the mode of constructing DOUBLE STOVES." Quebec, dated 13th October, 1852.

No. 379—MIDGLEY, (*Charles*,) of the City of Montreal, for "An Improved CHURN." Quebec, dated 27th October, 1852.

No. 380—MIDGLEY, (*Charles*,) of the City of Montreal, for "An Improved BEE HIVE." Quebec, dated 27th October, 1852.

No. 381—BROWN, (*William*,) of the City of Toronto, for "A new and useful improvement in making GRAIN RAKES." Quebec, dated 6th November, 1852.

No. 382—TIFFANY, (*Frederick*,) of the City of Toronto, for "A new and improved apparatus for warming air and for warming and ventilating HOUSES and other inhabited apartments." Quebec, dated 6th November, 1852.

No. 383—FLINN, (*Patrick*,) of the City of Montreal, for "A Compound Action WATER WHEEL." Quebec, dated 8th November, 1852.

No. 384—STACY, (*George*,) of the City of Montreal, for "A new and useful method of constructing SPIKE MACHINES." Quebec, dated 20th January, 1853.

No. 385—ALLCHIN, (*William*,) of the Village of Paris, in the County of Brant, for "An improved SCYTHE HOLDER." Quebec, dated 26th January, 1853.

No. 386—ANSLEY, (*George*,) of the Village of Vienna, in the County of Elgin, for "The Centrifugal and Centripetal CHURN." Quebec, dated 8th February, 1853.

No. 387—BURLEY, (*Ezekiel*,) of the Township of Clarke, in the County of Durham, for "An improvement on the WOODEN PLOUGH." Quebec, dated 14th February, 1853.

No. 388—HIGLEY, (*Peter Rowe*,) of the Village of Oshawa, in the Township of Whitby, in the County of Ontario, for "A new and improved Machine for cutting HAY and STRAW." Quebec, dated 7th March, 1853.

No. 389—WILDER, (*Arctus Andrews*,) of the Township of Sandwich, in the County of Essex, for "A new and useful Machine for PLANING, TONGUEING and GROOVING BOARDS." Quebec, dated 7th March, 1853.

No. 390—MANDIGO, (*Daniel*,) of the Village of St. John's, in the County of Chambly, for "A new and useful improvement in the construction of LIGHTNING RODS." Quebec, dated 16th February, 1853.

No. 391—ROUNDS, (*Albert*,) of the Village of St. John's, in the County of Chambly, for "A new and useful improvement in the construction of LIGHTNING CONDUCTORS." Quebec, dated 16th February, 1853.

No. 392—MURDOCH, (*Peter*,) of the Township of Ancaster, in the County of Wentworth, for "New and improved running GEAR for Vehicles." Quebec, dated 15th April, 1853.

No. 393—ANSLEY, (*George*,) of the Village of Vienna, in the County of Elgin, for "A Portable Hot Air FURNACE and Cooking STOVE." Quebec, dated 15th April, 1853.

No. 394—RUSSELL, (*James*,) of the Township of Ancaster, in the County of Wentworth, for "A new and useful machine for Crushing Grain, to be called RUSSELL'S CORN CRUSHER." Quebec, dated 15th April, 1853.

No. 395—MURDOCH, (*Peter*,) of the Township of Ancaster, in the County of Wentworth, for "A new and improved SEED DRILL to be attached to a Plough." Quebec, dated 15th April, 1853.

No. 396—LEMON, (*Charles*,) of the Township of Augusta, in the County of Grenville, for "An improvement in the construction of PLOUGHS." Quebec, dated 15th April, 1853.

No. 397—TETU, (*Charles Hilaire*,) of the Parish of Rivière Ouelle, in the County of Kamouraska, for "A new and useful process of manufacturing LEATHER from the Skin of the Whale or Porpoise." Quebec, dated 16th April, 1853.

No. 398—TETU, (*Charles Hilaire*,) of the Parish of Rivière Ouelle, in the County of Kamouraska, for "A new and useful mode of manufacturing WHALE and PORPOISE OILS." Quebec, dated 16th April, 1853.

No. 399—PARADIS, (*Joseph*,) of the City of Montreal, for "A useful improvement in the construction of THRESHING MACHINES." Quebec, dated 29th April, 1853.

No. 400—RUTTAN, (*William Consider*,) of the Township of Norwich, in the County of Oxford, for "An improved GUN BARREL and PROJECTILE." Quebec, dated 29th April, 1853.

No. 401—RICHARD, (*Edmond*,) of the Parish of St. Roch, in the County of Quebec, for "A Machine for sawing straight and crooked Wood of equal and unequal dimensions." Quebec dated 29th April, 1853.

No. 402—BELL, (*David*,) of the Parish of St. Roch, in the County of Quebec, for "A Press or Machine for the manufacture of Earthenware Pipes and Draining Tiles." Quebec, dated 29th April, 1853.

No. 402—PLAMONDON, (*Joseph*,) of the City of Quebec, for "A Machine for cutting Tobacco without moistening it." Quebec, dated 29th April, 1853.

No. 404—BRIGHAM, (*Daniel P.*,) of the Village of Oshawa, in the County of Ontario, for "A new and useful improvement in the construction of Fanning Mills." Quebec, dated 29th April, 1853.

No. 405—KENT, (*Asph Buck*,) of the Township of West Oxford, in the County of Oxford, for "A Self-Gigging, Self-Setting, and Self-Regulating Saw Mill." Quebec, dated 29th April, 1853.

No. 406—DEAN, (*John*,) of the Village of Vienna, in the County of Elgin, for "A Double-Reflector for Baking purposes." Quebec, dated 29th April, 1853.

No. 407—EVERITT, (*Zenas*,) of the Township of Flamborough West, in the County of Wentworth, for "An improved Ladder." Quebec, dated 12th May, 1853.

No. 408—HOLWELL, (*William Antrobus*,) of the City of Quebec, for "A new and useful improvement in the construction of Reins, or Bridles, to be called "The Duplex Safety Rein." Quebec, dated 12th May, 1853.

No. 409—MERRITT, (*Daniel Smith*,) of the Township of Houghton, in the County of Norfolk, for "A new and improved Carriage and Feeding, and Gigging Back Works for Steam and Water Saw Mills." Quebec, dated 11th May, 1853.

No. 410—WOODS, (*Joseph*,) of the Town of Chatham, in the County of Kent, for "A new and improved Cant Hook, for piling, and otherwise handling and disposing of Railway Iron Bars." Quebec, dated 28th May, 1853.

No. 411—TIBBITS, (*Benjamin F.*,) of the City of Quebec, for "An improved mode of constructing Steam Engines." Quebec, dated 11th June, 1853.

No. 412—ROCKWELL, (*Nirum Wildman*,) of the Township of Farnham, in the District of Montreal, for "A limited Horse Swing." Quebec, dated 11th June, 1853.

No. 413—SMITH, (*Charles Wesley*,) of the Township of Townsend, in the County of Norfolk, for "New and useful improvements in the construction of Harvesting Machines." Quebec, dated 20th June, 1853.

No. 414—MORLEY, (*John*,) of the Village of Thorold, in the County of Welland, for "An improved Mould Board for Ploughs." Quebec, dated 20th June, 1853.

No. 415—McINTYRE, (*Jackson*,) of the City of Kingston, for "A File Cutting Machine." Quebec, dated 20th June, 1853.

No. 416—RODIER, (*Charles Seraphin*,) of the City of Montreal, for "A new and useful improvement in the construction of Threshing Machines." Quebec, dated 20th June, 1853.

No. 417—ARMSTRONG, (*John W.*,) of the Township of Eramosa, in the County of Wellington, for "A new and useful improvement in the construction of Ploughs." Quebec, dated 21st June, 1853.

No. 418—HANDFORD, (*John*,) of the Township of Sandwich, in the County of Essex, for "An improved Threshing Machine." Quebec, dated 21st June, 1853.

No. 419—WALLBRIDGE, (*Alexander Solomon*,) of the Township of Stanbridge, in the District of Montreal, for "A new and useful machine for Sawing and Planing all Lumber by one operation." Quebec, dated 20th July, 1853.

No. 420—URQUHART, (*George*,) of the Township of Eaton, in the District of St. Francis, for "An improvement in the manufacture of Metallic Carriage Springs, to be called 'The Urquhart Elliptic Spring.'" Quebec, dated 20th July, 1853.

No. 421—LADD, (*Calvin Palmer*,) of the City of Montreal, for "A Metallic Burial Case." Quebec, dated 8th July, 1853.

22

No. 422—THOMAS, (*Robert,*) of the City of Toronto, for "A Paddle Box Tubular RAFT." Quebec, dated 19th July, 1853.

No. 423—SPENCE, (*William John,*) of the City of Quebec, for "A self-adjusting PADDLE WHEEL." Quebec, dated 26th July, 1853.

No. 424—ROBITAILLE, (*Alexis,*) of the City of Quebec, for "A new and improved apparatus for producing GAS from resin, oil, and other substances of like nature, and from the decomposition of water." Quebec, dated 2nd September, 1853.

No. 425—DEAN, (*John,*) of the Village of Vienna, in the County of Elgin, for "An improvement in the mode of constructing the DOUBLE REFLECTOR for baking purposes, invented by him and for which Letters Patent were granted to him on the 29th April, 1853. Quebec, dated 7th September, 1853.

No. 426—ANDERSON, (*Alexander,*) of the Township of Markham, in the County of York, for "A new and useful machine for planting POTATOES." Quebec, dated 26th Semptember, 1853.

No. 427—SOUTHWICK, (*Massa Branch,*) of the Parish of St. Hilaire, in the District of Montreal, for "A new and useful apparatus for CRUSHING, DRYING, and otherwise preparing potatoes and other vegetable substances, as well as fruits and meats for food." Quebec, dated 15th September, 1853.

No. 428—REESE, (*Lewis,*) of the Village of Oshawa, in the County of Ontario, for "A new and useful improvement in the manufacture of A STRAW CUTTING MACHINE." Quebec, dated 19th September, 1853.

No. 429—TURNBULL, (*Alexander,*) of the Town of Dundas, in the County of Wentworth, for "A new and useful improvement in the construction of the Canadian PLOUGH." Quebec, dated 15th October, 1853.

No. 430—BUCHANNAN, (*Nathan,*) of the City of Montreal, for "A new and useful apparatus for, and method of, desiccating LUMBER and other materials." Quebec, dated 1st October, 1853.

No. 431—MODELAND, (*Isaac,*) of the Township of Chinguacousy, in the County of Peel, for "Improvements in the construction of PLOUGHS." Quebec, dated 19th September, 1853.

No. 432—STEPHENS, (*Robert Emmet,*) of the Town of Owen Sound, in the County of Grey, for "A new and improved EXCAVATOR for cutting or excavating and moving clay, sand, gravel, or other substances." Quebec, dated 7th October, 1853.

No. 433—PARSONS, (*John,*) of the City of Toronto, for "An improved Machine for making BRICKS." Quebec, dated 6th October, 1853.

No. 434—PARSONS, (*John,*) of the City of Toronto, for "An apparatus for the purpose of cleansing or drawing off BEER from the fermenting tuns." Quebec, dated 13th October, 1853.

No. 435—CRAWFORD, (*Dalrymple,*) of the City of Toronto, for "Improved Machinery for arresting the progress of RAILWAY TRAINS." Quebec, dated 15th October, 1853.

No. 436—WOOD, (*Jacob,*) of the Village of Oshawa, in the Township of Whitby, in the County of Ontario, for "A new and useful improvement in the present mode of constructing CHURNS." Quebec, dated 2nd February, 1854.

No. 437—AMSBARY, (*Lewis,*) of the Village of Oshawa, in the Township of Whitby, in the County of Ontario, for "A new and useful improvement in the construction of CHURNS." Quebec, dated 2nd February, 1854.

No. 438—KWASNESKI, (*Stanislas,*) of the City of Montreal, for "The Prize Hot Air and COOKING FURNACE." Quebec, dated 8th February, 1854.

No. 439—DUNHAM, (*George,*) of the Town of Brockville, in the County of Leeds, for "An improved method of running PADDLE WHEELS." Quebec, dated 11th February, 1854.

No. 440—FORBES, (*Jacob Thaddeus,*) of the Township of Haldimand, in the County of Northumberland, for "An improved Elevating BEDSTEAD." Quebec, dated 2nd February, 1854.

No. 441—BOWMAN, (*William,*) of the City of Hamilton, for "Improvements in Railway CARS and CARRIAGES." Quebec, dated 2nd February, 1854.

No. 442—ST. JACQUES, (*Antoine,*) of the Parish of St. Antoine de la Rivière Chambly, District of Montreal, for "A new and useful improvement in the construction of POST AUGERS." Quebec, dated 22nd February, 1854.

No. 443—WINER. (*John*,) of the City of Hamilton, in the County of Wentworth, for " A new and useful improvement for healing air, for warming apartments by the waste heat of a stove, or fire grate, to be denominated WISER'S PYRO-PNEUMATIC FIRE GRATE." Quebec, dated 22nd March, 1854.

No. 444—COLE, (*Benjamin*,) of the City of Quebec, for "A new way of closing SHOP WINDOW SHUTTERS." Quebec, dated 23rd March, 1854.

No. 445—SCOVELL, (*Hiram*,) of the Village of Waterford, in the County of Norfolk, for "A CIDER MILL and PRESS." Quebec, dated 28th March, 1854.

No. 446—SOPER, (*William Harrison*,) of London, in the County of Middlesex, for "An improvement in the grooving and inside finish of RIFLE BARRELS." Quebec, dated 28th March, 1854.

No. 447—REESE, (*Lewis*,) of the Village of Oshawa, in the County of Ontario, for " A new and useful improvement in the construction of a machine for cutting HAY or STRAW." Quebec, dated 30th March, 1854.

No. 448—WILLISTON, (*George*,) of the City of Quebec, for "A new and improved Machine for STRAIGHTENING or CURVING RAILS." Quebec, dated 4th April, 1854.

No. 449—GAUVREAU, (*Pierre*,) of the City of Quebec, for "A new and useful cement, to be called by him GAUVREAU'S CANADIAN HYDRAULIC CEMENT." Quebec, dated 5th April, 1854.

No. 450—LEE, (*Jonas Philip*,) of Niagara, in the County of Lincoln, for "A new and useful improvement in a machine for knitting plain fabrics, such as shirts, drawers, stockings, &c., known as, and called, the DOUBLE ACTING KNITTING MACHINE." Quebec, dated 10th April, 1854.

No. 451—CHARNOCK, (*John Henry*,) of the City of Hamilton, for "A new and useful Machine for Moulding all descriptions of TILES, PIPES and BRICKS, for drainage, sewerage, building or other purposes, from clay or other plastic substances." Quebec, dated 17th April, 1854.

No. 452—MURDOCH, (*Peter*,) of the Township of Ancaster, in the County of Wentworth, for " A COMPOUND CARRIAGE, so constructed that all kinds of wheel carriages may be converted into sleighs." Quebec, dated 18th April, 1854.

No. 453—MURDOCH, (*Peter*,) of the Township of Ancaster, in the County of Wentworth, for "Improvements in the DOUBLE DASH CHURN." Quebec, dated 18th April, 1854.

No. 454—LOSSING, (*Richard*,) of the Town of Brantford, in the County of Brant, for "A ROLLING SCREEN FANNING MILL." Quebec, dated 21st April, 1854.

No. 455—PARSONS, (*John*,) of the City of Toronto, for an " Apparatus for cooking, for bakers' ovens, for drying and roasting molt and other vegetable produce, for seasoning lumber, also for a drying room, with self acting ventilator, for laundries, hatching poultry, heating Irons and keeping cooked provisions hot, by the application of GAS." Quebec, dated 28th April, 1854.

No. 456—HOWELL, (*Levi*,) of the Township of Ancaster, in the County of Wentworth, for " New and useful improvements in the construction of the CIDER MILL and PRESS." Quebec, dated 2nd February, 1854.

No. 457—WAIT, (*Benjamin*,) of Willoughby, in the County of Welland, for "A combination of machinery for the making of BARRELS, KEGS, TUBS, and other bilge works." Quebec, dated 14th June, 1854.

No. 458—SELDECK, (*Daily*,) of the Town of Prescott, in the County of Grenville, for "A new and useful improvement in the construction of CHURNS." Quebec, dated 14th June, 1854.

No. 459—HOYT, (*Ralph*,) of the City of Hamilton, for "An improved OBSTETRICAL SUPPORTER." Quebec, dated 29th June, 1854.

No. 460—SCOBELL, (*Joseph*,) of the City of Montreal, for "A new and improved method of manufacturing PEAT-BOG by drying, pressing and cooking, for fuel and other purposes." Quebec, dated 7th June, 1854.

No. 461—CHATTERTON, (*Richard Dover*,) of the Town of Cobourg, for "A floating Gangway, Boat Launch, and LIFE RAFT." Quebec, dated 19th June, 1854.

No. 462—THIRKELL, (*Joseph*,) of the Town of London, in the County of Middlesex, for

"Improvements in the forming, shaping and casting of IRON PLOUGHS." Quebec, dated 29th May, 1854.

No. 463—SCOBELL, (Joseph,) of the City of Montreal, for "A new and improved method of covering Roofs with SLATES." Quebec, dated 14th June, 1854.

No. 464—HUCKETT, (William J.,) of the City of Toronto, in the County of York, for "An improved SIGNAL LIGHT for Railways." Quebec, dated 30th June, 1854.

No. 465—MUCHALL, (Richard,) of the Township of Hamilton, in the County of Northumberland, for "A Machine for working irregular surfaces, so as to form a piece of TIMBER to any Required shape." Quebec, dated 13th July, 1854.

No. 466—MURGATROYD, (Thomas,) of Smithville, in the Township of Grimsby, County of Lincoln, for "New and useful improvements on CARRIAGES." Quebec, dated 21st July, 1854.

No. 467—BROWN, (John,) of the City of Toronto, in the County of York, for "A Seed Sower." Quebec, dated 21st July, 1854.

No. 468—PORTER, (D'Arcy,) of the City of Hamilton, in the County of Wentworth, for "A new and useful SEWING MACHINE." Quebec, dated 21st July, 1854.

No. 469—PYE, (John,) of the City of Quebec, for "A new and improved method of constructing WATER CLOSETS." Quebec, dated 14th August, 1854.

No. 470—ANDRES, (Stephen Redington,) of the Village of Chambly, for "The new art of manufacturing Paper from the Plant known by the Linnean Gineric name of 'GNAPHALIUM,' and vulgarly called 'CUDWEED, or LIFE EVERLASTING.'" Quebec, dated 25th August, 1854.

No. 471—EGAN, (Michael,) of the Town of Niagara, in the County of Lincoln, for "A new and improved mode of making and preparing MOULDS for Copper, Brass and Composition Castings." Quebec, dated 26th August, 1854.

No. 472—GATISS, (John H.,) of the Township of Barton, in the County of Wentworth, for "A new and useful improvement in the apparatus for cleaning and scouring WHEAT, RYE and BUCKWHEAT." Quebec, dated 28th August, 1854.

No. 473—HAYDEN, (Joel Babcock,) of the Town of Brantford, in the County of Brant, for "An improved HUB for Waggon and Carriage Wheels." Quebec, dated 4th September, 1854.

No. 474—NIXON, (William,) of the Township of Grimsby, in the County of Lincoln, for "A POTATO AND SEED DRILL." Quebec, dated 4th September, 1854.

No. 475—BROWN, (John,) of the City of Toronto, in the County of York, for "An improved STRAW CUTTER." Quebec, dated 4th September, 1854.

No. 476—CARPENTER, (Lewis Blackley,) of the City of Quebec, for "An improved HAND LANTERN." Quebec, dated 6th October, 1854.

No. 477—MILLER (Henry,) of the Township of Sandwich, in the County of Essex, for "A new and useful machine for expeditiously arresting the progress of railway cars by almost sudden STEAM BRAKES." Quebec, dated 19th September, 1854.

No. 478—STEPHENS, (Robert E.,) of the Town of Sydenham, in the County of Grey, for "An improved BEDSTEAD." Quebec, dated 20th October, 1854.

No. 479—GATISS, (John H.,) of the Township of Barton, in the County of Wentworth, for "A Central Discharge WATER WHEEL." Quebec, dated 28th October, 1854.

No. 480—LINDO, (Henry Charles,) of the City of Quebec, for "A new and useful process of depriving hides and skins of the hair, wool, fur or bristles preparatory to being TANNED." Quebec, dated 19th October, 1854.

No. 481—ROMAINE, (Robert,) of Peterborough, in the County of Peterborough, for "Certain improvements in the apparatus for effecting AGRICULTURAL OPERATIONS." Quebec, dated 19th October, 1854.

No. 482—WATEROUS, (Charles Horatio,) of the Town of Brantford, in the County of Brant, for "A machine for making NUTS and WASHERS from a heated bar of metal." Quebec, dated 8th November, 1854.

No. 483—DU BERGER, (Charles,) of the Parish of Eboulements, in the County of Saguenay, for "A new mode of preventing Railroad Cars from running off the track or rail, consisting of a SAFETY HOOK." Quebec, dated 7th November, 1854.

No 481—CUTTER, (*Samuel,*) of the City of Montreal, for "A new and improved method of making GAS, and applying it to and for the purpose of illumination, heating or any other use to which Gas is now applied; by the dry distillation of ripe sunflower seed, flax, castor oil, beans or seed, and all other seeds, all grains, and all nuts, whole or cracked, with or without hulls, husks, chaff, or shells." Quebec, dated 7th November, 1854.

No. 485—LEMIRE, (*Leyn Antoine,*) of the City of Quebec, for "A new Polishing Puff, called the WHEEL and HAND DUFF, for Daguerrotypic purposes." Quebec, dated 11th November, 1854.

No. 486—LOUNSBURY, (*Rodolphus,*) of the Township of Grimsby, and LYONS, (*Nathaniel Griffin,*) of the Township of Calstor, both in the County of Lincoln, for "A new and useful Machine, or Implement of Agriculture, entitled, THE CANADIAN THISTLE KILLER AND CULTIVATOR." Quebec, dated 8th December, 1854.

No. 487—THOMAS, (*Robert,*) of the City of Quebec, for "A Machine for clearing Snow from off Railway Tracks, to be called THOMAS' SNOW EXTERMINATOR." Quebec, dated 30th November, 1854.

No. 488—ANDERSON, (*Alexander,*) of the Township of Markham, in the County of York, for "A POTATO DIGGER." Quebec, dated 13th December, 1854.

No. 489—SMITH, (*James Blanchfield,*) of North Cayuga, in the County of Haldimand, for "A new and useful Improvement in the construction of Portable or Stationary Steam or Water SAW MILLS." Quebec, dated 6th December, 1854.

No. 490—HELM, (*John,*) of the Town of Port Hope, in the County of Durham, and WADE, (*John,*) of the Township of Hamilton, County of Northumberland, for a "Machine for boring HOLES in the ground for Fence Posts or other purposes." Quebec, dated 20th January, 1855.

No. 491—BROWN, (*H. P.,*) of the Town of Woodstock, in the County of Oxford, for an "Improvement on the CHAFF CUTTER or CUTTING BOX." Quebec, dated 19th January, 1855.

No. 492—ADAMS, (*R.,*) of the City of Toronto, in the County of York, for a "REVERSE COOKING STOVE." Quebec, dated 20th January, 1855.

No. 493—FITZPATRICK, (*W.,*) of the City of Montreal, in the County of Montreal, for "certain Improvements in NAIL MACHINE FEEDERS." Quebec, dated 20th January, 1855.

No. 494—OVERHOLT, (*J.,*) of the Township of Blandford, in the County of Oxford, for a "Horizontal SAWING MACHINE for cross-cutting logs of wood." Quebec, dated 20th January, 1855.

No. 495—McBETH, (*B.,*) of the Township of South Dorchester, in the County of Elgin, for a "Longitudinal motioned FANNING MILL." Quebec, dated 3rd February, 1855.

No. 496—COWING, (*H.,*) of the City of Toronto, in the County of York, for "Certain improvements upon MACHINERY." Quebec, dated 8th February, 1855.

No. 497—PINGLE, (*J.,*) of the Township of Markham, in the County of York, for a "POTATO DIGGER." Quebec, dated 8th February, 1855.

No. 498—ROBINSON, (*L.,*) of the Town of Sandwich, in the County of Essex, and WOODBRIDGE, (*J.,*) for a "Safety LEVER BUCKLE." Quebec, dated 13th March, 1855.

No. 499—McDOUGALL, (*J.,*) of the City of Toronto, in the County of York, for a "COOKING and BOILING Apparatus." Quebec, dated 6th March, 1855.

No. 500—FOX, (*Thos. S.,*) of the Town of Prescott, in the County of Grenville, for a "Self-acting apparatus applicable to Locomotive ENGINES and Railroad Cars, for making and adjusting their own tracks with safety upon Railroads, commonly called Switching." Quebec, dated 6th March, 1855.

No. 501—ANDERSON, (*A.,*) of the Township of Markham, in the County of York, for an "Improved CULTIVATOR." Quebec, dated 6th March, 1855.

No. 502—PALMER, (*A.,*) of the City of Toronto, in the County of York, for a "New and useful REAPING Machine." Quebec, dated 13th March, 1855.

No. 503—MARKLE, (*H.,*) of the Township of East Flamboro', in the County of Wentworth, for a "New and improved Double DASHER CHURN." Quebec, dated 15th March, 1855.

No. 504—PETCH, (*Charles,*) of the Town of Port Hope, in the County of Durham, Assignee of Reuben P. Benton, of the City of Toronto, for "Improvements in machinery for manufacturing Waggon Spokes and other articles irregular in their form." Quebec, dated 22nd March, 1855.

No. 505—ATKINSON, (J.,) of Pine Grove, in the Township of Vaughan, in the County of York, for an "Improvement upon the Drill and Broad-cast Sowing Machine." Quebec, dated 22nd March, 1855.

No. 506—CRAWFORD, (D.,) of the City of Toronto, in the County of York, for "Improved machinery for Filling Steam Boilers with Water." Quebec, dated 24th March, 1855.

No. 507—EGAN, (M.,) of the Town of Niagara, in the County of Lincoln, for a "New and improved method of oiling Car Journals." Quebec, dated 27th March, 1855.

No. 508—DARLING, (S.,) of the Village of Dunnville, in the County of Haldimand, for "The art of raising sunken vessels or other objects, by means of Buoys and Weights." Quebec, dated 5th April, 1855.

No. 509—STEERS, (A.,) of the City of Toronto, in the County of York, for a "New and improved method of manufacturing the Dye, Saccharine Salts, or extracts of vegetable substances, without the usual evaporation." Quebec, dated 21st April, 1855.

No. 510—STEERS, (A.,) of the City of Toronto, in the County of York, for a "New and improved method of Quick Tanning." Quebec, dated 20th April, 1855.

No. 511—DORION, (Charles,) of the Parish of St. Laurent, in the District of Montreal, for a "New and improved method of constructing Cutters, for the purpose of racing." Quebec, dated 10th April, 1855.

No. 512—WILLIAMS, (J.,) of the City of Montreal, for a "New and useful improvement in the blast of Locomotive Engines." Quebec, dated 21th April, 1855.

No. 513—MORSE, (S.,) of the Town of Milton, in the County of Halton, for an "Improved Plough." Quebec, dated 28th April, 1853.

No. 514—HOLBORN, (W.,) of the Village of Streetsville, in the County of Peel, for a "Washing Machine." Quebec, dated 28th April, 1855.

No. 515—JAMES, (J.,) and DENNIS, (J.,) of the Township of Whitchurch, in the County of York, for a "Washing Machine." Quebec, dated 4th May, 1855.

No. 516—YOUNG, (J. B.,) BROWN, (R. S.,) and DAVIS, (H.,) of the City of Hamilton, for a "New and useful invention for propelling Boats against the wind and in all directions with the same wind." Quebec, dated 9th May, 1855.

No. 517—HUNGERFORD, (E. B.,) of the Township of Westminster, in the County of Middlesex, for a "Cast-iron fastener for the putting together of posts and rails of Bedsteads." Quebec, dated 8th May, 1855.

No. 518—OGDEN, (J. G.,) of the Town of Three Rivers, for a "New and useful improvement in the construction of Water Wheels." Quebec, dated 15th May, 1855.

No. 519—BOWNAN, (W.,) of the City of Hamilton, for "A new and useful mode of constructing Railway Car Wheels." Quebec, dated 15th May, 1855,

No. 520—LACROIX, (N.,) of the City of Montreal, for "A new and improved Water Wheel called 'Turbine Helicoide.'" Quebec, dated 10th August, 1855.

No. 521—BOWMAN, (W.,) of the City of Hamilton, for "A new and useful improvement in the construction of Railway Cars." Quebec, dated 12th January, 1855.

No. 522—FITZPATRICK, (W.,) of the City of Montreal, for "New and useful improvements in Nail Machine Feeders." Quebec, dated 22nd March, 1855.

No. 523—JEWELL, (H.,) of the City of Quebec, for "A new and useful machine for picking Oakum." Quebec, dated 22nd March, 1855.

No. 524—COLE, (A. D.,) of the Town of Sherbrooke, in the District of St. Francis, for "A new and useful Water Wheel." Quebec, dated 10th April, 1855.

No. 525—HOOD, (Thomas D.,) of the City of Montreal, for "A new and improved method of constructing that part of the Pianoforte called the Hopper." Quebec, dated 10th August, 1855.

No. 526—POOLER, (R.,) of the City of Quebec, for "A new and useful improvement in the construction of a breech-loading FIRE ARM, either rifled or smooth bored." Quebec, dated 4th June, 1855.

No. 527—NIBLOCK, (W.,) Township of Elizabethtown, in the County of Leeds, for " An Improvement in the manner of constructing HORSE RAKES for raking hay." Quebec, dated 26th May, 1855.

No. 528—LEE, (J. P.,) of Niagara, in the County of Lincoln, for a " Round Rotary or Circular KNITTING LOOM." Quebec, dated 28th May, 1855.

No. 529—McDOUGALL, (R.,) of the City of Toronto, in the County of York, for an " Improved OIL BOX for oiling axles of Rail Car Wheels." Quebec, dated 8th June, 1855.

No. 530—RODIER, (Charles S.,) of the City of Montreal, for a " New and useful machine for SAWING WOOD." Quebec, dated 10th April, 1855.

No. 531—BARNES, (J.,) of the Village of Oakville, in the County of Halton, for a " Reciprocal acting PUMP." Quebec, dated 14th June, 1855.

No. 532—YOUNG, (J. B.,) BROWN, (R. S.,) DAVIS, (H.,) all in the City of Hamilton, for a " Self-opening RAILWAY GATE." Quebec, dated 14th June, 1855.

No. 533—FELL, (J.,) of the Township of Augusta, in the County of Grenville, one of the United Counties of Leeds and Grenville, for a " SEED MACHINE for the purpose of judiciously sowing clover, grass or other small seeds." Quebec, dated 7th July, 1855.

No. 534—DRISCOLL, (W.,) of the Township of Montague, in the County of Lanark, for a " New and useful BUTTER CHURN." Quebec, dated 7th July, 1855.

No. 535—MIGHT, (R.,) of the Village of Millbrook, in the Township of Cavan, in the County of Durham, for a " Portable vibrating and self-acting circular SAWING MACHINE." Quebec, dated 25th July, 1855.

No. 536—HIGLEY, (P. R.,) of the Village of Oshawa, in the County of Ontario, for an " Improved CARRIAGE SPRING." Quebec, dated 7th July, 1855.

No. 537—MURDOCH, (P.,) of the Village of Ancaster, in the County of Wentworth, for an " Improvement in AXLES and SPRINGS for Carriages." Quebec, dated 21st August, 1855.

No. 538—FORBES, (J. W.,) of the Village of Dunnville, in the County of Haldimand, for a " Self-acting and Self-adjusting RAILROAD SWITCH, and Alarm and Register." Quebec, dated 1st September, 1855.

No. 539—MURDOCH, (P.,) of the Village of Ancaster, County of Wentworth, for an " Improvement in the construction of double and single TREES." Quebec, dated 21st August, 1855.

No. 540—SELLECK, (D.,) of the Town of Prescott, in the County of Grenville, for a " New and useful Improvement in the construction of CHURNS." Quebec, dated 23rd August, 1855.

No. 541—MILLER, (J. J.,) of Dunnville, in the County of Haldimand, for an " Improved RUDDER." Quebec, dated 4th September, 1855.

No. 542—DELANEY, (W.,) of the Town of Port Hope, in the County of Durham, for an " Improved method of constructing the GEARING of Buggies and other Spring Vehicles." Quebec, dated 4th September, 1855.

No. 543—ANDERSON, (A.,) of the Township of Markham, in the County of York, for an " Improved WASHING MACHINE." Quebec, dated 4th September, 1855.

No. 544—DONAGHUE, (J.,) of Chippawa, in the County of Welland, for a " New and useful Improvement in the SLAB, PLATE PILLAR and COLUMN, usually placed at graves in memory of the dead." Quebec, dated 5th September, 1855.

No. 545—OATES, (Richard H.,) of the City of Toronto, in the County of York, for " An Instantaneous REEFER." Quebec, dated 5th September, 1855.

No. 546—OILL, (J.,) of the Town of St. Catharines, in the County of Lincoln, for " Improvements in the machinery of REAPING and MOWING MACHINES." Quebec, dated 6th September, 1855.

No. 547—DUNN, (J.,) of the City of Montreal, in the District of Montreal, for a " New and improved method of constructing alarms or signals, to be called DUNN'S AIR WHISTLE." Quebec, dated 12th September, 1855.

No. 548—CLARKE, (J. P.,) of the City of Toronto, in the County of York, for a " New Keyed

Musical Instrument named the "HYALIENA or GLASS ORGAN." Quebec, dated 18th September, 1855.

No. 549—FULLER (*Thomas*,) of the City of Toronto, in the County of York, for an "Improved PLOUGH." Quebec, dated 18th September, 1855.

No. 550—TAYLOR, (*J.*,) of the City of Toronto, in the County of York, for a "New method of manufacturing PRINTING PAPER from the straw of wheat, oats and rye, or from any other kind of straw." Quebec, dated 19th September, 1855.

No. 551—BRIGGS, (*G. C.*,) of the City of Hamilton, in the County of Wentworth, for an "Improved WASHING MACHINE." Quebec, dated 19th September, 1855.

No. 552—COE, (*Charles W.*,) of the Township of Sandwich, in the County of Essex, for a "Machine for DRILLING HOLES (and other operations) in Metals." Quebec, dated 19th September, 1855.

No. 553—GOSLIN, (*N. H.*,) and SELLECK, (*D.*,) of the Town of Prescott, in the County of Grenville, for an "Improvement in the construction of WASHING MACHINES." Quebec, dated 20th September, 1855.

No. 554—WILLSON, (*F. G.*,) of Ontario, in the County of Wentworth, for an "Improved HOT AIR FURNACE, Safety Register and system of Ventilation." Quebec, 21st September, 1855.

No. 555—MILLER, (*J.*,) of the Town of Picton, in the County of Prince Edward, for a "Machine for accelerating the process of tanning [HIDES." Quebec, dated 27th September, 1855.

No. 556—WIGGINS (*Thomas*,) of the Township of Eaton, in the County of Compton, for a "CHEESE PRESS." Toronto, dated 21st November, 1855.

No. 557—MARSH, (*J. F.*,) of the Town of Port Sarnia, for "Improvements in the construction of PLOUGHS." Quebec, dated 25th September, 1855.

No. 558—SMART, (*J.*,) of the Town of Brockville, for an "Improvement in the construction of PLATFORM SCALES." Quebec, dated 25th September, 1855.

No. 559—STAINTHORP, (*J.*,) of Stamford, in the County of Willard, for an "Improvement in machinery for the manufacture of CANDLES." Quebec, dated 24th September, 1855.

No. 560—HAMILTON, (*J.*,) of the Town of Peterborough, in the County of Peterborough, for an "Improved CLOTHES MANGLE." Quebec, dated 27th September, 1855.

No. 561—DENNIS, (*J.*,) of the Township of Whitchurch, in the County of York, for "Improvements in the construction of CHURNS." Toronto, dated 21st November, 1855.

No. 562—PORTER, (*D.*,) of the City of Hamilton, in the County of Wentworth, for an "Improved WASHING MACHINE." Toronto, 20th November, 1855.

No. 563—OILL, (*J.*,) of the Town of St. Catharines. in the County of Lincoln, for "New and useful improvements in the construction of MOWING and REAPING MACHINES." Toronto, dated 21st November, 1855.

No. 564—CONDELL, (*J.*,) of KEMPTVILLE, in the United Counties of Leeds and Grenville, for a "New plan or principle for the construction of an artificial LIMB." Toronto, 21st November, 1855.

No. 565—MATTHEW, (*D.*,) of the Township of Saltfleet, in the County of Wentworth, for "Improvements in the construction of LOCOMOTIVE ENGINES." Toronto, 21st November, 1855.

No. 566—FREEMAN, (*D.*,) of the Township of Burford, in the County of Brant, for a "New nd useful improvement in the manufacture of CARRIAGES." Toronto, dated 21st November 1855.

No. 567—FULLER, (*Thomas J.*,) of the City of Toronto, in the County of York, for a "KNITTING MACHINE." Toronto, dated 30th November, 1855.

No. 568—HULBERT, (*S.*,) of the Town of Prescott, in the County of Grenville, for an "Agricultural PLOUGH." Toronto, dated 3rd December, 1855.

No. 569—DEAN, (*Cyrus*,) of the City of Hamilton, for a "New and useful machines for making use of the water heat from any FURNACE." Toronto, dated 3rd December, 1855.

No. 570—KENDALL, (*A.*,) of the Village of Windsor, in the County of Essex, for a "New machine for making SHINGLES." Toronto, dated 3rd December, 1855.

No. 571—BEAR, (J.,) of the Township of Whitchurch, in the County of York, for an "Improvement in the manufacture of CHURNS." Toronto, dated 3rd December, 1855.

No. 572—HIBBERD, (A. A.,) of the Village of Oakville, in the County of Halton, for a "New and useful mode of conveying water into STEAM BOILERS." Toronto, dated 4th December, 1855.

No. 573—BINGHAM, (J.,) of the Township of Norwich, in the County of Oxford, for a "New and useful improvement in the manufacture of PLOUGHS." Toronto, dated 4th December, 1855.

No. 574—WILLARD, (H. E.,) of the City of Montreal, for a "New and improved method of scouring and polishing STONE, MARBLE and IRON." Toronto, dated 10th December, 1855.

No. 575—HAYDEN, (J. B.,) of Brantford, in the County of Brant, for a "Metallic improved Box and fastening for CARRIAGE WHEELS." Toronto, dated 15th December, 1855.

No. 576—McLELLAN, (J.,) of the Village of Windsor, in the Township of Sandwich, in the County of Essex, for a "New machine for the repairing of Iron rails and for Cars and Carriages to run upon RAILWAYS." Toronto, dated 15th December, 1855.

No. 577—BERGUE, (Charles L. A. de,) of the City of Montreal, for an "Apparatus for acting on WATER and other liquids so as to force, displace, or propel the same, or a body floating thereon." Toronto, dated 10th December, 1855.

No. 578—MANNING, (W.,) of the City of Montreal, for a "New and improved Wash Tub for clothes, denominated 'THE MONTREAL WASH TUB.'" Toronto, dated 10th December, 1855.

No. 579—BRIGHT, (L.,) of Brampton, in the County of Peel, for "Certain improvements in a WASHING MACHINE." Toronto, dated 15th December, 1855.

No. 580—ROSS, (J.,) of the Township of Nichol, in the County of Wellington, for an "Improved Leverage Power FIRE ENGINE." Toronto, dated 15th December, 1855.

No. 581—BOWEN, (P.,) of the Village of Port Ryerse, in the County of Norfolk, for a "Triple action vertical SCOURER and SEPARATOR for cleansing Wheat and other Grain." Toronto, dated 24th December, 1855.

No. 582—WATAROUS, (C. H.,) of the Town of Brantford, in the County of Brant, for "Useful improvements in the construction of Steam and Water Circular SAW MILLS." Toronto, dated 24th December, 1855.

No. 583—TANNER, (W.,) of Smithville, in the County of Lincoln, for "Improvements in the construction of Steam Engine BOILERS." Toronto, dated 5th January, 1856.

No. 584—PICAULT, (P. E.,) of the City of Montreal, for "A Medical Preparation called by him 'THE NURSE'S and MOTHER'S TREASURE." Toronto, dated 17th January, 1856.

No. 585—WAUDBY, (H.,) of the Village of Thornhill, in the County of York, for a "New Centre Force and Suction PUMP." Toronto, dated 17th January, 1856.

No. 586—TRUDEAU, (T.,) of the City of Montreal, for an "Improvement in the construction and mode of connecting RAILWAY CARRIAGES." Toronto, dated 17th January, 1856.

No. 587—ORD, (R.,) of the Town of Niagara, in the County of Lincoln, for "New and useful improvements in a machine for screwing BOLTS." Toronto, dated 23rd January, 1856.

No. 588—McINTOSH, (A.,) of the City of Toronto, County of York, for "New improvements in the composition of CEMENT for Roofing Houses, &c." Toronto, dated 5th February, 1856.

No. 589—ADAMS, (W. F.,) of the City of Toronto, in the County of York, for a "New semi-revolving cylinder STEAM ENGINE." Toronto, dated 11th February, 1856.

No. 590—WESTMAN, (J.,) of the City of Toronto, in the County of York, for a "New method of raising FRUIT TREES from the parent tree, without grafting or budding." Toronto, dated 11th February, 1856.

No. 591—ROSS, (J.,) of the Township of Nichol, in the County of Wellington, for "New improvements in the construction of PUMPS or FIRE ENGINES." Toronto, dated 11th February, 1856.

No. 592—TATE, (Charles M.,) of the City of Montreal, for a "New and improved method of constructing Links or couplings for Railway Carriages, called by him TATE'S SAFETY LINK." Toronto, dated 5th February, 1856.

No. 593—PORTER, (*D.*,) of the City of Hamilton, County of Wentworth, for a "Self-acting Rail Road or ENTRANCE GATE." Toronto, dated 15th February, 1856.

No. 594—MOFFATT, (*A.*,) of the Parish of St. Roch, in the County of Quebec, for a "SPRING for closing doors outside and inside." Toronto, dated 15th February, 1856.

No. 595—TANNER, (*W.*,) of Smithville, in the County of Lincoln, for "Improvements in the construction of STEAM ENGINE BOILERS." Toronto, dated 19th February, 1856.   •

No. 596—CHOATE, (*W. B.*,) of the Village of Galt, in the County of Waterloo, for an "Improvement in the manufacture of LANTERNS." Toronto, dated 17th January, 1856.

No. 597—LEMON, (*Charles*,) of the Township of Augusta, in the County of Grenville, for a "New and useful method of casting the mould Boards for PLOUGHS." Toronto, dated 23rd February, 1856.

No. 598—HAWKINS, (*F. R.*,) of the Town of Dundas, in the County of Wentworth, for "Improvements upon and in the construction of IDE'S GRAIN DRILL." Toronto, dated 23rd February, 1856.

No. 599—PORTER, (*D.*,) of the City of Hamilton, in the County of Wentworth, for a "Moving and self-acting CATTLE GUARD for Railway purposes." Toronto, dated 23rd February, 1856.

No. 600 - BROWN, (*J.*,) of the City of Toronto, in the County of York, for a "New OVEN for Baking purposes." Toronto, dated 23rd February, 1856.

No. 601—GOODENAW, (*M. L.*,) of the Township of Grantham, in the County of Lincoln, for a "New art for manufacturing PAINTS from a vegetable deposit of Bog Iron Ore and from Hydraulic Cement Rock." Toronto, dated 23rd February, 1856.

No. 602—CULL, (*J. A.*,) of the City of Toronto, for an "Improvement in the preparation of INDIAN CORN for the purposes of distillation." Toronto, dated 29th February, 1856.

No. 603—CULL, (*J. A.*,) of the City of Toronto, for an "Improvement in the manufacture of STARCH from Indian Corn." Toronto, dated 29th February, 1856.

No. 604—GOULD, (*Charles H.*,) of the City of Montreal, for an "Improved PLANING MACHINE." Toronto, dated 19th February, 1856.

No. 605—HEDLEY, (*E.*,) of the City of Toronto, in the County of York, for a "New and improved method of constructing SHINGLE MACHINES." Toronto, dated 5th March, 1856.

No. 606—WESTMAN, (*J.*,) of the City of Toronto, in the County of York, for "A Double action WASHING MACHINE." Toronto, dated 6th March, 1856.

No. 607—HUGILL, (*J.*,) of the Township of Beverly, in the County of Wentworth, for a "DIAGONAL WATER WHEEL." Toronto, dated 12th March, 1856.

No. 608—HICKOK, (*S. S.*,) of the Town of Whitby, in the County of Ontario, for "Certain improvements in the construction of CLOTHES HORSES." Toronto, dated 12th March, 1856.

No. 609—PETTIT, (*S.*,) of the Township of Pickering, in the County of Ontario, for a "Circular Shaving STRAW CUTTER." Toronto, dated 12th March, 1856.

No. 610—MUNSON, (*A. E.*,) of the Town of Cobourg, in the County of Northumberland, for "Certain improvements in the construction of CARRIAGES and other four-wheeled Vehicles." Toronto, dated 18th March, 1856.

No. 611—GOULD, (*D.*,) of the Township of Richmond, in the County of Lennox, for a "New and improved pressed BRICK for Building purposes." Dated 12th March, 1856.

No. 612—RITCHIE, (*Thomas*,) of the Township of Dumfries, in the County of Waterloo, for an "Improvement in the DRAFT applied to reaping, mowing or other Machines." Toronto, dated 20th March, 1856.

No. 613—FLANIGAN, (*J.*,) of the Town of Prescott, in the County of Grenville, for a "New and improved method of ventilating Rail Road CARS, STEAM BOATS, and other closely covered and rapidly moving vehicles, and of expelling at the same time cinders, smoke, dust and other disagreeables." Toronto, dated 12th March, 1856.

No. 614—HUFF, (*H.*,) of the Town of Cobourg, in the County of Northumberland, for a "New and useful machine for dovetailing in CABINET MAKING." Toronto, dated 27th March, 1856.

No. 615—FOWLER, (*H.*,) of the Town of Belleville, in the County of Hastings, for a " Reciprocating ENGINE." Toronto, dated 27th March, 1856.

No. 616—HEADLY, (*J. H.*,) of the Township of Walpole, in the County of Haldimand, for a " New method of manufacturing marbleized GRANITE." Toronto, dated 27th March, 1856.

No. 617—McLAUGHLIN, (*S.*,) of the City of Quebec, for a " Self-acting Railway collision PREVENTER." Toronto, dated 5th February, 1856.

No. 618—PHELPS, (*W.*,) of the Village of Brighton, in the County of Northumberland, for a " New and improved method of constructing BEE HIVES, called the Union BEE HIVE." Toronto, dated 5th April, 1856.

No. 619—SIDEY, (*G.*,) of the Village of Thorold, in the County of Welland, for a " New and useful machinery known as a horizontal revolving WIND POWER." Toronto, dated 5th April, 1856.

No. 620—DAVIS, (*J.*,) of the City of Hamilton, in the County of Wentworth, for a " Slabbing and rolling gang of circular saws for SAWING LUMBER or round logs into Boards or Planks." Toronto, dated 5th April, 1856.

No. 621—MORSE, (*Thomas G.*,) of the Village of Windsor, in the County of Essex, for an "Improved atmospheric CHURN." Toronto, dated 9th April, 1856.

No. 622—OLIVER, (*J. A.*,) of the Township of Westminster, in the County of Middlesex, for a " CORN PLANTER, or machine for Sowing Corn." Toronto, dated 14th April, 1856.

No. 623—PETTET, (*S.*,) of the Township of Pickering, in the County of Ontario, for a " Horizontal Rotary SHINGLE MACHINE." Toronto, dated 14th April, 1856.

No. 624—BLODGETT, (*S. S.*,) of the Town of Brockville, in the County of Leeds, for an " Improved OVEN for Baking and Cooking Meats or other articles." Toronto, dated 16th April, 1856.

No. 625—GILBERT, (*E. E.*,) of the City of Montreal, for a " New and improved machine for sawing, called by him Gilbert's STEAM SAWYER." Toronto, dated 22nd April, 1856.

No. 626—GOULD, (*Charles H.*,) of the City of Montreal, for a " New tension spring for CARRIAGES." Toronto, dated 24th April, 1856.

No. 627—HORNING, (*L.*,) of Simcoe, in the County of Norfolk, for a " CORN PLANTER, or Machine for sowing Corn." Toronto, dated 28th April, 1856.

No. 628—GILL, (*W.*,) of the Town of Dundas, in the County of Wentworth, for an " Improvement on STEAM ENGINES by variable cut off and expansion Gear for stationary or Marine Engines." Toronto, dated 30th April, 1856.

No. 629—LENT, (*J.*,) of the Township of Hamilton, in the County of Northumberland, for a " Machine for digging and picking POTATOES." Toronto, dated 30th April, 1856.

No. 630—MILLICHAMP, (*Thomas,*) of the City of Toronto, in the County of York, for an " Improved TAP for water and other liquids." Toronto, dated 12th May, 1856.

No. 631—McMURCHY, (*Thomas,*) of the Village of Weston, in the County of York, for a " Hot or Cold CYLINDER MANGLE." Toronto, dated 14th May, 1856.

No. 632—TOMKINS, (*W. G.*,) of the City of Hamilton, in the County of Wentworth, for a " Process for withdrawing the SAP from trees recently felled, and rendering the same both seasoned and dry in a very brief time, and in case of need imbuing the body of the tree with coloring matter, or inserting therein chemical substances in liquid form to prevent DRY-ROT, decay, or render the tree imcombustible." Toronto, dated 16th May, 1856.

No. 633—ANDERSON, (*A* ,) of the Township of Markham, in the County of York, for an " Improved revolving HAY RAKE and PEA PULLER." Toronto, dated 14th May, 1856.

No. 634—THOMPSON, (*J. M.*,) of the Township of Esquesing, in the County of Holton, for a " New and improved method of hanging a MULLY SAW." Toronto, dated 23rd May, 1856.

No. 635—BAUMAN, (*P.*,) of the Village of Preston, in the County of Waterloo, for an "Improved Portable CIDER MILL and PRESS." Toronto, dated 5th May, 1856.

No. 636—McFADDEN, (*R. C.*,) of the Township of Chatham, in the County of Kent, for certain ";Improvements upon a BOOT CRAMPING MACHINE." Toronto, dated 19th June, 1856.

No. 637—LAUNSBURY, (*R.*,) of the Township of Grimsby, in the County of Lincoln, for a "New and useful Improvement in CORN PLANTERS." Toronto, dated 19th June, 1856.

No. 638—HOWARD, (*W.*,) of the Village of Streetsville, in the County of York, for certain "Improvements on the concave HORSE SHOE." Toronto, dated 27th June, 1856.

No. 639—BRUCE, (*A. C.*,) of Ellen Morris, in the Count of Brant, for a "New CULTIVATOR." Toronto, dated 27th June, 1856.

No. 640—RICE, (*I. O.*,) of the Village of Dunnville, in the County of Haldimand, for "New and useful improvements in the manufacture of Springs for CARRIAGES." Toronto, dated 27th June, 1856.

No. 641—EMERSON, (*R.*,) of the Township of Norwich, in the County of Oxford, for an "Eccentric PRESS which can be prepared to apply as a cider press, a cheese press, &c." Toronto, dated 2nd July, 1856.

No. 642—SPENCER, (*E.*,) of the Town of Brockville, in the County of Leeds, for a "New and useful improvement in the manner of constructing common STOVES." Toronto, dated 2nd July, 1856.

No. 643—MALLERD, (W.,) of the City of Toronto, for an "Improved Steam Boiler FEEDER, a safety steam alarm and water indicator." Toronto, dated 10th July, 1856.

No. 644—DAVIS, (*N.*,) of the Village of Smithville, in the County of Lincoln, for a "Self-regulating SAW MILL." Toronto, dated 15th July, 1856.

No. 645—SHURTLEFF, (*J.*,) of the Town of Whitby, in the County of Ontario, for an "Improved stove pipe rim, called by him a FIRE PROOF ventilating Stove Pipe Rim." Toronto, dated 10th July, 1856.

No. 646—KILLAM, (*H.*,) of the Township of Townsend, in the County of Norfolk, for an "Improvement in the construction of PLOUGH CUTTERS." Toronto, dated 15th July, 1856.

No. 647—KILLAM, (*H.*,) of the Township of Townsend, in the County of Norfolk, for an "Improvement in the construction of wheeled cultivating GANG PLOUGHS." Toronto, dated 15th July, 1856.

No. 648—BURROWES, (*Thomas B.*,) of the City of Hamilton, in the County of Wentworth, for a "New Hydraulic Momentum and Gravitation WATER WHEEL." Toronto, dated 17th July, 1856.

No. 649—ADAMS, (*R.*,) of the City of Toronto, in the County of York, for a "New and improved STOVE for cooking and other purposes." Toronto, dated 25th July, 1856.

No. 650—WILCOX, (*A.*,) of the Township of Norwich, in the County of Oxford, for an "Improved method of constructing FRAMES for Barnes, Dwelling Houses and other Edifices." Toronto, dated 25th July, 1856.

No. 651—HARE, (*J. D.*,) of the Town of Dundas, in the County of Wentworth, for a "New and improved method of constructing WASHING MACHINES." Toronto, dated 8th August, 1856.

No. 652—BRANDER, (*W.*,) of the Village of Ingersoll, in the County of Oxford, for an "Improved Portable frame to be attached to a plunge CHURN." Toronto, dated 27th August, 1856.

No. 653—SUPPER, (*E. E.*,) of the Town of Cayuga, in the County of Haldimand, for a "SHINGLE MACHINE." Toronto, dated 27th August, 1856.

No. 654—ORD, (*D.*,) of the Town of Niagara, in the County of Lincoln, for an "Improved Rail Road CAR BRAKE." Toronto, dated 27th August, 1856.

No. 655—FITZMORRIS, (*N. E.*,) of the Township of Sandwich, in the County of Essex, for a "New and useful mode of lubricating (otherwise a new and improved mode of oiling,) the journals of Railway AXLES." Toronto, dated 27th August, 1856.

No. 656—BUCKNAM, (*J. A.*,) of the Township of Markham, in the County of York, for a "New and useful CLOTHES TREE." Toronto, dated 27th August, 1856.

No. 657—SARGENT, (*G. A.*,) of Bloomfield, in the County of Prince Edward, for an improved Loom, to be called the VICTORIA LOOM." Toronto, dated 29th August, 1856.

No. 658—BUTEAU, (*A*,) of the Parish of Berthier, in the County of Montmagny, for a "New mode of catching PORPOISES." Toronto, dated 29th August, 1856.

No. 659—ROMAINE, (*R.*,) of the Town of Peterborough, in the County of Peterborough, for the introduction into Canada of a "French Machine for BENDING Wood." Toronto, dated 13th June, 1856.

No. 660—TAYLOR, (*James*,) and TAYLOR, (*John*,) of the City of Toronto, in the County of York, for an "Improved Fire Proof Safe, to be called TAYLOR'S Provincial Salamander Fire Proof Safe." Toronto, dated 2nd September, 1856.

No. 661—THOMPSON, (*James*,) of the City of Toronto, in the County of York, for a "New WATER WHEEL." Toronto, dated 12th September, 1856.

No. 662 – *Cancelled.*

No. 663—WATSON, (*J.*,) of the Township of Norwich, in the County of Oxford, for certain "Improvements on PLOUGHS." Toronto, dated 19th September, 1856.

No. 664—WATSON, (*J.*,) of the City of Toronto, in the County of York, for the "Art of manufacturing Sugar and Spirit out of the Juice of Bulbous Roots, and converting a residue of the distillation into POTASH." Toronto, dated 19th September, 1856.

No. 665—STEVENS, (*Charles*,) of the Township of Compton, in the County of Compton, for an "Improved HORSE RAKE." Toronto, dated 23rd October, 1856.

No. 666—NORTON, (*A.*,) of the Township of Barnston, for a "New and Improved GRAIN SOWER." Toronto, dated 24th October, 1856.

No. 667—DUNN, (*Patrick*,) and SORNBERGER, (*S.*,) of the City of Montreal, for "New and useful Improvements in the manufacture of Nail Machine FEEDERS." Toronto, dated 24th October, 1856.

No. 668—PARSONS, (*J.*,) of the City of Toronto, in the County of York, for an "Improved machine for SHEARING SHEEP." Toronto, dated 9th October, 1856.

No. 669—PARSONS, (*J.*,) of the City of Toronto, in the County of York, for an "Apparatus for Cooking, Bakers' Ovens, drying and roasting Malt, &c., &c., &c." Toronto, dated 29th October, 1856.

No. 670—*Error in old book.*

No. 671—STANFIELD, (*Thomas*,) of Etobicoke, in the County of York, for a "COOKING STOVE with a Grate." Toronto, dated 29th October, 1856.

No. 672—COPP, (*W. J.*,) of the City of Hamilton, in the County of Wentworth, for an "Improved LINING for Refrigerators, Water Coolers and House Stove Pipe Rims." Toronto, dated 29th October, 1856.

No. 673—ROMAINE, (*R.*,) of the Town of Peterborough, in the County of Peterborough, in our said Province, for an "Improved machine for bending WOOD or other substances." Toronto, dated 29th October, 1856.

No. 674—GOING, (*H.*,) of Wolfe Island, in the County of Frontenac, for a "SPEED WHEEL and return or oscillating power." Toronto, dated 29th October, 1856.

No. 675—FORBES, (*D.*,) of the City of Toronto, in the County of York, for a "New composition for ROOFING." Toronto, dated 29th October, 1856.

No. 676—McCUAIG, (*J.*,) of the City of Toronto, in the County of York, for a "New and useful and improved Machine for Pressing, Smoothing and Shaping BONNETS." Toronto, dated 29th October, 1856.

No. 677—BURROWES, (*Thomas B.*,) of the City of Hamilton, in the County of Wentworth, for certain "Improvements in the construction of HARROWS." Toronto, dated 29th October, 1856.

No. 678—TOMKINS, (*W. G.*,) of the City of Hamilton, in the County of Wentworth, for certain "Improvements in his Patent process for withdrawing the SAP from Trees newly felled, &c." Toronto, dated 29th October, 1856.

No. 679—TOMKINS, (*W. G.*,) of the City of Hamilton, in the County of Wentworth, for certain "Improvements in grinding WHEAT and other Grains." Toronto, dated 29th October, 1856.

No. 680—GOULD, (*J. L.*,) of the Village of Uxbridge, in the County of Ontario, for a "New and improved CHURN." Toronto, dated 7th November, 1856.

No. 681—CARLETON, (G. W.,) of the Town of Cobourg, in the County of Northumberland, for a "SOUND TELEGRAPH." Toronto, dated 7th November, 1856.

No. 682—McVICAR, (D.,) of the City of London, in the County of Middlesex, for "Improvements on Brown's Patent STRAW CUTTER." Toronto, dated 7th November, 1856.

No. 683—FITZGIBBON, (A.,) of the City of Montreal, for an "Improved form of RAIL for Railway Tracks or for Tramways." Toronto, dated 20th November, 1856.

No. 684—AUBIN, (N.,) of the City of Quebec, and now of the City of Toronto, for a "New retort for generating illuminating GAS from saw dust, rosin, or other materials." Toronto, dated 10th December, 1856.

No. 685—WOOD, (G. W.,) and BEEMER, (J.,) of the Township of Windham, of Townsend, in the County of Norfolk, for an "Improvement in the art of taking and finishing Portraits and Pictures in Oil and Water colour PAINTS." Toronto, dated 31st October, 1856.

No. 686—PHILLIPS, (J.,) of the Township of York, in the County of York, for a "Machine for stuffing SAUSAGES." Toronto, dated 26th November, 1856.

No. 687—MITCHELL, (R.,) and COCKBURN, (A. F.,) of the City of Montreal, for a "New and improved method of constructing safety valves for HYDRANTS." Toronto, dated 11th December, 1856.

No. 688—MILLS, (I.,) of the Township of Flamboro' West, in the County of Wentworth, for a "New and valuable Fire and Water Proof TILE for covering Buildings." Toronto, dated 17th December, 1856.

No. 689—GOULD, (J. L.,) of the Village of Uxbridge, in the County of Ontario, for a "New method of cutting off the tops and digging TURNIPS by machinery and Horse power." Toronto, dated 17th December, 1856.

No. 690—SHEARMAN, (S.,) of the Village of Vankleckhill, in the County of Prescott, for a certain "New and useful Machine for the manufacture of BRICKS." Toronto, dated 19th December, 1856.

No. 691—BEACH, (A.,) and BEACH, (F. B.,) of the Township of South Gower, in the United Counties of Leeds and Grenville, for a "Horse power for drilling in the ROCK for Wells and other purposes." Toronto, dated 17th December, 1856.

No. 692—FULLER, (Thomas,) of the Village of Oshawa, in the County of Ontario, for a "New method of supporting School House SEATS and DESKS." Toronto, dated 4th December, 1856.

No. 693—DOYLE, (J. P.,) of the City of Montreal, in the District of Montreal, for "The Effluvia Sewer Grate, or STENCH TRAP." Toronto, dated 16th January, 1857.

No. 694—WAIT, (B.,) of Etobicoke, in the County of York, for a "CYLINDRICAL SAW AUGER, for boring Wooden tubes for Pumps, Water Courses, &c." Toronto, dated 19th January, 1857.

No. 695—BOTTOMLEY, (Thomas,) of Owen Sound, in the County of Grey, for a "New improved and useful method of Building Fire and Water Proof HOUSES and other structures." Toronto, dated 20th January, 1857.

No. 696—KELLUM, (J.,) of the Township of Townsend, in the County of Norfolk, for a "New improvement in the art of grinding or polishing PLOUGH CASTINGS." Toronto, dated 14th January, 1857.

No. 697—MAGEE, (W. H.,) of the Village of Merrickville, in the County of Grenville, one of the United Counties of Leeds and Grenville, for a "New and improved PLOUGH." Toronto, dated 20th January, 1857.

No. 698—GORTSHORE, (J.,) of the Town of Dundas, in the County of Wentworth, for certain "Improvements in the construction of SMUT MACHINES." Toronto, dated 21st January, 1857.

No. 699—McFARLAND, (Tarbell, A.,) of the Town of Stratford, in the County of Perth, for a "New Horizontal Iron WIND MILL." Toronto, dated 12th February, 1857.

No. 700—JUDSON, (L.,) of the Township of Yonge, in the County of Leeds, for a "New and useful method for making the TEETH for Horse Rakes." Toronto, dated 12th February, 1857.

No. 701—MESSER, (R.,) of the City of Toronto, in the County of York, for a "Self-acting Coupling for Railway CARRIAGES." Toronto, dated 12th February, 1857.

No. 702—GILL, (W.,) of the Village of Waterdown, in the County of Wentworth, for certain "Improvements in the construction of STEAM ENGINES." Toronto, dated 12th February, 1857.

No. 703—HICKOK, (S. S.,) of the Town of Whitby, in the County of Ontario, for a "New and useful mode of COUPLING Railway Carriages and other Cars." Toronto, dated 12th February, 1857.

No. 704—ODELL, (A.,) of the Village of Bowmanville, in the County of Durham, for a "New and improved method of constructing WASHING MACHINES." Toronto, dated 20th February, 1857.

No. 705—LYMAN, (R.,) of the Village of Orono, in the Township of Clarke, in the County of Durham, for a "SHOE PACK." Toronto, dated 23rd February, 1857.

No. 706—CULL, (J. A.,) of the City of Toronto, in the County of York, for certain "Improvements in the manufacture of Rotary PUMPS." Toronto, dated 23rd February, 1857.

No. 707—HASKIN, (U.,) of the Village of Oshawa, in the County of Ontario, for a "Self-acting cylindrical LATHE." Toronto, dated 23rd February, 1857.

No. 708—HAMILTON, (W.,) of the City of Toronto, in the County of York, for certain "Improved Spring machinery for closing SHOP and other doors." Toronto, dated 17th March, 1857.

No. 709—ELLIS, (J.,) of the Town of Port Hope, in the County of Durham, for a "Cheap unabsorbent, indestructible Building material termed artificial STONE." Toronto, dated 16th March, 1857.

No. 710—WHITNEY, (F. A.,) of the City of Toronto, in the County of York, for a "Rotory FIRE ENGINE." Toronto, dated 19th March, 1857.

No. 711—TOWERS, (Thomas,) of the Town of St. Catharines, in the County of Lincoln, for certain "Improvements in the construction of WINDLASSES for Vessels." Toronto, dated 30th March, 1857.

No. 712—LAFFERTY, (J.,) and JESPER, (E.,) of the City of Toronto, in the County of York, for a "Rotary REAPING and MOWING MACHINE." Toronto, dated 30th March, 1857.

No. 713—GOULD, (J. L., of the Township of Uxbridge, in the County of Ontario, for a "New and improved method of constructing HORSE RAKES." Toronto, dated 30th March, 1857.

No. 714—CLEMENT, (P. B.,) of the Township of Niagara, in the County of Lincoln, for a "New and improved method of constructing HORSE RAKES." Toronto, dated 30th March, 1857.

No. 715—MATTHEWS, (G.,) of the City of Montreal, for a "New Bank note Printing Ink called the Canada Bank Note PRINTING TINT." Toronto, dated 1st April, 1857.

No. 716—LYLE, (W.,) of the Town of Dundas, in the County of Wentworth, for an "Improved WATER WHEEL." Toronto, dated 7th April, 1857.

No. 717—ANDERSON, (A.,) of the City of London, in the County of Middlesex, and RANNEY, (Thomas,) of Adolphus Town, in the County of Lennox, for a "New and improved method of constructing GRIDIRONS." Toronto, dated 7th April, 1857.

No. 718—BINGHAM, (J.,) of the Township of Norwich, County of Oxford, for a "New and useful improvement in the construction of PLOUGHS." Toronto, dated 20th February, 1857.

No. 719—KELLUM, (J.,) of the Township of Townsend, in the County of Norfolk, for a useful improvement on CHURNS." Toronto, dated 7th April, 1857.

No. 720—SHERWOOD, (A.,) of the Town of Merrittville, in the County of Welland, for a "New and useful Article or OVEN for culinary purposes." Toronto, dated 7th April, 1857.

No. 721—CURTIS, (D. T.,) of the Village of Port Perry, in the County of Ontario, for a "New method of clamping frames, &c., by the double action eccentric LEVER CLAMP." Toronto, dated 7th April, 1857.

No. 722—DENNIS, (J.,) of the Township of Whitechurch, in the County of York, for a "Suction and Lifting PUMP combined." Toronto, dated 15th April, 1857.

No. 723—DENNIS, (J.,) of the Township of Whitechurch, in the County of York, for certain "Improvements in the common wood suction PUMP." Toronto, dated 15th April, 1857.

No. 724—ARCHER, (J.,) and REESLEY, (H.,) both of the City of Toronto, in the County of York, for certain "Improvements in the art of manufacturing Oils, called by them NON-CONGEALING OIL." Toronto, dated 16th April, 1857.

No. 725—HICKOK, (S. S.,) of the Town of Whitby, in the County of Ontario, for an "Improved Wheel Hub, termed Hickock's Improved WHEEL HUB." Toronto, dated 22nd April, 1857.

No. 726—BEVERLY, (H. L.,) of the City of Toronto, in the County of York, for a "New and Improved SHINGLE CUTTING MACHINE." Toronto, dated 28th April, 1857.

No. 727—MIRICK, (W.,) of the Village of Mirickville, in the County of Grenville, for a Wire GRAIN FORK." Toronto, dated 4th May, 1857.

No. 728—CANT, (A.,) and CANT, (J.,) of the Town of Galt, in the County of Waterloo, for a "New moveable SCAFFOLD." Toronto, dated 4th May, 1857.

No. 729—ADAMS, (J.,) of the Township of Hope, in the County of Durham, for a "Double Cylinder Clover THRESHER." Toronto, dated 7th May, 1857.

No. 730—BOTTOMLEY, (Thomas,) of the City of Toronto, in the County of York, for a "Broadcast SOWING MACHINE, for sowing all sorts of Grain and Seeds." Toronto, dated 13th May, 1857.

No. 731—HUDSON, (R. H.,) of the City of Toronto, in the County of York, for a "Self-acting CATCH, or FASTENER for the moveable backs of Chairs, Seats or Sofas, in Railway Cars, Steam Boats, &c., &c." Toronto, dated 7th May, 1857.

No. 732—ROBINSON, (Y. W.,) of the City of Hamilton, in the County of Wentworth, for a "Cast Steel Grass or CRADLE SCYTHE." Toronto, dated 7th May, 1857.

No. 733—STONE, (O.,) of the Village of Oshawa, in the County of Ontario, for a "Condensed atmospheric Air Bath, with Purifier and Medicator attached, to be called Stone's Atmospheric AIR BATH." Toronto, dated 12th May, 1857.

No. 734—HASKINS, (U.,) of the Village of Oshawa, in the County of Ontario, for a "New and improved Rotary STEAM ENGINE." Toronto, dated 12th May, 1857.

No. 735—OSGOOD, (H. A.,) of the Township of Niagara, in the County of Lincoln, for an "Improvement on the mode of fastening and securing the seats of Railway CARS." Toronto, dated 12th May, 1857.

No. 736—PTOLEMY, (J.,) of the Township of Saltfleet, in the County of Wentworth, for a "Corn Thrasher or CORN SHELLER." Toronto, dated 18th May, 1857.

No. 737—MARLATT, (H.,) of the Township of Thorold, in the County of Welland, for a "New revolving POWER, to be applied to Swing Bridges, Turn Tables, Revolving Cars, Tread Wheels, &c., &c." Toronto, dated 18th May, 1857.

No. 738—BRESSE, (W.,) of the Town of Brockville, in the County of Leeds, for an "Improved Machine for Raking and loading Hay by HORSE POWER." Toronto, dated 20th May, 1857.

No. 739—BRAID, (A.;) of the City of Hamilton, in the County of Wentforth, for an "Improvement in the Smoke Stacks and Spark Arresters to be used in Locomotive ENGINES." Toronto, dated 18th May, 1857.

No. 740—BERMIER, (H.,) of the Parish of Lotbinère, in the County of Lotbinière, for a "New and improved double STOVE." Toronto, dated 26th May, 1857.

No. 741—GAIGE, (W. W.,) of the Town of Whitby, in the County of Ontario, for a "New process for Tanning HIDES." Toronto, dated 29th May, 1857.

No. 742—WAY, (J. B.,) of the Township of Whitby, in the County of Ontario, for a "New Churn called the DRUM CHURN." Toronto, dated 30th May, 1857.

No. 743—NOBLE, (J.,) of the Town of St. Catharines, in the County of Lincoln, for a "New Revolving ROLLER Box, for Railway Cars, Steam Boats, &c., &c." Toronto, dated 2nd June, 1857.

No. 744—GAGNON, (I. G.,) of the City of Quebec, for an "Apparatus for preventing the

Explosion or Bursting of BOILERS of Steam Vessels from want of Water." Toronto, dated 2nd July, 1857.

No. 745—CLARKE, (J. P.,) of the City of Toronto, in the County of York, for an "Agricultural Implement called the Rotary PULVERIZER." Toronto, dated 20th June, 1857.

No. 746—HEADLEY, (J. H.,) of the Township of Walpole, in the County of Haldimand, for a "New and Improved Rotary Press for pressing Marbleized GRANITE." Toronto, dated 20th June, 1857.

No. 747—HUNTINGTON, of the Township of North Norwich, in the County of Oxford, for a "New and useful Improvement in the construction of Ploughs, termed the GAIN TWIST." Toronto, dated 20th June, 1857.

No. 748—IVORY, (W.,) of the Township of Clarke, in the County of Durham, for a "Circular Lever WASHING MACHINE." Toronto, dated 20th June, 1857.

No. 749—SPENCER, (E.,) of the Town of Brockville, in the County of Leeds, for a "New and useful WATER WHEEL." Toronto, dated 20th June, 1857.

No. 750—ALLISON, (B. J.,) of the Township of Tyendenaga, in the County of Hastings, for a "New and improved WASHING MACHINE." Toronto, dated 20th April, 1857.

No. 751—BAYES, (J.,) of the Town of Niagara, in the County of Lincoln, for an "Improved MOULD BOARD and LAND SIDE for Ploughs." Toronto, dated 30th June, 1857.

No. 752—GOING, (H.,) of Wolfe Island, in the County of Frontenac, for a "CRADLER and SELF-RAKER." Toronto, dated 2nd July, 1857.

No. 753—HECTOR, (Thomas,) of the City of Toronto, in the County of York, for a "Self-Regulating CANDLE SHADE." Toronto, dated 2nd July, 1857.

No. 754—CHAFFEE (E. M.,) of the City of Montreal, for a "New and useful Improvement in the preparing, coloring and applying India Rubber and Gutta Percha to cloth of all kinds, Leather and other articles, without the use of a solvent, under the name of Chaffee's Improvement in Rubber and GUTTA PERCHA." Toronto, dated 13th July, 1857.

No. 755—SHUTTLEWORTH, (Thomas,) and MODELAND (Thomas,) of the Township of Vaughan, in the County of York, for certain "Improvements in the construction of Mould Boards for PLOUGHS." Toronto, dated 23rd July, 1857.

No. 756—WRAY, (L.,) of the Town of Brantford, in the County of Brant, for a "Process for Producing and Manufacturing fine crystalized Sugar, Syrup, and Molasses, from the African and Chinese, and all other varieties of the "Holdeus SACCHARATUS of LINNOEUS." Toronto, dated 23rd July, 1857.

No. 757—BOLSTER, (G.,) of the City of Toronto, in the County of York, for a "Mastich-Canvas Fire and Water Proof CEMENT for Roofing." Toronto, dated 23rd July, 1857.

No. 758—MARR, (D. D.,) and CHESLEY, (E.,) both of the Township of Woodhouse, in the County of Norfolk, for an "Improvement in the construction of FIRE PLACES." Toronto, dated 23rd July, 1857.

No. 759—SPOFFORD, (W.,) of the Township of Markham, in the County of York, for a "New Tanning Process for Tanning HIDES, &c." Toronto, dated 23rd July, 1857.

No. 760—CHESLEY, (E,,) of the Township of Woodhouse, in the County of Norfolk, for an "Improvement in the construction of CARRIAGES." Toronto, dated 23 July, 1857.

No. 761—KIRKLAND, (H. A.,) and MILLINGTON, (L.,) both of the Town of Guelph, in the County of Wellington, for an "Accelerative and accommodating STRAW CUTTING MACHINE." Toronto, dated 23rd July, 1857.

762—CRAIG, (W.,) of the Township of Camden East, in the County of Addington, for a "Spinner double and Twister for the Manufacture of Twisted YARN." Toronto, dated 7th August, 1857.

No. 763—WILLOUGHBY, (Matthew,) of the City of Toronto, in the County of York, for a "STRAW CUTTER." Toronto, dated 7th August, 1857.

No 764—GREEN, (G. W.,) of the Township of West Flamboro', in the County of Wentworth, for the "DOUBLE SHUFFLE CHURN." Toronto, dated 7th August, 1857.

No.;765—WILKINSON, (J. A.,) of the Town of Cobourg, in the County of Northumberland, for an "Independent Lever Elongating Carriage, or BUGGY SPRING." Toronto, dated 7th August, 1857.

No. 766—PORTER, (D.,) and SCHNEIDER, (J. W.;H.,) both of the City of Hamilton, in the County of Wentworth,) for a "New and useful STRAW CUTTER." Toronto, dated 19th August, 1857.

No. 767—CAMPBELL, (G.,) of the City of Toronto, in the County of York, for the "Hecla Portable FORGE." Toronto, dated 19th August, 1857.

·No. 768—MOORE, (G. H.,) of the Township of Norwich, in the County of Oxford, for a "Self-loading CART." Toronto, dated 20th August, 1857.

No. 769—CUMMINGS, (G.,) of the Town of Niagara, in the County of Lincoln, for an "Improved Steam Engine SLIDE VALVE." Toronto, dated 20th August, 1857.

No. 770—O'HARA, (Charles,) of the Township of York, in the County of York, for an "Oscillating PADDLE for propelling Steam Vessels." Toronto, dated 20th August, 1857.

No. 771—CRAIG, (J. P.,) of the City of Montreal, for "IRON PIANOS, cast in a Single Piece." Toronto, dated 4th September, 1857.

No. 772—NEYLION, (M.,) of Richmond Hill, in the County of York, for a "Seeder to be attached to a Gang PLOUGH." Toronto, dated 19th August, 1857.

No. 773—MARKS, (J.,) of the City of Hamilton, in the County of Wentworth, for certain "Improvements in Spark Arresters, Chimney and Petticoat Pipes for LOCOMOTIVES." Toronto, dated 15th September, 1857.

No. 774—MORLEY, (I.,) of the Village of Thorold, in the County of Welland, Administrator of the Estate and effects of John Morley, deceased, in trust for John Morley, Wm. Henry Morley, Thomas George Morley and Alexander Morley, for an "Improved Mould Board for PLOUGHS." Toronto, dated 15th September, 1857.

No. 775—BOWEN, (W. R.,) of the Township of Cramahe, in the County of Northumberland, for a "Feed Works to be used in Saw Mills called Bowen's Rotary re-action FEED WORKS." Toronto, dated 15th September, 1857.

No. 776—MUNGER, (J. G.,) and HARRIS, (H.,) of the Township of Colchester, of the Township of Gosfield, both in the County of Essex, for a "New and improved method of constructing PUMPS." Toronto, dated 15th September, 1857.

No. 777—DEAN, (C.,) of the City of London, in the County of Middlesex, for a "New mode of effecting more perfect combustion, in the furnaces of STEAM BOILERS, and of saving fuel." Toronto, dated 15th September, 1857.

No. 778—HYSERT, (H.,) and FANNER, (Charles,) both of the Village of Smithville, in the Township of Grimsby, County of Lincoln, for a "SAWING MACHINE." Toronto, dated 15th September, 1857.

No. 779—TATE, (Charles M.,) of the City of Montreal, for an "Improvement in the construction of Knapp's Lamps for Burning ROSIN OIL." Toronto, dated 16th September, 1857.

No. 780—DEWITT, (H,) of the Parish of Chateauguay, in the County of Chateauguay, for "FURROW WHEELS to be attached to Reaping and Mowing Machines, and for other purposes." Toronto, dated 16th September, 1857.

No. 781—BRUCE, (D.,) of Paspebiac, in the County of Bonaventure, for a "New and Improved mode of and apparatus for making concentrated Animal MANURE." Toronto, dated 11th October, 1857.

No. 782—LE ROY, (J. B.,) of the Township of Murray, in the County of Northumberland, for a "Portable Farm Board FENCE." Toronto, dated 28th September, 1857.

No. 783—ARMSTRONG, (J.,) of the Township of Bathurst, in the County of Lanark, for a "New and improved HARROW." Toronto, dated 30th September, 1857.

784—YATES, (H., of the Town of Brantford, in the County of Brant, for an "Improvement in the FIRE Box of the Boilers of Locomotives, or other Steam Engines." Toronto, dated 12th October, 1857.

No. 785—YATES, (H.,) of the Town of Brantford, in the County of Brant, for an "Improvement in perfecting the consumption of SPARKS and parts and portions of unconsumed fuel in Locomotives and other Steam Engines." Toronto, dated 12th October, 1857.

No. 786—McLAREN, (*J. W.*,) of Lawville, in the County of Halton, for an "Improved Mould Board for PLOUGHS." Toronto, dated 12th October, 1857.

No. 787—McNAB, (*J.*,) of the Town of Owen Sound, in the County of Grey, for a "Horizontal Car COUPLER." Toronto, dated 12th October, 1857.

No. 788—JENNESS, (*D. M.*,) of the Township of Stanstead, in the County of Stanstead, for an "Improved Horse Rake, called by him Jenness' Improved HORSE RAKE." Toronto, dated 13th October, 1857.

No. 789—DRAYSON, (*H. E.*,) of the City of Hamilton, in the County of Wentworth, for a "New mode of manufacturing GUNPOWDER." Toronto, dated 7th November, 1857.

No. 790—YATES, (*H.*,) of the Town of Brantford, in the County of Brant, for an "Improved perforated FIRE GRATE, FEED WATER HEATER and DAMPER combined, for Locomotives and other Steam Engines." Toronto, dated 6th November, 1857.

No. 791—PARKES, (*P.*,) of Yorkville, in the County of York, for a "STEAM PRESS for making Bricks, Tiles, &c., from dry clay." Toronto, dated 6th November, 1857.

No. 792—PARKES, (*Charles R.*,) of the City of Toronto, in the County of York, for a "Brick Drain Pipe and Tile making MACHINE." Toronto, dated 6th November, 1857.

No. 793—TUTTLE, (*W. H.*,) of the Village of Canfield, in the County of Haldimand, for a "New and improved AUGER HANDLE." Toronto, dated 6th November, 1857.

No. 794—MANNING, (*W.*,) of the City of Montreal, for a "New and useful Machine for cutting or turning out HEADS for Barrels, Kegs, Casks, or any description of Coopers' Works." Toronto, dated 6th November, 1857.

No. 795—CUDNEY, (*D.*,) of the Town of St. Catharines, in the County of Lincoln, for a "VEGETABLE CUTTER." Toronto, dated 6th November, 1857.

No. 796—HALE, (*J.*,) of the Township of Vaughan, in the County of York, for a "Churn to be called Hale's Improved CHURN." Toronto, dated 6th November, 1857.

No. 797—HILL, (*B.*,) of the City of Toronto, in the County of York, for a "Radical Winged PROPELLER." Toronto, dated 6th November, 1857.

No. 798—McFARLAND, (*Farbell A.*,) of the Town of Stratford, in the County of Perth, for a "New and useful improvement in the construction of GATES." Toronto, dated 7th November, 1857.

No. 799—EATON, (*J.*,) of the Township of East Flamboro' in the County of Wentworth, for a "New method of constructing LAMPS." Toronto, dated 7th November, 1857.

No 800—HYSERT, (*H.*,) of the Village of Smithville, in the Township of Grimsby, County of Lincoln, for certain "Improvements in STUMP MACHINES." Toronto, dated 7th November, 1857.

No. 801—STIRER, (*W. C.*,) of the Township of Markham, in the County of York, for a "Hollow Flanged LIGHTNING ROD." Toronto, dated 7th November, 1857.

No. 802—TAYLOR, (*J. F.*,) of the Town of Windsor, in the County of Essex, for a "New and useful Machine for coupling Railway Cars, termed a SELF-COUPLER and COUPLING PIN SAVER." Toronto, dated 18th November, 1857.

No. 803—EMERY, (*R.*,) of the City of Toronto, in the County of York, for a "PRESS for the manufacture of Eave Troughs of Tin and Galvanized Iron." Toronto, dated 28th November, 1857.

No. 804—LABELLE, (*J.*,) of the City of Montreal, for a "THRESHING and WINNOWING MACHINE without Linen Apron." Toronto, dated 3rd March, 1857.

No. 805—CAMPBELL, (*D.*,) of the City of Toronto, in the County of York, for a "Revolving ANGLE JOINT." Toronto, dated 18th November, 1857.

No. 806—CRAWFORD, (*D.*,) in the County of York, for an "Improved SOAP." Toronto, dated 15th December, 1857.

No. 807—CROUTER, (*S. S.*,) of the Township of Whitby, in the County of Ontario, for a "Stump, Stone, Ship PULLER." Toronto, dated 15th December, 1857.

No. 808—CANT, (*A.*,) of the Town of Galt, in the County of Waterloo, for a "New ROOT CUTTING MACHINE." Toronto, dated 15th December, 1857.

No. 809—FOWLER, (*H.*,) of the Town of Belleville, in the County of Hastings, for an "Improved Apparatus for Washing and Wringing CLOTHES." Toronto, dated 12th January, 1858.

No. 810—LETTORE, (*G. R.*,) of the City of Montreal, for an "Improvement SEWING MACHINES." Toronto, dated 11th January, 1858.

No. 811—FRENCH, (*C.*,) and FRENCH, (*L.*,) of the Village of Eaton, in the County of Compton, for a "New and improved STRAW CUTTER." Toronto, dated 11th January, 1851.

No. 812—CLARKE, (*J. P.*,) of the City of Toronto, in the County of York, for a "Mode of propelling Steamboats, named Clarke's Series of PADDLES." Toronto, dated 8th February, 1858.

No. 813—THOMAS, (*J.*,) of Toronto, in the County of York, for a "New and improved PAD-DLE." Toronto, dated 8th February, 1858.

No. 814—GODFREY, (*J. S.*,) of the Village of Thamesford, in the County of Oxford, for a "New and improved WASHING MACHINE." Toronto, dated 12th February, 1858.

No. 815—FAREWELL, (*I. W.*,) of the Township of Whitby East, in the County of Ontario, for the "Excelsior STRAW FEEDER." Toronto, dated 13th February, 1858.

No. 816—OLIVER, (*W. G.*,) of the City of Toronto, in the County of York, for a "New and useful method of applying and using ELECTRICITY as an Anesthetic Agent in extracting Teeth and in other Surgical operations." Toronto, dated 16th March, 1858.

No. 817—MORRIS, (*J.*,) of the Village of Bradford, in the County of Simcoe, for a "New and improved Room and House HEATER." Toronto, dated 16th March, 1858.

No. 818—CRAWFORD, (*D*,) of the City of Toronto, in the County of York, for an "Improve-ment in the manufacture of SOAP." Toronto, dated 16th March, 1858.

No. 819—CRAWFORD, (*D.*,) Of the City of Toronto, in the County of York, for an "Improve-ment in the manufacture of SOAP." Toronto, dated 16th March, 1858.

No. 810 - CRAWFORD, (*D.*,) of the City of Toronto, in the County of York, for an "Improve-ment in the manufacture of SOAP." Toronto, dated 16th March, 1858.

No. 821—THOMSON, (*J.*,) of the Village of Yorkville, in the County of York, for a certain "New and improved method of constructing MANGLES." Toronto, dated 16th March, 1858.

No. 822—HICKS, (*B. M.*,) of the Town of Brantford, in the County of Brant, for a "New method of SLATING." Toronto, dated 16th March, 1858.

No. 823—TOULMIR, (*W. J. F.*,) of old Yonge Street, near Toronto, in the County of York, for a "Self-generating Gas Burner and LAMP." Toronto, dated 16th March, 1858.

No. 824—SOFER, (*J.*,) of the Township of Clarke, in the County of Durham, for an "Improved Clover SEPARATOR." Toronto, dated 16th March, 1858.

No. 825—BIGELAW, (*A.*,) of the City of Hamilton, in the County of Wentworth, for an "Endless Chain STEAM PLOUGH." Toronto, dated 16th March, 1858.

No. 826—WEBSTER, (*L.*,) of the Township of Hatley, in the County of Stanstead, for a "New and improved BEE HIVE." Toronto, dated 20th March, 1858.

No. 827—COOMBS, (*D.*,) of the City of Montreal, for a "Combined Churn and Cream FREEZER." Toronto, dated 31st March, 1858.

No. 828—BRYSON, (*Thomas M.*,) of the City of Montreal, for a "New and improved method of protecting the toes of BOOTS or SHOES." Toronto, dated 31st March, 1858.

No. 829—HICKS, (*G. A.*,) of the Town of Woodstock, in the County of Oxford, for an "Improved SILVERIC OIL or Self-generating non-explosive Gas Burner." Toronto, dated 20th April, 1858.

No. 830—JESSUP, (*J. J.*,) of the Township of Elizabethtown, in the County of Leeds, for a "New and useful Farming Implement, called a SOIL PULVERIZER." Toronto, dated 7th April, 1858.

No. 831—CLARKE, (*H.*,) of the Village of Thamesford, in the County of Oxford, for an "Improved Machine for CROSS-CUTTING Logs, cutting Firewood, &c." Toronto, dated 7th April, 1858.

No. 832—MELLING, (J.,) of the Township of Scarboro', in the County of York, for a "Machine for PRESSING or COMPRESSING Clay, or composition by rotary and reciprocating motion, into the form of Bricks, Tiles, Pipes, Artificial Stone, &c., &c." Toronto, dated 8th April, 1858.

No. 833—LAWRENCE, (L.,) of the Township of Granby, in the County of Shefford, for "WASHING and WRINGING Machine." Toronto, dated 1st May, 1858.

No. 834—BENNETT, (A.,) of Sutton, in the County of Brome, for a "New and Improved Bee House, called Bennett's Platform BEE HOUSE." Toronto, dated 1st May, 1858.

No. 835—GREEN, (Charles,) of Brantford, in the County of Brant, for a "Separating THRASHING Machine." Toronto, dated 7th April, 1858.

No. 836—DONER, (C.,) of the Village of Cashel, in the Township of Markham, County of York, for "Friction SASH HANGINGS and LOCK." Toronto, dated 14th May, 1858.

No. 837—FORBES, (L. W.,) of the Town of Windsor, in the County of Essex, for a "Combined Rocking STAVE and HEADING Machine." Toronto, dated 14th May, 1858.

No. 838—DAVIS, (R.,) of the Village of Yorkville, in the County of York, for an "Improvement in direct central discharge WATER-WHEEL and antifriction Circular Gates." Toronto, dated 8th June, 1858.

No. 839—SPENCER, (The Reverend J.,) of the City of Toronto, in the County of York, for a "Mailing PRESS and PAYING Machine." Toronto, dated 8th June, 1858.

No. 840—YATES, (H.,) of the Town of Brantford, in the County of Brant, for "Improvements in the WING RAILS of Railway Carriages." Toronto, dated 8th June, 1858.

No. 841—MILLER, (A.,) of the Town of Chatham, in the County of Kent, for a "Safety STEAM ALARM." Toronto, dated 8th June, 1858.

No. 842—SCHOFIELD, (F.,) of the Town of Woodstock, in the County of Oxford, for certain "Improvements in the method of constructing THRASHING Machines and SEPARATORS." Toronto, dated 8th June, 1858.

No. 843—LOUNSBURY, (R.,) of the Township of Grimsby, in the County of Lincoln, for a "New and useful HORSE RAKE." Toronto, dated 9th June, 1858.

No. 844—BARLOW, (G. F.,) of Eaton, in the County of Compton, for a "New and improved CHEESE PRESS." Toronto, dated 18th June, 1858.

No. 845—SMITH, (Charles W.,) of the City of Montreal, for a "Head Protector against Heat, Coup-de-soleil, &c." Toronto, dated 18th June, 1858.

No. 846—GARDINER, (J. J.,) of the Village of Newcastle, in the County of Durham, for a "Improved WASHING Machine." Toronto, dated 2nd July, 1858.

No. 847—WALBRIDGE, (A. S.,) of Stanbridge, in the County of Missisquoi, for an "Improved method of BENDING TIMBER." Toronto, dated 2rd July, 1858.

No. 848—GLEASON, (Thomas C.,) of the City of Hamilton, in the County of Wentworth, for an "Improved Grain Cleaner and SMUT MILL." Toronto, dated 9th June, 1858.

No. 849—WISHART, (J.,) of the Village of Waterdown, in the County of Wentworth, for an "Improved DRILL PLOUGH." Toronto, dated 2nd July, 1858.

No. 850—WEBSTER, (S. Thomas,) of the City of Montreal, for an "Improved LINK and DRAW BAR for coupling Railway Cars." Toronto, dated 3rd July, 1858.

No. 851—DICK, (The Reverend R.,) of the City of Toronto, in the County of York, for "A new System of Book-keeping, called Dick's ACCOUNTANT PATÉNT." Toronto, dated 26th July, 1858.

No. 852—DICK, (The Reverend R.,) of the City of Toronto, in the County of York, for a "New machine for the purpose of addressing papers and periodical parcels, for the PAGING of BOOKS, and for all similar operations of a recurrent nature by the application of Printed Stamps or labels to be called 'Dick's DISPATCH PATENT." Toronto, dated 26th July, 1858.

No. 853—COLE, (A. N.,) of the Town of Brockville, in the County of Leeds, for a "New and useful instrument, called Cole's Gravitating PLUMB and LEVEL." Toronto, dated 13th July, 1858.

No. 854—ADDISON, (J.,) of the City of Hamilton, in the County of Wentworth, for a "Wooden Spring Mattrass for BEDS." Toronto, dated 13th July, 1858.

No. 855—HURST, (*W.*) of the Town of Peterborough, in the County of Peterborough, for a " Bale Universal JOINT." Toronto, dated 13th July, 1858.

No. 856—THOMAS, (*J. H.*) of the Township of Whitby, in the County of Ontario, for a " Self-Oiling Box for CARRIAGE HUBS." Toronto, dated 13th July, 1858.

No. 857—McDONALD, (*G.*) of the City of Hamilton, in the County of Wentworth, for an " Improved AXLE Box and Journal Relieving Bearing. Toronto, dated 13th July, 1858.

No. 858—KEITH, (*D. S.*) of the City of Toronto, in the County of York, for a " Self-Acting Cistern FLAT VALVE." Toronto, dated 13th July, 1858.

No. 859—WESTMAN, (*W. D.*) of the Township of King, in the County of York, for a " Turnip or ROOT GRATER." Toronto, dated 16th July, 1858.

No. 860—THIRKELL, (*J.*) of the Village of Ingersoll, in the County of Oxford, for a certain " New and improved method of constructing SAWING Machines." Toronto, dated 26th July, 1858.

No. 861—EATON, (*J.*) of the Town of Belleville, in the County of Hastings, for a " Centrifugal Propelling and Steering BOXED WHEEL." Toronto, dated 26th July, 1858.

No. 862—MARSH, (*A.*) of the Town of Windsor, in the County of Essex, for an " Improved GAS GENERATOR." Toronto, dated 26th July, 1858.

No. 863—GREGORY, (*H.*) and DUNSTAN, (*R. W.*) both of the City of Hamilton, in the County of Wentworth, for a "Cooling, Warming, Dust Preventing and Air DISTRIBUTING VENTILATOR." Toronto, dated 26th July, 1858.

No. 864—STITT, *J.*) of the Town of Prescott, in the County of Grenville, for a "GRUBBING Machine." Toronto, dated 30th July, 1858.

No. 865—COLE, (*R.*) of the City of Quebec, for a " New Elevator and STUMP EXTRACTOR." Toronto, dated 16th August, 1858.

No. 866—MITCHELL, (*R.*) of the City of Montreal, for a " New and improved method of constructing STEAM HEATERS." Toronto, dated 26th August, 1858.

No. 867—SMYTH, (*W.*) of the City of Montreal, for the " Nonpareil BOOT and SHOE." Toronto, dated 28th August, 1858.

No. 868—THOMAS, (*W.*) of the Village of Orono, in the Township of Clarke, in the County of Durham, for a " Secret Self-protecting SCRUTOIRE." Toronto, dated 2th August, 1858.

No. 869—LOWE, (*J.*) of the City of Montreal, for a " Magnetic improved PRESSURE GAUGE." Toronto, dated 26th August, 1858.

No. 870—WRAY, (*J.*) of the City of Montreal, for a " New method of constructing COFFINS, to prevent infection." Toronto, dated 26th August, 1858.

No. 871—BOWEN, (*Charles A. A.*) of the Town of St. Catherines, in the County of Lincoln, for an " Improved GAS RETORT." Toronto, dated 25th August, 1858.

No. 872—KEITH, (*D. S.*) of the City of Toronto, in the County of York, for a "Sliding Tubular PUMP PLUNGER with Air Chamber." Toronto, dated 25th August, 1858.

No. 873—WOODCOCK, (*R.*) of the Town of Chatham, in the County of Kent, for a " Metal POLISHER." Toronto, dated 26th August, 1858.

No. 874—WAY, (*J. B.*) of the Township of Whitby, in the County of Ontario, for a " New combined or separate Clod-Crusher, Harrower, and ROLLER." Toronto, dated 25th August, 1858.

No. 875—COLBY, (*Charles C.*) of the Village of Stanstead, for a " Composition of matter for Agricultural uses, called the Canadian FERTILIZER." Toronto, dated 7th September, 1858.

No. 876—STILES, (*P. B. B.*) and MARRITT, (*J.*) of the Village of East Gwillimbury, in the County of York, for a " Pair of Rotating HARROWS." Toronto, dated 13th September, 1858.

No. 877—LOUNT, (*G.*) of the Township of Whitchurch, in the County of York, for a " Lever Elevating FARM GATE." Toronto, dated 13th September, 1858.

No. 878—TATE, (*Charles M.*) of the City of Montreal, for a " New and improved method of constructing CREEPERS." Toronto, dated 11th February, 1858.

No. 879—EDEY, (*H. F.*) of the City of Montreal, for a " Machine for the production of Wind called a new PNEUMATOPOIC." Toronto, dated 28th September, 1858.

No. 880—MATRE, (*M.*,) of the Village of Chippawa, in the County of Welland, for a "New Sporting Gun." Toronto, dated 18th September, 1858.

No. 881—NORTHCOTE, (*H.*,) and COOPER, (*F.*,) of the City of Toronto, in the County of York, for a "Double and reverse acting LIFT particularly adapted to Hanging Window Sashes.' Toronto, dated 28th September, 1858.

No. 882—GREEN, (*G. W.*,) of the Village of Greensville, in the Township of West Flamboro', County of Wentworth, for a "Hand-Sowing TURNIP MACHINE." Toronto, dated 30th September, 1858.

No. 883—HUNTER, (*A. J.*,) of the Township of Bayham, in the County of Elgin, for a "Self-generating GAS BURNER." Toronto, dated 18th September, 1858.

No. 884—CLARK, (*F.*,) of the Village of Thamesford, in the County of Oxford, for an "Improved Reaping and MOWING Machine." Toronto, dated 3rd November, 1858.

No. 885—COLLINS, (*D.*,) of the Village of Port Credit, in the County of Peel, for an "Improved LIGHT CARRIAGE." Toronto, dated 3rd November, 1858.

No. 886—HOGG, (*J.*,) of the City of Toronto, in the County of York, for a "Lever and Spring Dash-CHURN." Toronto, dated 3rd November, 1858.

No. 887—LAWRENCE, (*J.*,) of the Village of Palermo, in the County of Halton, for a "New application or arrangement of the Gearing to drive the Knife of a REAPING Machine." Toronto, dated 3rd November, 1858.

No. 888—SOPER, (*L. N.*,) of the Town of Woodstock, in the County of Oxford for an "Elastic Lock STITCH SEWING Machine." Toronto, 3rd November, 1858.

No. 889—VAN BROCKLIN, (*P. C.*,) of the Township of Brantford, in the County of Brant, for certain "New and useful improvements in the construction and operation of PUMPS for raising Fluids." Toronto, dated 3rd November, 1858.

No. 890—NOBLE, (*J.*,) of the Town of St. Catharines, in the County of Lincoln, for a "New and useful Machinery for making AXES." Toronto, dated 3rd November, 1858.

No. 891—CRAWFORD, (*D.*,) of the City of Toronto, in the County of York, for an "Improvement in preparing SOAP." Toronto, dated 15th November, 1858.

No. 892—CARPENTER, (*B.*,) of the Township of Ancaster, in the County of Wentworth, for a "Direct revolving flue Cooking STOVE." Toronto, dated 15th November, 1858.

No. 893—BLACK, (*N.*,) of the Village of Rockwood, in the County of Wellington, for an "Improved ARTIFICIAL LEG, with Universal Joint at the Ankle." Toronto, dated 15th November, 1858.

No. 894—McNELLIS, (*W. J.*,) of the Town of Belleville, in the County of Hastings, for an "Improved direct action and re-action WATER WHEEL." Toronto, dated 18th November, 1858.

No. 895—DICK, (*The Reverend R.*,) of the City of Toronto, in the County of York, for an "Accountant and DISPATCH Patent," Toronto, dated 1st December, 1858.

No. 896—BARRETT, (*E.*,) of the City of Toronto, in the County of York, for a "New and improved method of constructing HAND STAMP Printing Presses." Toronto, dated 29th November, 1858.

No. 897—VANDERVOORT, (*W.*,) of the Township of Sidney, in the County of Hastings, for a "Portable Board or Picket FENCE." Toronto, dated 18th November, 1858.

No. 898—HAUR, (*A. L.*,) of the Village of Waterloo, in the County of Welland, for an "Improved PLOUGH." Toronto, dated 18th November, 1858.

No. 899—RUTTAN, (*H.*,) of the Town of Cobourg, in the County of Northumberland, for a "New or improved method of WARMING and Ventilating Buildings, Railroad Cars and Vessels." Toronto, dated 29th November, 1858.

No. 900—IVORY, (*W.*,) of the Township of Clarke and Village of Newcastle and County of Durham, for a "Revolving Box Cylinder CHURN." Toronto, dated 3rd December, 1858.

No. 901—MERRILL, (*A.*,) of the Township of Houghton, in the County of Norfolk, for a "Platform PUMP." Toronto, dated 3rd December, 1858.

No. 902—HUCKETT, (*William John,*) of the City of Toronto, in the County of York, for "A Self-Acting WAGGON BRAKE." Toronto, dated 16th December, 1858.

G

No. 903—HICKOK, *(Samuel Sherman,)* of the City of Toronto, in the County of York, for "An improved Self-Acting SAFETY-CATCH or Fastener for Railway Car Seats." Toronto, dated 16th December, 1858.

No. 904—NOTTER, *(Thomas Walter,)* of the City of Toronto, in the County of York, for "A Gas Salvator BURNER." Toronto, dated 17th December, 1858.

No. 905—GARTH, *(George,)* of the City of Toronto, in the County of York, for "Preservative Vessels and HERMETIC COVERS." Toronto, dated 20th December, 1858.

No. 906—METHOT, *(E. E.,)* of the Parish of Lotbinière, in the County of Lotbinère, for "A new and improved Double Oven FAMILY STOVE." Toronto, dated 5th January, 1859.

No. 907—ARMSTRONG, *(James,)* of the Township of Bathurst, in the County of Lanark, for "A new and improved CHURN." Toronto, dated 30th December, 1858.

No. 908—POLYBLANK, *(William,)* of the City of Toronto, in the County of York, for "A useful Machine called a WASHING JENNY." Toronto, dated 10th January, 1859.

No. 909—CASH, *(David,)* of the Village of Markham, in the County of York, for "A new Gate called Cash's Self-closing FARMER'S GATE." Toronto, dated 11th January, 1859.

No. 910—GILBERT, *(E. E.,)* of the City of Montreal, for "An improved STEAM BOILER." Toronto, dated 20th January, 1859.

No. 911—RUTTAN, *(Henry,)* of the Town of Cobourg, in the County of Northumberland, for "A new or improved method of WARMING and Ventilating Buildings, Railroad Cars and Vessels." Toronto, dated 31st December, 1858.

No. 912—ARMOUR, *(John,)* of the Township of York, in the County of York, for "An improved straight portable or permanent FENCE and GATE POST." Toronto, dated 3rd February, 1859.

No. 913—MATTHEWS, *(William,)* of the City of Toronto, in the County of York, for "A Metallic equal tension PLATE for Cottage Piano Fortes." Toronto, dated 9th February, 1859.

No. 914—HILBORN, *(James,)* of the Township of Reach, in the County of Ontario, for "An improved WASHING MACHINE." Toronto, dated 9th February, 1859.

No. 915—BARKER, *(William,)* of the Township of Whitby, in the County of Ontario, for "A Fuel Saver and Hot Air CONDUCTOR." Toronto, dated 9th February, 1859.

No. 916—SAMPSON, *(J. H.,)* of the City of Montreal, for "An improvement in BOOT TREES." Toronto, dated 14th February, 1859.

No. 917—WORTHINGTON, *(J.,)* and BROWN, *(J.,)* both of the City of Toronto, in the County of York, for "A seam of Clay and its composition, with materials for the manufacture of drainage and sewerage TILE, or PIPE; also, Stone Crockeryware, or common Yellow Earthenware." Toronto, dated 9th February, 1859.

No. 918—WALKER, *(James H.,)* of the City of Hamilton, in the County of Wentworth, for "A Smoke consuming LANTERN and LAMP to burn coal and other Oils." Toronto, dated 14th February, 1859.

No. 919—METHOT, *(Edward E.,)* of the Parish of Lotbinière, in the County of Lotbinière, for "New and improved Models and designs for STOVE PLATES." Toronto, dated 26th February, 1859.

No. 920—GODLEY, *(Sidney,)* of the Township of Sandwich, in the County of Essex, for "An improved COOKING STOVE." Toronto, dated 1st March, 1859.

No. 921—JAMES, *(C. R.,)* of the City of Toronto, in the County of York, for "Certain improvements in the method of constructing STRAW CUTTERS." Toronto, dated 1st March, 1859.

No. 922—LEMON, *(Charles,)* of the Township of Augusta, in the County of Grenville, for "A new and useful Churn, termed Lemon's Oscillating DASH CHURN." Toronto, dated 1st March, 1859.

No. 923—GIRARDIN, *(Venuste,)* of Belle Rivière, in the Township of Rochester, in the County of Essex, for "A fluent equilibrating SLIDE VALVE for Locomotives and Steam Engines." Toronto, dated 1st March, 1859.

No. 924—WALSH, *(J. C.,)* of the City of Montreal, for "Walsh's Canadian Self-regulating GAS BURNER." Toronto, dated 8th March, 1859.

No. 925—GURNEY, (*E.,*) GURNEY, (*C.,*) and CARPENTER, (*A.,*) of the City of Hamilton, for "An improved Cooking Stove, called the PROTECTIONIST." Toronto, dated 11th March, 1859

No. 926—DONER, (*C.,*) of the Village of Cashel, in the Township of Markham, in the County of York, for "A Portable Counterpoise GATE." Toronto, dated 14th March, 1859.

No. 927—BRIGGS, (*Isaac,*) of Gananoque, in the County of Leeds, for "Certain Improvements in the manufacture of CUT NAILS and SPIKES." Toronto, dated 14th March, 1859.

No. 928—McDONALD, (*Allan,*) of the Town of Belleville, in the County of Hastings, for "A Portable GRIST MILL." Toronto, dated 16th March, 1859.

No. 929—HORNING, (*C. H.,*) of the Township of West Flamborough, in the County of Wentworth, for "An improved RAKE for Harvesters." Toronto, dated 16th March, 1859.

No. 930—MOWRY, (*Aldus,*) of the Village of Ashburnham, in the County of Peterborough, for "A CHOP GRINDER." Toronto, dated 16th March, 1859.

No. 931—GAIGE, (*Werden,*) of the Town of Whitby, in the County of Ontario, for "A new and improved method of TANNING LEATHER." Toronto, dated 24th March, 1859.

No. 932—LAW, (*James,*) of the Village of Scarborough, in the County of York, for "Law's Shingle and Barrel Heading SAWING MACHINE." Toronto, dated 24th March, 1859.

No. 933—RIDER, (*W. S.,*) of Bayfield, in the County of Huron, for "An improved HORSE POWER." Toronto, dated 26th March, 1859.

No. 934—DOANE, (*Henry,*) of the City of Toronto, in the County of York, for "An improved method of SWINGING Two Wheeled Vehicles." Toronto, dated 1st April, 1859.

No. 935—SIPES, (*J.,*) and SIPES, (*H.,*) both of the Township of Beverly, in the County of Wentworth, for "An improved CHURN." Toronto, dated 5th April, 1859.

No. 936—ABELL, (*John,*) of the Township of Vaughan, in the County of York, for "Certain improvements in the method of constructing THRASHING MACHINES." Toronto, dated 6th April, 1859.

No. 937—FORSYTH, (*Hiram,*) of the Township of Stamford, in the County of Welland, for "A new and improved GRINDING MILL." Toronto, dated 6th April, 1859.

No. 938—ARMSTRONG, (*Thomas,*) of the Village of Markham, in the County of York, for "An improved method of cutting and crimping BOOTS." Toronto, dated 5th April, 1859.

No. 939—MORSE, (*Samuel,*) of the Town of Milton, in the County of Halton, for an "Improved Combined REAPING and MOWING MACHINE." Toronto, dated 9th April, 1859.

No. 940—HORNING, (*C. H.,*) of the Township of West Flamborough, in the County of Wentworth, for "An improved Double FORCE PUMP." Toronto, dated 12th April, 1859.

No. 941—WILLIAMSON, (*W. J. T.,*) of the City of Toronto, in the County of York, for "The Williamson's GAS BURNER." Toronto, dated 21st April, 1859.

No. 942—TOURANGEAU, (*J. G.,*) of the City of Quebec, for "A DOUGH MAKER for Bread and Biscuits." Toronto, dated 2nd May, 1859.

No. 943—TOURANGEAU, (*J. G.,*) of the City of Quebec, for "A hot air OVEN for the baking of Bread and Biscuits." Toronto, dated 2nd May, 1859.

No. 944—LAVIN, (*L.,*) of the Town of Goderich, in the County of Huron, for "An improved Box for the Axles of Railroad Cars." Toronto, dated 28th April, 1859.

No. 945—TOMKINS, (*G.,*) of the Township of Malahide, in the County of Elgin, for "A certain improvement in the composition of the matter required in the manufacture of Percussion MATCHES." Toronto, dated 28th April, 1859.

No. 946—BRIKLY, (*Joseph,*) of the Township of South Dorchester, in the County of Elgin, for "A Self-revolving HAND LOOM." Toronto, dated 4th May, 1859.

No. 947—NORTON, (*David Eton,*) of the City of Toronto, in the County of York, for "An improved FANNING MILL." Toronto, dated 10th May, 1859.

No. 948—McKENZIE, (*T. H.,*) and HAWKINS, (*F. R.,*) both of the Town of Dundas, in the County of Wentworth, for "Certain improvements in Johnson's CHURN." Toronto, dated 11th May, 1859.

No. 949—POLLARD, (*W. D.,*) of the Town of Collingwood, in the County of Simcoe, for "A method of treating Bituminous Shale to obtain OILS containing paraffine therefrom." Toronto, dated 14th May, 1859.

No. 950—MARRITT, (John,) of Queensville, in the County of York, for "Improved draft and coupling Irons for Rotary HARROWS." Toronto, dated 23rd May, 1859.

No. 951—BARBER, (N. L.,) of the Township of McGillivray, in the County of Huron, for "The Norman AIR CHURN." Toronto, dated 23rd May, 1859.

No. 952—BROWN, (R.,) and BROWN, (J.,) of the Township of Caledon, in the County of Peel, for "A catenarian System of PRINTING." Toronto, dated 28th May, 1859.

No. 953—HAMILTON, (William,) of the City of Toronto, in the County of York, for "An improvement in the manufacture of CORES for Castings." Toronto, dated 27th May, 1859.

No. 954—TUTTLE, (Jacob,) of the Township of Delaware, in the County of Middlesex, for "A new TANNING COMPOSITION." Toronto, dated 23rd May, 1859.

No. 955—FERRY, (T. F.,) of the Village of Willington, in the Township of Hillier, in the County of Prince Edward, for "An improved PLOUGH." Toronto, dated 23rd May, 1859.

No. 956—DICKEY, (James,) of the City of Toronto, in the County of York, for "The Toronto HARROW and CULTIVATOR." Toronto, dated 1st June, 1859.

No. 957—EATON, (Richard,) of the City of Hamilton, in the County of Wentworth, for an "Apparatus for economising FUEL in Locomotives and other Steam Engines." Toronto, dated 26th May, 1859.

No. 958—HUFFMAN, (Jacob,) of the Township of Camden, in the County of Addington, for "An improved GRAIN FORK." Toronto, dated 1st June, 1859.

No. 959—HALL, (W. J.,) of Roxton Falls, in the County of Shefford, for "An improvement in the construction of Churns, called Hall's improved Labor-saving CHURN." Toronto, dated 28th June, 1859.

No. 960—MITCHELL, (A.,) of the City of Montreal, for an "Improvement in moulding and casting metal, called by him Mitchell's PROCESS." Toronto, dated 29th June, 1859.

No. 961—PILBEAM, (David,) of the City of Montreal, for "An improved Last called by him Pilbeam Perfectus LAST." Toronto, dated 29th June, 1859.

No. 962—LOWE, (J.,) of the City of Toronto, in the County of York, for a "FORCE PUMP and Feed Apparatus." Toronto, dated 1st June, 1859.

No. 963—LAMBKIN, (C. H.,) of the Village of Jordan, in the County of Lincoln, for "An improvement in Washing Machines,called the Revolving and Smooth WASHBOARD." Toronto, dated 1st June, 1859.

No. 964—STILLWELL, (Henry,) of Vienna, in the County of Elgin, for "An automaton GATE." Toronto, dated 8th June, 1859.

No. 965—EALES, (Walter,) of the City of Toronto, in the County of York, for a "New and improved PAINT." Toronto, dated 8th June, 1859.

No. 966—PALMER, (Dennis,) of the Township of Grimsby, in the County of Lincoln, for "New improvements in MOWING MACHINES." Toronto, dated 8th June, 1859.

No. 967—DERBY, (E. L.,) of the Village of Mowen, in the County of Addington, for a "Knuckle-Joint SCREW POWER for extracting Stumps, and for pressing Cheese, Cloth, Paper, Apples for Cider, &c." Toronto, dated 2nd June, 1859.

No. 968—HALL, (Samuel,) of the Township of Wellesley, in the County of Waterloo, for a "New Portable FENCE." Toronto, dated 22nd June, 1859.

No. 969—LALOR, (Thomas,) of the City of Hamilton, County of Wentworth, for "Two new Bank and Safe Lock GUARDS, of cast steel with Rollers." Toronto, dated 22nd June, 1859.

No. 970—WHITE, (George,) of the Village of New Market, in the County of York, for "An improved Machine for DRILLING IRON and other Metals." Toronto, dated 22nd June, 1859.

No. 971—LOMAX, (W. R.,) of the City of Montreal, for "An improved Steamboat Propeller, called Lomax's Compensating PROPELLER." Quebec, dated 29th September, 1859.

No. 972—LOMAX, (W. R.,) of the City of Montreal, for "An improved Stove Pipe BEND." Quebec, dated 29th September, 1859.

47

No. 973—MAXWELL, (*D.,*) and CONNELL, (*J.,*) both of the Town of Paris, in the County of Brant, for "An Improved Grain Drill FEEDER." Toronto, dated 5th July, 1859.

No. 974—BYER, (*Abraham,*) of the Township of Pickering, in the County of Ontario, for "A Stone DRESSER." Toronto, dated 18th July, 1859.

No. 975—FRASER, (*Hugh,*) of the Town of Collingwood, in the County of Simcoe, for "A New Rotating HARROW." Toronto, dated 18th July, 1859.

No. 976—THOMAS, (*Robert,*) of the City of Toronto, in the County of York, for Thomas' Anti-Friction Compound PUMP." Toronto, dated 18th July, 1859.

No. 977—HILL, (*B. L.,*) of the Town of Sandwich, in the County of Essex, for "A new and improved Method of TANNING HIDES and SKINS into ordinary Leather of the various sorts and kinds, as well as into Morocco Leather, by the admixture of a certain Composition of matter." Quebec, dated 30th September, 1859.

No. 978—FRYATT, (*Henry,*) of the Township of Pickering, in the County of Ontario, for "An Improved CHURN." Toronto, dated 18th July, 1859.

No. 979—McALPIN, (*A.,*) of the Town of Clifton, in the County of Welland, for "An Improved VENTILATOR for Railway Cars, or for Buildings." Quebec, dated 30th September, 1859.

No. 980—REINAGEL, (*George,*) of the Town of Brantford, in the County of Brant, for "Reinagel's improved FEED MILL." Quebec, dated 30th September, 1859.

No. 981—STEPHENS, (*John,*) of the Town of Port Hope, in the County of Durham, for "A new and improved Machine for WINNOWING and Cleaning Grain." Quebec, dated 30th September, 1859.

No. 982—O'DELL, (*Abiel,*) of the Town of Bowmanville, in the County of Durham, for "O'Dell's Fruit or Vegetable PICKER." Quebec, dated 5th October, 1859.

No. 983—RUSSELL, (*John,*) of the City of Toronto, in the County of York, for "An Improved Portable GRIST MILL." Quebec, dated 5th October, 1859.

No. 984—TOUT, (*William,*) of the City of Hamilton, in the County of Wentworth, for "An Improved FANNING MILL." Quebec, dated 5th October, 1859.

No. 985—GOODENOUGH, (*R. A.,*) of the City of Toronto, in the County of York, for "An Improved SHOE for Horses, Mules and Donkeys." Quebec, dated 6th October, 1859.

No. 986—AGNEW, (*J. L.,*) of the City of Toronto, in the County of York, for "A New Stump EXTRACTOR." Quebec, dated 6th October, 1859.

No. 987—ROTT, (*Henry,*) of the Township of Clinton, in the County of Lincoln, for "An improved Stump EXTRACTOR." Quebec, dated 7th October, 1859.

No. 988—KERN, (*J. W.,*) of the City of London, in the County of Middlesex, for "An Improved Mould Board for PLOUGHS." Quebec, dated 25th October, 1859.

No. 989—WEBSTER, (*Thomas,*) of the City of Toronto, in the County of York, for "An Improved Feed Motion for STRAW CUTTERS." Quebec, dated 21st October, 1859.

No. 990—ELLIS, (*William,*) of the Town of Prescott, in the County of Grenville, for "A Cask Steaming, Purifying and Drying APPARATUS." Toronto, dated 8th June, 1859.

No. 991—BAKER, (*William,*) of the Township of Whitby, in the County of Ontario, for "A New Method of Constructing VESSELS or Buildings." Toronto, dated 22nd June, 1859.

No. 992—TURNER, (*Sidney,*) of the City of Toronto, in the County of York, for the Turner Hand PRINTING PRESS." Toronto, dated 30th June, 1859.

No. 993—MARTIN, (*James.*) of the City of Toronto, in the County of York, for "A new and Improved Exhaust CHAMBER and Steam Surcharger, with Smoke Pipe attachments, for Locomotives and other ENGINES." Toronto, dated 5th July, 1859.

No. 994—MARTIN, (*James,*) of the City of Toronto, in the County of York, for "An Improved SLIDE VALVE." Toronto, dated 5th July, 1859.

No. 995—POLLARD, (*W. D.,*) and CONNELL, (*James,*) both of the Town of Collingwood, in the County of Simcoe, for "A Method of preparing Tanners' or Dyers' Bark of Oak, Hemlock Birch or Sumac Compressed for Portability termed COLLINGWOOD BARK for Dyer's or Tanner's use." Quebec, dated 7th October, 1859.

48

No. 996—INNES, (*Alexander*,) of the City of Montreal, for "A New Still called INNES' STILL." Quebec, dated 29th September, 1859.

No. 997—WHITEHEAD, (*Lewis*,) of the City of Toronto, in the County of York, for "A new and useful Compound called SPRING BRACE and Spiral Spring to be used in the Manufacture of Spring Mattresses, &c." Quebec, dated 6th October, 1859.

No. 998—McKENZIE, (*G. C.*,) of the Village of Georgetown, in the County of Halton, for "An improved STRAW CUTTER." Quebec, dated 7th October, 1859.

No. 999—BENNETT, (*George*,) and DALZELL, (*R.*,) both of the Town of Brockville, in the County of Leeds, for "A Screw Cutting Machine, termed "Bennett and Dalzell's little GIANT SCREW CUTTER." Quebec, dated 10th October, 1859.

No. 1000—HILBARD, (*Ashley*,) of the City of Montreal, for "A Canvas SHOE or BOOT united with India Rubber or Gutta Percha." Quebec, dated 13th October, 1859.

No. 1001—VINCELETTE, (*V.*,) VINCELETTE, (*C.*,) and COURTOIS, (*E.*,) of Iberville, for "An improvement in the construction of Stoves, called VINCELETTE and COURTOIS STOVE." Quebec, dated 20th October, 1859.

No. 1002—GROSS, (*John*,) of the Village of Clinton, in the County of Huron, for "A CHAIN HORSE POWER." Quebec, dated 21st October, 1859.

No. 1003—SMITH, (*Ananias*,) of the City of Toronto, in the County of York, for "A new Method of constructing LATHES for turning regular or irregular surfaces." Quebec, dated 26th October, 1859.

No. 1004—YATES, (*Henry*,) of the Town of Brantford, in the County of Brant, for "A variable and double annular BLAST Apparatus for Locomotives and other Steam Engines." Quebec, dated 31st October, 1859.

No. 1005—WOOD, (*Melvin*,) of the Village of Sparta, in the Township of Yarmouth, in the County of Elgin, for "An improved Straw Cutter, called Wood's STRAW CUTTER." Quebec, dated 9th November, 1859.

No. 1006—DOEL, (*W. H.*,) of the Town of Whitby, in the County of Ontario, for "A Portable COPYING PRESS, containing a Chamber for Writing Materials." Quebec, dated 9th November, 1859.

No. 1007—RYCKMAN, (*Samuel W.*,) of the Township of Howard, in the County of Kent, for "A new and improved Machine for SHELLING MAIZE or Indian Corn, from the Husk or Cob." Quebec, dated 26th October, 1859.

No. 1008—PATTISON, (*W. M.*,) of Frelighsburg, in the County of Missisquoi, for "An improved Fountain Pen-holder tube, called the Canadian FOUNTAIN PEN Holder." Quebec, dated 9th November, 1859.

No. 1009—HILBART, (*Ashley*,) of the City of Montreal, for "An improved EMERY WHEEL." Quebec, dated 9th November, 1859.

No. 1010—ANDERSON, (*A.*,) and GILMAN, (*R. L.*,) both of the City of London, in the County of Middlesex, for "Certain Improvements in the Method of constructing HAND RAKES." Quebec, dated 9th April, 1859.

No. 1011—CAMPBELL, (*J. A.*,) and VANDUSEN, (*C.*,) both of the Village of Georgetown, in the County of Halton, for "A MAILING Apparatus for the purpose of Printing on newspapers and other publications the names of Subscribers." Quebec, dated 9th November, 1859.

No. 1012—EDEY, (*Henry Farrel*,) of the City of Montreal, for "A Self-Acting Graduating Fire GRATE." Quebec, dated 17th November, 1859.

No. 1013—MAXWELL, (*E. J.*,) of the City of Montreal, for "A Double Action Flush Window BOLT." Quebec, dated 26th November, 1859.

No. 1014—McGAFFEY, (*I. W.*,) of the City of Hamilton, in the County of Wentworth, for certain new and useful improvements in "Straw and Feed CUTTERS." Quebec, dated 28th November, 1859.

No 1015—ANSLEY, (*George*,) of the Town of Guelph, in the County of Wellington, for a "Diagonal Vibrating STRAW CUTTER." Quebec, dated 26th November, 1859.

No. 1016—EASTWOOD, (*Willard*,) of the Village of Ingersoll, in the County of Oxford, Assignee of SADLER, (*Thomas*,) of North Dorchester, in the County of Middlesex, for "A now and improved Sawing Machine, called Willard Eastwood's New and Improved SAWING MACHINE." Quebec, dated 1st December, 1859.

No. 1017—WATSON, (*William,*) of the Town of Vaughan, and EMERY, (*T. W.,*) of Toronto, for the " American GAS RETORT." Quebec, dated 1st December, 1859.

No. 1018—ANDERSON, (*Alexander,*) of the City of London, in the County of Middlesex, for " An improved STRAW CUTTER." Quebec, dated 9th December, 1859.

No. 1019—COLLARD, (*Henry,*) of the Township of Leeds, in the County of Leeds, for " An improved CULTIVATOR." Quebec, dated 19th December, 1859.

No. 1020—CUNNINGHAM, (*J. W.,*) of Gananoque, in the County of Leeds, for "A BUTTER WORKER." Quebec, dated 13th December, 1859.

No. 1021—CRAWSHAW, (*J.,*) of the Town of Cobourg, in the County of Northumberland, for "A certain improvement in POWER LOOMS." Quebec, dated 17th January, 1860.

No. 1022—DALES, (*Robert Pinny,*) of the Village of Drayton, in the County of Wellington, for " An improved FORCE PUMP." Quebec, dated 17th January, 1860.

No. 1023—McMURTRY, (*William,*) of the Township of Hope, in the County of Durham, for "A certain Washing and CHURNING Machine." Quebec, dated 17th January, 1860.

No. 1024—McLAREN, (*James William.*) of the Village of Lowville, in the County of Halton, for "An improved MOULD BOARD for Ploughs." Quebec, dated 25th January, 1860.

No. 1025—STITT, (*James,*) of Prescott, in the County of Grenville, for " A new and improved Method of Manufacturing COAL OIL by a Rotating Retort." Quebec, dated 27th January, 1860.

No. 1026—PARK, (*Shubael,*) of the City of Hamilton, in the County of Wentworth, for " A Self-Locomotive Ditch EXCAVATOR." Quebec, dated 28th January, 1860.

No. 1027—ARMSTRONG, (*William,*) of the City of Toronto, in the County of York, for "A FUEL LOADER." Quebec, dated 25th January, 1860.

No. 1028—McGAFFEY, (*I. W.,*) of the City of Hamilton, in the County of Wentworth, for "An improved Fluid GAS LIGHT Apparatus." Quebec, dated 6th February, 1860.

No. 1029—EMERSON, (*Ralph,*) of North Norwich, in the County of Oxford, for "A LAPPED TONGUED Siding and Roofing." Quebec, dated 25th January, 1860.

No. 1030—PARK, (*Shubael,*) of the City of Hamilton, in the County of Wentworth, for "A Self-Locomotive Steam Plough and CULTIVATOR." Quebec, dated 1st February, 1860.

No. 1031—HILBORN, (*James,*) of the Township of Reach, in the County of Ontario, for " A certain POTATO PLANTER." Quebec, dated 6th February, 1860.

No. 1032—TATE, (*C. M.,*) of the City of Quebec, for "The Act of extracting OIL from Peat." Quebec, dated 12th January, 1860.

No. 1033—DYSON, (*Arthur,*) of the City of Quebec, for a " New and improved instrument for opening Oysters, to be called Dyson's OYSTER OPENER." Quebec, dated 12th January, 1860.

No. 1034—TUCK, (*Samuel,*) of the Town of Sherbrooke, in the District of St. Francis, for " A new and improved Cast Iron Plough SHARE with Steel Point." Quebec, dated 12th January, 1860.

No. 1035—HUNTINGTON, (*Gideon,*) of the Township of North Norwich, in the County of Oxford, for "A certain GAUGE Plough, Cultivator and Sowing Machine combined." Quebec, dated 18th February, 1860.

No. 1036—MONTGOMERY, (*John,*) of the City of Kingston, in the County of Frontenac, for "An Anti-Combustible SOLUTION or Mixture." Quebec, dated 18th February, 1860.

No. 1037—LAMBERT, (*John Y.,*) of the Township of Fullarton, in the County of Perth, for "An improved WASHING MACHINE." Quebec, dated 18th February, 1860.

No. 1038—WILLIAMSON, (*William,*) of Smith's Falls, in the County of Lanark, for "A certain Barrel Head MACHINE." Quebec, dated 18th February, 1860.

No. 1039—McKENZIE, (*George,*) of the Town of Goderich, in the County of Huron, for "A certain BUSH ENGINE." Quebec, dated 24th February, 1860.

No. 1040—MULHOLLAND, (*Andrew,*) of the City of Quebec, for " A Vertically Rotating and Stationary BREAK CHURN." Quebec, dated 24th February, 1860.

No. 1041—TRENHOLM, (*Edward*,) of the Town of Kingsey, in the County of Drummond, for "A Machine for Clearing Snow or other obstruction from a Railroad Track, to be called Trenholm's Railroad Track Cleaner." Quebec, dated 27th January, 1860.

No. 1042—MILLIGAN, (*Francis*,) of the City of Quebec, for "An improvement in the Action of Vertical Pianofortes." Quebec, dated 23rd March, 1860.

No. 1043—WATSON, (*Joseph*,) of the Township of Norwich, in the County of Oxford, for "An improved Churn." Quebec, dated 13th December, 1859.

No. 1044—WATEROUS, (*Charles Horatio*,) of the Township of Brantford, in the County of Brant, for "An improvement in the application of Steam Power, and in the manner of making such application, for the purposes of moving and working Steam Ploughs, Steam Fire Engines, &c., &c., &c." Quebec, dated 27th January, 1860.

No. 1045—CLEMO, (*Ebenezer*,) of the City of Montreal, for "A new process of manufacturing Pulp, for the manufacture of paper and parchment, from straw and other vegetable substances." Quebec, dated 27th January, 1860.

No. 1046—TUCK, (*Samuel*,) of the Town of Sherbrooke, for "A new and useful manufacture, styled Tuck's Cast Iron Sugar Boiler." Quebec, dated 2nd March, 1860.

No. 1047—COHN, (*Louis*,) of the City of Toronto, in the County of York, for "An improved Self-Binder for papers." Quebec, dated 7th March, 1860.

No. 1048—ELVIDGE, (*Charles*,) of Newmarket, in the County of York, for "A certain Sewing Machine." Quebec, dated 7th March, 1860.

No. 1049—JEBB, (*Thomas A.*,) of the Township of West Gwillimbury, in the County of Simcoe, for "An improved Churn." Quebec, dated 7th March, 1860.

No. 1050—MAYNARD, (*George*,) of the City of Toronto, in the County of York, for "An Erie Aquatic Propeller." Quebec, dated 7th March, 1860.

No. 1051—SCOTT, (*Thomas*,) of Newburg, in the County of Addington, for "A new Cultivator." Quebec, dated 7th March, 1860.

No. 1052—GAGE, (*Arnold*,) of the Township of Burford, in the County of Brant, for "An improved Churn." Quebec, dated 13th March, 1860.

No. 1053—WORTMAN, (*Charles Henry*,) of the Village of Colbrook, in the County of Addington, for "An improved Eave Trough Machine." Quebec, dated 13th March, 1860.

No. 1054—LUSH, (*David*,) of the Village of Newmarket, in the County of York, for "A Blower for cleaning Grain." Quebec, dated 13th March, 1860.

No. 1055—WHITE, (*George William*,) of the City of Montreal, for "An improvement in the making of Boots and Shoes." Quebec, dated 14th March, 1860.

No. 1056—HENRY, (*Matthew*,) of the Township of Compton, in the County of Compton, for "A useful manufacture, styled Henry's concave Sugar Boiler." Quebec, dated 19th March, 1860.

No. 1057—COCHRANE, (*William Fraser*,) of the Village of Port Bruce, in the County of Elgin, for "An Atmospheric Flour Bolting Chest." Quebec, dated 27th March, 1860.

No. 1058—HOLMES, (*Charles*,) of the Town of St. Catharines, in the County of Lincoln, for "An improved Grain Separator." Quebec, dated 27th March, 1860.

No. 1059—PERRY, (*Samuel V.*,) of the Township of Karuesttown, in the County of Addington, for "A new and improved Machine for Thrashing, Separating and Cleaning Grain." Quebec, dated 29th March, 1860.

No. 1060—MARSH, (*Alfred*,) of the Town of Windsor, in the County of Essex, for "A new and useful improvement in the manufacture of Illuminating Gas." Quebec, dated 4th February, 1860.

No. 1061—MILL, (*George B.*,) of the City of Toronto, in the County of York, for "A Pressure Check Gas Burner." Quebec, dated 9th February, 1860.

No. 1062—McLAREN, (*Hugh*,) of Lowville, Township of Nelson, in the County of Halton, for "An improved Straw Cutter." Quebec, dated 9th February, 1860.

No. 1063—DEVINEY, (*William*,) and HIBBON, (*James*,) both of the Township of Reach, in the County of Ontario, for ".A Double Action Crank." Quebec, dated 18th February, 1860.

No. 1064—McKENZIE, (*Daniel*,) of the Town of Belleville, in the County of Hastings, for "An improved Apparatus for the manufacture of GAS, for illuminating purposes." Quebec, dated 18th February, 1860.

No. 1065—VAN BROCKLIN, (*Philip C.*,) of the Town of Brantford, in the County of Brant, for "An Expansive Tubular Stove, or FIRE BOX." Quebec, dated 25th February, 1860.

No. 1066—BROCKENSHIRE, (*John*,) of Bowmanville, in the County of Durham, for "A Double Action Wooden Suction PUMP." Quebec, dated 27th March, 1860.

No. 1067—CINNAMON, (*James*,) of the Village of Oshawa, in the County of Ontario, for "An improved Washing MACHINE." Quebec, dated 27th February, 1860.

No. 1068—McCLARY, (*William*,) of the City of London, in the County of Middlesex, for "A new and improved method of constructing Queen Posts, Adjustable Dragonal Braces, and iron or wooden angle or Brace Blocks for BRIDGES." Quebec, dated 4th April, 1860.

No. 1069—WALLACE, (*Alexander*,) of the City of Quebec, for "A Railway Car VENTILATOR." Quebec, dated 17th April, 1860.

No. 1070—HULBERT, (*Samuel*,) of the Town of Prescott, in the County of Grenville, for "Air Pump Dash CHURN." Quebec, dated 19th April, 1860.

No. 1071—PATCHING, (*Joseph*,) of the City of Hamilton, in the County of Wentworth, for "A new article, Patching's CAR VENTILATOR." Quebec, dated 19th April, 1860.

No. 1072—SOPER, (*Lewis Nelson*,) of the Town of Woodstock, in the County of Oxford, for "An improved SEWING Machine." Quebec, dated 19th April, 1860.

No. 1073—THORPE, (*Thomas*,) of the Town of Guelph, in the County of Wellington, for "An Air-tight outfitting Spring Sash WINDOW." Quebec, dated 19th April, 1860.

No. 1074—GRANT, (*Robert W.*,) of the Town of Brockville, in the County of Leeds, for "An improved Churn, styled Grant's Eccentric Double Dash CHURN." Quebec, dated 29th April, 1860.

No. 1075—HUNTER, (*William R.*,) of the City of Hamilton, in the County of Wentworth, for Hunter's continuous T Rail for use on RAILWAYS." Quebec, dated 29th April, 1860.

No. 1076—WALSH, (*Michael*,) of the Town of Perth, in the County of Lanark, for "An improved CHURN." Quebec, dated 27th March, 1860.

No. 1077—VAN BROCKLIN, (*P. C.*,) of the Town of Brantford, in the County of Brant, for "A Combined Seed Drill CULTIVATOR and Horse Hoe." Quebec, dated 29th April, 1860.

No. 1078—HOTTON, (*William*,) of the Township of Harwich, in the County of Kent, for "An improved Mould Board for PLOUGHS." Quebec, dated 10th April, 1860.

No. 1079—DODD, (*John*,) of West Flamboro', in the County of Wentworth, for "A Steelyard or WEIGHING Machine." Quebec, dated 29th April, 1860.

No. 1080—FRYATT, (*Henri*,) of the Village of Aurora, in the County of York, for "An improved Method of opening and shutting GATES." Quebec, dated 19th April, 1860.

No. 1081—MAGEE, (*William H*,) of the Village of Merrickville, in the County of Grenville, for "A new Method of constructing PLOUGHS." Quebec, dated 19th April, 1860.

No. 1082—MACINTOSH, (*Joseph J*,) of the Township of Yonge, in the County of Leeds, for "A Grain Separator, styled Macintosh's Patent Fluc Grain SEPARATOR." Quebec, dated 29th April, 1860.

No. 1083—WARD, (*Alexander F.*,) of the Gore of Camden, in the County of Kent, for "A Self-acting Anti-friction Steam SLIDE VALVE." Quebec, dated 25th January, 1860.

No. 1084—MILLARD, (*Joseph*,) of the Village of New Market, in the County of York, for "A Screw Regulating CHEESE PRESS." Quebec, dated 11th May, 1860.

No. 1085—MORTON (*Thomas*,) of the City of Hamilton, in the County of Wentworth, for "A new Self-acting COUPLER and uncoupler for Railway Carriages." Quebec, dated 9th May, 1860.

No. 1086—BOYS, (*Henry, R. A.*,) of the Town of Barrie, in the County of Simcoe, for "A SCREW METER." Quebec, dated 9th May, 1860.

No. 1087—PARK, (*John C.*,) of the Town of Brantford, in the County of Brant, for "A new and improved combined Machine for WELDING, and otherwise repairing the iron rails used

7

for Cars to run upon Railways by the application of Steam Power." Quebec, dated 9th May, 1860.

No. 1088—CAMPBELL, (*Hugh Sym*,) of the City of Toronto, in the County of York, for "An improved CHURN." Quebec, dated 11th May, 1860.

No. 1089—COMBS, (*Horace A.*,) and ASHMAN, (*P.*,) both of the Village of Ontario, in the County of Wentworth, for "An improved Double Acting CHURN." Quebec, dated 11th May, 1860.

No. 1090—THOMSON, (*James E.*,) and KEITH, (*David S.*,) both of the City of Toronto, in the County of York, for "A circulating Tubular Jacked BOILER." Quebec, dated 11th May, 1860.

No. 1091—McDOUGAL, (*John C.*,) of the City of Toronto, in the County of York, for "An Octagonal CHURN." Quebec, dated 11th May, 1860.

No. 1092—NICOL, (*Thomas*,) of the Town of Whitby, in the County of Ontario, for "A Portable Cross-Cut SAWING Machine, with parallel movements." Quebec, dated 9th May, 1860.

No. 1093—JAMES, (*Josiah*,) of the Township of Whitchurch, in the County of York, for "A universal Joint Walking for CHURNS and other Machinery." Quebec, dated 29th April, 1860.

No. 1094—YATES, (*Henry*,) of the Town of Brantford, in the County of Brant, for "An Improvement in Machinery for Coupling, Shaping and renewing the surfaces of METAL BARS." Quebec, dated 9th May, 1860.

No. 1095—CONGER, (*W. S.*,) of the Town of Peterborough, in the County of Peterborough, and ASHFORD, (*James*,) of the Township of Hope, in the County of Durham, Assignees of LEWIS, (*S.*,) of the Town of Port Hope, in the County of Durham, for "A new and Improved Machinery or Apparatus for the purpose of extracting a Polishing substance commonly known as TRIPOLI from SHELL or SHALE MARL." Quebec, dated 22nd May, 1860.

No. 1096—STROTWELL, (*John I.*,) of the Township of Yarmouth, in the County of Elgin, for "The EXCELSIOR Churn." Quebec, dated 29th May, 1860.

No. 1097—ROBINSON, (*John Bernard*,) of Drummondville, in the County of Willard, and JEGO, (*John*,) of Mulmur, in the County of Simcoe, for "An Article Styled the Robinson and Jego improved Method of BOLTING FLOUR." Quebec, dated 30th May, 1860.

No. 1098—HARRIS, (*Alanson*,) of the Village of Beamsville, in the County of Lincoln, for "A combined Corn Sheller and ROOT CUTTER." Quebec, dated 30th May, 1860.

No. 1099—BOWMAN, (*William*,) of the City of London, in the County of Middlesex, for "An Improved FIRE GRATE for Locomotives and other purposes." Quebec, dated 30th May, 1860.

No. 1100—SIMON, (*George H.*,) of the Township of Etobicoke, in the County of York, for "A new PROPELLING Arrangement." Quebec, dated 30th May, 1860.

No. 1101—CONGER, (*W. S.*,) of the Town of Peterborough, in the County of Peterborough, and ASHFORD, (*James*,) of the Township of Hope, in the County of Durham, Assignees of LEWIS, (*S.*,) of the Town of Port Hope, in the County of Durham, for "A Discovery in SHELL or SHALE MARL of a polishing substance, commonly known as TRIPOLI." Quebec, dated 22nd May, 1860.

No. 1102—JONES, (*John*,) of the City of Quebec, for "Jones' Velocipede and HAND CARRIAGE." Quebec, dated 1st June, 1860.

No. 1103—ST. GERMAIN, (*Joseph*,) of the City of St. Hyacinthe, in the County of St. Hyacinthe, for "A Balance Wheeled HORSE RAKE." Quebec, dated 1st June, 1860.

No. 1104—MAXWELL, (*E. John*,) of the City of Montreal, for "Maxwell's Excelsior WINDOW BOLT." Quebec, dated 1st June, 1860.

No. 1105—KERBY, (*Abraham*,) of the Town of Brantford, in the County of Brant, for "A Self-acting and detaching CAR COUPLING." Quebec, dated 14th June, 1860.

No. 1106—SUTHERLAND, (*D. T.*,) of the Town of Guelph, in the County of Wellington, for an "Improved Railway CAR COUPLING." Quebec, dated 15th June, 1860.

No. 1107—FENCH, (*Charles*,) of the Township of King, in the County of York, for "A Portable Worm FENCE." Quebec, dated 15th June, 1860.

No. 1108—HASKER, (*Edward*,) and HARDAKER, (*James*,) both of the Town of Paris, in the County of Brant, for "An Improved Churn, styled Queen's CHURN." Quebec, dated 15th June, 1860.

53

No. 1109—PARADIS, (*Louis II. E.,*) of the Parish of St. Antoine, in the County of Vercheres, Universal Legatee of PARADIS, (*Henry Amable,*) for Paradis Iodine HAIR RESTORATIVE." Quebec, dated 1st June, 1800.

No. 1110—CAMPBELL, (*James A.,*) of Georgetown, in the County of Halton, for "A CARD PRESS and MAILING MACHINE." Quebec, dated 4th July, 1800.

No. 1111—BOWMAN, (*William,*) of the City of London, in the County of Middlesex, for "An Iron Surface bearing FISH or JOINT PLATES for Railways." Quebec, dated 4th July, 1860.

No. 1112—MORSE, (*Samuel,*) of the Town of Milton, in the County of Halton, for " An improved combined Reaping and Mowing MACHINE." Quebec, dated 4th July, 1860.

No. 1113—CARLETON, (*Charles* and *Joshua,*) both of the Township of York, in the County of York, for "An Improved Seaming CULTIVATOR." Quebec, dated 4th July, 1860.

No 1114—WORTHINGTON, (*John,*) and BROWN, (*John,*) for "A Composition for the manufacture of FIRE BRICKS." Quebec, dated 4th July, 1860.

No. 1115—MARSH, (*Alfred,*) of the Town of Windsor, in the County of Essex, for "An improved GAS GENERATOR." Quebec, dated 28th June, 1860.

No. 1116—SPENCER, (*James,*) of the City of Toronto, in the County of York, for "A Machine for PRINTING words, names, numbers, dates, or addresses upon paper, pages,

No. 1117—MEADOWS, (*Charles,*) of the Township of East Zorra, in the County of Oxford, for "An improved machine for Sawing FIREWOOD from the log." Quebec, dated 6th July, 1860.

No. 1118—ECKARETT, (*Philip D.,*) of Unionville, in the Township of Markham, in the County of York, for "A ROOT SLICER." Quebec, dated 9th July, 1860.

No. 1119—GRIGGS, (*Henry P.,*) of the Town of Port Hope, in the County of Durham, for "An Empire Thermometer CHURN." Quebec, dated 9th July, 1860.

No. 1120—BROWN, (*Charles B.,*) of the Town of St. Thomas, in the County of Elgin, for " A Plaster, Dry Manure and Grain SOWER." Quebec, dated 23rd July, 1860.

No. 1121—KELSO, (*Samuel John,*) of Chicoutimi, in the County of Chicoutimi, for "An aqua-gravitation ENGINE." Quebec, dated 26th July, 1860.

No. 1122—PALSER, (*Joseph B.,*) of the City of Montreal, for "An improved and useful article of manufacture, termed and denominated by him STAPLE FIBRE." Quebec, dated 26th July, 1860.

No. 1123—MAXWELL, (*Edward John,*) of the City of Montreal, for "A double-action Flush WINDOW BOLT." Quebec, dated 25th July, 1860.

No. 1124—HOUSE, (*Lewis,*) of the Village of Beamsville, in the County of Lincoln, for " A CORN SHELLER." Quebec, dated 2nd August, 1860.

No. 1125—YATES, (*Henry,*) of the Town of Brantford, in the County of Brant, for "An improved Perforated FIRE GRATE, Feed Water Heater, and Damper combined, for Steam Engines." Quebec, dated 2nd August, 1860.

No. 1126—BRIDGE, (*Andrew,*) of West Brook, in the Township of Kingston, in the County of Frontenac, for " A self-acting CHURN." Quebec, dated 2nd August, 1860.

No. 1127—BROADBENT, (*Hiram,*) of the City of Hamilton, in the County of Wentworth, for "Improved STOP COCKS, PLUGS and VALVES, for the passage of Water and other Fluids." Quebec, dated 2nd August, 1860.

No. 1128—WELCH, (*William,*) of the City of Hamilton, in the County of Wentworth, for "A Spark ANNIHILATOR." Quebec, dated 2nd August, 1860.

No. 1129—WHITE, (*George,*) of the Village of New Market, in the County of York, for "An improved Straw Cutting Box." Quebec, dated 7th August, 1860.

No. 1130—PALSER, (*Joseph B.,*) of the City of Montreal, for "An improved Apparatus to be used in the manufacture of PAPER PULP from straw and other fibrous material." Quebec, dated 8th August, 1860.

No. 1131—SCOTT, (*C. G.,*) and LOCKWOOD, (*S. D.,*) both of the Township of Camden, in the County of Addington, for " An improved Harvesting FORK." Quebec, dated 25th September, 1860.

No. 1132—MARLATT. (*Hiram,*) of the Village of Thorold, in the County of Welland, for "A FRUIT PICKER." Quebec, dated 25th September, 1860.

No. 1133—SMITH, (*J. T.,*) of the Town of Belleville, in the County of Hastings, for "Smith's perfect system of Mill Stone DRESSING by a Diamond." Quebec, dated 25th September, 1860.

No. 1134—BROWN, (*Horace,*) of the Township of Bastard, in the County of Leeds, for "A now method of Balancing MILL STONES." Quebec, dated 25th September, 1860.

No. 1135—WILSON, (*Charles,*) of the Village of St. Mary's, in the County of Perth, for "A Grain SEPARATOR." Quebec, dated 25th September, 1860.

No. 1136—DAVIS, (*John,*) of the Town of Chatham, in the County of Kent, for "An Hydraulic BELLOWS." Quebec, dated 25th September, 1860.

No. 1137—CLARKE, (*J. Paton,*) of the City of Hamilton, in the County of Wentworth, for "A Reaping and Mowing Machine, termed the Scythe Reaper and Mower." Quebec, dated 25th September, 1860.

No. 1138—FINDLAY, (*James,*) of the City of Toronto, in the County of York, for "A Branch Rail, termed Findlay's Branch RAIL." Quebec, dated 25th September, 1860.

No. 1139—SCHNEIDER, (*J. W. H.,*) of the Township of Barton, in the County of Wentworth, for "A Safety Check for the more effectual management of kicking, runaway, and otherwise unruly HORSES." Quebec, dated 25th September, 1860.

No. 1140—LANGSTAFF. (*John,*) of the Township of Markham, in the County of York, for "A wooden cave trough or water CONDUCTOR." Quebec, dated 25th September, 1860.

No. 1141—WATEROUS, (*Charles H.,*) of the Town of Brantford, in the County of Brant, for "A new mode of Packing and Preserving Hops." Quebec, dated 25th September, 1860.

No. 1142—MIGHT, (*Robert,*) of the Village of New Hamburg, in the County of Waterloo, for "An improved mode of constructing Thrashing MACHINES." Quebec, dated 25th September, 1860.

No. 1143—FOWELL, (*Thomas,*) of the Township of Seneca, in the County of Haldimand, and GUNSON, (*William,*) of the Township of Glandford, in the County of Wentworth, for "An improved Cultivator and THISTLE CUTTER." Quebec, dated 25th September, 1860.

No. 1144—McKENZIE, (*George,*) of the Town of Goderich, in the County of Huron, for "An improved PIPE BUSH." Quebec, dated 25th September, 1860.

No. 1145—YERKS, (*John,*) of Charlotteville, in the County of Norfolk, for "An improved ROOT CUTTER." Quebec, dated 25th September, 1860.

No. 1146—MORSE, (*Samuel,*) of the Town of Milton, in the County of Halton, for "An improved THRASHING MACHINE." Quebec, dated 25th September, 1860.

No. 1147—JAMES, (*William,*) of Mariposa, in the County of Victoria, for "A Double Action Dash CHURN." Quebec, dated 25th September, 1860.

No. 1148—WEIR, (*William,*) of the City of Montreal, for "An improvement in the manufacture of FAPER PULP, from Straw and other vegetable substances." Quebec, dated 2nd October, 1860.

No. 1149—WEBSTER, (*Norman L.,*) of Richmond, in the County of Richmond, for "A new and improved Furnace, to be called Webster's FURNACE." Quebec, dated 2nd October, 1860.

No. 1150—PARADIS, (*Joseph,*) of the Parish of St. Jude, in the County of St. Hyacinthe, for "An improved WATER WHEEL." Quebec, dated 3rd October, 1860.

No. 1151—PALSER, (*Joseph B.,*) in the City of Montreal, for "Certain new and useful improvements in the Manufacture of PAPER PULP from Straw and other fibrous materials." Quebec, dated 3rd October, 1860.

No. 1152—MOODY, (*Matthew,*) of the Parish of Terrebonne, for "An accommodating Joint working on two centre bearings, applied to MOWING and REAPING Machines." Quebec, dated 4th October, 1860.

No. 1153—BROOKS, (*Charles,*) of the Township of Ascot, for "A Self-acting Carriage BRAKE." Quebec, dated 4th October, 1860.

No. 1154—LANE, (*Frederick,*) of the City of Montreal, for "A new and improved Galvanic Battery and ELECTRIC HELIX." Quebec, dated 6th October, 1860.

No. 1155—ACKERMAN, (*Francis M.,*) of the Village of Morven, in the County of Addington, for "An Article termed the Ackerman WASHING Machine." Quebec, dated 12th October, 1860.

No. 1156—COOPER, (*Eugene.*) of the Township of Oneida, in the County of Haldimand, for "A STUMPING Machine." Quebec, dated 22nd October, 1800.

No. 1157—BUCKLER, (*David,*) of Garafraxa, in the County of Wellington, for "A Chair or Lounge termed the LAZY MAN'S FRIEND." Quebec, dated 25th September, 1860.

No. 1158—TEES, (*David,*) of the City of Montreal, for "An Air-tight Coffin or burial Case, denominated by him, Tees' Air-tight COFFIN or Burial CASKET." Quebec, dated 25th October, 1860.

No. 1159—KLEIN, (*David,*) of the City of Quebec, for "A Floating BRIDGE." Quebec, dated 13th December, 1860.

No. 1160—KIRK, (*George,*) of the Town of Chatham, in the County of Kent, for "A new and improved Method of INDEXING Books." Quebec, dated 6th November, 1860.

No 1161—SUDWORTH, (*William,*) of the Town of Woodstock, in the County of Oxford, for "An improved process of Balling and TANNING HIDES and SKINS." Quebec, dated 2nd November, 1860.

No. 1162—GRANGE, (*Thomas,*) of the Township of Richmond, in the County of Lennox and Addington, for "An Improved HARROW TOOTH." Quebec, dated 2nd November, 1860.

No. 1163—HAMILTON, (*James,*) of the Town of Peterborough, in the County of Peterborough, for "An Improved Grain Sower and CULTIVATOR, combined." Quebec, dated 21st December, 1860.

No. 1164—LEONARD, (*Elijah,*) of the Town of London, in the County of Middlesex, for "A SAWING MACHINE for cross-cutting Timber." Quebec, dated 21st December, 1860.

No. 1165—LAWLOR, (*John D.,*) of Fort Erie, in the County of Welland, for "An Improved SAWING MACHINE." Quebec, dated 21st December, 1860.

No. 1166—KIMBALL, (*Nelson,*) of the Township of London, in the County of Middlesex, for "An Improved CULTIVATOR." Quebec, dated 31st December, 1860.

No. 1167—MARKS, (*Joseph,*) of the City of Hamilton, in the County of Wentworth, for "A New system of Lubricating Valves, Pistons, Cylinders, Piston Rods and Valve Spindles of Locomotives and other ENGINES" Quebec, dated 21st December, 1860.

No. 1168—MARKINS, (*George H.,*) of the City of Hamilton, in the County of Wentworth, and MILLS, (*Isaac,*) of the Township of Flamboro' West, in the County of Wentworth, for "An Article for counting, and testing the quality of EGGS." Quebec, dated 21st December, 1860.

No. 1169—TAYLOR, (*Thomas H.,*) of the Town of Chatham, in the County of Kent, for "A Self-acting CLEANER for a Plough." Quebec, dated 21st December, 1860.

No. 1170—MURPHY, (*Thomas,*) of the Village of Clifton, in the County of Welland, for "A New and Improved LAMP for burning coal oil and other Hydro-carbon liquids without a glass chimney." Quebec, dated 21st December, 1860.

No. 1171—STILES, (*Peter B. B.,*) of the Village of Beaverton, in the County of Ontario, for "A LIFTING GATE." Quebec, dated 21st December, 1860.

No. 1172—BRIGHT, (*William,*) and COLLINS, (*James,*) both of the Town of Guelph, in the County of Wellington, for "A Clothes AIRER." Quebec, dated 21th December, 1860.

No. 1173—FELL, (*David,*) of the Town of Cornwall, in the County of Stormont, for "A New and Improved Rotary Lever CHURN." Quebec, dated 16th January, 1861.

No. 1174—SHATTUCK, (*Chester,*) of the City of Toronto, in the County of York, for "A new composition of matter for Tanning LEATHER." Quebec, dated 7th January, 1861.

No. 1175—MAXWELL, (*Edward J.,*) of the City of Montreal, for "A Spring Latch to be called Maxwell's Spring LATCH." Quebec, dated 25th January, 1861.

No. 1176—GILL, (*William,*) of the City of Toronto, in the County of York, for "A certain improvement in the FLUES of Steam Boilers." Quebec, dated 21st December, 1860.

No. 1177—KINNEY, (*Cyrus,*) of the Township of Dereham, in the County of Oxford, Assignee of KINNEY, (*Israel,*) of the Town of Simcoe, in the County of Norfolk, for "A new mode of applying Power to any Machinery by combining Rotary Motion with the inclined PLANE." Quebec, dated 10th January, 1861.

No. 1178—CHURCHILL (Z.,) of the Township of Pickering, in the County of Ontario, for "A Stump EXTRACTOR." Quebec, dated 16th January, 1861.

No. 1179—LLOYD, (Ferdinand D.,) of the City of Toronto, in the County of York, for "Lloyd's Patent Broadcast SEED SOWER." Quebec, dated 12th January, 1861.

No. 1180—SHORTS, (Samuel D.,) of the Township of Richmond, in the County of Lennox, for "A Machine for the Manufacture of Cheese and Butter, termed the DAIRY MAID." Quebec, dated 16th January, 1861.

No. 1181—RODGERS, (Frederick,) of the City of Hamilton, in the County of Wentworth, for "An improved CAM for working the under needle or Catch Pin of Sewing Machines." Quebec, dated 16th January, 1861.

No. 1182—ARMSTRONG, (James,) of the Township of Bathurst, in the County of Lanark, for "A new and improved Churn, termed the JENNY LIND CHURN." Quebec, dated 16th January, 1861.

No. 1183—PALMER, (Henry,) of the City of London, in the County of Middlesex, for "A new Electro-voltaic POCKET BATTERY." Quebec, dated 16th January, 1861.

No. 1184—ERVIN, (Francis,) and BEEMER, (William,) both of the Township of Brantford, in the County of Brant, for "A Horizontal Lever WASHING Machine." Quebec, dated 24th January, 1861.

No. 1185—SKINNER, (Sylvester,) of the Village of Gananoque, in the County of Leeds, for "A Machine for BENDING Hame Timber, Plough Handles, &c., by end pressure." Quebec, dated 1st February, 1861.

No. 1186—CRAWFORD, (Eliza Ann,) of the City of Toronto, in the County of York, Assignee of CRAWFORD, (Arthur,) of the aforesaid City, for "Self-acting FIRE LIGHTER, for lighting fire in Wood or Coal Stoves, Grates, Ovens, Fire-places, &c." Quebec, dated 1st February, 1861.

No. 1187—RUSS, (Cyrus,) of the Village of Smithville, in the County of Lincoln, for "A POTATO DIGGER." Quebec, dated 1st February, 1861.

No. 1188—BRUSH, (George,) of the City of Montreal, for "An Improved Hydraulic Press, to be called Brush's HYDRAULIC PRESS." Quebec, dated 4th March, 1861.

No. 1189—BELL, (David,) of St. Nicholas, in the County of Levis, for "A New SNOW PLOUGH." Quebec, dated 19th March, 1861.

No. 1190—GALL, (Warren,) of the Township of Stanstead, in the County of Stanstead, for "A new and useful STRAW CUTTER." Quebec, dated 19th March, 1861.

No. 1191—TASSE, (Damase,) of the Parish of Ste. Scholastique, in the County of Two Mountains, for "A SPRING to open a Horse's Foot." Quebec, dated 19th March, 1861.

No. 1192—KEMPLIN, (Cornelius,) and GOFF, (P. D. H.,) Assignees of BLANCKENSEE, (Julius,) all of the Town of Woodstock, in the County of Woodstock, for "A Motific Hydragogue ENGINE." Quebec, dated 4th March, 1861.

No. 1193—BROWN, (William R.,) of the Town of Bowmanville, in the County of Durham, for "An Improved ROOT CUTTER." Quebec, dated 4th March, 1861.

No. 1194—CATHCART, (John,) of the Village of Beaverton, in the County of Ontario, for "Cathcart's RULE for Cutting Boots and Shoes." Quebec, dated 4th March, 1861.

No. 1195—EMERY, (Thomas W.,) and CLAYTON, (James,) both of the City of Toronto, in the County of York, for "A Gas Regulator, Purifier and COOLER." Quebec, dated 7th February, 1861.

No. 1196—FORREST, (James,) of the Village of Ontario, in the County of Wentworth, for "A Self-Acting Cattle GUARD." Quebec, dated 4th March, 1861.

No. 1197—DAVIDSON, (Thomas,) of the Township of York, in the County of York, for "A Combined Grain and Seed DRILL." Quebec, dated 4th March, 1861.

No. 1198—LUSK (David,) of the Village of New Market, in the County of York, for "A Combined Blower and FANNING MILL." Quebec, dated 4th March, 1861.

No. 1199—McNISH, (*James,*) of the Township of Yonge, in the County of Leeds, for " A n ew form of Mould Board for PLOUGHS." Quebec, dated 4th March, 1861.

No. 1200—ROBINSON, (*John S.*,) of the City of London, in the County of Middlesex, for "A Double Acting Suction and FORCE PUMP with Ball Valves." Quebec, dated 4th March, 1861.

No. 1201—WATEROUS, (*Charles H.*,) of the Town of Brantford, in the County of Brant, for " A Water DRAWER." Quebec, dated 4th March, 1861.

No. 1202—YATES, (*Edwin,*) of Morisson, in the County of Victoria, for " A Combined Washing, Wringing and MANGLING Machine." Quebec, dated 4th March, 1861.

No. 1203—DART, (*Charles,*) in the Town of Brockville, in the County of Leeds, for " An Improved WASHING Machine." Quebec, dated 5th March, 1861.

No. 1204—CUNNINGHAM, (*John W.*,) of Gananoque, in the County of Leeds, for " An Elastic Self-Acting Lamp Chimney WIPER." Quebec, dated 11th March, 1861.

No. 1205—RANDALL, (*William,*) of the Township of Uxbridge, in the County of Ontario, for " An EXCAVATOR, for excavating earth." Quebec, dated 6th March, 1861.

No. 1206—JOSLYN, (*Hubbard,*) of the Township of Stanstead, in the County of Stanstead, for " An Improved Machine for Wringing Clothes to be called Joslyn's Improved CLOTHES WRINGER." Quebec, dated 4th April, 1861.

No. 1207—PARK. (*John Carter,*) of the Town of Brantford, in the County of Brant, for " A Machine for removing SNOW and ICE from Railway Tracks." Quebec, dated 9th April, 1861.

No. 1208—COCKBURN, (*Alexander F.*,) of the City of Montreal, for " A Compression Swivel Action WATER-COCK." Quebec, dated 11th March, 1861.

(*Void by Judgment of the Superior Court, dated 28th April, 1862.*)

No. 1209—TETU, (*David Henri,*) of Rivière Ouelle, in the County of Kamouraska, for " A FISHING Apparatus in Deep Water." Quebec, dated 18th April, 1861.

No. 1210—HANNUM, (*John A. B* ,) of the Town of Cornwall, in the County of Stormont, for " A CHURN POWER." Quebec, dated 25th April, 1851.

No. 1211—YATES, (*Henry,*) of Brantford, Assignee for the residue of the unexpired period of a certain Patent granted to one McLENNAN, (*James,*) on the 15th December, A. D. 1855, for " A new Machine for the repairing of IRON RAILS, used for Cars and Carriages to run upon Railways." Quebec, dated 6th February, 1861.

No. 1212—GRAVES, (*Lorenzo,*) of the Township of Barnston, in the County of Stanstead, for " A Double Pressure Clothes WRINGER." Quebec, dated 10th May, 1861.

No. 1213—WESTMAN, (*W. D.*,) of the Township of King, in the County of York, for " An Improved SCREEN for Fanning Mills." Quebec, dated 12th March, 1861.

No. 1214—OSTRUM, (*H. W.*,) and SUTTON, (*Joseph,*) both of the Township of Sidney, in the County of Hastings, for " An Improved FANNING MILL." Quebec, dated 12th March, 1861.

No. 1215—OSTRUM, (*H. W.*,) and SUTTON, (*Joseph,*) both of the Township of Sidney, in the County of Hastings, for " An Improved CHURNING GEAR." Quebec, dated 12th March, 1861.

No. 1216—WATSON, (*William,*) of the Township of Vaughan, in the County of York, for " An Improvement in the manufacture of OIL GAS." Quebec, dated 23rd March, 1861.

No. 1217—FULLER, (*Albert O.*,) of the Township of Erin, in the County of Wellington, for " A new and portable labour saving Machine for cutting MORTICES in carriage and all other Hubs by hand." Quebec, dated 21st March, 1861.

No. 1218—BROWN, (*William,*) and WEAVER, (*Jesse,*) both of the Township of Malahide, in the County of Elgin, for " An Evaporating FURNACE." Quebec, dated 23rd March, 1861.

No. 1219—SMITH, (*Richard,*) of the Town of Sherbrooke, in the District of St. Francis, for " An Improved Extension AUGER." Quebec, dated 8th May, 1361.

No. 1220—SMITH, (*Richard,*) of the Town of Sherbrooke, in the District of St. Francis, for " A new and Improved BELT LINK." Quebec, dated 8th May, 1861.

No. 1221—COLE, (*L. M.*,) of the City of Montreal, for " A Metallic HEEL for Boots and Shoes." Quebec, dated 8th May, 1861.

No. 1222—HIBBARD, (*Ashley,*) of the City of Montreal, for " VENTILATING India Rubber Boots and Shoes." Quebec, dated 11th May, 1861.

58

No. 1223—BENTLEY, (C.,) of the Township of Perkins, in the County of Ontario, for "An Eave Trough and Finish." Quebec, dated 21st March, 1861.

No. 1224—HINTON, (G. H.,) of the City of Montreal, for "New and useful Improvements in the Manufacture of Saws." Quebec, dated 8th May, 1861.

No. 1225—Error in the old Book, repetition of Patent marked No. 1213.

No. 1226—PARK, (A. J.,) of the Village of Norwichville, in the County of Oxford, for "An Improved Process of Tanning and Manufacturing Leather." Quebec, dated 20th May, 1861.

No. 1227—STEWART, (James,) of the City of Hamilton, for "A new and improved Pattern or Design for Cooking Stoves." Quebec, dated 20th May, 1861.

No. 1228—HILL, (Richard,) of the Town of Port Hope, in the County of Durham, for "An improved Plough." Quebec, dated 17th April, 1861.

No. 1229—ROBINSON, (George,) of Drummondville, in the County of Welland, for "An improved Extension Clothes Horse." Quebec, dated 10th April, 1861.

No. 1230—COSSITT, (G. M.,) COSSITT, (N.,) and YOUNG, (Alexander,) of the Village of Smith's Falls, in the County of Lanark, for "An improved Reaper Attachment." Quebec, dated 10th April, 1861.

No. 1231—IVES, (George,) of the Town of Windsor, in the County of Essex, for "An improved Saw Horse." Quebec, dated 10th April, 1861.

No. 1232—PHILIP, (John Read,) of the Town of Cobourg, in the County of Northumberland, for "An improved mode of Lowering Boats from the Davits of Ships." Quebec, dated 22nd April, 1861.

No. 1233—LEMAN, (Henry,) of the Township of Reach, in the County of Ontario, for "The Farmer's improved Hay Rake." Quebec, dated 17th April, 1861.

No. 1234—VERNON, (Elias,) of the City of Hamilton, in the County of Wentworth, for "An Economical Hot Air Apparatus." Quebec, dated 30th April, 1861.

No. 1235—DAVISON, (James,) of Belleville, in the County of Hastings, for "An improved Power for Churning, Pumping and Washing." Quebec, dated 20th April, 1861.

No. 1236—COOLEY, (William,) Assignee of PERKINS, (E. S,) of the City of Montreal, for "A new and useful Improvement in the ordinary Two Arm Saw Set." Quebec, dated 3rd June, 1861.

No. 1237—KNOWLTON, (A. A,) of the Township of Brome, in the County of Brome, for "A Washing Machine." Quebec, dated 18th July, 1861.

No. 1238—JAMES, (Josiah,) of the Township of Whitchurch, in the County of York, for "A Superficial Wedge Power." Quebec, dated 20th April, 1861.

No. 1239—THOMAS, (John,) of the City of Toronto, in the County of York, for "An improvement in the construction of the Piano Forte." Quebec, dated 21st May, 1861.

No. 1240—HAZLETON, (Heman,) of the Township of Townsend, in the County of Norfolk, for "An improved Self-propelling Gate." Quebec, dated 21st May, 1861.

No. 1241—WHYTOCK, (Andrew,) of the City of Quebec, for "Improvements in coating Sheets of Metal with other Metals and other Substances." Quebec, dated 27th August, 1861.

No. 1242—O'DELL, (Abiel,) of the Town of Bowmanville, in the County of Durham, for "A Self Regulating Spiral Spring Mangle and Washing Machine." Quebec, dated 3rd August, 1861.

No. 1243—WARE, (Paul T.,) of the City of Toronto, in the County of York, for "An improved Sewing Machine." Quebec, dated 9th August, 1861.

No. 1244—NORTH, (D. E.,) of the Town of Bowmanville, in the County of Durham, for "An improved Churn, termed Norton's Horizontal Screw Dash Churn." Quebec, dated 10th August, 1861.

No. 1245—McKELVEY, (James,) of the Town of St. Catharines, in the County of Lincoln, for "A Refrigerator termed 'The Prince of Wales Cupboard Refrigerator.'" Quebec, dated 25th June, 1861.

No. 1246—CLAIR, (*Michael,*) of the Township of Sophiasburgh, in the County of Prince Edward, for " The Excelsior WASHER." Quebec, dated 4th June, 1861.

No. 1247—Error in the old Book, same Patent as No. 1261.

No. 1248—FOGG, (*Thomas,*) of the Town of Brantford, in the County of Brant, for " A Ballasting CAR." Quebec, dated 21st May, 1861.

No. 1249—WELTE, (*Silas,*) of the Village of Princeton, in the County of Oxford, for " An improved Churn, termed the ' Blenheim CHURN.' " Quebec, 22nd May, 1861.

No. 1250—KERR, (*Robert,*) of the Township and County of Waterloo, for " A Grain and Seed Broad Cast SOWER." Quebec, dated 25th May, 1861.

No 1251—PARKES, (*Charles R.,*) of the City of Toronto, in the County of York, for " An improved CHURN." Quebec, dated 30th July, 1861.

No. 1252 - DAVIS, (*Thomas,*) of the Village of Marysville, in the Township of Wolfe Island and County of Frontenac, for " A Sub-Marine BUOY Purchase." Quebec, dated 27th May, 1861.

No. 1253—CARMAND, (*George A.,*) of the Village of Morrisburg, in the County of Dundas, for " A Vegetable Root CUTTER." Quebec, dated 28th May, 1861.

No. 1254—YOUNG, (*Adam,*) of the Township of Crowland, in the County of Welland, for " An Improved MILL SAW." Quebec, dated 9th July, 1861.

No. 1255—PIKE, (*John,*) of Prescott, in the County of Grenville, as Assignee of FRASER, (*John G.,*) of the aforesaid place, for " An Improved CHURN." Quebec, dated 30th July, 1861.

No. 1256—PATTERSON, (*John,*) of the Village of Ingersoll, in the County of Oxford, for " A DRILL for Drilling Holes in Rock." Quebec, dated 17th July, 1861.

No. 1257—BRUCE, (*David,*) of the City of London, in the County of Middlesex, for " An Improved SAWING Machine." Quebec, dated 17th July, 1861.

No. 1258—VANDERWATER, (*Elias,*) of the Township of Sidney, in the County of Hastings, for " An Improved REAPING and MOWING Machine." Quebec, dated 17th July, 1861.

No. 1259—HILLMAN, (*Armaleeh,*) of Stratford, in the County of Perth, for " Spring Cushioned SEAT for Waggons and other Vehicles." Quebec, dated 17th July, 1861.

No. 1260—FRYATT, (*Henry,*) of Aurora, in the County of York, for " A Rotatory TOOTH for Harrows." Quebec, dated 17th July, 1861.

No. 1261—DOLBRY, (*James,*) and DOLBRY, (*Isaac,*) both of the Township and County of York, for " A new and improved LATH Cutting Machine." Quebec, dated 17th July, 1861.

No. 1262—HILBARD, (*James,*) of the Township of Reach, in the County of Ontario, for " A Steam LOCOMOTIVE for Travelling upon Public Highways." Quebec, dated 17th July, 1861.

No. 1263—DEANS, (*George,*) of the Town of Port Dover, in the Coun.y of Norfolk, for " A CHALLENGE Washing Machine." Quebec, dated 18th July, 1861.

No. 1264—McEWEN, (*Peter,*) of Russell, in the County of Russell, for " An Improved PLOUGH." Quebec, dated 30th July, 1861.

No. 1265—POWERS, (*John,*) of the Town of Stratford, in the County of Perth, for " The Victoria WASHING Machine." Quebec, dated 3rd August, 1861.

No. 1266—OATES, (*Richard H.,*) of the City of Toronto, in the County of York, for " A Self Revolving WIND MILL House with Circular Foundations." Quebec, dated 9th August, 1861.

No. 1267—BIGELOW, (*Albert,*) of the City of Hamilton, in the County of Wentworth, for " A new and improved ROCK DRILL." Quebec, dated 10th August, 1861.

No. 1268—DORWIN, (*Jebediah H.,*) of the City of Montreal, for " An Improved Mercurial BAROMETER." Quebec, dated 18th September, 1861.

No. 1269—WEBBER, (*Robert,*) of the Township of East Zorra, in the County of Oxford, for " Webber's Scarifier or Field CULTIVATOR." Quebec, dated 20th September, 1861.

No. 1270—SLATER, (*Samuel,*) of London, in the County of Middlesex, for " An Adjusting LAST." Quebec, dated 20th August, 1861.

No. 1271—WALKER, (*William,*) and WALKER, (*Thomas,*) both of the Township of Chinguacousey, in the County of Peel, for " The Ocean Wave WASHING Machine." Quebec, dated 29th November, 1861.

No. 1272—SHANNON, (*C. S.*,) of the City of Hamilton, for "An Improved Driving REIN." Quebec, dated 29th November, 1831.

No. 1273—DODD, (*Henry,*) of the Township of Goderich, in the County of Huron, for "Improved SEIVES or Screens for Fanning Mills." Quebec, dated 29th November, 1861.

No. 1274—O'BRIEN, (*Volney,*) of the Town of Guelph, in the County of Wellington, for "The Excelsior CHURN." Quebec, dated 29th November, 1861.

No. 1275—BOWERMAN, (*Amos,*) of the Township of Whitchurch, County of York, BOWERMAN, (*Jacob C.*,) and BOWERMAN, (*Willis D.*,) both of the Township of Whitby, in the County of Ontario, for "Bowerman's Improved CARDING Machine." Quebec, dated 29th November, 1861.

No. 1276—THOMPSON, (*James G.*,) of the Town of Peterborough, for "An Automatic GATE." Quebec, dated 29th November, 1861.

No. 1277—FOOTE, (*A. J.*,) of the Village of Tilsonbury, in the County of Oxford, for "A new and useful Washing and Scouring MACHINE." Quebec, dated 29th November, 1861.

No. 1278—McLAREN, (*Hugh,*) of Louisville, in the County of Halton, for "A Combined Seed Drill and CULTIVATOR." Quebec, dated 29th November, 1861.

No. 1279—McILROY, (*Thomas,*) of Brampton, for "An Improved Inlaid BEDSTEAD." Quebec, dated 29th November, 1861.

No. 1280—NUTTING, (*N. H.*,) of the Township of Marysburg, in the County of Prince Edward, for "The Ontario WASHING Machine." Quebec, dated 29th November, 1861.

No. 1281—DEPEW, (*William,*) of Paris, in the County of Brant, for "A Balance GATE." Quebec, dated 29th November, 1861.

No. 1282—ASHE, (*Edward D.*,) for "A new and improved method of constructing Steam ENGINES to be called SHAFT Engines." Quebec, dated 2nd December, 1861.

No. 1283—SEYMOUR, (*H.*,) of the City of Montreal, for "A Composition to be named Seymour's Concentrated FUEL." Quebec, dated 2nd December, 1861.

No. 1284—SOUTHWICK, (*M. B.*,) of Mont St. Claire, in the County of Rouville, for "A new and useful Machine for Separating Shives, Chaff, and Dust from the Tow of Flax, Hemp, and to be called 'Southwick's Tow CLEANER.'" Quebec, dated 5th December, 1861.

No. 1285—DOUGALL, (*James,*) of the Parish of Montreal, for "A Composition of MATTER for the Packing of Axle Boxes of Locomotives, Engines, Tenders, and Railway Cars." Quebec, dated 5th December, 1861.

No. 1286—HENRY, (*Matthew,*) of the Township of Compton, in the County of Compton, for "An Improved FANNING MILL." Quebec, dated 9th December, 1861.

No. 1287—RAY, (*Stillman,*) of the Township of Stanstead, in the County of Stanstead, for "Ray's Improved TUB and PAIL Machines." Quebec, dated 18th December, 1861.

No. 1288—HUTCHINS, (*William F.*,) of the City of Montreal, for "A RIVET Machine." Quebec, dated 10th December, 1861.

No. 1289—SMITH, (*Edward,*) of the Township of Edwardsburg, in the County of Grenville, for "Egyptian GAS." Quebec, dated 29th November, 1861.

No. 1290—PARENT, (*Etienne Henri,*) of the City of Quebec, for the introduction of a certain Machine, called "Air Expansion Motion POWER, produced by the Combustion of Gases, by means of the Electric Spark." Quebec, dated 30th November, 1861.

No. 1291—WALLBRIDGE, (*A. S.*,) of Bedford, in the County of Missisquoi, for "An improved mode of operating Variable Expansion Steam Cut-off Valves." Quebec, dated 28th November, 1861.

No. 1292—HENRY, (*M.*,) of the Township of Compton, in the County of Compton, for "A new Plough to be called 'Henry's Complete PLOUGH.'" Quebec, dated 9th December, 1861.

No. 1293—McLAREN, (*James William,*) of Lowville, in the County of Halton, for "An Improved Feed GEAR for Straw Cutters." Quebec, dated 26th November, 1861.

No. 1294—COMER, (*Lewis,*) of the Township of Hinchinbroke, in the County of Frontenac, for "An Improved BEE HIVE." Quebec, dated 26th November, 1861.

No. 1295—CHAMBERS, (*William,*) of London, in the County of Middlesex, for "An Improved Carriage HUB." Quebec, dated 29th November, 1861.

No. 1290—TAYLOR, (*Augustus E.*,) of the Town of Brockville, in the County of Leeds, for " An Improved Door Bell." Quebec, dated 29th November, 1861.

No. 1297—LAWSON, (*Henry*), of the Town of Peterborough, in the County of Peterborough, for " A Combined Retort for generating GAS from Carbon Oil." Quebec, dated 29th November, 1861.

No. 1298—BLANTON, (*Thomas*,) of Drummondville, in the County of Welland, for " An Improved Broad Cast Sower and Drag." Quebec, dated 29th November, 1861.

No. 1299—McDOUGALL, (*William*,) of the Township and County of York, for " A Self-Acting Brake for Sawing Machines." Quebec, dated 29th November, 1861.

No. 1300—HARPER, (*Thomas William*,) of the Town of Cobourg, in the County of Northumberland, for " A new Wash Tub." Quebec, dated 29th November, 1861.

No. 1301—LANGS, (*Edwin K.*,) of the Township of Brantford, in the County of Brant, for " A Portable and Substantial Fence-Post and Fence." Quebec, dated 29th November, 1861.

No. 1302—VAN BROCKLIN, (*Philip C.*) of the Town of Brantford, in the County of Brant, for " An Improved Grain Drill Cultivator and Horse Hoe." Quebec, dated 29th November, 1861.

No. 1303—WORSWICK, (*Thomas*,) of the Town of Guelph, in the County of Wellington, for " An Improved Switch for Railroads." Quebec, dated 29th November, 1861.

No. 1304—FLEMING, (*John*,) of Petrolia, in the County of Lambton, for " A Double Acting Well." Quebec, dated 4th December, 1861.

No. 1305—HASTINGS, (*Thomas H.*,) of the City of London, in the County of Middlesex, for " A new Machine for obtaining Rotary Motion for Driving Machinery." Quebec, dated 16th December, 1861.

No. 1306—HOWELL, (*James*,) of the Township of Dereham, in the County of Oxford, for " An Iron Die for Mouldings and Casting Plough Shares." Quebec, dated 16th December, 1861.

No. 1307—MOHAFFY, (*William*,) of the Town of Brampton, in the County of Peel, for " An Improved Plough." Quebec, dated 16th December, 1861.

No. 1308—SHAW, (*H. N.*,) of Cooksville, in the County of Peel, for " An improved Dome Petroleum Separator." Quebec, dated 16th December, 1861.

No. 1309—MEAKINS, (*George H.*,) of the City of Hamilton, in the County of Wentworth, for " A Combined Universal Hemmer and Binder." Quebec, dated 26th December, 1861.

No. 1310—TOMLINSON, (*James*,) of the Township of Pickering, in the County of Ontario, for " A Bevelled Sawn Hoof." Quebec, dated 27th December, 1861.

No. 1311—MARTIN, (*Samuel S.*,) of the City of Toronto, in the County of York, Assignee of CULL (*John Angell*,) the Assignee of Cull (*Edward Lefroy*,) the Inventor for " Auxiliary Spring Improvements for Sewing Machines." Quebec, dated 27th December, 1861.

No. 1312—KEACHIE, (*G. C.*,) of the Town of Brantford, in the County of Brant, for " An Improved Strapless Skate." Quebec, dated 27th December, 1861.

No. 1313—FISHER, (*Arthur*,) of the City of Montreal, for " A Hollow Brick." Quebec, dated 7th February, 1862.

No. 1314—WEAGANT, (*H. F.*,) of Morrisburg, in the County of Dundas, for " A Tripod Churning Machine." Quebec, dated 8th February, 1862.

No. 1315—McKENZIE, (*A. D.*,) of Augusta, County of Grenville, and McGAFFY, (*J. W.*,) of the City of Hamilton, County of Wentworth, for " Improvements in Gas Generators and Burners." Quebec, dated 4th January, 1862.

No. 1316—ADAMS, (*A.*,) of the City of Montreal, for " A new and useful Machine for Splitting Sticks for Matches." Quebec, dated 4th March, 1862.

No. 1317—MUNRO, (*George*,) of the Town of Peterborough, for " Munro's Patent Model Grist Mill." Quebec, dated 29th November, 1861.

No. 1318—GODERICH, (*Charles*,) of the Town of St. Thomas, in the County of Elgin, for " An Anti-friction Railroad Car Box." Quebec, dated 8th January, 1862.

No. 1319—PELLS, (*Isaac Thompson*,) of the City of Toronto, in the County of York, for "An Article known or described as Baking Powder." Quebec, dated 9th January, 1862.

No. 1320—YOUNG, (*W. A.*,) of the Town of Dundas, in the County of Wentworth, for "A Boot TREEING Machine." Quebec, dated 15th January, 1862.

No. 1321—FLEMING, (*David*,) of the City of Toronto, in the County of York, for "A new kind of Farm FENCE." Quebec, dated 15th January, 1862.

No. 1322—YOUNG, (*William A.*,) of Dundas, in the County of Wentworth, for "An Improvement on a Boston Patented Boot CRIMPING Machine." Quebec, dated 15th January, 1862.

No. 1323—KINNEY, (*Israel*,) of the Town of Simcoe, in the County of Norfolk, for "An Improved CHURN Attachment." Quebec, dated 28th January, 1862.

No. 1324—AUSTIN, (*John*,) of the Town of Fergus, in the County of Wellington, for "The Mill Stone ASSISTANT." Quebec, dated 19th February, 1862.

No. 1325—LOCKMAN, (*Christopher*,) of the City of Hamilton, in the County of Wentworth, for "An improvement in Shuttle SEWING Machines, termed the "Family Shuttle SEWING Machine." Quebec, dated 19th February, 1862.

No. 1326—MYERS, (*William*,) of the Township of Williamsburgh, in the County of Dundas, for "A new and improved Fanning MILL and Machine, for Separating Oats, Cockle, and other Seeds from Wheat." Quebec, dated 19th February, 1862.

No. 1327—MANNER, (*G. A.*,) of the Township of Innisfil, in the County of Simcoe, for "A Double Lever Power, or an improvement to the Lever Power on BULL Wheels." Quebec, dated 28th February, 1862.

No. 1328—KERR, (*Robert*,) of the Township of Waterloo, in the County of Waterloo, for "An Improved Grain and Seed Broad Cast SOWER." Quebec, dated 28th February, 1862.

No. 1329—MILLAR, (*J. W.*,) and MILLAR, (*J. F.*,) of the Village of Morrisburgh, in the County of Dundas, for "An improved Moulding Flask for making the Mould Boards of PLOUGHS without Sand." Quebec, dated 12th March, 1862.

No. 1330—WATSON, (*Reuben*,) and OVERTON, (*John*,) both of the Township of Moore, in the County of Lambton, for "An improved Plough, called the "Lincolnshire Plough Boy." Quebec, dated 14th March, 1862.

No. 1331—CLENDENING, (*Smith J.*,) of the Township of Malahide, in the County of Elgin, for "A Portable Clothes DRIER." Quebec, dated 17th March, 1862.

No. 1332—BOCEKII, (*Charles*,) of the City of Toronto, in the County of York, for "A Lamp Chimney CLEANER." Quebec, dated 17th March, 1862.

No. 1333—TRENHOLM, (*Edward*, of Trenholmville, in the Township of Kingsley, in the County of Drummond, for "An improved Snow Plough and Flange CLEANER." Quebec, dated 20th March, 1862.

No. 1334—FAUNCE, (*Alba*,) of the Town of Sherbrooke, in the District of St. Francis, for "A Vegetable Root CUTTER." Quebec, dated 21st March, 1862.

No. 1335—YORK, (*Edson*,) of the Township of Stanstead, in the County of Stanstead, for "A new and improved Vegetable Cutter, called ' York's Vegetable CUTTER." Quebec, dated 2nd April, 1862.

No. 1336—YORK, (*Edson*,) of the Township of Stanstead, in the County of Stanstead, for "A new and improved Churn, called York's Rotary CHURN." Quebec, dated 2nd April, 1862.

No. 1337—ROBERTSON, (*W. C.*,) of Belleville, in the County of Hastings, for "An Improved Garment DELINEATOR." Quebec, dated 8th March, 1862.

No. 1338—MOODIE, (*J. W. D.*,) of Belleville, in the County of Hastings, for "A Rotary Interest INDICATOR." Quebec, dated 8th March, 1862.

No. 1339—TOMLINSON, (*James*,) of the Township of Pickering, in the County of Ontario, for "A Steam Coiled Hoop, for all kinds of Cooper's Work." Quebec, dated 8th March, 1862.

No. 1340—MILLS, (*Isaac*,) of the Township of Flamboro' West, in the County of Wentworth, for "A Double and Single Dash, Hinge and Crank Churn, called Mills' Victoria CHURN." Quebec, dated 8th March, 1862.

No. 1341—VAN BROCKLIN, (*P. C.*,) of the Township of Brantford, in the County of Brant, for "A new and useful improvement called, Van Brocklin's Two Horse Wheeled CULTIVATOR." Quebec, dated 11th March, 1862.

No. 1342—SEYMOUR, *(Henry,)* of the City of Montreal, for "A new mode of Preserving WOOD from the effects of Damp or Rot, to be called Seymour's System of Preserving WOOD." Quebec, dated 26th December, 1861.

No. 1343—STEAD, *(E.,)* of the City of Toronto, in the County of York, for "A Composition of matter to clarify and Deodrize Canadian Rock Oil and Coal OIL." Quebec, dated 26th March, 1862.

No. 1344—THOMSON, *(James E.,)* and HIND, *(Henry Y.,)* both of the City of Toronto, in the County of York, for "An Apparatus for the Manufacture of Illuminating GAS from Crude Petroleum, or Rock Oil." Quebec, dated 28th March, 1862.

No. 1345—THOMSON, *(James E.,)* and HIND, *(Henry,)* both of the City of Toronto, in the County of York, for "A process for the Manufacture of Illuminating GAS from Crude Petroleum or Rock Oil." Quebec, dated 28th March, 1862.

No. 1346—ROE, *(G. C.,)* of the Town of Brantford, in the County of Brant, for "A Horizontal Endless Chain or Rope Horse POWER." Quebec, dated 10th April, 1862.

No. 1347—MARDIN, *(J. A.,)* of the Township of Barnston, in the District of St. Francis, for "A new and improved Punching Machine, called 'Mardin's PUNCHING Machine.'" Quebec, dated 22nd April, 1862.

No. 1348—LONG, *(Edward,)* of the City of Montreal, for "A new method of Preparing Signs and Plates designated, Edward Long's Adjustable Letters and FIGURES." Quebec, dated 22nd April, 1862.

No. 1349—ROGERS, *(Richard,)* of the City Montreal, for "A new Composition of MATTER to be used in the Manufacture of Blacking Pots, Pomatum Pots or similar Articles." Quebec, dated 22nd April, 1862.

No. 1350—ARMSTRONG, *(J. R.,)* of the City of Toronto, in the County of York, for "A new Design of a Cooking Stove, styled The MAPLE LEAF." Quebec, dated 29th November, 1861.

No. 1351—CONOVER, *(Samuel,)* of the City of Toronto, in the County of Peel, for "An article called the Victoria Concave WASHING Machine." Quebec, dated 12th April, 1862.

No. 1352—NORTON, *(E. C.,)* of the Town of Bowmanville, in the County of Durham, for "A new and improved Straw Cutter, called Norton's Diamond Straw CUTTER." Quebec, dated 12th April, 1862.

No. 1353—WALMSLEY, *(John,)* of the Village of Berlin, in the County of Waterloo, for "A Machine called 'A Combined Sower and CULTIVATOR.'" Quebec, dated 12th April, 1862.

No. 1354—BODLEY, *(Charles,)* of Mount Forrest, for "An improved Sifter Fanning Mill and ELEVATOR." Quebec, dated 12th April, 1862.

No. 1355—FORSTER, *(M.,)* of the Village of Glen William, in the County of Halton, for "An improved Safety WHIPPLE TREE and Spring closed hold backs." Quebec, dated 12th April, 1862.

No. 1356—GAGE, *(James Lorenzo,)* of the Village of Dacotah, in the County of Halton, for a "BAG FASTENER." Quebec, dated 12th April, 1862.

No. 1357—PARR, *(Robert,)* of the Township of Darlington, in the County of Durham, for "A Hair and Feather Cleanser and RENOVATOR." Quebec, dated 15th April, 1862.

No. 1358—DALGAMO, *(James,)* of Chatham, in the County of Kent, for "An Instantaneous Adjustment WRENCH." Quebec, dated 15th April, 1862.

No. 1359—MARTINAU *(Ulric Joseph,)* of the Parish of Longueil, for "An improved Metal ROOF made with Galvanized Iron and other Metals" Quebec, dated 29th May, 1862.

No. 1360—BURBANK, *(James R.,)* of the Village of Danville, in the County of Richmond, for "A new and improved Washing and WRINGING Machine." Quebec, dated 18th June, 1862.

No. 1361—GRAVES, *(Lorenzo,)* and CLARK, *(Hollis,)* both of the Township of Barnston, for "A New SAWING Machine." Quebec, dated 18th June, 1862.

No. 1362—MORRILL, *(R. T.,)* of the Township of Stanstead, for "An improved THRESHING Machine." Quebec, dated 18th June, 1862.

No. 1363—LEWIS, *(Richard,)* of Melbourne, County of Richmond, for "A new and improved CHURN," Quebec, dated 18th June, 1862.

No. 1364—TODD, (*David,*) of the Town of Windsor, in the County of Essex, for "A Railway Brake or Gauge FRUSTRATOR." Quebec, dated 27th May, 1862.

No. 1365—ROMBOUGH, (*Reverend J. H.,*) of the Township of Osnabruck, in the County of Stormont, for "A Self-feeding THRASHING Machine, Improved Separator and Fanning MILL." Quebec, dated 27th May, 1862.

No. 1366—ROBSON,(*Thomas,*) of the Township of Brantford, in the County of Brant, for "An improved Feed Mill, a Machine to a fine State Bark, India Corn in the Ear and other Substances, and for Cracking for Feed Coarse GRAINS." Quebec, dated 27th May, 1862.

No. 1367—MITCHELL, (*J. E.,*) and DEPEW, (*William,*) both of the Town of Paris, in the County of Brant, for "An improved Balance GATE." Quebec, dated 3rd June, 1862.

No. 1368—WARNER, (*J. S.,*) of Cornwall, in the County of Stormont, for "A Churn called The People's Self-Acting CHURN." Quebec, dated 3rd June, 1862.

No. 1369—METCALFE, (*Robert,*) of the Village of Carleton Place, in the County of Lanark, for "Certain Improvements in the construction of CHURNS." Quebec, dated 3rd June, 1862.

No. 1370—SCOTT, (*A. H.,*) of the Village of Tilsonbury, in the County of Oxford, for "A new mode of applying Power to Machinery by means of Rotary Motion with a Slide LEVER." Quebec, dated 3rd June, 1862.

No. 1371—MARTIN, (*George,*) of the Village of Oshawa, in the County of Ontario, ior "A New Fanning Mill or Wheat Separator, called Martin's Improved Wheat SEPARATOR." Quebec, dated 3rd June, 1862.

No. 1372—WATEROUS, (*Charles H.,*) of the Township of Brantford, in the County of Brant, for "A Centripetal Churn and Centripetal Agitator, for Refining and fitting for use Rock Oil, or Petroleum and COAL OIL." Quebec, dated 6th June, 1862.

No. 1373—DREW, (*H. C.,*) of the Township of Whitby, in the County of Ontario, for "An Improved Waggon and CARRIAGE." Quebec, dated 9th June, 1862.

No. 1374—BIGELOW, (*Albert,*) of the City of Hamilton, for "A new and improved Compression COCK." Quebec, dated 9th June, 1862.

No. 1375—NORTHEY, (*Thomas,*) of the City of Hamilton, for "An improved Expansion Steam ENGINE." Quebec, dated 9th June, 1862.

No. 1376—WEAVER, (*Samuel,*) of the Township of Humberstone, in the County of Welland, for "A new Process for taking Photographs, called Weaver's PROCESS." Quebec, dated 9th June, 1862.

No. 1377—MARKS. (*Joseph,*) and EATON, (*Richard,*) both of the City of Hamilton, for "An Improved Smoke Stack and Spark Arrester for Locomotives and other Steam ENGINES." Quebec, dated 9th June, 1862.

No. 1378—WHITE, (*Robert,*) of the City of Kingston, for "An Adjustable Concave CLEANER." Quebec, dated 9th June, 1862.

No. 1379—MORGAN, (*H. B.,*) of the Township of Tilsonbury, in the County of Oxford, for "A Bee Hive and Miller DESTROYER." Quebec, dated 9th June, 1862.

No. 1380—ROGERS, (*Richard,*) of the Town of Whitby, in the County of Ontario, for "A Double attached Clothes WRINGER." Quebec, dated 20th June, 1862.

No. 1381—LIVERGOOD, (*H. J.,*) of the Township of Brantford, in the County of Brant, for "An Improved Bee Hive, styled 'Livergood's BEE HIVE.'" Quebec, dated 7th July, 1862.

No. 1382—McNEAL, (*J. B.,*) of the Township of Westminster, in the County of Middlesex, for "A New and useful improvement in the Manufacture of REFRIGERATORS." Quebec, dated 7th July, 1862.

No. 1383—HOLT, (*William,*) of York Mills, in the County of York, for "A Ploughing, Ridging, Drilling, Sowing and Rolling MACHINE." Quebec, dated 7th July, 1862.

No. 1384—GREGORY, (*Thomas,*) of the Township of King, in the County of York, for "An improved STRAW CUTTING Machine." Quebec, dated 7th July, 1862.

No. 1385—PHILLIPS, (*James,*) of the City of Toronto, in the County of York, for "An improved Self-heating Box Smoothing IRON." Quebec, dated 7th July, 1862.

No. 1386—SIMMONS, (*Nelson,*) of the Township of Sophiasburgh, in the County of Prince Edward, for "A Revolving Float CHURN." Quebec, dated 8th July, 1862.

No. 1387—HANNUM, (*J. A. B.,*) of the Town of Cornwall, in the County of Stormont, for " A Double Dasher Churn POWER." Quebec, dated 8th July, 1862.

No. 1388—BENNETT, (*John,*) of the Township of Madoc, in the County of Hastings, for "A Combination SIEVE." Quebec, dated 8th July, 1862.

No. 1389—CLENCH, (*L. M.,*) of the Village of St. Mary's, in the County of Perth, for a " Hydropult, to be called the Pneumatic repeating HYDROPULT." Quebec, dated 8th July, 1862.

No. 1390—WARD, (*D. C.,*) of Streetville, in the County of Peel, for a " New method of constructing Washing Machines with WRINGER attached." Quebec, dated 8th July, 1862.

No. 1391—BOTTOMLEY, (*Thomas H.,*) of the City of Toronto, in the County of York, for a " Metallic Carriage and Waggon HUB." Quebec, dated 8th July, 1862.

No. 1392—WATEROUS, (*Charles L.,*) of Brantford, in the County of Brant, for an " Improved machine for manufacturing the SHOES of horses and other animals." Quebec, dated 8th July, 1862.

No. 1393—TAYLOR,(*Emerson,*) of the Village of Springfield, in the County of Peel, for "New and improved method of constructing Straw DUSTERS." Quebec, dated 8th July, 1862.

No. 1394—WATSON, (*Zemas,*) of the Township of Howard, in the County of Kent, for a " Machine for planting and drilling SEEDS." Quebec, dated 8th July, 1862.

No. 1395—McGILL, (*John,*) and CHANTLER, (*Henry,*) both of the City of Toronto, for a " New article for watering the STREETS, called a Hydrosperser." Quebec, dated 8th July, 1862.

No. 1396—HALL, (*Charles P.,*) of Ingersoll, in the County of Oxford, for an " Improved spring attachment for closing Doors and GATES, and for balancing Window Sashes." Quebec, dated 8th July, 1862.

No. 1397—GOLDIE, (*William,*) of the Township of Guelph, in the County of Wellington, for a " Wheat Cleaning MACHINE." Quebec, dated 14th July, 1862.

No. 1398—PERRY, (*Samuel,*) of the City of Montreal, for a " New and improved mode of manufacturing HOUSE SHOES by machinery." Quebec, dated 19th July, 1862.

No. 1399—MACFARLANE, (*Henry H.,*) of Sorel, in the County of Richelieu, for "A new and improved Sounding APPARATUS." Quebec, dated 19th July, 1862.

No. 1400—KIMPTON, (*Marshall,*) of the Township of Stanstead, County of Stanstead, for " A new and improved WATER DRAWER." Quebec, dated 19th July, 1862.

No. 1401—GAULD, (*George,*) of the Township of Onondaga, County of Brant, for the " Archimedean CHURN." Quebec, dated 21st July, 1862.

No. 1402—O'DELL, (*Abiel,*) of the Town of Bowmanville, in the County of Durham, for " A new and improved Clothes Wringer, called O'Dell's self-adjusting and self-fastening CLOTHES WRINGER." Quebec, dated 31st July, 1862.

No. 1403—RUMOHR, (*Frederick,*) of the Village of Markham, in the Township of Markham, County of York, for " An improved two-horse CULTIVATOR." Quebec, dated 21st July, 1862.

No. 1404—MORRILL, (*Benjamin Thrasher,*) of the Township of Stanstead, County of Stanstead, for "A Metallic MILK COOLER." Quebec, dated 23rd July, 1862.

No. 1405—GOULD, (*Charles Hubbard,*) of the City of Montreal, for " A new and useful improvement in FRICTIONAL GEARING." Quebec, dated 21st August, 1862.

No. 1406—STEPHENSON, (*William Duncan,*) of the City of Montreal, for " An improved SPRING BED." Quebec, dated 1st August, 1862.

No. 1407—McKILLOPP, (*Archibald,*) of the Township of Inverness, County of Megantic, for " A self-acting security GATE." Quebec, dated 5th August, 1862.

No. 1408—COCKBURN, (*Alexander Fraser,*) of the City of Montreal, for " A compression swivel action WATER-COCK." Quebec, dated 19th July, 1862.

No. 1409—DOUGLAS, (*Thomas Sholto,*) of the City of Montreal, for "The discovery of Benzine Copal VARNISH." Quebec, dated 21st August, 1862.

No. 1410—RUTTAN, (*David William,*) and YORK, (*Richard,*) both of the Village of North Port, in the County of Prince Edward, for " A Spring Power Boot CRIMPER." Quebec, dated 22nd August, 1862.

No. 1411—FRYATT, (*Henry*,) of the Village of Aurora, in the County of York, for "An Improved SCRUBBING MACHINE." Quebec, dated 22nd August, 1862.

No. 1412—DOYLE, (*Thomas*,) of the Village of Sweaburg, in the Township of Oxford, in the County of Oxford, for "A CHAIR and SOFA Combined." Quebec, dated 22nd August, 1862.

No. 1413—O'DELL, (*Abiel*,) or the Town of Bowmanville, in the County of Durham, for "A Saw Set and Clamp, called O'Dell's portable combined SAW SET and SAW CLAMP." Quebec, dated 22nd August, 1862.

No. 1414—BAGULEY, (*Joseph James*,) of the Village of Allandale Mills, County of Peterborough, for "A Musical Modulator, styled Baguley's Singing School Mechanical MODULATOR." Quebec, dated 25th August, 1862.

No. 1415—SOULES, (*John*,) of Mount Pleasant, Township of Brantford, County Brant, for "A new and improved Grain and Grass Drill, designated Soule's upright rotary Grain and GRASS DRILL." Quebec, dated 25th August, 1862.

No. 1416—CANT, (*Fracis*,) of the Town of Galt, County of Waterloo, for "An improved Cam for working the under-needle or catch-pin of SEWING MACHINES." Quebec, dated 25th August, 1862.

No. 1417—HEAD, (*Thomas*,) of the Township of Beverley, in the County of Wentworth, for "A Machine applied to every kind of CHURN for more efficient and speedy way of making Butter." Quebec, dated 25th August, 1862.

No. 1418—NORTH, (*Michael*,) of the Town of Brantford in the County of Brant, for "An invention called Michael North's Cheap and Economical MANGLE." Quebec, dated 25th August, 1862.

No. 1419—PARIZEAU, (*Joseph*,) and PARIZEAU, (*Stanislas*,) both of the Parish of St. Martin, in the County of Laval, for "A new and improved CHURN." Quebec, dated 2nd September, 1862.

No. 1420—CHASE, (*James*,) of Brooklin, County of Ontario, for a "TILE DITCHER." Quebec, dated 7th July, 1862.

No. 1421—MARRITT, (*John*,) of the Township of King, in the County of York, for "A CLOTHES WASHER." Toronto, dated 25th August, 1862.

No. 1222—FARRELL, (*William*,) of Carleton Place, in the County of Lanark, for "An apparatus for working a Common CHURN." Quebec, dated 25th August, 1862.

No. 1423—ROSS, (*George*,) of the City of Kingston, in the County of Frontenac, for "A portable frost-proof FENCE." Quebec, dated 25th August, 1862.

No. 1424—ADDISON, (*John*,) of the City of Hamilton, in the County of Wentworth, for "A Spring MATTRASS." Quebec, dated 25th August, 1862.

No. 1425—DREW, (*H. C.*,) of the Township of Whitby, in the County of Ontario, for "A new and improved Water Conductor and ELEVATOR." Quebec, dated 2nd September, 1862.

No. 1426—DREW, (*Eldred*,) and JOHNS, (*David*,) both of the Township of Usborne, in the County of Huron, for "A Churning Machine to be called the Economist CHURN." Quebec, dated 2nd September, 1862.

No. 1427—FORFAR, (*Thomas*,) of the City of London, in the County of Middlesex, for "An improved STRAW CUTTER." Quebec, dated 2nd September, 1862.

No. 1428—CAMPBELL, (*James*,) and GROBB, (*George*,) both of the Town of St. Catharines, County of Lincoln, for "A portable Mill Stone COOLER." Quebec, dated 2nd September, 1862.

No. 1429—FLETCHER, (*James*,) of the Town of Woodstock, County of Oxford, for "An improved Circular rotary HARROW." Quebec, dated 2nd September, 1862.

No. 1430—DUCHESNE, (*Epiphanc*,) of the Parish of L'Acadie, in the County of St. John's, for "A Double Action RAKE." Quebec, dated 11th September, 1862.

No. 1431—SANDFORD, (*Gelston*,) of the City of Quebec, for "New and useful improvements in Machinery for separating FIBRES from the stalks and leaves of fibre yielding Plants." Quebec, dated 12th September, 1862.

No. 1132—SHEARS, (*Eben B.*,) of the Town of Clifton, in the County of Welland, for "A process or mode by which GAS made from crude earth or rock oils of Canada, known as

Petroleum, may be made to burn without emitting Smoke." Quebec, dated 15th September, 1862.

No. 1433—HOLMES, (Edward,) of the City of Hamilton, for "A new and improved STAVE DRESSING Machine." Quebec, dated 15th September, 1862.

No. 1434—HOLMES, (Edward,) of the City of Hamilton, for "New useful improvements in Machine for JOINTING Staves." Quebec, dated 15th September, 1862.

No. 1435—HOLMES, (Edward,) of the City of Hamilton, for "A new and improved Hoop Driving and STAVE CROZING Machine." Quebec, dated 15th September, 1862.

No. 1436—ANDERSON, (Robert,) of the Township of Peel, County of Wellington, for "A new MOULD BOARD for a Plough." Quebec, dated 17th September, 1862.

No. 1437—FREEMAN, (Peter Wesley,) of the Township of Loughborough, County of Frontenac, for "A Lever and ROLLER GATE." Quebec, dated 17th September, 1862.

No. 1438—LAWSON, (Edward,) of the City of Toronto, in the County of York, for "A Double Dash Rotary CHURN." Quebec, dated 20th September, 1862.

No. 1439—DORWIN, (Jedediah Hubbell,) of the City of Montreal, for "An improved Portable Mercurial BAROMETER." Quebec, dated 24th September, 1862.

No. 1440—AUDIN, (Aimé Nicolas Napoleon,) of Beloeil, in the County of Vercheres, for "A new and improved HYDROMETER." Quebec, dated 10th October, 1862.

No. 1441—WALTON, (Richard N.,) of the City of London, in the County of Middlesex, for "An Article designated Walton's Economical CLOTHES DRYER." Quebec, dated 17th September, 1862.

No. 1442—CAMPBELL, (George,) of the City of Toronto, in the County of York, for "A FIRE ESCAPE." Quebec, dated 20th September, 1862.

No. 1443—COULTHARD, (Joseph,) of the City of Montreal, for "A Cross Anglo Sliding Combination WHEEL." Quebec, dated 18th October, 1862.

No. 1444—HILMAN, (Abimelech,) and CAMPBELL, (Nathan,) both of the Town of Stratford, County of Perth, for an improved Churn, to be called the "PRINCE CHURN." Quebec, dated 22nd August, 1862.

No. 1445—MILLER, (Hugh,) of the City of Toronto, County of York, for an Illuminating Oil, to be called "Miller's ILLUMINATOR." Quebec, dated 9th October, 1862.

No. 1446—ROSE, (David Allen,) of the Township of Ernestown, County of Lennox and Addington, for "An Improvement of a CHURN for making Butter." Quebec, dated 10th October, 1862.

No. 1447—WORTMAN, (Charles Henry,) of the Township of Camden East, County of Addington, for a Force and Suction Pump, called Wortman's Combined Force and SUCTION PUMP." Quebec, dated 17th October, 1862.

No. 1448—McCONNELL, (John,) of Cornwall, County of Wentworth, for "A Shifting HINGE, Joint or Coupling." Quebec, dated 17th October, 1862.

No. 1449—PORTER, (D'Arcy,) of the City of Toronto, County of York, for "A Railroad CAR ROOF." Quebec, dated 23rd October, 1862.

No. 1450—ROBINSON, (Michael,) of the Town of Oakville, County of Halton, for "An improved Boot Treeing Machine, to be known as 'Robinson's BOOT TREE.'" Quebec, dated 23rd October, 1862.

No. 1451—POWELL (Charles,) of the Township and County of York, for "An improved Double Action Swing FORCE PUMP." Quebec, dated 24th October, 1862.

No. 1452—HILBORN, (James,) of the Township of Beach, County of Ontario, for "A Door, Table and Counter BELL." Quebec, dated 24th October, 1862.

No. 1453—SCHNEIDER, (John William Henry,) of the Township of Thorold, County of Welland, for "New and useful improvements on Straw or Hay Cutting Boxes." Quebec, dated 24th October, 1862.

No. 1454—PORTER, (D'Arcy,) of the City of Toronto, County of York, for "A Depilating Compound for SKINS and HIDES." Quebec, dated 24th October, 1862.

No. 145—CULL, (John Angell,) Assignee of CULL, (Edward Lefroy,) both of the City of

Toronto, County of York, for an Article styled the "FOREST CULTIVATOR." Quebec, dated 6th October, 1862.

No. 1456—PORTER, (*D'Arcy*,) of the City of Toronto, County of York, for "A WRINGING Machine." Quebec, dated 25th October, 1862.

No. 1457—PRITCHARD, (*Thomas*,) of the Village of Aurora, County of York, for "A COLOURING Machine, to be used in the Tanning of Leather." Quebec, dated 27th October, 1862.

No. 1458.—THOMPSON, (*William Linton*,) of the Township and County of Stanstead, for "A new and improved Window and Blind FASTENER." Quebec, dated 30th October, 1862.

No. 1459—RODGERS, (*David*,) of the Village of St. Eustache, County of Two Mountains, for "An INSTRUMENT for measuring unknown distances." Quebec, dated 30th October, 1862.

No. 1460—LEWIS, (*Richard*,) of Melbourne, County of Richmond, for "New and improved HANGING Gates." Quebec, dated 30th October, 1862.

No. 1461—BOOTH, (*Henry*,) of the City of Toronto, County of York, for "A CHIMNEY for Coal Oil or other Lamps." Quebec, dated 17th November, 1862.

No. 1462—MORRIS, (*Thomas*,) of the Town of Brantford, County of Brant, for "Morris's RAIL Repairing Machine." Quebec, dated 25th November, 1862.

No. 1463—GLENDILLEN, (*Elijah*,) of the Township of North Dorchester, County of Middlesex, for "A WASHING Machine." Quebec, dated 17th November, 1862.

No. 1464—HILLMAN, (*Abimelech*,) of the Town of Stratford, County of Perth, for "An improved Churn, to be called Hillman's up and down Self-acting Rotary reversible Dash CHURN." Quebec, dated 25th November, 1862.

No. 1465—STILWELL, (*Edward Lounsbury*,) of the Village of Klineburgh, County of York, for "A Self-setting RAT TRAP." Quebec, dated 27th November, 1862.

No. 1466—CAMPBELL, (*Nathan*,) of Stratford, County of Perth, for "Certain improvements on the PRINCE CHURN." Quebec, dated 20th November, 1862.

No. 1467—LEACH, (*Reverend J.*,) of Goderich, County of Huron, for "A non-freezing PRINTING INK." Quebec, dated 1st December, 1862.

No. 1468—PANNABAKER, (*Lewis*,) of the Township of Normanby, County of Grey, for "A Grain Cradle Finger ADJUSTER." Quebec, dated 1st December, 1862.

No. 1469—RANDALL, (*William*,) of the Township of Uxbridge, County of Ontario, for "A new and useful improvement in Saw Mills, called 'The Excelsior SAW MILL.'" Quebec, dated 9th December, 1862.

No. 1470—BRIKLY, (*Joseph*,) of the Township of South Dorchester, County of Elgin, for "A Self-acting HAND LOOM." Quebec, dated 9th December, 1862.

No. 1471—TRENHOLM, (*Edward*,) of Trenholmville, Township of Kingsey, County of Drummond, for "A new and improved Apparatus for Cooling Grain, Coal or other articles kept in bulk on Shipboard or in Stores, to be called 'Trenholm's APPARATUS for Cooling Grain, Coal, &c.'" Quebec, dated 13th December, 1862.

No. 1472—MILLER, (*William*,) of the Township of Markham, County of York, for "An improved geared box CHURN." Quebec, dated 10th December, 1862.

No. 1473—SHERROT, (*Richard James*,) of the City of London, County of Middlesex, for "A CLOTHES HORSE for airing and drying Linen or Clothes within doors." Quebec, dated 16th December, 1862.

No. 1474—MILLAR, (*Warren*,) of the City of Montreal, for "A new and useful LOOP CHECK in Sewing Machines using a rotating hook." Quebec, dated 16th December, 1862.

No. 1475—LAMB, (*Peter Rothwell*,) Joint Inventor and Assignee of Richard Hornbroke of Toronto, of the City of Toronto, County of York, for "A Machine to be called Lamb's Cutting, Flanging and EMBOSSING Machine." Quebec, dated 19th December, 1862.

No. 1476—MITCHELL, (*Valentine*,) of the Township of Cavan, in the County of Durham, for "A WOOD CUTTING Machine." Quebec, dated 12th January, 1863.

No. 1477—WEBSTER, (*Thomas*,) of the Village of Brampton, in the County of Peel, for "Improved Feed motion for STRAW CUTTERS." Qubbec, dated 12th January, 1863.

No. 1478—SCOTT, (*Aaron Hawley,*) of the Township of Dereham, in the County of Oxford, for "A Table Leaf SUPPORTER." Quebec, dated 12th January, 1863.

No. 1479—HUGHES, (*Joel,*) of the Township of West Gwillimbury, in the County of Simcoe, for "A Cheese Press to be known as 'Hughes' Double CHEESE PRESS.'" Quebec, dated 12th January, 1863.

No. 1480—OATES, (*Richard H.,*) of the City of Toronto, in the County of York, for "A Vertical Post rising Clothes DRYER." Quebec, dated 12th January, 1863.

No. 1481—AIKMAN, (*John,*) of the Township of North Norwich, in the South Riding of the County of Oxford, for "A ROCKER for the more convenient pouring of liquids out of large Pots or Vessels, known as "Aikman's Rocker." Quebec, dated 12th January, 1863.

No. 1482—DAY, (*Sylvester,*) of the Township of Brantford, in the County of Brant, for "A Two Wheeled HAY RAKE." Quebec, dated 12th January, 1803.

No. 1483—McENERY, (*James Francis,*) of the City of Quebec, for "A Salt Water Vapour CONDENSER and Ship Masters' Fresh Water Supplyer." Quebec, dated 17th January, 1863.

No. 1484—WILSON, (*Walter Scott,*) of the City of Montreal, for "New and useful improvements in the construction of SMOOTHING IRONS." Quebec, dated 21st January, 1863.

No. 1485—MURRAY, (*Donald,*) of the Village of St. Mary's, in the County of Perth, for "An improved WOOD Sawing Machine." Quebec, dated 21st January, 1863.

No. 1486—SHAFER, (*Oscar F.,*) of the Village of Thamesford, in the County of Oxford, for "A BAG Holding and Weighing Machine." Quebec, dated 4th February, 1863.

No. 1487—CAMPBELL, (*George,*) of the City of Toronto, for "A Ladies SKIRT LIFTER." Quebec, dated 22nd January, 1863.

No. 1488—McCORMICK, (*Levi Willson,*) of the Township of West Flamborough, in the County of Wentworth, for "A Root Seed DRILL." Quebec, dated 4th February, 1863.

No. 1489—PENTON, (*Thomas,*) of the Township of South Dumfries, in the County of Brant, for "A Regulating SEED Drill." Quebec, dated 4th February, 1863.

No. 1490—SUTTON, (*William,*) of the Town of Brantford, in the County of Brant, for "An Improved GRAIN DRYER." Quebec, dated 5th February, 1863.

No. 1491—BACON, (*Avery D.,*) of the Township of Malahide, in the County of Elgin, for "An Improved BEEHIVE." Quebec, dated 11th February, 1863.

No. 1492—BENOIT, (*Damase,*) of the Town of St. Hyacinthe, for "A new and useful Gas Purifier and REGULATOR." Quebec, dated 5th March, 1863.

No. 1493—MARKS, (*Joseph,*) of the City of Montreal, for "An Anti-incrustation POWDER for the removal of Silica deposit off the internal surface of Steam Generating Boilers." Quebec, dated 5th March, 1863.

No. 1494—HEALY, (*Richard,*) of the Village of Bedford, in the County of Missisquoi, for "A Machine for Rossing Tan Bark." Quebec, dated 5th February, 1863.

No. 1495—BROWN, (*John,*) of the Township of Waterloo, in the County of Waterloo, for "Improvements in Machinery for the Manufacture of FLOUR." Quebec, dated 11th March, 1863.

No. 1496—SANDERSON, (*Burton,*) of the Township of Stanstead, for "A BIT for Tapping Sugar Maples." Quebec, dated 13th March, 1863.

No. 1497—BLOOMFIELD, (*Robert,*) of the City of Montreal, and GOTHWAITE, (*William,* of the City of Montreal, for "An Improved Steam Valve PISTON. Quebec, dated 13th March, 1863.

No. 1498—PETTINGILL, (*John,*) of Coaticook, in the County of Stanstead, for "A new and useful improvement in machines for DIGGING Potatoes." Quebec, dated 13th March, 1863.

No. 1499—PARSONS, (*Alonzo Henry,*) of the Village of Stanstead Plain, in the County of Stanstead, for "A new and useful Beehive, to be called the Improved Platform BEEHIVE." Quebec, dated 16th March, 1863.

No. 1500—ROSS, (*Alexander,*) of the City of Montreal, for "A Thermo-Electric Fire ALARM and Heat Detector." Quebec, dated 16th March, 1863.

No. 1501—MARTIN, (*John Robert,*) of the Town of Cayuga, in the County of Haldimand, for "An Improved FIELD ROLLER." Quebec, dated 17th March, 1863.

No. 1502—TRETHEWEY, (*Samuel*,) of the Village of Muskoka Falls, in the County of Victoria, for "A BALANCE Piston." Quebec, dated 18th March, 1863.

No. 1503—OSTRUM, (*Henry Wellington*,) of the Township of Sidney, in the County of Hastings, for "A Broad Cast Grain Sower, known as the "Excelsior Grain SOWER." Quebec, dated 21st March, 1863.

No. 1504—GLENDILLEN, (*William*,) of the Township of North Oxford, in the County of Oxford, for "A WASHING Machine." Quebec, dated 21st March, 1863.

No. 1505—BROOKES, (*Thomas*,) of the City of Toronto, for "A Funnel MEASURE." Quebec, dated 21st March, 1863.

No. 1506—SHUPE, (*Eli*,) of the Village 'of St. George, in the Township of Dumfries and County of Brant, for "A combined REAPING and Mowing Machine." Quebec, dated 23rd March, 1863.

No. 1507—PAYNE, (*Edward*,) of the Town of Cobourg, in the County of Northumberland, for "Improvements in the Apparatus or machinery used in the process of distilling Thickwash or BEER." Quebec, dated 24th March, 1863.

No. 1508—BOWERMAN, (*Willett Dorlet*,) of Whitby, in the County of Ontario, for "A Friction Roll and Roping Belt Box and GUDGEON." Quebec, dated 24th March, 1863.

No. 1509—FOURDRINIER, (*George Henry*,) of the Village of Lyn, in the County of Leeds, for "A Revolving DESSICATOR for Drying and Improving Grain and for Manufacturing Malt." Quebec, dated 24th March, 1863.

No. 1510—ARLESS, (*James*,) of the City of Montreal, for "A New and useful Steam GANGWAY, for loading and unloading Vessels." Quebec, dated 30th March, 1863.

No. 1511—FLECK, (*Alexander*,) of the City of Montreal, for "Improvements in the Tyler WATER WHEEL." Quebec, dated 31st March, 1863.

No. 1512—McGLOGHLAN, (*William D.*,) of Newbury, in the County of Middlesex, for "A Boot, Shoe and STOVE POLISHER." Quebec, dated 30th March, 1863.

No. 1513—TINDALL, (*John William Ward*,) late of Liverpool in England, now a resident of Sarnia, for "A Process of Deodorizing Paraffine, Coal, Pitch, Rock and other like Oils and HYDRO-CARBONS." Quebec, dated 24th March, 1863.

No. 1514—SUTTON, (*William Henry*,) and GIBSON, (*James John*,) both of the Town of Brantford, County Brant, for "A Combined Hot and Cold Air Mechanical GRAIN DRYER." Quebec, dated 6th April, 1863.

No. 1515—MITCHELL, (*George*,) of the City of Toronto, for "A Self inflating Water-Proof Floating BAG, intended for Mail and other purposes." Quebec, dated 6th April, 1863.

No. 1516—BURKHOLDER, (*Michael*,) of Pickering, in the County of Ontario, for "An improved Wheeled Steel Toothed HORSE RAKE." Quebec, dated 8th April, 1863.

No. 1517—NORTH, (*Michael*,) of the Town of Brantford, in the County of Brant, for "An Economical Drum HEATER." Quebec, dated 10th April, 1863.

No. 1518—ARNOLD, (*William Saxon*,) of the Town of Chatham, in the County of Kent, for "An improvement in a Wood SAWING Machine, being a Crank attached to a Pitman of the saw and a self-adjusting Gauge for raising or lowering the Saw 'when in motion." Quebec, dated 10th April, 1863.

No. 1519—RANDALL, (*William*,) of the Township of Uxbridge, in the County of Ontario, for "An improvement in MECHANICAL movements for regulating the speed of Machinery, called the 'REGULATOR.'" Quebec, dated 13th April, 1863.

No. 1520—RANDALL, (*William*,) of the Township of Uxbridge, in the County of Ontario, for "An improvement in Straw Cutters called the Eccentric STRAW CUTTER." Quebec, dated 13th April, 1863.

No. 1521—NOXON, (*Freeman Clark*,) of Bloomfield, in the County of Prince Edward, for "An improved CULTIVATOR." Quebec, dated 17th April, 1863.

No. 1522—RICHARDSON, (*William Cuthro*,) of the City of Quebec, for "A Cough and Cold MIXTURE, called "Syrup of Canada Balsam." Quebec, dated 20th April, 1863.

No. 1523—BYRON, (*Edward L.*,) of the Township of Compton, in the County of Compton, for "A new and useful Improvement on a REEL and SWIFT combined." Quebec, dated 24th April, 1863.

No. 1524—HENDERSON, *William Henry,*) of the Town of Brockville, in the County of Leeds, for "Henderson's Canadian Air CHURN." Quebec, dated 28th April, 1863.

No. 1525—DOUSON, *(Edward,)* of the Township of Clarke, in the County of Durham, for "A ROOT CUTTER." Quebec, dated 13th May, 1863.

No. 1526—ROBINSON, *(John S.,)* of the City of London, in the County of Middlesex, for "A Tanner's OIL." Quebec, dated 19th May, 1863.

No. 1527—JONES, *(Charles,)* of the Village of Palermo, in the County of Halton, Assignee of Samuel Morse, of the Town of Milton, in the County of Halton, for "Improvements to Fraser's CHURN." Quebec, dated 19th May, 1863.

No. 1528—BETHUNE, *(Donald,)* of the Town of Port Hope, in the County of Durham, for "A Ship Collision GUARD." Quebec, dated 19th May, 1863.

No. 1529—SUTTON, *(Robert Twiss,)* of the Town of Lindsay, in the County of Victoria, for "A Machine or Apparatus for drying and cooling GRAIN." Quebec, dated 19th May, 1863.

No. 1530—MONTGOMERY, *(John,)* of the City of Toronto, for "A SOLUTION for the prevention of fire, and the preservation of wood from decay." Quebec, dated 21st May, 1863.

No. 1531—COURTOIS, *(Edward,)* of the Town of Iberville, for "A portable and self adjusting FENCE." Quebec, dated 1st June, 1863.

No. 1532—SEYMOUR, *(Harry,)* of the City of Montreal, for "A chemical compound white and body PAINT." Quebec, dated 1st June, 1863.

No. 1533—BACCIRINI, *(Gaetano,)* and FILIPPI, *(Pasquale,)* of the City of Montreal, for "An Improved Portland CEMENT." Quebec, dated 1st June, 1863.

No. 1534—MAHLER, *(Maurice,)* of the City of Montreal, for "A Seamless HAT." Quebec, dated 1st June, 1863.

No. 1535—WARD, *(Samuel James,)* of the Town of Belleville, in the County of Hastings, for "A Roller and WASH BOARD." Quebec, dated 3rd June, 1863.

No. 1536—HENNESSEY, *(Hugh,)* of the City of Hamilton, in the County of Wentworth, for "A self-acting COUPLER for coupling Railway Cars." Quebec, dated 3rd June, 1863.

No. 1537—NELSON, *(John,)* of the Town of Napanee, in the County of Lennox and Addington, for "A mode of constructing wrought iron Thrashing CYLINDERS." Quebec, dated 3rd June, 1863.

No. 1538—JAMES, *(Josiah,)* of Whitechurch, in the County of York, for "An improvement in PUMPS." Quebec, dated 4th June, 1863.

No. 1539—COREY, *(Randolph P ,)* of Hillier, in the County of Prince Edward, for "An Apple GRINDER." Quebec, dated 9th June, 1863.

No. 1540—SYLVESTER, *(Richard,)* of the Township of Scarboro,' in the County of York, for "An Improved CRADLE." Quebec, dated 3rd June, 1863.

No. 1541—BENDER, *(George,)* LEWIS, *(Zenas B.,)* and MILWARD, *(Mathew,)* of the Village of Clifton, in the County of Welland, for "Improvements in Wood Sawing MACHINES." Quebec, dated 4th June, 1863.

No. 1542—ELLSWORTH, *(O. Hamilton,)* of the Village of Bayfield, in the County of Huron, for "Ellsworths' Patent Lever Power or endless INCLINED PLANE." Quebec, dated 9th June, 1863.

No. 1543—RICHMOND, *(Francis T.,)* and THOMAS, *(William,)* both of the City of London, in the County of Middlesex, for "The Locomotive Crosscut SAWING MACHINE." Quebec, dated 9th June, 1863.

No. 1544—BENNETT, *(Richard Benson,)* of the Town of Belleville, in the County of Hastings, for "An Improved STAINTON PLOUGH." Quebec, dated 17th June, 1863.

No. 1545—KINNEY, *(Israel,)* of the Town of Brantford, in the County of Brant, for "A new and useful MOTIVE POWER." Quebec, dated 17th June, 1863.

No. 1546—THOMPSON, *(William,)* of Ashburnham, in the County of Peterborough, for "The Victoria Lever POWER for Hand Machinery." Quebec, dated 22nd June, 1863.

72

No. 1517—McDOUGALL, (*John Cameron*,) of Fort Erie, in the County of Welland, for "New and useful Improvements in HARVESTING Machines." Quebec, dated 22nd June, 1863.

No. 1548—INGLIS, (*William*,) of the City of Montreal, for "A new and useful improved Vertical STEAM BOILER." Quebec, dated 2nd July, 1863.

No. 1549—SANDFORD, (*Gelston*,) of the City of Quebec, for "Additional new and useful improvements in the Machine for breaking and cleaning FLAX, HEMP, and other like fibre yielding plants." Quebec, dated 3rd July, 1863.

No. 1550—THORPE, (*Thomas*,) of the City of Ottawa, for "The Tri-section of any rectilineal ANGLE." Quebec, dated 1st July, 1863.

No. 1551—CHATTERTON, (*Richard Dover*,) of the Town of Cobourg, in the County of Northumberland, for "A Platform ELEVATOR for loading heavy bodies, such as wood, coal, freight, &c., into Railway Trucks, Tenders, and other Carriages, called the 'Cobourg Platform ELEVATOR.'" Quebec, dated 15th June, 1863.

No. 1552—CAMPBELL, (*George*,) of the City of Toronto, for "A Galvanic Magnetic Toilet COMB." Quebec, dated 25th June, 1863.

No. 1553—CHATTERTON, (*Richard Dover*,) of the Town of Cobourg, in the County of Northumberland, for "A Railway Buffer and Collision Brake, called the Cobourg Railway Train PROTECTOR." Quebec, dated 16th June, 1863.

No. 1554—CHAPMAN, (*William*,) of the Township of Nottawasaga, in the County of Simcoe, for "A new and useful improvement in Furniture CASTORS." Quebec, dated 1st July, 1863.

No. 1555—SOPER, (*John*,) of the Village of Vienna, in the County of Elgin, for "A new and improved BEE HIVE." Quebec, dated 1st July, 1863.

No. 1556—BELL, (*George Waters*,) of Stanstead, for "An improved self-closing Gate to be called Bell's improved self-closing GATE fixtures." Quebec, dated 3rd July, 1863.

No. 1557—TRENHOLM, (*Edward*,) of Trenholmville, in the Township of Kingsey, in the County of Drummond, for "New and improved machinery for the purpose of loading and unloading ships with flour in barrels or any article contained in barrels, cases, bundles, or loose pieces, to be called 'Trenholm's Barrel LOADING Machine.'" Quebec, dated 3rd July, 1863.

No. 1558—ALISON, (*Robert James*,) of the City of Montreal, for "An improved machine for rossing TAN-BARK." Quebec. dated 3rd July, 1863.

No. 1559 McKILLOP, (*Archibald*,) of the Township of Inverness, in the County of Megantic, for "A Suspension Gate and BARN Door, called 'The Farmer's Rolling Gate.'" Quebec, dated 8th June, 1863.

No. 1560—KENDALL, (*Oren*,) of the Village of Coaticook, in the County of Stanstead, for "An improvement in Water Wheels, to be called 'O. Kendall's Improved TURBINE.'" Quebec, dated 3rd July, 1863.

No. 1561—DUNN, (*Alexander*,) of the City of Montreal, for "A new and improved apparatus for the better ventilation of PUBLIC Buildings, Houses and the like." Quebec, dated 3rd July, 1863.

No. 1562—McDONALD, (*Alexander*,) of the City of Montreal, for "A new and improved apparatus for hoisting and lowering BARRELS into and out of Ships." Quebec, dated 3rd July, 1863.

No. 1563—RAGG, (*Richard Benjamin*,) of the City of Montreal, and EMERY, (*Thomas William*,) of the same place, for "A new and improved Ventilator, to be called 'Ragg and Emory's VENTILATOR.'" Quebec, dated 7th July, 1863.

No. 1564—WALMSLEY, (*John*,) of the Village of Berlin, in the County of Waterloo, for "Improvements in Agricultural Implements for pulverizing and cleaning the soil and casting SEED and other substances thereon." Quebec, dated 18th June, 1863.

No. 1565—McGAFFEY, (*Ives Wallingsford*,) of the City of Hamilton, in the County of Wentworth, for "A Regulating DAMPER." Quebec, dated 2nd July, 1863.

No. 1566—ANDERSON, (*James Elijah*,) of the Town of Port Dover, in the County of Norfolk, for "Anderson's GIG." Quebec, dated 2nd July, 1863.

No. 1567—MORSE, (*Samuel*,) of the Town of Milton, in the County of Halton, for "A means of giving motion to certain parts of a THRESHING Machine and Separator." Quebec, dated 8th July, 1863.

No. 1568—CRAWFORD, (*Dalrymple,*) of the City of Toronto, for " Improvements in Oils and fats." Quebec, dated 8th July, 1863.

No. 1569—WRAY, (*Joseph,*) of the City of Montreal, for "A Refrigerator for the preservation of DEAD bodies." Quebec, dated 13th July, 1863.

No. 1570—BERRY, (*William,*) of the City of Montreal, for "An anti-friction loop stopper for SEWING Machines." Quebec, dated 11th July, 1863.

No. 1571—STEPHENSON, (*William Duncan,*) of the City of Montreal, for " A new and useful Tube and Valve atmospheric CHURN Dasher." Quebec, dated 17th July, 1863.

No. 1572—COLLEY, (*Edward William,*) of St. Mary's, in the County of Perth, for " An Eavetrough and Metallic MOULDING Machine." Quebec, dated 28th July, 1863.

No. 1573—BEEBE, (*George F.,*) of Sophiasburgh, in the County of Prince Edward for " A Stump EXTRACTOR." Quebec, dated 28th July, 1863.

No. 1574—MILO, (*Francis,*) of Kingston, in the County of Frontenac, for "A TRANS-PLANTER." Quebec, dated 28th July, 1863.

No. 1575—CHASE, (*James,*) of Brooklin, in the County of Ontario, for " A machine for sinking Field DRAINS." Quebec, dated 31st July, 1863.

No. 1576—BOWERMAN, (*Levi V.,*) of Hallowell, in the County of Prince Edward, for "A WAGGON Box." Quebec, dated 31st July, 1863.

No. 1577—McKAY, (*Marshall,*) of the City of London, for "A SLAT Splitting Machine." Quebec, dated 31st July, 1863.

No. 1578—BRICE, (*George Byron,*) of Ingersoll, in the County of Oxford, for " A Sulkey and Seat Spring called ' Brice's SULKEY and Seat Spring.'" Quebec, dated 3rd August, 1863.

No. 1579—RODD, (*Walter James Handscome,*) and LOVELL, (*James,*) both of the City of Toronto, for "A process for the manufacture of paper and textile fabrics from the Heltanthus or SUNFLOWER." Quebec, dated 3rd August, 1863.

No. 1580—DRISCOLL, (*William,*) of Merrickville, in the County of Grenville, for "A double crank churning and Horizontal BORING Machine." Quebec, dated 6th August, 1863.

No. 1581—MEAKING, (*George Henry,*) of Belleville, in the County of Hastings, for " An improved SEWING MACHINE." Quebec, dated 12th August, 1863.

No. 1582—HURLBUT, (*James,*) of the Township of Reach, in the County of Ontario, for " A Water METER." Quebec, dated 7th August, 1863.

No. 1583—LISTER, (*David,*) of the City of Toronto, in the County of York, for " A new and useful hopper shaped Fire GRATE for Locomotive Engines." Quebec, dated 18th August, 1863.

No. 1584—RODDEN, (*William Henry,*) of the City of Toronto, in the County of York, for " A sled Snow SHOVEL." Quebec, dated 22nd August, 1863.

No. 1585—GOOD, (*James,*) of the City of Toronto, in the County of York, for " An ash box for the description of stove known as the ALBANIAN radiating Stove." Quebec, dated 25th August, 1863.

No. 1586—BOWEN, (*William Renslow,*) of the Township of Haldimand, in the County of Northumberland, for "A machine for the shrinking of WAGGON tires." Quebec, dated 22nd August, 1863.

No. 1587—CHASE, (*James,*) of Brooklin, in the County of Ontario, for "A window curtain roller fixture, called ' Chase's Magic Curtain FIXTURE.'" Quebec, dated 25th August, 1863.

No. 1588—SLATER, (*George,*) of Mount Forest, in the County of Grey, for "An article called a Weather STRIP to be attached to outside doors." Quebec, dated 26th August, 1863.

No. 1589—FAIRMAN, (*Warren,*) of the Township of Pittsburg, in the County of Frontenac, for "An improved Fence called 'Fairman's FENCE." Quebec, dated 21st August, 1863.

No. 1590—ROBLIN, (*Edwin,*) of the Township of Sophiasburgh, in the County of Prince Edward, for "An improved SNAITH." Quebec, dated 31st August, 1863.

No. 1591—WAGNER, (*William*,) of the City of Montreal, for "A new and improved KILN or OVEN for burning bricks, tiles, &c." Quebec, dated 11th September, 1863.

No. 1592—TULLEY, (*Kivas*,) of the City of Toronto, for "A valve PROPELLER." Quebec, dated 12th September, 1863.

No. 1593—CHURCHILL, (*Jehiel*,) and CHURCHILL, (*Thomas*,) both of the Township of Pickering, in the County of Ontario, for "A machine for the fabrication of BASKETS." Quebec, dated 22nd September, 1863.

No. 1594—McDONALD, (*Charles*,) of the Village of Embro, in the Township of West Zorra, in the County of Oxford, for "An improvement to the double or wool custom carding MACHINE." Quebec, dated 28th September, 1863.

No. 1595—DEAN (*Cyrus*,) of the Town of St. Catharines, in the County of Lincoln, for "A machine for effecting more perfect combustion of fuel in the furnaces of LOCOMOTIVES." Quebec, dated 28th September, 1863.

No. 1596—SHEPARD, (*Daniel*,) of the Village of Waterdown, in the County of Wentworth, for "The Slave Cross CUTTER." Quebec, dated 2nd October, 1863.

No. 1597—SHAW, (*Arthur*,) Assignee of Jonathan H. Havens, both of the Village of Queenston, in the County Lincoln, for "A new and useful Window LOCK." Quebec, dated 5th October, 1863.

No. 1598—CRANDELL, (*Charles Newton*,) of the Township of Onondaga, in the County of Brant, for "An improved Bee-hive, called 'Crandell's patent moveable comb and miller catcher BEE-HIVE.'" Quebec, dated 7th October, 1863.

No. 1599—FEAR, (*John*,) of the Village of Washington, in the Township of Blenheim, in the County of Oxford, for "An improved Pump, called 'The Balance PUMP.'" Quebec, dated 8th October, 1863.

No. 1600—SOPER, (*Alpha*,) of the Village of Orono, in the Township of Clarke, in the County of Durham, for "An apparatus for the raising of sunken vessels, called 'Soper's portable submarine air TANKS.'" Quebec, dated 15th October, 1863.

No. 1601—CHAMBERS, (*William*,) of the City of London, in the County of Middlesex, for "A combined Cultivator and grain and seed DEPOSITOR." Quebec, dated 15th October, 1863.

No. 1602—MILNER, (*Thomas*,) of the City of Montreal, for "A new and useful CORDER." Quebec, dated 26th October, 1863.

No. 1603—JENKS, (*Sylvester B.*,) of the Town of Sherbrooke, for "A new and improved EGG-BEATER." Quebec, dated 26th October, 1863.

No. 1604—LEVEQUE, (*Adolphe*,) of the City of Montreal, for "A sub-marine Elevating BAG." Quebec, dated 27th October, 1863.

No. 1605—INGLIS, (*William*,) of the City of Montreal, for "Improvements in the valve gear of the steam engine, to be called Inglis' improved Water tube BOILER." Quebec, dated 27th October, 1863.

No. 1606—PAINCHAUD, (*Charles Francois*,) of the Parish of Ste. Anne de Varennes, for "An improved HORSE RAKE." Quebec, dated 27th October, 1863.

No. 1607—LYMBURNER, (*Marcel E.*,) of the City of Montreal, for "A new and improved SKIRTLIFTER." Quebec, dated 27th October, 1863.

No. 1608—KURCZYN, (*Frederick H.*,) of the City of Montreal, for "A new water proof CEMENT for paths, roofings, floorings, cisterns and water tanks." Quebec, dated 27th October, 1863.

No. 1609—WOOD, (*Henry*,) and KINNOND, (*Margaret Lighton*,) of the City of Montreal, and FOURDRINIER, (*George Henry*,) of the Village of Lyn, in Upper Canada, for "A new and useful EXCELSIOR DESICCATOR, and other apparatus for curing damaged grain, and for the manufacture of malt." Quebec, dated 27th October, 1863.

No. 1610—BELL, (*John*,) and BELL, (*David*,) of the Parish of St. Nicholas, in the County of Levis, for "A Reversible WING for railway crossings." Quebec, dated 26th November, 1863.

No. 1611—HIGHET, (*Robert*,) of the Town of Cobourg, in the County of Northumberland, for "An improved Iron AXLE TREE, to be called Highet's patent iron Axle Tree." Quebec, dated 2nd November, 1863.

No. 1612—COLEMAN, (*John,*) of the Village of Oshawa, in the County of Ontario, for "A Machine called a Nulling GAGE." Quebec, dated 28th November, 1863.

No. 1613—CHATTERTON, (*Richard Dover,*) of the Town of Cobourg, in the County of Northumberland, for "A safety coupling apparatus called Chatterton's Safety COUPLING for carriages, railway cars, &c." Quebec, dated 29th November, 1863.

No. 1614—JEPSON, (*John Vivian,*) of the City of Montreal, for "A new and improved Steam Pressure GAUGE." Quebec, dated 5th November, 1873.

No. 1615—KITCHEN, (*William W.,*) of the Township of Grimsby, in the County of Lincoln, for "A double SINGLE-TREE." Quebec, dated 5th November, 1863.

No. 1616—SMITH, (*Samuel,*) of the Village of Acton, in the County of Halton, for "An improved machine for the jointing of staves for Barrels, called 'Smith's STAVE-JOINTER.'" Quebec, dated 23rd November, 1863.

No. 1617—LEE, (*Walter M.,*) of Oshawa, in the County of Ontario, for "An improved Bee-Hive, called 'Lee's Dividing BEE-HIVE.'" Quebec, dated 23rd November, 1863.

No. 1618—BRYAN, (*Thomas,*) and ASHMAN, (*Mark,*) both of the Township of London, in the County of Middlesex, for "An improved Cradle for the cutting of grain, called 'The Economic Mulcy CRADLE.'" Quebec, dated 23rd November, 1863.

No. 1619—ROE, (*Cyrenius Chapin,*) of the Town of Brantford, in the County of Brant, for "A Horse Power, called the 'Canadian HORSE POWER.'" Quebec, dated 24th November, 1863.

No. 1620—LOCKMAN, (*Christopher,*) of the City of Hamilton, in the County of Wentworth, for "An ATTACHMENT for Sewing Machines for ruffling." Quebec, dated 24th November, 1863.

No. 1621—SUTTON, (*Frederick E.,*) Assignee of SUTTON, (*Walter Jee,*) of the Village of Oshawa, in the County of Ontario, for "An improved Rat-trap, called 'Sutton's Canadian RAT-TRAP.'" Quebec, dated 24th November, 1863.

No. 1622—WALKER, (*Robert Edwin,*) of the Town of Stratford, in the County of Perth, for "An improved Straw Carrier, called 'The Folding Straw CARRIER.'" Quebec, dated 28th November, 1863.

No. 1623—BLETCHER, (*Thomas,*) of the Town of Peterborough, in the County of Peterborough, for "A Wood Sawing MACHINE." Quebec, dated 24th November, 1863.

No. 1624—WARD, (*James,*) of the Township of Bury, in the County of Compton, for "A new and improved Flax PULLER." Quebec, dated 1st December, 1863.

No. 1625—CARRIER, (*Henry,*) of Roxton Falls, in the County of Shefford, for "A new and improved BEE HIVE." Quebec, dated 3rd December, 1863.

No. 1626—PRINGLE, (*Thomas,*) of the City of Montreal, for "A Tidal Grain ELEVATOR." Quebec, dated 3rd December, 1863.

No. 1627—GALLACHER, (*John McAuley,*) of the City of Montreal, for "A new and useful compound, to be called 'Gallacher's fertilizing COMPOUND.'" Quebec, dated 3rd December, 1863.

No. 1628—SUMMERS, (*Hyatt,*) of the Township of Thorold, in the County of Welland, for "An improved Horse Rake, called Summers' 'Duplicate HORSE RAKE.'" Quebec, dated 9th December, 1863.

No. 1629—SNIDER, (*Daniel,*) of the Township of Vaughan, in the County of York, for "An improved Churn, called 'Snider's Lever handle and flap dash CHURN.'" Quebec, dated 10th December, 1863.

No. 1630—SAMPSON, (*James Henry,*) of the Village of Belmont, in the County of Middlesex, for "An improved Boot Tree, called 'Sampson's BOOT TREE.'" Quebec, dated 14th December, 1863.

No. 1631—AUBIN, (*Aimé Nicholas Napoleon,*) of Béloeil, in the County of Verchères, for "A new and improved safety RUNNER for winter Vehicles." Quebec, dated 16th December, 1863.

No. 1632—PROWSE, (*George Roger,*) of the City of Montreal, for "A new and improved Steam RADIATOR." Quebec, dated 19th December, 1863.

No. 1633—HAVENS, (*Jonathan Hilton,*) of the Town of Guelph, in the County of Wellington, for "An improved COUPLING for Railroad Cars." Quebec, dated 22nd December, 1863.

No. 1634—HARRISON, (*James Edward,*) of the Village of Bridgewater, and WOLFE,

George,) of the same place, for "An improved machine for the Extracting of stumps, called the 'Bridgewater STUMP Machine.'" Quebec, dated 5th January, 1864.

No. 1635—CLEMENT, (*Richard,*) of the Township of Stamford, in the County of Welland, for "An improved clothes wringer, called "Clement's Clothes WRINGER." Quebec, dated 8th January, 1864.

No. 1636—CAMERON, (*John,*) of the Township of Pickering, in the County of Ontario, for "A churn and washing machine combined which is applicable to rubbing, sifting and gratting purposes, called 'Cameron's combined circular CHURN and Washing Machine.'" Quebec, dated 9th January, 1864.

No. 1637—CHATTERTON, (*Richard Dover,*) of the Town of Cobourg, in the County of Northumberland, for "A new and useful coupling for carriages on Railways and common Roads, called 'Chatterton's improved safety COUPLING.'" Quebec, dated 25th January, 1864.

No. 1638—HARRIS, (*John,*) of the City of Montreal, for "A new and useful lever PADDLE for propelling and steering vessels." Quebec, dated 13th January, 1864.

No. 1639—KENDALL, (*William C.,*) of Buckingham, in the County of Ottawa, for "A new and improved water wheel, to be called 'Kendall's simple DISCHARGE water wheel.'" Quebec, dated 13th January, 1864.

No. 1640—GINGRAS, (*Edward D.,*) of the City of Quebec, for "A new and improved apparatus for attaching SEATS to sleighs and other vehicles either for winter or summer use." Quebec, dated 13th January, 1864.

No. 1641—MATTHEWS, (*George,*) of the City of Montreal, Assignee of Thomas Sterry Hunt, of the same place, for "An insoluble and indestructing printing Ink, to be called 'The Patent Lake TINT.'" Quebec, dated 13th January, 1864.

No. 1642—PARKIN, (*Edward Cullen,*) of Valcartier, in the County of Quebec, for "A new and useful material, to be called 'LUPULANE, (to be used in Manufacture of Paper.)'" Quebec, dated 19th January, 1864.

No. 1643—DARVILL, (*David,*) of the City of London, in the County of Middlesex, for "An improved LEVER-POWER Machine." Quebec, dated 3rd February, 1864.

No. 1644—COLEMAN, (*John,*) of the Village of Oshawa, in the County of Ontario, for "A nulling and spiral Gauge, called 'Coleman's nulling and spiral GAUGE.'" Quebec, dated 3rd February, 1864.

No. 1645—O'HARA, (*James,*) of the Village of Brockton, in the Township and County of York, for "Improved wheels for the propelling of ships and other vessels, called O'Hara's Diagonal Sculling WHEELS." Quebec, dated 3rd February, 1864.

No. 1646—McKINNON, (*Donald,*) of the Township of Markham, in the County of York, for "An improved Thrashing Machine, called 'McKinnon's THRASHING Machine.'" Quebec, dated 3rd February, 1864.

No. 1647—FORSYTH, (*John,*) of the Town of Dundas, in the County of Wentworth, for "An improvement on the valves of double action FORCE PUMPS, (including the particular kind of pump patented by one Waters)." Quebec, dated 3rd February, 1864.

No. 1648—STOVEL, (*Samuel,*) of the Township of Minto, in the County of Wellington, and STOVEL, (*Ebenezer,*) of the same Township, for "A self-adjusting Snow GATE." Quebec, dated 3rd February, 1864.

No. 1649—McLIM, (*John,*) of the Village of Scotland, in the Township of Oakland, in the County of Brant, for "A screw concave CHURN-DASH." Quebec, dated 3rd February, 1864.

No. 1650—CANT, (*Hugh,*) of the Town of Galt, in the County of Waterloo, for "An improved form or description of Steam Engine, called 'Cant's rotary ENGINE.'" Quebec, dated 11th February, 1864.

No. 1651—SMITH, (*Joel,*) of the Township of Haldimand, in the County of Northumberland, for "A machine for shrinking or upsetting the tires of Wheels of Waggons and other vehicles, called and known as 'Smith's tire SHRINKING Machine.'" Quebec, dated 12th September, 1863.

No. 1652—LAWSON, (*Edward,*) of Melbourne, in the County of Richmond, for "A new and useful machine for separating and sorting Ores and other matter." Quebec, dated 29th February, 1861.

No. 1653—DOUGALL, (James,) of the City of Montreal, for " An improved system of Drainage." Quebec, dated 28th February, 1861.

No. 1654—LAWRENCE, (Samuel,) of the Township of Stanstead, in the County of Stanstead, for " A new and improved Churn." Quebec, dated 25th February, 1861.

No. 1655—PETERSON, (Norris Conrad,) of the Town of Sarnia, in the County of Lambton, for " A machine for upsetting and fitting Ties for wheels and other Irons." Quebec, dated 26th February, 1861.

No. 1656—HUNTINGTON, (Gedeon,) of Norwichville, in the Township of Norwich, in the County of Oxford, for " An improved machine for upsetting the ties of wheels of carriages, waggons and other vehicles, called Huntington's improved Upsetting machine." Quebec, dated 28th February, 1861.

No. 1657—ANSLEY, (Ozias,) of the township of Port Dover, in the County of Norfolk, for " A Ventilating Stove." Quebec, dated 1st March, 1861.

No. 1658—BLANCHARD, (Louis,) of the Township of Cornwall, in the County of Stormont, for " A new description of gate, called 'Blanchard's improved Gate.'" Quebec, dated 2nd March, 1861.

No. 1659—PAYNE, (Edward,) of the City of Montreal, for " A new and useful apparatus or instrument for ascertaining the gravity of liquids, to be called 'Payne's Spiritometer.'" Quebec, dated 8th March, 1861.

No. 1660—GRAY, (George,) of the City of London, in the County of Middlesex, for " A new and improved mould-board for ploughs, called Gray's Mould Board No. 5." Quebec, dated 18th February, 1861.

No. 1661—MILLER, (James,) of the Parish of St. Pie, in the County of Bagot, for "The discovery of the art of manufacturing from tan-bark a substance for tanning or dying purposes, to be called ' Miller's Extract of Tan-Bark.'" Quebec, dated 12th March, 1861.

No. 1662—McCARTER, (Alexander,) of the Village of Walkerton, in the County of Bruce, for " A new and useful improvement in boxing-machine for Carriage and Waggon Wheels." Quebec, dated 16th March, 1861.

No. 1663—CUNNINGHAM, (Henry,) of the City of Kingston, in the County of Frontenac, for "A new and useful double top, and return flue heating and smoke consuming Stove." Quebec, dated 16th March, 1861.

• No. 1664—LOFTUS, (Robert George,) of the Township of Enniskillen, in the County of Lambton, for " A new and useful process by which the sulphuric acid used in refining distilled petroleum coal oil, naptha, and other products of the distillation of petroleum and coal, can be recovered and made equal to the acid in its original state for the Refining of the aforesaid articles." Quebec, dated 21st March, 1861.

No. 1665—RICHARDSON, (David,) of the Township of Brantford, in the County of Brant, for "An article called ' Richardson's Churn.'" Quebec, dated 21st March, 1861.

No. 1666—WILSON, (Samuel,) of the Village of Norwood, in the County of Peterborough, and McGEE, (James H.,) of the Town of Port Hope, in the County of Durham, for " A new and improved method of constructing Elbows for stove-pipes, the Elbow as improved being called ' McGee & Wilson's stove-pipe Elbow.'" Quebec, dated 4th April, 1861.

No. 1667—LEONARD, (Elijah,) of the City of London, in the County of Middlesex, for "An improved sawing machine for the cross cutting of Timber." Quebec, dated 4th April, 1861.

No. 1668—CULL, (John Angell,) of the City of Toronto, in the County of York, for "An improvement in the form and arrangement of the teeth and tines of a certain agricultural instrument, called ' The Forest Cultivator,' as also of those of all other cultivators or harrows, the shanks of which are used in a position either slanting or curved or sloping backwards, after the manner of the teeth or tines of the said 'Forest Cultivators.'" Quebec, da'ed 4th April, 1861.

No. 1669—CARPENTER, (Alexander,) of the City of Hamilton, in the County of Wentworth, for " A hot water drum, to be attached in the second or third stories of dwelling houses, for cooking and other stoves for the purpose of heating water for BATH and other purposes." Quebec, dated 4th April, 1864.

No. 1670—TAYLOR, (*Philip,*) of the Village of Oshawa, in the County of Ontario, for "An article for the heating of cutters and carriages, called 'Taylor's cutter and carriage HEATER.'" Quebec, dated 4th April, 1864.

No. 1671—GLEASON, (*Alvirus,*) of the Township of Walnfleet, in the County of Welland, for "Certain new and useful improvements in Thrashing machines and Grain Separators, the machine as improved being called 'Gleason's FANNING Mill and Grain Separator.'" Quebec, dated 4th April, 1864.

No. 1672—McGINNES, (*Timothy,*) of the Township of Ameliasburgh, in the County of Prince Edward, for "An improved apparatus for the drawing of water, called 'McGinnes' Water DRAWER.'" Quebec, dated 30th March, 1864.

No. 1673—PICHETTE, (*François Xavier,*) of the City of Quebec, for "A new and improved carriage SHAFT coupling." Quebec, dated 13th April, 1864.

No. 1674—NADEAU, (*Francois,*) of the City of Quebec, for "A new and improved Coal Oil Street LAMP." Quebec, dated 13th April, 1864.

No. 1675—WATSON, (*Joseph,*) of the Township of Norwich North, in the County of Oxford, for "A MACHINE for the sowing of all kinds of grain and of plaster, &c., broadcast with or without a harrow or cultivator attached to it; and for sowing all kinds of grain in drills, and for plating corn by means of furrow and covering teeth combined and attached to the axle or box." Quebec, dated 4th April, 1864.

No. 1676—JONES, (*Charles,*) of the Village of Brant, in the County of Halton, for "An improved clothes-dryer and clothes-horse, called the Victoria Clothes-Dryer and CLOTHES-HORSE." Quebec, dated 4th April, 1864.

No. 1677—WARD, (*James,*) of the Township of Bury, in the County of Compton, for "A new and useful instrument denominated a Butter worker and Bread MOULDER." Quebec, dated 13th April, 1864.

No. 1678—WILLIAMS, (*John,*) of the City of Montreal, for "An improved Cinder CEMENT for lining puddling furnaces." Quebec, dated 13th April, 1864.

No. 1679—GOUDIE, (*David Roy,*) of the City of Montreal, for "An improvement in the manufacture of fly and vermin paper, to be called 'Goudie's Fly and Vermin ANNIHILATOR.'" Quebec, dated 13th April, 1864.

No. 1680—PARADIS, (*Joseph,*) of the City of Montreal, for "A new and improved escapement HAMMER." Quebec, dated 22nd April, 1864.

No. 1681—DUNN, (*Alexander,*) of the City of Montreal, for "A new and improved self-acting WATER-CLOSET." Quebec, dated 22nd April, 1864.

No. 1682—MACLEA, (*William James,*) of the City of Toronto, in the County of York, for "A new soldering iron, called 'Maclea's gas-heating SOLDERING IRON.'" Quebec, dated 2nd May, 1864.

No. 1683—FOGG, (*Thomas,*) of Richmond, in the County of Richmond, for "An improved CHAIR for preventing bolts or nuts used in bracing and joining together iron rails from becoming loose or insecure." Quebec, dated 2nd May, 1864.

No. 1684—ROWF, (*Horace E.,*) of the Village of Napanee, in the County of Lennox, one of the United Counties of Frontenac, Lennox and Addington, for "A new and useful coffee-pot, called 'The Royal COFFEE-POT.'" Quebec, dated 2nd May, 1864.

No. 1685—CLAYTON, (*James,*) of the Town of Whitby, in the County of Ontario, for "A new and useful machine for planting seed and distributing manure, called the 'Root seed and plaster DISTRIBUTER.'" Quebec, dated 2nd May, 1864.

No. 1686—ANDERSON, (*Alexander,*) of the City of London, in the County of Middlesex, for "A new and useful Harrow, called the 'Universal elastic reversable Harrow." Quebec, dated 2nd May, 1864.

No. 1687—OTTON, (*Demas,*) of the Township of Sophiasburgh, in the County of Prince Edward, for "A new and improved ROLLER (iron headed)." Quebec, dated 2nd May, 1864.

No. 1688—THOMAS, (*J. H.,*) of the Village of Brooklin, in the County of Ontario, for "A

79

new and useful Bee-hive, called 'Thomas' combined movenble comb Bee Palace and BEE-HIVE.'" Quebec, dated 2nd May, 1864.

No. 1689—STUART, (James,) of the City of Hamilton, in the County of Wentworth, for "An article which he calls a 'Township Indicator.'" Quebec, dated 17th May, 1864.

No. 1690—HAVEN, (Jonathan Hilton,) of the Town of Guelph, in the County of Wellington, for "A new and useful Chair, called 'Haven's Sewing CHAIR.'" Quebec, dated 2nd May, 1864.

No. 1691—SHAW, (John,) of the Village of Oshawa, in the County of Ontario, for "A Butter working machine, called 'Shaw's Butter working MACHINE.'" Quebec, dated 2nd May, 1864.

No. 1692—NOXON, (Samuel,) of the Village of Ingersoll, in the County of Oxford, for "A new and useful cultivator, called 'Noxon's CULTIVATOR.'" Quebec, dated 2nd May, 1864.

No. 1693—RILEY, (James,) of the Town of Windsor, in the County of Essex, for "A machine called 'Riley's straw hay stalk and root CUTTE.'" Quebec, dated 2nd May, 1864.

No. 1694—FLETCHER, (Thomas,) of the Township of Beverly, in the County of Wentworth, for "A new and useful BEAM and Mould-board, respectively, for ploughs." Quebec, dated 5th May, 1864.

No. 1695—FULLER, (Richard,) of the City of Hamilton, in the County of Wentworth, for "A new and useful method of impregnating and preserving wood with PETROLEUM or the extracts thereof." Quebec, dated 6th May, 1864.

No. 1696—HANNUM, (Silas Pomeroy,) of the Town of L'Orignal, in the County of Prescott, and HAMILTON, (William,) of the same place, for "An improved GOLD-WASHING machine." Quebec, dated 1st June, 1864.

No. 1697—MOODY, (John,) of the Town of Terrebonne, for "Additional new and useful improvements in the machine for breaking and cleaning FLAX, Hemp and other like fibre yielding plants." Quebec, dated 27th May, 1864.

No. 1698—OAKELY, (William,) of the Town of Goderich, in the County of Huron, for "A new and useful Life Preserver, called 'Oakely's Polyzone LIFE PRESERVER.'" Quebec, dated 30th May, 1864.

No. 1699—STOVEL, (George,) of the Township of Minto, in the County of Wellington, for "A new and useful Hay ELEVATOR." Quebec, dated 31st May, 1864.

No. 1700—PERKS, (George,) of the Town of Port Hope, in the County of Durham, for "An improvement in Lamps, which he calls the FAN BLAST." Quebec, dated 31st May, 1864.

No. 1701—HARRIS, (Alanson,) of the Village of Beamsville, in the County of Lincoln, for "A new and useful improvement in Land ROLLERS." Quebec, dated 1st June, 1864.

No. 1702—KEFFER, (Benjamin,) of the Township of Vaughan, in the County of York, for "A new and useful Churn, called 'The British American CHURN.'" Quebec, dated 1st June, 1864.

No. 1703—COUPLAND, (Samuel,) of the Township of Blanshard, in the County of Perth, and ADAIR, (John,) of the Town of St. Mary's, in the same County, for "A new and improved machine, called Coupland and Adair's combined Cultivator and Seed SOWER." Quebec, dated 1st June, 1864.

No. 1704—PATTERSON, (Alexander,) of the Village of Gananoque, in the County of Leeds, for "A machine called Patterson's Excelsior Mattrass Filling CUTTER." Quebec, dated 1st June, 1864.

No. 1705—CALCUTT, (Henry,) of the Village of Ashburnham, in the County of Peterborough, for "A compound liquid cooler and heater for cooling and heating liquids of every description, to be called "Calcutt's compound Liquid Cooler and HEATER." Quebec, dated 3rd June, 1864.

No. 1706—CLARKE, (Hugh,) of the Village of Orono, in the County of Durham, for "A new CULTIVATOR." Quebec, dated 1st June, 1864.

No. 1707—JAMES, (William,) of the Township of South Norwich, in the County of Oxford, for "A new and improved carriage JACK." Quebec, dated 4th June, 1864.

No. 1708—BOYCE, (George W.,) of the Village of Addison, in the Township of Elizabethtown, in the County of Leeds, for "An improved CHURN." Quebec, dated 4th June, 1864.

No. 1709—MOSIMAN, (*John Frederick*,) of the City of Toronto, in the County of York, for "An improved Hot Air Stove or Furnace." Quebec, dated 9th June, 1864.

No. 1710—WHIFTY, (*Philip*,) of the City of Quebec, for "A new and useful gold mining Pick, called ' Whitty's solid eye mining Pick.' " Quebec, dated 16th June, 1864.

No. 1711—BEATY, (*John J*,) of the Village of Streetsville, in the County of Peel, for "An Egg Beater." Quebec, dated 13th June, 1864.

No. 1712 -KINNEY, (*Israel*,) of the Township of Oakland, in the County of Brant, for "An improved Box and Axle, called "Kinney's anti-friction Box and Axle." Quebec, dated 14th June, 1864.

No 1713—MILLE ?, (*Abraham P.*,) of the Village of Norwich, in the County of Oxford, for "A new and useful Hydrostatic Engine." Quebec, dated 14th June, 1864.

No. 1714—CHASE, (*James*,) of the Village of Brooklin, in the County of Ontario, for "A new and useful Reaper Attachment." Quebec, dated 17th June, 1864.

No. 1715 VANDYKE, (*John*,) of Grimsby, in the County of Lincoln, for "A new and useful boring Machine." Quebec, dated 17th June, 1864.

No. 1716—HENDERSON, (*William II.*,) of Brockville, in the County of Leeds, for "An improved Roof, called "Henderson's non-leaking Roof." Quebec, dated 20th June, 1864.

No. 1717—McKINNON, (*Duncan*,) of the Township of Markham, in the County of York, for "The Double Scribe." Quebec, dated 20th June, 1864.

No. 1718—BENTLEY, (*William*,) of the Village of Mount Forest, in the County of Grey, and IRELAND, (*Isaac*,) of the same place, for "A new and useful combined Hoop and Lath Machine." Quebec, dated 21st June, 1864.

No. 1719—HART, (*John*,) of the Township of Granby, District of Bedford, for "A new and improved Gas Stove for the consumption of coal oil as fuel." Quebec, dated 11th July, 1864.

No. 1720—BLACK, (*James Fitzgibbon David*,) of the City of Montreal, for "An improved Rail and Arch for strengthening and arching Vessels." Quebec, dated 16th July, 1864.

No. 1721—NICKLESON, (*Moses Charman*,) of the Town of Port Dover, in the County of Norfolk, for "A new and useful compound chemical Soap." Quebec, dated 21st June, 1864.

No. 1722—ORTON, (*William*,) of the Village of Aurora, in the County of York, for "A new and useful combined Hay-Maker and hay-raker." Quebec, dated 21st June, 1864.

No. 1723—UNWIN, (*Walker*,) of the Township of Blanshard, County of Perth, for "An improved Plough, called ' Unwin's Adjustable Plough." Quebec, dated 5th July, 1864.

No. 1724—CONDELL, (*John*,) of the Town of Brockville, County of Leeds, for "An improved Artificial Leg." Quebec, dated 23rd July, 1864.

No. 1725—COLEMAN, (*David*,) of Castleton, County of Northumberland, for "A new and useful Draft Neck-Yoke." Quebec, dated 26th July, 1864.

No. 1726—BROWN, (*Henry*,) of the City of Kingston, County of Frontenac, for "The Art of Manufacturing a Pulp from the Bark of the Cedar Tree, furnishing a fit and proper material for a new and useful composition of matter for the manufacture of Paper, called ' Cedar Bark Paper Pulp.' " Quebec, dated 23rd July, 1864.

No. 1727—CONDELL, (*John*,) of the Town of Brockville, County of Leeds, for "An improved Artificial Limb, called ' Condel's Artificial Limb.' " Quebec, dated 23rd July, 1864.

No. 1728—HORTON, (*Cyrus*,) of the Township of Southwold, County of Elgin, for "A new and useful Combined Drill and Sowing Machine." Quebec, dated 26th July, 1864.

No. 1729—COOK, (*Edward*,) of the Township of West Zorra, County of Oxford, for "A new and useful Safety Rail-Coupling." Quebec, dated 5th August, 1864.

No. 1770—MALPUSS, (*Samuel*,) of Middleton Centre, County of Norfolk, for "A new and useful Shingle-Jointer" Quebec, dated 16th August, 1864.

No. 1731—TAYLOR, (*William*,) of the Township of Malahide, County of Elgin, for an improvement in Carriage Springs, called "The Taylor Carriage Spring." Quebec, dated 17th August, 1864.

No. 1732—VANDUSEN, (*Conrad,*) of the Town of Milton, County of Halton, for "A machine which he calls 'The Champion Clothes Dryer.'" Quebec, dated 17th August, 1864.

No. 1733—DUNKAR, (*Henry Dennison,*) of the Village of Oshawa, County of Ontario, for "A new and useful Self-Adjusting Steam Piston-Packing." Quebec, dated 17th August, 1864.

No. 1734—McFARLANE, (*John,*) of the Township of Etobicoke, County of York, and McFARLANE, (*Daniel,*) of the same Township, for "An improved Mechanical Contrivance or Machine for opening and closing any ordinary Gate, called and known as the 'McFarlane Self-Acting Gate.'" Quebec, dated 17th August, 1864.

No. 1735—MERRILL, (*Abel,*) of the Township of Houghton, in the County of Norfolk, for "An improved Keel for Vessels." Quebec, dated 17th August, 1864.

No. 1736—GALLOWAY, (*Andrew,*) of the Township of Glanford, in the County of Wentworth, for "A new and useful discovery, which he calls 'Galloway's portable combination single and double Ladder.'" Quebec, 17th August, 1864.

No. 1737—THOMPSON, (*Thomas,*) of the City of Quebec, for "An improved Smoking Pipe." Quebec, dated 24th September, 1864.

No. 1738—THOMPSON, (*Thomas,*) of the City of Quebec, for "A new and useful Purifier." Quebec, dated 24th September, 1864.

No. 1739—GAMACHE, (*Isaac,*) of the Town of Levis, for a new and useful apparatus for loading and unloading Vessels." Quebec, dated 24th September, 1864.

No. 1740—SMITH, (*Richard,*) of the Town of Sherbrooke, in the District of St. Francis, for "A new and improved Tobacco-cutter, to be called 'Smith's Eureka Tobacco-cutter.'" Quebec, dated 24th September, 1864.

No. 1741—GIBSON, (*John,*) of the Town of St. Mary's, in the County of Perth, for "A new Mill-Pick, called 'Gibson's Mill-Pick.'" Quebec, dated 20th September, 1864.

No. 1742—MOYER, (*Isaac Allbright,*) of the Township of Clinton, County of Lincoln, for "A new and useful Meat-chopper, called the 'Empire Meat-chopper.'" Quebec, dated 27th September, 1864.

No. 1743—THAYER, (*Joseph,*) of the Town of Belleville, in the County of Hastings, for "A new and useful Guide-head for Lathes, called 'Thayer's eccentric Guide-head.'" Quebec, dated 27th September, 1864.

No. 1744—PAYNE, (*Frederick John,*) of the Township of Southwold, in the County of Elgin, for "A new and useful field Cultivator." Quebec, dated 26th September, 1864.

No. 1745—THOMSON, (*James E.,*) of the City of Toronto, in the County of York, for "An improved Safety-Lock." Quebec, dated 24th September, 1864.

No. 1746—QUACKENBUSH, (*Alonzo,*) of the Village of Port Dalhousie, County of Lincoln, for "An improved Churn." Quebec, dated 28th September, 1864.

No. 1747—STOVEL, (*Ebenezer,*) of the Village of Mount Forest, County of Grey, for "A new and useful Self-Regulating Snow Gate." Quebec, dated 28th September, 1864.

No. 1748—DONNELLY, (*William Clark,*) of the Township of Walpole, County of Haldimand, and PARKER, (*Jesse,*) of the same Township, for "A Safety Carriage Spring." Quebec, dated 4th October, 1864.

No. 1749—YEAGER, (*Henry,*) of the Township of West Flamborough, County of Wentworth, for "A new and useful machine which he calls a 'The Upsetting Machine.'" Quebec, dated 24th October, 1864.

No. 1750—LAMAIN, (*Charles,*) of the Township of Hamilton, County of Northumberland, for "A new and useful Seed-Sowing Machine." Quebec, dated 24th October, 1864.

No. 1751—HENDERSON, (*Joseph C.,*) of the Town of Brockville, County of Leeds, for "An improved Coal Stove, called 'Henderson's New Coal-Burner.'" Quebec, dated 24th October, 1864.

No. 1752—VAN BUSKIRK, (*William C.,*) of the Town of St. Thomas, County of Elgin, for "A new and useful Draining Plough." Quebec, dated 25th October, 1864.

No. 1753—JOHNS, (*David,*) of the Village of Exeter, County of Huron, for "A new and useful machine for moulding Eave-Troughs." Quebec, dated 26th October, 1864.

82

No. 1754—ASKEW, (John,) of the Township of Raleigh, County of Kent, for "A cast-iron ARM to apply to wrought-iron axle-trees." Quebec, dated 26th October, 1864.

No. 1755—DUTTON, (William,) of the Township of Vespra, County of Simcoe, for "A new and useful system of dressing mill-stones, called 'The Auxiliary Mill-Stone DRESS.'" Quebec, dated 25th October, 1864.

No. 1756—RICHARDSON, (William K.,) of the City of Hamilton, County of Wentworth, for "The Magic self-compressing clothes wringing MACHINE." Quebec, dated 9th November, 1864.

No. 1757—ROBLIN, (Edwin,) of the Township of Sophiasburgh, County of Prince Edward, for "A new and useful Churn POWER." Quebec, dated 9th November, 1864.

No. 1758—WASHBURN, (Stephen,) of the Township of South Dumfries, County of Brant, for "An improved Portable Fence, called the 'Portable Picket Worm FENCE.'" Quebec, dated 15th November, 1864.

No. 1759—HANFORD, (John,) of the Town of Windsor, County of Essex, for "An improved Saw-Setter, to be known as 'Hanford's SAW-SETTER.'" Quebec, dated 18th November, 1864.

No. 1760—VAN NORMAN, (Joseph,) of the Township of Dereham, County of Oxford, for "A new and useful improvement in the construction of Furnaces for the melting of metals, and in the art of melting metals therein, to be known as 'Joseph Van Norman's improved Furnace for the Melting of METALS.'" Quebec, dated 18th November, 1864.

No. 1761—WEAVER, (Jesse,) of the Township of Malahide, County of Elgin, and RULE, (Robert W.,) of the same place, for "A Ditching MACHINE." Quebec, dated 19th November, 1864.

No. 1762—FRYATT, (Henry,) of the Village of Aurora, Township of Whitchurch, County of York, for "An improved Sawing MACHINE." Quebec, dated 21st November, 1864.

No. 1763—GOOLD, (Franklin P.,) of the Town of Brantford, County of Brant, for "A new and useful improved Churn and BUTTER-WORKER." Quebec, dated 21st November, 1864.

No. 1764—LAMBERT, (Samuel,) of the City of Kingston, County of Frontenac, for "A new and useful Rail-Joint Fastening for RAILWAYS." Quebec, dated 22nd November, 1864.

No. 1765—PARSON, (William,) of the City of Toronto, County of York, for "A new and useful machine for forcing oil and water from the bottom of wells, and water from mines, to be called 'Parson's Oil EJECTOR.'" Quebec, dated 22nd November, 1864.

No. 1766—COLLINS, (James,) of the Town of Guelph, County of Wellington, for "An improved Self-Delivering Attachment for Reaping MACHINES." Quebec, dated 22nd November, 1864.

No. 1767—BEANES, (Edward,) of the City of Toronto, County of York, for "A new and useful process for improvements in the Preparing or Treating of Animal CHARCOAL." Quebec, dated 24th November, 1864.

No. 1768—HONEY, (Richard Charles,) of the Village of Newtonville, in the Township of Clarke, County of Durham, for "A new and useful improved WHEEL-HUB." Quebec, dated 24th November, 1864.

No. 1769—ANDERSON, (Alexander,) of the City of London, County of Middlesex, for "A new and useful Straw-Cutter, to be called and known as 'Anderson's STRAW-CUTTER.'" Quebec, dated 28th November, 1864.

No. 1770—GOODWIN, (Flavius Gustavus,) of the Township of Dereham, in the County of Oxford, for "An improved Seed DRILL." Quebec, dated 9th December, 1854.

No. 1771—ROBINSON, (John S.,) of the City of London, for "A new and useful Currier's OIL." Quebec, dated 10th December, 1864.

No. 1772—ROBSON, (Thomas,) of the Town of Brantford, in the County of Brant, for "A new and useful Flour Drier, to be called 'The Steam Flour DRIER.'" Quebec, dated 10th December, 1864.

No. 1773—CARTER, (Henry,) of the Township of Malahide, County of Elgin, for "A new and useful Hydrostatic ENGINE." Quebec, dated 10th December, 1864.

No. 1774—KILLAM, (Hervey,) of the Village of Waterdown, County of Norfolk, for "A new and useful MOULD-BOARD for Ploughs." Quebec, dated 10th December, 1864.

No. 1775—MITCHELL, (*James E.*,) of the Town of Paris, County of Brant, for "A new and useful matching machine, to be called 'Mitchell's non-paralleled Matching MACHINE.'" Quebec, dated 10th December, 1864. ·

No. 1776—DARLING, (*George Lacey*,) of the Town of Simcoe, in the County of Norfolk, for "A new and useful machine to be called 'Darling's Lever Power and Vertical Sawing MACHINE.'" Quebec, dated 29th November, 1864.

No. 1777—LAMAIN, (*Charles*,) of the Township of Hamilton, in the County of Northumberland, for "A new and useful Double Mould-board Drilling PLOUGH." Quebec, dated 10th January, 1865.

No. 1778—McARTHUR, (*John*,) of the Village of Fergus, in the County of Wellington, for "A new and useful MOULD-BOARD Plough." Quebec, dated 10th December, 1864.

No. 1779—VAHEY, (*William*,) of the Village of Arkona, in the County of Lambton, for "An improved Weather STRIP." Quebec, dated 20th December, 1864.

No. 1780—PARADIS, (*Joseph*,) of the City of Montreal, for "A new and useful PRESS for compressing hay, cotton, tobacco, &c." Quebec, dated 16th January, 1865.

No. 1781—RYAN, (*Cornelius*,) of the City of Montreal, for "A new and useful improvement in STOVES and Heating Apparatus." Quebec, dated 16th January, 1865.

No. 1782—HUNTER, (*Richard S.*,) of the Township of Stanstead, in the District of St. Francis, for "A new and useful Metallic THRESHOLD and outside Door Attachment." Quebec, dated 16th January, 1865.

No. 1783—HODGES, (*James*,) of the Township of Bulstrode, in the District of Arthabaska, for "A new and useful MACHINE for manufacturing Fuel from Peat, for excavating Canals and other purposes." Quebec, dated 16th January, 1865.

No. 1784—WELLS, (*Reuben Trumbull Monroe*,) of the Township of Stanbridge, in the District of Bedford, for "A new and useful Machine for starting CARS." Quebec, dated 16th January, 1865.

No. 1785—CRAWFORD, (*Joshua*,) of the City of Toronto, in the County of York, for "An Abdominal SUPPORTER." Quebec, dated 17th January, 1865.

No. 1786—LINTON, (*Aaron*,) of the Town of Brockville, in the County of Leeds, for "An improved Mill PICK." Quebec, dated 21st January, 1865.

No. 1787—FEELY, (*John C.*,) of the Town of Brantford, in the County of Brant, for "A new and useful Horse RAKE." Quebec, dated 23rd January, 1865.

No. 1788—TOMLINSON, (*William*,) of the Township of Brantford, in the County of Brant, for "The Economical THRESHING MACHINE." Quebec, dated 3rd February, 1865.

No. 1789—ARMSTRONG, (*James Rogers*,) of the City of Toronto, in the County of York, for "A new and useful Cooking Stove, called 'The ARMSTRONG.'" Quebec, dated 3rd February, 1865.

No. 1790—WESTCOTT, (*Isaac*,) of the Town of Bowmanville, in the County of Durham, for "A new and useful machine, called 'Westcott's CULTIVATOR.'" Quebec, dated 3rd February, 1865.

No. 1791—WORT (*John*,) and CLAYTON, (*Peter*,) both of the Township of Malahide, in the County of Elgin, for "A new and improved Washing Machine, called 'Wort and Clayton's Improved WASHING Machine.'" Quebec, dated 8th February, 1865.

No. 1792—BRUCE, (*David*,) of the City of London, in the County of Middlesex, for "A new and useful improved SAWING Machine." Quebec, dated 8th February, 1865.

No. 1793—WHITMORE, (*Samuel Mowe*,) of the Parish of St. François du Lac, in the County of Yamaska, for "A new and useful improvement in the art of TANNING." Quebec, dated 10th October, 1864.

No. 1794—MITCHELL, (*Robert*,) of the City of Montreal, for "A new and improved Steam RADIATOR." Quebec, dated 14th February; 1865.

No. 1795—HOBART, (*George Savage*,) of the City of Kingston, in the County of Frontenac, and ENSLEY, (*John Israel*,) of the same place, for "A new and useful combined Burner and CHIMNEY, with non-conducting wick tube of Lamps." Quebec, dated 14th February, 1865.
11

No. 1796--RITCHIE, (*John*,) of Etchemin, in the County of Levis, for "A new and useful MACHINE for holding Saw Logs, to be called 'Ritchie's patent attached Sawmill Chairs.'" Quebec, dated 15th February, 1865.

No. 1797—PAYNE, (*Edward*,) of the City of Montreal, for "A new and useful Staple CLAMP for supporting and insulating over ground telegraph wires." Dated 15th February, 1865.

No. 1798—LIBBY, (*Mark*,) of the Township of Bolton, C. E.; for "A new and useful MACHINE for raising alluvium, muck and soft earth, from swamps, ponds, marshes, beds of rivers, or any other place." Quebec, dated 15th February, 1865.

No. 1799—DAIGNEAU, (*Jeremiah*,) of Roxton Pond, in the County of Shefford, for "A new and useful Stove REGISTER." Quebec, dated 15th February, 1865.

No. 1800—LEGGO, (*William Augustus*,) and DESBARATS, (*George Edward*,) of the City of Quebec, for "A new and useful Art of Photo-Electrotyping, to be called "LEGGOTYPING." Quebec, dated 22nd February, 1865.

No. 1801—REEKIE, (*David*,) of the Township of Georgina, in the County of York, for "A new and useful LIFTING-GATE." Quebec, dated 4th March, 1865.

No. 1802—WIGGINS, (*William Augustus*,) of the Town of Belleville, in the County of Hastings, for "A new and useful Trap Hook, called 'Wiggins' TRAP HOOK.'" Quebec, dated 4th March, 1865.

No. 1803—BROWN, (*John*,) of the City of Toronto, in the County of York, for "A new and useful Horse Rake, called 'John Brown's Horse Rake.'" Quebec, dated 16th March, 1865.

No. 1804—HINMAN, (*Derrick Jay*,) of the Township of Haldimand, in the County of Northumberland, for "A new and improved BROOM." Quebec, dated 22nd March, 1865.

No. 1805—NORTHEY, (*Thomas*,) of the City of Hamilton, in the County of Wentworth, for "A new and improved Differential Governor for Steam ENGINES." Quebec, dated 22nd March, 1865.

No. 1806—EQUI, (*Giovanni Bartolomeo*,) of the City of Toronto, in the County of York, for "A new and improved process for preparing Hemp and Flax, so that either may be spun and wove by the same machinery that is commonly used for spinning and weaving COTTON.' Quebec, dated 23rd March, 1865.

No. 1807—EQUI, (*Giovanni Bartolomeo*,) of the City of Toronto, in the County of York, for "A process of manufacturing and refining white and brown sugar and syrup out of Indian CORN and other Cereals." Quebec, dated 23rd March, 1865.

No. 1808—BLACK, (*George*,) of the City of Hamilton, in the County of Wentworth, for "A new and useful AIR heating apparatus." Quebec, dated 22nd March, 1865.

No. 1809—THOMAS, (*John Hopkins*,) of the Village of Brooklin, in the County of Ontario, for "A combined moveable Comb and doubled boarded BEE-HIVE." Quebec, dated 22nd March, 1865.

No. 1810—SHUPE, (*Eli*,) of the Village of St. George, in the Township of Dumphries, in the County of Brant, for "The Reel and Finger-board motion, being an improvement on "Shupes combined Reaping and Mowing MACHINE, and others." Quebec, dated 22nd March, 1865.

No. 1811—HOUTON, (*James*,) of the Town of Dundas, in the County of Wentworth, for "Certain new and useful improvements in the manufacturing, building and working of the Excelsior combined reaping and mowing machine, called 'The improved Excelsior combined Reaping and Mowing MACHINE.'" Quebec, dated 23rd March, 1865.

No. 1812—ANDERSON, (*Alexander*,) of the City of London, in the County of Middlesex, for "A new and useful Anderson's even-balanced vibrating CULTIVATOR." Quebec, dated 23rd March, 1865.

No. 1813—CHASE, (*James*,) of the Village of Brooklin, in the County of Ontario, for "A new and useful improved Spring BED-BOTTOM." Quebec, dated 27th March, 1865.

No. 1814—SHAVER, (*William Robert*,) of Ancaster, in the County of Wentworth, for "A safety CAP for covering the joints of connecting rods in Threshing and other machines." Quebec, dated 27th March, 1865.

No. 1815—WILLIAMS, (*John*,) of the City of Montreal, for "An improved Puddling FURNACE." Quebec, dated 11th April, 1865.

No. 1816—JULIEN, (*Henri,*) of the City of Quebec, for "A new and improved Printing PRESS." Quebec, dated 11th April, 1865.

No. 1817—FINDLAY, (*James,*) of the City of Toronto, in the County of York, for "A new Spring, called 'Findlay's SPRING.'" Quebec, dated 17th April, 1865.

No. 1818—WEALCH, (*George Henry,*) of the Village of Blenheim, in the County of Kent, for "A new and improved Spinning WHEEL." Quebec, dated 17th April, 1865.

No. 1819—LEONARD, (*David,*) of the Township of Onondaga, in the County of Brant, for "A new and useful Wheel for creating a motive power by Horse power called 'Leonard's Inclined WHEEL.'" Quebec, dated 17th April, 1865.

No. 1820—WOOD, (*James,*) of the Township of Grimsby, in the County of Lincoln, for "A new and useful Slide Door for Oil-lamp Burners." Quebec, dated 17th April, 1865.

No. 1821—PETRIMOULX, (*Henry,*) of the Township of Sandwich, in the County of Essex, for "A new and improved Portable CRANE." Quebec, dated 17th April, 1865.

No. 1822—OAKLEY, (*Frederick,*) of the City of Toronto, in the County of York, for "A new and useful improvement in Lamp BURNERS." Quebec, dated 17th April, 1865.

No. 1823—DONER, (*Christopher,*) of the Village of Aurora, in the County of York, for "A reversable saturated WASH-BOARD." Quebec, dated 17th April, 1865.

No. 1824—HOCKIN, (*William,*) of the Town of Guelph, in the County of Wellington, for "A stave chamfering and Crozing MACHINE." Quebec, dated 17th April, 1865.

No. 1825—McGEE, (*John,*) of the City of Toronto, Assignee of William Hickin, of the Township of Draper, in the County of Victoria, for "A new and useful DIE for stamping sheet metal for bottoms of Kettles, Boilers, &c." Quebec, dated 19th April, 1865.

No. 1826—GORDON, (*John Hamilton,*) and TAYLOR, (*Richard,*) Assignees of Michael Judge, all of the City of Toronto, in the County of York, for "A new and useful process for the manufacture of Boiler and Kettle Bottoms (known as a collar for Dies used in stamping sheet metal); also a duplicate collar-die, and also a new application of Ball and Socket to the upper or cameo die, and also a process of trimming Sheet METAL." Quebec, dated 19th April, 1865.

No. 1827—KITCHEN, (*William Whitney,*) of the Township of Grimsby, in the County of Lincoln, for "A new and useful Knuckle-Rubbing Clothes WASHER." Quebec, dated 24th April, 1865.

No. 1828—WELCH, (*James,*) of the Township of Dunwich, in the County of Elgin, for "A self-acting Portable CHEESE PRESS." Quebec, dated 21st April, 1865.

No. 1829—POCOCK, (*Stephen,*) of the Town of Woodstock, in the County of Oxford, for "An improved Window Blind, called 'the Oxford Window BLIND.'" Quebec, dated 24th April, 1865.

No. 1830—COUSIN, (*James M.,*) of the City of London, in the County of Middlesex, for "A self-acting Cattle PUMP." Quebec, dated 25th April, 1865.

No. 1831—DION, (*Charles,*) of the City of Montreal, for "A new and useful Fire Alarm, to be called 'Sonnerie d'Alarme DION.'" Quebec, dated 17th January, 1865.

No. 1832—BEVIER, (*Edwin,*) of the City of Hamilton, in the County of Wentworth, for "A new and useful CHURN, called 'The Ladies' Friend.'" Quebec, dated 1st May, 1865.

No. 1833—BIRCH, (*Thomas John,*) of the Town of Stratford, in the County of Perth, for "A new and useful article called 'Birch's Lock-seam Eave-trough and FORMER.'" Quebec, dated 1st May, 1865.

No. 1834—DION, (*Charles,*) of the City of Montreal, for "A new and improved Fire Alarm, to be called 'SONNERIE d'Alarme Dion.'" Quebec, dated 3rd May, 1865.

No. 1835—WATSON, (*Clark,*) of Coaticook, in the County of Stanstead, for "A new and useful WASHING Machine." Quebec, dated 3rd May, 1865.

No. 1836—RIDER, (*William,*) of the Township of Stanley, in the County of Huron, for "A new and useful RIDER's Horse Power." Quebec, dated 3rd May, 1865.

No. 1837—KNICKERBOCKER, (*Theophilus,*) of the Township of North Norwich, in the County of Oxford, for "A new and useful Fruit PICKER." Quebec, dated 5th May, 1865.

No. 1838—HALL, (*Aaron C.*,) of Stanstead, in the District of St. Francis, for " A new and useful Tubular SAP-BOILER." Quebec, dated 5th May, 1865.

No. 1839—RYAN, (*Cornelius,*) of the City of Montreal, for " Improvements in Coal Burning Cooking STOVES." Quebec, dated 16th May, 1865.

No. 1810—SLEEPER, (*Lewis,*) of the Village of Coaticook, in the County of Stanstead, for " A new and improved Axle for Railway Carriages, to be called 'Sleeper's Patent Double Curve AXLE.'" Quebec, dated 19th May, 1865.

No. 1841—SLEEPER, (*Lewis,*) of the Village of Coaticook, in the County of Stanstead, for " A new and useful Improved Rail for Railway purposes, to be called 'Sleeper's Patent Continuous RAIL.'" Quebec, dated 22nd May, 1865.

No. 1842—BENNETT, (*John,*) of the Town of Belleville, in the County of Hastings, for " A new and useful Double-action Fanning Mill, called 'Bennett's Double-action FANNING MILL.'" Quebec, dated 17th May, 1865.

No. 1843—NUNN, (*William Coe,*) of the Town of Whitby, in the County of Ontario, for "A new and Improved Railway SIGNAL." Quebec, dated 30th May, 1865.

No. 1844—HAGGERT, (*John,*) of the Village of Brampton, in the County of Peel, for " A new and useful Axle NUT, or mode of securing wheels to their axles." Quebec, dated 17th May, 1865.

No. 1845—PIGEON, (*Narcisse,*) of the City of Montreal, for " A new and useful Art of manufacturing Crystallized SUGAR, similar to cane sugar and syrup, from Indian Corn or other cereal grains or roots." Quebec, dated 14th June, 1865.

No. 1846—COMBS, (*Horace A.*,) of the Township of Saltfleet, in the County of Wentworth, for " A new and useful CHURN-DASH, for the old fashioned or round Churn." Quebec, dated 12th June, 1865.

No. 1847—MACEY, (*William Couch,*) of the Village of Richmond Hill, in the County of York, for " A new and useful improvement in Doors, the Door as improved to be called 'Macey's Air-tight DOOR.'" Quebec, dated 16th June, 1865.

No. 1848—JOHNSTON, (*John,*) of the Township of Howard, in the County of Kent, for " A new and useful self-supporting and Portable Farm Fence, to be called 'Johnston's self-supporting and Portable Farm FENCE.'" Quebec, dated 19th June, 1865.

No. 1849—TERWILLIGER, (*John W.*,) of the Township of Ameliasburg, in the County of Prince Edward, for " A new and useful Auger, called 'the Farmer's Easy BORER.'" Quebec, dated 20th June, 1865.

No. 1850—SMITH, (*Samuel,*) of the Town of Guelph, in the County of Wellington, for " A machine for cutting the locks of barrel and other hoops, to be called 'Smith's Hoop Locking MACHINE.'" Quebec, dated 26th June, 1865.

No. 1851—WOOD, (*Henry,*) of the City of Montreal, for " A new and useful improved Valve for clearing the condensed water from the cylinders of steam engines." Quebec, dated 1st July, 1865.

No. 1852—TAFT, (*Andrew B.*,) of the City of Montreal, for " An Automatic Safety Car COUPLING." Quebec, dated 6th July, 1865.

No. 1853—SMITH, (*Richard,*) of the Town of Sherbrooke, in the District of St. Francis, for " A new and useful Flour SIFTER." Quebec, dated 6th July, 1865.

No. 1854—CERAT, (*Jean Baptiste,*) of the City of Montreal, for " A Composition of Matter, to be called 'Composition CERAT.'" Quebec, dated 6th July, 1865.

No. 1855—MYLIUS, (*Rudolf,*) of the Town of Berlin, in the County of Waterloo, for " A new and useful GUN LOCK, to be applied to the Breech-Loading Needle Gun, the gun with the addition of such improved lock to be called 'Mylius' Breech-Loading Needle Gun.'" Quebec, dated 7th July, 1865.

No. 1856—MYLIUS, (*Rudolf,*) of the Town of Berlin, in the County of Waterloo, for " A new and useful composition of Matter consisting of an inflammable substance for igniting by friction, with an iron or steel Needle, the powder in a Cartridge, the said composition to be called ' Mylius' PRIMER.'" Quebec, dated 7th July, 1865.

No. 1857—LISTER, (*David,*) of the City of Toronto, in the County of York, for " A new and useful improved Steam Packing for PISTONS." Quebec, dated 7th July, 1865.

No. 1858—LAMBERT, (Richard,) of the City of Quebec, for "A machine for operating and working Bored Oil Wells." Quebec, dated 18th July, 1865.

No. 1859—GIBSON, (William,) of the Township of Granby, in the County of Shefford, for "A new and useful Bag String or Tie." Quebec, dated 19th July, 1865.

No. 1860—WALTON, Brooks W.,) of the Village of Kettleby, in the Township of King, in the County of York, for "A new and useful Drill and Cultivator combined," Quebec, dated 15th July, 1865.

No. 1861—ROBERTS, (Mathew L.,) of the Village of Smithville, in the County of Lincoln, for "A new and useful Spade or Instrument for digging Post holes and other holes." Quebec, dated 24th July, 1865.

No. 1862—SNIDER, (Henry,) of the Township of Sophiasburg, in the County of Prince Edward, for "A new and useful Clothes Dryer, to be called 'Snider's suspension Clothes Dryer.' " Quebec, dated 25th July, 1865.

No. 1863—BAINES, (Hugh,) of the City of Montreal, for "A new and useful machine for making Railroad Points and for bracing the heels of the Points with Steel, as also the ends of all Railroad Rails." Quebec, dated 27th July, 1865.

No. 1864—LAWLOR, (Thomas,) of the City of Toronto, in the County of York, for "A new and useful Latch and Side-bolt Lock for Gaol purposes for Cell and Corridor Gates." Quebec, dated 4th August, 1865.

No. 1865—AIKINS, (William Thomas,) of the City of Toronto, in the County of York, for "A process for the manufacture of Sugar and Syrup from Indian Corn and other Cereals, and from all amylaceous or saccharine Bulbs or Roots and from Starch, prepared from these or any other sources, the said process to be called 'Simple and direct method of manufacturing Sugar and Syrup from Cereals and Roots and.Starch.' " Quebec, dated 4th August, 1865.

No. 1866—HUNT, (Thomas Sterry,) of the City of Montreal, for "A Composition for Furnace Linings and Fire Bricks." Quebec, dated 10th August, 1865.

No. 1867—PECKHAM, (Charles S.,) of the Village of Stanstead Plain, in the County of Stanstead, for "A new and useful Inproved Metallic Threshold and Outside Door Attachment." Quebec, dated 10th August, 1865.

No. 1868—McSTRAVICK, (Henry,) of the City of Hamilton, in the County of Wentworth, for "A new and useful Metallic or Gutta Percha Shoulder-cap for fastening the Broom Corn, without winding the same, with wire or twine, to the handle of the Broom." Quebec, dated 9th August, 1865.

No. 1869—ANDERSON, (George William,) of the City of Montreal, for "A new and useful Universal Needle Threader." Quebec, dated 12th August, 1865.

No. 1870—WATSON, (John,) of the Village of Air, in the County of Waterloo, for "Certain new and useful Improvements in Reaping and Mowing Machines." Quebec, dated 15th August, 1865.

No. 1871—CLARK, (James,) of the Township of Caledon, in the County of Peel, for "A new and useful machine for working an ordinary Dash Churn." Quebec, dated 15th August, 1865.

No. 1872—EDMONDS, (John,) of the Village of Smithville, in the County of Lincoln, for "A new and useful improvement on the plan now in use. for the setting, placing, or inserting the Tubes in Boilers for the purpose of generating Steam." Quebec, dated 16th August, 1865.

No. 1873—CAULFIELD, (Edward,) of the Town of Brockville, in the County of Leeds. for "Certain new and useful improvements in that class of apparatus which relates to the increase of the illuminating powers of Gas, such as is used for lighting cities and dwellings." Quebec, dated 16th August, 1865.

No. 1874—FERGUSON, (George,) of the City of Toronto, in the County of York, for "A Fire Lighting Attachment." Quebec, dated 16th August, 1865.

No. 1875—CEREDO, (Paul,) of the City of Montreal, for "A machine called the 'Cinderella Sifting Machine,' for sitting and separating coal, ashes, and for other purposes." Quebec, dated 16th August, 1865.

No. 1876—HENNEBERG, (Frederick,) of the Village of Washington, in the Township of Blenheim, in the County of Oxford, and BECHTEL, (Menno,) of the Township of Wilmot, in the County of Waterloo, for " A new and useful machine, which they call ' Henneberg's Rotatory Flax PULLER.' " Quebec, dated 18th August, 1865.

No. 1877—HARRINGTON, (*Jacob,*) of the Township of East Zorra, in the County of Oxford, for " A new and useful Flax PULLER, called and known as ' The Canadian Flax Puller." Quebec, dated 18th August, 1865.

No. 1878—COPP, (*William J.,*) of the City of Hamilton, in the County of Wentworth, for "An improved Cooking STOVE, known as ' The Prince of Wales Cooking Stove.' " Quebec, dated 18th August, 1865.

No. 1879—BARNETT, (*Samuel Herbert,*) of the City of Montreal, for "A new and usefu ALARM, to be called ' Barnett's Electro Burglar and Fire Detector.' " Quebec, dated 19th August, 1865.

No. 1880—HILL, (*Robert,*) of the Town of Barrie, in the County of Simcoe, for " A new and useful Improved Side Gearing for THRESHING Machines." Quebec, dated 22nd August, 1865.

No. 1881—MILLER, (*James,*) of Upton, in the County of Bagot, District of St. Hyacinthe, for " A new and useful Improvement in the manufacture and preparation of a Concentrated Extract of Tan-bark, to be called ' Miller's Concentrated Extract of TAN-BARK.' " Quebec, dated 25th August, 1865.

No. 1882—THOMPSON, (*William Linton,*) of the Township of Stanstead, in the County of Stanstead, for " A new and useful improved PEAT Manufacturer." Quebec, dated 25th August, 1865.

No. 1883—HIBBARD, (*William Ritchie,*) of the City of Montreal, for "An improved Cachet or Safety SEAL for Trunks." Quebec, dated 25th August, 1865.

No. 1884—SAUNDERS, (*William,*) of the Township of Pickering, in the County of Ontario, for " Saunder's Improved WASHING Machine." Quebec, dated 26th August, 1865.

No. 1885—CURTIS, (*William,*) of the Town of Belleville, in the County of Hastings, and RAMFORD, (*William,*) of the same place, for " A new and useful Lifting Pump, known as ' Curtis and Bamford's Lifting Pump.' " Quebec, dated 28th August, 1865.

No. 1886—COX, (*John Hutching,*) and MURPHY, (*John,*) of the City of Montreal, for " A new and useful Speed REGULATOR for Fluids or Spiritometer." Quebec, dated 29th August, 1865.

No. 1887—HILTMAYER, (*Nicholas,*) of the Village of Omemee, in the County of Victoria, and MORRISON, (*George,*) of the same place, for " A new and useful Car COUPLING Life Saver." Quebec, dated 1st September, 1865.

No. 1888—HEATH, (*Ansley,*) of the Township of Townsend, in the County of Norfolk, for "A new and useful Implement of Husbandry to be called ' Heath's Plaster SOWER.' " Quebec, dated 1st September, 1865.

No. 1889—DANIELS, (*Cyrus,*) of the Township of Barnston, in the County of Stanstead, for "A new and useful improved BEE-HIVE." Quebec, dated 4th September, 1865.

No. 1890—CHAMPION, (*Alexander,*) of the Town of Stratford, in the County of Perth, for "New and useful improvements in Reaping MACHINES." Quebec, dated 6th September, 1865.

No. 1891—ROGERS, (*Thomas,*) of the City of Toronto, in the County of York, for " A new and useful BINDER for Sewing Machines." Quebec, dated 6th September, 1865.

No. 1892—WOODBURY, (*Edwin.*) of the City of London, in the County of Middlesex, for " A new and useful Woodbury's Bag HOLDER." Quebec, dated 6th September, 1865.

No. 1893—SMITH, (*Samuel,*) of the Town of Guelph, in the County of Wellington, for " A new and useful Smith's improved combined STAVE Machine." Quebec, dated 12th September, 1865.

No. 1894—TREFFRY, (*Henry,*) of the Village of Howick, in the County of Huron, for " A new and useful Fence, called ' Treffry's Portable Angular Board FENCE.' " Quebec, dated 12th September, 1865.

No. 1895—HORN, (*Francis Judd,*) of the Township of East Whitby, in the County of Ontario, for " A new and useful Broad-cast SEED SOWER and Cultivator." Quebec, dated 10th May, 1865.

No. 1896—PORTER, (*D'Arcy,*) of the City of Toronto, in the County of York, for "Certain new and useful improvements in SEWING Machines." Quebec, dated 10th September, 1865.

No. 1897—HENRY, (*Albert N.,*) of the Village of Oshawa, in the County of Ontario, for " A new and useful BEE-HIVE." Quebec, dated 19th September, 1865.

No. 1898—COLLARD, (*Henry,*) of the Township of Leeds, in the County of Leeds, for " A new and useful Pea HARVESTER." Quebec, dated 22nd September, 1865.

No. 1899—FOX, (*John Conrad,*) of the City of Kingston, in the County of Frontenac, for " An improved Sounding BOARD for Pianos." Quebec, dated 23rd September, 1865.

No. 1900—KERR, (*James,*) of the Town of Galt, in the County of Waterloo, for " A new and useful Grain Separator, called 'Kerr's improved Grain SEPARATOR.'" Quebec, dated 23rd September, 1865.

No. 1901—HALL, (*Chester Frederick,*) of the City of Toronto, in the County of York, for " A new and useful improvement in the construction of Lumber WAGGONS, designed especially for use in mill and lumber yards, the object of which is to facilitate the discharge of their loads." Quebec, dated 23rd September, 1865.

No. 1902—WHITEFIELD, (*Edwin,*) of the City of Montreal, for " A new and useful Indellible PRINTING Ink." Ottawa, dated 25th October, 1865.

No. 1903—KIRKUP, (*Lancelot,*) of the City of Montreal, for " A new and useful Double BOLT Rivet and Spike Machine." Ottawa, dated 25th October, 1865.

No. 1904—VARNEY, (*Samuel,*) of the Township of Brompton, in the District of St. Francis, for " A new and improved Double Acting Force PUMP." Ottawa, dated 25th October, 1865.

No. 1905—HOUSTON, (*John,*) of the Township of Stanstead, in the County of Stanstead, for " A new and improved CHURN." Ottawa, dated 25th October, 1865.

No. 1906—KIRKUP, (*Lancelot,*) of the City of Montreal, for " A new and useful improved Split Railroad SPIKE." Ottawa, dated 25th October, 1865.

No. 1907—HALL, (*John,*) of the Township of Leeds, in the County of Megantic, for " A new and useful Vertical Double Acting Mill Stone and Feeding GEAR." Ottawa, dated 25th October, 1865.

No. 1908—JANNARD, (*Mathias,*) of the City of Montreal, for " A new and improved Air Tight Metal COFFIN." Ottawa, dated 25th October, 1865.

No. 1909—PORTER, (*Alexander Forbes,*) of the City of Montreal, for " A new and useful Electric Steam BATTERY." Ottawa, dated 14th November, 1865.

No. 1910—CARD, (*Ephraim D.,*) of the Township of Haldimand, in the County of Northumberland, for " A new and useful Self-acting BRAKE for Carriages." Ottawa, dated 31st October, 1865.

No. 1911—ROBINSON, (*William Apsley,*) of the City of Hamilton, in the County of Wentworth, for " Certain new and useful improvements in Locomotives, the first thereof being in that part called the 'Safety Valve,' and the other in the mode of counter-weighing or balancing that part called the 'Link Motion or Slide-valve GEAR.'" Ottawa, dated 23rd November, 1865.

No. 1912—PETTIT, (*Miles,*) of the Township of Hallowell, in the County of Prince Edward, for " A new and useful Spinning and Quilling machine, called 'Pettet's Shuttlehead Spinning and Quilling MACHINE.'" Ottawa, dated 23rd November, 1865.

No. 1913—PITTS, (*Joseph Nelson,*) of the Town of Port Dover, in the County of Norfolk, for " A Turbine Water WHEEL." Ottawa, dated 23rd November, 1865.

No. 1914—BOLTON, (*Henry,*) of the Township of Eramosa, in the County of Wellington, for " A new and useful Pig's Nose Cartilage DIVIDER." Ottawa, dated 23rd November, 1865.

No. 1915—DEWITT, (*Thomas,*) of the Village of Morpeth, in the County of Kent, for " A new and useful Spring-jack and Coupling for Wheel CARRIAGES." Ottawa, dated 23rd November, 1865.

No. 1916—CARTER, (*Henry,*) of the Township of Malahide, in the County of Elgin, for " A new and useful machine, called 'Carter's Balance CHAIN.'" Ottawa, dated 23rd November, 1865.

No. 1917—FRASER, (*George Corwin,*) of the Township of Pickering, in the County of Ontario, for " An improved apparatus for the Coupling or Joining together of Railroad Cars, called 'The Universal SELF-COUPLER.'" Ottawa, dated 23rd November, 1865.

No. 1918—VANHORN, (*William*,) of the Township of Pittsburg, in the County of Frontenac, for " A new and useful Portable Foot Carriage Warmer." Ottawa, dated 23rd November, 1865.

No. 1919—KINNEY, (*Cyrus*,) of the Township of Dereham, in the County of Oxford, for " A Portable Combined Sheep-Rack and Shed." Ottawa, dated 23rd November, 1865.

No. 1920—PILKEY, (*Alfred*,) of the Town of Stratford, in the County of Perth, for " A new and useful Compound to be used in connection with the Liquor of Hemlock Bark, for the Tanning of Leather." Ottawa, dated 23rd November, 1865.

No. 1921—DARLING, (*George Lacey*,) of the Town of Simcoe, in the County of Norfolk, and GARDINER, (*Samuel*,) of the same place, for " A new and useful Machine or Implement for Boring in Rock, called 'The Combination Rock Drill.'" Ottawa, dated 23rd November, 1865.

No. 1922—PITTS, (*Joseph Nelson*,) of the Town of Port Dover, in the County of Norfolk, for " A Universal Loom-Head." Ottawa, dated 23rd November, 1865.

No. 1923—PITTS, (*Joseph Nelson*,) of the Town of Port Dover, in the County of Norfolk, for " A Ventilating Drum Stove." Ottawa, dated 23rd November, 1865.

No. 1924—NEVILLE, (*Anthony*,) of the Township of Ernesttown, in the County of Lennox and Addington, for " An Improvement in Lamps." Ottawa, dated 23rd November, 1865.

No. 1925—JAMES, (*Josiah*,) of the Township of Whitechurch, in the County of York, for " A new and useful Improvement in the Tire of Carriage Wheels; the Wheel with the improvement being called 'The Eureka Carriage Wheel.'" Ottawa, dated 24th November, 1865.

No. 1926—KINNEY, (*Israel*,) of the Township of Oakland, in the County of Brant, for " A new and useful appliance for securing Doors against the weather, called 'Israel Kinney's Weather Door Leaf.'" Ottawa, dated 24th November, 1865.

No. 1927—TAYLOR, (*Charles*,) of Bonaventure, in the District of Gaspé, for " A new and useful Machine for Deepening and Sharpening the Teeth of Saws." Ottawa, dated 25th November, 1865.

No. 1928—HODGES, (*James*,) of the Township of Bulstrode, in the District of Arthabaska, for " A new and useful improved Machine for Pulping and Manufacturing Peat Fuel." Ottawa, dated 27th November, 1865.

No. 1929—GORDON, (*Alexander*,) of the City of Hamilton, in the County of Wentworth, for " A new and useful improved Bee-Hive." Ottawa, dated 28th November, 1865.

No. 1930—O'DELL, (*Abiel*,) of the Town of Bowmanville, in the County of Durham, for " A new and useful improved Washing Machine, called the 'The Ariston.'" Ottawa, dated 28th November, 1865.

No. 1931—WHITE, (*William*,) of the City of Ottawa, in the County of Carleton, for " A new and useful Art for Preserving Eggs, called 'White's Novel Egg Preserving Art.'" Ottawa, dated 30th November, 1865.

No. 1932—PERRY, (*Edward*,) of the City of Montreal, for " A new and useful Trunk Hasp." Ottawa, dated 15th December, 1865.

No. 1933—WOODWARD, (*Alfred*,) of the City of Montreal, for " A new and useful Apparatus for Carburretting Gas." Ottawa, dated 15th December, 1865.

No. 1934—INCE, (*Thomas Henry*,) of the City of Toronto, in the County of York, for " Certain new and useful Improvements in Shoeing Horses." Ottawa, dated 19th December, 1865.

No. 1935—DION, (*Charles*,) of the City of Montreal, for "A new and useful improved Domestic Fire Alarm." Ottawa, dated 21st December, 1865.

No. 1936—MILLS, (*Minard*,) of the Township of Yarmouth, in the County of Elgin, for " A new and useful machine, called 'Mills's Beef Steak Mangler.'" Ottawa, dated 19th December, 1865.

No. 1937—MORNINGSTAR, (*Jesse*,) of the Village of Waterloo, in the County of Waterloo, for " A new and useful Grain Separator, called 'The self-regulating Grain Separator.'" Ottawa, dated 19th January, 1866.

No. 1938—THERRIEN, (*Louis Chrysanthe*,) of the City of Montreal, for "A new and improved Stop-Cock." Ottawa, dated 23rd January, 1866.

No. 1939—HOUGH, (*Charles*,) of the City of Quebec, for " A new and useful Strap to prevent horses from moving when left alone." Ottawa, dated 23rd January, 1866.

No. 1940—BAINES, (*Hugh*,) of the City of Montreal, for "A new, useful and easy Railroad TRACK." Ottawa, dated 23rd January, 1866.

No. 1941—GOULD, (*Ira*,) of the City of Montreal, for "A new and useful drain Stench prevention TRAP." Ottawa, dated 23rd January, 1866.

No. 1942—HILL, (*Archelaus W.*,) of the Township of Stanstead, for "A new and useful Rotatory HARROW." Ottawa, dated 23rd January, 1866.

No. 1943—WOOD, (*Henry*.) of the City of Montreal, for "An improved Machinery for producing extract of hemlock, oak or other bark, and for manufacturing tan-bark SUGAR." Ottawa, dated 23rd January, 1866.

No. 1944—TAYLOR, (*Henry S.*,) of Stanstead, in the County of Stanstead, for "A new and useful superheated STEAM Generator. Ottawa, dated 26th January, 1866.

No. 1945—SWEENEY, (*Peter*,) of the Town of Windsor, in the County of Essex, for "A new and useful Rock-boring Machine." Ottawa, dated 11th January, 1866.

No. 1946—HALL, (*William S.*,) of the Township of Stanstead, for "A new and useful improved Rotary HARROW." Ottawa, dated 30th January, 1866.

No. 1947—ROTTON, (*Otto*,) of the City of Kingston, in the County of Frontenac, for "A new and useful apparatus for extracting Coal Oil or Petroleum from Wells or Reservoirs by means of Hydraulic pressure, which apparatus he calls 'Otto Rotton's Adjustable Hydraulic Tubing for OIL WELLS.'" Ottawa, dated 30th January, 1866.

No. 1948—PORTER, (*D'Arcy*,) of the City of Toronto, in the County of York, for "A new and useful improvement in RIP SAWS." Ottawa, dated 31st January, 1866.

No. 1949—VALIQUET, (*Thomas*,) of St. Hilaire, in the County of Rouville, for "An improved Bee-hive, to be called 'The Canadian Farmer's BEE-HIVE.'" Ottawa, dated 31st January, 1866.

No. 1950—HALE, (*Charles*,) of the Village of Bobcaygeon, in the County of Victoria, for "A new and useful method of tanning, named the 'Eclectic method of Tanning." Ottawa, dated 31st January, 1866.

No. 1951—CLENCH, (*Leon Moses*,) of the Town of St. Mary's, in the County of Perth, and NIVEN, (*Alexander*,) of the same place, for "The application of compressed atmospheric air to the braking of speed or stopping of railway trains and railway cars, (the same being under the immediate control of the Engine Driver thereof) together with a plan for the above mentioned purpose, to be called 'The Atmospheric Railway CAR BRAKE.'" Ottawa, dated 31st January, 1866.

No. 1952—JOHNS, (*Francis*,) of the Township of Ascot, for "A new and useful manufacture, to be called 'Johns' Patent Waterproof Safety FUSE.'" Ottawa, dated 31st January, 1866.

No. 1953—HALL, (*John*,) of the City of Toronto, in the County of York, for "A certain new and useful improvement in Granaries and FRUIT HOUSES." Ottawa, 2nd February, 1866.

No. 1954—PIGEON, (*Narcisse*,) of the City of Montreal, for "The Introduction of the art of the Revivification of Animal CHARCOAL by a Watery process," of which he has obtained a knowledge while in his travels in France. Ottawa, dated 13th February, 1866.

No. 1955—PRENTICE, (*Edward Alexander*,) of the City of Montreal, for "A new and useful apparatus for Carbonizing WOOD, &c., &c." Ottawa, dated 19th February, 1866.

No. 1956—STEVENS, (*Samuel*,) of the Town of Belleville, in the County of Hastings, for "A new and useful APPARATUS for distilling Petroleum, Alcohol, Turpentine, and other things." Ottawa, dated 9th February, 1866.

No. 1957—LAMONTAGNE, (*François Auguste*,) of the City of Montreal, for "A new and useful Visiting card case, to be called 'Lamontagne's improved CARD CASE." Ottawa, dated 6th March, 1866.

No. 1958—EATON, (*Richard*,) of the City of Montreal, for "An improved Fire Grate and Ash pan suitable for locomotive ENGINES." Ottawa, dated 6th March, 1866.

No. 1959—LAIRD, (*Robert W.*,) of the Village of Stanstead, in the County of Stanstead, for "A new and useful composition of matter to be called 'Laird's patent composition for welding and refining steel and IRON." Ottawa, dated 6th March, 1866.

No. 1960—FOGG, (*Thomas*,) of the City of Montreal, for "An improved and useful Railway SWITCH." Ottawa, dated 6th March, 1866.

No. 1961—WATEROUS, (*Charles Horatio*,) of the Town of Brantford, in the County of Brant, for "A new and useful improvement in the Steam Engine, known as 'Waterous' combined Portable and Stationery ENGINE.'" Ottawa, dated 23rd February, 1866.

No. 1962—MORNINGSTAR, (*Jesse*,) of the Village of Waterloo, in the County of Waterloo for "A new and useful Mower and Reaper Knife, called 'The Tension Mower and Reaping KNIFE.'" Ottawa, dated 23rd February, 1866.

No. 1963—WOODS, (*George*,) of the City of Ottawa, in the County of Carleton, for "A new and useful medicine, which he has named 'Woods' unrivalled Pain KILLER.'" Ottawa, dated 23rd February, 1866.

No. 1964—MORNINGSTAR, (*Jesse*,) of the Village of Waterloo, in the County of Waterloo for "A new and useful invention, called 'The Revolving Steam GENERATOR.'" Ottawa, dated 23rd February, 1866.

No. 1965—KIRK, (*Andrew*,) of the Village of Kincardine, in the County of Bruce, for "A new and useful Cultivator TOOTH." Ottawa, dated 23rd February, 1866.

No. 1966—CALDWELL, (*Leslie B.*,) of the Village of Myrtle, in the County of Ontario, for "A new and useful Equalizing SPRING." Ottawa, dated 23rd February, 1866.

No. 1967—MORNINGSTAR, (*Jesse*,) of the Village of Waterloo, in the County of Waterloo, for "A new and useful machine, called 'Morningstar's oscillating reaction CHURN.'" Ottawa, date 1 23rd February, 1866.

No. 1968—ROTTON (*Otto*,) of the City of Kingston, in the County of Frontenac, for "A new and useful composition of cementing barrels or other vessels and preventing leakage of petroleum and its distilled products from barrels or other vessels so cemented, called 'The Compound Silicate Barrel CEMENT.'" Ottawa, dated 23rd February, 1866.

No. 1969—ROTTON, (*Otto*,) of the City of Kingston, in the County of Frontenac, for "A machine for Cementing Petroleum and other Barrels or Vessels, called 'The Centrifugal Barrel CEMENTER.'" Quebec, dated 23rd February, 1866.

No. 1970—ROTTON, (*Otto*,) of the City of Kingston, in the County of Frontenac, for "A new and useful Cement for rendering barrels or other vessels impervious to Alcohol and its extracts, and wines, colognes, fixed oils and water, with its extracts as also some kinds of Petroleum, the said invention to be known as 'The Paraffine Barrel CEMENT.'" Ottawa, dated 23rd February, 1866.

No. 1971—HATCH, (*Richard*,) of the Town of Whitby, in the County of Ontario, for "A new and useful central pipe and damper for DUMB-STOVES." Ottawa, dated 23rd February, 1866.

No. 1972—STEVENSON, (*Thomas*,) of the City of Hamilton, in the County of Wentworth, for "A new and improved method of casting the threads or screws and the ends of AXLES." Ottawa, dated 23rd February, 1866.

No. 1973—AIKMAN, (*Daniel Thomas*,) of the Township of Dumfries, in the County of Brant, for "The Dairy-Queen CHURN Motion." Ottawa, dated 23rd February, 1866.

No. 1974—HORNER, (*Daniel F.*,) of the Township of Markham, in the County of York, for "A new and useful machine for making BUTTER into rolls of any required weight." Ottawa, dated 23rd February, 1866.

No. 1975—LOGAN, (*George Washington*,) of the United Townships of Sherbrooke and Moulton, in the County of Haldimand, for "A new and useful bored or drove WELL." Ottawa, dated 23rd February, 1866.

No. 1976—ROTTON, (*Otto*,) of the City of Kingston, in the County of Frontenac, for "A new and useful Composition of matter for the purpose of Cementing barrels or other vessels and rendering them impervious to Petroleum or other fluids impregnated with water or otherwise as the case may be, called 'The Resistant Gluten COMPOUND.'" Ottawa, dated 23rd February, 1866.

No. 1977—DAWSON, (*David*,) of the Township of Blandford, in the County of Oxford, for "A new and useful Root-Cutter, called 'The Woodstock Swing BOOT-CUTTER.'" Ottawa, dated 23rd February, 1866.

No. 1978—HAVEN, (*Jonathan Hilton*,) of the Village of Queentown, in the County of Lincoln, for "An improved Motive Power." Ottawa, dated 24th February, 1866.

No. 1979—ACRES, (*Jonathan William*,) of the Town of Paris, in the County of Brant, for "Certain new and improved means of preventing the bursting of water Pipes." Ottawa, dated 23rd February, 1866.

No. 1980—WILSON, (*George*,) of the Village of Warwick, in the County of Lambton, for "A new and improved method of procuring a well of Water." Ottawa, dated 24th February, 1866.

No. 1981—CRAWFORD, (*Dalrymple*,) of the City of Toronto, in the County of York, for "Certain new and useful improvements in the preparation and use of Palm-Oil." Ottawa, dated 24th February, 1866.

No. 1982—BRINGHAM, (*Bela Brewster*,) of the City of London, for "A new and useful improvement in the sinking of Well-Tubes." Ottawa, dated 24th February, 1866.

No. 1983—POWERS, (*Thomas Hart*,) of the Township of North Fredericksburgh, in the united Counties of Lennox and Addington, for "A new and useful improvement in Brooms and Brushes." Ottawa, dated 23rd February, 1866.

No. 1984—STEVENSON, (*Thomas*,) of the City of Hamilton, in the County of Wentworth, for "A new and useful machine for moulding and casting the thread or screw in Nuts." Ottawa, dated 23rd February, 1866.

No. 1985—TUTTLE, (*Eben Clarke*,) of the Township of East Whitby, in the County of Ontario, for "A new and useful machine for rolling out and forming Hoes, Spades, Scythes, Forks and other articles made of Iron and Steel and partly of both materials, called 'Tuttle's Patent Rolling Mill.'" Ottawa, dated 23rd February, 1866.

No. 1986—HOUGHTON, (*James*,) of the Town of Dundas, in the County of Wentworth, for "Certain new and useful improvements in the manufacturing, building and working of the improved Excelsior combined Reaping and Mowing Machine." Ottawa, dated 23rd February, 1866.

No. 1987—FRYATT, (*Henry*,) of the Village of Aurora, in the County of York, and FITZGERALD, (*James Charles*,) of the same Village of Aurora, for "An improved Sawing Machine." Ottawa, dated 23rd February, 1866.

No. 1988—LUCAS, (*William James*,) of the City of London, in the County of Middlesex, and LYONS, (*Henry W.*,) of the Township of London, in the same County, for "A new and useful Spinning wheel called 'The Victoria Spinning Wheel.'" Ottawa, dated 23rd February, 1866.

No. 1989—RAILTON, (*George*,) of the Village of Bothwell, in the County of Kent, for "An Oil Well and Artesian Drill." Ottawa, dated 23rd February, 1866.

No. 1990—BROWN, (*Lester Bruce*,) of the Town of Simcoe, in the County of Norfolk, but now residing temporarily at Storey Farm, in the County of Venango, in the State of Pennsylvania, in the United States of America, for "A new and useful machine for washing clothes, called 'Brown's Vacuum and Wabbler Washer and Churn.'" Ottawa, dated 23rd February, 1866.

No. 1991—STUTT, (*James*,) of the Township of York, in the County of York, for "A new and useful machine called 'Stutt's Machine for preparing wood for paper Pulp.'" Ottawa, dated 23rd February, 1866.

No. 1992—SUTTON, (*Robert T.*,) of the Town of Lindsay, in the County of Victoria, for "Certain new and useful improvements in drying and cleaning Grain." Ottawa, dated 23rd February, 1866.

No. 1993—GORDON, (*Alexander*,) of the City of Hamilton, in the County of Wentworth, for "A new and useful composition of matter which he denominates 'Compound Petroleum Paint-Oil.'" Ottawa, dated 24th February, 1866.

No. 1994—CHASE, (*James*,) of the Village of Brooklin, in the County of Ontario, for "A new and useful wood lathe Attachment." Ottawa, dated 28th February, 1866.

No. 1995—HIGLEY, (*Peter Row*,) of the Village of Oshawa, in the County of Ontario, for "A new and useful Mop-Head, called 'Higley's Mop-Head.'" Ottawa, dated 2nd March, 1866.

No. 1996—TUITLE, (*Eben Clarke,*) of the Township of East Whitby, in the County of Ontario, for "An improved socket for Hoes, Forks and Spades, called 'Tuttle's Improved SOCKET.'" Ottawa, dated 2nd March, 1866.

No. 1997—HANNAFORD, (*Edward Phillips,*) of the City of Montreal, for "A new and useful Railway Rail JOINT and expansion and contraction movement." Ottawa, dated 2nd March, 1866.

No. 1998—YATES, (*Henry,*) of the City of Montreal, for "An improved Railway Joint CHAIR." Ottawa, dated 6th March, 1866.

No. 1999—KIRKWOOD, (*Alexander,*) of the City of Ottawa, in the County of Carleton, for "A new and improved chemical process for the production of a material for the manufacture of PAPER from wood shavings or wood saw-dust." Ottawa, dated 14th March, 1866.

No. 2000—AUBIN, (*Aimé Nicholas Napoleon,*) of the Parish of Beloeil, in the County of Verchères, for "An apparatus for impregnating illuminating GAS or atmospheric air with hydrocarbon vapor." Ottawa, dated 23rd March, 1866.

No. 2001—SCOTT, (*James George,*) of the City of Quebec, for "A side RUBBER for Vessels." Ottawa, dated 23rd March, 1866.

No. 2002—KIRKWOOD, (*Alexander,*) of the City of Ottawa, in the County of Carleton, for "A new and useful combination or combinations of materials to produce a vendible substance or substances, for use as FUEL." Ottawa, dated 19th March, 1866.

No. 2003—OSTROM, (*Henry Wellington,*) of the Township of Sidney, in the County of Hastings, for "A treble faced RAIL for use on Railways, together with chairs and keys for the said rail." Ottawa, dated 23rd March, 1866.

No. 2004—MOODIE, (*William,*) of the City of Montreal, for "A new and useful Tap." Ottawa, dated 28th March, 1866.

No. 2005—ROBINSON, (*Orpheus,*) of the Town of Brantford in the County of Brant, for "A new and useful Improvement in the structure of Bridges and other Fabrics, called 'the extended TRUSS.'" Ottawa, dated 23rd March, 1866.

No. 2006—FIELD, (*William Amosa,*) of the Town of St. Catharines, in the County of Lincoln, for "A new and useful Improvement in PUMPS." Ottawa, dated 23rd March, 1866.

No. 2007—WALMSLEY, (*John,*) of the Town of Berlin, in the County of Waterloo, for "A new and useful Implement, called 'Walmsley's Potato RAISER.'" Ottawa, dated 23rd March, 1866.

No. 2008—KINNY, (*Jesse,*) of the Village of Drumbo, of the Township of Blenheim, in the County of Oxford, for "A new and useful Root Cutter, called 'The Dollar ROOT CUTTER.'" Ottawa, dated 23rd March, 1866.

No. 2009—MACEY, (*William Couch,*) of the Village of Richmond Hill, in the County of York, for "A new and useful composition of matter or material for building purposes." Ottawa, dated 23rd March, 1866.

No. 2010—HOPKINS, (*Samuel Joseph,*) of the City of Toronto, in the County of York, for "A new and useful Sash FASTENER." Ottawa, dated 23rd March, 1866.

No. 2011—DOTY, (*John,*) of the City of Hamilton, in the County of Wentworth, for "A new and useful machine for tapping nuts, called 'Doty's nut Tapping MACHINE.'" Ottawa, dated 23rd March, 1866.

No. 2012—FORFAR, (*Thomas,*) of the Township of Scarboro, in the County of York, for "A new and useful double or single action Washing MACHINE." Ottawa, dated 24th March, 1866.

No. 2013—MOUNTCASHELL, (*The Right Honorable Stephen, Earl of,*) of Lobo-House, in the County of Middlesex, for "A new and useful Double Window, called 'The Mountcashell DOUBLE WINDOW.'" Ottawa, dated 24th March, 1866.

No. 2014—PRINCE, (*John,*) of the Township of Ascot, in the County of Compton, for "A new and useful Sap FEEDER." Ottawa, dated 21st April, 1866.

No. 2015—FLEMING, (*Horatio Nelson,*) of the Township of Compton, in the County of Compton, for "A new and useful double dash CHURN." Ottawa, dated 21st April, 1866.

No. 2016—POWELL, (*Charles,*) of the Township of York, in the County of York, for "A rod coupling or joint for securing and fastening together wood or iron Rods for pumps or oth r purposes." Ottawa, dated 13th April, 1866.

No. 2017—TAYLOR, (*James,*) of the Township of Blanchford, in the County of Oxford, for "A new and useful improvement in the REGULATOR for Tue-Irons, known as 'Barrett's Patent Tuyer,' the said improvement to be called 'Taylor's improved Tue-Iron Regulator.'" Ottawa, dated 13th April, 1866.

No. 2018—SPARLING, (*Richard,*) of the Township of Mosa, in the County of Middlesex, for "A new and useful MACHINE for digging potatoes, called the 'Canadian Potato Digger.'" Ottawa, dated 14th April, 1866.

No. 2019—WEST, (*William,*) of the Town of Peterborough, in the County of Peterborough, for "An improved Grain SEPARATOR." Ottawa, dated 14th April, 1866.

No. 2020—FULLER, (*Richard,*) of the City of Hamilton, in the County of Wentworth, for "A new and useful invention for reducing Bamboo Cane into PULP, for making paper cordage and twine." Ottawa, dated 30th April, 1866.

No. 2021—LAZIER, (*John,*) of the Town of Belleville, in the County of Hastings, for "A new and useful Wool Spinner, designated as 'Lazier's Domestic SPINNER.'" Ottawa, dated 30th April, 1866.

No. 2022—HIGGINS, (*James Munroe,*) of the Town of Belleville, in the County of Hastings, for "A new and useful Perforated Pipe, for the purpose of sinking wells, called 'Higgins' Excelsior Well PIPE.'" Ottawa, dated 30th April, 1866.

No. 2023—McGREGOR, (*David Carruthers,*) of the Town of St. Mary's, in the County of Perth, for "An Axle SETT for Carriage and other wheels, to be called 'McGregor's Axle Sett.'" Ottawa, dated 1st May, 1866.

No. 2024—BOTTOMLEY, (*Thomas Henry,*) of the City of Toronto, in the County of York, for "A new and useful Double CULTIVATOR." Ottawa, dated 3rd May, 1866.

No. 2025—PATTERSON, (*Alexander,*) of the Village of Gananoque, in the County of Leeds, for "A new and useful combined Yarn REEL and Cloth-holder." Ottawa, dated 30th April, 1866.

No. 2026—DOOLITTLE, (*Moses C.,*) of the Township of Malahide, in the County of Elgin, for "A new and useful SPINNING Machine, called 'Doolittle's improved Spinning Machine.'" Ottawa, dated 3rd May, 1866.

No. 2027—MURPHY, (*William,*) of the Town of Paris, in the County of Brant, for "A new and useful improved Double Cheque SPIRIT-METER." Ottawa, dated 3rd May, 1866.

No. 2028—OTTLEY, (*Thomas M.,*) of the Village of Fort Erie, in the County of Welland, for "A new and improved method of LUBRICATING the Axles of Carriages." Ottawa, dated 3rd May, 1866.

No. 2029—GORDON, (*Alexander,*) of the City of Hamilton, in the County of Wentworth, for "Certain new and useful improvements in the working mechanism for DRILLING oil-wells and for raising oil from the same." Ottawa, dated 3rd May, 1866.

No. 2030—OTTLEY, (*Thomas M.,*) of the Village of Fort Erie, in the County of Welland, for "A new and improved mode of constructing WELLS, which he denominates 'The Subterranean Reservoir Well.'" Ottawa, dated 3rd May, 1866.

No. 2031—WARD, (*Jacob,*) of the Village of Morpeth, in the County of Kent, for "Certain new and useful improvements in the Corn PLANTER, such implement with the said improvements to be called 'Ward's improved Corn Planter.'" Ottawa, dated 3rd May, 1866.

No. 2032—DEWITT, (*Thomas,*) of the Village of Morpeth, in the County of Kent, for "A certain improvement called 'DeWitt's improvement on the THIMBLE SKEIN for Lumber Waggons.'" Ottawa, dated 3rd May, 1866.

No. 2033—POPE, (*Robert,*) of the Village of Newcastle, in the County of Durham, for "A new and useful Main-line and Siding-protecting SWITCH." Ottawa, dated 3rd May, 1866.

No. 2034—COCHRANE, (*William Fraser,*) of the Township of Malahide, in the County of Elgin, for "A new and useful improvement in the FEEDING of the Meal to the bolting Reel in Flouring Mills." Ottawa, dated 3rd May, 1866.

No. 2035—OTTLEY, (*Thomas M.,*) of the Village of Fort Erie, in the County of Welland, for "A new and improved SURCINGLE." Ottawa, dated 3rd May, 1866.

No. 2036—MIALL, (*Edward*,) of the Village of Oshawa, in the County of Ontario, for "A new and useful Dove-tailing machine, called 'Miall's DOVE-TAILER.'" Ottawa, dated 3rd May, 1866.

No. 2037—SELLS, (*Hugh*,) of the Village of Vienna, in the County of Elgin, for "A new and useful improved Cider Mill." Ottawa, dated 9th May, 1866.

No. 2038—CENTERS, (*Martin*,) of the Township of Longuell, in the County of Prescott, for "A certain new and useful improvement in the Rotary Dash Churn, called 'Centers' improved CHURN.'" Ottawa, dated 10th May, 1866.

No. 2039—GORDON, (*Alexander*,) of the City of Hamilton, in the County of Wentworth, for "A certain improvement in the operating of the Walking-beam for Oil WELLS." Ottawa, dated 10th May, 1866.

No. 2040—NEVILLE, (*Anthony*,) of the Township of Ernest-town, in the united Counties of Lennox and Addington, for "A certain improvement in LAMPS." Ottawa, dated 14th May, 1866.

No. 2041—DELL, (*Solomon*,) of the Village of Strathroy, in the County of Middlesex, for "A new and useful Lever Spinning WHEEL." Ottawa, dated 15th May, 1866.

No. 2042—TROYER, (*Michael*,) of the Township of Houghton, in the County of Norfolk, for "A new and useful Cane MILL." Ottawa, dated 15th May, 1866.

No. 2043—SMITH, (*Richard*,) of the Town of Sherbrooke, for "A new and useful improvement in Tobacco Cutters and Nut CRACKERS." Ottawa, dated 23rd May, 1866.

No. 2044—ETON, (*Richard*,) of the City of Montreal, for "A new and improved Fire GRATE for Locomotives and other Furnaces." Ottawa, dated 23rd May, 1866.

No. 2045—ETON, (*Richard*,) of the City of Montreal, for "Improvements in the construction of Railway Freight CARS." Ottawa, dated 23rd May, 1866.

No. 2046—HAGGERT, (*John*,) of the Village of Brampton, in the County of Peel, for "A new and useful Axle-nut or mode of securing Wheels to their AXLES." Ottawa, dated 9th May, 1866.

No. 2047—AUBIN, (*Aimé Nicholas Napoléon*,) of Belœil, in the County of Verchères, for "A new and useful Hydrostatic BLOWER, to be called 'Aerophos.'" Ottawa, dated 23rd May, 1866

No. 2048—PROWSE, (*George R.*,) of the City of Montreal, for "An improved REFRIGERATOR." Ottawa, dated 23rd May, 1866.

No. 2049—CHASE, (*Orlando Darwin*,) of the Township of Sutton, in the County of Brome, for "An improved Washing and Churning MACHINE." Ottawa, dated 29th May, 1866.

No. 2050—CHATTERTON, (*Richard Dover*,) of the Town of Cobourg, in the County of Northumberland, for "A new and improved self-acting Coupler for Railway Carriages, called 'Chatterton's self-acting BAR or BOSS-coupler.'" Ottawa, dated 30th May, 1866.

No. 2051—HUNT, (*Thomas Sterry*,) of the City of Montreal, for "Certain improvements in the manufacture of vegetable extracts for Tanning and DYEING." Ottawa, dated 2nd June, 1866.

No. 2052—AUBIN, (*Aimé Nicholas Napoléon*,) of Belœil, in the County of Verchères, for "A Safety CAN, called 'Burette de sûreté.'" Ottawa, dated 5th June, 1866.

No. 2053—LAZIER, (*James Bogart*,) of the Township of Reach, in the County of Ontario, for "A new and useful Barley Fork, called 'Lazier's improved Barley FORK.'" Ottawa, dated 30th April, 1866.

No. 2054—FAREWELL, (*Abraham*,) of the Village of Oshawa, in the County of Ontario, for "A new process for the preparation of lubricating oil from crude rock and Mineral OILS; for the Deodorization of all rock and mineral oils, and for rendering refined oils, obtained from the same, non-explosive, up to about one hundred and fifty degrees of Fahrenheit, by the application of certain chemicals, steam and heat." Ottawa, dated 27th June, 1866.

No. 2055—ENSLEY, (*John Israel*,) of the City of Toronto, in the County of York, for "A new and useful Apparatus for the purpose of Manufacturing Gas, Bone-black, Phosphorus, Ammonia, Pyroligneous acid, Turpentine, Tar and other useful substances from refuse of animal and vegetable matter, called 'The Economical GAS Works.'" Ottawa, dated 31st May, 1866.

No. 2056—HAYCOCK, (*Samuel Hatt*,) of the City of Ottawa, in the County of Carleton, for "A conical-headed BALL for firing Guns and Ordnance." Ottawa, dated 1st June, 1866.

No. 2057—HAND, (*Ekens,*) of the Town of Cobourg, in the County of Northumberland, for "An improved PISTON for Pump." Ottawa, dated 2nd June, 1866.

No. 2058—DAVIS, (*Charles,*) of the Village of Wallaceburg, in the County of Kent, for "A new and useful hollow GRATE or Furnace-Bars." Ottawa, dated 7th June, 1866.

No. 2059—BAINES, (*Hugh,*) of the City of Toronto, in the County of York, for "A new and useful reversible Forge-rolling MACHINE for manufacturing all kinds of Malleable metals." Ottawa, dated 7th June, 1866.

No. 2060—ROTTON, (*Otto,*) of the City of Kingston, in the County of Frontenac, for "A new and useful art or method of rendering barrels or other vessels impervious to penetrating fluids, by forcing cement between barrels or other vessels made double, called 'The Union CEMENTING process for cementing petroleum and other barrels and vessels.'" Ottawa, dated 13th June, 1866.

No. 2061—FULLER, (*Richard,*) of the City of Hamilton, in the County of Wentworth, for "Certain new and useful Improvements in the construction of Grain and Hay RAKES." Ottawa, dated 14th June, 1866.

No. 2062—STEERS, (*Thomas, Jr.,*) of Melbourne, in the County of Richmond, for "A new and useful APPARATUS for manufacturing Dye, Saccharine Salts, or extracts of vegetable substance." Ottawa, dated 18th June, 1866.

No. 2063—LEMON, (*Alfred James,*) of the Township of Beverly, in the County of Wentworth, for "A POTATO-DIGGER." Ottawa, dated 18th June, 1866.

No. 2064—COMSTOCK, (*Levi Richardson,*) of the City of Ottawa, for "A Revolving Flue RADIATOR." Ottawa, dated 31st May, 1866.

No. 2065—DELL, (*William Henry,*) of the Township of Adelaide, in the County of Middlesex, for "A PENDULUM Spinning Wheel." Ottawa, dated 11th June, 1866.

No. 2066—MILLOY, (*Hugh,*) of the Village of Erin, in the County of Wellington, for "An improved MOULD Board for Ploughs, to be called and known as 'The Wellington Mould-Board.'" Ottawa, dated 13th June, 1866.

No. 2067—KIRK, (*Andrew,*) of the Township of Kincardine, in the County of Bruce, for "A Self-acting CULTIVATOR." Ottawa, dated 20th June, 1866.

No. 2068—MARR, (*James,*) of the Township of Woodhouse, in the County of Norfolk, for "A new and useful PLOUGH-GUIDE and Holder." Ottawa, dated 21st June, 1866.

No. 2069—DICK, (*Joseph,*) of the Village of Oshawa, in the County of Ontario, for "Certain new and useful improvements in the Self-Raking REAPER, the said improvements being embodied in a machine, to be called 'Dick's Harvester.'" Ottawa, dated 21st June, 1866.

No. 2070—WINTER, (*Joseph,*) of the Village of Aylmer, in the County of Elgin, for "A new and useful Discovery to be called 'Winter's improved method of manufacturing POTASH.'" Ottawa, dated 3rd July, 1866.

No. 2071—DOYLE, (*John,*) of the Village of Sweabergh, in the County of Oxford, for "A new and useful self-shooting Burglary Battery, to be called 'Doyle's self-shooting Burglary BATTERY.'" Ottawa, dated 3rd July, 1866.

No. 2072—McINTOSH, (*John,*) of the City of Hamilton, in the County of Wentworth, for "A new and useful Portable Steam Engine Boiler called 'The McIntosh Portable Steam BOILER.'" Ottawa, dated 3rd July, 1866.

No. 2073—GIBBS, (*Elijah,*) of the City of Toronto, in the County of York, for "A new and useful Last Block FASTENER." Ottawa, dated 3rd July, 1866.

No. 2074—BARTHOLOMEW, (*Dennis,*) of the Township of East Zorra, in the County of Oxford, for "A new and useful Field Roller to be called 'The Excelsior Field ROLLER.'" Ottawa, dated 5th July, 1866.

No. 2075—HENDERSON, (*Joseph Clinton,*) of the Town of Brockville, in the County of Leeds, for "A new and useful Bituminous Coal Burner, called 'Henderson's new Bituminous Coal BURNER.'" Ottawa, dated 18th May, 1866.

No. 2076—HEATHFIELD, (*Mathew Wathrock,*) of the City of London, in the County of Middlesex, for "A new and useful compound which he names 'Salmoni's English White OIL.'" Ottawa, dated 6th July, 1866.

98

No. 2077—STEELE, (John,) of the City of Montreal, for "A new and improved Brick Making MACHINE." Ottawa, dated 16th July, 1866.

No. 2078—ETCHES, (Philip,) of the Village of Bothwell, in the County of Kent, for "A new and useful Improved Stop-COCK." Ottawa, dated 31st July, 1866.

No. 2079—PIERCE, (George,) of the Village of Kingsville, in the Township of Gosfield, in the County of Essex, for "A Corn Sheller and SEPARATOR." Ottawa, dated 31st July, 1866.

No. 2080—WOOD, (Samuel Silas,) of the Township of Blenheim, in the County of Oxford, for "An Improved Bolt CUTTER." Ottawa, dated 31st July, 1866.

No. 2081—OVERHOLT, (George Henry,) of the Township of Grimsby, in the County of Lincoln, for "A new and useful reading and writing FRAME." Ottawa, dated 31st July, 1866.

No. 2082—WILSON, (John Crampton,) of the Township of Oro, in the County of Simcoe, for "A new and useful MULTIPLIER." Ottawa, dated 31st July, 1866.

No. 2083—ROBINSON, (Joseph William,) of the Village of Bridgewater, in the County of Hastings, for "The Axe-Rolling and Swagging Machine for Making Chopping AXES." Ottawa, dated 31st July, 1866.

No. 2084—BARRETT, (Michael,) of the City of Toronto, in the County of York, for "A new and useful art for the revivification of Sulphuric Acid spent in the refining of Coal OIL." Ottawa, dated 31st July, 1866.

No. 2085—D'ARCY, (George Joseph,) of the Village of Oil Springs, in the County of Lambton, for "A new and useful mode of extracting Gas, Lubricating Oil, Burning Oil and Tar from Shale ROCK." Ottawa, dated 31st July, 1866.

No. 2086—KIRKWOOD, (Alexander,) of the City of Ottawa, in the County of Carleton, for "A new and useful kind of paper called 'Mellotus PAPER.'" Ottawa, dated 8th August, 1866.

No. 2087—CARTER, (Henry,) of the Township of Malahide, in the County of Elgin, for "A new and useful Machine called Carter's combined Ditching and Sod and Turf CUTTER." Ottawa, dated 18th August, 1866.

No. 2088—LAMB, (John,) of the City of Ottawa, in the County of Carleton, for "A new and useful Water WHEEL." Ottawa, dated 23rd August, 1866.

No. 2089—VAN CAMP, (Lewis,) of the Town of Berlin, in the County of Waterloo, for "A certain new and useful improvement in instruments for the application of Fluids for the production of topical anasthesia, called 'Van Camp's Patent SPRAY-TUBE.'" Ottawa, dated 23rd August, 1866.

No. 2090—WATSON, (John,) of the Town of Guelph, in the County of Wellington, for "A certain new and useful improvement in the Turbine Water WHEEL." Ottawa, dated 23rd August, 1866.

No. 2091—ATHERTON, (Calvin,) of the Village of Union, Township of Yarmouth, County of Elgin, for "Atherton's Union Carriage SPRINGS." Ottawa, dated 31st August, 1866.

No. 2092—RODDEN, (William Henry,) of the City of Toronto, in the County of York, for "A new and improved system of PIPING for water cisterns." Ottawa, dated 31st August, 1866.

No. 2093—BURKE, (John,) of the Town of Belleville, in the County of Hastings, for "An improvement in Breech-loading FIRE-ARMS." Ottawa, dated 11th September, 1866.

No. 2094—INGLIS, (Joseph James,) and SPENCE, (David,) Assignees of Thomas Wilkinson, for "A Composition of matter for ILLUMINATING or other purposes." Ottawa, dated 31st August, 1866.

No. 2095—COLLET, (Martin,) of the City of Toronto, in the County of York, for "Collet's method of slaughtering and preserving MEAT." Ottawa, dated 11th September, 1866.

No. 2096—CORBIN, (Charles Ingersoll,) of the Township of East Oxford, in the County of Oxford, for "A certain new and useful improvement on the revolving Horse-Rake, the so improved rake to be called 'Corbin's improved Revolving HORSE-RAKE.'" Ottawa, dated 13th September, 1866.

No. 2097—SPENCER, (Elihu,) of the City of Ottawa, in the County of Carleton, for "A certain new and useful improvement in the manner of inserting India Rubber Elastic into leather BOOTS and SHOES." Ottawa, dated 13th September, 1866.

No. 2098—RAINER, (*Joseph Frederick*,) of the Town of Whitby, in the County of Ontario, for "A new and useful style of PIANO, known as 'Rainer's new Elliptic Piano.'" Ottawa, dated 13th September, 1866.

No. 2099—AYRES, (*Parley Jabez*,) of the Town of Peterboro', in the County of Peterboro', for "A new and useful Auger Handle, called 'Ayres' magic AUGER-HANDLE.'" Ottawa, dated 13th September, 1866.

No. 2100—CLENCH, (*Leon Moses*,) of the Town of St. Mary's in the County of Perth, for "An Elbow needle-bar, silent motion and oscillating feeding attachment for sewing machines, to be called 'Clench's Elbow NEEDLE-BAR, silent motion and oscillating feed attachment for Sewing Machines.'" Ottawa, dated 13th September, 1866.

No. 2101—AYRES, (*Parley Jabez*,) of the Town of Peterboro', in the County of Peterboro' for "A new and useful tire upsetting machine, called "Ayres' improved TIRE upsetting Machine.'" Ottawa, dated 13th September, 1866.

No. 2102—HILL, (*Robert*,) of the Village of Nobleton, in the County of York, for "Certain improvements in the side gearing for Threshing MACHINES," in addition to those for which he has already obtained Letters Patent of Invention in Canada, bearing date the 2nd day of August, A.D., 1865. Ottawa, dated 13th September, 1866.

No. 2103—BAINES, (*Hugh*,) of the City of Toronto, in the County of York, for "A new and useful steel-cased axle and SHAFT with steel bushed wheels and bearings for all kinds of Rolling-Stock and Machinery." Ottawa, dated 13th September, 1866.

No. 2104—HENDRY, (*Thomas*,) of the Township of Whitechurch, in the County of York, for "An improved PLOUGH, certain improvements in which are new and useful. Ottawa, dated 13th September, 1866.

No. 2105—KENNEDY, (*John Alexander*,) of the Township of Blenheim, in the County of Oxford, for "A new and useful improved Waggon JACK." Ottawa, dated 17th September, 1866.

No. 2106—BUNTIN, (*Alexander*,) of the City of Montreal, for the introduction of "A new and useful invention known as 'Henrich's Valter's machine for PULPING WOOD for the manufacture of PAPER.'" Ottawa, dated 19th September, 1866.

No. 2107—BUNTIN, (*Alexander*,) of the City of Montreal, for the introduction of "A new and improved machinery for the Pulping of Wood for the manufacture of PAPER." Ottawa, dated 20th September, 1866.

No. 2108—ROTTON, (*Otto*,) of the City of Kingston, in the County of Frontenac, for "A new, useful and improved STILL, called 'The Double Exhaust Conical Still or Evaporator.'" Ottawa, dated 17th September, 1866.

No. 2109—ROTTON, (*Otto*,) of the City of Kingston, in the County of Frontenac, for "A new and useful improved Still, called 'The Acephaloid STILL.'" Ottawa, dated 17th September, 1866.

No. 2110—ROTTON, (*Otto*,) of the City of Kingston, in the County of Frontenac, for "A new and useful method of applying CEMENT within closed barrels or other vessels, called 'The Direct Force Cementing Process.'" Ottawa, dated 17th September, 1866.

No. 2111—McDOWELL, (*Daniel*,) of the City of Montreal, for "A new and useful apparatus for cleaning flues of Steam BOILERS." Ottawa, dated 18th September, 1866.

No. 2112—McEVILLA, (*William*,) of the Village of Roxton Falls, in the County of Shefford, for "A Pocket Watch SAFE." Ottawa, dated 19th September, 1866.

No. 2113—SAWYER, (*Horace*,) of the Township of Eaton, in the County of Compton, for "A new and useful improvement in the manufacture of Extract of TAN BARK and other materials." Ottawa, dated 19th September, 1866.

No. 2114—CAMPBELL, (*Oliver*,) of the Township of Compton, in the County of Compton, for "A new and useful Water WHEEL and Curb." Ottawa, dated 19th September, 1866.

No. 2115—WALKER, (*Henry*,) of the Village of Buckingham, in the County of Ottawa, for "A Vice Mill Stone PICK." Ottawa, dated 19th September, 1866.

No. 2116—MEYER, (*Edward B.*,) of the City of Quebec, for "New and useful improvements in DRILLING Machines." Ottawa, dated 19th September, 1866.

No. 2117—FELL, (*Thomas Mara*,) and FELL, (*Ambrose George*,) of the City of Montreal, for

" Certain new and useful improvements in the manufacture of WHITE LEAD." Ottawa, dated 19th September, 1866.

No. 2118—MAGOON, (*Aaron,*) of the Township of Stanstead, in the County of Stanstead, for " A new and improved Rotary HARROW." Ottawa, dated 25th September, 1866.

No. 2119—SCOTT, (*George,*) of the City of Montreal, for " A new and improved Bedstead FASTENER." Ottawa, dated 25th September, 1866.

No. 2120—LAMAIN, (*Charles,*) of the Township of Hamilton, in the County of Northumberland, for " A new and useful CULTIVATOR." Ottawa, dated 29th September, 1866.

No. 2121—BARCLAY, (*Robert,*) of the Town of Paris, in the County of Brant, for " A certain new and useful improvement in Sewing MACHINES." Ottawa, dated 29th September, 1866.

No. 2122—ALEXANDER, (*Alexander Gale,*) of the City of Hamilton, in the County of Wentworth, for " A new and useful means and apparatus for generating Hydrocarbon VAPORS and continuing an uniform flow thereof." Ottawa, dated 29th September, 1866.

No. 2123—JONES, (*John,*) of the City of Kingston, in the County of Frontenac, for " A Horse-hay FORK." Ottawa, dated 29th September, 1866.

No. 2124—TENCH, (*William Eastwood,*) of the Town of Clifton in the County of Welland, for " A new and useful Pump apparatus for superseding Bags in Artesian WELLS." Ottawa, dated 29th September, 1866.

No. 2125—LEWIS, (*Coridon,*) of the Village of Salford, in the Township of Dereham, in the County of Oxford, for " A new and useful Dairyman's CHURN." Ottawa, dated 29th September, 1866.

No. 2126—LYONS, (*Charles,*) of the Town of Simcoe, in the County of Norfolk, for " A Steel Headed Railway RAIL, also a method by which steel can be welded on or in the head of a railway rail so that it cannot be loosened and rendered useless until the head is completely worn down." Ottawa, dated 3rd October, 1866.

No. 2127—LOUDON, (*Robert,*) of the Village of Bothwell, in the Township of Zone, in the County of Kent, for " A certain new and useful improvement in the construction of Steam Boilers and ENGINES to control the Draught and dispense with the Blast-pipe, in combination with the new invention by one J. G. Shirts for the use of Petroleum as fuel." Ottawa, dated 3rd October, 1866.

No. 2128—MARAIS, (*Felicite,*) of the City of Montreal, for " A composition of matter, to be called ' English Cleansing FLUID of F. Marais." Ottawa, dated 4th October, 1866.

No. 2129—YEAGER, (*Henry,*) of the City of Hamilton, in the County of Wentworth, for " A new and useful machine for Pitching and Loading Hay and Straw, called ' Yeager's Revolving Hay PITCHER.' " Ottawa, dated 4th October, 1866.

No. 2130—GILL, (*William,*) of the City of Toronto, in the County of York, and DUFF, (*James,*) of the same place; for " A new and useful machine for the safer and better management of Steam BOILERS." Ottawa, dated 5th October, 1866.

No. 2131—BRUTON, (*Charles Frederick,*) of the Town of Napanee, in the County of Lennox and Addington, for " An improved Flannel cloth and yarn MIXTURE." Ottawa, dated 9th October, 1866.

No. 2132—ENSLEY, (*John Israel,*) of the City of London, in the County of Middlesex, for " A new and useful method of fastening HOOPS." Ottawa, dated 12th October, 1866.

No. 2133—EAKINS, (*John Henry,*) of the Township of Enniskillen, in the County of Lambton, for " A new and useful improvement in the VALVES used in pumping OIL WELLS." Ottawa, dated 12th October, 1866.

No. 2134—DURRANT, (*Revd. John,*) of the Town of Stratford, in the County of Perth, for " A new and useful flexible cleaner for Lamp Chimnies and glass GLOBES." Ottawa, dated 30th October, 1866.

No. 2135—WILSON, (*James,*) of the Township of Nelson, in the County of Halton, for " A new and useful improvement on the Steam Engine, known as ' The Central Application Non-Friction VALVE." Ottawa, dated 13th October, 1866.

No. 2136—SHERBURNE, (*Elijah Burton,*) of the Township of East Williams, in the County of Middlesex, for "A Flax-extending Drove |Exterminating Miller and Robber Proof BEE-HIVE." Ottawa, dated 3rd July, 1866.

No. 2137—BOOLE, (*Leonard Hoffman,*) of the City of Ottawa, in the County of Carleton, for "A new and useful manner of preserving Eggs in a granulated or compact form, to be known as 'Boole's Granulated EGGS.'" Ottawa, dated 18th October, 1866.

No. 2138—WILLIS, (*Thomas,*) of the Township of Blanchard, in the County of Perth, for "A new and useful improved Horse POWER." Ottawa, dated 18th October, 1866.

No. 2139—ROGERS, (*Robert,*) of the City of Montreal, for "A new and useful Gas Stove Furnace and RANGE." Ottawa, dated 25th October, 1866.

No. 2140—BAKER, (*George James,*) of Town of Oakville, in the County of Halton, for "A new and useful method of fastening buckles in harness, bridles, reins, martingales and stirrup leathers, and for the fastening of all other straps used about HARNESSES." Ottawa, dated 30th October, 1866.

No. 2141—BEMIS, (*Benjamin Bowman, Jr.,*) of the Village of Winterbourne, in the County of Waterloo, for "A new and useful machine for the drying of grain, called 'Bemis's Canadian Grain DRYER.'" Ottawa, dated 30th October, 1866.

No. 2142—BROOKS, (*Mott Billings,*) of the Town of Brockville, in the County of Leeds, for "A new and useful machine, which he has named 'Brook's Patent Ribbon ROLLER and self-measuring machine." Ottawa, dated 30th October, 1866.

No. 2143—CLUTE, (*Charles Clarke,*) of the Town of Picton, in the County of Prince Edward, for "A new and useful apparatus for purifying and enriching common illuminating GAS." Ottawa, dated 31st October, 1866.

No. 2144—HOULGRAVE, (*John,*) of the Town of St. Catharines, in the County of Lincoln, for "A new and useful Spring Bed BOTTOM." Ottawa, dated 30th October, 1866.

No. 2145—ALEXANDER, (*Alexander Gale,*) of the City of Hamilton, in the County of Wentworth, for "A new and useful method of Generating or increasing the Power of Hydro-carbon GAS." Ottawa, dated 18th October, 1866.

No. 2146—DAVIS, *James William,*) of the Town of Galt, in the County of Waterloo, for "A Mould BOARD, called 'The Maple Leaf.'" Ottawa, dated 7th November, 1866.

No. 2147—DAVIS, (*Thomas,*) of the Village of Portsmouth, in the County of Frontenac, for "A new and useful Friction Wedge POWER." Ottawa, dated 9th November, 1866.

No. 2148—WALTON, (*Joseph N.,*) of the Town of Sherbrooke, Assignee of Richard Smith, of the same place, for "A new and useful machine, called 'Smith's EGG BEATER.'" Ottawa, dated 12th November, 1866.

No. 2149—WYATT, (*Matthew T.,*) of the City of Quebec, for a new and useful Butting MACHINE." Ottawa, dated 12th November, 1866.

No. 2150—WYATT, (*Matthew T.,*) of the City of Quebec, for "A new and useful Combined Butting, Splitting, and Lath making Saw BENCH." Ottawa, dated 13th November, 1866.

No. 2151—DAVIDSON, (*Thomas,*) of the City of Montreal, for "An improved Bottom or Top of sheet Metal VESSELS." Ottawa, dated 13th November, 1866.

No. 2152—WARREN, (*Samuel Russell,*) of the City of Montreal, for "An improved Minia-ture ORGAN." Ottawa, dated 13th November, 1866.

No. 2153—BOOLE, (*Leonard Hoffman,*) of the City of Ottawa, in the County of Carleton, for "A new and useful combination of Machinery, to be hereafter known as 'Booles' DRYING Machine.'" Ottawa, dated 4th December, 1866.

No. 2154—HAMILTON, (*William,*) of the City of Toronto, in the County of York, for "A new and useful improvement in the fastening of Nuts on Railway and other BOLTS." Ottawa, dated 13th November, 1866.

No. 2155—PRITCHARD, (*Henry C.,*) of the City of Toronto, in the County of York, and LATHAM, (*Samuel,*) of the same City, for "A new and useful Shoe TRIMMER." Ottawa, dated 15th November, 1866.

No. 2156—FOSTER, (*Archibald McDonald,*) of the City of Hamilton, in the County of Went-worth, for "A new and useful Anti-incrustation POWDER for Boilers." Ottawa, dated 15th November, 1866.

No. 2157—JELLET, (*Robert Patteyson,*) of the Town of Belleville, in the County of Hastings, for " A new and useful Telescopic Jointed GUN." Ottawa, dated 15th November, 1866.

No. 2158—THOMPSON, (*William,*) of the City of Toronto, in the County of York, for " An improved apparatus for Carbonating Illuminating GASES." Ottawa, dated 19th November, 1866.

No. 2159—OLIVER, (*John Price,*) of the Village of Kingsville, in the County of Essex, and DRAKE, (*William Malott,*) of the same Village, for " A new and useful QUILTING FRAME." Ottawa, dated 21st November, 1866.

No. 2160—HALL, (*James Johnson,*) of the Town of St. Mary's, in the County of Perth, for " A new illuminating Oil, to be known as 'Hall's Illuminating OIL.'" Ottawa, dated 22nd November, 1866.

No. 2161—McBEAN, (*John,*) of the Village of Corunna, in the Township of Moore, in the County of Lambton, for " A new and useful Pavement, called 'The Improved McBeth PAVEMENT.'" Ottawa, dated 22nd November, 1866.

No. 2162—HALL, (*James Johnson,*) of the Town of St. Mary's, in the County of Perth, for " A new and useful Spirit GAS." Ottawa, dated 22nd November, 1866.

No. 2163—HOPKINS, (*Robert,*) of the Township of East Williams, in the County of Middlesex, for " A Lamp, known as 'The Victoria OIL LAMP.'" Ottawa, dated 23rd November, 1866.

No. 2164—HENDERSON, (*Joseph Clinton,*) of the Town of Brockville, in the County of Leeds, for " A new and useful Joint for the Rails of Railways, called 'Henderson's Patent Rail JOINT.'" Ottawa, dated 24th November, 1866.

No. 2165—FERL, (*Peter Henry,*) of the Town of Windsor, in the County of Essex, for " A new and useful deep water Fishing Machine, called ' Peter H. Ferl's vertical deep water FISHING Machine.'" Ottawa, dated 24th November, 1866.

No. 2166—LEMON, (*William,*) of the Village of Lynden, in the County of Wentworth, for " A new and useful method of altering the Enfield Rifle, or any other Muzzle-loading Rifle into a Breech-loader, to be known as 'Lemon's Breech-loading RIFLE.'" Ottawa, dated 27th November, 1866.

No. 2167—OAKLEY, (*Frederick,*) of the City of Toronto, in the County of York, for " A new and useful Egg and Cream Beater, known as 'Oakley's Egg and Cream BEATER.'" Ottawa, dated 27th November, 1866.

No. 2168—OTTLEY, (*Thomas M.,*) of the Village of Fort Erie, in the County of Welland, for " A new and improved Feed CUTTER." Ottawa, dated 27th November, 1866.

No. 2169—COLLINS, (*Thomas Coxton,*) of the City of Toronto, in the County of York, Assignee of Frederick Oakley, of the same place, for " A new and improved Burglar-alarm and Door-FASTENER combined." Ottawa, dated 28th November, 1866.

No. 2170—WATSON, (*John,*) of the Town of Guelph, in the County of Wellington, for " A certain new and useful BRICK Machine, for making or pressing bricks of clay or other suitable materials." Ottawa, dated 28th November, 1866.

No. 2171—SCHOMBERG, (*Henry Alexander,*) of the City of Toronto, in the County of York, for " Certain new and useful improvements in a Combined MOP and Scrubber, made by one Alma Clematus Racon." Ottawa, dated 1st December, 1866.

No. 2172—SMITH, (*Richard,*) of the Town of Sherbrooke, in the District of St. Francis, for " A new and useful improvement in Machines for the manufacture of PAPER, to be called 'Smith's Steam Regulator for Paper Machines.'" Ottawa, dated 3rd December, 1866.

No. 2173—HOWELL, (*William James Shee,*) of the City of Quebec, for " A new and useful Elastic Roller SASH, spring for sliding windows in Railway cars, houses, &c., with self-adjusting and screw adjusting appliance for regulating pressure of Roller." Ottawa, dated 4th December, 1866.

No. 2174—JAMIESON, (*William,*) of the Township of Lochiel, in the County of Glengarry, for " A new and useful Machine for lifting and removing STONES." Ottawa, dated 11th December, 1866.

No. 2175—ROWE, (*Edward,*) of the Village of Lyn, in the Township of Elizabethtown, in the County of Leeds, for " A new and useful Pump-GEARING." Ottawa, dated 10th December, 1866.

No. 2176—GRAHAM, (Simon Peter,) of the Village of Springford, in the County of Oxford, for " An Iron BUGGY BODY." Ottawa, dated 11th December, 1866.

No. 2177—CHRISTIE, (Miss Mary Hercus,) of the City of Toronto, in the County of York, for " A new and useful Hinged Pan and Sifter combined, to be called and known as 'The Toronto SIFTER.'" Ottawa, dated 17th December, 1866.

No. 2178—HUNT, (Robert,) of the Village of Plattsville, in the County of Oxford, for " A new, useful and improved Reverse Twisting and Double Action Apparatus for Spinning Machines, called 'Hunt's Reverse Twist Spinning GEARS.'" Ottawa, dated 19th December, 1866.

No. 2179—SUTTON, (Hughbert James,) of the City of London, for " A new and useful Solidified Oil or Lubricating GREASE." Ottawa, dated 20th December, 1866.

No. 2180—JOHNSON, (John,) of the City of Toronto, in the County of York, for " A new and useful process or method for rendering unexplosive Benzole and other hydro-carbon liquids, and for generating and illuminating gas therefrom, the compound so produced to be called ' Patent GAS OIL.'" Ottawa, dated 11th December, 1866.

No. 2181—REID, (Charles,) of the Town of St. Catharines, in the County of Lincoln, for " A new and useful Stove pipe SHELF." Ottawa, dated 14th December, 1866.

No. 2182—MATHER, (John,) of Gatineau Mills, in the County of Ottawa, for " A new and useful Slab CUTTER." Ottawa, dated 20th December, 1866.

No. 2183—BRINZER, (Casper,) of the Village of Yorkville, in the County of York, for " A new and useful Chair and Step Ladder, called 'The Brinzer CHAIR and Step Ladder combined.'" Ottawa, dated 9th January, 1866.

No. 2184—TAYLOR, (Charles,) of the County of Bonaventure, in the District of Gaspé, for " A new and useful Stone and Quartz BREAKER." Ottawa, dated 11th December, 1866.

No. 2185—LAZIER, (John,) of the Town of Belleville, in the County of Hastings, for " A new and useful Domestic SPINNER." Ottawa, dated 17th December, 1866.

No. 2186—YEMEN, (John,) of the Village of Mitchell, in the County of Perth, for " A Heel Plate, called 'Yemen's Reversable HEEL PLATE.'" Ottawa, dated 11th December, 1866.

No. 2187—WOOD, (Henry,) of the City of Montreal, for " An improvement in the manufacture of Paper STOCK from straw, flag, grass and other fibrous vegetable matter." Ottawa, dated 11th December, 1866.

No. 2188—WOOD, (Henry,) of the City of Montreal, for " An improvement in the manufacture of FIBRE from Indian Corn or Maize Plant, fibrous Grasses, Canes, Bamboos, Seeds and other fibrous vegetable matter." Ottawa, dated 11th December, 1866.

No. 2189—PAYNE, (Moses A.,) of the Township of Yarmouth, in the County of Elgin, for " A new and useful machine, called ' Moses A. Payne's Force Sand PUMP.'" Ottawa, dated 31st December, 1866.

No. 2190—CUMMINGS, (John,) of the Township of East Zorra, in the County of Oxford, and HARRINGTON, (Hiram,) of the said Township, for "An improved Threshing MACHINE." Ottawa, dated 31st December, 1866.

No. 2191—CUMMINGS, (Matthew,) of the Village of Bridgewater, in the County of Hastings, for " A new and useful dog-power Washing MACHINE." Ottawa, dated 5th January, 1867.

No. 2192—BARNES, (Jacob,) of the Town of Oakville, in the County of Halton, for "A new useful and improved Box STOVE or Furnace with tubulated smoke and improved heat conductors, with open draft regulator and atmospherical pressure pump." Ottawa, dated 7th January, 1867.

No. 2193—ALEXANDER, (Thomas,) of the City of Hamilton, in the County of Wentworth, for " A new and useful apparatus for generating Hydro-Carbon VAPOURS." Ottawa, dated 7th January, 1867.

No. 2194—BURN, (Richard,) of the City of Ottawa, in the County of Carleton, for " A new and useful PROJECTILE, which he terms ' A Sword Shot.'" Ottawa, dated 7th January, 1867.

No. 2195—BEECHER, (*William Fordyce,*) of the Town of Brockville, in the County of Leeds, for "A new and useful improved RADIATOR." Ottawa, dated 12th December, 1865.

No. 2196—ROTTON, (*Otto,*) of the City of Kingston, in the County of Frontenac, for "A new and useful Still or Evaporator, called 'The non-destructive Vapour STILL.'" Ottawa, dated 13th December, 1866.

No. 2197—PERRY, (*Edward,*) of the City of Montreal, for "A new and useful Pivot HINGE." Ottawa, dated 17th December, 1866.

No. 2198—GAUVREAU, (*Louis Pierre,*) of the City of Quebec, for "A new and useful Cement, to be called 'Gauvreau's Orleans Hydraulic CEMENT." Ottawa, dated 18th December, 1866.

No. 2199—BORDEN, (*Elias W.,*) of Bedford, in the County of Missisquoi, for "A new and useful double-action CHURN." Ottawa, dated 20th December, 1866.

No. 2200—HENDERSON, (*Joseph Clinton,*) of the Town of Brockville, in the County of Leeds, for "A new and useful Radiator or Dumb Stove, which he has called "Henderson's Impro ed RADIATOR." Ottawa, dated 22nd December, 1866.

No. 2201—MARRITT, (*John,*) of Aurora, in the County of York, for "Marritt's Aurora FLAX PULLER." Ottawa, dated 22nd December, 1866.

No. 2202—CLAPHAM, (*James Henry,*) of the City of Quebec, for "A new and useful Drilling and Pumping MACHINE." Ottawa, dated 18th December, 1866.

No. 2203—SMITH, (*Charles Joseph,*) of the Town of Brantford, in the County of Brant, for "A new and useful improvement in Fire GRATE Bars for Furnaces." Ottawa, dated 30th January, 1867.

No. 2204—LAWLOR, (*Richard,*) of the Village of Hawkesbury, in the County of Prescott, for a new and useful CHURN and Butter-worker." Ottawa, dated 7th January, 1867.

No. 2205—WILSON, (*Thomas L.,*) of the City of Montreal, for "A new and useful Steam Jet CUPOLA, for smelting metals." Ottawa, dated 21st January, 1867.

No. 2206—WOOD, (*Henry,*) of the City of Montreal, for "A new and useful improvement in the manufacture of FIBRE and paper stock from fibrous vegetable matter, as canes, bamboos, Indian corn or maize plant, reeds, grasses, rice plant, straw, flax, hemp and other such vegetable materials, for the purpose of obtaining fibre for the manufacture of textile materials, &c., and paper stock, by treatment with chemicals and steam, and for bleaching the same, both operations being performed under pressure or in vacuo." Ottawa, dated 21st January, 1867.

No. 2207—WATT, (*George,*) of Beauharnois, in the District of Beauharnois, for "An improved double-action HINGE." Ottawa, dated 21st January, 1867.

No. 2208—WOOD, (*Henry,*) of the City of Montreal, for "A new and useful improved Retainer BOILER and moveable Furnace for treating or disintegrating vegetable matter, bleaching, &c., and for desulphurising and amalgamating all kinds of ores, materials, &c., all under pressure or in vacuo." Ottawa, dated 21st January, 1867.

No. 2209—MILLS, (*Mortimer Birdsill,*) of the Village of Sparta, in the County of Elgin, for "A new and useful triangle CHURN." Ottawa, dated 31st December, 1866.

No. 2210—STOAKES, (*John Taylor,*) of the Parish of St. Bernard de Lacolle, in the County of St. Johns, in the District of Iberville, for "A new and useful lateral acting self coupling buffer for Railroad CARS." Ottawa, 21st January, 1867.

No. 2211—WALLIS, (*Elias,*) of the Township of Elgin, in the County of Huntingdon, for "A new and useful Farmer's labor saving MACHINE combined." Ottawa, dated 23rd January, 1867.

No. 2212—MORSE, (*William,*) of the Township of Trafalgar, in the County of Halton, for "A GATE." Ottawa, dated 24th January, 1867.

No. 2213—ROWE, (*Jonas Henry,*) of the Township of King, in the County of York, for "A new and useful Spinning Wheel, called 'The improved Self-returning Spindle Carrier, or Champion Spinning WHEEL.'" Ottawa, dated 24th January, 1867.

No. 2214—HODGES, (*James,*) of the Township of Bulstrode, in the District of Arthabaska, for "New and useful improvements in the manufacture of IRON, COPPER and other metals, by Incorporating their ores when in a pulverized state, with or without a flux, with pulped peat as a fuel for smelting or reduction." Ottawa, dated 31st December, 1866.

No. 2215 - HIBBARD, (*Ashley*,) of the City of Montreal, for "Cirée BELTING." Ottawa, dated 31st December, 1866.

No. 2216—SLATER, (*Erastus*,) of the City of Toronto, in the County of York, for " A new and useful Extension LADDER." Ottawa, dated 24th January, 1867.

No. 2217—ROTTON, (*Otto*,) of the City of Kingston, in the County of Frontenac, for " A new and useful STILL, called 'The Spray Still.' " Ottawa, dated 24th January, 1867.

No. 2218—BOWMAN, (*William*,) of the City of London, in the County of Middlesex, for " A Crude Petroleum BURNER." Ottawa, dated 24th January, 1867.

No. 2219—CRANE, (*John*,) of the Town of Woodstock, in the County of Oxford, for "A new and useful Truss, to be known as 'Crane's Self Adjusting Truss.' " Ottawa, dated 24th January, 1867.

No. 2220—SWAIN, (*P.*,) and POWERS, (*D. E.*,) Assignees of B. H. Rose, for "A new and useful Improvement in the Cross Cut SAW and Buck Saw respectively." Ottawa, dated 25th January, 1867.

No. 2221—RYKERT, (*George Zachariah*,) of the Township of Grantham, in the County of Lincoln, for " A new and useful Gate, called 'The Grantham GATE.' " Ottawa, dated 26th January, 1867.

No. 2222—DUFFY, (*Charles*,) of the Village of Collingwood, in the County of Simcoe, for " A new and useful Spring Bed BOTTOM." Ottawa, dated 28th January, 1867.

No. 2223—LYONS, (*Robert Charles*,) of the Town of Simcoe, in the County of Norfolk, for " An improved rail PILE." Ottawa, dated 28th January, 1867.

No. 2224—NOTMAN, (*William*,) of the City of Montreal, for "A new and useful ART of taking photographic pictures representing winter scenes, by artifical means, with or without figures." Ottawa, dated 28th January, 1867.

No. 2225—GALVIN, (*Bartholomew Clifford*,) of the city of Ottawa, in the County of Carleton, for " A Portable SWITCH and Railway Engine Car lifter combined, to be used in connection with railway tracks, whereby the shunting of Railway Cars may be effected without the aid of permanent switches, and with or without the aid of Locomotive Engines, and whereby also, such Engines or Railway Cars may be put on or off the track when desired." Ottawa, dated 31st January, 1867.

No. 2226—PENDLETON, (*Harvey Smith*,) of the Township of Dereham, in the County of Oxford, for " A new and useful CEMENT or composition of matter for covering roofs, forming pavements, and for other purposes. Ottawa, dated 31st January, 1887.

No. 2227—PENDLETON, (*Harvey Smith*,) of the Township of Dereham, in the County of Oxford, for " A new and useful art of making BUTTER from the liquids separated from the solids during the process of manufacturing Cheese." Ottawa, dated 31st January, 1867.

No. 2228—STEVENSON, (*Michael*,) of the Town of St. Mary, in the County of Perth, for "A new and useful DRILLING Machine, called 'A double hole hand drilling machine for Railroad Iron." Ottawa, dated 2nd February, 1867.

No. 2229—MANNING, (*Samuel Howe*,) of the City of London, in the County of Middlesex, for "A new and useful Land Roller, called 'Mannin's Improved Land ROLLER." Ottawa, dated 16th February, 1867.

No. 2230—MARSTON, (*William Philip*,) of the City of Toronto, in the County of York, for " Certain new and useful Improvements in Breech loading RIFLES, specially adapted to the altering of Muzzle loading Enfield, and other Rifles, to Breech Loaders." Ottawa, dated 31st January, 1867.

No. 2231—DOUD, (*Bernard Sproul*,) of the Township of Pakenham, in the County of Lanark, for "A new and improved Composition CEMENT." Ottawa, dated 4th February, 1867.

No. 2232—KREIGHOFF, (*Ernest*,) of the City of Toronto, in the County of York, for " Certain new and useful Improvements in Spring Mattrasses, Sofas, CHAIRS, applicable to any other article which is now or might be provided with elastic stuffing." Ottawa, dated 4th February, 1867.

No. 2233—HULBERT, (*Samuel*,) of the Town of Prescott, in the County of Grenville, for "Certain Improvements in the Agricultural PLOUGH. Ottawa, dated 4th February, 1867.

No. 2234—LECKIE, (*Robert*,) of Actonvale, in the County of Bagot, for "A new and useful improvement in the manufacture of Sulphuric ACID, Sulphate of Metals, Copper, Nickel and Oxide of Cobalt." Ottawa, dated 4th February, 1867.

No. 2235—LECKIE, (*Robert*,) and MACFARLANE, (*Thomas*,) of Actonvale, in the County of Bagot, for "A new and useful improvement of Sulphuric ACID, Hydrochloric Acid, Sulphate of Soda, Gold, Silver, and Copper, Oxide of Copper, of Nickel and of Cobalt." Ottawa, dated 5th February, 1867.

No. 2236—WILLSON, (*Alfred*,) of Bell Ewart, in the Township of Innisfil, in the County of Simcoe, for "A new and useful self-acting Car COUPLER and Uncoupler in (case of accidents) and hand uncoupler." Ottawa, dated 6th February, 1867.

No. 2237—DOUD, (*Bernard Sproul*,) of the Township of Pakenham, in the County of Lanark, for "A new and improved Sleigh BRAKE." Ottawa, dated 8th February, 1867.

No. 2238—DEWE, (*John*,) of the City of Toronto, in the County of York, for "A new and useful STAMP Improver." Ottawa, dated 8th February, 1867.

No. 2239—ROBERTS, (*Mathew Lyman*,) of the Village of Smithville, in the County of Lincoln, for "A new and useful improved PLOUGH." Ottawa, dated 12th February, 1867.

No. 2240—HIBBARD, (*Ashley*,) of the City of Montreal, for "A new and useful improvement in the manufacture of 'Cirée BELTING.'" Ottawa, dated 13th February, 1867.

No. 2241—LAWRIE, (*Thomas*,) of the City of Hamilton, in the County of Wentworth, for "A new and useful Compound adjustable revolving Grain DRYING MACHINE." Ottawa, dated 14th February, 1867.

No. 2242—STEPHENS, (*Robert Erratt*,) of the Town of Owen Sound in the County of Grey, for "A new and useful Breech Loading Fire Arm, called 'The Stephens GUN.'" Ottawa, dated 11th February, 1867.

No. 2243—FOYE, (*Benjamin Birdwood*,) of the City of Toronto, in the County of York, for "A new and useful Automatic REPEATER for use in Telegraph Lines." Ottawa, dated 14th February, 1867.

No. 2244—VICKERS, (*William*,) of the Township of Blanchard, in the County of Perth, for "A Swivel GATE." Ottawa, dated 14th February, 1867.

No. 2245—GREEN, (*James Adams*,) of the City of Hamilton, in the County of Wentworth, for "A new and useful improved method of Casting Iron ARMS for Waggon Axletrees and the nuts used in connection therewith." Ottawa, dated 19th February, 1867.

No. 2246—MOORE, (*Honble. Philip H.*,) for "A new method of Manufacturing PEAT into Coal, by process of Steam," under Special Act, Cap. 161, 29 & 30 Vict. Ottawa, dated 26th February, 1867.

No. 2247—DOUD, (*Bernard Sproul*,) of the Township of Pakenham, in the County of Lanark, for "A new and useful Hand Grain RAKE." Ottawa, dated 6th February, 1867.

No. 2248—ANCTIL, (*Eusèbe*,) of the Parish of Ste. Anne de la Pocatière, in the Province of Canada, and ANCTIL, (*François Xavier*,) of the same place, for "A new and improved Printing PRESS, to be called 'Presse Anctil.'" Quebec, dated 20th February, 1867.

No. 2249—LYONS, (*Robert Charles*,) of the Town of Simcoe, in the County of Norfolk, for "A new and useful improvement in ROLLS for the rolling of steel headed Railway Rails." Ottawa, dated 23rd February, 1867.

No. 2250—MACKENZIE, (*Daniel*,) of the Town of Belleville, in the County of Hastings, for "A new and useful GAS GENERATOR and Carburetter." Ottawa, dated 23rd February, 1867.

No. 2251—WIARD, (*Norman*,) of the Village of Ancaster, in the County of Wentworth, for "Certain improvements in the means of preventing, indicating and correcting an undue degree of the super-heating of STEAM in Steam Boilers, and for promoting an equality of temperature in the parts for the more economical working thereof, and for the prevention of explosions." Ottawa, dated 23rd February, 1867.

No. 2252—THOMSON, (*George Montayn*,) of the City of Ottawa, in the County of Carleton, for " A certain new and useful improvement in Machines for crushing, cutting and pressing Hay, and other similar substances, called " The Roller Hay PRESS." Ottawa, dated 25th February, 1867.

No. 2253—SCHOFIELD, (*Harmon Stevens*,) of the Town of Brockville, in the County of Leeds, for " A new and useful BLOTTER and Eraser combined." Ottawa, dated 26th February, 1867.

No. 2254—BARRY, (*Charles Walker*,) of the City of Montreal, for " A new useful apparatus for generating heat and light by the decomposition of Coal or other OILS." Ottawa, dated 27th February, 1867.

No. 2255—PHRAYNE, (*Jonathan Beaumont*,) of the City of Montreal, for "An Improved Self-adjusting Carriage STEP." Ottawa, dated 4th March, 1867.

No. 2256—ANDERSON, (*Charles F.*,) of the Township of Stanstead, in the County of Stanstead, for " A new and useful Washing Machine and Ironing TABLE combined." Ottawa, dated 4th March, 1867.

No. 2257—FRASER, (*Hugh*,) of the Village of Clarksburg, in the County of Grey, and PERRIN, (*Abraham*,) of the same place, for " A new and useful oscillating Planking SCREW." Ottawa, dated 7th March, 1867.

No. 2258—HARRIS, (*Philip Pearson*,) for the introduction of a Patent under cap. 157, 29 & 30 Vict. " A Machine for refining and deodorizing Crude Petroleum OIL." Ottawa, dated 7th March, 1867.

No. 2259—WALBANK, (*Samuel Seddon*,) of the Town of Iugersol, in the County of Oxford, for "A new and useful Coal Oil and Petroleum DEODORIZER." Ottawa, dated 9th March, 1867.

No. 2260—WILSON, (*Arthur Gates*) of the Township of Kingsey, in the County of Drummond, for " A new and useful improvement in the manufacture of Carriage and Harness TRIMMINGS." Ottawa, dated 9th March, 1867.

No. 2261—ANDERSON, (*Charles F.*,) of the Township of Stanstead, in the County of Stanstead, for " A new and useful Lamp Chimney CLEANER and Household Conveniencer." Ottawa, dated 4th March, 1867.

No. 2262—THOMSON, (*James Edward*,) of the City of Toronto, in the County of York, for " An Improved Seal LOCK." Ottawa, dated 7th March, 1867.

No. 2263—KINNEY, (*Israel*) of the Town of Woodstock, in the County of Oxford, for "A new and useful WASHBOARD, to be known as 'The Paragon Washboard." Ottawa, dated 4th March, 1867.

No. 2264—PENDLETON, (*Harvey Smith*,) of the Township of Dereham, in the County of Oxford, for " A new and useful apparatus, called 'The Canadian Dish WASHER." Ottawa, dated 4th March, 1867.

No. 2265—McCARTHY, (*George*,) of the Town of Barrie, in the County of Simcoe, for " A Foot Warmer and LANTERN combined." Ottawa, dated 7th March, 1867.

No. 2266—NICHOL, (*Thomas*,) of the Town of Chatham, in the County of Kent, for " A Breech Loading RIFLE." Ottawa, dated 7th March, 1867.

No. 2267—CREVIER, (*Toussaint*,) and POITRAS, (*Edouard*,) of the City of Montreal, for " A new and useful improved Hot Air FURNACE." Ottawa, dated 11th March, 1867.

No. 2268—WARK, (*James*,) of the City of Montreal, for "An improved apparatus for producing Steam in boilers by the use of Coal Oil or Crude Petroleum as FUEL." Ottawa, dated 11th March, 1867.

No. 2269—CODD, (*Donald*,) of the City of Ottawa, in the County of Carleton, for "An Improved Corn SHELLER." Ottawa, dated 12th March, 1867.

No. 2270—MERILL, (*Horace*,) of the City of Ottawa, in the County of Carleton, for " A new and useful Slab CUTTER." Ottawa, dated 12th March, 1867.

No. 2271—INGLES, (*Joseph James*,) of the Town of Brantford, in the County of Brant, for "A new and useful composition of matter for Roofing and Side Walks and other purposes, known as 'Ingles' fire proof CEMENT for Roofing and Side Walks." Ottawa, dated 14th March, 1867.

14

No. 2272—MOORE, (*Cyrus,*) of the town of Brantford, in the County of Brant, for " A new and useful Lubricating GREASE." Ottawa, dated 14th March, 1867.

No. 2273—BEVAN, (*Owen Theophilus,*) of the Village of Petrolia, in the County of Lambton, for " A new and useful forced and Crude Petroleum Steam GENERATOR." dated 13th March, 1867.

No. 2274—SUMMERS, (*William,*) of the Village of Woodbridge, in the County of York, for " Certain new and useful Improvements in grain crushing or chopping Mills, and in the method of making the fluted Iron ROLLERS for the same." Ottawa, dated 14th March, 1867.

No. 2275—VAN BUSKIRK, (*William Campbell,*) of the Town of St. Thomas, in the County of Elgin, for " A new and useful Draining PLOUGH." Ottawa, dated 14th March, 1867.

No. 2276—MOORE, (*Cyrus,*) of the Town of Brantford, in the County of Brant, for " A new and useful Lubricating OIL." Ottawa, dated 14th March, 1867.

No. 2277—MARRITT, (*John,*) of the Village of Aurora, in the County of York for " A new and useful Machine to be called ' Marritt's Economic KNIFE Cleaner." Ottawa, dated 15th March, 1867.

No. 2278—BARRY, (*Charles Walker,*) of the City of Montreal, for " A new and useful Improved combined Gas Stove and FURNACE." Ottawa, dated 18th March, 1867.

No. 2279—MEILLEUR, (*Antoine Auguste,*) of the City of Montreal, for " An Improved REFRIGERATOR." Ottawa, dated 18th March, 1867.

No. 2280—CREVIER, (*Toussaint,*) and POITRAS, (*Edouard,*) of the City of Montreal, for " New and useful Improvements in REFRIGERATORS." Ottawa, dated 18th March, 1867.

No. 2281—MAGOON, (*Aaron,*) of the Township of Stanstead, in the County of Stanstead, for " A new and useful Lime KILN." Ottawa, dated 18th March, 1867.

No. 2282—LOCKHART, (*Robert,*) of the Town of Walkerton, in the County of Bruce, for " A new and useful Hub and Felloe BORING Machine for the use of Wheel-Wrights." Ottawa, dated 20th March, 1867.

No. 2283—LOCKHART, (*Robert,*) of the Town of Walkerton, in the County of Bruce, for " A new and useful self Centering FACE SETT for the use of Wheelwrights." Ottawa, dated 20th March, 1867.

No. 2284—INCE, (*Thomas Henry,*) of the City of Toronto, in the County of York, for " The Introduction of a new and useful composition of matter, called 'The Agricultural FERTILIZER.' " Ottawa, dated 23rd March, 1867.

No. 2285—MILLER, (*John Robert,*) of the Town of Stratford, in the County of Perth, for " A new and useful and Improved PLOUGH mould-board." Ottawa, dated 23rd March, 1867.

No. 2286—CRANDELL, (*Benjamin,*) of the Village of Borelia, in the County of Ontario, for " A self-acting BRAKE on the front wheels of a Waggon, that may be applied to all vehicles drawn by animals." Ottawa, dated 23rd March, 1867.

No. 2287—HUNTER, (*Thomas,*) of the City of Toronto, in the County of York, for " A new and improved Creasing and Sleeking Machine for LEATHER WORK." Ottawa, dated 23rd March, 1867.

No. 2288—DUNNING, (*William Justus,*) of the Village of Demorestville, in the County of Prince Edward, for " A new and useful Suction and Force PUMP." Ottawa, dated 23rd March, 1867.

No. 2289—REYNOLDS, (*Lorenzo Dow,*) of the Town of St. Catharines, in the County of Lincoln, for " A new and useful Invention, called ' Reynolds' Renovating FLUID." Ottawa dated 27th March, 1867.

No. 2290—MEMBERY, (*Frederick,*) of the Township of Ernestown, in the County of Lennox and Addington, for " A new and useful Axle OILER, called 'The Expert Axle Oiler.' " Ottawa, dated 27th March, 1867.

No. 2291—HARVEY, (*Urson Adolphus,*) Assignee of Luther Dunn, of the Village of St. David's, in the County of Lincoln, for " A new and useful machine for the stretching of LEATHER to be used for Belting, and in Saddlery and Harness making." Ottawa, dated 23rd March, 1867.

No. 2292—HARVEY, (*Urson Adolphus*,) Assignee of Luther Dunn, of the Village of St. David's, in the County of Lincoln, for "A new and useful machine for the Edging, Cutting and marking of Leather Belting and other material." Ottawa, dated 23rd March, 1867.

No. 2293—PIPER, (*Edward Spencer*,) of the City of Toronto, in the County of York, for "A new and useful Ventilator and Smoke Conductor, called 'The improved Archimedean Ventilator and Smoke Conductor.'" Ottawa, dated 1st April, 1867.

No. 2294—COOK, (*Frederick*,) of the Village of Oil Springs, in the Township of Enniskillen, in the County of Lambton, for "A new and useful apparatus for burning, as fuel, Petroleum, or Fluids made from it." Ottawa, dated 1st April, 1867.

No. 2295—PRATT, (*Moses*) of the Town of Windsor, in the County of Essex, for "A Grain Separator." Ottawa, dated 1st April, 1867.

No. 2296—YIELDING, (*Richard*,) of the Town of Windsor, in the County of Essex, for "A new and useful Invention, called 'Richard Yielding's Apparatus for burning, as Fuel, Petroleum, and other kindred Fluids.'" Ottawa, dated 3rd April, 1867.

No. 2297—PATTERSON, (*Peter*), of the City of Toronto, in the County of York, for "A new and useful Concave Tire and Tire Coupling." Ottawa, dated 5th April, 1867.

No. 2298—KENNY, (*Israel*,) of the Town of Woodstock, in the County of Oxford, for "A new and useful Seat for Buggies and other Vehicles." Ottawa, dated 5th April, 1867.

No. 2299—WOOD, (*Melvin*,) of the Township of Yarmouth, in the County of Elgin, for "A new and useful Churn, called 'The Quakeress Churn.'" Ottawa, dated 10th April, 1867.

No. 2300—COPELAND, (*Joseph*,) of the Township of Yarmouth, in the County of Elgin for "A new and useful Farm Gate, known as 'The Copeland Gate.'" Ottawa, dated 10th April, 1867.

No. 2301—CLIFF, (*George*,) of the Town of Sarnia, in the County of Lambton, for "A new and useful Improved self-acting Hand Loom." Ottawa, dated 10th April, 1867.

No. 2302—DIMON, (*Henry Wood*,) of the Township of Charlotteville, in the County o' Norfolk, for "A self-acting Waggon and wheeled Vehicle Brake, called 'Dimon's Self-Acting Waggon Brake.'" Ottawa, dated 10th April, 1867.

No. 2303—ROBINSON, (*John Smith*,) of the City of London, in the County of Middlesex, for "A new and useful Composition of Matter which is an improved method of deodorizing Petroleum or Rock Oil." Ottawa, dated 10th April, 1867.

No. 2304—LUCAS, (*Robert Land*,) of the Township of Trafalgar, in the County of Halton for "A new and useful Farm and Railway Elevating Gate." Ottawa, dated 13th April 1867.

No. 2305—DUNCAN, (*John*,) of the Town of Port Dover, in the County of Norfolk, for "A new and useful and improved Hay Elevator." Ottawa, dated 13th April, 1867.

No. 2306—BAKER, (*Francis*,) of the Village of Kilbride, in the Township of Nelson, in the County of Halton, for "A new and useful Rotary and non-exhaust Steam Engine." Ottawa, dated 16th April, 1867.

No. 2307—McGARRY, (*James*,) of the Village of Drummondville, in the County of Lincoln, for "Certain new and useful improvements for Carburetting Air." Ottawa, dated 17th April, 1867.

No. 2308—WILKES, (*George Samuel*,) of the Town of Brantford, in the County of Brant for "A certain new and useful improvement in Mowing and Reaping Machines." Ottawa, dated 10th April, 1867.

No. 2309—BATCHELDER, (*Greenleaf W.*,) of the City of Montreal, for "A new and useful Hay Press." Ottawa, dated 2nd April, 1867.

No. 2310—WARREN, (*Samuel Russell*,) of the City of Montreal, for "An improved Organ Wind Chest Slide." Ottawa, dated 11th April, 1867.

No. 2311—MERRIAM, (*Charles Rolland*,) of the Town of Sherbrooke, for "A new and useful Tin Sap Spout." Ottawa, dated 11th April, 1867.

No. 2312—HOUSTON, (*John*,) of the Township of Barnston, in the County of Stanstead, for "A new and useful Rocking Churn." Ottawa, dated 16th April, 1867.

No. 2313—BROWN, (*George Augustus,*) of the Town of Belleville, in the County of Hastings, for "A new and useful Spring Reach CARRIAGE." Ottawa, dated 16th April, 1867.

No. 2314—AUBIN, (*Aimé Nicholas Napoléon,*) of Beloeil, in the County of Verchères, for "An apparatus for lighting Villages or Towns, by means of Air and Hydrocarburetted STEAM." Ottawa, dated 16th April, 1867.

No. 2315—TAYLOR, (*Homer,*) of the City of Montreal, for "A new and improved apparatus for generating heat by the Combustion of Crude Petroleum, Coal OIL, &c., &c." Ottawa, dated 16th April, 1867.

No. 2316—PIERCE, (*George Henry,*) of the Village of Richmond, in the County of Richmond, for "An improved Fire Proof Mastic CEMENT for Roofing, and for other purposes." Ottawa, dated 18th April, 1867.

No. 2317—VERNON, (*John M.,*) of the City of Montreal, for "A new and useful improved composition for COATING Wood, Cloth, Metals, Stone, Brick, making lining for Journal Boxes, Roofing, Pavements, Side Walks, &c., &c." Ottawa, dated 26th April, 1867.

No. 2318—HUGHES, (*Charles,*) of the City of Montreal, for "A Portable Self-Connecting Fence." Ottawa, dated 29th April, 1867.

No. 2319—UTLEY, (*Maurice Howell,*) of the City of Montreal, for "A new and Improved Vacuo Vacua Electro APPARATUS for the treatment and cure of Diseases." Ottawa, dated 29th April, 1867.

No. 2320—BUCHANAN, (*James Ray,*) of the Township of Colchester, In the County of Essex, for "A new and useful Well Sinker and Tubular WELL, known as 'Buchanan's Well Sinker and Tubular Well.'" Ottawa, dated 18th April, 1867.

No. 2321—THOMPSON, (*Robert,*) of the Township of Oro, in the County of Simcoe, for "A new and useful Log ELEVATOR." Ottawa, dated 23rd April, 1867.

No. 2322—RAYMOND, (*Jonathan B.,*) of the Township of Yarmouth, in the County of Elgin, for "A new and useful Metallic BELTING, called 'Raymond's Metallic Belting.'" Ottawa, dated 25th April, 1867.

No. 2323—BRUNTON, (*William Youngman,*) of the City of London, in the County of Middlesex, for "A new and useful Founders Facing or DUST." Ottawa, dated 25th April, 1867.

No. 2324—STEVENS, (*Samuel,*) of the Town of Belleville, in the County of Hastings, for "Certain new and useful improvements in Cheese VATS." Ottawa, dated 7th May, 1867.

No. 2325—SMITH, (*Robert,*) of the City of Toronto, in the County of York, for "Certain new and useful improvements in the construction of Amalgamating TABLES for separating Gold from pulverized Ore and in the apparatus connected therewith." Ottawa, dated 7th May, 1867.

No. 2326—FORFAR, (*Thomas,*) of the Township of East Flamboro', in the County of Wentworth, for "A new and useful CHURN, to be called 'The Dairy Churn." Ottawa, dated 7th May, 1867.

No. 2327—BARCLAY, (*Robert,*) of the Town of Paris, in the County of Brant, for "A certain new and useful Improvement in the construction of SEWING Machines." Ottawa, dated 7th May, 1867.

No. 2328—GLENDILLEN, (*William,*) of the Township of North Oxford, in the County of Oxford, for "A new and useful Spinning WHEEL." Ottawa, dated 7th May, 1867.

No. 2329—CHATTERTON, (*Richard Dover,*) of the Town of Cobourg, in the County of Northumberland, for "A new mode of Propelling Vessels by means of a Machine or Apparatus, which he has named 'Chatterton's Hydro Momentum PROPELLER.'" Ottawa, dated 7th May, 1867.

No. 2330—BRADLEY, (*William Harden,*) of the Township of Haldimand, in the County of Northumberland, for "A new and useful improved CULTIVATOR." Ottawa, dated 16th May, 1867.

No. 2331—JOHNSON, (*John,*) of the City of Toronto, in the County of York, for "A LAMP to be called 'The Cotton Packed Safety Lamp.'" Ottawa, dated 7th May, 1867.

No. 2332—BRUSH, (*George S.,*) of the City of Montreal, for "A Double Acting Steam PUMP." Ottawa, dated 9th May, 1867.

No. 2333—MUNGER, (*John Girty,*) of the Township of Colchester, in the County of Essex, for "An improved adjustable Friction Roller Farm GATE." Ottawa, dated 13th May, 1867.

No. 2334—HENWOOD, (*Reginald,*) of the Town of Brantford, in the County of Brant, for · ' A new and improved Sewer GUARD, called 'The Air-tight Sewer Guard.'" Ottawa, dated 13th May, 1867.

No. 2335—KENNEDY, (*Charles E.,*) of the Township of Hatley, in the District of St. Francis, for "A new and useful Sap HEATER." Ottawa, dated 9th May, 1867.

No. 2336—BERTRAND, (*Jean Baptiste,*) of the City of Quebec, for "A LEVER Apparatus for changing the position of the rabbet of doorways or other openings." Ottawa, dated 9th May, 1867.

No. 2337—COOK, (*Frederick,*) of the Village of Oil Springs, in the County of Lambton, for "A new and useful Improvement in Apparatus for burning Petroleum, and fluids made from it." Ottawa, dated 13th May, 1867.

No. 2338—HARDING, (*George,*) of the City of Toronto, in the County of York, for "Certain new and useful Improvements in TRAPS for Water Closets, or Slop Closets, especially adapted for use in Jails, Hospitals, Asylums and other Public Institutions." Ottawa, dated 13th May, 1867.

No. 2339—McINTYRE, (*John,*) of the Town of Windsor, in the County of Essex, for a "Lateral SAW, called ' McIntyre's Patent Lateral SAW.'" Ottawa, dated 13th May, 1867.

No. 2340—PATON, (*James B.,*) of the Township of Waterloo, for "A new and useful Knife and Scissors SHARPENER." Ottawa, dated 11th May, 1867.

No. 2341—STUART, (*William,*) of the Township of Osnabruck, in the County of Stormont, for "A new and useful Self-Cleaning Plough COULTER, called 'Stuart's Self-Cleaning Plough COULTER.'" Ottawa, dated 14th May, 1867.

No. 2342—FINDLAY, (*Robert,*) of the Town of Windsor, in the County of Essex, for "A new and useful Improved double Acting PUMP." Ottawa, dated 17th May, 1867.

No. 2343—LABOUGLIE, (*Louis,*) of Buckingham, in the County of Ottawa, for "An improvement in the Art of purifying ORES." Ottawa, dated 17th May, 1867.

No. 2344—MARKS, (*Joseph,*) of the City of Montreal, for "A new and useful Improved Compound Self-packing Balance Globe VALVE." Ottawa, dated 17th May, 1867.

No. 2345—WOOD, (*Henry,*) of the City of Montreal, for "A new and useful improvement in the manufacture of WHITE LEAD from Metallic Lead, Litharge and Ores of Lead." Ottawa, dated 27th May, 1867.

No. 2346—WOODWARD, (*Henry,*) of the City of Montreal, for "A new and useful improved apparatus for Carbureting Coal GAS." Ottawa, dated 4th June, 1867.

No. 2347—LEWIS, (*Richard,*) of Melbourne, in the County of Richmond, for "A new and useful Economical Gate HANGING." Ottawa, dated 8th June, 1867.

No. 2348—REECE, (*John,*) of the Township of Stanstead, for "An improved Pegging MACHINE." Ottawa, dated 14th June, 1867.

No. 2349—DALY, (*Joseph Henry,*) of the City of Montreal, "For the introduction of improvements in Railway WHEELS and TIRES, and in casting the same, and other articles requiring a hard surface, combined with strength and toughness." Ottawa, dated 14th June, 1867.

No. 2350—MUIR, (*William,*) of the City of Toronto, in the County of York, "For the introduction of Compounding or Combining Mineral COAL with Mineral OILS, PETROLEUM and other Hydro Carbon substances, or the residue thereof after distillation for producing an illuminating Gas by the process of Heat." Ottawa, dated 23rd May, 1867.

No. 2351—WAGNER, (*Alexander H.,*) of the Town of Windsor, in the County of Essex, for "Wagner's statutable outward opening Door for Churches and Public Buildings." Ottawa, dated 6th June, 1867.

No. 2352—GZOWSKI, (*Casimir Stanislaus,*) and MACPHERSON, (*David Lewis,*) (by Special Act, Cap. 162, 29th and 30th Vic.,) for "Certain improvements in treating certain Ores and

Alloys, and in obtaining METALS and other products therefrom." Ottawa, dated 23rd June, 1867.

No. 2353—GZOWSKI, (*Casimir Stanislaus,*) and MACPHERSON, (*David Lewis,*) (by Special Act, Cap. 162, 29th and 30th Vic ,) for "Certain improvements in treating certain Ores and Alloys, and in obtaining METALS and other products therefrom." Ottawa, dated 23rd June, 1867.

No. 2354—CHASE, (*James,*) of the Village of Brooklin, in the County of Ontario, for "A new, useful and Barrel Head TURNER." Ottawa, dated 6th June, 1867.

No. 2355—BIGELOW, (*Silas,*) of the Town of Lindsay, in the County of Victoria, for "A useful Water or Boat Wheel, called 'The Extension Pulley Water WHEEL.'" Ottawa, dated 17th May, 1867.

No. 2356—CLAY, (*William Thomas,*) of the Village of Thornhill, in the County of York, for "A new and useful machine, styled 'Clay's Canadian Bolt Feed for Grist and Merchant MILLS.'" Ottawa, dated 6th June, 1867.

No. 2357—CHASE, (*James,*) of the Village of Brooklin, in the County of Ontario, for "A new, useful and improved Shingle and Heading SAWING Machine." Ottawa, dated 6th June, 1867.

No. 2358—WILSON, (*John Midien,*) of the City of Ottawa, in the County of Carleton, for "A new and useful Repeating Suction and Force PUMP." Ottawa, dated 6th June, 1867.

No. 2359—HARTLEY, (*William,*) of the Village of Mount Forest, in the County of Wellington, for "Certain new and useful improvements in the Sawing MACHINE." Ottawa, dated 13th May, 1867.

No. 2360—ROBINSON, (*John S.,*) of the City of London, in the County of Middlesex, for "A new and useful improvement in the Improved Method of Deodorizing Petroleum or Rock OILS." Ottawa, dated 6th June, 1867.

No. 2361—McLENNAN, (*Alexander,*) of the Township of Lancaster, in the County of Glengarry, for "A new and useful Hay FORK, called 'The Javelin Hay Fork.'" Ottawa, dated 6th June, 1867.

No. 2362—HODGENS, (*Thomas Daniel,*) of the City of London, in the County of Middlesex, for "A new and useful 'Hodgens' improved fastening for thimble Skeins for WAGGONS.'" Ottawa, dated 6th June, 1867.

No. 2363—DOWD, (*Bernard Sproule,*) of the Village of Pakenham, in the County of Lanark, for "A new and useful Patent Loading WAGGON for facilitating loading hay, grain and articles in Bulk." Ottawa, dated 6th June, 1867.

No. 2364—MILNE, (*James,*) of Innisfil, in the County of Simcoe, for "A new and improved COUPLING for Railway Cars." Ottawa, dated 6th June, 1867.

No. 2365—WALKER, (*Levi,*) of the Village of Kincardine, in the County of Bruce, for "A new and useful Water POWER, which he calls 'Walker's Economical Water Power.'" Ottawa, dated 14th June, 1867.

No. 2366—CRYDERMAN, (*Ezra Benson,*) of the Town of Darlington, in the County of Durham, for "A new and useful invention for the purpose of extracting Honey from the Comb, to be called 'The Canadian Honey EXTRACTOR.'" Ottawa, dated 14th June, 1867.

No. 2367—BETHUNE, (*Donald,*) of the Town of Port Hope, in the County of Durham, for "A certain new and useful Machine or Apparatus by which Railway Brakes are made self-acting, called 'Bethune's Self-acting Railway BRAKE.'" Ottawa, dated 14th June, 1867.

No. 2368—HORNER, (*Michael,*) of the Township of Markham, in the County of York, for "A new and improved Self-Shutting GATE." Ottawa, dated 14th June, 1867.

No. 2369—STEVENS, (*Samuel,*) of the Town of Belleville, in the County of Hastings, for "A new and useful improvement in distilling PETROLEUM." Ottawa, dated 14th June, 1867.

No. 2370—WYNN, (*Henry,*) of the City of London, in the County of Middlesex, for "A new and useful Wynn's Fountain PEN." Ottawa, dated 14th June, 1867.

No. 2371—TAYLOR, (*Francis Daniel,*) of the City of Montreal, for "New and useful Improvements in machinery for crushing and pulverizing QUARTZ and other ore-bearing substances." Ottawa, dated 27th June, 1867.

No. 2372—DUTTON, (*Walter*,) of the Town of Ingersoll, in the County of Oxford, for "A new and useful method of Cutting and Crimping Boots and Shoes for Men, Women and Children, called 'The Dutton Boot.'" Ottawa, dated 24th June, 1867.

No. 2373—BISHOP, (*Thomas Barnes*,) of the City of Montreal, for "A vulcanized rubber heel CAP for boots and shoes." Ottawa, dated 27th June, 1867.

No. 2374—HORSKIN, (*Horatio*,) of Stanbridge, in the District of Bedford, for "A new and useful COUPLING for attaching Shafts to Vehicles." Ottawa, dated 27th June, 1867.

No. 2375—JULL, (*Orange*,) of the Village of Orangeville, in the County of Wellington, for "A Grain CLEANER." Ottawa, dated 6th June, 1867.

No. 2376—TAFT, (*Andrew B.*,) of the City of Montreal, for "A new and useful improvement in the Nicholson PAVEMENT." Ottawa, dated 15th June, 1867.

No. 2377—BISHOP, (*Thomas Barnes*,) of the City of Montreal, for "A new and useful India Rubber Cushion or Elastic Horse Shoe." Ottawa, dated 15th June, 1867.

No. 2378—HOSKINGS, (*Gilbert Marcus*,) of the City of London, in the County of Middlesex, for "A new and useful foot MORTICING Machine." Ottawa, dated 26th June, 1867.

No. 2379—HUNTLEY, (*Francis Stevens*.) of the City of Toronto, in the County of York, for "A new and useful Farm and Stock GATE." Ottawa, dated 26th June, 1867.

No. 2380—LOCKMAN, (*Christopher*,) of the City of Hamilton, in the County of Wentworth, for "A new and useful SEWING Machine." Ottawa, dated 27th June, 1867.

No. 2381—HILLMAN, (*Abimelech*,) of the Town of Stratford, in the County of Perth, for "A Self-acting Car COUPLER." Ottawa, dated 27th June, 1867.

No. 2382—HECTOR, (*Thomas*.) of the City of Ottawa, in the County of Carleton, for "A new and useful improved HOE." Ottawa, dated 28th July 1867.

No. 2383—POWELL, (*Charles*,) of the Village of Newton, in the County of York, for "Certain new and useful improvements to Pumps and Hose attachments to PUMPS." Ottawa, dated 28th June, 1867.

No. 2384—HIBBARD, (*Henry Nobles*,) of Point Abino, in the County of Welland, for "A new and useful tube-well called 'Hibbard's improved TUBE-WELL.'" Ottawa, dated 28th June, 1867.

No. 2385—WARNER, (*Joel Sylvester*,) of the Town of Prescott, in the County of Grenville, for "A new and useful composition by which House-Ashes and Pot-Ash may be converted into PEARL-ASH." Ottawa, dated 28th June, 1867.

No. 2386—CARNIE, (*John*,) of the Township of South Dumfries, in the County of Brant, for "A new and useful Hot Air FURNACE." Ottawa, dated 19th June, 1867.

No. 2387—McGILL, (*George W.*,) of the Village of Fort Erie, in the County of Welland, for "A new and useful Fastener for Paper, Parchment, Cloth, Leather, or other Fabrics, called 'McGill's Metallic FASTENER.'" Ottawa, dated 18th June, 1867.

No. 2388—DOBBIN, (*William Comstock*,) of the Village of Bridgeport, in the County of Waterloo, for "Certain new and useful improvements in the Machine called and known as "Dobbin's one-horse CULTIVATOR for turnips, corn, potatoes, and all crops required to be cultivated in Drills or Rows.'" Ottawa, dated 19th June, 1867.

No. 2389—EVANS, (*William C.*,) of the City of Kingston, in the County of Frontenac, for "A new and useful Mineral CEMENT." Ottawa, dated 19th June, 1867.

No. 2390—THOMAS, (*John B.*,) of the Township of Ernestown, in the County of Lennox and Addington, for "A new and useful Invention, called "The Metallic Hame FASTENING.'" Ottawa, dated 19th June, 1867.

No. 2391—AUSTIN, (*Grimmon*,) of the Town of Perth, in the County of Lanark, for "A new and useful Improvement in Cheese VATS." Ottawa, dated 24th June, 1867.

No. 2392—PARSON, (*William Jr.*,) of the City of Toronto, in the County of York, for "New and useful improvements in manufacturing GAS from spirits of Petroleum." Ottawa, dated 24th June, 1867.

No. 2393—BETHUNE, (*Donald*,) of the Town of Port Hope, in the County of Durham, for 'Bethune's Railway Train STOPPER.'" Ottawa, dated 24th June, 1867.

No. 2391—ROTTON, (Otto,) of the City of Kingston, in the County of Frontenac, for "New and useful Deodorizers, called 'The Safe DEODORIZERS." Ottawa, dated 25th June, 1867.

No. 2395—HUNTLEY, (Francis Stevens,) of the City of Toronto, in the County of York, for "A new and useful Portable Lamp Shade HOLDER." Ottawa, dated 26th June, 1867.

No. 2396—WHITE, (Solomon,) of the Town of Windsor, in the County of Essex, Assignee of Samuel H. Cain, of the same place, for "A new and improved motion for vertical SAW or method of giving an upright Saw (single or gangs,) the oscillating, reciprocating or whip saw or rocking motion." Ottawa, dated 28th June, 1867.

No. 2397—WHELPLEY, (James Davenport,) and STORER, (Jacob Jones,) by Special Act, 29 and 30 Vic., Cap. 163, for "A new and useful CRUSHER and Pulveriser, for reducing to powder, by a novel and improved method, metallic and mineral substances including fuel." Ottawa, dated 28th June, 1867.

No. 2398—WHELPLEY, (James Davenport,) and STORER, (Jacob Jones,) by Special Act, 29 and 30 Vic., Cap. 163, for "New and useful improvements in the application of pulverised fuel as a combustible for the generation of Heat and LIGHT." Ottawa, dated 28th June, 1867.

No. 2399—WHELPLEY, (James Davenport,) and STORER, (Jacob Jones,) by Special Act, 29 and 30 Vic., Cap. 163, for "A new and useful process for the treatment of Metallic ORES and fuel pulverized in a peculiar furnace and a subsequent operation in the reduction of metal thus treated." Ottawa, dated 28th June, 1867.

No. 2400—WHELPLEY, (James Davenport,) and STORER, (Jacob Jones,) by Special Act, 29 and 30 Vic., Cap. 163, for "A Spray WHEEL for melting down and precipitating dust and noxious gas from furnaces." Ottawa, dated 28th June, 1867.

No. 2401—OWEN, (William,) of the City of Toronto, in the County of York, for "A new and useful Reversible Rotary Steam ENGINE." Ottawa, dated 3rd January, 1868.

No. 2402—CURRIE, (Neil,) of the City of Toronto, and CURRIE, (James,) of the City of Toronto, and OWEN, (William,) of the same City of Toronto, for "A new and useful Steam INJECTOR for injecting water into Steam Boilers or Tanks, without the aid of Pumps ; for lift-and hoisting purposes ; for driving water wheels, and for supplying Reservoirs with water." Ottawa, dated 3rd January, 1868.

No. 2403—WILSON, (Alfred,) of the Village of Belle Ewart, in the County of Simcoe, for "A new and useful Self-acting Car COUPLER." Ottawa, dated 7th January, 1868.

No. 2404—WALES, (Henry Benedict,) of St. Andrews, in the County of Argenteuil, for "A new and useful drilling, planting, cultivating and Potato-Digging machine combined, called ' Wales' Combined Drilling, Planting, Cultivating and Potato-Digging MACHINES." Ottawa, dated 7th January, 1868.

No. 2405—McMICHAEL, (Lafayette D.,) of the Township of Townshend, in the County of Norfolk, for "A new and useful apparatus for the Carburetting and regulating the flow of GAS." Ottawa, dated 7th January, 1868.

No. 2406—GEROLAMY, (William Augustus,) of the Village of Tara, in the Township of Arran, in the County of Bruce, for "An improved Fanning-MILL." Ottawa, dated 7th January, 1868.

No. 2407—THOMPSON, (John,) of the Town of Woodstock, in the County of Oxford, for "Certain new and useful Improvements in the Gang PLOUGH." Ottawa, dated 8th January, 1868.

No. 2408—MARCH, (William W.,) of the Town of Lindsay, in the County of Victoria, for "A new and useful Improvement in HARVESTERS." Ottawa, dated 9th January, 1868.

No. 2409—ADAM, (John,) of the Town of Chatham, in the County of Kent, for "A new and useful improvement in the mechanism of Fanning MILLS, such improvement consisting in the peculiar arrangement of the Shaft and Pinions therein,—whereby the speed of the vibration of the shoe, screens and riddles is increased without the motion of the fans being at the same time increased." Ottawa, dated 9th January, 1868.

No. 2410—GEISS, (William,) of the Town of Paris, in the County of Brant, for "A new and useful Lever for Sewing Machines (for taking up the slack thread therein), called "The Positive take-up LEVER." Ottawa, dated 8th January, 1868.

No. 2111—JACKSON, (*Henry*,) of the Town of Chatham, in the County of Kent, for "A new and useful double Cooking STOVE." Ottawa, dated 9th January, 1868.

No. 2112—HARRIS, (*David*,) of the Town of Ingersoll, in the County of Oxford, for "A Curd DRYER." Ottawa, dated 10th January, 1868.

No. 2113—EVANS, (*Frank*,) of the Village of Orillia, in the County of Simcoe, for "A new and useful Trifoliate HINGE, opening both inwards and outwards." Ottawa, dated 10th January, 1868.

No. 2114—REYNOLDS, (*Patrick*,) of the Township of Sarnia, in the County of Lambton, for "A new and useful improved Horse RAKE." Ottawa, dated 10th January, 1868.

No. 2115—JOHNSON, (*Jacob Smith*,) of the Town of Picton, in the County of Prince Edward, for "A new and useful Hay and Manure FORK, called 'The Dominion Fork." Ottawa, dated 11th January, 1868.

No. 2116—CLEMENTS, (*William*,) of the Village of Newbury, in the County of Middlesex, for "A new and useful Veneer KNIFE." Ottawa, dated 11th January, 1868.

No. 2117—LENHARD, (*George*,) of the City of Toronto, in the County of York, for "A new and useful method of arranging springs for BEDS, Mattrasses, Seats of Sofas, Chairs and Ottomans." Ottawa, dated 13th January, 1868.

No. 2118—SMITH, (*Wesley*,) of the Town of Brantford, in the County of Brant, for "A new and useful composition for the tanning of Hides and SKINS." Ottawa, dated 13th January, 1868.

No. 2119—EASTMAN, (*Sandford Moore*,) of the Town of St. Mary's, in the County of Perth, for "A new and useful combined Foot STOVE and Lantern, called 'Eastman's Combined Foot Stove and Lantern." Ottawa, dated 13th January, 1868.

No. 2120—PIKE, (*John*,) Assignee of Thomas Orsen Spencer, of the City of Ottawa, in the County of Carleton, for "A new and useful Washing MACHINE." Ottawa, dated 14th January, 1868.

No. 2121—DEEN, (*Cyrus*,) of the Village of Port Robinson, in the County of Welland, for "A new and useful Force and Lift PUMP combined, to be called and known as 'Dean's Force and Lift Pump.'" Ottawa, dated 14th January, 1868.

No. 2122—ASH, (*George*,) of the Township of Brantford, in the County of Brant, for "Ash's Canadian Horse Grappling Fork." Ottawa, dated 14th January, 1868.

No. 2123—CLARK, (*Barnabas*,) of the Town of St. Catharines, in the County of Lincoln, for "A new, useful and improved Corn PLANTER." Ottawa, dated 14th January, 1868.

No. 2124—HUGHES, (*John Watson*,) of the Village of Schomberg, in the Township of King, in the County of York, for "Certain new and useful improvements in Foot WARMERS." Ottawa, dated 14th January, 1868.

No. 2125—VAUGHAN, (*Joseph John*,) of the City of Ottawa, in the County of Carleton, for "A new and useful Railroad Car COUPLING." Ottawa, dated 14th January, 1868.

No. 2126—MINOR, (*Uriah Wesley*,) of the Village of Port Colborne, in the County of Welland, for "A new and useful removeable Folding Clothes DRYER." Ottawa, dated 14th January, 1868.

No. 2127—MATER, (*Michael*,) of the Village of Chippewa, in the County of Welland, for "A new and useful Breech Loading Rifle and GUN." Ottawa, dated 15th January, 1868.

No. 2128—LAND, (*Andrew Gordon*,) of the Town of Brantford, in the County of Brant, for "A new and useful Elevator, to be known as 'A. G. Land's Hydraulic ELEVATOR." Ottawa, dated 15th January, 1868.

No. 2129—ROBINSON, (*William Aspley*,) of the City of Hamilton, in the County of Wentworth, for "A new and useful Valve Motion GRADUATOR." Ottawa, dated 16th January, 1868.

No. 2130—ELLERSHAUSEN, (*Francis*,) of the City of Montreal, for "Certain new and useful improvements in the manufacture of Cast Malleable IRON." Ottawa, dated 16th January, 1868.

No. 2131—ABEL, (*Thomas*,) of the City of Montreal, for "A new and useful Fly Wheel Copying PRESS." Ottawa, dated 20th January, 1868.

No. 2432—BETHUNE, (*Donald*,) of the Town of Fort Hope, in the County of Durham, for " A new and useful discovery, called ' Bethune's new and improved mode of working Railway BRAKES." Ottawa, dated 20th January, 1868.

No. 2433—LAMOUREUX, (*Damase*,) of the City of Montreal, for " A certain new and useful improvement in the manufacture of substances made from a mixture of Tar or Asphalte and Broken Stones and analogous substances, to be called ' The Concrete Tar COMPOSITION.' " Ottawa, dated 22nd January, 1868.

No. 2434—HOWARD, (*James*,) of the City of Hamilton, in the County of Wentworth, for " A new and useful Apparatus for applying Petroleum and other oils as FUEL, which he calls ' The Hydropyroleon.' " Ottawa, dated 22nd January, 1868.

No. 2435—ROBERTS, (*Matthew Lyman*,) of the Village of Smithville, in the County of Lincoln, for " A new and useful Hay and Straw ELEVATOR." Ottawa, dated 17th January, 1868.

No. 2436—EVES, (*James*,) of the City of Toronto, in the County of York, for " A new and useful Nectar Cream Mineral WATER." Ottawa, dated 17th January, 1868.

No. 2437—MURGATROYD, (*Thomas*,) of the Village of Smithville, in the County of Lincoln, for " A new and useful Carriage WHEEL." Ottawa, dated 17th January, 1868.

No. 2438—PIERCE, (*Henry*,) the of Village of Chippewa, in the County of Welland, for " A new and useful Steamer and Plate WARMER." Ottawa, dated 17th January, 1868.

No. 2439—KIRKUP, (*Lancelot*,) of the City of Montreal, in the District of Montreal, for " A certain new and useful Railway Spike and NAIL." Ottawa, dated 17th January, 1868.

No. 2440—COOK, (*Neil*,) of the Town of Prescott, in the County of Grenville, for " A new and useful Door and Gate SPRING." Ottawa, dated 17th January, 1868.

No. 2441—EADIE, (*George W.*,) of the City of Montreal, for " A new and useful improvement in SPADES." Ottawa, dated 17th January, 1868.

No. 2442—COOK, (*Solon Martin*,) of the Town of Brantford, in the County of Brant, for " A new and useful machine for the Sharpening of Horse SHOES." Ottawa, dated 17th January, 1868.

No. 2443—PEASE, (*Guy Carleton*,) of the City of Ottawa, in the County of Carleton, for " A new and useful GATE." Ottawa, dated 11th January, 1868.

No. 2444—ALEXANDER, (*Thomas*,) of the Village of Glenwilliams, in the County of Halton, for " A new and useful improvement in HARROWS." Ottawa, dated 15th January, 1868.

No. 2445—LEMON, (*Alfred James*,) of the Township of Beverly, in the County of Wentworth, for " A new and useful Potato DIGGER and Turnip Puller." Ottawa, dated 16th January, 1868.

No. 2446—LEEMING, (*Sarah Coates*,) of the City of Montreal, in the District of Montreal, the wife of John Leeming, of the same City of Montreal, for " The introduction of certain improvements in BRICK making Machines." Ottawa, dated 16th January, 1868.

No. 2447—DAMUDE, (*Jacob*,) of Fonthill, in the County of Welland, for " A new and improved GATE, to be called ' The New Dominion Gate.' " Ottawa, dated 17th January, 1868.

No. 2448—INCE, (*Thomas Henry*,) of the City of Toronto, in the County of York, for " The introduction of a new and useful apparatus for extinguishing fires, called ' L'Extincteur or Portable FIRE ENGINE.' " Ottawa, dated 18th January, 1868.

No. 2449—LARUE, (*François Alexandre Hubert*,) of the City of Quebec, and DUQUET, (*Cyrille*,) of the same City of Quebec, for " A new and useful PURIFIER of Magnetic Sand, (Purificateur du Sable Magnétique)." Ottawa, dated 20th January, 1868.

No. 2450—GARRETT, (*James*,) of the Township of Malahide, in the County of Elgin, for " A new and useful Manure and Hay Elevating Horse FORK." Ottawa, dated 20th January, 1868.

No. 2451—McMURRAY, (*James Saurin*,) of the City of Toronto, in the County of York, for "A certain new and useful method of Coupling Railway Cars, Carriages and Waggons by means of a Self-acting Coupler, and of uncoupling without the necessity of going in between the same, and to be called ' Murray's Improved Car COUPLER.' " Ottawa, dated 20th January, 1868.

No. 2452—WORTHEN, (*Sanborn*,) of Coaticook, in the Township of Barnston, in the County of Stanstead, for "Certain new and useful improvements in the Hand Loom." Ottawa, dated 20th January, 1868.

No. 2153—MURPHY, (John,) of the Township of Hinchinbrooke, in the County of Huntingdon, for "A new and useful Stove Polish, named 'The Liquid Lightning Stove Polish.'" Ottawa, dated 20th January, 1868.

No. 2154—WHITE, (Henry Augustus,) of the City of Hamilton, in the County of Wentworth, for "A new and useful article, called 'White's Magic Clothes Sprinkler.'" Ottawa, dated 22nd January, 1868.

No. 2155—AUBIN, (Aim Nicholas Napoleon,) of the City of Montreal, in the District of Montreal, for "A new and useful Portable Mill, for the Cutting, Grinding and Moulding of Peat." Ottawa, dated 22nd January, 1868.

No. 2156—TURNER, (William,) of the Town of Port Dover, in the County of Norfolk, for "A new and useful Hay Lifter." Ottawa, dated 22nd January, 1868.

No. 2157—MASON, (William,) of the Town of Windsor, in the County of Essex, for "A new and useful Erasive Liquid Soap." Ottawa, dated 22nd January, 1868.

No. 2158—CHOATE, (William B.,) of the Town of Galt, in the County of Waterloo, for "A new and useful Heat Radiator." Ottawa, dated 23rd January, 1868.

No. 2159—CAMPBELL, (Nathan,) of the Village of Brooklin, in the County of Ontario, for "A new and useful Clothes Dryer." Ottawa, dated 23rd January, 1868.

No. 2160—ROXBURGH, (James,) of the Township of Downie, in the County of Perth, for "A new and useful combined Hay Rake and Elevator." Ottawa, dated 23rd January, 1868.

No. 2161—CAMPBELL, (Nathan,) of Whitby, in the County of Ontario, Assignee of James Chase, of the Village of Brooklin, in the said County of Ontario, for "A new and useful Window Curtain Roller Fixture." Ottawa, dated 23rd January, 1868.

No. 2162—FAIRFIELD, (Henry Billings,) of the City of Toronto, in the County of York, for "A new and useful improvement in Churn Dashers." Ottawa, dated 25th January, 1868.

No. 2163—GROSS, (Ferdinand,) of the City of Montreal, in the District of Montreal, for "Certain useful improvements in Artificial Legs." Ottawa, dated 25th January, 1868.

No. 2164—MACQUISTEN, (Patrick,) of the City of Montreal, in the District of Montreal, for "A certain new and useful composition for footpaths, road-ways and cellar floors, called 'The Montreal Composition.'" Ottawa, dated 25th January, 1868.

No. 2165—COOK, (Frederick,) of the Town of Sarnia, in the County of Lambton, for "Certain new and useful improvements in the Art of vaporizing and burning Hydro-carbon Fluids as Fuel." Ottawa, dated 26th January, 1868.

No. 2166—FENNACY, (Albert R.,) of the Town of Windsor, in the County of Essex, for "A new and useful Steam Cooking apparatus." Ottawa, dated 27th January, 1868.

No. 2167—PATTISON, (Ambrose F.,) of the Township of Pelham, in the County of Welland, for "A new, useful and improved Horse Rake." Ottawa, dated 27th January, 1868.

No. 2168—LAPMAN, (Henry,) of the Township of East Oxford, in the County of Oxford, for "A new and useful Leather Creasing Machine." Ottawa, dated 28th January, 1868.

No. 2169——HEARLE, (William,) of the Village of Beamsville, in the Township of Clinton, in the County of Lincoln, for "A new and useful Heating Apparatus or Drum Stove." Ottawa, dated 28th January, 1868.

No. 2170—MUNGER, (John Girly,) of the Township of Colchester, in the County of Essex, for "A new and useful improvement on a Water Lifter, called 'Munger's Improved Water Lifter.'" Ottawa, dated 28th January, 1868.

No. 2171—INGLIS, (Joseph James,) of the Town of Brantford, in the County of Brant, for "A new and useful Churn, called 'The Highland Mary Churn.'" Ottawa, dated 28th January, 1868.

No. 2172—TAYLOR, (Francis Daniel,) of the City of Montreal, in the District of Montreal, for "A new and useful process for amalgamating Ores and desulphurizing the same, and also an apparatus or machinery for carrying out said process." Ottawa, dated 29th January, 1868.

No. 2173—KINNEY, (Israel,) of the Town of Woodstock, in the County of Oxford, for "A new and useful HARROW, to be known as 'The Ontario Harrow.'" Ottawa, dated 30th January, 1868.

No. 2174—ROBINSON, (*George King*,) of the Village of Kingsville, in the County of Essex, or "A certain improvement in the Stove, known as 'The Petroleum GAS STOVE.'" Ottawa, dated 31st January, 1868.

No. 2175—CARTER, (*Henry*,) of the Township of Malahide, in the County of Elgin, for "A new and useful Hay LIFTER." Ottawa, dated 3rd February, 1868.

No. 2176—CORNWALL, (*William*,) of the Village of Rockport, in the County of Leeds, for "A new and useful combined Wire and Picket FENCE." Ottawa, dated 3rd February, 1868.

No. 2177—COOK, (*Frederick*,) of the Town of Sarnia, in the County of Lambton, for "A new and useful art of vaporizing and burning Hydro Carbon Fluids as FUEL." Ottawa, dated 3rd February, 1868.

No. 2178—BOUGHNER, (*John Henry*,) of the Village of Beamsville, in the Township of Clinton, in the County of Lincoln, for "A new and useful Stove Drum HEATER." Ottawa, dated 3rd February, 1868.

No. 2179—COOK, (*Frederick*,) of the Town of Sarnia, in the County of Lambton, for "An improved art of vaporizing and burning Hydro Carbon Fluids as FUEL." Ottawa, dated 3rd February, 1868.

No. 2480—LEIGHTON, (*William*,) of the Town of Windsor, in the County of Essex, for "A new and improved method of manufacturing Steel Headed RAILS, the improved Rail being called 'Leighton's Steel Headed Rail.'" Ottawa, dated 4th February, 1868.

No. 2481—YEAGER, (*Henry*,) of the Town of Berlin, in the County of Waterloo, for "An improved Combination Water WHEEL, which he calls 'The Empire Water Wheel.'" Ottawa, dated 4th February, 1868.

No. 2482—McSHERRY, (*Andrew*,) of the Village of Erin, in the County of Wellington, for "Certain new and useful improvements in PLOUGHS." Ottawa, dated 4th February, 1868.

No. 2483—MITCHELL, (*Samuel Henry*,) of the Town of St. Mary's in the County of Perth, for "A new and useful combined HIVE and Bee House.'" Ottawa, dated 5th February, 1868.

No. 2484—LEDUC, (*Jean Baptiste*,) of the Parish of Ste. Cécile, in the County of Beauharnois, for "A combined Mop Self-wringer and Scrubbing Machine." Ottawa, dated 5th February, 1868.

No. 2485—JAMIESON, (*William Murray*,) of the City of Toronto, in the County of York, for "A new and useful BRICK Machine, called 'The Douglas improved Canada Brick Machine.'" Ottawa, dated 7th February, 1868.

No. 2486—DRUMMOND, (*Robert*,) of the Village of Meaford, in the Township of St. Vincent, in the County of Grey, and STEPHENS, (*Alexander Rolph*,) of the same Village of Meaford, for "A new and useful Spring Bed BOTTOM." Ottawa, dated 7th February, 1868.

No. 2487—WEIR, (*David Hughes*,) of the Township of West Nissouri, in the County of Middlesex, for "A new and useful description of Lamp BURNER, called 'The Dominion Illuminator and Gas Condensing Coal Oil Burner.'" Ottawa, dated 10th February, 1868.

No. 2488—CAMERON, (*James McAlpine*,) of the Township of Derby, in the County of Grey, for "A certain new and useful Machine, named 'Cameron's new motion Flax PULLER.'" Ottawa, dated 11th February, 1868.

No. 2489—HAMMOND, (*Thomas Munro*,) of the City of Montreal, in the District of Montreal, for "A new and useful Carbon or Charcoal Pipe." Quebec, dated 12th February, 1868.

No. 2490—PHELPS, (*Oscar Clark*,) of the Town of Sherbrooke, in the County of Compton, for "Certain improvements in the manufacture of Hoop Skirts, the skirt with the improvements in question to be called 'The Collapsing North Star SKIRT.'" Ottawa, dated 12th February, 1868.

No. 2491—KELLEY, (*William F.*,) of the Village of Thamesford, in the County of Oxford, for "A certain new and useful Composition for Black BOARDS." Ottawa, dated 12th February, 1868.

No. 2492—COWLING, (*Eben Landon*,) of the City of Montreal, in the District of Montreal, for "Certain new and useful improvements in the art of treating WOOD for its preservation by super-heated Steam in combination with various Chemicals." Ottawa, dated 12th February, 1868.

No. 2493—HAWLEY, (*Richard,*) of the Village of Park Hill, in the Township of West Williams, in the County of Middlesex, for "A new and useful Carriage Spring, to be called 'Hawley's Excelsior Buck Board Spring.'" Ottawa, dated 12th February, 1868.

No. 2494—MATHESON, (*Samuel,*) of the Township of East Zorra, in the County of Oxford, and CAISTER, (*Israel,*) of the same place, for "Certain new and useful improvements in the plans of constructing Harrows; the harrow, as improved, to be called 'The Excelsior Seed Grain Harrow.'" Ottawa, dated 12th February, 1868.

No. 2495—ROBINSON, (*Oscar George,*) of the Town of Bothwell, in the County of Kent, for "A new and useful medical compound for the cure of Ring Bone Spavin." Ottawa, dated 14th February, 1868.

No. 2496—HOLLIDAY, (*John,*) of the City of Quebec, in the District of Quebec, for "A new and useful Glaciarum." Ottawa, dated 14th February, 1868.

No. 2497—EHRHARDT, (*Louis Henry Gustavus,*) of the City of Montreal, in the District of Montreal, for "A new and useful explosive compound for Blasting and for other analogous objects." Ottawa, dated 17th February, 1868.

No. 2498—LENHARDT, (*George,*) of the City of Toronto, in the County of York, for "A new and useful method of fastening or securing Springs in mattrasses, beds, sofas, chairs and ottoman bottoms, and other articles to which such springs may be applied." Ottawa, dated 18th February, 1868.

No. 2499—TURNER, (*William,*) of the Town of Port Dover, in the County of Norfolk, for "A new and useful double leverage Hay and Farley Fork." Ottawa, dated 19th February, 1868.

No. 2500—MARENGO, (*Joseph,*) of the Parish of St. Athanase, in the County of Iberville, for "A new and useful mode of Decorative Painting, which he calls 'Calcomanie.'" Ottawa, dated 20th February, 1868.

No. 2501—JAMES, (*Christopher Retallick,*) of the City of Toronto, in the County of York, for "A new and useful improvement in the means of working Stamps and Hammers." Ottawa, dated 20th February, 1868.

No. 2502—McKAY, (*John,*) of the Town of Woodstock, in the County of Oxford, for "A new and useful Trace Buckle, to be called 'The improved Trace Buckle.'" Ottawa, dated 22nd February, 1868.

No. 2503—BEATY, (*George,*) of the Village of Beamsville, in the County of Lincoln, for "A new and useful Cast Metallic Boot and Shoe Heel.'" Ottawa, dated 28th February, 1868.

No. 2504—BEST, (*Joseph,*) of the Town of Brockville, in the County of Leeds, for "A new and useful Damper, which he calls 'Best's Patent Damper.'" Ottawa, dated 28th February, 1868.

No. 2505—COPE, (*Henry Culp,*) of the Township of Brantford, in the County of Brant, for "A new and useful Churn Dasher, called 'The Atmospheric Churn Dasher.'" Ottawa, dated 28th February, 1868.

No. 2506—IRWIN, (*Thomas,*) of the Town of Brockville, in the County of Leeds, for "A new and useful apparatus or machine for radiating hot air and economising fuel to be used in connection with an ordinary stove, the said apparatus to be known as 'The Dominion Hot Air and Radiating Fuel Economizer.'" Ottawa, dated 28th February, 1868.

No. 2507—ELLSWORTH, (*Eliza*) now of the Village of Ashburnham, in the County of Peterborough, widow of Oren Hamilton Ellsworth, late of the Village of Kincardine, in the County of Bruce, for "A certain new and useful machine, known as 'Ellsworth's Patent Lever Power or Endless inclined Plane.'" Ottawa, dated 28th February, 1869.

No. 2508—LEEMING, (*John,*) of the City of Montreal, for "The introduction of new and useful annular Ovens, known as 'Hoffman and Litch's annular Ovens for the continuous burning of Minerals, Lime, Bricks, Tiles, Salt, Glaze Stone Ware, Pottery and other things.'" Ottawa, dated 29th February, 1868.

No. 2509—EATON, (*Richard,*) of the City of Montreal, in the District of Montreal, for "Certain new and useful improvements in Stoves and Furnaces." Ottawa, dated 2nd March, 1868.

No. 2510—RUETTEL, (John,) of the Village of Kincardine, in the County of Bruce, for " A new and useful Hay PULLER." Ottawa, dated 4th March, 1868.

No. 2511—HAMLIN, (George Dalon,) of the Town of Dunnville, in the County of Haldimand, for "A certain new and useful improvement in FENCES, the Improved Fence to be called ' Hamlin's Moveable Braced FENCE.' " Ottawa, dated 3rd March, 1868.

No. 2512—MARENGO, (Alexander,) of the Parish of St. Athanase, in the County of Iberville, and MARENGO, (Joseph,) of the same Parish, for "A new and useful machine for cigar and cigarette making, called ' The Cigarette MAKER.' " Ottawa, dated 4th March, 1868.

No. 2513—FAINT, (John,) of the Village of Brooklin in the County of Ontario, for "A new and useful method of making and fastening STOVE-PIPES." Ottawa, dated 4th March, 1868.

No. 2514—SCOTT, (William,) of t e Town of Windsor, in the County of Essex, for "A new and useful Seat Spring, called ' William Scott's Improved Seat SPRING." Ottawa, dated 5th March, 1868.

No. 2515—ROBERTSON, (William,) of the City of Montreal, for "A new and useful combined Ladder and TABLE." Ottawa, dated 5th March, 1868.

No. 2516—PONTON, (Jean Baptiste,) of Marieville, in the County of Rouville, in the District of St. Hyacinthe, for " An improved Ferry BOAT (Betau Traversier)." Ottawa, dated 6th March, 1868.

No. 2517—SPARROW, (Thomas West,) of the Town of Galt, in the County of Waterloo, for " A new and useful Self-Adjusting Rain Water CONDUCTOR." Ottawa, dated 9th March, 1868.

No. 2518—MARKS, (Joseph,) of the City of Montreal, in the District of Montreal, for " A new and useful Grate BAR for Steam boiler and other Furnaces." Ottawa, dated 10th March, 1868.

No. 2519—WILLIAMS, (Joseph,) of the Township of Blenheim, in the County of Oxford, for "A new and useful Economizing HEATER for wood, coal, and other fuel, to be called ' Williams' Economizing Heater." Ottawa, dated 10th March, 1868.

No. 2520—SCHOFIELD, (Levi,) of the Township of Woolf Island, in the County of Frontenac, for" Certain new and useful improvements in LOOMS." Ottawa, dated 10th March, 1868.

No. 2521—MEAD, (Isaiah,) of the Town of Dundas, in the County of Wentworth, for " A machine for the manufacture of Ribbon PEGS." Ottawa, dated 11th March, 1868.

No. 2522—FICK, (Lewis Wesley,) of the Township of Houghton, in the County of Norfolk for "A new and useful Heat RADIATOR." Ottawa, dated 11th March, 1868.

No. 2523—CHOATE, (Zaccheus Burnham,) of the Township of Blanford, in the County of Wentworth, for "A new and useful BEDSTEAD for Invalids." Ottawa, dated 11th March, 1868.

No. 2524—METCALFE, (William,) of the Township, of Augusta, in the County of Grenville, for "A new and useful Window Stop or FASTENER, which he calls ' Metcalfe's Patent Sash Supporter and Fastener." Ottawa, dated 13th March, 1868.

No. 2525—PALMER, (Joseph,) of the City of Ottawa, in the County of Carleton, for " A new and useful method of manufacturing Heads for Elliptic SPRINGS, to be known as ' Palmer's new and improved method of manufacturing Heads for Elliptic Springs.' " Ottawa, dated 13th March, 1868.

No. 2526—HOWARD, (James,) of the City of Hamilton, in the County of Wentworth, for " A new and useful tri-colored Signal LAMP." Ottawa, dated 13th March, 1868.

No. 2527—INCE, (Thomas Henry,) of the City of Toronto, in the County of York, for " A new and useful REST for fire-arms." Ottawa, dated 13th March, 1868.

No. 2528—WARD, (Alexander Field,) of the Township of the Gore of Camden, in the County of Kent, for " A new and useful Steam Engine and Frame combined with improved Valve Gear for Cross-cutting LOGS." Ottawa, dated 13th March, 1868.

No. 2529—COPELAND, (Benjamin Gilbert,) of the City of Montreal, in the District of Montreal, for " A new and useful safety water-proof Blasting CARTRIDGE." Ottawa, dated 13th March, 1868.

2530—BURNEY, (*John Land*,) of the City of Toronto, in the County of York, for "A new and useful art or process for the Cooling and preserving of MILK." Ottawa, dated 13th March, 1868.

No. 2531—KINNEY, (*Cyrus*,) of Paris, in the County of Brant, for "A new and useful HARROW." Ottawa, dated 13th March, 1868.

No. 2532—BOISSONNAULT, (*Nicholas Ferdinand*,) of the City of Ottawa, for an Apparatus for Locking Printing Type in the Form, called "Le SERRE-FORME Boissonnault." Ottawa, dated 14th March, 1868.

No. 2533—WILSON, (*John William*,) of the Township of Williams, in the County of Middlesex, for "A new and useful FIELD-ROLLER." Ottawa, dated 14th March, 1868.

No. 2534—WILDER, (*Mathew Euphratus*,) of the Township of Onondaga, in the County of Brant for "A new and useful PAINT-OIL used in the grinding and mixing of paints." Ottawa, dated 16th March, 1868.

No. 2535—MICHAUD, (*Charles Edward*,) of the City of Ottawa, in the County of Carleton, for "A new Steam Turbine and Rotary Engine, called 'TURBINE-VAPEUR-MICHAUD.' Ottawa, dated 17th March, 1868.

No. 2536—RICHARDSON, (*William Riley*,) of the Town of Prescott, in the County of Grenville, for "A new and useful Washing Machine, called 'The Ladies FRIEND.'" Ottawa, dated 21st March, 1868.

No. 2537—SMITH, (*Richard*,) of the Town of Sherbrooke, in the County of Compton, in the District of St. Francis, for "A new and useful art for the manufacture of Seamless BOXES from paper pulp." Ottawa, dated 23rd March, 1868.

No. 2538—SHERMAN, (*Simeon*,) of Vankleek Hill, in the Township of Hawkesbury, in the County of Prescott, for "A new and useful apparatus for boring the hubs of wheels, called 'Sherman's HUBBORING apparatus,'" Ottawa, dated 23rd March, 1868.

No. 2539—LEWIS, (*Richard*,) of the Township of Melbourne, in the County of Richmond, for "A new and useful Swivel and Slide GATE." Ottawa, dated 23rd March, 1868.

No. 2540—HAMILTON, (*William*,) of the City of Toronto, in the County of York, and HAMILTON, (*William*,) the younger, of the same place, for "A new and useful improvement in the Manufacture of Railway Crossing POINTS." Ottawa, dated 23rd March, 1868.

No. 2541—ROW, (*Michael Horton*,) of the Village of Kentville, in the County of Grenville, for "New and useful over-action extension arm for the spindle-head of Spinning Machines to be called 'The Conqueror Spindle-Head Extension ARM." Ottawa, dated 23rd March, 1868.

No. 2542—McLAREN, (*John Cummings*,) of the City of Montreal, in the District of Montreal, for "A new and useful Belt Splice Point FINISHER." Ottawa, dated 27th March, 1868.

No. 2543—HINTON, (*George Henry*,) of the City of Montreal, in the District of Montreal, and STEVENS, (*Darwin*,) of the same place, for "A new and useful FURNACE and apparatus for simultaneously tempering and straightening saws and steel plates." Ottawa, dated 27th March, 1868.

No. 2544—HENRY, (*James*,) of the Town of Collingwood, in the County of Simcoe, for "A certain new and useful improvement in Paper NECK-TIES." Ottawa, dated 27th March, 1868.

No. 2545—PERRY, (*Samuel*,) in the City of Montreal, in the District of Montreal, for "A new and useful Hydro-Carbon BURNER and Gas Generator for creating heat and steam; also, for generating permanent illuminating Gas." Ottawa, dated 30th March, 1868.

No. 2546—BARKER, (*Jacob*,) of the Township of Windham, in the County of Norfolk, for "A new and useful Rack SEPARATOR for the thrashing of Corn." Ottawa, dated 30th March, 1868.

No. 2547—OAKLEY, (*Frederick*,) of the City of Toronto, in the County of York, for "A new and useful machine for cooling and sweetening milk and for cooling beer, called 'Oakley's Mechanical cooler and DEODORIZER." Ottawa, dated 30th March, 1868.

No. 2548—PIERCE, (*George Henry*,) of the Village of Richmond, in the Township of Cleveland, in the District of St. Francis, for "Certain new and useful improvements in VENEERING when applied to Walls, Floors, Lamp shades, Window shades and other analogous substances." Ottawa, dated 30th March, 1868.

122

No. 2549—MUDGE, (*Ashel Hurlburt,*) of the Township of Blenheim, in the County of Oxford, for "A new and useful Spring BRACE for Spring Waggons, Buggies and other Carriages." Ottawa, dated 30th March, 1868.

No. 2550—BARCLAY, (*Robert,*) of Paris, in the County of Brant, for "A certain new and useful improvement in the construction of Sewing MACHINES." Ottawa, dated 1st April, 1868.

No. 2551—LAMOUREUX, (*Damase,*) of the City of Montreal, in the District of Montreal, for "A new and useful Curb for Pavements, to be known as 'The Canada Pavement CURB.'" Ottawa, dated 1st April, 1868.

No. 2552—ANDERSON, (*Charles F.,*) of the Village of Stanstead, in the County of Stanstead, for "A certain new and useful improvement in Spring Bed BOTTOMS." Ottawa, dated 1st April, 1868.

No. 2553—PEART, (*Jacob*) of the Township of Nelson, in the County of Halton, for "A new and useful application to the Land Wheel of Marr's Patent Plough HOLDER." Ottawa, dated 1st April, 1868.

No. 2554—LAMBERT, (*Richard,*) of the Township of Bayham, in the County of Elgin, for "A new and useful machine for making a continuous roping (in place of the short pieces made by the machines now in use,) to be used with the ordinary Wool Carding Machine, to be called 'Lambert's Improvement in the Domestic Wool Carding MACHINE.'" Ottawa, dated 2nd April, 1868.

No. 2555—JAY, (*Pierre Eymard,*) of the City of Montreal, in the District of Montreal, for "A new and useful Machine, which he calls 'Appareil SUCON.'" Ottawa, dated 3rd April, 1868.

No. 2556—DOBSON, (*Isaac,*) of the Town of Goderich, in the County of Huron, for "A new and useful BROOM, to be known as 'Isaac Dobson's turned and Banded Broom.'" Ottawa, dated 1st April, 1868.

No. 2557—SHUPE, (*Isaac,*) of the Township of Waterloo, in the County of Waterloo, for "A certain new and useful improvement in the construction of Waggon BRAKES." Ottawa, dated 3rd April, 1868.

No. 2558—FINIGAN, (*Thomas Dunham,*) of the City of Quebec, in the District of Quebec, for "A new and useful Rotary Steam ENGINE, called 'The Improved Rotary Steam Engine.'" Ottawa, dated 6th April, 1868.

No. 2559—TUBBS, (*Joseph Shepherd,*) of the Township of Cramahe, in the County of Northumberland, for "A new and useful combined Drill Seed Sower and CULTIVATOR." Ottawa, dated 6th April, 1868.

No. 2560—CLARKE, (*James Paton,*) of the Village of Yorkville, in the County of York, for "A new and useful Machine, which he calls 'The Domestic Saw MILL.'" Ottawa, dated 8th April, 1868.

No. 2561—WALTERS, (*Henry Thomas,*) of the City of Ottawa, in the County of Carleton, for "A new and useful FORGING Machine." Ottawa, dated 8th April, 1868.

No. 2562—TAYLOR, (*Homer,*) of the City of Montreal, in the District of Montreal, and EATON, (*Richard,*) of the same City of Montreal, for "A new and useful apparatus for the economically utilizing Petroleum and other Hydro Carbon substances in the generation and combustion of the GASES contained therein." Ottawa, 15th April, 1868.

No. 2563—ALGUIRE, (*Sterling,*) of the Township of Yonge, in the County of Leeds, for "A new and useful machine, which he calls 'Alguire's Improved Patent Milk AGITATOR.'" Ottawa, dated 15th April, 1868.

No. 2564—GROOM, (*George,*) of the City of Toronto, in the County of York, for "A new and useful CHURN." Ottawa, dated 15th April, 1868.

No. 2565—CHADWICK, (*Benjamin Brock,*) of the City of Hamilton, in the County of Wentworth, Assignee of Lewis Baxter, of the Village of Ridgeway, in the County of Welland, for "A new and useful Petroleum Gas FURNACE." Ottawa, dated 15th April, 1868.

No. 2566—BLAKE, (*George,*) of the Town of Whitby, in the County of Ontario, for "A new and useful oscillating RAKE to be used in connection with Reaping Machines." Ottawa, dated 15th April, 1868.

No. 2567—MUNGER, (*John Girty,*) of the Township of Colchester, in the County of Essex, and MUNGER, (*Theodore,*) of the same Township of Colchester, for " A new and useful GATE, to be called 'Munger's Automatic Gate.' " Ottawa, dated 15th April, 1868.

No. 2568—WILSON, (*Alfred,*) of the Village of Bell Ewart, in the Township of Innisfil, in the County of Simcoe, for " Certain improvements in the construction of Iron CASKS." Ottawa, 15th April, 1868.

No. 2569—POWELL, (*Joseph Francis,*) of the City of Montreal, in the District of Montreal, for " A new and useful machine for the making of BRICKS." Ottawa, dated 15th April, 1868.

No. 2570—YOCOM, (*John,*) of the Village of Dunville, in the County of Haldimand, for " A new and useful Draining PLOUGH." Ottawa, dated 16th April, 1868.

No. 2571—DICKHOUT, (*Richard,*) of the Village of Salford, in the County of Oxford, for " A new and useful Machine, known as 'The New Dominion CHURN and Packing Machine.' " Ottawa, dated 16th April, 1868.

No. 2572—ABELL, (*John,*) of the Village of Woodbridge, in the County of York, for " A new and useful Jointed RAKE for Reaping Machines." Ottawa, dated 16th April, 1868.

No. 2573—CHESTERMAN, (*Edwin,*) of the City of Montreal, in the District of Montreal, for " Certain new and useful improvements in BOOTS, Shoes, Overalls and other things by providing suitable ventilation, and at the same time retaining more perfectly the natural warmth of the feet." Ottawa, dated 16th March, 1868.

No. 2574—SMITH, (*Schuyler,*) of the Township of Stanstead, in the County of Stanstead, in the District of St. Francis, for " A new and useful Hames FASTENER." Ottawa, dated 17th April, 1868.

No. 2575—MANNING, (*Thomas,*) of the Village of Strathroy, in the County of Middlesex, for " A new and useful Boot and SHOE-TIP with protecting edge." Ottawa, dated 16th April, 1868.

No. 2576—O'DELL, (*Abiel,*) of the Town of Port Hope, in the County of Durham, for " A new and useful Clothes WRINGER, called ' O'Dell's Royal Canadian Clothes Wringer.' " Ottawa, dated 17th April, 1868.

No. 2577—EVANS, (*John Henry,*) and PULLAN, (*William Gibbon,*) of the City of Montreal, Assignees of Amédée Fontaine, of the same place, for " Certain new and useful improvements in the machinery for manufacturing PINS." Ottawa, dated 17th April, 1868.

No. 2578—RICHARDS, (*Leonard Moir,*) of the Township of Glanford, in the County of Wentworth, for " A new and useful Apparatus for lifting and depositing HAY, STRAW and other substances, which he calls 'The Canadian Giant.' " Ottawa, dated 17th April, 1868.

No. 2579—DERY, (*Louis,*) of the City of Quebec, in the District of Quebec, for " A new and useful BOLT or fastening, for the French Window (Targette de chassis à mortaise à battant à côte.") Ottawa, dated 18th April, 1868.

No. 2580—OSTROM, (*Henry Wellington,*) of the Town of Belleville, in the County of Hastings, for " A new and useful subsoil PLOUGH and attachment, called ' Ostrom's Subsoil Plough and attachment.' " Ottawa, dated 21st April, 1868.

No. 2581—STEVENS, (*Samuel,*) of the Town of Belleville, in the County of Hastings, for " Certain new and useful improvements in Horse HAY-FORKS." Ottawa, dated 22nd April, 1868.

No. 2582—WALKER, (*James,*) of the Township of Whitby, in the County of Ontario, for " Certain new and useful improvements in the PLOUGH, the Plough with such improvements added to be denominated ' Walker's New Dominion General Purpose Plough.' " Ottawa, dated 22nd April, 1868.

No 2583—JACKSON, (*Walter,*) of the Town of St. Mary's, in the County of Perth, for " A new and useful Eave TROUGH, to be called and known as 'The Groove Seam Eave Trough.' " Ottawa, dated 23rd April, 1868.

No. 2584—LESSER, (*Mona,*) of the City of Montreal, in the County of Hochelaga, for " A new and useful article of women's wearing apparel, to wit, ' an appendage to the SKIRT.' " Ottawa, dated 23rd April, 1868.

No. 2585—McKELCAN, (*Frederick Payne,*) of the City of Montreal, in the County of Hoche-

16

laga, for "A new and useful STOVE, called 'The Ultimatum Stove.'" Ottawa, dated 23rd April, 1868.

No. 2586—SENN, (*Mark Anthony,*) of the Township of South Cayuga, in the County of Haldimand, and HAGNEY, (*Cornelius,*) of the same Township of South Cayuga, for "A new and useful CHURN, called 'The Ontario Queen Churn.'" Ottawa, dated 25th April, 1868.

No. 2587—THOMPSON, (*Alexander,*) of the Township of Wawanosh, in the County of Huron, for "A new and useful Steam Rock DRILL and stone dressing Machine." Ottawa, dated 30th April, 1868.

No 2588—HAMILTON, (*William,*) of the City of Toronto, in the County of York, and HAMILTON, (*William, Jr.,*) of the same City of Toronto, for "A new and useful Machine for pressing Plug TOBACCO." Ottawa, dated 2nd May, 1868.

No. 2589—GOING, (*Henry,*) of Wolfe Island, in the County of Frontenac, for "A new and useful combined Mowing and Reaping MACHINE." Ottawa, dated 2nd May, 1868.

No. 2590—WEAGANT, (*Henry Ludwick,*) of the Village of Morrisburgh, in the County of Dundas, for "A new and useful machine for cutting SLATS, called 'The Slat Cutter.'" Ottawa, dated 2nd May, 1868.

No. 2591—HEALY, (*Jesse Martin,*) of the City of Ottawa, in the County of Carleton, for "Certain new and useful improvements in the Spokes and Hubs of WHEELS." Ottawa, dated 2nd May, 1868.

No. 2592—REID, (*Robert Gerald,*) of the Township of Walsingham, in the County of Norfolk, for "A new and useful Washing MACHINE, named 'The Dominion Steam Washing Machine.'" Ottawa, dated 5th May, 1868.

No. 2593—ROCHFORD, (*George Benjamin,*) of the Town of Bowmanville, in the County of Durham, for "A new and useful Self-Heating Smoothing IRON, called 'Rochford's Self-heating Smoothing Iron.'" Ottawa, dated 6th May, 1868.

No. 2594—GOODALL, (*Charles,*) of the City of Toronto, in the County of York, for "A new and useful Inclined Groove Stove Pipe FASTENER." Ottawa, dated 6th May, 1868.

No. 2595—RELYEA, (*George Van Nest,*) of the Town of Belleville, in the County of Hastings, for "A new and useful TRUSS for Hernia, to be known as 'The Relyea Truss.'" Ottawa, dated 7th May, 1868.

No. 2596—CORNWALL, (*Joshua Starr,*) of the Township of Beverly, in the County of Wentworth, for "A new and useful Water ELEVATOR." Ottawa, dated 11th May, 1868.

No. 2597—STEPHENSON, (*William,*) of the Village of Knatchbull, in the County of Halton, for "A new and useful Wrought Iron Plough SHARE." Ottawa, dated 11th May, 1868.

No. 2598—LAKE, (*Isaac Spencer,*) of the Village of Hullsville, in the County of Haldimand, for "A new and useful GATE, to be called 'The Dominion Gate.'" Ottawa, dated 11th May, 1868.

No. 2599—WALTON, (*Charles,*) of the Township of Haldimand, in the County of Northumberland, for "New and useful improvements in the Farming Implement called 'The CULTIVATOR.'" Ottawa, dated 22nd May, 1868.

No. 2600—CLARK, (*William Warner,*) of the Town of Ingersoll, in the County of Oxford, for for "A new and useful composition of matter for Washing purposes, called 'Clarke's Excelsior WASHING COMPOSITION.'" Ottawa, dated 13th May, 1868.

No. 2601—FARLEY, (*John Sidney,*) of the Township of Sidney, in the County of Hastings, for "A new and useful FORK, called 'The Sidney Barley Fork.'" Ottawa, dated 13th May, 1868.

No. 2602—GLENDILLON, (*Elijah,*) of the Township of North Dorchester, in the County of Middlesex, for "A certain new and useful improvement in Spinning WHEELS, the Wheel with such improvement to be called 'The King of the Dominion Spinning Wheel.'" Ottawa, dated 14th May, 1868.

No. 2603—PIKE, (*John,*) of the City of Toronto, in the County of York, for "A new and useful CHURN." Ottawa, dated 18th May, 1868.

No. 2604—BADGEROW, (*Abraham,*) of the Township of Scott, in the County of Ontario, for "Certain new and useful improvements on the ordinary Lever or Log PUMP, the Pump with such improvements added to be called and known as ' The Revolving Crank Pump.' " Ottawa, dated 22nd May, 1868.

No. 2605—HILLMAN, (*Abimelech,*) of the Town of Stratford, in the County of Perth, for " A new and useful Self-Acting Machine or Apparatus for coupling together Railway Cars or Carriages." Ottawa, dated 22nd May, 1868.

No. 2606—CAMERON, (*Donald,*) of the Township of Ramsay, in the County of Lanark, for "Certain new and useful Improvements in an Agricultural Machine or Implement, to wit: the HARROW." Ottawa, dated 23rd May, 1868.

No. 2607—SHAFER, (*Oscar Frederick,*) of the Village of Thamesford, in the County of Oxford, for "A new and useful Machine, to wit: An Abdominal and uterine SUPPORTER." Ottawa, dated 25th May, 1868.

No. 2608—WATEROUS, (*Charles Horatio,*) of the Town of Brantford, in the County of Brant, for "A new and useful machine for Sawing Logs and Cants into Lumber." Ottawa, dated 26th May, 1868.

No. 2609 –SCOTT, (*Jacob,*) of the Village of Richmond, in the Township of Cleveland, in the District of St. Francis, for "Certain new and useful improvements in the ' Force Pump,' the Pump with such improvements being also adapted for use in connection with Fire Engines." Ottawa, dated 27th May, 1868.

No. 2610—FOLEY, (*James,*) of the City of Montreal, for "A new and useful Composition of matter obtained from Rice plant and other substances for the manufacture of Paper and Paper Stock." Ottawa, dated 27th May, 1868.

No. 2611—PONTON, (*Jean Baptiste,*) of Marieville, in the County of Rouville, for "A new and useful Thermometer Fire ALARM." Ottawa, dated 27th May, 1868.

No. 2612—MANNY, (*Eugene,*) of the Town of Beauharnois, in the District of Beauharnois, for "Certain new and useful improvements in those portions of the Steam Engines known as the ' Slide VALVES.' " Ottawa, dated 27th May, 1868.

No. 2613—BEEMER, (*William,*) of the Town of Brantford, in the County of Brant, for "Certain new and useful improvements in the Wick-burning Oil LAMP." Ottawa, dated 29th May, 1868.

No. 2614—FOLEY, (*James,*) of the City of Montreal, in the District of Montreal, for "A new and useful machine for the manufacture of the EXTRACT from Hemlock, Oak and other Barks for tanning purposes, and as a mordant for Printers and Dyers' use." Ottawa, dated 30th May, 1868.

No. 2615—WHITMER, (*David Wanner,*) of the Township of Blenheim, in the County of Oxford, for " A new and useful machine, namely: A combined Rotary PRESS and Mill for Cider or other Sap." Ottawa, dated 30th May, 1868.

No. 2616—LEGGO, (*William,*) of the City of Montreal, in the District of Montreal, for "Certain new and useful improvements in a certain machine or apparatus, called ' The Backing PAN,' used in the process of Electrotyping." Ottawa, dated 2nd June, 1868.

No. 2617—CHATTERTON, (*Richard Dover,*) of the Town of Cobourg, in the County of Northumberland, for " A new and useful Machine for removing snow from Railways, Highways and other roads, called ' Chatterton's Snow CLEARER.' " Ottawa, dated 4th June, 1868.

No. 2618—WATERHOUSE, (*George Washington,*) of the Village of Fort Erie, in the County of Welland, for "A new and useful machine or apparatus for making of GAS from Petroleum." Ottawa, dated 4th June, 1868.

No. 2619—NICHOL, (*James,*) of the Township of Nelson, in the County of Halton, for " A new and useful Machine or apparatus for cleaning the Boilers of Steam ENGINES." Ottawa, dated 30th May, 1868.

No. 2620—ANDERSON, (*Robert,*) of the City of Toronto, in the County of York, for " A new and useful machine or apparatus, for the coupling of the fore and hind parts of carriages, intended to supersede what is sometimes called the ' Fifth Wheel ' thereof, and the king bolt, to be called and known as ' Anderson's Safety COUPLING.' " Ottawa, dated 4th June, 1868.

No. 2621—MILLS, (*Mortimer Birdsell,*) of the Village of Sparta, in the County of Essex, for

"A new and useful machine for stitching Harness, to be called 'Mills' Improved Stitching Horse.'" Ottawa, dated 13th June, 1868.

No. 2622—LECKIE, (*Robert,*) of Acton Vale, in the County of Bagot, for "A new and useful machine or apparatus used for producing Illuminating Gas from Crude Petroleum or other similar substances." Ottawa, dated 4th June, 1868.

No. 2623—GRANT, (*Robert Walker,*) of the Town of Brockville, in the County of Leeds, for "A new and useful article of manufacture, that is to say, a box for holding Cheese, named 'Grant's Paper Cheese Box.'" Ottawa, dated 4th June, 1868.

No. 2624—BULMER, (*Henry.*) of the City of Montreal, in the District of Montreal, in the Province of Quebec, one of the Provinces of Canada, and SHEPPARD, (*Charles,*) of the same City of Montreal, for "A certain new and useful machine, that is to say, an Automatic Machine for the Making of Bricks." Ottawa, dated 4th June, 1868.

No. 2625—COLBURN, (*Justin L.,*) of the Township of Magog, in the County of Stanstead, for "A new and useful Machine, for the more readily and effectually working, washing and salting Butter." Ottawa, dated 5th June, 1868.

No. 2626—BIGELOW, (*Albert,*) of the City of Hamilton, in the County of Wentworth, for "A new and useful Machine or Apparatus, namely, a Joint and Coupling for the Driving Shaft of Machinery, which he calls 'Bigelow's Universal Joint and Coupling.'" Ottawa, dated 5th June, 1868.

No. 2627—MILLER (*James,*) of the Township of Kincardine, in the County of Bruce, for "Certain new and useful improvements in Gates, and which he calls 'Miller's Improved Farm Gate.'" Ottawa, dated 5th June, 1868.

No. 2628—WOODWARD, (*Henry,*) of the City of Montreal, in the District of Montreal, for "A new and useful machine for cleaning Knives." Ottawa, dated 8th June, 1868.

No. 2629—ANDERSON, (*Alexander,*) of the City of London, in the County of Middlesex, for "A new and useful Machine or Apparatus, namely, a Joint for connecting or coupling together the links of Stove Pipes, and also the several portions of conducting pipes, to be called 'Anderson's Patent Stove Pipe Coupling.'" Ottawa, dated 13th June, 1868.

No. 2630—CLINE, (*Horace,*) of the Township of Trafalgar, in the County of Halton, for "A new and useful machine for Thrashing and Cleaning Peas, to be called 'The Pea Thrasher and Separator.'" Ottawa, dated 13th June, 1868.

No. 2631—DONAVAN, (*William,*) of the Township of Lochiel, in the County of Glengarry, for "A new and useful Gate, to be called 'The Glengarry Gate.'" Ottawa, dated 13th June, 1868.

No. 2632—WING, (*Francis Bond Head,*) of the Township of Blenheim, in the County of Oxford, for "A new and useful article of manufacture, the same being 'a Female periodical Bandage.'" Ottawa, dated 13th June, 1868.

No. 2633—BURBANK, (*James Bontell,*) of the Village of Danville, in the District of St. Francis, for "Certain new and useful improvements in the article of manufacture from India Rubber, (commonly called a 'Weather Strip') applied to doors and also to the windows of Houses and railway coaches, for the purpose of excluding the weather and dust." Ottawa, dated 18th June, 1868.

No. 2634—BELL, (*Cyrus Sumner,*) of the Town of Chatham, in the County of Kent, for "A new and useful machine or apparatus for the double purpose of boring and morticing wood, to be called 'The Combined Boring and Morticing Machine.'" Ottawa, dated 18th June, 1868.

No. 2635—NORTON, (*John,*) of the Township of Yarmouth, in the County of Elgin, for "A new and useful machine or Apparatus for sawing and boring timber, called 'Norton's Sawing and Boring Machine.'" Ottawa, dated 18th June, 1868.

No. 2636—DAYFOOT, (*John Bullock,*) of the Village of Georgetown, in the County of Halton, for "A new and useful Stove for the purpose of Buring spent Tan Bark." Ottawa, dated 5th June, 1868.

No. 2637—VASBINDER, (*Samuel,*) of the Township of South Cayuga, in the County of Haldimand, Assignee of Mahlon Doan, of the same place, for "A certain new and useful improvement on a certain machine for extracting Stumps for which machine Letters Patent of Invention were issued to one Eugene Cooper, bearing date on the 22nd of October, 1860. Ottawa, dated 12th June, 1868.

No. 2638—CASWELL, (Asa,) of the Village of Aylmer, in the County of Elgin, and McGEOCH, (John,) of the same place, for " A new and useful machine for forming Metal Eave TROUGHS." Ottawa, dated 13th June, 1868.

No. 2639—HEWKEY, (John,) of the Village of Park Hill, in the County of Middlesex, for "A certain new and useful improvement in Carriage SPRINGS, the improved Spring to be called 'Hawkey's Semi-circular Carriage Spring.'" Ottawa, dated 13th June, 1868.

No. 2640—DEWE, (John,) and HARDING, (George,) Assignees of Bartholomew Lalor, all of the City of Toronto, in the County of York, for " A new and useful PADLOCK, to be called and known as 'The Detector Lock.'" Ottawa, dated 19th June, 1868.

No. 2641—KLINGENMEIER, (John Mathias,) of the Town of St. Catharines, in the County of Lincoln, for " A new and useful article of manufacture, the same being a Kneading TROUGH or Table and Cabinet for the Storage of flour, food and other domestic articles, and which is called 'Klingenmeier's House Keeper Safe or Kitchen Cabinet.'" Ottawa, dated 19th June, 1868.

No. 2642—MARENGO, (Joseph,) of the Parish of St. Athanase, in the County of Iberville, for " A certain new and useful machine or apparatus intended to diminish the usual friction between the axles and boxes in the hubs of wheels in wheeled vehicles, and between shafts and their Journals in MACHINERY." Ottawa, dated 15th June, 1868.

No. 2643—HUFFMAN, (George,) of the Township of Bertie, in the County of Welland, for " A new and useful Machine or Apparatus for binding Hay and Straw, the same being intended to be used in connection with the Elevating Hay Forks now in use, and which is called 'Huffman's Hay and Straw BINDER.'" Ottawa, dated 20th June, 1868.

No. 2644—HIGHET, (Robert,) of the Town of Cobourg, in the County of Northumberland, for "Certain new and useful improvements in the manufacture of Wheeled VEHICLES." Ottawa, dated 20th June, 1868.

No. 2645—GIBSON, (Alexander,) of the Township of Barford, in the County of Kent, for "A new and useful Machine for dressing or putting the necessary face on Mill Stones, to be known as 'Gibson's Improved Mill Stone DRESSER.'" Ottawa, dated 20th June, 1868.

No. 2646—WESTLICK, (John,) of the Township of Hope, in the County of Durham, for "A new and useful Agricultural Machine or Implement for sowing seed and artificial Manure at the same time, called 'Westlick's Canadian Combined Seed DRILL.'" Ottawa, dated 20th June, 1868.

No. 2647—GAGE, (Robert,) of the City of Kingston, in the County of Frontenac, for " A certain new and useful improvement in the Machines or Apparatus used for the purpose of quilting, and commonly called 'Quilting FRAMES.'" Ottawa, dated 20th June, 1868.

No. 2648—PATRICK, (George Morrison,) of the City of Ottawa, in the County of Carleton, for " A new and useful Machine or Apparatus to be applied to SLEIGHS, Railway Dumping Cars and other Carriages for carrying dead weight, for the purpose of facilitating the unloading thereof." Ottawa, dated 24th June, 1868.

No. 2649—BAKER, (George James,) of the Town of Oakville, in the County of Halton, for " A new and improved Washing MACHINE." Ottawa, dated 5th June, 1868.

No. 2650—COPP, (William Joseph,) of the City of Hamilton, in the County of Wentworth, for " A certain new and useful improvement in FIRED. gs and Ovens of Cooking Stoves, Cooking Stoves with the said improvement to be called ' Copp's cold air Firedog and self-ventilating hot air Oven.'" Ottawa, dated 20th June, 1868.

No. 2651—ELLERSHAUSEN, (Francis,) of the City of Montreal, in the District of Montreal, for " A new and useful process for the manufacture of CAST STEEL and Malleable Iron from Cast Iron." Ottawa, dated 26th June, 1868.

No. 2652—JAMES, (William,) of the Village of Springford, in the County of Oxford, for " A new and useful GATE to be worked by Lever Power." Ottawa, dated 26th June, 1868.

No. 2653—HUTTON, (Albert,) of the Town of Windsor, in the County of Essex, for " A new and useful machine or apparatus for the cooling of Liquor." Ottawa, dated 26th June, 1868.

No. 2654—RAINER, (*Joseph Frederick,*) of the Town of Whitby, in the County of Ontario, for "Certain new and useful improvements in the PIANO-FORTE, for the better arrangement of the scale, the increasing the power, and the securing the greater durability of the tune thereof, to be called 'Rainer's New Dominion Grand Piano.'" Ottawa, dated 26th June, 1868.

No. 2655—ELLERSHAUSEN, (*Francis,*) of the City of Montreal, in the District of Montreal, for "A new and useful furnace for the manufacture of Cast STEEL from pig iron in conjunction with wrought iron, or iron ore, and for the purpose of smelting blistered steel in large quantities, or re-smelting metals in general." Ottawa, dated 26th June, 1868.

No. 2656—DOUD, (*Bernard Sproule,*) of the City of Ottawa, in the County of Carleton, for "A new and useful WHEEL, which he calls 'Doud's Patent Improved Waggon WHEEL.'" Ottawa, dated 26th June, 1868.

No. 2657—MEEK, (*William,*) of the Village of Orangeville, in the County of Wellington, for "A new and useful CHURN." Ottawa, dated 26th June, 1868.

No. 2658—WHITE, (*Andrew,*) of the Township of North Dumfries, in the County of Wellington, for "A new and useful Machine or Apparatus for lifting HAY." Ottawa, dated 26th June, 1868.

No. 2659—DICK, (*Joseph Jr.,*) of the Village of Oshawa, in the County of Ontario, for "A certain new and useful improvement in the rake, in ordinary use, in connection with the Reaping Machine, for removing the Grain, as cut from the table thereof, to be called 'Joseph Dick's, Junior, Improved Harvester RAKE.'" Ottawa, dated 26th June, 1868.

No. 2660—SOLOMON, (*William,*) of the Town of Cobourg, in the County of Northumberland, for "A new and useful Machine for the raising of Heavy Weights, called 'So'omon's Rotary Extension Lever POWER." Ottawa, dated 27th June, 1868.

No. 2661—ROBERTS, (*Francis,*) of of the Township of West Gwillimbury, in the County of Simcoe, for "A new and useful Machine for cutting and destroying Thistles or other noxious weeds; the said machine being used in connection with and attached to the implement of husbandry in ordinary use, and known as the 'CULTIVATOR.'" Ottawa, dated 7th July, 1868.

No. 2662—CROWNOVER, (*Thomas,*) of the Town of St. Catharines, in the County of Lincoln, for "A new and useful Machine or Apparatus for Measuring Carriage Bows." Ottawa, dated 27th June, 1868.

No. 2663—HEROUX, (*Joseph,*) of Yamachiche, in the County of St. Maurice, for "A new and useful ROWING Machine or Apparatus." Ottawa, dated 27th June, 1868.

No. 2664—GRANGER, (*John,*) of the Town of Brooklin, in the County of Ontario, in the Province of Ontario, for "A new and useful machine or apparatus for the purpose of Smoking Meat, called 'Granger's Portable Smoke HOUSE.'" Ottawa, dated 27th June, 1868.

No. 2665—ROBBINS, (*Robert Davis,*) of the Township of Bastard, in the County of Leeds, for "A new and useful Horse Hay Fork, called 'Robbin's Lyon Claw Horse Hay Fork.'" Ottawa, dated 3rd July, 1868.

No. 2666—GORDON, (*Ebenezer,*) of the Town of Belleville, in the County of Hastings, for "A new and useful Washing Machine, called 'Gordon's WASHING Machine.'" Ottawa, dated 3rd July, 1868.

No. 2667—COLLETT, (*Martin,*) of the City of Toronto, in the County of York, for "A new and useful preparation for preserving meat, fish, and other provisions, called 'Collett's Bisulphate of SODA.'" Ottawa, dated 9th July, 1868.

No. 2668—MERRILL, (*Charles Lee,*) of the City of London, in the County of Middlesex, for "A new and useful Machine for boring wells, to be called or known as 'Merrill's Horse-Power Rock and Earth DRILL.'" Ottawa, dated 10th July, 1868.

No. 2669—LAWRENCE, (*Jacob,*) of the Village of Palermo, in the County of Halton, for "A certain new and useful improvement in the Cutter BARS of Reaping and Mowing Machines." Ottawa, dated 10th July, 1868.

No. 2670—BROWN, (*Edward,*) of the Village of Dunnville, in the County of Haldimand, for 'Certain new and useful improvements in TUBE-WELLS." Ottawa, dated 10th July, 1868.

No. 2671—WARNER, (*Henry,*) of the City of Quebec, in the District of Quebec, for "A new and useful Machine or APPARATUS, namely, 'a combined Wheel and Chain Tiller attachment for the working of the Rudders of Vessels, called 'Warner's Steering Apparatus.'" Ottawa, dated 13th July, 1868.

No. 2672—GORDON, (*William Cumming,*) of the Village of Oshawa, in the County of Ontario, for "A new and useful MACHINE for regulating the delivery of the Meal into the Bolts of Mills in the process of the Manufacture of Flour." Ottawa, dated 6th July, 1868.

No. 2673—HENDERSHOT, (*Abram,*) of the Township of Beverley, in the County of Wentworth, in our Province of Ontario, one of the Provinces of Canada, and CLEMENT, (*Firman,*) of the Township of Ancaster, in the said Province of Ontario, for "A new and useful MACHINE, the same being 'a Revolving Plough-Coulter.'" Ottawa, dated 10th July, 1868.

No. 2674—CODY, (*Charles Grandeson,*) of the Township of Dereham, in the County of Oxford, for "A new and useful MACHINE for cooling, airing and deodorizing of Milk and other liquids." Ottawa, dated 10th July, 1868.

No. 2675—KEELER, (*Daniel,*) of the Village of Spencerville, in the Township of Edwardsburgh, in the County of Grenville, for "A new and useful MACHINE for Churning Butter to called 'The Dominion Churn.'" Ottawa, dated 20th June, 1868.

No. 2676—DEAN, (*John,*) of the Village of Aylmer, in the County of Elgin, assignee of Charles Corey, of the same place, for "A new and useful MACHINE for holding driving reins." Ottawa, dated 20th June, 1868.

No. 2677—WILSON, (*Sophia,*) of the Town of Windsor, in the County of Essex, wife of Harris Wilson, of the same place, for "A new and useful ART or METHOD of making or manufacturing from one pint of milk with other ingredients, and producing therefrom one pound of butter." Ottawa, dated 14th July, 1868.

No. 2678—McMILLAN, (*Willam,*) of the City of London, in the County of Middlesex, for "A new and useful OIL, called 'McMillan's lubricating Oil.'" Ottawa, dated 14th July, 1868.

No. 2679—SISSONS, (*Joseph,*) of the City of Montreal, in the District of Montreal, for "A new and useful MACHINE for freezing Ice-cream, to be called 'The Arctic Ice-Cream Freezer." Ottawa, dated 15th July, 1868.

No. 2680—FANNING, (*John,*) of the Town of Petrolia, in the County of Lambton, for "A new and useful MACHINE for washing clothes, called 'The Improved Washing Machine.'" Ottawa, dated 15th July, 1868.

No. 2681—MERRILL, (*Charles Lee,*) of the City of London, in the County of Middlesex, for "A new and useful MACHINE for pumping liquids, to be called 'Merrill's Counterbalance Combined Suction and Force Pump.'" Ottawa, dated 15th July, 1868.

No. 2682—JAMES, (*Charles Henry,*) of the Town of Cornwall, in the County of Stormont, for "A new and useful MACHINE or APPARATUS for facilitating the replacing on railway tracks of locomotives and other railway carriages, to be called 'The Dominion Reverse Repeating Rail.'" Ottawa, dated 16th July, 1868.

No. 2683—MISENER, (*Henry Moe,*) of the Township of Dumfries, in the County of Brant, for "A certain new and useful Improvement on a MACHINE for raising hay, to be called 'Misener's Improved Screw Hay Fork.'" Ottawa, dated 16th July, 1868.

No. 2684—CLARKE, (*Adam Elijah,*) of the City of Montreal, in the District of Montreal, for "Certain new and useful Improvements in SKATE fastening." Ottawa, dated 17th July, 1868.

No. 2685—THOMPSON, (*William Linton,*) of the Township of Stanstead, in the County of Stanstead, for "A new, useful and improved method of preparing the Laminæ of wood, to be used for covering the walls of HOUSES." Ottawa, dated 17th July, 1868.

No. 2686—PLATT, (*Samuel,*) of the Town of Goderich, in the County of Huron, for "A new and useful MACHINE for making Salt, to be called 'A Salt Evaporator.'" Ottawa, dated 17th July, 1868.

No. 2687—O'BRIEN, (*Denis Cornelius,*) of the Village of Richmond Hill, in the County of York, for "A new and useful MACHINE for the manufacture of Salt, to be called 'O'Brien's Brine Evaporator.'" Ottawa, dated 22nd July, 1868.

No. 2688—LEGGO, (*William Augustus,*) of the City of Montreal, in the County of Montreal, for "A new and useful METHOD, called 'Leggo's Moulding process' for obtaining moulds for electrotyping purposes.'" Ottawa, dated 17th July, 1868.

No. 2689—JONES, (*Benjamin Potter*,) of the City of Ottawa, in the County of Carleton, for "A new and useful Enclosed BEDSTEAD, to be called 'Jones' Patent Enclosed Bedstead.'" Ottawa, dated 20th July, 1868.

No. 2690—GRANT, (*James Alexander*,) of the City of Ottawa, in the County of Carleton, and PERRY, (*James*,) of the same place, for "A certain new and useful improvement in the art of manufacturing Illuminating GAS, namely, the making of it from Crude Petroleum and Wood." Ottawa, dated 1st August, 1868.

No. 2691 -FOSTER, (*Charles*,) of the Township of Metcalf, in the County of Middlesex, for "A new and useful MACHINE or APPARATUS for the purpose of utilizing Waste-Steam in the manufacture of Potash, Salt, Sugar and all other art c es requiring the process of evaporation by heat in their manufacture, to be called ' Foster's Waste-Steam Utilizer.'" Ottawa, dated 17th July, 1868.

No. 2692—CARR, (*George*,) of the Township of Sidney, in the County of Hastings, for "Certain new and useful improvements in HARROWS." Ottawa, dated 17th July, 1868.

No. 2693—JONES, (*Charles Wesley*,) of the Township of Percy, in the County of Northumberland, for "A new and useful CHURN, called 'The Drum Churn.'" Ottawa, dated 3rd July, 1868.

No. 2694—FORD, (*David*,) of the Township of Bertie, in the County of Welland, for "A certain new and useful improvement on 'Henderson and Ford's Patent Spring BED-BOTTOM,' patented in the United States of America, on 22nd May, 1866." Ottawa, dated 21th July, 1868.

No. 2695—MASECAR, (*Charles Henry*,) of the Township of Townsend, in the County of Norfolk, for "A new and useful HARROW." Ottawa, dated 25th July, 1868.

No. 2696—MORRIS, (*Thomas*,) of the Town of Brantford, in the County of Brant, for "A new and useful WRENCH, to be known as 'Morris Improved Wrench.'" Ottawa, dated 24th July, 1868.

No. 2697—WARD, (*Jonothan*,) of the Township of Dorchester, in the County of Middlesex, for "A new and useful SAW TOOTH and GUMMING, to be called 'Ward's Imperial Saw Tooth and Gumming." Ottawa, dated 24th July, 1868.

No. 2698—BACH, (*Valentine*,) of the Village of Morriston, in the County of Wellington, for "A new and useful MACHINE for churning butter, to be called 'The Double Acting Lever Churn." Ottawa, dated 24th July, 1868.

No. 2699—METCALF, (*Robert*,) of the Village of Carleton Place, in the County of Lanark, for "A new and useful MACHINE for working butter, called 'Metcalf's Butter Worker." Ottawa, dated 24th July, 1868.

No. 2700—HOGAN, (*Harvey*,) of the Township of Dereham, in the County of Oxford, for "A certain new and useful improvement on the HAY-FORK, known as ' Blodgett's Hay-fork." Ottawa, dated 27th July, 1868.

No. 2701—JOHNSON, (*Thomas Richard*.) of the City of Montreal, in the District of Montreal, for "A new and useful self-ventilating HAT, for wearing in warm weather, to be called 'Johnson's Improved Self-ventilating Hat.'" Ottawa, dated the 28th July, 1868.

No. 2702—MAY, (*Samuel*,) of the City of Toronto, in the County of York, for "Certain new and useful improvements in the CUSHIONS of Billiard Tables." Ottawa, dated the 28th July, 1868.

No. 2703—BRA T, (*Joseph*,) of the Township of Moulton, in the County of Haldimand, for "A new and useful BEE HIVE to be called 'The Standard Hive.'" Ottawa, dated the 31st, July, 1868.

No. 2704—WILLIAMS, (*David*,) of the Town of Peterborough, in the County of Peterborough, for "A new and useful art or mode of dressing MILL-STONES, called 'Williams's Improved Mill-Stone Dress.'" Ottawa, dated the 8th July, 1868.

No. 2705—PELLOW, (*William Hearn*,) of the Village of Oshawa, in the County of Ontario, for "A new and useful MACHINE, for the rapidly heating of water, to be called 'Pellow's Circulating Vat Heater.'" Ottawa, dated the 24th July, 1868.

2706—CRANDELL, (*Stephen Elmore*,) of the Village of Borella, in the Township of Reach, in the County of Ontario, for "A new and useful Spiral Combined SPRING, to be called 'The Combined Spiral Spring.'" Ottawa, dated the 24th July, 1868.

No. 2707—BOA, (*William,*) of the City of Montreal, in the District of Montreal, for " A new and useful MACHINE for automatically counting or enregistering articles of merchandise, and other things, to be called ' Boa's Improved Tallying Machine.' " Ottawa, dated the 24th July, 1868.

No. 2708—WILSON, (*Thomas Laverick,*) of the City of Montreal, in the District of Montreal, and McDOUGALL, (*John,*) of the same place, for "A new and useful TRUCK for Railway-Cars." Ottawa, dated the 24th July, 1868.

No. 2709—BROWN, (*Alden Veranus,*) of Sweetsburgh, in the County of Missisquoi, in the District of Bedford, for " A new and useful Hydraulic ENGINE, for giving motion to machinery, to be called or known as ' Brown's Hydraulic Engine.' " Ottawa, dated the 29th July, 1868.

No. 2710—WALKER, (*Thomas,*) of the Township of Chinguacousy, in the County of Peel, and WALKER, (*William, Jr.,*) of the same place, for " A new and useful MACHINE for the purpose of guiding ploughs when ploughing, to be called ' T. and W. Walker's Plough Guide.' " Ottawa, dated the 3rd August, 1868.

No. 2711—PENDLETON, (*Harvey Smith,*) of the Township of Dereham, in the County of Oxford, for "A new and useful REFLECTOR for Lamps." Ottawa, dated the 3rd August, 1868.

No. 2712—CORNWALL, (*William,*) of Rockport, in the Township of Escott, in the County of Leeds, for " A new and useful MANUFACTURE, to wit: A Bit for Horse, to be called ' The Pulley Bit.' " Ottawa, dated the 4th August, 1868.

No. 2713—ANGER, (*Alexander,*) of the Township of Bertie, in the County of Welland, for " A new and useful MACHINE or APPARATUS for the Heating and Ventilating of Railroad Cars, Houses and Buildings and Kilns for drying purposes." Ottawa, dated the 5th August, 1868.

No. 2714—PRESTON, (*Porter,*) of the Village of Bethany, in the Township of Manvers, in the County of Durham, for " A new and useful MACHINE or WATER WHEEL for Mill-driving purposes, to be called ' Preston's Direct Pressure Voluted Conoid Turbine Wheel.' " Ottawa, dated the 10th August, 1868.

No. 2715—BOWERMAN, (*Isaac Beadell,*) of the Township of South Norwich, in the County of Oxford, for " A new and useful MACHINE or TOOL, namely, a VICE, to be known as ' The Universal Adjustable Vice.' " Ottawa, dated the 10th August, 1868.

No. 2716—LAMBKIN, (*Philo,*) of the Village of Riceburg, in the District of Bedford, for "A new and useful Portable Self-adjusting FENCE." Ottawa, dated 10th August, 1868.

No. 2717—ROBERTS, (*Francis,*) of the Township of West Gwillimbury, in the County of Simcoe, for " A new and useful Machine or Apparatus for the purpose of cutting and destroying Thistles and other weeds, such Machine or Apparatus to be attached to and used in connection with any ordinary plough either by means of a shear bearer or shear point, such Machine or Apparatus to be called ' Robert's Thistle CUTTER No. 3.' " Ottawa, dated 17th August, 1868.

No. 2718—DOTY, (*John,*) of the Town of Oakville, in the County of Halton, for " A new and useful Machine for the upsetting of AXLES." Ottawa, dated 19th August, 1868.

No. 2719—PEARCE, (*Stephen Theodore,*) of the Village of Buckingham, in the County of Ottawa, for " A certain new and useful improvement in the art of mechanically separating from each other without the use of water, air, or any fluid, particles of mineral or other substances which may be mixed together and having specific gravities differing from each other, the said improvement to be called ' Pearce's Improved method of Dry DRESSING;' and also for two certain new and useful machines, the use of which are necessary to the carrying out and effecting of such improvement; the first of which said machines is to be called or known as ' Pearce's Centrifugal SEPARATOR,' and the second thereof as ' Pearce's Cone SEPARATOR.' " Ottawa, dated 4th August, 1868.

No. 2720—GILFILLAN, (*William,*) of the Township of Marmora, in the County of Hastings, for " A new and useful machine namely: a Spring for the doors of Railway Cars or Carriages, to be called ' The Reverse Pressure Car Door Spring.' " Ottawa, dated 24th August, 1868.

17

No. 2721—MARKLE, (*Isaac Brock*,) of the Village of Elmira, in the County of Waterloo, for "A certain new and useful improvement in ploughs, namely: In the attaching of the points to the shares thereof, to be called 'The Universal Moveable Plough Share POINT.'" Ottawa, dated 24th July, 1868.

No. 2722—LEWIS, (*Richard*,) of Melbourne, in the County of Richmond, for "A new and useful GATE, namely: 'An Inclined or self-closing Gate.'" Ottawa, dated 12th August, 1868.

No. 2723—GILFILLAN, (*William*,) of the Township of Marmora, in the County of Hastings, for "A new and useful Machine, namely: a spring for doors and gates, to be called "the Double Acting reverse Pressure Door and Gate SPRING.'" Ottawa, dated 24th July, 1868.

No. 2724—FERGUSON, (*David Cameron*,) of the Town of Scarboro', in the County of York, for "Certain new and useful improvements in the suction Pump for raising water, the Pump with such improvements to be called 'Ferguson's improved PUMP.'" Ottawa, dated 24th July, 1868.

No. 2725—ST. JACQUES, (*Antoine*,) of the Parish of St. Anne d'Yamachiche, in the County of St. Maurice, for "A certain new and useful composition of matter forming a BALM for the relief of Coughs, called 'Baume adoucissant pour la toux.'" Ottawa, dated 24th July, 1868.

No. 2726—GREEN, (*Freeman*,) of the Township of Saltfleet, in the County of Wentworth, for "A certain new and useful improvement on the Spinning WHEEL, to be called or [known as 'Freeman Green's Canadian Spinning Wheel.'" Ottawa, dated 30th July, 1868.

No. 2727—KEEFER, (*Michael, Jr.*,) of the Township of Vaughan, in the County of York, for "A certain new and useful improvement in instruments for unloading or otherwise removing hay, straw, corn and other such like produce; the Hay-fork with such improvement added to be called 'Keefer's Harpoon HAY-FORK.'" Ottawa, dated 10th August, 1868.

No. 2728—LEAN, (*Roderick*,) of the Township of Easthope, in the County of Perth, for "A new and useful machine, namely: 'A Punching DIE.'" Ottawa, dated 5th August, 1868.

No. 2729—GENTESSE, (*Camille*,) of the City of Montreal, in the District of Montreal, for "A new and useful Machine or Agricultural implement for sowing seeds and grains, harrowing the land at the same time, to be called 'Semeuse à Sas.'" Ottawa, dated 10th August, 1868.

No. 2730—DAVIS, (*Adolphus*,) of the City of Montreal, in the District of Montreal, for "A new and useful Self-COUPLER for Railway Cars, to be called 'Davis' Self-Coupler for Railway Cars.'" Ottawa, dated 20th August, 1868.

No. 2731—BLAKE, (*George*,) of the Town of Whitby, in the County of Ontario, for "A new and useful self-acting SEMAPHORE for Railway purposes." Ottawa, dated 22nd August, 1868.

No. 2732—CLOTHER, (*Richard Henry*,) of the Village of Kemptville, in the County of Grenville, for "A new and useful Machine for the purpose of drying clothes, said machine to be called 'The Excelsior Clothes HANGER.'" Ottawa, dated 22nd August, 1868.

No. 2733—BENTLEY, (*George Washington*,) of the Township of Pickering, in the County of Ontario, for "A new and useful Machine for Gumming SAWS, to be called 'Bentley's Saw Gummer, Grinder and Upset.'" Ottawa, dated 22nd August, 1868.

No. 2734—HAMMOND, (*John Yale*,) of the Town of St. John's, in the District of Iberville, for "A new and useful Machine for raising water, to be called 'The Common Sense PUMP.'" Ottawa, 22nd August, 1868.

No. 2735—LARARD, (*Reginald*,) of the Village of Oshawa, in the County of Ontario, for "A new and useful improvement in the method of securing spring heads in the construction of spring mattrasses and other articles where spiral springs are used, to be called 'Larard's Patent Button Head ATTACHMENT.' " Ottawa, dated 26th August, 1868.

No. 2736—COONE, (James,) of the Village of Manilla, in the County of Victoria, for "Certain new and useful Improvements in Hay RAKES." Ottawa, dated 27th August, 1868.

No. 2737—STEPHENS, (Robert Errett,) of the Town of Owen Sound, in the County of Grey, for "A new and useful Improvement in the manner of hanging and fastening Gates, to be called 'Stephen's self-locking adjustable Hinge and LATCH.' " Ottawa, dated 27th August, 1868.

No. 2738—McCALL, (Edwin Robert,) of the Township of Charlotteville, in the County of Norfolk, for "A new and useful Machine for the purpose of gauging the depth of furrow in ploughing land, to be called 'McCall's Improved Plough GAUGE.' " Ottawa, dated 27th August, 1868.

No. 2739—MARR, (James,) of the Township of Woodhouse, in the County of Norfolk, for "A certain new and useful Improvement to his 'Plough Guide and Holder,' for which he obtained Letters Patent for the Province of Canada, bearing date the 21st day of June, in the year 1866." Ottawa, dated 28th August, 1868.

No. 2740—BENTLEY, (Randall,) of the Township of Normanby, in the County of Grey, for "A new and useful Machine for the purpose of making ditches, the said Machine to be called 'Bentley's Excelsior Ditching Machine.' " Ottawa, dated 28th August, 1868.

No. 2741—CANT, (Adam,) and CANT, (Hugh,) both of the Town of Galt, in the County of Wentworth, Assignees of Adam Cant, of the same place, for "A new and useful Machine or apparatus for heating air, to be called 'Cant's Air HEATER.' " Ottawa, dated 17th August, 1868.

No. 2742—STEPHEN, (Richard,) of the Township of Woodhouse, in the County of Norfolk, for "A new and useful Harrow, to be called 'Stephen's Rough and Ready HARROW.' " Ottawa, dated 22nd August, 1868.

No. 2743—HOPKINS, (John Kelsey,) of the Township of West Flamboro, in the County of Wentworth, and RASBERRY, (William) of the same place, for "A new and useful Manufacture of stove pipe thimbles, by the means of the composition of matter for the manufacture of an article, to be called 'The Fire Proof Stove Pipe Thimbles.' " Ottawa, dated 26th August, 1868.

No. 2744—BECKETT, (John Clark,) of the Township of Franklin, in the County of Huntingdon, for "A new and useful machine for the purpose of drawing manure, tan bark, gravel, dirt and other things, to be called 'Beckett's new and useful Dumping WAGGON.' " Ottawa, dated 27th August, 1868.

No. 2745—NEALE, (John,) of the Township of Barrie, in the County of Frontenac, for "A new and useful machine and art for separating the Metals from auriferous and argentiferous rock, the said machine and art to be called 'The Electrical cylinder for separating the metals from auriferous and argentiferous rocks.' " Ottawa, dated 28th August, 1868.

No. 2746—EWING, (Charles Eldon,) of the Village of Grafton, in the Township of Haldimand, in the County of Northumberland, for "Certain new and useful improvements in the art or method of lubricating the axles of vehicles by a tube passing through the hub and box, and also of a means whereby the box of axles is prevented from working loose in the hub, to be called or known as 'Ewing's Improved combined lubricator and axle box FASTENER.' " Ottawa, dated 31st August, 1868.

No. 2747—BUCHANAN, (Andrew,) of the Township of Colchester, in the County of Essex, for "A new and useful Machine for the purpose of cleaning wheat and other grain for milling purposes, to be called 'Buchanan's Grain SEPARATOR.' " Ottawa, dated 22nd August, 1868.

No. 2748—GILPIN, (Richard Thomson,) of the Town of St. Mary, in the County of Perth, for "A new and useful Machine, namely, an attachment to Waxed-thread Sewing Machines for the purpose of keeping waxed-thread pliable by heat, to be called ' Gilpin's Hot Air Waxed Thread HEATER.' " Ottawa, dated 27th August, 1868.

No. 2749—MARIt, (*James*,) of the Township of Woodhouse, in the County of Norfolk, for " A new and useful Machine for racking all kinds of grain off, of and from Reaping Machines, to be called ' James Marr's self-acting RAKE.' " Ottawa, dated 3rd September, 1868.

No. 2750—CORDINGLY, (*Solomon*,) of the Township of Trafalgar, in the County of Halton, for "A new and useful Machine for the purpose of boring Fence Caps, to be called 'Cordingly's Fence Cap BORER.' " Ottawa, dated 4th September, 1868.

No. 2751—YELLAND, (*William*,) of the Town of Peterborough, in the County of Peterborough, for "A new and useful Harrow, to be called ' Yelland's Improved Patent HARROW." ' Ottawa, dated 4th September, 1868.

No. 2752—COOPER, (*Cornelius*,) of Strathroy, in the County of Middlesex, for " A new and useful Horse SHOE for resisting and overcoming the tendency of snow and mud to accumulate and adhere to the hoofs and shoes of horses during the snowy and muddy seasons, to be called Cooper's Convex HORSE SHOE.' " Ottawa, dated 4th September, 1868.

No. 2753—JOHNSON, (*Robert Wellington*,) of Tilsonbury, in the Township of Dereham, in the County of Oxford, for "A new and useful tackle and Lever Power Stump Extracting Machine, to be called ' Johnson's tackle Lever Power Stump MACHINE." Ottawa, dated 8th August, 1868.

No. 2754—VASS, (*David*,) of the City of Montreal, for " A new and useful Telescopic Fire Escape LADDER for rescuing the inmates of burning houses, to be called ' Vass' Telescopic Fire Escape Ladder. Ottawa, dated 24th July, 1868.

No. 2755—PROWSE, (*George Roger*,) of the City of Montreal, in the District of Montreal, for " A new and useful improved Washing BOILER for the purpose of cleaning or removing impurities from clothes, by the rapid circulation of boiling water through the boiler, called ' Prowse's Improved Washing Boiler." Ottawa, dated 28th August, 1868.

No. 2756—CUMMINGS, (*George Washington*,) of the City of Toronto, in the County of York, for " A new and useful Machine for the purpose of making Bricks, to be called ' The New Dominion Brick PRESS.' " Ottawa, dated 4th September, 1868.

No. 2757—ANDERSON, (*James Way*,) of the Township of Ameliasburgh, in the County of Prince Edward, for "A new and useful wire and slat Fence with equal wire tension windlass, to be called ' The Dominion Fence.' " Ottawa, dated 4th September, 1868.

No. 2758—LAWRENCE, (*Jacob*,) of the Village of Palmermo, in the County of Halton, for " A new and useful improvement on Reaping and Mowing Machines, namely, the addition of a geared windlass thereto, for raising and lowering the Cutter Bar ADJUSTER.' " Ottawa, dated 5th September, 1868.

No. 2759—CORDINGLEY, (*William George*,) of the City of Ottawa, in the County of Carleton, for " A new and useful Machine or Apparatus for cooking meat or vegetables by either steaming or boiling." Ottawa, dated 7th September, 1868.

No. 2760—BLACK, (*Norris*,) of the City of Toronto, in the County of York, for " A new and useful Hand Shuttle Sewing Machine, which he calls ' Black's Sewing MACHINE.' " Ottawa, dated 7th September, 1868.

No. 2761—JONES, (*Benjamin Potter*,) of the City of Ottawa, in the County of Carleton, for " A new and useful Window HOLDER or support dispensing with cords and weights now in ordinary use, to be called ' Jones' Improved Sash Press and Holder.' " Ottawa, dated 8th September, 1868.

No. 2762—ROBERGE, (*David*,) of the City of Montreal, in the District of Montreal, for "A new and useful improved HORSE SHOE, for curing and preventing lameness in Horses.' " Ottawa, dated 9th September, 1868.

No. 2763—HAMILTON, (*William*,) of the City of Toronto, in the County of York, for "A new and useful Improved Varnish PAINT." Ottawa, dated 9th September, 1868.

No. 2764—GALIBERT, (*Theodore*,) of the City of Montreal, in the District of Montreal, for the introduction of " A new and useful Respiring Apparatus permitting the wearer to penetrate and remain without danger, in places where ordinary breathing is impossible either from foul air or smoke, called 'Galibert's RESPIRING Apparatus or ' Appareils Respiratoires.' " Ottawa, dated 12th September, 1868.

No. 2765—DIMMA, (*Thomas*,) of the Township of Scott, in the County of Ontario, for "A new and useful Lever spinning Wheel for the purpose of spinning WOOL. Ottawa, dated 4th September, 1868.

No. 2766—PARSON (*William*,) of the City of Toronto, in the County of York, for " A new and useful method by which to connect together the peg fount and stand of Glass LAMPS without the use of cement." Ottawa, dated 7th September, 1868.

No. 2767—ANDERSON, (*Alexander*,) of the City of London, in the County of Middlesex, for " A new and useful Machine for raking Hay and pulling peas, to be called 'Anderson's Patent Hay Rake and Pea PULLER.' " Ottawa, dated 11th September, 1868.

No. 2768—HALLAM (*John*,) of the Village of Bruce Mines, in the District of Algoma, for " A new and useful Machine for churning and for washing clothes, to be called ' Hallam's New Dominion Churn and WASHER.' " Ottawa, dated 12th September, 1868.

No. 2769—WILKINSON, (*George*,) of the Village of Gormley, in the County of York, for " A certain new and useful improvement in the construction of ploughs; the plough with such improvement added to be called ' Wilkinson's Dominion PLOUGH.' " Ottawa, dated 11th September, 1868.

No. 2770—ELLIOT, (*James*,) of the City of Montreal, in the District of Montreal, for " A new and useful machine for the stopping of runaway horses, to be called Elliot's Horse BRAKE.' " Ottawa, dated 11th September, 1868.

No. 2771—PIKE, (*John*,) of the City of Toronto, in the County of York, for " A new and useful Machine for cutting roots or vegetables for feeding STOCK." Ottawa, dated 15th September, 1868.

No. 2772—FORFAR, (*Thomas*,) of the Village of Waterdown, in the County of Wentworth, for " A new and useful metallic frame and toothed apparatus or gearing for application to any description of clothes wringer, the purposes of which are to prevent the Machine being thrown out of gear on account of the separation of the rollers by the passage of heavy articles between them." Ottawa, dated 11th September, 1868.

No. 2773—McCONKEY, (*Thomas*,) of the City of Toronto, in the County of York, for " A new and useful art for the manufacture of Embossed, Etched, relief Glass Letters and Figures for Signs, Windows, Door PLATES, &c." Ottawa, dated 15th September, 1868.

No. 2774—BUTTERFIELD, (*Lonson*,) of the Village of Bradford, in the County of Simcoe, for " A new and useful Gang Plough for cultivating land, to be called ' The improved Gang PLOUGH.' " Ottawa, dated 15th September, 1868.

No. 2775—BROWN, (*Charles Frederick*,) of the Town of Berlin, in the County of Waterloo, for " A new and useful Spring MATTRASS, to be ' Brown's Superior Spring Mattrass.' " Ottawa, dated 16th September, 1868.

No. 2776—HARRIS, (*Edward Marshall*,) of the Town of St. John's, in the County of St. John's, for " A new and useful process and Mach 'e for refining spirituous hydro-carbon and other liquids, thereby imparting to them that 1 'encss and quality which they would not otherwise acquire than by being kept for ma v years, such Machine to be called ' Apparatus for refining Spirituous Hydro-Carbon and ther LIQUIDS.' " Ottawa, dated 18th September, 1868.

No. 2777—CAMPBELL, (*George*,) of the City of Toronto, in the County of York, for " A new and useful Blower and Damper, Stove-pipe Fastener and House REODORIZER." Ottawa, dated 17th September, 1868.

No. 2778—LEUGH, (*John*,) of the Village of Buckingham, in the County of Ottawa, for " A new and useful improvement in SAW TEETH, and in the apparatus for forming the same, to be called ' Leugh's improvement in SAW TEETH and an apparatus for forming the same,' " Ottawa, dated 18th September, 1868.

No. 2779—RUSSELL; (*Calvin Follett,*) of the Township of Horton, in the County of Renfrew, for "A new and useful machine, to be called 'The Extension FIRE LADDER.'" Ottawa, dated 18th September, 1868.

No. 2780—LUSTER, (*Samuel,*) of the Township of Cleveland, in the County of Richmond, in the District of St. Francis, for "A new and useful composition of matter for the tanning of LEATHER, called 'Luster's composition for TANNING LEATHER.'" Ottawa, dated 18th September, 1868.

No. 2781—TILLY, (*William Edward,*) in the Village of Hampton, in the Township of Darlington, in the County of Durham, for "A new and useful Quilting FRAME, to be called 'The Ontario Quilting Frame.'" Ottawa, dated 18th September, 1868.

No. 2782—ROBERTS, (*Francis,*) of the Township of West Gwillimbury, in the County of Simcoe, for "A new and useful machine for CUTTING THISTLES.'" Ottawa, dated 21st September, 1868.

No. 2783—MILLER, (*John Robert,*) of the Town of Stratford, in the County of Perth, for "A new and useful improved HAY-FORK, to be called 'Miller's Hay-Fork.'" Ottawa, dated 22nd September, 1868.

No. 2784—McLAREN, (*Hugh,*) of the Village of Strathroy, in the County of Middlesex, and McLAREN, (*Andrew,*) of the same place, for "A new and useful art or method of manufacturing artificial LEGS and ARMS from Vulcanite Rubber or Vulcanizable Gum, to be called 'McLaren's RUBBER LIMB.'" Ottawa, dated 22nd September, 1868.

No. 2785—ROBERTSON, (*Hugh,*) of Thorold, in the County of Welland, for "A new and useful art or mode of HITCHING HORSES." Ottawa, dated 22nd September, 1868.

No. 2786—PEDERSON, (*Christian,*) of the City of Montreal, in the District of Montreal, for "A new and useful SNOW SHOE, to be called 'Pederson's improved SNOW-SHOE.'" Ottawa, dated 22nd September, 1868.

No. 2787—LECKIE, (*Robert,*) of Acton Vale, in the County of Bagot, for "A new and useful STOREHOUSE, for the preservation of fruit, vegetables and other organic substances.'" Ottawa, dated 29th September, 1868.

No. 2788—McCLOSKEY, (*Charles James,*) of the Township of Rochester, in the County of Essex, for "A new, useful and improved HAY-FORK, to be called 'The Elevating HAY-FORK.'" Ottawa, dated 29th September, 1868.

No. 2789—TREMBLE, (*Frederick,*) of the Town of Amherstburgh, in the County of Essex, for "A new and useful Spoke Trimmer, to be called 'The Rotary Spoke TRIMMER.'" Ottawa, dated 22nd September, 1868.

No. 2790—JACKSON, (*John,*) of the Town of Simcoe, in the County of Norfolk, and JACKSON, (*George,*) of the same place, for "A new and useful Mangle for Mangling clothes, to be called or known as 'Jackson's MANGLE.'" Ottawa, dated 22nd September, 1868.

No. 2791—POWER, (*William,*) of the City of Montreal, in the District of Montreal, for "A new and useful Boiler CLEANER, to be called 'Power's Improved apparatus for cleaning and removing sediment from boilers by the use of Steam.'" Ottawa, dated 22nd September, 1868.

No. 2792—PENELTON, (*James,*) of the Town of Guelph, in the County of Wellington, for "A new and useful improved Window SASH, to be called 'the Counter Balance Window SASH.'" Ottawa, dated 22nd September, 1868.

No. 2793—BRIGGS, (*Absolom.*) of the Township of Wolfe Island, in the County of Frontenac, for "A certain new and useful improvement in Machines for Reaping GRAIN." Ottawa, dated 23rd September, 1868.

No. 2794—TUTTLE, (*Eben Clark,*) of the Village of Oshawa, in the County of Ontario, for "A new and useful SCYTHE, to be called 'Tuttle's improved Dominion Scythe.'" Ottawa, dated 25th September, 1868.

No. 2795—SHIPMAN, (*Sylvanus Keeler,*) of the Village of Almonte, in the County of Lanark, for "A new and useful Machine for fastening the sashes of windows when either raised or lowered, to be called, The Counter Balance Cam FASTENER.'" Ottawa, dated 28th September, 1868.

No. 2796—DINNING, (*Robert Strong*,) of the Town of Woodstock, in the County of Oxford, for "A new and useful improvement in the Feed ROLLER to be attached to Riley's straw, hay, stock and root cutter." Ottawa, dated 29th September, 1868.

No. 2797—ASPDEN, (*Thomas*,) of the Town of Perth, in the Township of Drummond, in the County of Lanark, for "A new and useful art or method of obtaining by compression the LIQUOR for making a concentrated extract or tanning liquor from the stems or branches of wood and leaves of Hemlock, oak and other trees." Ottawa, dated 25th September, 1868.

No. 2798—ASPDEN, (*Thomas*,) of the Town of Perth, in the Township of Drummond, in County of Lanark, for "A new and useful art of obtaining Phosphorus from Apatite or mineral Phosphate of LIME." Ottawa, dated 25th September, 1868.

No. 2799—ASPDEN, (*Thomas*,) of the Town of Perth, in the Township of Drummond, in the County of Lanark, and MORRIS, (*William John*,) of the same place, for "A new and useful Machine or Apparatus for obtaining by compression, the Tanning LIQUOR from the bark of Hemlock, Oak, and analogous trees." Ottawa, dated 25th September, 1868.

No. 2800—KINNEY, (*Israel*,) of the Town of Woodstock, in the County of Oxford, for "A new and useful improvement to be known as 'An Improved system of constructing Cultivators and Gang PLOUGHS.'" Ottawa, dated 29th September, 1868.

No. 2801—McLACHLAN, (*John*,) of the Town of Galt, and KAY, (*Adam*,) of the same place, for "A new and useful MANDREL, to be used in connection with a turning lathe, to be called 'The Expanding Mandrel.'" Ottawa, dated 29th September, 1868.

No. 2802—ALLEN, (*George*,) of the Township of North Oxford, in the County of Oxford, for "A new and useful improvement on Whipple Trees, to be called 'Allan's Improved Three Horse Double TREE.'" Ottawa, dated 30th September, 1868.

No. 2803—LONG, (*Asa Edmund*,) of the Township of Dungannon, in the County of Hastings, for "A new and useful Gold Separator and FILTERER, to be called 'Long's Patent Gold Separator and Filterer.'" Ottawa, dated 29th September, 1868.

No. 2804—McLAWS, (*David*,) of the Village of Wallacetown, in the County of Elgin for "A new and useful BRAKE for Vehicles, called 'McLaws' Waggon Brake.'" Ottawa, dated 9th October, 1868.

No. 2805—JENKINS, (*William Henry*,) of the City of Hamilton, in the County of Wentworth, for "A new and useful Hand LIFTER, to be called 'Jenkins' Patent Improved Lifter.'" Ottawa, dated 9th October, 1868.

No. 2806—HOVEY, (*George Alonzo*,) of the Township of Hatley, in the County of Stanstead, for "A new and useful Machine for cleaning and renovating Feathers, to be called or known as 'The Feather RENOVATOR.'" Ottawa, dated 9th October, 1868.

No. 2807—HARRISON, (*Thelismar*,) of the Township of Marysburgh, in the County of Prince Edward, for "A new and useful composition of matter for mixing Paint, to be called 'Harrison's compound Oil for mixing PAIN..'" Ottawa, dated 30th September, 1868.

No. 2808—GOKEY, (*Peter*,) of the Village of Everton, in the County of Wellington, for "A new and useful machine for hanging clothes on to dry, to be called 'The Dominion Clothes HORSE.'" Ottawa, 7th October, 1868.

No. 2809—DIMON, (*Harvey Wood*,) of the Village of Victoria, in the County of Norfolk, for "A new and useful Self-adjusting Waggon BRAKE." Ottawa, dated 8th October, 1868.

No. 2810—DEBLOIS, (*Onezime*,) of the City of Montreal, in the District of Montreal, for "A new and useful COAL SCUTTLE, to be called 'Seaux Deblois.'" Ottawa, dated 8th October, 1868.

No. 2811—EVANS, (*Thomas*,) of the City of London, in the County of Middlesex, for "A new and useful CHAIN DRILL for agricultural purposes, to be called 'Evans' Patent Chain Drill.'" Ottawa, dated 8th October, 1868.

No. 2812—McDONALD, (John Duncan,) of the Township of Sombra, in the County of Lambton, and McDONALD, (John Frasher,) of the same place, for "A certain new, useful and improved PUMP, to be called 'The Victoria Pump.'" Ottawa, dated 1st October, 1868.

No, 2813—LIKENS, (James Charles,) of the Township of Reach, in the County of Ontario, for "A certain new, useful and Improved WAGGON JACK, called 'Likens' Improved Dominion Waggon Jack.'" Ottawa, dated 6th October, 1868.

No. 2814—MORTON, (James,) the younger, of the Village of Everton, in the County of Wellington, for "A new and useful hay, manure or earth ELEVATOR, to be called 'The Ontario Elevator.'" Ottawa, dated 6th October, 1868.

No. 2815—DeGUISE, (Joseph Balthazar,) of the City of Montreal, for "A new and useful TOBACCO CUTTER, to be called 'The New Mill for Cutting Tobacco,'" Ottawa, 6th October, 1868.

No. 2816—CUMMINGS, (George Washington,) of the City of Toronto, in the County of York, for "A certain new and useful improvement in certain descriptions of COOKING STOVES." Ottawa, dated 15th October, 1868.

No. 2817—WHITESIDE, (Henry,) the younger, of the City of Ottawa, in the County of Carleton, for "A certain new, useful and improved SPRING BED, to be called 'The Whiteside Spring Bed.'" Ottawa, dated 14th October, 1868.

No. 2818—SHELLY, (William,) of the City of Montreal, in the District of Montreal, for "A new and useful CARRIAGE WHEELS RIM JOINT SUPPORTER, to be called and known as 'Shelly's Improved Rim Joint Supporter for Carriage Wheels.'" Ottawa, dated 15th October, 1868.

No. 2819—PAYNE, (Edward,) in the City of Montreal, in the District of Montreal, for "A new and useful composition for feed for cattle, to be called 'Payne's improved composition for CATTLE FEED.'" Ottawa, dated 15th October, 1868.

No. 2820—APPLETON, (Edwin,) of the Village of Vienna, in the County of Elgin, for "A new and useful HORSE SHOE for expanding contracted or foundered hoofs." Ottawa, dated 15th October, 1868.

No. 2821—BOWMAN, (Daniel Martin,) of the City of London, in the County of Middlesex, for "A new and useful manufacture or composition of matter for making COPYING INK, to be called 'The Canadian non-corrosive sympathetic Copying Ink.'" Ottawa, dated 15th October, 1868.

No. 2822—BOWRON, (Addison,) of Hamilton, in the County of Wentworth, for "A new and useful article for heating rooms, to be called 'Bowron's Tubulated STOVE PIPE.'" Ottawa, dated 15th October, 1868.

No. 2823—SMITH, (Edgar Russell,) of the Town of St. John's, in the County of St. John's, for "A new, useful and improved MATTRASS, to be called 'The Improved Sponge Mattrass corrugated or tufted.'" Ottawa, dated 19th October, 1868.

No. 2824—IVES, (Lorenzo,) of the Township of Hatley, in the County of Stanstead, for "A new and useful Valve, to be called 'Ives Patent Stationery VALVE.'" Ottawa, dated 20th October, 1868.

No. 2825—BETHUNE, (Donald,) of the Town of Port Hope, in the County of Durham, for "A certain new, useful and improved Car Coupler, to be called 'Bethune's improved self-acting CAR COUPLER.'" Ottawa, dated 23rd October, 1868.

No. 2826—READ, (James Kempt,) of the Village of Burritt's Rapids, in the Township of Oxford, in the County of Grenville, for "Certain new and useful improvements in a composition of matter used for the covering of ROOFS of Buildings." Ottawa, dated 26th October, 1868.

No. 2827—LEWIS, (Coridon,) of the Village of Salford, in the County of Oxford, for "A new and useful Dash Churn, to be called 'The Excelsior Lever CHURN.'" Ottawa, dated 23rd October, 1868.

No. 2828—MCMILLAN, (John,) of the Town of Petrolea, in the County of Lambton, for "A new and useful art of treating, (in course of refining) crude, distilled or refined Petroleum, coal or shale oil, with air, or steam, or water, to be called ' Patent Carbonized KEROSENE.'" Ottawa, dated 23rd October, 1868.

No. 2829—COLEMAN, (David,) of the Village of Castleton, in the County of Northumberland, for "A new and useful Draught Harness, to be called 'D. Coleman's Improvement on Draught HARNESS.'" Ottawa, dated 23rd October, 1868.

No. 2830—IVES, (Lorenzo,) of the Township of Hatley, in the County of Stanstead, for "A new and useful Machine for conducting the Sap from Maple Trees into buckets or other holders, to be called 'Ives' Patent Circular Nail SPOUT.'" Ottawa, dated 24th October, 1868.

No. 2831—LEAN, (Roderick,) of the Town of Stratford, in the County of Perth, for "A new, useful and improved Agricultural Implement, to be called 'R. Lean's Combined Gang Plough and CULTIVATOR.'" Ottawa, dated 26th October, 1868.

No. 2832—MANEER, (Samuel,) of Craigvale, in the County of Simcoe, for "A new and useful Metallic DASHBOARD for Carriages." Ottawa, dated 28th October, 1868.

No. 2833—GROOM, (George,) of the City of Toronto, in the County of York, for ": A new and useful Soap, to be called 'The Toronto Patent SOAP.'" Ottawa, dated 30th October, 1868.

No. 2834—SHOURDS, (Ephraim Hammond,) of the Village of Thorold, in the County of Welland, for "A new and useful art or process for preserving, in their natural state, Fruits and Meats of all kinds, to be called or known as 'The New Dominion PROCESS for Preserving Fruits and Meats.'" Ottawa, dated 26th October, 1868.

No. 2835—REAMAN, (Samuel,) of the Village of Ringwood, in the County of York, for "Certain new, useful and improved Horse Hay Forks or ELEVATORS." Ottawa, dated 26th October, 1868.

No. 2836—JACKSON, (John,) of the City of Toronto, in the County of York, for "A new, useful and improved Solartype Heating Stove, to be called 'Jackson's Improvement in Solartype Heating STOVES.'" Ottawa, dated 26th October, 1868.

No. 2837—CUMMINGS, (George Washington,) of the City of Toronto, in the County of York, for "A new and useful Mopping and Scrubbing Machine, to be called 'The Combined Mop and Scrub Brush HOLDER.'" Ottawa, dated 26th October, 1868.

No. 2838—MCFARLANE, (John,) of the Village of Otterville, in the County of Oxford, for "A new and useful CARRIAGE SPRING, to be called 'The Improved Elliptic Solid Cast Steel Carriage Spring.'" Ottawa, dated 27th October, 1868.

No. 2839—FISHER, (Adam,) of the Township of Woodhouse, in the County of Norfolk, for "A new and useful Agricultural Machine for tilling or cultivating land, to be called 'Fisher's Improved CULTIVATOR.'" Ottawa, dated 30th October, 1868.

No. 2840—ENGHOLM, (Otto,) of the City of Montreal, in the District of Montreal, for the introduction of "A new and useful art of cutting and dressing Mill Stones, by means of hard stones, to be called or known as 'Golay's art of cutting and dressing MILL STONES, by means of hard stones, particularly the diamond, with the apparatus for executing the same.'" Ottawa, dated 26th October, 1868.

No. 2841—ALLEN, (Charles,) of the Village of Waterloo, in the District of Bedford, for "A new and useful AIR-TIGHT DOUBLE STOVE, to be called 'Allen's Improved Air-tight Double Stove.'" Ottawa, dated 30th October, 1868.

No. 2842—HOULE, (William,) of the City of Montreal, in the District of Montreal, and BOUDREAU, (Mathurin,) of the same place, for "A new and useful pattern for CUTTING the leather of BOOTS, to be called 'Patron de bottes sans crampage.'" Ottawa, dated 30th October, 1868.

No. 2843—KELLY, (Alfred John,) of the Town of Bowmanville, in the County of Durham, for "A new and useful improvement on WIRE SPRINGS and their attachments for

18

beds, sofas, chairs, lounges, &c., to be called 'Kelly's Improvement on Wire Springs and their attachments, for beds, sofas, chairs, lounges, &c.'" Ottawa, dated 30th October, 1868.

No. 2841-GIBSON, (Adam McCutchin,) of the Township of Reach, in the County of Ontario, for "A new and useful art or method of connecting the links of STOVE PIPES, to be called 'The spring connecting and self-locking stove pipe joint.'" Ottawa, dated 4th November, 1868.

No. 2845—ROCKEY, (Emmanuel,) of the Township of Malahide, in the County of Elgin, for "A new and useful machine for making DITCHES, to be called 'The Rock Ditcher.'" Ottawa, dated 6th November, 1868.

No. 2846—EWING, (Charles Eldon,) of the Village of Grafton, in the Township of Haldimand, in the County of Northumberland, for "Certain new and useful improvements in the art or method of lubricating AXLES OF VEHICLES, called or known as 'Ewing's Improved Combined Lubricator and Axle-Box Fastener.'" Ottawa, dated 6th November, 1868.

Re-issue of No. 2746.

No. 2847—COLLINS, (Thomas Cozen,) of the City of Toronto, in the County of York, for "A certain new and useful Sleigh BRAKE, to be called 'Collins' Self-acting Sleigh Brake.'" Ottawa, dated 1st December, 1868.

No. 2848—FERGUSON, (Stephen B.,) of the Township of Hollowell, in the County of Prince Edward, for "A new and useful Washing Machine, to be called 'The Railroad Washing MACHINE.'" Ottawa, dated 1st December, 1868.

No. 2849—ANDREWS, (John Stanley,) of the Town of Brantford, in the County of Brant, for "A new and useful BUCKLE, to be called 'The Buckeye Buckle.'" Ottawa, dated 1st December, 1868.

No. 2850—STEPHENSON, (John,) of the Township of Markham, in the County of York, and STEPHENSON, (William,) of the Township of East Gwillimbury, in the said County of York, for "A certain new, useful and improved PUMP, to be called 'Stephenson's Eccentric Spring Pump.'" Ottawa, dated 1st December, 1868.

No. 2851—THOMPSON, (John Henry,) of the Village of Streetsville, in the County of Peel, for "A certain new and useful Mill Stone FEEDER, to be called 'Thompson's Patent Middlings Feeder.'" Ottawa, dated 1st December, 1868.

No. 2852—WILLIAMSON, (George Thomas,) of the City of Toronto, in the County of York, for "A new and useful improvement, on the art or method of fastening or securing Plank Walks, Flooring and other things, to be called 'Williamson's Improved method of fastening or securing Plank WALKS, Floorings and other things.'" Ottawa, dated 1st December, 1868.

No. 2853—WHITE, (William,) of the Village of Uxbridge, in the County of Ontario, for "A new and useful machine for raising, lifting and drawing of water from wells, aqueducts and reservoirs, to be called 'The self-acting and Magic Pump.'" Ottawa, dated 1st December, 1868.

No. 2854—BATES, (Jasper,) of the Village of Clarksburgh, in the Township of Collingwood, in the County of Grey, for "A new and useful Fence GATE, to be called 'Bates' sliding, balance, suspension and swing Gate.'" Ottawa, dated 1st December, 1868.

No. 2855—BROWNELL, (Myron Socrates,) of the Village of Vienna, in the County of Elgin, for "A new and useful Machine for Scroll SAWING." Ottawa, dated 1st December, 1868.

No. 2856—BROWNELL, (Myron Socrates,) of the Village of Vienna, in the County of Elgin, for "A new and useful CASTER for Furniture and moveable effects, to be called 'The Turntable Caster.'" Ottawa, dated 1st December, 1868.

No. 2857—WARNER, (John Johnson,) of the Village of Otterville, in the Township of Norwich, in the County of Oxford, for certain new, useful and improved Carriage SPRINGS, to be called 'Warner's Improved Elliptic Carriage Springs.'" Ottawa, dated 1st December' 1868.

No. 2858—HURD, (*Luther Harnden*,) of the City of Hamilton, in the County of Wentworth, for "A new and useful Bed Bottom, to be called 'Hurd's Excelsior Bed BOTTOM.'" Ottawa, dated 1st December, 1868.

No. 2859—FARMER, (*William Washington*,) of the Township of Reach, in the County of Ontario, for "A new and useful improved SAW-SET, to be called 'Farmer's Patent Lever Saw-Set.'" Ottawa, dated 1st December, 1868.

No. 2860—FAIRLIE, (*Robert Francis*,) of the City of Montreal, in the District of Montreal, for "Certain new and useful improvements in Railway Locomotive ENGINES and BOILERS, and the adaptation of locomotives to the carriage of goods and passengers, to be called 'Fairlie's new and useful improvements in locomotive engines and boilers, and the adaptation of locomotives for the carriage of goods and passengers.'" Ottawa, dated 1st December, 1868.

No. 2861—WASHBURN, (*Stephen*,) of the Village of St. George, in the County of Brant, for "A new and useful SNOW GATE with hinges and fastenings." Ottawa, dated 1st December, 1868.

No. 2862—McCARTHY, (*Jeremiah*,) of the Village of Petrolia, in the County of Lambton, for "A new and useful machine for the purpose of separating from Petroleum and other kindred oils the gas commonly united with those oils, to be called 'McCarthy's GAS SEPARATOR.'" Ottawa, dated 1st December, 1868.

No. 2863—ENGHOLM, (*Otto*,) of the City of Montreal, for "Certain new and useful improvements on COPYING PRESSES, to be called 'Engholm's new and useful improvements on Copying Presses for Letters.'" Ottawa, dated 1st December, 1868.

No. 2864—THAIN, (*Francis Andrew*,) of the City of Montreal, in the District of Montreal, for "Certain new and useful improvements in the manufacture of ALBUMEN, and on the furnace and apparatus used therefor, to be called 'Thain's new and useful improvements on the manufacture of Albumen, and on the furnace and apparatus used therefor.'" Ottawa, dated 1st December, 1868.

No. 2865—SMITH, (*Martin Luther*,) of the Village of Springfield, in the County of Elgin, for "A new and useful WEIGHING MACHINE, to be called 'Smith's Platform Scale.'" Ottawa, dated 1st December, 1868.

No. 2866—GARDINER, (*William*,) of the Township of Cavan, in the County of Durham, for "A new and useful LAND ROLLER, to be called "Gardiner's separate self-adjusting Triplicate Land Roller." Ottawa, dated 1st December, 1868.

No. 2867—CUSSON, (*Alfred*,) of the Village of Longueuil, in the County of Chambly, for "A certain new and useful improvement in the flues of DOUBLE STOVES, to be called 'Conduits améliorés du feu et de la fumée dans les poêles doubles par A. Cusson." Ottawa, dated 1st December, 1868.

No. 2868—FAIRLIE, (*Robert Francis*,) of the City of Montreal, in the District of Montreal, for "Certain new and useful improvements in the construction and coupling of Railway CARS.'" Ottawa, dated 1st December, 1868.

No. 2869—HENDRY, (*Christian*,) of the Village of Waterloo, in the County of Waterloo, for "A new and useful STOVE PIPE DAMPER, to be called 'Hendry's Canadian Wood Saver.'" Ottawa, dated 1st December, 1868.

No. 2870—TROTT, (*John*,) of the Village of Wingham, in the County of Huron, for "A new, useful and improved Air-Heating Apparatus, to be called 'Trott's AIR-HEATING and DAMPER DRUM." Ottawa, dated 1st December, 1868.

No. 2871—TURNER, (*Richard*,) of the City of Quebec, for "A new, useful and improved BROOM, to be called 'Turner's The Mistress' Friend." Ottawa, dated 2nd December, 1868.

No. 2872—WHITE, (*James*,) of the Township of Yarmouth,) in the County of Elgin, for "A new, useful and improved WAGGON-BRAKE, to be called or known as 'White's Self-acting Waggon-Brake.'" Ottawa, dated 1st December, 1868.

No. 2873—NESBITT, (*Samuel*,) of the City of Toronto, in the County of York, for "A new and useful machine for making MATCHES, to be called 'The Electric Match Maker.'" Ottawa, dated 1st December, 1868.

No. 2874—WARNER, (*Lewis*,) of the Town of St. Thomas, in the County of Elgin, for "A new and useful improvement in the art of heating buildings with hot air, to be called ' Warner's improved method of HEATING Buildings.' " Ottawa, dated 1st December, 1868.

No. 2875—CLEMENTS, (*William*,) of the Village of Newsbury, in the County of Middlesex, for "A new and useful combined undulated SPRING for Railroad Cars, Waggons and Carriages." Ottawa, dated 1st December, 1868.

No. 2876—JANSON, (*Charles*,) of the Township of East Gwillimbury, in the County of York, and ARNOLD, (*James*,) of the same place, for "A certain new, useful and improved Force or Suction Pump, to be called ' Janson and Arnold's doubled actioned Suction or Force PUMP.' " Ottawa, dated 1st December, 1868.

No. 2877—HAMILTON, (*William*,) of the City of Toronto, in the County of York, and HAMILTON, (*William Jr.*,) of the same place, for "A new, useful and improved Rotary ENGINE, to be called ' Hamilton's Improved Balanced Rotary Engine.' " Ottawa, dated 1st December, 1868.

No. 2878—VANDRY, (*Hoppolyte*,) of Shefford Mountain, in the County of Shefford, for "A certain new, useful and improved FENCE, to be called ' Clôture portative, à fermeture mobile et à l'épreuve des animaux.' " Ottawa, dated 3rd December, 1868.

No. 2879—SPENCER, (*Robert*,) of the City of Montreal, in the District of Montreal, for "A new and useful composition of matter for LUBRICATING purposes." Ottawa, dated 3rd December, 1868.

No. 2880—PRIOR, (*Hiram*,) of the Town of Woodstock, in the County of Oxford, for "A new and useful Stove DRUM, to be called ' Prior's Drum.' " Ottawa, dated 2nd December, 1868.

No. 2881—BRAMMER, (*Robert*,) of the Village of Sharon, in the County of York, for "A new and useful Machine for loading and unloading Hay, Straw of any kind or description, to be called ' Brammer's Needle Cylinder Hay FORK.' " Ottawa, dated 2nd December, 1868.

No. 2882—MOORE, (*Cyrus Sumner*,) of the Town of St. Catharines, in the County of Lincoln, for "A new and useful composition of matter for the making of Lubricating Oil, to be called ' Moore's Improved Lubricating OIL.' " Ottawa, dated 2nd December, 1868.

No. 2883—MARTIN, (*James Walter*,) of the Township of London, in the County of Middlesex, for "A new, useful and improved Waggon SEAT, to be called ' Martin's Horizontal Revolving Seat.' " Ottawa, dated 2nd December, 1868.

No. 2884—HIGHET, (*Robert*,) of the Town of Cobourg, in the County of Northumberland, for "A new, useful and improved BUCK SAW HANDLE, to be called ' The Canadian single or double Brace Saw Stretcher.' " Ottawa, dated 2nd December, 1868.

No. 2885—SHAW, (*John*,) of the Town of Whitby, in the County of Ontario, for "A new useful and improved WASHING MACHINE, to be called ' Shaw's Improved Washing Machine.' " Ottawa, dated 2nd December, 1868.

No. 2886—CALCOTT, (*John*,) of the Township of Yarmouth, in the County of Elgin, in our Province of Ontario, one of the Provinces of Canada, and CALCOTT, (*Christopher*,) of the same place, for "A new, useful and improved GATE, to be called ' Calcott's Screw Raising Metallic Post Gate.' " Ottawa, dated 4th December, 1868.

No. 2887—FRASER, (*William*,) of the Village of Glenwilliam, in the County of Halton, for "A new and useful machine for raising and conveying HAY or MERCHANDISE." Ottawa, dated 2nd December, 1868.

No. 2888—CRAIG, (*James Peter*,) of the City of Montreal, in the District of Montreal, for "Certain new and useful improvements in the construction of PIANO-FORTES ; such improvements to be called ' Piano système Craig.' " Ottawa, dated 4th December, 1868.

No. 2889—MACFARLANE, (*Thomas*,) of the Village of Acton Vale, in the County of Bagot, in the District of St. Hyacinthe, for "Certain new and useful improvements on the art of extracting COPPER from its ores, by the humid process, to be called ' Macfarlane's new and useful improvement on the art of Extracting Copper from its ores by the humid process.' " Ottawa, dated 4th December, 1868.

No. 2890—JUDD, (*William Simmonds*,) of ;the Town of Napanee, in the County of Lennox

143

and Addington, for " A new and useful machine for making TINT PHOTOGRAPHS, to be called 'Judd's Pearl Tint Printing Apparatus.'" Ottawa, dated 4th December, 1868.

No. 2891—OAKLEY, (*Frederick,*) of the City of Toronto, in the County of York, for " A new and useful machine for Ventilating Rooms through flues or stove pipes, to be called 'Oakley's CONE VENTILATOR.'" Ottawa, dated 4th December, 1868.

No. 2892—HOLDEN, (*Moses,*)of the Village of Strathroy, in the County of Middlesex, for "Certain new and useful improvements in ladders used for gathering Fruit, Painting and Papering in Buildings, House-cleaning and Renovating, Bill-posting and other such like purposes, to be called 'Holden's Improved FRUIT LADDER." Ottawa, dated 7th December, 1868.

No. 2893—DOYLE, (*Richard Judson,*) of Owen Sound, in the County of Grey, for " A new and useful FENCE, to be called 'Doyle's Double Lock Portable Fence and Trellis.'" Ottawa, dated 9th December, 1868.

No. 2894—HETHERINGTON, (*James,*) of the Village of Orono, in the County of Durham, for "Certain new and useful improvements on a machine, namely, a CULTIVATOR for farming or agricultural purposes, the improved machine to be called 'The Dominion Cultivator.'" Ottawa, dated 9th December, 1868.

No. 2895—FICK, (*Lewis Wesley,*) of the Township of Houghton, in the County of Norfolk, for " A new and useful Railway CAR SPRING, to be called 'Fick's Car Spring.'" Ottawa, dated 11th December, 1868.

No. 2896—MEADOWS, (*Samuel,*) of the City of Toronto, in the County of York, for " A new and useful machine for concentrating and reflecting artificial light, to be called 'Meadow's Corrugated GLASS REFLECTORS.'" Ottawa, dated 11th December, 1868.

No. 2897—SHEELY, (*Christopher,*) in the Township of Reach, in the County of Ontario, for " A new, useful and improved machine or implement for Cutting Wood, to be called 'Sheely's Improved Self-fastening SAW HANDLE.'" Ottawa, dated 11th December, 1868.

No. 2898—FOLEY, (*James,*) of the City of Montreal, in the District of Montreal, for " A new and useful manufacture, namely, making PAPER STOCK or PULP, for the manufacture of paper from the fibres obtained from the leaves, stalks and roots of the plant commonly known as the Wild Rice plant, a perennial known by the botanical name 'Oryza.'" Ottawa, dated 11th December, 1868.

No. 2899—BYRON, (*Edward Low,*) of the Township of Compton, in the County of Compton, for " A new, useful and improved HORSE RAKE, to called 'Byron's Planotooth Horse Rake.'" Ottawa, dated 12th December, 1868.

No. 2900—STROHM, (*Gilbert,*) of the Township of North Cayuga, in the County of Haldimand, for " A new and useful art or method of lifting Waggon Racks loaded with hay or grain, to be called 'Strohm's RACK and GRAIN LIFTER.'" Ottawa, dated 12th December, 1868.

No. 2901—HARRISON, (*Robert,*) of the City of Toronto, in the County of York, in our Province of Ontario, one of the Provinces of Canada, and CALDWELL, (*William Macauley,*) of the same place, for " A certain new and useful improvement in the construction of the Amalgamator, a machine for extracting minerals from ore, to be called 'Harrison and Caldwell's improved AMALGAMATOR.'" Ottawa, dated 12th December, 1868.

No. 2902—CAMPBELL, (*Peter,*) of the Town of Woodstock, in the County of Oxford, for "A new and useful machine for renovating Feathers, to be called 'Campbell's FEATHER RENOVATOR.'" Ottawa, dated 12th December, 1868.

No. 2903—DIMMER, (*Thomas,*) of the Township of Scott, in the County of Ontario, for " A new and useful mechanical combination for the purpose of applying to any machine, where a combination of a rotary and reciprocating motion is required, or where it may be desirable to convert a rotary into a reciprocating motion, such combination to be called 'Dimmer's Mechanical COMBINATION.'" Ottawa, dated 12th December, 1868.

No. 2904—BENTLEY, (*Randall*,) of the Township of Normandy, in the County of Grey, for "New and useful improvements on Bentley's Excelsior DITCHING MACHINE, the said machine, with such improvements added, to be called 'Bentley's Improved Excelsior Ditching Machine.'" Ottawa, dated 12th December, 1868.

No. 2905—MURMANN, (*Eugene A.*,) of St. Clements, in the County of Waterloo, for "A new and useful improvement in BOOTS and SHOES, consisting of Metallic Counters therefor." Ottawa, dated 14th December, 1868.

No. 2906—MANN, (*James Walter*,) of the Town of Port Dover, in the County of Norfolk, for "A new and useful improvement in using HORSE FORKS." Ottawa, dated 11th December, 1868.

No. 2907—BEAUDRY, (*Timothée*,) of the Parish of St. Flavien, in the County of Lotbinière, for "A new and useful series of SAWS, (commonly called 'A Gang of Saws,') with different sets, to be known as 'Série de Scies à plusieurs sets de Beaudry.'" Ottawa, dated 16th December, 1868.

No. 2908—DAVY, (*John*,) of the Township of Dereham, in the County of Oxford, for "A new and useful machine for tightening clothes lines, to be called 'Davy's Clothes Line TIGHTENER.'" Ottawa, dated 16th December, 1868.

No. 2909—DEMERS, (*Cyrille*,) of the Parish of St. Flavien, in the County of Lotbinère, for "A new and useful machine for the coupling and uncoupling of Railway Cars, to be called 'Demers's new and useful Machine for the coupling of Railway CARS.'" Ottawa, dated 16th December, 1868.

No. 2910—STIMSON, (*James*,) of the Village of St. George, in the Township of South Dumfries, in the County of Brant, for "A certain new, useful and improved VELOCIPEDE, to be called 'Stimson's Velocipede.'" Ottawa, dated 16th December, 1868.

No. 2911—SELLS, (*Hugh*,) of the Village of Vienna, in the County of Elgin, for "A new and useful Butter Churn, to be called 'Counter Balance Rocking CHURN.'" Ottawa, dated 16th December, 1868.

No. 2912—WHITESIDE, (*Henry, Jr.*,) of the City of Ottawa, in the County of Carleton, for "A certain new, useful and improved Clothes DRYER, to be called 'Whiteside's Patent Clothes Dryer.'" Ottawa, dated 17th December, 1868.

No. 2913—HOWARD, (*Henry*,) of the Town of St. John's, in the County of Iberville, for "A new and useful improvement on a machine for Ventilating Hospitals, Barracks, Schools, Prisons, Asylums, Private Houses, Steamboats, and Railroad Cars; the machine with such improvement, to be called 'Howard's VENTILATOR.'" Ottawa, dated 18th December, 1868.

No. 2914—COMBS, (*John*,) of the Township of Saltfleet, in the County of Wentworth, for "A new and useful Machine for fastening doors of Barns, and other things, to be called or known as 'The Dominion Door FASTENER.'" Ottawa, dated 18th December, 1868.

No. 2915—RIDDY, (*Robert Samuel*,) of the Town of Windsor, in the County of Essex, for "A new and useful composition of matter for rendering light and agreeable cakes, puddings and fancy breads of all kinds, to be called 'Egg Substitute or Excelsior EGG POWDER.'" Ottawa, dated 18th December, 1868.

No. 2916—COLLEY, (*Edward William*,) of St. Mary's, in the County of Perth, for "A new and useful Force PUMP for forcing water for the purpose of extinguishing fire and for other purposes, to be called 'Colley's Patent Fire Engine.'" Ottawa, dated 18th December, 1868.

No. 2917—HURD, (*Prosper Armstrong*,) of the City of Hamilton, in the County of Wentworth, for "A new and useful Washing MACHINE, called 'The Ontario Washing Machine.'" Ottawa, dated 18th December, 1868.

No. 2918—GORDON, (*James Kent*,) of the City of Hamilton, in the County of Wentworth, for " A new and useful Stove DRUM for heating rooms, to be called ' Gordon's Mammoth Hot Air Drum.' " Ottawa, dated 18th December, 1868."

No. 2919—McMINN, (John,) of the Village of Schomberg, in the County of York, for ".A. new and useful Stove Pipe DAMPER, to be called ' McMinn's Stove Pipe Damper and Regulator.' " Ottawa, dated 18th December, 1868.

No. 2920—GILMORE, (Robert,) of the City of Hamilton, in the County of Wentworth, for " A new and useful improvement in the manufacture of Corn BROOMS and Brushes; the Broom with such improvement added to be called ' Gilmore's Improved Shifting Handle.' " Ottawa, dated 18th December, 1868.

No. 2921—EWING, (Franklin,) of the Township of Percy, in the County of Northumberland, for " A new and useful CHURN, to be called ' Ewing's four dash Churn.' " Ottawa, dated 18th December, 1868.

No. 2922—ABRAMS, (George William,) of the Township of Pittsburg, in the County of Frontenac, for " A new and useful improvement on the Horse Hay FORK, to be called ' Abram's improvement on the Horse Hay Fork.' " Ottawa, dated 18th December, 1868.

No. 2923—McLACHLAN, (John,) of the Village of Newmarket, in the County of York, for " A new and useful Sleigh BRAKE, to be called ' McLachlan's Dominion Sleigh Brake.' " Ottawa, dated 23rd December, 1868.

No. 2924—PICKLES, (John,) of the City of Montreal, in the District of Montreal, for " A new and useful art or process of solidifying the LIQUID or Semi-liquid concentrated extract of Hemlock, Oak and other barks for tanning, dyeing and other purposes, and also, of a new and useful machine for effecting such process." Ottawa, dated 23rd December, 1868.

No. 2925—BLACKBURN, (Stephen,) of the City of London, in the County of Middlesex, for ' A certain new, useful and improved STEAM CONDENSER." Ottawa, dated 23rd December, 1868.

No. 2926—CLOW, (Holmes Purdee,) of the Town of Napanee, in the County of Lennox and Addington, for " Certain new and useful improvements in the machine known as the Horse Hay RAKE; the rake, with such improvements, to be called ' Clow's Self-delivering Wheel-horse Rake.' " Ottawa, dated 23rd December, 1868.

No. 2927—BREACK, (Joseph,) of the Township of Markham, in the County of York, for " A new and useful machine for the applying of lever power to machinery, such machine to be called ' Breack's Application of Lever Power to MACHINERY.' " Ottawa, dated 23rd December, 1868.

No. 2928—SMITH, (Thomas,) of the City of Ottawa, in the County of Carleton, for " A new and useful machine for lifting hay, to be called ' The Excelsior HAY FORK.' " Ottawa, dated 23rd December, 1868.

No. 2929—NAYLON, (John Joseph,) of the Village of Newmarket, in the County of York, for ' A new, useful and improved POTATO DIGGER, to be called ' Naylon's Improved Potato Digger.' " Ottawa, dated 23rd December, 1868.

No. 2930—OSBORNE, (Philo Tanner,) of the Village of Colborne, in the County of Northumberland, for " A new and useful machine for Wringing Mops, to be called ' Osborne's MOP WRINGER.' " Ottawa, dated 23rd December, 1868.

No. 2931—CAMPBELL, (George,) of the City of Toronto, in the County of York, for " A new and useful Steam Washing MACHINE." Ottawa, dated 24th December, 1868.

No. 2932—ENGHOLM, (Otto,) of the City of Montreal, in the District of Montreal, in our Province of Quebec, one of the Provinces of Canada, for the introduction of " A new and useful machine for preserving caught fish alive, to be called ' Engholm's new and useful machine for preserving CAUGHT FISH alive for a number of days during transport to market and afterwards; also for use in the manufacture of malt.' " Ottawa, dated 24th December, 1868.

No. 2933—FRY, (John Sharland,) of the City of Quebec, in the District of Quebec, one of the Provinces of Canada, for the introduction of "A new and useful art of purifying and deodorizing PETROLEUMS and other liquid and solid HYDRO-CARBONS, animal and vegetable oils, fats and fatty acids, to be called 'Lamb and Steny's new and useful art of purifying and deodorizing petroleums and other liquid and solid hydro-carbons, animal and vegetable oils, fats and fatty acids.'" Ottawa, dated 24th December, 1868.

No. 2934—STUART, (*Henry,*) in the Township of Hay, in the County of Huron, for "A new and useful machine for Boring holes in the ground for fence-posts, to be called 'Stewart s fence post HOLE-BORER.'" Ottawa, dated 26th December, 1868.

No. 2935—WORKMAN, (*George,*) of the village of Mount Pleasant, in the County of Durham, for "A new and useful HARROW, to be called 'Workman's Improved Harrow.'" Ottawa, dated 26th December, 1868.

No. 2936—BARNES, (*Thomas,*) of the Township of Harwich, in the County of Kent, for "A new, useful and improved FENCE to be called 'Barnes' portable and stationary fence combined.'" Ottawa, dated 26th December, 1868.

No. 2937—HALL, (*Samuel Stillman,*) of the City of Montreal, in the District of Montreal, for "A new and useful machine or apparatus for holding together securely the posts and side rails or ends or side bars of bedsteads, to be called 'Hall's improved BEDSTEAD FASTENER.'" Ottawa, dated 26th December, 1868.

No. 2938—RIPLEY, (*Albert Forster,*) of the Village of Thurso, in the Township of Lochaber, in the County Ottawa, for "A certain new, useful and improved SPINNING WHEEL, to be called or known as 'Ripley's Improved Spinning Wheel.'" Ottawa, dated 29th December, 1868.

No. 2939—BROWNELL, (*Myron Socrates,*) of the Village of Vienna, in the County of Elgin, for "Certain new and useful improvements in the machine used for agricultural purposes, and called or known as 'The Combined Sower, Cultivator and ROLLER.'" Ottawa, dated 29th December, 1868.

No. 2940—WALMSLEY, (*John,*) of the Town of Berlin, in the County of Waterloo, in our Province of Ontario, one of the Provinces of Canada, and ZIEGLER, (*Enoch,*) of the same place, for "A certain new, useful and improved PLOUGH SHARE, to be called or known as 'The Ontario Improved Plough Share.'" Ottawa, dated 29th December, 1868.

No. 2941—SMITH, (*Richard,*) of the Town of Sherbrook, in the District of Saint Francis, for "A new and useful machine for making seamless boxes or other hollow articles from PULP.'" Ottawa, dated 29th December, 1868.

No. 2942—ROCHFORD, (*George Benjamin,*) of the Town of Bowmanville, in the County of Durham, for "A certain new, useful and improved Stove Pipe DAMPER, to be called 'Rochford's Ventilator and Damper combined.'" Ottawa, dated 29th December, 1868.

No. 2943—HURST, (*William,*) of the Village of Coldwater, in the County of Simcoe, for "A new and useful CHURN, to be called or known as the 'Excelsior Churn.'" Ottawa, dated 29th December, 1868.

No. 2944—POWELL, (*John George,*) of the Township of East Oxford, in the County of Oxford, for "A certain new and useful improvement in the manufacture of TUE-IRONS; the tue-iron, with such improvements added, to be called or known as 'Powell's Improved Tue-Iron.'" Ottawa, 29th December, 1868.

No. 2945—LANGWORTH, (*John,*) of the Village of Queenstown, in the County of Lincoln, for "A certain new, useful and improved HAY-FORK, to be called or known as 'Langworth's Double Harpoon Hay Fork.'" Ottawa, dated 29th December, 1868.

No. 2946—REED, (*George Spear,*) of the City of Toronto, in the County of York, for "A certain new and useful article of manufacture, namely, a shelf to be attached to the Smokepipes of STOVES, to be called or known as 'The adjustable self-sustaining and extension stove shelf.'" Ottawa, dated 30th December, 1868.

No. 2947—DEMPSEY, (P.C.,) of Ameliasburgh, Ont., for "An Improvement in Churn Dashers." Ottawa, dated 7th January, 1869.

No. 2948—STEWART, (T. A.,) of Lucan, and FERGUSON, (R.), of London, Ont., for "A machine for the destruction of Thistles, Wild Oats and other Weeds." Ottawa, dated 7th January, 1869,

No. 2949—BETHUNE, (D.,) of Port Hope, Ont., for "A Lightening Preserver." Ottawa, dated 7th January, 1869.

No. 2950—LUTZ, (M. C.,) of Galt, Ont., for "A Heater and Radiator." Ottawa, 5th January, 1869.

No. 2951—SIMPSON, (A ,) of Brighton, Ont., for "A Car-Coupler." Ottawa, dated 8th January, 1869.

No. 2952—BARNES, (T.,) and RIDLEY, (W.,) of Harwich, Ont., for "A Hay Lifter." Ottawa, dated 8th January, 1869.

No. 2953—MINCHIN, (G.,) of North East Hope, Ont., for "An Axle-Gauge." Ottawa, dated 8th January, 1869,

No. 2954—GAUVREAU, (L.P.,) of Quebec, Que., for "A Machine for the purifying of Magnetic Minerals." Ottawa, dated 11th January, 1869.

No. 2955—LARUE, (F. A. H.,) of Quebec, Que., for "A Magnetic Sand separator." Ottawa dated 11th January, 1869.

No. 2956—LARUE, (F. A. H.,) and AUDET, (O.,) of Quebec, Que., for "A Magnetic Sand separator." Ottawa, dated 11th January, 1869.

No. 2957—BURNELL, (M.,) of Toronto, Ont., for "A Boot and Knife Cleaner." Ottawa dated 14th January, 1869.

No. 2958—WOODS, (S. L.,) and HAZARD, (W. E.,) of Richmond, Ont., for "A Washing Machine." Ottawa, dated 14th January, 1869.

No. 2959—McLINN, (J.,) of Scotland, Ont., for "A Buggy Seat." Ottawa, dated 14th January, 1869.

No. 2960—DAVIS, (S.,) of Clinton, Ont., for "A Brace for Eave-Troughs." Ottawa, dated 14th January, 1869.

No. 2961—HUNT, (T. S.,) of Montreal, and DOUGLAS, (J.,) of Quebec, Que., for "Art of extracting Copper from its ores." Ottawa, dated 14th January, 1869.

No. 2962—BARTLETT, (E.,) ef Pagot, Ont., for "A Rotary Steam Engine." Ottawa, dated 14th January, 1869.

No. 2963—O'BRIAN, (G.,) of Eldorado, Ont., for "A Machine for extracting Gold or Silver from rock and earth." Ottawa, dated 14th January, 1869.

No. 2964—ELLERSHAUSEN, (F.,) of Montreal, Que., for "An improvement in the manufacture of Iron." Ottawa, dated 14th January, 1869.

No. 2965—McNAUGHTON, (J. C.) of Port Hope, Ont , for "A Carding Machine Spring Shell." Ottawa, dated 15th January, 1869.

No. 2966—WESTLICK, (J.,) of Hope, Ont., for "A Hay-Fork." Ottawa, dated 15th January, 1869.

No. 2967—LAZIER, (J. B.,) of Reach, Ont., for "An improved Revolving Horse Hay Rake." Ottawa, dated 15th January, 1860.

No. 2968—O'DELL, (A.,) of Port Hope, Ont, for "A clothes Drying Machine." Ottawa, dated 15th January, 1869.

No. 2969—LEGGO, (W. F.,) of Ottawa, Ont., for "A chemical Process for preparing Hides for Tanning." Ottawa, dated 15th January, 1869.

No. 2970—COCHRANE, (J.,) of Cramahe, Ont., for "A Churn." Ottawa, dated 15th January, 1869.

No. 2971—YOCOM, (J.,) of Dunnville, Ont., for "A hot air Stove." Ottawa, dated 15th January, 1869.

19

No. 2972—GROTE, (*G.* II.,) of Toronto, Ont., for "An Invalid and Fracture COUCH." Ottawa, dated 15th January, 1869.

No. 2973—McLEAN, (*T. Ferguson,*) of Goderich, Ont., for "A process for manufacturing SALT from Brine, and apparatus therefor." Ottawa, dated 15th January, 1869.

No. 2974—PIERCE, (*G. H.,*) of Richmond, Que., for "A Rock Drill HOLDER." Ottawa, dated 15th January, 1869.

No. 2975—LEGGE, (*C.,*) of Montreal, Que., for "Electric CLOCKS." Ottawa, dated 27th January, 1869.

No. 2976—McLEAN, (*G. N.,*) of Brockville, Ont., for "A self CAR-COUPLER." Ottawa, dated 27th January, 1869.

No. 2977—MILNER, (*W.,*) of Strathroy, Ont., for "An improvement in Waggon GEARS." Ottawa, dated 27th January, 1869.

No. 2978—STEAD, (*J. G.,*) of Newmarket, Ont., for "A DRAUGHT Regulator and Ventilator." Ottawa, dated 28th January, 1869.

No. 2979—BUTLER, (*J.,*) of Goderich, Ont., for "A Brine Evaporator and Salt DRYER." Ottawa, dated 15th January, 1869.

No. 2980—ANDERSON, (*J. E.,*) of Port Dover, Ont., for "A HORSE FORK." Ottawa, dated 15th January, 1869.

No. 2981—BELLEW, (*H. P.,*) of Quebec, Que., for "Railway CAR-WHEELS." Ottawa, dated 23rd January, 1869.

No. 2982—LAROCHELLE, (*A. H.,*) of St. Anselme, Que., for "An apparatus for drying Ore and Magnetic SAND." Ottawa, dated 23rd January, 1869.

No. 2983—FOSTER, (*J.,*) of Montreal Que., for "Permanent ways for Wooden RAILWAYS." Ottawa, dated 25th January, 1869.

No. 2984—NORTHAY, (*T.,*) of Hamilton, Ont., for "A KNITTING Machine." Ottawa, dated 25th January, 1869.

No. 2985—WISMER, (*L.,*) of Roseville, Ont., for "A Portable Angular Web FENCE." Ottawa, dated 28th January, 1869.

No. 2986—GADSBY, (*T.,*) of St. Thomas, Ont., for "A CHURN." Ottawa, dated 28th January, 1869.

No. 2987—PTOLEMY, (*J.,*) and PTOLEMY, (*R. A.,*) of Tapleytown, Ont., for "A Rotary Steam ENGINE." Ottawa, dated 16th January, 1869.

No. 2988—FOSTER, (*J.,*) of Montreal, Que., for "An improvement on apparatus for Separating and Extracting Magnetic substances from SAND, Ores and Rock." Ottawa, dated 18th January, 1869.

No. 2989—ASHBURY, (*G.,*) and WIMPERLEY, (*J.,*) of Belleville, Ont., for "Phosphate Bone MANURE." Ottawa, dated 18th January, 1869.

No. 2990—FINNIGAN, (*P. D.,*) of Quebec, Que., for "An improvement in the method of repairing TUBES in tubular boilers." Ottawa, dated 19th January, 1869.

No. 2991—MALLORY, (*A. W.,*) of Yonge, Ont., for "A Self-Loader Hay and Straw FORK." Ottawa, dated 29th January, 1869.

No. 2992—OSBORNE, (*W.,*) of Galt, Ont., for "The Art of preparing Meal from Wheat." Ottawa, dated 29th January, 1869.

No. 2993—GARDNER, (*F. A.,*) of Hamilton, Ont., for "A KNITTING Machine." Ottawa, dated 23rd January, 1869.

No. 2994—VAN WAGNER, (*P. S.,*) of Saltfleet, for "An improvement on WHIPPLETREE-HOOKS." Ottawa, dated 23rd January, 1869.

No. 2995—WILKINSON, (*J.,*) of Goderich, Ont., for "Improvements on machinery for Evaporating BRINE." Ottawa, dated 25th January, 1869.

No. 2996—BOTTOMLEY, (*T. H.,*) of Toronto, Ont., for "An EDGE-TOOL Grinding machine." Ottawa, dated 25th January, 1869.

No. 2997—WHITE, (*W.,*) and KELLY, (*J.,*) of Uxbridge, Ont., for " A Method of manufacturing SHEETING and LATHING for buildings." Ottawa, dated 2nd February,¡1869.

No. 2998—HIGHET, (*R.,*) of Cobourg, Ont., for " An improvement in the Art of building the boxes or bodies of Carriages." Ottawa, dated 3rd February, 1869.

No. 2999—DE WITT, (*T.,*) of Morpeth, Ont., for " A PUNCHING Machine." Ottawa, dated 3rd February, 1869.

No. 3000—DE WITT, (*T.,*) of Morpeth, Ont., for " A WASHING Machine." Ottawa, dated 3rd February, 1869.

No. 3001—HALES, (*C.,*) assignee of Hales, T., of Otonabee, Ont., for " An improvement on BOB-SLEIGHS." Ottawa, dated 3rd January, 1869.

No. 3002—HALES, (*C.,*) assignee of Hales, T., of Otonabee, Ont., for " A Pressure PUMP." Ottawa, dated 3rd February, 1869.

No. 3003—PARKER, (*J. O.,*) and PARKER, (*J. G.,*) assignees of Watson, J., of Toronto, Ont., for " A Steam RADIATOR." Ottawa, dated 4th February, 1869.

No. 3004—GILBERT, (*E. E.,*) of Montreal, Que., for " Improvements on STEAM Engines and BOILERS." Ottawa, dated 6th February, 1669.

No. 3005—BUCHANAN, (*J. A.,*) of Burford, Ont., for " A portable gang circular Saw MILL." Ottawa, dated 8th January, 1869.

No. 3006—CONWAY, (*G. O. S.,*) of Whitby, Ont., for " Improvements on RAKES to be attached to Reaping Machines." Ottawa, dated 8th February, 1869.

No. 3007—BENSEN, (*H. V.,*) of Borella, Ont., for " A CHURN." Ottawa, dated 8th February, 1869.

No. 3008—SMITH, (*M. L.,*) of Springfield, Ont., for " Improvements in platform LADDERS." Ottawa, dated 9th February, 1869.

No. 3009—HARRIS, (*J.,*) of Montreal, Que., for " An improvement on the apparatus for Heating or Cooling FLUIDS." Ottawa, dated 9th February, 1869.

No. 3010—GRIFFIN, (*R. A.,*) of Montreal, Que., for " A process for Curing or Drying PEAT." Ottawa, dated 11th February, 1869.

No. 3011—ASPDEN, (*T.,*) of Perth, Ont., for " The Art of Cleansing Tannin extract and apparatus therefor." Ottawa, dated 11th February, 1869.

No. 3012—WALKER, (*T.,*) and WALKER, (*W.,*) of Chinguacousy, Ont., for " An apparatus for Guiding PLOUGHS." Ottawa, dated 11th February, 1869.

No. 3013—FRASER, (*A. F.,*) of Chatham, Ont., for " Hame FASTENER or Hame Tie." Ottawa, dated 11th February, 1869.

No. 3014—WYATT, (*W. T.,*) of Simcoe, Ont., for " Mineral Printing INK." Ottawa, dated 12th February, 1869.

No. 3015—McNEIL, (*J.,*) of Lobo, Ont., for " A Pruning SAW." Ottawa, dated 13th February, 1869.

No. 3016—PRINCE, (*O.,*) assignee of Radcliffe, J., of Windsor, Ont., for " A double combination improved VELOCIPEDE." Ottawa, dated 13th February, 1869.

No. 3017—SELLS, (*H.,*) of Vienna, Ont., for " A WASHING Machine." Ottawa, dated 16th February, 1869.

No. 3018—RUTTAN, (*H. I.,*) of Cobourg, Ont., for " A Ventilating and Warming Apparatus." Ottawa, dated 16th February, 1869.

No. 3019—PENELTON, (*J.,*) of Guelph, Ont., for " An Improvement in the Art of balancing WINDOW SASHES." Ottawa, dated 19th February, 1869,

No. 3020—CHAFFEY, (*G.,*) of Kingston, Ont., for " Adjustable propelling SCREWS and RUDDERS." Ottawa, dated 19th January, 1869.

No. 3021—ALLCHIN, (*W.,*) of Paris, Ont., for " A hot air DRUM." Ottawa, dated 19th February, 1869.

No. 3022—VAN WAGNER, (*P. S.,*) of Saltfleet, Ont., for " An improvement on REAPING and MOWING Machines." Ottawa, dated 20th February, 1869.

No. 3023—COOK, (J.,) of Smith Ville, Ont., for "A Horse Hay Fork." Ottawa, dated 22nd January, 1869.

No. 3024—DICK, (P.,) of Invernay, Ont., for "An improvement in Grain CRADLES." Ottawa, dated 22nd February, 1869.

No. 3025—DRAKE, (W.,) of North Dumfries, Ont., for "A Revolving Clothes RACK ' Ottawa, dated 22nd February, 1869.

No. 3026—FERGUSON, (S.,) o. Hollowell, Ont., for "A Clothes Rack and Ironing TABLE combined." Ottawa, dated 22nd February, 1869.

No. 3027—BOOTH, (H.,) of Toronto, Ont., for "A Stove Pipe Damper and VENTILATOR." Ottawa, dated 22nd February, 1869.

No. 3028—WADE, (W.,) and MORREY, (J. F.,) of Ingersoll, Ont., for "A Portable FENCF." Ottawa, dated 22nd February, 1869.

No. 3029—MINOR, (B.,) of Walnfleet, Ont., for "A portable Clothes DRYER." Ottawa, dated 23rd February, 1869.

No. 3030—HARRIS, (P. P.,) of Quebec, Que., for "A Process or apparatus for Distilling spirituous Liquors in vacuo." Ottawa, dated 23rd February, 1869.

No. 3031—CAMERON, (A.,) of Kingston, Ont., for "A HAY-RAKE." Ottawa, dated 23rd February, 1869.

No. 3032—STEREMEN, (G. L,) of Aurora, Ont., for "Improved Hoof Cushion SPUR." Ottawa, dated 12th February, 1869.

No. 3033—CROOKS, (C. J.,) of Woodstock, Ont., for "A Corn PLANTER." Ottawa, dated 3rd February, 1869.

No. 3034—FURBER, (C.,) of Montreal, Que., for "Improvements on Dressing Glass Reflectors." Ottawa, dated 24th February, 1869.

No. 3035—TELFER, (J. C.,) of Montreal, Que , for "Railway CAR Couplings" Ottawa, dated 24th February, 1869.

No. 3036—HUMPHREY, (H.,) of Townsend, Ont., for "A CAR-COUPLER." Ottawa, dated 24th February, 1869.

No. 3037—IRVIN, (J.,) of Oshawa, Ont., for "A Heating and Cooking Apparatus." Ottawa dated 24th February, 1869.

No. 3038—PEDLAR, (G. H.,) of Oshawa, Ont,, for "A Heating Apparatus." Ottawa, dated 24th February, 1869.

No. 3039—BROOKS,[(G.,) of Picton, Ont., for "A machine for Shaving WOOD." Ottawa, dated 24th February, 1869.

No. 3040—GRANT, (P.,) of Morriston, Ont., for "A Potato PLANTER." Ottawa, dated 24th February, 1869.

No. 3041—WHITE, (M.,) of Ottawa, Ont., for "An improved Walking BOOT." Ottawa, dated 25th February, 1869.

No. 3042—COONEY, (J.,) of Emily, Ont., for "A Horse POWER." Ottawa, dated 26th February, 1869.

No. 3043—JONES, (C.,) assignee of Anderson, A., of London Township, Ont., for "A Damper and VENTILATOR." Ottawa, dated 26th February, 1869.

No. 3044—GRANT, (G.,) of Goderich, Ont., for "A Salt EVAPORATOR." Ottawa, dated 2nd March, 1869.

No. 3045—PILGRIM, (R. A.,) and MEAKINS, (G. H.,) of Hamilton, Ont., for "A machine for the manufacture of SODA WATER." Ottawa, dated 4th March, 1869.

No. 3046—VAN WAGNER, (P. S.,) of Saltfleet, Ont., for "A Tire Setting Machine." Ottawa, dated 4th March, 1869.

No. 3047—CLEMENT, (J. S.,) of Niagara, Ont., for "A Horse Hay FORK." Ottawa, dated 5th March, 1869.

No. 3048—YOUNG, (H.,) of Hamilton, Ont., for "An improvement in Tallow CUPS." Ottawa, dated 5th March, 1869.

151

No. 3049—DEAN, (*J.,*) of Oshawa, Ont., for " A Churn." Ottawa, dated 5th March, 1869.

No. 3050—JOHNSTON, (*J.,*) of Lindsay, Ont., for "A Weather Strip." Ottawa, dated 6th March, 1860.

No. 3051—BLOOMER, (*J.,*) of Hamilton, Ont., for ".A Gas and Smoke Consumer." Ottawa, dated 8th March, 1869.

No. 3052—GRIFFITH, (*J.,*) of Port Robinson, Ont., for " A combined Heel and Edge Shave." Ottawa, dated 9th March, 1869.

No. 3053—JOHNS, (*F.,*) of Sherbrooke, Que., for " A Window Lock." Ottawa, dated 9th March, 1869.

No. 3054—ROCKEY, (*E.,*) of Malahide, Ont., for "A machine for Cleaning the Coulters of Ploughs." Ottawa, dated 9th March, 1869.

No. 3055—MITCHELL, (*R.,*) of Montreal, Que., for " An Improved Peat Valve." Ottawa, dated 9th March, 1860.

No. 3056—SIMPSON, (*C. G. C.,*) and ENGHOLM, (*O.,*) of Montreal, Que., for "A Copying Press." Ottawa, dated 9th March, 1869.

No. 3057—DICK, (*J.,*) of Oshawa, Ont., for "A Velocipede." Ottawa, dated 9th March, 1869.

No. 3058—REIOL, (*R. J.,*) of Walsingham, Ont., for " A Washing Machine." Ottawa, dated 10th March, 1869.

No. 3059—REID, (*R.J.,*) of Walsingham, Ont., for "A Horse Collar." Ottawa, dated 10th March, 1869.

No. 3060—FRYATT, (*H.,*) of Aurora, Ont, for " A Bag Holder and Carrier." Ottawa, dated 10th March, 1869,

No. 3061—GRAHAM, (*E. P. C.,*) of Hallowell, Ont., for "Improvements in Bee Hives." Ottawa, dated 10th March, 1869.

No. 3062—DUFF, (*M.,*) of Hamilton, Ont., for " A composition of matter for the manufacture of Butter." Ottawa, dated 10th March, 1869.

No. 3063—DENISON, (*W. S.,*) of Richmond, Ont., for "A Washing Machine." Ottawa, dated 11th March, 1869.

No. 3064—WALTON, (*W.,*) of Trafalgar, Ont., for "A Machine for Mopping and Cleaning Floors." Ottawa, dated 11th March, 1869.

No. 3065—LLOYD, (*G.,*) of Whitchurch, Ont., for "A Washing Machine." Ottawa, dated 11th March, 1869.

No. 3066—COMSTOCK, (*W. H.,*) of Brockville, Ont., for "A Gas Apparatus." Ottawa, dated 11th March, 1869.

No. 3067—TOUHNIN,(*W. J,,*)of Toronto, for "A Chain Pump." Ottawa, dated 13th March, 1869.

No. 3068—FOSTER, (*J.,*) of Montreal, Que., for " A Refrigerator." Ottawa, dated 13th March, 1869.

No. 3069—VAN WAGNER, (*P. S.,*) of Saltfleet, Ont., for " An Improvement on Whiffletree Hooks." Ottawa, dated 15th March, 1869.

No. 3770—HARRIS, (*I. A.,*) of Herrwood, Ont., for "A Churn." Ottawa, dated 15th March, 1869.

No. 3071—ENGHOLM, (*O.,*) of Montreal, Que., for "A Furnace and Apparatus for Generating Steam." Ottawa, dated 24th March, 1869.

No. 3072—TOTMAN, (*E.,*) of Hamilton. Ont., for "A Horse Power." Ottawa, dated 20th March, 1869.

No. 3073—EMERY, (*T. W.;*) of Montreal, Que., for " A Broom-Holder." Ottawa, dated 20th March, 1869.

No. 3074—BRODIE, (*H.,*) of Ameliasburg, Ont., for ' A Milking Stool." Ottawa, dated 24th March, 1869.

No. 3075—CLARK, (*W.*,) of Montreal, Que., for "An improvement on Easy Chairs." Ottawa, dated 24th March, 1869.

No. 3076—FORSTER, (*A. G.*,) of Streetsville, Ont., for "A Portable Oven." Ottawa, dated 24th March, 1881.

No. 3077—SLADE, (*J.*,) of Chatham, Ont., for "A Weaving Machine." Ottawa, dated 24th March, 1869.

No. 3078—LORIMER, (*J.*,) of Hamilton, Ont., for "Improvements in Brooms." Ottawa, dated 20th March, 1869.

No. 3079—SIMPSON, (*C. G. C.*,) of Montreal, Que., for "An improvement on Paddle Wheels of Steamboats." Ottawa, dated 20th March, 1869.

No. 3080—HAWKINS, (*J.*,) of Trafalgar, Ont., for "A Tire Upsetting Machine." Ottawa, dated 22nd March, 1869.

No. 3081—YATES, (*H.*,) of Brantford, Ont , for " A Method of strengthening and preserving the Rails of iron and wooden Railways." Ottawa, dated 22nd March, 1869.

No. 3082—FENSOM, (*J.*,) of Toronto, Ont., for "An improvement on Copying Presses." Ottawa, dated 22nd March, 1869.

No. 3083—BACH, (*E.*,) of Toronto, Ont., for " An improvement in Breast Collars." Ottawa, dated 23rd March, 1869.

No. 3084—HUNT, (*J. H.*,) of Kingston, Ont., for "An improvement in Chimney Tops." Ottawa, dated 23rd March, 1869.

No. 3085—RUSSELL, (*W. G.*,) and RUSSELL, (*S.*,) of Millbrook, Ont., for " Improvements in Velocipedes." Ottawa, dated 24th March, 1869.

No. 3086—BRODIE, (*H.*,) of Ameliasburg, Ont., for "A Grinding Stone Attachment." Ottawa, dated 24th March, 1869.

No. 3087—PAGE, (*A. E. O.*,) of Point Abino, Ont., for " Improvements in Plough Coulters." Ottawa, dated 24th March, 1869.

No. 3088—ADAMS, (*T.*,) of Montreal, Que., for "Improvements on slide Valves, Pistons and Glands." Ottawa, dated 18th March, 1869.

No. 3089—WYATT, (*M. T.*,) of Quebec, Que., for " A Floating Saw Mill." Ottawa, dated 24th March, 1869.

No. 3090—BANER, (*H.*,) of Hamilton, Ont., for "An improvement in Peat or Turf Cutting Machines." Ottawa, dated 27th March, 1869.

No. 3091—BOWMAN, (*M.*,) of Montreal, Que., for "A Medicinal Compound." Ottawa, dated 18th March, 1869.

No. 3092—CLARK, (*G.*,) of Toronto, Ont., for " A Drying Grain Apparatus." Ottawa, dated 20th March, 1869.

No. 3093—BUCK, (*W.*,) of Otonabee, Ont., for "A Plough Cleaner." Ottawa, dated 20th March, 1869.

No. 3094—IRWIN, (*J.*,) of Oshawa, Ont., for " A Machine for condensing the waste Steam from Engines for the re-supply of the Boilers for heating and purifying water." Ottawa, dated 20th March, 1869.

No. 3095—LOVE., (*C.*,) of Strathroy, Ont., for "A Brick Machine." Ottawa, dated 20th March, 1869.

No. 3096—TOWNSLEY, (*W.*,) of Yorkville, Ont., for "An improvement on Machines for making Bricks." Ottawa, dated 20th March, 1869.

No. 3097—FLETT, (*J. H.*,) of Reach, Ont., for "Shoeing and Veterinary Stocks." Ottawa, dated 20th March, 1869.

No. 3098—LENT, (*M.*,) of Hamilton, Ont., for " A Composition for covering Roofs of Buildings." Ottawa, dated 29th March, 1869.

No. 3099—FORRESTER, (*W. H.*,) of Cannifton, Ont,, for "A Clothes and Fruit Dryer." Ottawa, dated 29th March, 1869.

No. 3100—MULHOLLAND, (*R.*,) of Ellice, Ont., for "Improvements in Sluice Mill Gates." Ottawa, dated 29th March, 1869.

No. 3101—SHERWIN, (*W.*,) of Ailsa Craig, Ont , for "A Machine for Pressing Cheese." Ottawa, dated 30th March, 1869.

No. 3102—ERSKINE, (*W. C. C.*,) of Eugenia, Ont., for "A Railway Ticket Holder." Ottawa, dated 30th March, 1869.

No. 3103—ERSKINE, (*W. C. C.*,) of Eugenia, Ont , for "A Machine for holding open the lid or cover of any kind of Box or Trunk." Ottawa, dated 30th March, 1869.

No. 3104—TWEDDLE, (*J.*,) of Esquesing, Ont., for "A Swing Churn." Ottawa, dated 30th March, 1869.

No. 3105—BELLEW, (*H. F.*,) of Quebec, Que., for "A Rail Car Brake." Ottawa, dated 30th March, 1869.

No. 3106—McEACHRAN, (*D.*,) of Montreal, Que., for "A Veterinary Bit." Ottawa, dated 30th March, 1869.

No. 3107—ERSKINE, (*W. C. C.*,) of Eugenia, Ont , for "Velocipedes." Ottawa, dated 30th March, 1869.

No. 3108—VANDEWATER, (*D. G.*,) of South Fredericksburgh, Ont , for "Improvements on Plough Coulters." Ottawa, dated 30th March, 1869.

No. 3109—THORN, (*C.*,) of Reach, Ont., for "An Interfering Hoof Pad." Ottawa, dated 30th March, 1869.

No. 3110—STEPHENS, (*R. E.*,) of Owen Sound, Ont., for "A Reversible Door Lock. ' Ottawa, dated 30th March, 1869.

No. 3111—BOWRON, (*A.*,) of Hamilton, Ont., for "A Hot Air Furnace." Ottawa, dated 30th March, 1869.

No. 3112—McPHERSON, (*A.*,) of Woodville, Ont., for "A Land Roller." Ottawa, dated 31st March, 1869.

No. 3113—GROSS,(*F.*,) of Montreal, Que,, for "A Truss." Ottawa, dated 2nd April, 1869.

No. 3114—SISSONS, (*J.*,) of Montreal, Que., for "An Ice Cream Freezer." Ottawa, dated 3rd April, 1869.

No. 3115—BROOKS, (*J.*,) of Coaticook, Que., for "A Process for making Gasoline or Benzine." Ottawa, dated 3rd April, 1869.

No. 3116—CAMPBELL, (*J*,) of Clarksburgh, Ont., for "A Swing Churn." Ottawa, dated 3rd April, 1869.

No. 3117—PATRIC, (*C. E.*,) of Oshawa, Ont., for "An Improved Grain and Seed Drill." Ottawa, dated 3rd April, 1869.

No. 3118—JACOBS, (*J. W.*,) of Port Perry, Ont., for "An Apparatus for producing an Oscillating Motion." Ottawa, dated 4th April, 1869.

No. 3119—ELSON, (*P.*,) of the Township of London, Ont., for "A Hay and Grain Rack and Unloader." Ottawa, dated 4th April, 1869.

No. 3120—BRANDRETH, (*W.*,) of Adelaide, Ont., for "Improvements in Scythe Snaiths." Ottawa, dated 7th April, 1869.

No. 3121—MILLER, (*A.*,) of Waterloo, Ont., for "A Hay and Grain Unloader." Ottawa, dated 7th April, 1869.

No. 3122—ORTH, (*J.*,) and HOUSEBERGER, (*M.*,) of Clinton, Ont., for "An Improvement on Plough Shares." Ottawa, dated 7th April, 1869.

No. 3123—MINIELY, (*A.*,) of Adelaide, and WALLACE, (*A. H.*,) of Warwick, Ont., for "Improvements on Bee Hives." Ottawa, dated 7th April, 1869.

No. 3124—WELCH, (*W.*,) of Montreal, Que., for "A Feather Bed Renovator." Ottawa, dated 10th April, 1869.

No. 3125—FORBES, (*J. W.*,) of Windsor, Ont., for "A Steam Balance Valve." Ottawa dated 10th April, 1869.

No. 3126—MORSE, (J.,) of Fingal, Ont., for "An Improvement on Thrashing Machines" Ottawa, dated 2nd April, 1869.

No. 3127—BLAKESLEY, (C. D.,) of Waterford, Ont., for "A Spring Bed Bottom." Ottawa dated 2nd April, 1869.

No. 3128—MOIR, (J.,) CURRY, (B. S.,) and ALSOP, (R ,) of Montreal, Que., for "An improvement in Gas Apparatus." Ottawa, dated 2nd April, 1869.

No. 3129—KIRK, (A.,) of Kincardine, Ont., for "An improvement on Spinning Wheels.' Ottawa, dated 2nd April, 1869.

No. 3130—CARROLL, (R.,) of Toronto, Ont , for "Improvements in Hoisting Machines or Apparatus." Ottawa, dated 3rd April, 1869.

No. 3131—LUTZ, (M. C.,) assignee of PRALL, (W.,) of Galt, Ont., for " An improvement for adjusting pinions on Horse Powers and other Machinery." Ottawa, dated 8th April, 1869.

No. 3132—CAMPBELL, (P.,) of South Norwich, Ont., for "An improvement on Churn Dashers." Ottawa, dated 9th April, 1869.

No. 3133—LOCKMAN, (C.,) of Hamilton, Ont., for " An improvement on Sewing Machines." Ottawa, dated 9th April, 1869.

No. 3134—MURPHY, (H.,) of Montreal, Que., for "Improvements in Horse Hay Rakes." Ottawa, 9th April, 1869.

No. 3135—TRUDEAU, (M.,) of Montreal, Que., for "An improvement on Carriage Tops." Ottawa, 9th April, 1869.

No. 3136—WALKER, (J.,) of Whitby, Ont., for " An improvement on Ploughs." Ottawa, 8th April, 1869.

No. 3137—GRANT, (P.,) of Clinton, Ont., for "A Hay Elevator." Ottawa, 12th April, 1869.

No. 3138—BRIGGS, (G. C.,) of Hamilton, Ont., for "A Milk Can Cooler and Strainer." Ottawa, 12th April, 1869.

No. 3139—CLAPP, (G.,) of Marysburgh, Ont., for "Improvements in Pumps." Ottawa, 12th April, 1869.

No. 3140—DENNIS, (J.,) of Newmarket, Ont , for "An improvement in the art of constructing Barns." Ottawa, 12th April, 1869.

No. 3141—CALDER, (W. M.,) and WILCOX, (S.,) of Glanford, Ont., for "Improvements on Triple Land Rollers." Ottawa, 13th April, 1869.

No. 3142—BECKETT, (T. G.,) of Hamilton, Ont., for "An improvement on Iron Still Bottoms." Ottawa, 13th April, 1869.

No. 3143—WARD, (W. H.,) of Thorold, Ont., for "Improvements in Rolling Mills." Ottawa, 14th April, 1869.

No. 3144—WARD, (W. H.,) of Thorold, Ont., for "Improvements in Harvesting Reapers." Ottawa, 14th April, 1869.

No. 3145—BAINES, (H.,) of Toronto, Ont., for "Improvements on Railroad Carriage Wheels and Crossings." Ottawa, 15th April, 1869.

No. 3146—THOMPSON, (H.,) of Newmarket, and HASTINGS, (C.,) of Darlington, Ont., for "Improvements in Gates." Ottawa, 15th April, 1869.

No. 3147—MARR, (D. D.,) of Woodhouse, Ont., for "A Waggon Jack." Ottawa, 16th April, 1869.

No. 3148—FOGAL, (H.,) of Whitchurch, Ont., for "An improvement on Land Rollers." Ottawa, 16th April, 1869.

No. 3149—STONE, (B.,) of Bond Head, Ont , for "An improvement in the construction of Bee Hives." Ottawa, 17th April, 1869.

No. 3150—SHOFF, (R.,) of the Township of London, Ont., for "An Adjustable Axle Pattern." Ottawa, 17th April, 1869.

No. 3151—WARMINTON, (R.,) of Montreal, Que., for "Improvements in Railway Snow Ploughs." Ottawa, 19th April, 1869.

No. 3152—WRIGHT, (D. D.,) of Oakville, Ont., for "A Car-Coupler." Ottawa, 16th April, 1869.

No. 3153—CALDER, (J.,) of Fergus, Ont., for "A Waggon Brake." Ottawa, 16th April, 1869.

No. 3154—WILLAN, (T. M.,) of South Monoghan, Ont., for "An improvement on Field Roller and Grass Seed Sower." Ottawa, 16th April, 1869.

No. 3155—McCULLOUGH, (D.,) of Oxford, Ont., for "A Corn Planter." Ottawa, 16th April, 1869.

No. 3156—MOORE, (J.,) of Brantford, Ont., for "An Improvement in Stove Grates and Furnaces." Ottawa, 19th April, 1869.

No. 3157—HECKADON, (F.,) of Humberstone, Ont , for "Improvements in Lubricators." Ottawa, 19th April, 1869.

No. 3158—REIF, (C.,) of Chatham, Ont., for "A Churn Dasher." Ottawa, 19th April, 1869.

No. 3159—FARLEY, (J. S,) of Sidney, Ont., for "An improvement in Steel Shears." Ottawa, 19th April, 1869.

No. 3160—SCOTT, (G.,) of Montreal, Que., for "An improvement on Racks." Ottawa, 19th April, 1869.

No. 3161—GROOM, (G.,) of Brockville, Ont., for "Improvements on Washing Machine." Ottawa, 19th April, 1869.

No. 3162—BRIMSON, (E. A.,) of Montreal, Que., "Improvement in Cork-cutting Machine." 2ith April, 1869.

No. 3163—THOMAS, (A.,) of Montreal, Que., for "An improvement in Clothes Dryers." Ottawa, 22nd April, 1869.

No. 3164—CHOATE, (T.,) of Glandford, Ont., for "Improvements in Gates." Ottawa, 22nd April, 1869.

No. 3165—ALLEN, (C.,) of Woodstock, Ont., for "Improvements in Field Roller and Seed or Plaster Roller." Ottawa, 22nd April, 1869.

No. 3166—McMILLAN, (W. G.,) of Erucefield, Ont., for "An improvement in Horse Shoes." Ottawa, 22nd April, 1869.

No. 3167—CROSS, (J.,) of Oakville, Ont., for "A Machine for the more easily and rapidly manufacturing of Baskets." Ottawa, 22nd April, 1869.

No. 3168—BECKETT, (F. G.,) of Hamilton, Ont., for "An Improvement in Gas Burners." Ottawa, 23rd April, 1869.

No. 3169—JOHNS, (D.,) of Exeter, Ont., for "Improvements in Hot Air Drums." Ottawa, 22nd April, 1869.

No. 3170—BARTER, (G. E.,) of London Township, Ont., for "An Improvement on Clothes Boilers." Ottawa, 1st May, 1869.

No. 3171—HEWTON, (R.,) of Harrington, Ont., for "Improvement on Waggon Jack." Ottawa, 1st May, 1869.

No. 3172—WILLIAMS, (Z.,) of Sandwich, Ont., for "Sower and Cultivator." Ottawa, 1st May, 1869.

No. 3173—STEVENS, (S.,) of Brockville, Ont., for "Improvements in Tea and Coffee Pots." Ottawa, 7th May, 1869.

No. 3174—MURRAY, (P.,) of Levis, Que., for "An Improvement on Coal Burning Grates." Ottawa, 1st May, 1869.

No. 3175—BAKER, (W. R..) of Wellington Square, Ont., for "Improvements on Veloci-pedes." Ottawa, 1st May, 1869.

No. 3176—LANCASTER, (J.,) of Ottawa, Ont., for "Improvements in Shingle Machine." Ottawa, 1st May, 1869.

No. 3177—LUNDY, (S. J.,) of Uxbridge, Ont., for "A Grain Drill." Ottawa, 1st May, 1869.

No. 3178—MAYNARD, (W.,) of Montreal, Que., for "An Evaporating Apparatus." Ottawa, 11th May, 1869.

No. 3179—HARRIS, (P. P.,) of Quebec, Que., for "A Process and Apparatus for Distilling, Refining and Deodorizing Petroleum and other oils in vacuo." Ottawa, 12th May, 1869.

No. 3180—COWLES, (H. D.,) of Hamilton, Ont., for "Improvements in the Art or Process of manufacturing Horse-shoe Nails." Ottawa, 12th May, 1869.

No. 3181—BARSALOUX, (J.,) of Saint Sebastien, Que., for "Improvements in Hay Press." Ottawa, 12th May, 1869.

No. 3182—MALLORY, (A. W.,) of Yonge, Ont., for "A Grappling Machine." Ottawa, 12th May, 1869.

No. 3183—PEPLER, (J.,) of Toronto, Ont., for "A Millstone Test." Ottawa, 12th May, 1869.

No. 3184—BUCK, (W.,) of Otonabee, Ont., for "Improvements in Harrow." Ottawa, 12th May, 1869.

No. 3185—FLEURY, (J.,) of Aurora, Ont., for "Improvements in Gang Ploughs." Ottawa, 12th May, 1869.

No. 3186—HERRISON, (J. D.,) of Toronto, Ont., for "Improvements on Railway Car Couplings." Ottawa, 12th May, 1869.

No. 3187—DEWE, (J.,) of Toronto, Ont., for "A Machine for Fastening and Labelling Bags." Ottawa, 13th May, 1869.

No. 3188—LOWE. (J. C.,) of Maryborough, Ont., for "An Improvement on Horse Poke." Ottawa, 12th May, 1869.

No. 3189—JURY, (T.,) of Adelaide, Ont., for "A Fruit Gatherer." Ottawa, 12th May, 1869.

No. 3190—TURNER, (A.,) of Brockville, Ont., for "A composition of matter for converting Raw Linseed Oil into superior Drying oil." Ottawa, 12th May, 1869.

No. 3191—BUCK, (W.,) of Otonabee, Ont., for "A Clasp for securing the Blades of Cross-cut Saws to their Handles." Ottawa, 12th May, 1869.

No. 3192—HILMAN, A., of Stratford, Ont., for "Improvements in Stove-pipe Ventilators." Ottawa, 28th April, 1869.

No. 3193—COWLES, (H. D.,) of Hamilton, Ont., for "An Improvement in Skates." Ottawa, 12th May, 1869.

No. 3194—VAN WAGNER, (P. S.,) of Saltfleet, Ont., for "An Improvement in Holdback for Carriage Thills or Poles." Ottawa, 12th May, 1869.

No. 3195—McCANNEL, (A.,) of Caledon. Ont., for "An Improvement on Machines for Spinning Yarn." Ottawa, 12th May, 1869.

No. 3196—POWLEY, (J.,) of Peel, Ont., for "An Improvement on the Shaker and Riddle for separating grain from chaff." Ottawa, 12th May, 1869.

No. 3197—LANCASTER, (J. J.,) of London, Ont., for "An Improvement on Tube Wells." Ottawa, 12th May, 1869.

No. 3198—JEFFERSON, (H.,) of Toronto, Ont., for "An Artificial Stone." Ottawa, 12th May, 1869.

No. 3199—AINSLIE, J., of North Dumfries, Ont., for "A Machine for Cleaning and Polishing Lamp Glasses, Chimneys, &c." Ottawa, 14th May, 1869.

No. 3200—AUGER, (J. E.,) of Bertie, Ont., for "A Hay and Straw Elevator." Ottawa, 17th May, 1869.

No. 3201—COLGAN, (J.,) of Tecumseth, Ont., for "A Revolving Sower." Ottawa, 7th May, 1869.

No. 3202—SMITH, (D.,) of Lakefield, Ont., for "A Saw Mill Swedger. Ottawa, 17th May, 1869.

No. 3203—McCALLUM, (A. A.,) of Hungerford, Ont., for "A Machine for Bandaging, Curing and Boxing Cheese." Ottawa, 17th May, 1869.

No. 3204—CLARK, (T. S.,) of Toronto, Ont., for "A Mouse and Rat Trap." Ottawa, 21st May, 1869.

No. 3205—GOING, (H.,) of Wolfe Island, Ont., for "An Improvement in the manufacture of Pails or Buckets." Ottawa, 21st May, 1869.

No. 3206—YOUNG, (J.,) of Brant, Ont., for "An Improvement in Churns." Ottawa, 22nd May, 1869.

No. 3207—YATES, (H.,) of Brantford, Ont., for "An Improvement on Railway Track Crossing." Ottawa, 22nd May, 1869.

No. 3208—MACKINTOSH, (C. H.,) of Strathroy, Ont., for " Improvements in Machines for Sowing Grain." Ottawa, 22nd May, 1869.

No. 3209—BEATTY, (G.,) of Beamsville, Ont., for "Improvements in the manufacture of Boots and Shoes." Ottawa, 22nd May, 1869.

No. 3210—WALMSLEY, (J.,) and ZIEGLER, (E.,) of Berlin, Ont., for "An Improvement on Plough Share." Ottawa, 24th May, 1869.

No. 3211—GARTH,(C.,) of Montreal, Que., for "Improvements on Hot Water Furnaces." Ottawa, 25th May, 1869.

No. 3212—CLARK, (T. S.,) of Toronto, Ont., for "Tuyère." Ottawa, 25th May, 1869.

No. 3213—THOMPSON, (H.,) of Waterdown, Ont., for "An Improvement on Traces." Ottawa, 25th May, 1869.

No. 3214—DEIL, (S.,) of Strathroy, Ont., for "A Thumble Churn." Ottawa, 27th April, 1869.

No. 3215—MILLS, (I.,) of Hamilton, Ont., for "Improvements on Stove-pipe Safe for Chimneys." Ottawa, 22nd May, 1869.

No. 3216—BRADSHAW, (I. H.,) ROBINSON, (E.,) of Peterborough, Ont., for "Improvements on Hay and Grain Rakes." Ottawa, 22nd May, 1869.

No. 3217—McKIM, (N. W.,) of Portland, Ont., for "An improvement on the Wheel Horse Rake." Ottawa, 25th May, 1869.

No. 3218—GRAHAM, (E. B.,) of South Monaghan, Ont., for "A Combined Seeder, Cultivator and Roller." Ottawa, 25th May, 1869.

No. 3219—POWER, (W.,) of Montreal, Que., for "An improvement in the art and mode of constructing Steam or Sailing Vessels, &c. Ottawa, 25th May, 1869.

No. 3220—TODD, (G. M.,) of Guelph, Ont., for "An improvement on Ventilators and Dampers combined." Ottawa, 25th May, 1869.

No. 3221—McPHERSON, (A.,) of Clinton, Ont., for "An improvement on Thrashing Machine." Ottawa, 25th May, 1869.

No. 3222—STEER, (T.,) of Millbrook, Ont., for "Improvements on Gates." Ottawa, 29th May, 1869.

No. 3223—SCOTT, (G.,) of Montreal, Que., for "An improvement in the manufacture of Cast Iron Columns." Ottawa, 31st May, 1869.

No. 3224—CONNOR, (J.,) of Oakville, Ont., for "Improvements in Window Blinds." Ottawa, 31st May, 1869.

No. 3225—MUNZINGER, (J. M.,) of Hamilton, Ont., for "A Self-binding Portfolio." Ottawa, 31st May, 1869.

No. 3226—BELL, (T.,) of Seaforth, Ont., for "Improvements in Spring Bed Bottoms." Ottawa, 31st May, 1869.

No. 3227—BARILLIER, (C.,) of Chatham, Ont., for "A Cooking and Washing Apparatus." Ottawa, 31st May, 1869.

No. 3228—SHORTS, (S. D.,) of Richmond, Ont., for "Improvements on Washing Machines." Ottawa, 31st May, 1869.

No. 3229—CAVAN, (J.,) of Oakville, Ont., for "Improvements on Churns." Ottawa, 31st May, 1869.

No. 3230—HARRISON, (T.,) of Marysburgh, Ont., for "Scrubbing Machine." Ottawa, 31st May, 1869.

No. 3231—BRASH, (J.,) Assignee and Co-inventor with Bennett, T., and Singer, G., of Linwood, Ont., for "A machine for the manufacture of Horse Shoes." Ottawa, 31st May, 1869.

No. 3232—FORBES, (I. W.,) of Windsor, Ont., for "Improvements in Valve Gear." Ottawa, 1st June, 1869.

No. 3233—LAWLER, (J. D.,) of Montreal, Que., for "Improvements on Sewing Machines." Ottawa, 2nd July, 1869.

No. 3234—McKENZIE, (W.,) of Morrisburgh, Ont., for "Improvements on Fanning Mill and Separator." Ottawa, 2nd June, 1869.

No. 3235—MALLORY, (*A. W.*,) of Yonge, Ont., for "Improvements on Washing Machines." Ottawa, 2nd June, 1869.

No. 3236—SWITZER, (*T.*,) of Norwich, Ont., for "Improvements on the Combined Roller, Grass Seed and Plaster Sower." Ottawa, 2nd June, 1869.

No. 3237—DUNN, (*P.*,) of Cote St. Paul, Que., for "Improvements on a Machine for Extracting Spikes and Nails." Ottawa, 2nd June, 1869.

No. 3238—HIGH, (*P.*,) of Mosa, Ont., for "Improvement on Fanning Mills." Ottawa, 2nd June, 1869.

No. 3239—FORBES, (*I. W.*,) Windsor, Ont., for "Improvements on Steam Chest." Ottawa, 1st June, 1869.

No. 3240—McMICKEN, (*G.*,) of Windsor, and MARTIN, (*O.*,) of Ottawa, Ont., for "Improvements in the art of evaporating Brines in the manufacture of Salt." Ottawa, 1st June, 1869.

No. 3241—STEWART, (*C. H.*,) of Montreal, Que., for "Improvements on Velocipedes." Ottawa, 2nd June, 1869.

No. 3242—RICHARDS, (*A. W.*,) Hamilton, Ont., for "Improvements on Field Rollers." Ottawa, 2nd June, 1869.

No. 3243—CHAPMAN, (*H.*,) of Ainleyville, Ont., for "Improvements on Churns." Ottawa, 2n1 June, 1869.

No. 3244—McGILL, (*J.*,) of Montreal, Que., for "Improvements on the art of manufacturing Liquids and Gases for extinguishing Fire, and for rendering clothes and other things inflammable. Ottawa, 2nd June, 1869.

No. 3245—HINTON, (*G.*,) and WOLSTENCROFT, (*C.*,) of Ancaster, Ont., for "Improvements on Water Power." Ottawa, dated 2nd June, 1869.

No. 3246—NICHOLSON, (*G.*,) of Fort Erie, Ont., for "Improvements on the ordinary Farm Gate." Ottawa, dated 7th June, 1869.

No. 3247—SIMPSON, (*C. O. C.*,) of Montreal, Que., for "An Air Brake." Ottawa, dated 21st May, 1869.

No. 3248—HOLLIDAY, (*J.*,) assignee of Fraser, (*A.*,) of Quebec, Que., for "A machine for freezing and keeping Fish, &c., &c." Ottawa, dated 7th June, 1869.

No. 3249—DION, (*J. H.*,) of Quebec, Que., for "The Art or Process of moulding the bouches for pulleys." Ottawa, dated 7th June, 1869.

No. 3250—MORRILL, (*E. W.*,) of Stanstead, Que., for "A machine for polishing knives, forks and spoons." Ottawa, dated 7th June, 1869.

No. 3251—SOULES, (*J.*,) of Queensville, Ont., for "Improvements on saw tangs for crosscut saws." Ottawa, dated 7th June, 1869.

No. 3252—LEWIS, (*C.*,) of Salford, Ont., for "An improvement in the art or mode of hanging farm and other gates" Ottawa, dated 7th June, 1869.

No. 3253—PARENT, (*J. B.*,) of Quebec, Que., for "A machine for separating Indian corn from the cob." Ottawa, dated 7th June, 1869.

No. 3254—MARTIN, (*C.*,) of Montreal, Que., for "Improvements on Paper Fylers." Ottawa, dated 7th June, 1869.

No. 3255—ROBBIN, (*E.*,) of Sophiasburgh, Ont., for "A Turning Machine." Ottawa, dated 7th June, 1869.

No. 3256—CULP, (*H.*,) of Louth, Ont., for "Improvements on Sowing Machines." Ottawa, dated 7th June, 1869.

No. 3257—LIDDELL, (*R. D.*,) and KERN, (*J. W.*,) of London, Ont., for "An improvement in fire grates for the use of Locomotive and stationary Engines, and of Boilers, Furnaces, and Arches." Ottawa, dated 7th June, 1869.

No. 3258—STROHM, (*G.*,) of North Cayuga, Ont., for "Improvements on Rack and Grain Lifter." Ottawa, dated 7th June, 1869.

No. 3259—ANDERSON, (*L.*,) and ANDERSON, (*J. W.*,) of Ameliasburg, Ont., for "Improvements on Horse Shovel." Ottawa, dated 7th June, 1869.

No. 3260—STONE, (*H. C.,*) of Picton, Ont., for "An improvement in the Art or Process of dressing and dyeing Furs, Wools, Hairs and Skins." Ottawa, dated 8th June, 1869.

No. 3261—DEWE, (*J.,*) of Toronto, Ont., for "A machine for fastening straps, scaling railway cars, mail bags, &c.." Ottawa, dated 8th June, 1869.

No. 3262—McDONNELL, (*J. W.,*) of Durham, Out., for "An improvement on Gates." Ottawa, dated 9th June, 1869.

No. 3263—COSLEY, (*J.,*) of Oakville, Ont , for "Improvements on breech-loading rifles and guns." Ottawa, dated 9th June, 1869.

No. 3264—WAIT, (*A.,*) of Augusta, Ont., for "Improvements in Horse Hay Forks." Ottawa, dated 10th June, 1869.

No. 3265—HUTSON, (*E.,*) of Hamilton, Ont., for "A machine for moving railway cars." Ottawa, dated 10th June, 1869.

No. 3266—MEAGHER, (*T. F.,*) of Montreal, Que., for "Improvements in Locks for Drawers and other things." Ottawa, 11th June, 1869.

No. 3267—BARTLEY, (*W. P.,*) of Montreal, Que., for "Improvements on Steam Engines and Pumps." Ottawa, dated 11th June, 1869.

No. 3268—BERTRAND, (*H.,*) of St. Placide, Que., for "A machine for the renewing and purifying of air in buildings." Ottawa, dated 15th June, 1869.

No. 3269—GROVES, (*J.,*) of Fitzroy, Ont , for "A Machine for holding bags." Ottawa, dated 15th June, 1869.

No. 3270—DUNKLEY, (*H. O.,*) of Sterling, Ont., for "Improvements on Pumps." Ottawa, dated 17th June, 1869.

No. 3271—BEECHER, (*W. F.,*) of Brockville, Ont , for "A Liquid Cooler." Ottawa, dated 17th June, 1869.

No. 3272—WRAY, (*W.,*) and TOE, (*A. H.,*) for "A Bee Hive." Ottawa, dated 17th June, 1869.

No. 3273—HUMPIDGE, (*F. A.,*) of Strathroy, Ont., for "Improvements on Hollow Mandrels." Ottawa, dated 17th June, 1869.

No. 3274—CHANTELOUP, (*E.,*) of Montreal, Que., for "Improvements in Fluid Taps." Ottawa, dated 11th June, 1869.

No. 3275—LYONS, (*J.,*) of Aurora, On'., for "A Chaff Separator." Ottawa, dated 14th June, 1869.

No. 3276—WRIGHT, (*T.,*) of South Norwich, Ont., for "An improvement in Spinning Wheel," Ottawa, dated 16th June, 1869.

No. 3277—YOUNG, (*C.,*) of Windsor, Ont., for "Improvements on Refrigerators or Ice Boxes." Ottawa, dated 16th June, 1869.

No. 3278—EVOY, (*R.,*) of Adelaide, Ont., for "Improvements in the construction of houses for Hogs, and the appurtenances and apparatus belonging thereto." Ottawa, dated 17th June, 1869.

No. 3279—SMITH, (*A. J.,*) of Harwich, Ont., for "A Grain Drill." Ottawa, dated 18th June, 1869.

No. 3280—CLIFF, (*C. F.,*) of Hespeler, Ont., for "An improved discharge for steam heating Pipes." Ottawa, dated 19th June, 1869.

No. 3281—WARNER, (*H.,*) of Quebec, Que., for "A Pump " Ottawa, dated 18th June, 1869.

No. 3282—PARKINS, (*T. C.,*) of West Farnham, Ont., for "A Sewing Machine." Ottawa, dated 26th June, 1869.

No. 3283—PICKLES, (*J.,*) of Montreal, Que., for "Improvements in the art of creating and producing the circulation of liquids in certain processes of manufacture, viz.: First, in the boiling or treating of fibrous materials or other substances in the various operations of paper pulp manufacture; second, in the boiling or leaching of barks and dye woods for the separation of the tannin, dyeing and coloring extracts; third, in the circulation of liquids in mash tubs and other vessels used in brewing and distilling, as also in the machinery or apparatus for carrying out and effecting such improved arts respectively." Ottawa, dated 2nd June, 1869

No. 3284—EATON, (R.,) of Montreal, Que., for "Improvements on cooking stoves, kitchen ranges and air furnaces." Ottawa, dated 23rd June, 1869.

No. 3285—FILION, J., of St. Eustache, Que., for "A machine for sharpening and repairing the teeth of saws." Ottawa, dated 23rd June, 1868

No. 3286—FOSTER, (A. M.,) of Hamilton, Ont., for "A Lubricating Cup." Ottawa, dated 23rd June, 1869.

No. 3287—ADAMS, (J. F.,) of Owen Sound, Ont., for "A Pressure Photograph Receptacle and display case." Ottawa, dated 23rd June, 1869.

No. 3288—MORNINGSTAR, (S.,) of Arkond, Ont., for "Improvements on the self-acting Hand Loom." Ottawa, dated 23rd June, 1869.

No. 3289—GUSTIN, (I. S.,) of Madoc, Ont., for "Improvements on Pumps." Ottawa, 23rd June, 1869.

No. 3290—DRAPER, (T.,) of Petrolia, Ont., for "Improvements in the manufacture of working barrels for pumps, for oil, and other wells." Ottawa, 24th June, 1869.

No. 3291—PLAXTON, (J.,) of Barrie, Ont., for "Improvement in the joining and fixing together the links of stovepipes by means of a thread or screw." Ottawa, 24th June, 1869.

No. 3292—EATON, (R.,) of Montreal, Que., for "Improvements in Locomotives and other Steam Engines." Ottawa, 24th June, 1869.

No. 3293—DOYLE, (R. J.,) of Owen Sound, Ont., for "Improvement on Sleighs and wheeled vehicles." Ottawa, 24th June, 1869.

No. 3294—STRUTHERS, (W.,) of Derby, Ont., for "A machine for sowing grain." Ottawa, 24th June, 1869.

No. 3295—FORBES, (J. W.,) of Windsor, Ont, for "Improvements on Balance Valve." Ottawa, 24th June, 1869.

No. 3296—DICKEY, (J. I.,) DICKEY, (J. N,) and DICKEY, (N.,) Assignees of SULLY, (K.,) of Toronto, Ont., for "A machine for raising and lowering Window Sashes." Ottawa, 25th May, 1869.

No. 3297—METCALF, (W.,) of North Augusta, Ont., for "Churns." Ottawa, 26th June, 1869.

No. 3298—SCATCHARD, (T.,) of Weyton, Ont., for "Syphon Water Vacuum and Steam Engine Condenser." Ottawa, 26th June, 1869.

No. 3299—BLACKBURN, (S.,) of London, Ont., for "Improvements on Steam Condenser and Oil Separator." Ottawa, 26th June, 1869.

No. 3300 —DAVIDSON, (L.,) of Brantford, Ont., for "Improvement in the construction and use of Railroad Car Wheels and Crossings." Ottawa, 28th June, 1869.

No. 3301—FAHRLAND, (T.,) of Montreal, Que., for "Improvement on Wool Dressers." Ottawa, 28th June, 1869.

No. 3302—WHITE, (S.,) Assignee of CAIN, (S. H.,) of Windsor, Ont., for "Improvements in Saw Mills." Ottawa, 28th June, 1869.

No. 3303—JACKSON, (J. S.,) of Stratford, Ont., for "Improvements in Waggon Jack." Ottawa 29th June, 1869.

No. 3304—JACKSON, (J. S.,) of Stratford, Ont., for "Improvements in Churns." Ottawa, 29th June, 1869. .

No. 3305—JACKSON, (J. S.,) of Stratford, Ont., for "Improvements in the art of hanging fence gates." Ottawa, 29th June, 1869.

No. 3306—DENNIS, (J.,) of Newmarket, Ont, for "Hay and Grain Elevator." Ottawa, 29th June, 1869.

No. 3307—HEWES, (W.,) of Toronto, Ont., for "Improvements in Washing Machines." Ottawa, 29th June, 1869.

No. 3308—TAYLOR, (*M.*,) of Wallace, Ont., for "Process of manufacturing cheese from sour milk." Ottawa, 29th June, 1869.

No. 3309—MILLER, (*A.*,) of Wilmot, Ont., for "A Hay Fork." Ottawa, 29th June, 1869.

No. 3310—ADAMS, (*T.*,) of Montreal, Que., for "Improvements in Slide Valves and Piston Packing. Ottawa, 29th June, 1869.

No. 3311—REID, (*R. J.*,) of Walsingham, Ont., for "Improvements in Washing Machine." Ottawa, 30th June, 1869.

No. 3312—MAYNARD, (*W.*,) of Montreal, Que., for "Improvements on the machine or apparatus for extracting the juices of hemlock and other barks, for tanning and other purposes." Ottawa, dated 3rd September, 1869.

No. 3313—CLEVELAND, (*S.*,) of Coaticook, Que., for "A machine for upsetting and bending tires, punching metals and gumming saws." Ottawa, dated 20th August, 1869.

No. 3314—MORRIS, *W. J.*, and ASPDEN, (*T.*,) of Perth, Ont., for "An improvement in the manufacture of salt and in apparatus therefor." Ottawa, dated 3rd September, 1869.

No. 3315—PLATT, (*S.*,) of Goderich, Ont., for "Improvements in the manufacture of salt." Ottawa, dated 23rd October, 1869.

No. 3316—ANDERSON, (*A.*,) of London, Ont., for "A Pea Harvester." Ottawa, dated 30th June, 1869.

No. 3317—WEBSTER, (*W.*,) of Montreal, Que., for "Improvements on Screw Propellers for Vessels." Ottawa, dated 13th June, 1869.

No. 3318—WILKINSON, (*J. A.*,) of Simcoe, Ont., for "A Railway Guard." Ottawa, dated 30th June, 1869.

No. 3319—WHITESIDE, (*H.*,) of Ottawa, Ont., for "An improvement in Portable Beds." Ottawa, dated 30th June, 1869.

No. 3320—EATON, (*R.*,) of Montreal, Que., for "Improvements in Railway Cars." Ottawa, dated 30th June, 1869.

No. 3321—DAVIDSON, (*L.*,) of Brantford, Ont., for "Improvements on Railway Trucks." Ottawa, dated 30th June, 1869.

No. 3322—MOORE, (*A. T.*,) of Markham, Ont., for "Improvements on Well Pumps." Ottawa, dated 30th June, 1869.

No. 3323—LAMBE, (*F.*,) of Montreal, Que., for "Improvements in the art of treating and purifying Paraffine." Ottawa, dated 30th June, 1869.

No. 3324—CRANDELL, (*B.*,) of Reach, Ont., for "A machine for opening and shutting gate." Ottawa, dated 7th July, 1870.

No. 3325—YOUNG, (*C.*,) of Windsor, Ont. for "A Washing Machine." Ottawa, dated 7th August, 1871.

PATENTS ISSUED FOR FIVE YEARS,

UNDER PATENT ACT OF 1869.

No. 1—W. HAMILTON, of Toronto, Ont., for " A machine for measuring liquids." Ottawa, dated 18th August, 1869.

No. 2—D. J. ELLIS, of Southwold, Ont., for " A composition for the destruction of the Canada Thistle." Ottawa, dated 18th August, 1869.

No. 3—H. KIMBALL, of Toronto, Ont., for " A machine for preventing boiler explosions." Ottawa, dated 18th August, 1869.

No. 4—J. KELLY, of Oakville, Ont., for " A machine for grappling, fastening upon, and drawing or moving weights." Ottawa, dated 18th August, 1869.

No. 5—J. WILSON, of St. Catharines, Ont., for "The art of distilling whiskey." Ottawa, dated 18th August, 1869.

No. 6—H. WANDBY, of Toronto, Ont., for " A Mustard or Ketchup Bottle." Ottawa, dated 18th August, 1869.

No. 7—T. L. SIMPSON, of Shediac, N.B., for " A method of making Soap." Ottawa, dated 19th August, 1869.

No. 8—F. OAKLEY, of Toronto, Ont., for " An improvement on a machine for bolting and fastening together two or more portions of machinery." Ottawa, dated 19th August, 1869.

No. 9—T. DIMMA, of Aurora, Ont., for " A Potato and Apple Parer." Ottawa, dated 19th August, 1869.

No. 10—T. BASSETT, of Collingwood, Ont., for " A Hay Fork." Ottawa, dated 19th August, 1869.

No. 11—T. MACKIE, of Melbourne, Que., for " A process of separating Copper and Silver from the ores." Ottawa, dated 19th August, 1869.

No. 12—E. E. ABBOTT, of Gananoque, Ont., for " An improvement on Lathes' Chucks.' Ottawa, dated 19th August, 1869.

No. 13—J. BLACKLOCK and W. T. SMITHETT, of Hastings, Ont., for " Improvements in Machines for Boiling and Washing Clothes." Ottawa, 19th August, 1869.

No. 14—W. MILNER, of Strathroy, Ont., for " Improvements in Waggons for holding the waggon box to the Bolsters." Ottawa, 19th August, 1869.

No. 15—J. P. JOHNSTON, of Oshawa, Ont., for " A machine for Coupling Railway Carriages." Ottawa, 20th August, 1869.

No. 16—G. J. BAKER, of Oakville, Ont., for " A Carriage Rub Iron." Ottawa, 19th August, 1869.

No. 17—F. A. H. LARUE, of Quebec, Que., for " Improvements in the manufacture of cast-iron and steel." Ottawa, 19th August, 1869.

No. 18—J. F. CASS, of L'Orignal, Ont., for " Improvements on Screw Wrenches." Ottawa 21th August, 1869.

No. 19—S. H. WILLIAMS, of Saltfleet, Ont., for " Improvements on Adjuster for raising or lowering the platform of Reapers." Ottawa, 20th August, 1869.

No. 20—W. MILNER, of Strathroy, Ont., for "Improvement in Sleighs and Cutters for supporting the sleigh or cutter box. Ottawa, 20th August, 1869.

No. 21—J. W. DeCASTRO, of Montreal, Que., for " Improvement in Filtering Machines." Ottawa, 27th August, 1869.

21

No. 22—J. S. JACKSON, of Stratford, Ont., assignee of A. FRECHETTE, Ottawa, Ont., for " Improvements in the Gig Saw." Ottawa, 25th August, 1869.

No. 23—C. W. SALADEE, of St. Catharines, assignee of G. E. SMITH, of Toronto, Ont., for " Improvement in machine Buck Saws." Ottawa, 25th August, 1869.

No. 24—C. BOECKH, of Toronto, Ont., for " Improvements in Paint or Varnish Brushes.' Ottawa, 27th August, 1869.

No. 25—B. T. MORRILL, of Rock Island, Que., for "Improvements on Ploughs." Ottawa, 27th August, 1869.

No. 26—A. KENNEDY, of East Zorra, Ont., for " A Land Roller " Ottawa, 7th September, 1869.

No. 27—J. STRAIN, of Artemesia, Ont., for " Improvement on Spinning Wheel." Ottawa, 7th September, 1869.

No. 28—G. McLEAN, of Aberfoyle, Ont., for " Improvements in Bee-hives. Ottawa, 7th September, 1869.

No. 29—J. NELSON, of Belleville, Ont., for " Improvements in Thrashing Machines. Ottawa, 7th September, 1869.

No. 30—J. W. JACOBS, of Reach, Ont., for "Improvements in Locks." Ottawa, 7th September, 1869.

No. 31—W. BENTLEY and C. MEE, of Normanby, Ont., for " Improvements in Locks." Ottawa, 7th September, 1869.

No. 32—A. G. BATSON, of Brantford. Ont., for " Improvement on Bedsteads." Ottawa, 8th September, 1869.

No. 33—A. CAMPBELL, of Badenoch Settlement, Ont , for " A machine for pulling and dressing Turnips." Ottawa, 8th September, 1869.

No. 34—J. DOTY, of Oakville, Ont., for " An Improvement in the manufacture of Carriage Axles." Ottawa, 8th September, 1869.

No. 35—J. MARRITT, of Aurora. Ont., for " Improvements in bag holders." Ottawa, 8th September, 1869.

No. 36—C. ALLEN, of Waterloo, Que., for " Improvements in Stoves " Ottawa, dated 8th September, 1869.

No. 37—E. LAVIGNE, of Quebec, Que., for "A Swing." Ottawa, dated 11th September, 1869.

No. 38—W. R. BURRAGE, of Toronto, Ont., for "A Horse Yoke." Ottawa, dated 11th September, 1869.

No. 39—W. L. KINMOND, of Montreal, Que., for "Improvements in Railway Car and Engine Trucks." Ottawa, dated 11th September, 1869.

No. 40—D. W. DOAN, of Aurora, Ont., for "A portable fire-proof ash safe Leach and Smoke House combined.' Ottawa, dated 11th September, 1869.

No. 41—H. W. OSTRAM, of Sidney, Ont., and R. HALL, of West Flamborough, Ont., for " Improvements in Cultivators and Gang Ploughs." Ottawa, dated 11th September, 1869.

No. 42—R. MITCHELL, of Montreal, Que., for " Improvements on Stair Steps." Ottawa, dated 11th September, 1869.

No. 43—M' R. MEIGS, of Bedford, Que., for " Improvements in Invalid and Fracture Beds." Ottawa, dated 11th September, 1869.

No. 44—G. LUCAS, of Sarnia, Ont, for " A Feather Renovator." Ottawa, dated 11th September, 1869.

No. 45—J. H. OSBORNE, of Guelph, Ont., for " An Improvement on Sewing Machines." Ottawa, dated 11th September, 1869.

No. 46—R. F. HEDDEN, of Toronto, Ont., for "Improvements on a certain machine for preventing boiler explosions." Ottawa, dated 11th September, 1869.

No. 47—W. H. AISTORP, of Blanshard, Ont., for " Improvements in Pea-harvesters and Hay-rakes." Ottawa, dated 11th September, 1869.

No. 48—J. MACDONALD, of Petrolia, Ont., for "An apparatus for burning potroleum tar." Ottawa, dated 11th September, 1869.

No. 49—T. W. RITCHIE, of Montreal, Quebec, for "The art of protecting bonds." Ottawa, dated 13th September, 1869.

No. 50—J. TROUT, of St. Vincent, Ont., for "An Improvement on]Farm Gates." Ottawa, dated 13th September, 1869.

No. 51—W. G. CORDINGLEY and M. DEROCHE, of Ottawa, Ont., for "Improvements in Dumb Stoves." Ottawa, dated 13th September, 1869.

No. 52—W. BRANDRETH, of Adelaide, Ont., for "An Improvement on framed soythe snaith." Ottawa, dated 13th September, 1869.

No. 53—F. CHAMBERS, of Walnfleet, Ont., for "Improvements on Bee Hives." Ottawa, dated 13th September, 1869.

No. 54—J. H. CAMERON, of Lochlel, Ont., for "Improvements in Chain Pumps." Ottawa, dated 13th September, 1869.

No. 55—N. S. CARD, of Normandale, Ont., for "A Fruit Drier." Ottawa, dated 15th September, 1869.

No. 56—R. LEWIS, of Melbourne, Que., for "Improvements on Churns." Ottawa, dated 15th September, 1869.

No. 57—W. CURTIS, of Belleville, Ont., for "Improvements on Turbine Water Wheel." Ottawa, dated 15th September, 1869.

No. 58—T. FOGG, of St. Mary's, Ont., for "Improvements in Railway Switches." Ottawa, dated 15th September, 1869.

No. 59—A. J. LEMON, of Beverly, and F. CLEMENT, of Ancaster, Ont., for "Improvement on revolving Plough Coulter." Ottawa, dated 15th September, 1869.

No. 60—J. B. P. STACY, of Hamilton, Ont., for "A Washing Machine." Ottawa, dated 15th September, 1869.

No. 61—W. A. LEGGO, of Montreal, Que., for "An Improvement in Photographic Camera." Ottawa, dated 15th September, 1869.

No. 62—R. BEEDLE, of Dunwich, Ont., for "An Improvement on Hinges." Ottawa, dated 18th September, 1869.

No. 63—T. THOMAS, of Bowmanville, Ont., for "An Improvement on Oil Cans." Ottawa, dated 18th September, 1869.

No. 64—D. S. CORNELL, of Warwick, Ont., for "An Improvement in Hanging Gates." Ottawa, dated 18th September, 1869.

No. 65—R. EATON, of Montreal, Que., for "The art and apparatus for manufacturing lubricating oil from Petroleum Oil." Ottawa, dated 18th September, 1869.

No. 66—J. B. PIKE, of Raleigh, Ont., for "An Improvement in Inserted Saw Teeth." Ottawa, dated 18th September, 1869.

No. 67—W. A. LEGGO, of Montreal, Que., for "An Improvement in Photography." Ottawa, dated 18th September, 1869.

No. 68—C. McCALLUM, of Toronto, Ont., for "Improvement in Chopping Mill." Ottawa, dated 18th September, 1869.

No. 69—M. GARDNER, of Hespeler, Ont., for "An Improvement in the Furnaces of Steam Engine Boilers." Ottawa, dated 18th September, 1869.

No. 70—H. BAINES, of Toronto, Ont., for "Improvements in reworking old railway iron or rails or bars." Ottawa, dated 18th September, 1869.

No. 71—C. HOLLANDS, of Mitchell, Ont., for "An Improvement in the construction of Rotary Engines." Ottawa, dated 27th September, 1869.

No. 72—I. KINNEY, of Woodstock, Ont., for "An Improvement in the manufacture of Bolt Heads, Nuts and Washers for Railway." Ottawa, dated 27th September, 1869.

No. 73—J. WOODLEY, of Quebec, Que., for "Improvements in Boot and Shoe Heels." Ottawa, dated 27th September, 1869.

No. 74—E. PRICE, of Bayham, Ont., for "An improvement on Straw Cutter." Ottawa, dated 27th September, 1869.

No. 75—C. MYERS, of Oshawa, Ont., for "Improvements on Churn." Ottawa, dated 27th September, 1869.

No. 76—F. CULHAM, of Widder Station, Ont., for "Improvements on Thrashing Machines." Ottawa, dated 27th September, 1869.

No. 77—J. SAILES, of Little Britain, Ont., for "A machine for bending timber for Sleigh Runners." Ottawa, dated 27th September, 1869.

No. 78—F. J. GOODING, of Montreal, Que., for "The art of drying Peat." Ottawa, dated 27th September, 1869.

No. 79—W. MILNER, of Strathroy, Ont., for "An improvement in Waggons." Ottawa, dated 27th September, 1869.

No. 80—R. BROWN, of Stratford, Ont., for "An Elastic Shafting to prevent Back Lash." Ottawa, dated 27th September, 1869.

No. 81—W. DYSON, of London, Ont., for "The art of heating Vats and their contents in the manufacture of Cheese." Ottawa, dated 27th September, 1869.

No. 82—H. M. McKAY, of Woodstock, Ont., for "A Washing Machine." Ottawa, dated 27th September, 1869.

No. 83—P. BUTLER, of Walsingham, Ont., for "Improvements on Door and Gate Hinges." Ottawa, dated 1st October, 1869.

No. 84—A. A. McCALLUM, of Tweed, Ont., for "A machine for boxing, shipping, and preserving Cheese." Ottawa, dated 1st October, 1869.

No. 85—J. GRENVILLE, of Thorold, Ont., for "An improvement on Door and Gate Fasteners." Ottawa dated 1st October, 1869.

No. 86—I. KINNEY, of Woodstock, Ont., for "An improvement in the manufacture of springs for buggies, buck-boards and other wheeled vehicles." Ottawa, dated 1st October, 1869.

No. 87—G. SCOTT, of Montreal, Que., for "A machine for grinding sad irons." Ottawa, dated 1st October, 1869.

No. 88—A. McARTHUR, of Elora, Ont., for "An improvement on Horse Rakes." Ottawa, dated 1st October, 1869.

No. 89—H. CARTER, of Malahide, Ont., for "Improvements in Ditching Machines." Ottawa, dated 1st October, 1869.

No. 90—C. H. WATEROUS, of Brantford, Ont., for "A Set Gauge for Sawing Machines." Ottawa, dated 1st October, 1869.

No. 91—W. BAKER, of Arnprior, Ont., for "A machine for moulding and carrying bricks." Ottawa, dated 9th October, 1869.

No. 92—C. W. MUGRIDGE, of Hamilton, Ont., for "Improvements in the manufacture of Brooms and Brushes." Ottawa, dated 9th October, 1869,

No. 93—M. PRUE, of Walsingham, Ont., for "Improvement on Rotating Harrow." Ottawa, dated 9th October, 1869.

No. 94—W. MUIR, of Montreal, Que., for "Improvements on Multiple Sewing Machine." Ottawa, 15th October, 1869.

No. 95—G. GROOM, of Brockville, Ont., for "Improvements in Churns." Ottawa, 17th October, 1869.

No. 96—F. B. SPARKS, of Toronto, assignee of G. W. SYLVESTER, Dundas, Ont., for "A machine or apparatus for Deodorizing, Decolorizing Crude Petroleum, &c." Ottawa, 17th October, 1869.

No. 97—F. B. SPARKS, of Toronto, assignee of G. W. SYLVESTER, of Dundas, Ont., for "A machine or apparatus for Burning Animal Charcoal and other Carbons." Ottawa, 17th October, 1869.

No. 98—F. B. SPARKS, of Toronto, assignee of G. W. SYLVESTER, of Dundas, Ont., for

"An apparatus for extracting from and cleansing any filtering or macerating medium of any soluble matter remaining therein." Ottawa, 17th October, 1869.

No. 99—A. ST. JACQUES, of Yamachiche, Que., for "A composition of matter for the treatment and cure of sore throat." Ottawa, 17th October, 1869.

No. 100—J. BONATHAN, of Bowmanville, Ont., for "Improvements on a Bending Apparatus.' Ottawa, 15th October, 1869.

No. 101—J. BOWES, of Warnick, Ont., for "Improvements on machines for Churning." Ottawa, 15th October, 1869.

No. 102—S. BUSCHLEN, of Port Elgin, Ont., for "Improvements on Clothes Dryer." Ottawa, 15th October, 1869.

No. 103—B. W. WALTER, of Keltleby, Ont., for "A comb'ned Cultivator and Grain Drill." Ottawa, 15th October, 1869.

No. 104—A. DOUGLAS, of Ottawa, Ont., for "An apparatus to support Poles of Waggons, &c." Ottawa, 15th October, 1869.

No. 105—U. PHELPS, of Beachville, Ont., for "A machine for Shoeing Horses." Ottawa, 15th October, 1869.

No. 106—J. MORNINGSTAR, of Waterloo, Ont., for "Improvements in machines for Cultivating Land." Ottawa, 15th October, 1869.

No. 107—A. SLUTHOUR, of Brockville, Ont., for "A Force Pump." Ottawa, 15th October, 1869.

No. 108—C. MEE, of Toronto, Ont., for "A Bag Tie." Ottawa, 21st October, 1869.

No. 109—J. L. O. VIDAL, of St. Louis, Que., for "An improvement in Ploughs." Ottawa, 21st October, 1869.

No. 110—B. P. SNIDER, of Bertie, Ont., for "A machine for the purpose of Sawing Wood." Ottawa, 21st October, 1869.

No. 111—J. H. OSBORN, of Guelph, Ont., for "An Improvement on the Single Thread Sewing Machine for looping the Stitch." Ottawa, 21st October, 1869.

No. 112—J. H. SWEAZEY, of Ancaster, Ont., for "Improvements on 'Hay Lifters." Ottawa, 21st October, 1869.

No. 113—J. MUNSON, of Collingwood, Ont., for "Improvements in Beehives." Ottawa, 23th October, 1869.

No. 114—S. S. PHILLIPS, of St. Catharines, Ont., for "A machine for Running Boats." Ottawa, 28th October, 1869.

No. 115—W. DALES, of Cookstown, Ont., for "A Horse Hay Fork." Ottawa, 28th October, 1869.

No. 116—P. J. PILKEY, of Burford, Ont., for "Improvements in Waggon Racks." Ottawa, 28th October, 1869.

No. 117—L. LARIVÉE, of Montreal, Que., for "A composition of matter for preventing the falling off of hair and facilitating its growth, &c." Ottawa, 28th October, 1869.

No. 118—J. J. WARNER, of Otterville, Ont., for "A Whiffletree Snap." Ottawa, 30th October, 1869.

No. 119—G. McMICKEN, of Windsor, Ont., for "Salt Evaporator." Ottawa, 30th Oct., 1869.

No. 120—D. B. GARTON, of Barrie, Ont., for "A Washing Machine." Ottawa, 30th October, 1869.

No. 121—J. ALLEN, of Kerwood, Ont., for "Improvement on Churns." Ottawa, 30th October, 1869.

No. 122—J. FOSTER, of Montreal, Que., for "An improvement on apparatus for removing Snow from Railway Tracks." Ottawa, 30th October, 1869.

No. 123—J. L. MORDEN, of London, Ont., for "Improvements on Reaping Machines." Ottawa, 1st November, 1869.

No. 124—A. SLUTHOUR, of Brockville, Ont., for "Pumps." Ottawa, 1st November, 1869.

No. 125—P. ROUTLEDGE, of King, Ont., for "A machine for Punching Horse Shoes." Ottawa, 1st November, 1869.

No. 126—H. G. ABBOTT, of London Ont., for "An improvement on Vehicle Spring." Ottawa, 1st November, 1869.

No. 127—D. L. REY, of Montreal, Que., for "Improvements in the construction of Clocks." Ottawa, dated 1st November, 1869.

No. 128—C. HOUGH, of Quebec, Que., for "An improvement on Horse Shoes." Ottawa, dated 1st November, 1869.

No. 129—J. VESSOT, sen., and S. VESSOT, jun., of Joliette, Que., for "Sowing and Harrowing Machines." Ottawa, dated 1st November, 1869.

No. 130—G. W. CORBITT, of Toronto, Ont., for "A machine for applying treadle power to Sewing and other Machines." Ottawa, dated 1st November, 1869.

No. 131—G. A. MASSON, of Charlottenburgh, Ont., for "An improvement on Carriages." Ottawa, dated 5th November, 1869.

No. 132—I. KINNEY. of Woodstock, Ont., for "A Washing Machine." Ottawa, dated 5th November, 1869.

No. 133—G. HEAL, of Toronto, Ont , for "The art or process for preparing Sheep Skins." Ottawa, dated 8th November, 1869.

No. 134—J. FLINT, of St. Catharines, Ont., for "An Improvement in Cross-Cut Saws." Ottawa, dated 8th November, 1869.

No. 135—J. FLINT, of St. Catharines, Ont , for "An improvement in Saw Handles." Ottawa, dated 8th November, 1869.

No. 136—J. H. YOUNG, of Hamilton, Ont., for "An improvement on Churns." Ottawa, dated 8th November, 1869.

No. 137—J. K. BECKWITH, of Hillsburg, N.S., for "A Wind Wheel." Ottawa, dated 8th November, 1869.

No. 138—J. MURPHY, of St. John, N. B., for "An improvement in the manufacture of Scrubbing Brushes." Ottawa, dated 8th November, 1869.

No. 139—W. H. DART and J. S. DART, of Spryfield, N.S., for "An improvement on Coasting Sleighs and Steering Apparatus." Ottawa, dated 12th November, 1869.

No. 140—C. TROYER, of Stayner, Ont., for "Improvements on Car Coupler." Ottawa, dated 12th November, 1869.

No. 141—J. WRIGHT, of Hamilton, Ont., for "An improvement on Clothes Pin." Ottawa, dated 12th November, 1869.

No. 142—C. IRVIN, of Belleville, Ont., for "Improvements on Sowing Machines." Ottawa, dated 12th November, 1869.

No. 143—S. F. HUMPHREY, of Wardsville, Ont., for "Improvements in Sulkies." Ottawa, dated 12th November, 1869.

No. 144—W. H. GOODALE, of Toronto, Ont., for "A Washing Machine." Ottawa, dated 18th November, 1869.

No. 145—W. SYKES, of Toronto, Ont., for "An improvement in the art of tunnelling under rivers with alluvial beds." Ottawa, dated 18th November, 1869.

No. 146—M. HOWLES, of Hamilton, Ont., for "An improvement on Dampers for Stoves, Ovens, &c." Ottawa, dated 18th November, 1869.

No. 147—J. W. KING, of Shubenacadie, N.S., for "Improvements in machines by which fish are enabled to surmount and pass dams, cascades and other obstructions in water." Ottawa, dated 18th November, 1869.

No. 148—S. McPHERSON, of Ottawa, Ont., for "A Foot Warmer Lantern." Ottawa, dated 18th November, 1869.

No. 149—C. H. GUARD, of London, Ont., for "Improvements on Fifth Wheel and Spring Supporter." Ottawa, dated 18th November, 1869.

No. 150—H. B. CASGRAIN, of Ottawa, Ont., for "Improvements in the art of arranging Records and Documents in Fyles." Ottawa, dated 20th November, 1869.

No. 151—S. DE VEAUX, of Woodruff, St. Catharines, assignee of C. DEAN, of Crowland, Ont., for "A Washing Machine." Ottawa, dated 25th November, 1869.

No. 152—C. DEAN, of Port Robinson, Ont., for "Lamps and Lanterns." Ottawa, dated 25th November, 1869.

No. 153—E. F. AUSTIN, of Ottawa, Ont., for "A universal Lifter, Hammer, Screw Wrench, and Driver." Ottawa, dated 22nd November, 1869.

No. 154—A. W. MALLORY, of Yonge, Ont., for "Improvemen's in Hay Lifters." Ottawa, dated 22nd November, 1869.

No. 155—E. F. AUSTIN, of Ottawa, Ont., for "A machine for pounding Beef Steaks." Ottawa, dated 22nd November, 1869.

No. 156—C. BARBER, of Meaford, Ont., for "A Water Turbine." Ottawa, dated 25th November, 1869.

No. 157—J. DELGARNO, of Chatham, Ont., for "A composition for Shaft Bearings or Journal Boxes." Ottawa, 25th November, 1869.

No. 158—A. W. MALLORY, of Yonge, Ont , for "Improvements in Carriage Brace." Ottawa, 25th November, 1869.

No. 159—H. McININCH, of Belleville, Ont., "Improvement on Horse Shoes." Ottawa, dated 25th November, 1869.

No. 160—L. NIGHTINGALE, of Windsor, Ont., for "Improvements in Spring Bed Bottoms." Ottawa, dated 25th November, 1869.

No. 161—W. McDONALD, of Galt, for "An improvement in Hay Forks." Ottawa, dated 25th November, 1869.

No. 162—J. B. DEGUISE, of Montreal, Que., for "A machine for Chopping Meat." Ottawa, 26th November, 1869.

No. 163—A. DUNBAR, of Woodstock, Ont., for "Improvement in Horse Collars and Harness." Ottawa, 27th November, 1869.

No. 164—A. DUNBAR, of Woodstock, Ont., for "An Insole for Boots and Shoes." Ottawa, 27th November, 1869.

No. 165—J. W. WRIGHT, of Montreal, Que., for "Improvements on machines for Carving Wood, etc." Ottawa, 26th November, 1869.

No. 166—S. J. LYMAN, of Montreal, Que., for "Improvements on Railway Cars." Ottawa, 26th November, 1869.

No. 167—W. F. BEECHER, of Brockville, Ont., for "Improvements on Coal Stoves." Ottawa, 26th November, 1869.

No. 168—A. NEVILLE, of Napanee, Ont., for "Oil or Grease Extractor." Ottawa, 26th November, 1869.

No. 169—E. J. ROBINSON and W. ROBINSON, of Whitby, Ont., for "A machine for holding Window Blinds." Ottawa, 26th November, 1869.

No. 170—G. SEGER, of Humberstone, Ont., for "Improvement on a machine for Husking Corn." Ottawa, 6th December, 1869.

No. 171—J. DILWORTH and J. C. HODGINS, of Toronto, Ont., for "Improvements in apparatus for condensing the steam of high-pressure Steam Engines." Ottawa, 6th December, 1869.

No. 172—W. WELCH, of Montreal, Que., for "A Vapor Fumigator." Ottawa, 6th December, 1869.

No. 173—S. KINNEY, of Ottawa, Ont., for "A Saw Swage." Ottawa, 6th December, 1869.

No. 174—E. HAINES, of Cheltenham, Ont., for "An improvement on Spinning Wheels." Ottawa, 12th December, 1869.

No. 175—J. F. SHOEMAKER, of Waterloo, Ont., for "Improvements on Rakes." Ottawa, 12th December, 1869.

No. 176—W. J. WRIGHT, of London, Ont., for " Improvements on Bob Sleighs." Ottawa, 12th December, 1869.

No. 177—C. W. MUGRIDGE, of Hamilton, Ont., for ' Improvements in the manufacture of Brooms." Ottawa, 12th December, 1869.

No. 178—J. F. MOSSIMAN, of Toronto, Ont., for " Improvements in Coal Scuttles." Ottawa, 12th December, 1869.

No. 179—W. CRAIG, of Brampton, Ont., for " A process of enamelling Photographs." Ottawa, 12th December, 1869.

No. 180—E. L. FENERTY, of Halifax, N. S., for Skates." Ottawa, 12th December, 1869.

No. 181—S. CLEVELAND, of Coaticook, Que., for " A machine for Upsetting Tires, &c." Ottawa, 12th December, 1869.

No. 182—T. SCATCHARD, of Wyton, Ont., for " An improvement in Steam Engine Condenser." Ottawa, 12th December, 1869.

No. 183—J. TOMLINSON, of Pickering, Ont., for " Steam Coiled Hoop." Ottawa, 12th December, 1869.

No. 184—J. D. LAWLER, of Montreal, Que., for " Sewing Machines." Ottawa, 12th December, 1869.

No. 185—G. ANSLEY, of Guelph, Ont., for " Washing Machines." Ottawa, 17th December, 1869.

No. 186—J. B. ARMSTRONG, of Guelph, Ont., for " Improvements in Cutters." Ottawa, 17th December, 1869.

No. 187—R. SINCLAIR, of Toronto, Ont., for " A machine for producing a complete circulation of the water in Steam Boilers." Ottawa, 17th September, 1869.

No. 188—F. A. HUMPIDGE, of Strathroy, Ont., for " Improvements in Sawing Machines." Ottawa, 17th December, 1869.

No. 189—B. R. DEACON, of Montreal, Que , for " Improvements in Coal Safe." Ottawa, 17th December, 1869.

No. 190—A. CLIMENHEGG, of Adelaide, Ont., for " Improvements on Gates." Ottawa, 17th December, 1869.

No. 191—H. WATERS, of London, Ont., for " Improvements on Railway Chair and Couch." Ottawa, 20th December, 1869.

No. 192—G. HUNTINGTON, of Brantford, Ont., for " Washing Machines." Ottawa, 20th December, 1869.

No. 193—R. G. NASH, of Morrisburgh, Ont., for " A machine for Reducing Wood into Pulp." Ottawa, 20th December, 1869.

No. 194—W. M. SOMERVILLE, of Ottawa, Ont., for " A Stumping Machine." Ottawa, 20th December, 1869.

No. 195—R. STANDING, of Chinquacgusy, Ont., for " A machine for Cleaning out Stables." Ottawa, 20rd December, 1869.

No. 196—J. BROKENSHIRE, of Kingston, Ont., for " Improvements in Pumps." Ottawa, 23rd December, 1869.

No. 197—L. BRIGHT and J. T. MULLIN, of Brampton, Ont., for " Car Coupler." Ottawa, 23rd December, 1869.

No. 198—J. LAWRENCE, of Pickering, Ont , for " Improvements on Pitch Fork." Ottawa, dated 23rd December, 1869.

No. 199—J. R. CURRY, of Windsor, Ont., for " Flour Bolts." Ottawa, dated 23rd December, 1869.

No. 200—J. FOSTER, of Montreal, Que., for " Improvements in the construction of Rails for Wooden Railways." Ottawa, dated 23rd December, 1869.

No. 201—E. S. RUPERT, of Centreville, Ont., for " Improvements in Drum Heaters for Stoves." Ottawa, dated 23rd December, 1869.

No. 202—P. W. S. HAVILL, of Paris, Ont , for " Improvements in Furnace and Heaters." Ottawa, dated 23rd December, 1809.

No. 203—W. FRAZER, of Esquising, Out., for "Improvements in a machine for raising and conveying Hay or Merchandize." Ottawa, dated 27th December, 1869.

No. 204—T. GREENLESS, of Seaforth, Ont., for " A Pruning Knife." Ottawa, dated 27th December, 1869.

No. 205—J. FOSTER, of Montreal, Que., for " An Improvement on Permanent Ways for Wooden Railways." Ottawa, dated 5th January, 1870.

No. 206—A. MINOR, of Walnfleet, Ont., for "A Cutter Bar." Ottawa, dated 5th January, 1870.

No. 207—A. F. WARD, of Chatham, Ont., for " A Heat Regulator." Ottawa, dated 5th January, 1870.

No. 208—R. HENWOOD, of Brantford, Ont., for " Improvements in Fire Grate." Ottawa, dated 5th January, 1870,

No. 209—S. KINNEY, of Ottawa, Ont., for "Improvement in Saws." Ottawa, dated 5th January, 1870.

No. 210—J. MARR, of Woodhouse, Ont., for " An Improvement on Stove Pipe Shelves." Ottawa, dated 3rd January, 1870.

No. 211—C. McHAFFIE, of Hamilton, Ont., for "Improvements on common Stove Pipes." Ottawa, dated 3rd January, 1870.

No. 212—F. G. POKORNY and D. MOORE, of Montreal, Que., for " Improvements in Slate and File Squaring Machine." Ottawa, dated 3rd January, 1870.

No. 213—M. I. WILKINS, of Halifax, N.S., for "Improvements in Taps." Ottawa, dated 3rd January, 1870.

No. 214—R. SCARLETT, of Mooretown, Ont., for " An Improvement in the construction of Sleigh Knees." Ottawa, dated 3rd January, 1870.

No. 215—A. J. GUSTIN, of Toronto, Ont., for " Improvements in a machine 'for binding rails." Ottawa, dated 3rd January, 1870.

No. 216—E. GURNEY and C. GURNEY, of Hamilton, Out., for " Improvements in Heating Stoves." Ottawa, dated 3rd January, 1870.

No. 217—G. OTT, of Warwick, Ont., for "Improvements in Bee Hives." Ottawa, dated 3rd January, 1870.

No. 218—G. WIGGINS, of Hillier, Ont., for " A machine for Dovetail Tenons." Ottawa, dated 12th January, 1869.

No. 219—W. BROWN, of Augusta, Ont., for " A Swing and Rotary Gate Hanger." Ottawa, dated 12th January, 1870.

No. 220—T. WALSH, of Montreal, Que., for " Improvements on Steam Pumping Engines." Ottawa, dated 12th January, 1870

No. 221—P. DE WITT, of Bleuheim, Ont., for " An Improvement on, Pumps." Ottawa, dated 12th January, 1870.

No. 222—P. C. VANBROCKLIN, of Paris, Ont., for "An Improvement on Heaters." Ottawa, dated 12th January, 1870.

No. 223—J. BAKER, of Trenton, Ont., for " A machine for scooping up and lifting flour by hand." Ottawa, dated 12th January, 1870.

No. 224—A. ANDERSON, of London, Ont., for " Improvements in Cultivator." Ottawa, dated 12th January, 1870.

No. 225—A. BRIGGS, of Wolfe Island, Ont., for "Improvements in the construction of Knives for Reaping and Mowing Machines." Ottawa, dated 12th January, 1870.

No. 226—F. COLEMAN, of Mitchell, Ont., for " An Iron Cutter." Ottawa, dated 19th January, 1870.

No 227—H. MERRILL, of Ottawa, Ont., for " An Improvement in Saws." Ottawa, dated 19th January, 1870.
22

No. 228—T. L. WILSON, of Montreal, Que., for " Improvements on Stoves and Furnaces." Ottawa, dated 19th January, 1870.

No. 229—W. J. PURCEL, of Strathroy, Ont., for " A machine for moistening a number of Sheets in a Letter Book." Ottawa, dated 19th January, 1870.

No. 230—R. J. REID, of Walsingham, Ont., for " Improvements in Washing Machine." Ottawa, dated 20th January, 1870.

No. 231—P. E. JAY and A. RAFTER, of Montreal, Que., for " An improvement in the art of manufacturing Steel." Ottawa, dated 22nd January, 1870.

No. 232—R. WALL, of Montreal, Que., for " Improvements in the manufacture of Hose." Ottawa, dated 22nd January, 1870.

No. 233—J. BROWN, of Woodbridge, Ont., for " Improvements in Straw Cutting Machine." Ottawa, dated 22nd January, 1870.

No. 234—O. CORNELL, of Oneida, Ont., for " Improvements on Pruners." Ottawa, dated 22nd January, 1870.

No. 235—R. BUSTIN, of St. John, N.B., for " Improvements on Snow Ploughs." Ottawa, dated 22nd January, 1870.

No. 236—J. REITH, of Paris, Ont., for " Improvements on Hot Air Furnaces." Ottawa, dated 25th January, 1870.

No. 237—H. HOWARD, of Belleville, Ont,, for " A Butter Worker." Ottawa, dated 25th January, 1870.

No. 238—J. GROSS, of Jordan, Ont., for " Improvements on Drum Heaters." Ottawa, dated 25th January, 1870.

No. 239—H. TOTTON, of Paris, Ont., for " A machine for generating and carburetting gas." Ottawa, dated 25th January, 1870.

No. 240—E. W. RANSFORD, of Brantford, Ont., for " A machine for Hitching Post and Carriage Steps." Ottawa, dated 25th January, 1870.

No. 241—B. DUFFY, of Cobourg, Ont., for " Improvements in constructing the joining section of Stove Pipes." Ottawa, dated 25th January, 1870.

No. 242—F. HILL and J. GOULD, of Montreal, Que., for " Improvements on Pianofortes." Ottawa, dated 25th January, 1870.

No. 243—W. S. HOUGH, of Widder Station, Ont., for " A machine for Fumigating Bees." Ottawa, dated 9th February, 1870.

No. 244—H. and F. E. WADLEIGH of Hatley, Que., for " Improvements in machines for wringing Mops." Ottawa, dated 9th February 1870.

No. 245—J. CROWE, of Guelph, Ont., for " Improvements in Sewing Machines." Ottawa, dated 9th February, 1870.

No. 246—E. HIPKINS, of Burford, Ont., for " An improvement on Railway Car Trucks." Ottawa, dated 9th February, 1870.

No. 247—R. BROWN, of Stratford, Ont., for " An improvement in Elastic Shafting to prevent backlash." Ottawa, dated 9th February, 1870.

No. 248—D. B. PICKERTON, of Schombergh, Ont., for " Improvements on Carriages and Waggons." Ottawa, dated 9th February, 1870.

No. 249—A. GRAY, of Woodstock, Ont., for " A machine for regulating the temperature of Kilns." Ottawa, dated 9th February, 1870.

No. 250—G. SCOTT, of Montreal, Que., for " Improvements in Mop Heads and Scrubbing Brushes." Ottawa, dated 9th February, 1870.

No. 251—M. FISHER, of Hamilton, Ont., for " An apparatus for the manufacture of Salt from Brine," Ottawa, dated 9th February, 1870.

No. 252—J. A. STEVENSON, of Aurora, Ont., for " An improvement on Horse Hay Forks." Ottawa, dated 14th February, 1870.

No. 253—R. W. JAMES, of Bowmanville, Ont., for " Improvements on Fanning Mill." Ottawa, dated 14th February, 1870.

No. 254–P. E. JAY and J. A. RAFTER, of Montreal, Que., for "Improvements in the art of manufacturing Malleable Cast Iron." Ottawa, dated 14th February, 1870.

No. 255–W. P. BARTLEY, of Montreal, Que., for "Improvements on Steam Engines and Pumps." Ottawa, dated 18th February, 1870.

No. 256–T. SULLIVAN, of Belleville, Ont., for "A machine for shortening the Tires of Carriages." Ottawa, dated 23rd February, 1870.

No. 257.–J. F. WILLIAMS, of Niagara, Ont., for "An improvement in the art of lacing Boots and Shoes." Ottawa, dated 23rd February, 1870.

No. 258–F. LEONARD, of Goulbourne, Ont., for "Improvements in Scrubbing Machine." Ottawa, dated 25th February, 1870.

No. 259–H. BOLTON, of Elizabethtown, Ont., for "An improvement on a certain machine to be used in connection with a Churn." Ottawa, dated 5th March, 1870.

No. 260–J. SHAW, of Whitby, Ont., for "Improvements on Tables for making Pastry." Ottawa, dated 5th March, 1870.

No. 261–J. MOORE, of Brantford, Ont., for "An improvement in Grates." Ottawa, dated 5th March, 1870.

No. 262–B. LOZEE. of Cobourg, Ont., for "A Bee Hive." Ottawa, dated 5th March, 1870.

No. 263–T. TUNE, of Brantford, Ont., for "A machine for preserving Corks." Ottawa, dated 5th March, 1870.

No. 264–A. B. MACKAY, of Napier, Ont., for "Improvements on Quilting Frames." Ottawa, dated 5th March, 1870.

No. 265–G. C. WOOD, of Morpeth, Ont., for "A machine for Harvesting Beans and other similar products." Ottawa, dated 5th March, 1870.

No. 266–J. H. WILLIAMS, of Saltfleet, Ont., for "Improvements in Reaping Machines." Ottawa, 5th March, 1870.

No. 267–C. C. JORDESON, of Montreal, Que., for "An improvement on Windlasses." Ottawa dated 5th March, 1870.

No. 268–W. PEARSON, of Mulmur, Ont., for "Improvements in Churns." Ottawa, dated 5th March, 1870.

No. 269–J. LAMB, of Ottawa, Ont., for "A machine for separating groats from other grain." Ottawa, 5th March, 1870.

No. 270–G. WHITELY, of Seaforth, Ont., for "A machine for Turning Saw Logs on the carriage in a Saw Mill." Ottawa, 5th March, 1870.

No. 271–E. S. RUPERT, of Centreville, Ont., for "Improvements in Stoves." Ottawa, 5th March, 1870.

No. 272–S. SEWELL, East Whitby, Ont., for "Improvement on Ploughs." Ottawa, 5th March, 1870.

No. 273–J. CAMPBELL, assignee of C. H. GUARD, of Mount Forest, Ont., for "A machine for manufacturing Wheels." Ottawa, 5th March, 1870.

No. 274–H. CALCUTT, of Ashburnham, Ont., for "Improvement on Stove Drum." Ottawa, 10th March, 1870.

No. 275–E. A. BRIMSON, of Montreal, Que., for "Improvement in Cork Cutting Machine." Ottawa, 15th March, 1870.

No. 276–R. YOUNG, of Glasgow, Scotland, for "Improvements in machines for Dressing, Millstones." Ottawa, 15th March, 1870.

No. 277–J. B. WILLS, of Montreal, Que., for "Improvements on Horse Shoe Nail Machinery." Ottawa, 15th March, 1870.

No. 278–H. FOLLIOTT, of Temperanceville, Ont., and J. W. FOLLIOTT, of Bolsover, Ont., for "Land Roller." Ottawa, 15th March, 1870.

No. 279–J. E. ANDERSON, of Port Dover, Ont., for "Improvement in Wooden Hubs for Wheels." Ottawa, 15th March, 1870.

No. 280—J. MARR, of Woodhouse, Ont., for "An improvement on **Reaping Machines.**" Ottawa, 15th March, 1870.

No. 281—J. R. TEMPLE, of Hamilton, Ont , for "Improvements on a **machine for Churn-ing or Making Butter.**" 15th March, 1870.

No. 282—W. W. MASON, of Cartwright, Ont., for "Improvements in Churns," Ottawa, 15th March, 1870.

No. 283—T. BARNES, of Harwich, Ont., for "Improvements on Churns." Ottawa, 15th March, 1870.

No. 284—F. GREENE, of Montreal, Quebec, for "Hot Water Heating Apparatus." Ottawa, 15th March, 1870.

No. 285—G. H. MEAKINS, of Hamilton, Ont., for "An improvement in a Butter Churn." Ottawa, 15th March, 1870.

No. 286—G. BLAKE, of Whitby, Ont., for " A machine for Cutting Round Iron Pipes, &c." Ottawa, 15th March, 1870.

No. 287—C. I. CORBIN, of East Oxford, Ont , for "An improvement on Revolving Horse Rake." Ottawa, 15th March, 1870.

No. 288—E. SLEVIN, of Eboulements, Que., for "Improvements in the art or process of reducing refractory Iron Ores." Ottawa, 18th March, 1870.

No, 289—J. F. WILLIAMS, of Niagara, Ont., for "A Buckle for Fastening Straps and Bands." Ottawa, 18th March, 1870.

No. 290—R. HOGG, of Bothwell, Ont., for "A Packing for excluding water and air from the veins of Oil and other deep Wells." Ottawa, 18th March, 1870.

No. 291—D. McINTOSH, of Westminster, Ont., for "A machine for making Tiles and Bricks." Ottawa, 18th March, 1870.

No. 292—G. A. MULHOLLAND, of Eagle, Ont., for "Improvements on Churns. Ottawa, 18th March, 1870.

No. 293—T. MILNE, of Capetown, Ont., for "An improvement on Stovepipe." Ottawa, 18th March, 1870.

No. 294—N. Leech, of Howick, Ont., for "Improvements in Stoves." Ottawa, 18th March, 1870.

No. 295—J. W. MYERS, of Hamilton, Ont., for " A machine for Stretching or Expanding Boots and Shoes." Ottawa, 18th March, 1870.

No. 296—J. G. COVEY, of St. John, N. B., for "Chemical Composition for Re cutting Files." Ottawa, 18th March, 1870.

No. 297—T. SWITZER, of Norwich, Ont., for " A Brace Bit for Boring and Countersinking Holes." Ottawa, 18th March, 1870.

No. 298—A. FORSYTH, of Claremont, Ont., for "An improvement in the construction of the Running Gear for Buggies, &c." Ottawa, 18th March, 1870.

No. 299—F. M. ADAMS, of Perth, Ont., for " A machine for Enumerating and Registering Numbers in Tallying." Ottawa, 18th March, 1870.

No. 300—J. A. WILKINSON, of Simcoe, Ont., for "A Sickle Grinder." Ottawa, 22nd March, 1870.

No. 301—H. ELLIOTT, of Florenceville, Ont., for "Machinery for the manufacture of Barrels, Casks, &c." Ottawa, 22nd March, 1870.

No. 302—D. D. SLADE, of East Whitby, assignee of E. MIALL, Jr., of Oshawa, Ont., for "Improvements in Dovetailing Machines." Ottawa, 22nd March, 1870.

No. 303—H. D. LUNDY, of Aurora, Ont., for "Improvements on Rakes." Ottawa, 22nd March, 1870.

No. 304—H. KIMBALL, of Toronto, Ont., for "Improvements n Low Water Indicators." Ottawa, 22nd March, 1870.

No. 305—R. S. JARVIS, of Woodstock, Ont., for "Improvements on Quilting Frames." Ottawa, dated 22nd March, 1870.

No. 306—J. B. LENT, of Baltimore, Ont., for "Improvements on Spinning Wheels." Ottawa, dated 22nd March, 1870.

No. 307—P. DUPUIS, of Chateauguay, Que., for "A machine for cleaning all kinds of Grain." Ottawa, dated 22nd March, 1870.

No. 308—E. F. AUSTIN, of Ottawa, Ont., for "Improvements in Stove Pipe Shelves." Ottawa, dated 22nd March, 1870.

No. 809—A. ROBINSON, of Aurora, Ont., for "A machine for wringing Mops." Ottawa, 22nd March, 1870.

No. 310—J. H. ORCHARD, of Reach, Ont., for "A machine for preventing nuts from becoming unscrewed from their bolts." Ottawa, 22nd March, 1870.

No. 311—A. W. LAKE, of Storrington, Ont., for "An apparatus for regulating the fermentation of ale, beer and other liquors." Ottawa, 22nd March, 1870.

No. 312—J. SHIELS, of Kingston, Ont., for "Improvements on Lamp Chimneys and Burners." Ottawa, 22nd March, 1870.

No. 313—D. M. POTTER and J. KNETCHTEL, of Elora, Ont., for "Improvements on Grain Threshers and Separators." Ottawa, 22nd March, 1870.

No. 314—J. R. HAGGART and F. CLARKE, assignees of F. M. Carrol, of Woodstock, Ont., "Improvements on Brackets." Ottawa 22nd March, 1870.

No. 315—H. B. RATHBUN and E. W. RATHBUN, Mill Point, assignees of J. W. Herrington, of Richmond, Ont., for "Improvements in machines for cutting the heading of barrels." Ottawa, 22nd March, 1870.

No. 316—S. McPHERSON, of Ottawa, Ont., for "A Waggon Jack." Ottawa, 29th March, 1870.

No. 317—T. HODGSON, of Amherst, N.S., for "A Circular Saw Guard." Ottawa, 29th March, 1870.

No. 318—J. M. FARWELL, of Waterloo, Que., for "A Churn." Ottawa, 29th March, 1870.

No. 319—S. N. CHURCH, of Port Hope, Ont., for "An improvement on Wire Clothes Pins." Ottawa, 29th March, 1870.

No. 320—B. ARMSTRONG, of Sheffield, Ont., for "An Improvements in Churns." Ottawa, 29th March, 1870.

No. 321—C. A. GREGORY, of Quebec, Que., for "Improvements on apparatus for filling Bottles, Vials and other vessels and gauging their contents." Ottawa, 29th March, 1870.

No. 322—G. HOWSON, of Morrisburg, Ont., for "An improvement to a Steam Washing Boiler." Ottawa, 29th March, 1870.

No. 823—G. W. SCRIBNER, of Chatham, Ont., for "Improvements in Reed Organs." Ottawa, 29th March, 1870.

No. 324—J. SMITH, of Brantford, Ont., for "The art or method of utilizing waste heat from Fire Grates and Chimneys." Ottawa, 29th March, 1870.

No. 325—W. GARVEY, of Morrisburgh, Ont., for "An improvement in Steam Washing Machines." Ottawa, 29th March, 1870.

No. 326—J. SMITH, of Brantford, Ont., for "Improvements in Drums for Heating purposes." Ottawa, 29th March, 1870.

No. 327—J. S. MARTIN and J. MARTIN, jun., of Toronto, Ont., for "An Upright Boiler." Ottawa, dated 29th March, 1870.

No. 328—S. DITSON, of Notawasaga, Ont., for "Improvements in Churns." Ottawa, 29th March, 1870.

No. 329—B. F. DORSEY, of Brantford, Ont., for "A Fruit Gatherer." Ottawa, 1st April, 1870.

No. 330—C. YOUNG, of Windsor, Ont., for "A Furnace." Ottawa, 1st April, 1870.

No. 331—F. R. ELLIOT and W. D. WEBSTER, of Brantford, Ont., for "A Clothes Dryer and Quilting Frame." Ottawa, 1st April, 1870.

No. 332—H. L. WEAGANT, of Morrisburg, Ont., for "Improvements in a Spring Bed." Ottawa, 1st April, 1870.

No. 333—J. BORER, of West Flamboro, Ont., for "An improvement on Cultivator or Gang Plough." Ottawa, 1st April, 1870.

No. 384—G. CARPENTER, of Saltfleet, Ont., for "Improvements in Heating Stoves." Ottawa, 1st April, 1870.

No. 335—J. FERGUSON, of St. John, N.B., for "Improvements in the construction of railway carriages." Ottawa, 1st April, 1870.

No. 336—J. DUNLOP, of East Zorra, Ont., for "An improvement on Waggon Brakes." Ottawa, 1st April, 1870.

No. 337—E. FITCH, of St. Catharines, Ont., for "Improvements in Gates." Ottawa, 1st April, 1870.

No. 338—J. H. JOHNSON, of Newmarket, Ont., for "Improvements in Fanning Mill or Grain Separator." Ottawa, 1st April, 1870.

No. 339—H. L. WEAGANT, of Morrisburg, Ont., for "A machine for washing Potatoes." Ottawa, 1st April, 1870.

No. 340—J. SMITH, of Brantford, Ont , for "Improvements in Stoves and Fire Grates." Ottawa, 1st April, 1870.

No. 341—E. BEANES, of Toronto, Ont., for "Improvements in Browing." Ottawa, 1st April, 1870.

No. 342—L. CONADEAU, of Montreal, Que., for " A machine for destroying Rats." Ottawa, 1st April, 1870.

No. 343—T. RICHARDSON, of Hamilton, Ont., for "Improvements on Stove Pipes." Ottawa, 5th April, 1870.

No. 344—D. F. SMITH, of Hamilton Ont., for "Washing Machines." Ottawa, 5th April, 1870.

No. 345—J. TROTT, of Oakville, Ont., for "Improvements on a machine for making Coffee, &c." Ottawa, 5th April, 1870.

No. 346—C. LOCKMAN, of Hamilton, Ont., for "Sewing Machines." Ottawa, 5th April 1870.

No. 347—R. LOUNSBURY, of Morpeth, Ont., for "Washing Machines." Ottawa, 5th April, 1870.

No. 348—C. G. FOX, of Kingston, Ont., for "Improvement in Lamp Shades." Ottawa, 5th April, 1870.

No. 349—R. C. BECKETT, of Delta, Ont., for "Reel and Swifts." Ottawa, 5th April, 1870.

No. 350—W. S. TORRIE, of Moncton, N. B., for "An improvement in the manufacture of Soap." Ottawa, 5th April, 1870.

No. 351—W. McPHERSON, assignee of J. C. McPHERSON, Whitby, Ont., for "Burglar's Alarm." Ottawa, 5th April, 1870.

No. 352—E. COOK, of Petrolea, Ont., for "Improvements in Pump Rods." Ottawa, 5th April, 1870.

No. 353—J. MACK, of Hamilton, Ont., for "An Improvement in Steam Heaters." Ottawa, 5th April, 1870.

No. 354—E. HORSEY, of Kingston, Ont., for "Improvements in a Suction and Force Pump." Ottawa, 8th April, 1870.

No. 355—J. F. SWITZER, and L. CHEYNE, of Toronto, Ont., for "Improvements on machines for unloading Hay and Grain." Ottawa, 8th April, 1870.

No. 356—P. NICOLLE, of Lindsay, Ont., for "An improvement in Bee Hives." Ottawa, 8th April, 1870.

No. 357—T. and C. HOLLADAY, of Aurora, Ont., for " An improvement in a machine for Cutting Meat. Ottawa, 8th April, 1870.

No. 358—P. CEREDO, of Montreal, Que., for "Improvements on Hair Pins." Ottawa, 13th April, 1870.

No. 359—N. AGNEW, of Caradoc, Ont., for "Improvements on Coffee Pots." Ottawa, 13th April, 1870.

No. 360—J. VANATTER, of Stratford, Ont., for "Improvements in Churns." Ottawa, 13th April, 1870.

No. 361—S. BARNETT, of Clifton, Ont, for "An improvement on a ButterMould." Ottawa, 13th April, 1570.

No. 362—J. FRENCH, of Chatham, Ont., for "A machine for Cross-cutting Wood." Ottawa, 13th April, 1870.

No. 363-I. MILLS, of Hamilton, Ont., for "Improvements on Weather Leaf and Door Valve." Ottawa, 13th April, 1870.

No. 364—G. M. BRADFORD, of Chatham, Que., for "Improvements in the manufacture of Whips—"Bradford's Whip." Ottawa, 13th April, 1870.

No. 365—A. KERBY, of Napanee, Ont., for "Improvements in Horse Rakes." Ottawa, 13th April, 1870.

No. 366—J. E. CRANE, of Woodstock, Ont., for "Washing Machines." Ottawa, 13th April, 1870.

No. 367—J. H. WAY, of Bowmanville, and J. DOWNING, of Clark, Ont., for "Improvements in machines for Mangling Clothes." Ottawa, 13th April, 1870.

No. 368—P. MERRILL, of Florence, Ont., for "A machine for Clamping Saws." Ottawa, 13th April, 1870.

No. 369—S. MORNINGSTAR, of Arkona, Ont., for "Improvements in Looms." Ottawa, 13th April, 1870.

No. 370—T. THOMAS, of Bowmanville, Ont., for "Improvement in Reaping and Mowing Machines." Ottawa, 23rd April, 1870.

No. 371—T. YEANDLE, of Stratford, Ont., for "An improvement in Mould-board for Ploughs." Ottawa, 23rd April, 1870.

No. 372—G. SPARLING, of Dunnville, Ont., for "An improvement on Wine Coolers." Ottawa, 23rd April, 1870.

No. 373—E. HOLLINGSHEAD, of Toronto, Ont., for "An improvement on a machine for filling Barrels." Ottawa, 23rd April, 1870.

No. 374—J. CARR, of Toronto. Ont., for "An improvement in Snow Ploughs." Ottawa, 23rd April, 1870.

No. 375—T. ROBERTSON, of Toronto, Ont., for "An improvement in the construction of a machine for holding Biscuits, Cigars, &c." Ottawa, 23rd April, 1870.

No. 376—G. JONES, of Hamilton, Ont., for "An improvement in Churns." Ottawa, 25th April, 1870.

No. 377—J. WADDELL, of Goderich, Ont., for "An improvement in roofing Building Composition.." Ottawa, 25th April, 1870.

No. 378—H. B. CROSBY, of St. John, N.B., for "Improvements in Kilns for the manufacture of Lime, Plaster of Paris, &c." Ottawa, 25th April, 1870.

No. 379—R. KEMP, of Clinton, Ont., for "A machine for removing scum and other impurities from boilers of steam engines." Ottawa, 25th April, 1870.

No. 380—T. BARNES, of Harwich, Ont., for "Improvements on Gates,." Ottawa, 25th April, 1870.

No. 381—E. BARRETT, of Windsor, Ont., for "An improvement in Potato Diggers." Ottawa, 25th April, 1870.

No. 382—J. S. ROWSE, of Bath, assignee of P. Winskel, of Windham, Ont., for "A machine for unloading Hay, &c." Ottawa, 25th April, 1870.

No. 383—M. S. BROWNELL, of Vienna, Ont., for "A method of making a liquid tight joint in wood." Ottawa,, 25th April, 1870.

No. 384—C. G. HAMPTON, of Seaforth, Ont., for "An improvement on Sad and Fluting Irons." Ottawa, 25th April, 1870.

No. 385—J. FINDLAY, of Toronto, Ont , for "An improvement in Lift and Force Pumps." Ottawa, 25th April, 1870.

No. 386—G. O. FREEMAN, of Chatham, Ont., for "An improvement on a Steam Cooking Apparatus." Ottawa, 25th April, 1870.

No. 387—T. and R. ABBOTT, of Walsingham, Ont., for "An improvement in Mouse and Rat Traps." Ottawa, 25th April, 1870.

No. 388—W. FRASER, of Strathroy, Ont., for "Improvements in Clothes' Dryers." Ottawa, 2nd May, 1870.

No. 389—C. HACKETT, of Truro, N.S., for "An art for the casting of Waggon Pipes and Plough Shares." Ottawa, 4th May, 1870.

No. 390—J. G. BAILEY, of Galt, Ont., for "Improvement on Horse Hay Fork." Ottawa, 4th May, 1870.

No. 391—R. L. HAIGHTON, of Hamilton, Ont., for "An improvement in Instep Spring Supporters for Boots and Shoes." Ottawa, 3rd May, 1870.

No. 392—C. B. PARKER, of Caradoc, Ont., for "Improvements on Lumber Waggons." Ottawa, 3rd May, 1869.

No. 393—I. COLE, of Woolwich, Ont., for "Improvements on Rail Fences." Ottawa, 4th May, 1870.

No. 394—N. and H. TOTTEN, of Paris, Ont., for "An improvement on machinesfor generating into Gas for illuminating purposes, the light oils of the Petroleum series." Ottawa, 4th May, 1870.

No. 395—J. ABELL, of Woodbridge, Ont., for "An improvement in a machine for coupling the horse power to Threshing Machine Gearing." Ottawa, 4th May, 1870.

No. 396—D. J. WAGGONER, of Kingston, Ont., for "An improvement in machines for grappling to the beams and rafters of building for suspending Horse Hay Forks." Ottawa, 4th May, 1870.

No. 397—H. F. HOWELL, of St. Catharines, Ont., for "An improvement in Stills for petroleum and other oils." Ottawa, 4th May, 1870.

No. 398—J. R. GILL, of Hamilton, Ont., for "Improvements on Door Handles or Knobs." Ottawa, 4th May, 1870.

No. 399—J. W. ELLIOT, of Toronto, Ont., for "An improvement on a machine for removing Snow from Railway Trucks." Ottawa, 4th May, 1870.

No. 400—G. COMMANDER, of Toronto, Ont., for "An improvements in Handles for Tubs." Ottawa, 4th May, 1870.

No. 401—J. J. MURPHY, of Montreal, Que., for "Improvements on Portable Petroleum Gas Light." Ottawa, 4th May, 1870.

No. 402—L. COTÉ, of St. Hyacinthe, Que , for "A Sole Trimming and Finishing Machine." Ottawa, 4th May, 1870.

No. 403—S. INMAN, of Downie, Ont., for "Improvements on Horse Rake." Ottawa, 4th May, 1870.

No. 404—E. S. GEROW and A. T. WILCOX, of Athol, Ont., for "Improvements in the Saw and feeding works used in saw mills." Ottawa, 4th May, 1870.

No. 405—J. C. BAKER, of Brock, Ont., for "A Car Coupler." Ottawa, 4th May, 1870.

No. 406—C. BAWTINHIMER, of Wolverton, Ont., for "Improvements in Bolt Cutter." Ottawa, 4th May, 1870.

No. 407—C. GOODEN, of Amherst Shore, N. S., for "A Churn." Ottawa, 4th May, 1870.

No. 408—J. COVE, of Amherst, N. S., for "A Clothes Dryer." Ottawa, 4th May, 1870.

No. 409—E. KRIEGHOFF, and E. P. KRIEGHOFF, Jr., of Toronto, Ont., for "Improvements in Spring Mattresses." Ottawa, 17th May, 1870.

No. 410—J. NEIL, of Toronto, Ont., for "An improvement on machine for Setting Logs to the Saw." Ottawa, 17th May, 1870,

179

No. 411—R. D. CHATTERTON, of Bath, Eng., for " Rail and Carriage Couplings." Ottawa, 17th May, 1870.

No. 412—W. T. FARRE, of Montreal, Que., for "Improvements on a machine for Scroll Sawing." Ottawa, 17th May, 1870.

No. 413—C. ELLSWORTH, of Florence, Ont.. for " Improvements in Springs for vehicles." Ottawa, 17th May, 1870.

No. 414—J. LOUGH, of Buckingham, Que., for " Improvements in apparatus for forming Saw Teeth by pressure. Ottawa, 17th May, 1870.

No. 415—E. G. SCOVIL, of St. John, N. B., for "A machine for the charging of heavy piles into heating furnaces for heating iron preparatory to rolling." Ottawa, 17th May, 1870.

No. 416—E. S. MOORE, of Windsor, Ont., for "Mats." Ottawa, 17th May, 1870.

No. 417—W. S. CHILDS, of Montreal, Que., for "A method of laying Slates." Ottawa, 17th May, 1870.

No. 418—S. HALL, of Toronto, Ont., for " An improvement in a Churn Dash." Ottawa, 17th May, 1870.

No. 419—C. DUQUET, of Quebec, Que., for " A machine for ascertaining the steadiness and assiduity of Watchmen." Ottawa, 20th May, 1870.

No. 420—J. MILNE, of Hamilton, Ont., for "An improvement on Hay Fork Pulleys." Ottawa, 27th May, 1870.

No. 421—D. A. McDONELL, of Charlottenburg, Ont., for "Improvements on a certain machine now in ordinary use for hauling and drawing Timber, Cord Wood, Stones and other heavy commodities." Ottawa, 27th May, 1870.

No. 422—J. W. MADDIN, of Thamesville, Ont., for "An improvement in a Scaffold Bracket." Ottawa, 27th May, 1870.

No. 423 -J. FINDLAY, of Chambly, Que., for " Improvements on Cooking Stove." Ottawa, 27th May, 1870.

No. 424—H. D. BULMER, of Sackville, N. B., for "An improvement on Clothes Dryer." Ottawa, 27th May, 1870.

No. 425—J. B. WARNER, of Rainham, Ont., for "A machine for hoisting and unloading Hay and Grain." Ottawa, 27th May, 1870.

No. 426—A. WEIR, of Wellesley, Ont., for "Improvements in portable Fences." Ottawa, 27th May, 1870.

No. 427—J. BENNETT, of Belleville, Ont., for "An improvement in Threshing Machines and Separators." Ottawa, 27th May, 1870.

No. 428—J. SPARKS, of Gloucester, Ont., for "An improvement on Gates." Ottawa, 27th May, 1870.

No. 429—E. A. BRIMSON, of Montreal, Que., for "Turning Apparatus." Ottawa, 27th May, 1870.

No. 430—J. EDE, of Woodstock, Ont., for " An improvement on Draft Equalizer and Indicator. ' Ottawa, 27th May, 1873.

No. 431—E. CHAMBERS, of Marshville, Ont., for "Improvements in Lamp Burners." Ottawa, 27th May, 1870.

No. 432—J. THOMAS, of Clements Port, N. S., for "Soap." Ottawa, 27th May, 1870.

No. 433—J. B. DeGUISE, of Montreal, Que., for " A machine for Crimping Collars or other toilet articles." Ottawa, 27th May, 1870.

No. 434—R. SCOTT, of Murray, Ont., for " Improvements in machine for lifting and wheeling Stone, &c." Ottawa, 31st May, 1870.

No. 435—J. FENSON, of Toronto, Ont., for "An improvemement on Copying Presses." Ottawa, 31st May, 1870.

No. 436—J. O'MALLEY, of Knowlton, Que., for " Improvements on warming and drying Stove-pipe Grate." Ottawa, 31st May, 1870.

No. 437—F. ROBERTS, of West Gwillimbury, Ont., for "A machine for Pulling Fruit." Ottawa, 31st May, 1870.

No. 438—E. R. McCALL, of Charlotteville, Ont., for "Harvester Rake." Ottawa, 31st May, 1870.

No. 439—R. G. LEAKIE, of Montreal, Que., for "Improvements on the art of manufacturing Iron and Steel." Ottawa, 31st May, 1870.

No. 440-C. E. CLANCEY, of Camden, Ont., for "A machine for working Butter." Ottawa, 31st May, 1870.

No. 441—J. P. MAYER, assignee of J. W. WRIGHT, of Montreal, Que., for "Improvements on machine for Sawing Wood, &c." Ottawa, 31st May, 1870.

No. 442—C. POWELL, of Newton Brook, Ont., for "An improvement in Carriage Shaft Couplings." Ottawa, 31st May, 1870.

No. 443-II. WOODWARD, of Toronto, Ont., for "A machine for Carbonizing Gas." Ottawa, 31st May, 1870

No. 444—E. WHITE, of Arcona, Ont., for "Improvements on cutting bar Grinding Guide." Ottawa, 31st May, 1870.

No. 445-II. W. AS1ROM, of Hamilton, Ont., for "An improvement in a Plough." Ottawa, 31st May, 1870.

No. 446—J. K. BOSWELL, of Quebec, Que., for "Improvements in machines for regulating the fermentation of Beer and other liquors." Ottawa, 31st May, 1870.

No. 447—F. McCALL, of Charlotteville, Ont., for "Gates." Ottawa, 31st May, 1870.

No. 448—F. A. GARDNER, of Hamilton, Ont., for "Improvements on Sewing Machines." Ottawa, 31st May, 1870.

No. 449—S. TRUAX, of Hamilton, Ont., for "A Horse-power Fastener." Ottawa, 31st May, 1870.

No. 450—C. MEE, of Toronto, Ont., for "An improvement on Spring and Easy Chairs." Ottawa, 7th June, 1870.

No. 451—F. B. SPARKS, of Dundas, Ont., for "A process for the manufacture of Paraffine Oil from Petroleum." Ottawa, 7th June, 1870.

No. 452—W. GOODWIN, of Admaston, Ont., for "Improvements in Railway." Ottawa, 7th June, 1870.

No. 453—W. L. PARK, of Towsend, and J. S. ROTT, of Erin, Ont., for "Improvements in the section and section bar of Reaping or Mowing Machines." Ottawa, 7th June, 1870.

No. 454—A. KIRKWOOD, of Toronto, Ont., "for "Soup Biscuit." Ottawa, 7th June, 1870.

No. 455—H. E. DANGER, of Windsor, Ont., for "Improvement on the Hold-back for Carriage Thills or Poles." Ottawa, 7th June, 1870.

No. 456—J. KINNEY, of London, Ont., for "An improvement on a certain machine for a Coulter for a Plough." Ottawa, 17th June, 1870.

No. 457—L. WARNER, of St. Thomas, Ont., for "An improvement in the art of heating buildings with Hot Air." Ottawa, 17th June, 1870.

No. 458—F. ELLIOTT and D. SNIDER, of Woodbridge, Ont., for "A Washing Machine." Ottawa, 17th June, 1870.

No. 459—O. S. FERGUSON and F. A. GUNN, of St. Catharines, Ont., for "Improvements on Dampers or Heat Retainers." Ottawa, 17th June, 1870.

No. 460—D. D. MARR, of Woodhouse, Ont., for "A machine for Pruning." Ottawa, 17th June, 1870.

No. 461—D. M. LAMB, of Strathroy, Ont., for "Improvements in Ploughs." Ottawa, 17th June, 1870.

No. 462-G. R. ROWSE, of Montreal, Que., for "Improvements on Mangle for Clothes, for occupying less space." Ottawa, 17th June, 1870.

No. 463—J. BLASDELL, of Beverley, Ont., for "Improvements on a Revolving Plough Coulter." Ottawa, 17th June, 1870.

No. 464—E. HUTSON, of Hamilton, Ont., for "Improvements in machines for Sawing Laths." Ottawa, 17th June, 1870.

No. 465—J. BARETT, of Belleville, Ont., for "Sewing Machines." Ottawa, 17th June, 1870.

No. 466—C. GLENDENNING, of Caledon, Ont., for "An improvement in Weaving Looms," Ottawa, 17th June, 1870.

No. 467—F. CULHAM, of Widder Station, Ont , for "Improvements on Gates." Ottawa, 17th June, 1870.

No. 468—R. WILLIAMSON, of West Oxford, Ont., for "A machine for Holding Bags while being filled. Ottawa, 17th June, 1870.

No. 469—D. D. VAN NORMAN, of Simcoe, Ont., for "An Improvement on machines for Sharpening Scythes and Sickles." Ottawa, 17th June, 1870.

No. 470—W. S. ARNOLD, of Harwich, Ont., for "Improvements in Ploughs." Ottawa, 17th June, 1870.

No. 471—F. G POKORNY, of Montreal, Que., for "A composition of matter for giving Wood the appearance of Marble." Ottawa, 23rd June, 1870.

No. 472—D. LISTER, of Toronto, Ont., for "An improvement on the art or process of Welding Iron and Steel." Ottawa, 23rd June, 1870.

No. 473—W. H. HENDERSHOT, of Wainfleet, Ont., for "Improvements in Wood Pavement." Ottawa, 20th June, 1870.

No. 474—N. H. SHAW, of Bedford, Que., for "Improvement in Plough Coulters." Ottawa, 30th June, 1870.

No. 475—J. FLETCHER, of East Gwillimbury; Ont., for "A Rising Swing Gate." Ottawa, 30th June, 1870.

No. 476—G. ELMS, of West Farnham, Que., for "Improvements in machines for sawing Shingles." Ottawa, 30th June, 1870.

No. 477—R. and N. OLIVER of Eldorado, Ont., for "An improvement in Gates." Ottawa, 30th June, 1870.

No. 478—P. J. PILKEY, of Burford, Ont., for "Improvements in the straw carrying attachment of Threshing Machines." Ottawa, 30th June, 1870.

No. 479—G. L. MACKELCAN, of Hamilton, Ont., for "An Improvement in Portable and Marine Boilers." Ottawa, 30th June, 1870.

No. 480—J. L. TAYLOR, of Barton, Ont., for "Improvements on Reaping and Mowing Machines." Ottawa, 30th June, 1870.

No. 481—P. BRODIE, of Mount Unlacke, and W. WILSON, of Falmouth, N.S., for "Improvements on Machines for pulverizing or grinding metallic ores." Ottawa, 30th June, 1870.

No. 482—J. A. CULL, of Toronto, Ont., for "An Indestructible Paint." Ottawa, 30th June, 1870.

No. 483—D. ARNOT, of Aultsville, Ont., for "Improvements in Derricks." Ottawa, 30th June, 1870.

No. 484—W. FARMER, of Hamilton, Ont., for "The act of supplying oil to the burners of lamps and to feed furnaces." Ottawa, 6th July, 1870.

No. 485—W. C. SHOREY, of Napanee, Ont., for "Improvements in Horse Hay Knives and Forks." Ottawa, 6th July, 1870.

No. 486—J. GRAY, of Yorkville, Ont., for "Improvements in Springs for doors, vehicles, &c.." Ottawa, 6th July, 1870.

No. 487—J. LOCKWOOD, of Seguille, N.S, for "An improvement on Whiffletrees." Ottawa, 6th July, 1870.

No. 488- D. PHILIPS, of Tamworth, Ont., for "An improvement on Milk Pan." Ottawa, 6th July, 1870.

No. 489—M. A. BROADWELL, of Paris, Ont., for "A Composition for strengthening medicine and tonic to women during pregnancy." Ottawa, 6th July, 1870.

No. 490—W. STAFFORD, of Montreal, Que., for "An Improvement in Furnace Grate Bars for the use of steam boiler and other furnaces." Ottawa, 6th July, 1870.

No. 491—P. E. JAY and J. A. RAFTER, of Montreal, Que., for "A Machine for letting passengers on board of railway cars." Ottawa, 6th July, 1870.

No. 492—T. CUNNINGHAM and J. DORAN, of Ops, Ont., for "A machine for unloading Hay from waggons or other vehicles." Ottawa, 11th July, 1870.

No. 493—W. DECATOR, of St. Catharines, Ont., for "Improvements in the art of Distilling." Ottawa, 11th July, 1870.

No. 494—J. BATES, of Thornbury, Ont., for "An Improvement in the Dasher Shaft of Churns." Ottawa, 11th July, 1870.

No. 495—F. McAULEY, of Berlin, Ont , for "Improvements in Vehicles." Ottawa, 11th July, 1870.

No. 496—D. D. SCHRAG, of East Hope, South, Ont., for "Improvements in machines for Sowing Seeds." Ottawa, dated 11th July, 1870.

No. 497—H. McRAE, of Tiverton, Ont., for "A Churn Flange." Ottawa, 11th July, 1870.

No. 498—A. D. COLE, of Toronto, Ont., for "Improvements on Turbine Water Wheel." Ottawa, 12th July, 1870.

No. 499—F. L. SANBORN, of Montreal, Que., for "A Combined Planing and Splitting or Ripping Circular Saw," Ottawa, 12th July, 1870.

No. 500—G. and C. R. SCOTT, of Montreal, Que., for "Improvements on Metal Type." Ottawa, 12th July, 1870.

No. 501—J. LAW, of London, Ont., for "Improvements on a machine now in use for oil and spirit Cans." Ottawa, 12th July, 1870.

No. 502—J. FILION, of St.|Eustache, Que., for "A Stumping Machine." Ottawa, 12th July 1870.

No. 503—W. W. TURVER, of Toronto, Ont., for "Improvements in Spring Bed." Ottawa, 13th July, 1870.

No. 504—W. B. JACKSON, of London, Ont., for "An improvement on a machine for Hose Reels." Ottawa, 13th July, 1870.

No. 505—J. H. McNAIRN, of Toronto, Ont., for "Improvements on a machine for discharging Earth into closets." Ottawa, 13th July, 1870.

No. 506—D. D. SCHRAG, of East Hope, South, Ont., for "A machine for cutting Carrots, turnips, and other esculent roots." Ottawa, 13th July, 1870.

No. 507—H. L. ROOT, of Sherbrooke, Ont., for "Improvements on Revolving Harrows." Ottawa, 15th July, 1870.

No. 508—R. STANDING, of Chinguacousy, Ont., for "A machine for raising weights in a perpendicular position and afterwards sliding them in a horizontal position." Ottawa, 15th July, 1870.

No. 509—D. A. JONES, of Tecumseth, Ont , for "An improvement on Bee Hives." Ottawa, 15th July, 1870.

No. 510—C. W. SALADEE, of St. Catharines, Ont., for "An Improvement in Gates." Ottawa, 15th July, 1870.

No. 511—J. HUNTER, of Pittsburg, Ont., for "A machine for erecting and sustaining rail or board fences." Ottawa, 15th July, 1870.

No. 512—J. C. COOPER, of Strathroy, Ont., for "Improvement in Buggies and Carriages for coupling the shaft or pole to the axle." Ottawa, 15th July, 1870.

No. 513—W. MATTHEWSON, of Brooklin, Ont., for "An improvement in Washing and Wringing Machine." Ottawa, 16th July, 1870.

No. 514—R. FIELDS, of Blanchard, Ont., for "An Improvement in Churns." Ottawa, 16th July, 1870.

No. 515—M. MURPHY, of Morse Mills, St. Stephen, N.B., for "An improvement in the manufacture of Washing Barrels for Pumps." Ottawa, 16th July, 1870.

No. 516—H. C. PALMER, and D. NOBLE, of Montreal, Que., for "An improvement in Wool Pulling Machines." Ottawa, 19th July, 1870.

No. 517—R. W. McKIM, of Portland, Ont., for "Improvements in Horse Rakes." Ottawa, 19th July, 1870.

No. 518—G. F. THOMPSON, of St. John, N.B., for "Improvements in the mode of propelling any Steam or other Ferry Boat or Vessel." Ottawa, 19th July, 1870.

No. 519—H. T. DUNBURY, of Cobourg, Ont., for "An improvement in Vapour Burners." Ottawa, 19th July, 1870.

No 520—D. MONASTESSE and H. DESMARAIS, of Verchères, Que., for "An improvement in Churns." Ottawa, 19th July, 1870.

No. 521—G. BELL, of Orangeville, Ont., for "Improvements in Waggons and Sleighs." Ottawa, 27th July, 1870.

No. 522—J. FINDLAY, of Toronto, Ont., for "Vices." Ottawa, 27th July, 1870.

No. 523—C. ESTABROOKS, of Milltown, N.B., for "A machine to contain article of food when being cooked." Ottawa, 27th July, 1870.

No. 524—F. LAMBE, of London, Ont., for "Improvements in the art of treating and purifying Petroleums, Coal, and Shale Oils, &c." Ottawa, 27th July, 1870.

No. 525—J. WARREN, of Kingston, Ont., for "Improvements in the Fire Chambers of Steam Oilers.". Ottawa, 27th July, 1870.

No. 526—L. COTÉ, of St. Hyacinthe, Que., "Improvements on apparatus for trimming and finishing the Soles and Heels of Boots and Shoes." Ottawa, 27th July, 1870.

No. 527—C. H. GUARD, of London, Ont., for "Improvements on machine for Vehicles." Ottawa, 27th July, 1870.

No. 528 - J. R. ANNETT, of Montreal, Que., for "Improvements on convertible Sleeping Cars." Ottawa, 27th July, 1870.

No. 529—J. GIBSON, of Marys, Ont., for "A Hay Fork." Ottawa, 27th July, 1870.

No. 530—T. SMART, of Brockville, Ont., for "An improvement in Axle Skeins and Boxes." Ottawa, 1st August, 1870.

No. 531—J. McKELVERY, of St. Catharines, Ont, for "A machine for holding milk to raise the cream." Ottawa, 1st August, 1870.

No. 532—J. A. WAY, of Amellasburgh, Ont., for "Improvements in the manufacture of Hay Sacks." Ottawa, 1st August, 1870.

No. 533—L. L. VIGER, of Montreal, Que., for "An improvement in the manufacture of Cast Steel." Ottawa, 1st August, 1870.

No. 534—H. MARTIN, of Wallaceburgh, Ont., for "Improvements in Gates." Ottawa, 1st August, 1870.

No. 535—J. SMART, of Brockville, Ont., for "Improvements on Pulleys." Ottawa, 1st August, 1870.

No. 536—E. H. CARVER and J. M. ELLSWORTH, of Humberstone, Ont., for "A Corn Husker." Ottawa, 3rd August, 1870.

No. 537—C. G. C. SIMPSON, of Montreal. Que., for "Improvements on Railway Car Wheel." Ottawa, 3rd August, 1870.

No. 538—H. G. POOL, of Hatley, Que., for "An improvement on Safety Breech Hook." Ottawa, 3rd August, 1870.

No. 539—T. R. JOHNSON, of Montreal, Que, for "An improvement on Self Ventilating Hat." Ottawa, 3rd August, 1870.

No. 540—W. FARMER, of Hamilton, Ont., for "An improvement in Gas Fittings and Oil Lamps." Ottawa, 3rd August, 1870.

No. 541—D. A. ROSS, of Montreal, Que, for "Improvements on Car Couplings." Ottawa, 3rd August, 1870.

No. 542—J. F. LATIMER, of Port Stanley, Ont., for "Improvement in Water Elevators' Ottawa, 3rd, August, 1870.

No. 543—T. L. STEELE, of Montreal, Que., for "An improvement on the art of making Foot Pavements." Ottawa, 3rd August, 1870.

No. 544—T. L. STEELE, of Montreal, Que., for "A foundation for Wood Paving." Ottawa, 3rd August, 1870.

No. 545—W. HARVEY, of Danville, and G. H. KENDALL, of Montreal, Que., for Slate and Clay Paint." Ottawa, 3rd August, 1870.

No. 546—J. FINDLAY, of Toronto, Ont., for "Steam Boiler." Ottawa, 3rd August, 1870.

No. 547—J. H. HOUSE, of St. Catharines, Ont., for "Improvements on a machine for Fastening Window Sashes." Ottawa, 10th August, 1870.

No. 548—A. ROBERTSON, of Guelph, Ont., for "A machine or apparatus for running Petroleum for generating Steam, &c." Ottawa, 10th August, 1870.

No. 549—C. P. TREADWELL, of L'Orignal, Ont., for "An improvement in the manner of constructing Wooden Railways." Ottawa, 11th August, 1870."

No. 550—G. B. PATTEE, of Ottawa, Ont., for "Improvements in machines for swaging the Teeth of Saws." Ottawa, 12th August, 1870.

No. 551—I. KINNEY, of Woodstock, Ont., for "An improvement in the manufacture of Wheels for Buggies." 'Ottawa, 11th August, 1870.

No. 552—T. IRWIN, of Hamilton, Ont., for "A machine for Heating Water." Ottawa, 11th August, 1870.

No. 553—L. PINKERTON, of Schomberg, Ont., for "Improvements in gearing for imparting motion." Ottawa, 11th August, 1870.

No. 554—E. D. ASHE, of Quebec, Que., for "Improvements in Lamp Chimneys." Ottawa, 12th August, 1870.

No. 555—H. M. FARR, of Hespeler, Ont., for "Improvements in Carding Machine." Ottawa, 11th August, 1870.

No. 556—T. NORTLEY, of Hamilton, Ont., for "Improvements in a low-water Alarm." Ottawa, 11th August, 1870.

No. 557—C. CARPENTER, of Hamilton, Ont., for "A Knob for Locks, Bells, Pulls, &c." Ottawa, 11th August, 1870.

No. 558—J. MOODY, of St. Stephen, N. B., for "Improvements in Suction and Lift Pumps." Ottawa, 11th August, 1870.

No. 559—W. JAMES, of Springfield, Ont., for "Improvements in Fanning Mills." Ottawa, 11th August, 1870.

No. 560—T. L. STEELE, of Montreal, Que., for "Improvements on concrete for Roofing and Paving." Ottawa, 11th August, 1870.

No. 561—C. LEVEY, of Toronto, Ont., for "Improvements on Wood Working Machinery." Ottawa, 12th August, 1870.

No. 562—R. MANNING and D. JOHNS, of Exeter, Ont., for "Improvements on apparatus for Cooling Milk." Ottawa, 18th August, 1870.

No. 563—W. MILNER, of Strathroy, Ont., for "An improvement in Sleigh for supporting the cross-beam." Ottawa, 18th August, 1870.

No. 564—W. JAMES and W. JAMES, Jr., of Montreal, Que., for "Improvements on Hot Air Furnaces." Ottawa, 18th August, 1870.

No. 565—W. H. SHORT, of Montreal, Que., for "Improvements on Fire-proof Iron Safes." Ottawa, 25th August, 1870.

No. 566—J. E. LEMON, of Townsend, Ont., for "An improvement on Portable Fences." Ottawa, 25th August, 1870.

No. 567—D. G. URQUHART, of West Zorra, Ont., for "Improvements in the manufacture of Hay, Grain and Straw Elevators." Ottawa, 25th August, 1870.

No. 568—W. H. BARKER, of Windsor, N. S., for "Improvements in the construction of Skates." Ottawa, 25th August, 1870.

No. 569—W. MILNER, of Strathroy, Ont., for "An Improvement in Waggons." Ottawa, 25th August, 1870.

No. 570—J. KENDRICK, Sr., of Avening, Ont., for "An Improvement in Churn Gear." Ottawa, 25th August, 1870.

No. 571—J. A. WILKINSON, of Simcoo, Ont., for "A machine for Picking Apples, Pears and other fruit." Ottawa, 26th August, 1878.

No. 572—S. C. HALL, of Harwick, and A. L. BISNETT, of Blenheim, Ont., for "Improvements on Animal Pokes." Ottawa, 26th August, 1870.

No. 573—J. WRIGHT, of Pembroke, Ont., for " A machine for Sawing Shingles." Ottawa, 26th August, 1870.

No. 574—W. STEPHENSON, of East Gwillimbury, Ont., for "An improvement on Steam Engine." Ottawa, 26th August, 1870.

No. 575—J. WRIGHT, of Pembroke, Ont., for "Improvements in machines for Sawing Shingles." Ottawa, 26th August, 1870.

No. 576—W. H. BARKER, of Windsor, N S., for " Improvements on machinery for securing Anchors to the cat-heads of ships." Ottawa, 31st August, 1870.

No. 577—C. B. PARKER, of Caradoc, Ont., for "Improvements on Gate Hinges." Ottawa, 31st August, 1870.

No. 578—J. ROGERS, of Peel, Ont., for " Improvements on Gates." Ottawa, 31st August, 1870.

No. 579—W. W. KITCHIN, of Grimsby, Ont., for "Improvements in the manner of fastening Fences." Ottawa, 31st August, 1870.

No. 580—G. BEATTY, of Beamsville, Ont., for " A Cast Metallic Boot and Shoe Heel." Ottawa, 31st August, 1870.

No 581—A. DION, of Hull, Que., for " An Improvement in the construction of Reverberatory Lanterns." Ottawa, 5th September, 1870.

No. 582—T. CHEVIER, of Montreal, Que , for " Improvements on Refrigerators." Ottawa, 5th September, 1870.

No 583—G. PEDLER, of Exeter, Ont., for "Improvements on a machine for producing Musical Sounds." Ottawa, 5th September, 1870.

No. 584—M. CHARLESWORTH, of Seaforth, Ont., for "Improvements in machinery for feeding Middlings." Ottawa, 5th September, 1870.

No. 585—J. DOWNING, of Mount Vernon, Ont., for " Improvements in Stove Pipe Dampers." Ottawa, 5th September, 1870.

No. 586—B. B. TOYE, of Toronto, Ont., for "A Telegraph Relay." Ottawa, 5th September, 1870.

No. 587—J. G. COVEY, of St. John, N.B., for " A Steam Cooking Apparatus." Ottawa, 5th September, 1870.

No. 588 P. C. VAN BROCKLIN, of Paris, Ont., for "Improvements on Bag Holders." Ottawa, 5th September, 1870.

No. 589—C. H. CRANDON, of Brantford, Ont., for " Churns." Ottawa, 5th September, 1870.

No. 590—C. D. VAN ALLEN, of West Farnham, Que., for "Improvements on Combined Churns and Washers." Ottawa, 5th September, 1870.

No. 591—A. J. GUSTEN, of Toronto, Ont., for "Improvements on a machine for binding Rails together." Ottawa, 5th September, 1870.

No. 592—W. VOLLAR, of Montreal, Que., for " The art of Flooring. &c.." Ottawa, 5th September, 1870.

No. 593—H. WALFORD, of Prescott, Ont , for "Improvements in Railroad Tracks," Ottawa, 5th September, 1870.

No. 594—R. C. HARRIS, of Dalhousie, N.B., for " A machine for clearing Snow from Railway Tracks." Ottawa, 5th September, 1870,

No. 595—J. H. NUTE, of New Glasgow. N.S., for " Improvements on a Hand Machine for Spinning." Ottawa, 5th September, 1870.

No. 596—E. L. BYRON, of Compton, Que., for "Improvements in a Horse Rake." Ottawa, 5th September, 1870.

No. 597—C. HOUGH, of Quebec, Que., for " Improvements on Elastic Spring Horse Shoes. ' Ottawa, 8th September, 1870.

No. 598—S. PALING, of Woodstock, Ont., for " Improvements on Window Blind and Curtain Rollers." Ottawa, 14th September, 1870.

No. 599—A. A. WOOD, of Belleville, Ont., for " An improvement on a machine for Cooking Meat." Ottawa, 14th September, 1870.

No. 600—J. O Cooper, Lynn, Ont., "Composition of matter for Stuffing Leather or for improving or preserving it." 14th September, 1870.

No. 601—H. A. STRINGER and A. F. WARD, Chatham, Ont., " Improvement in Self-Rakes for Harvesters." 14th September, 1870.

No. 602—J. J. LAPPIN, Toronto, Ont., " Improvement on a machine for Threshing Grain." 14th September, 1870.

No. 603—H. WANDBY, Toronto, Ont., " Improvement on a certain machine for making Stove Pipe Stone Mould." 14th September, 1870.

No. 604—D. S. MILLS, Simcoe, Ont., " Improvement on a machine for gathering Fruit." 14th September, 1870.

No. 605—S. DUNSEITH, Montreal, Que., "Composition for Tanning Hides, Skins, &c." 14th September, 1870.

No. 606—G. GROOM, Brockville, Ont., " Improvement in Churn Dashers." 14th September, 1870.

No. 607—J. ARMSTRONG, Guelph, Ont., and J. THOMPSON. of the same place, "Improvement on the machine for Elevating Hay. 11th September, 1870.

No. 608—J DENNIS, New Market, Ont., " Machinery for use in Framing Timber." 15th September, 1870.

No. 609—J. H. DICKSON, Toronto, Ont., " Improvement on a certain art for Preserving Fruit." 15th September, 1870.

No. 610—J. SHOPLAND, London, Ont., " Improvement on Steam Washers." 15th September, 1870.

No. 611—T. FORFAR, Waterdown, Ont., "Improvement in Churns. 15th September, 1870.

No. 612—L. PAYETTE, Montreal, Que., " Improvements on Pontoons for raising sunken vessels." 15th September, 1870.

No. 613—J. BROKENSHIRE, Kingston, Ont., " Improvement on Ship Pumps." 22nd September, 1870.

No. 614—A. LAW, Kingston, Ont., " Improvement on the art of Electro-Plating Iron or Steel with gold or silver. 22nd September, 1870.

No. 615—C. BAILLIE, Montreal, Que., " Improvement on Water Closets' Basin Sluice, &c. 22nd September, 1870.

No. 616—W. H. RODDEN, Toronto, Ont., " Improvements in Ferrules or Sockets for Hoe-Fork, Weeder Rake or Chisel Handles." 22nd September, 1870.

No. 617—S. HALL, Toronto, Ont., " Harrow for harrowing and breaking Sods of earth and for covering Seeds." 22nd September, 1870.

No. 618—B. J. TEFT, Conestogo, Ont., " Improvement in the Rail fence." 22nd September, 1870.

No. 619—J. N. TARBOX, Hamilton, Ont , " Improvements on Sewing Machines." 26th September, 1870.

No. 620—F. ROURK, Montreal, Que., " Apparatus for the working of Velocipedes." 26th September, 1870.

No. 621—G. D. FERRIER, W. M. MOONEY and J. B. WILLS, Montreal, Que., "Steel Horse Shoe Nail." 26th September, 1870.

No. 622—W. H. DOEL, Toronto, Ont., "Machine for catching Cockroaches, Beetles, &c." 28th September, 1870.

No.623—M. SELWAY, Toronto, Ont., "Improvements in Boot Trees." 28th September, 1870.

No. 624—P. C. VAN BROCKLIN, Paris, Ont, "Improvement in rigid and flexible Pipe Bend." 28th September, 1870.

No. 625—J. DENNIS, Newmarket, Ont., "Machine for unloading Hay and Grain." 28th September, 1870.

No. 626—W. McLEAN, Petrolia, Ont., "Machine for enlarging the Bow of a well called ' Expanding Reamer Bit.' " 28th September, 1870.

No. 627—J. A. MACKINNON, Sandwich, Ont., "Improvements on Whiffletrees." 29th September, 1870.

No. 628—A. HILTON, Strathroy, Ont., "Washing Machine." 29th September, 1870.

No. 629—A. KIRKWOOD, Toronto, Ont., "Improvement in the composition of matter called ' Kirkwood's Soup Biscuit.' " 29th September, 1870.

No. 630—G. H. MEAKINS, Hamilton, Ont., and D. S. NOBLE, of the same place, " Im provements in Pumps." 29th September, 1870.

No. 631—C. C. BENNETT, Montreal, Que., "Improvements on Self-Adjusting Muff Blocks." 29th September, 1870.

No. 632—D. MAXWELL, Paris, Ont., and A. WHITELAW, of the same place, " Improve ments in Horse Power machines." 29th September, 1870.

No. 633—B. G. BATTRAM, Shakespeare, Ont., "Machine for punching Iron Harrow Bars." 29th September, 1870.

No. 634—M. B. SOUTHWICK, Mont St Hilaire, Que, "Improvements on machinery for breaking the straw of flax." 30th September, 1870.

No. 635—W. S. GRAHAM, Manilla, Ont., "Improvements in Table Leaf supporters." 30th September, 1870.

No. 636—W. TOUT, St. Mary's Ont., " Rack and Lever Jack." 1st October, 1879.

No. 637—D. S. MILLS, Simcoe, Ont , "Pruner." 1st October, 1870.

No. 638—E. HIPKINS, Berford, Ont., "Improvement on machines for carrying Railroad Cars." 1st October, 1870.

No. 639—W. G. C. MASTERSON, Hinchinbrooke, Que., "Improvements on Turbine Water Wheels." 1st October, 1870.

No. 640—E. GURNEY, Hamilton, Ont., and C. GURNEY, of the same place, " Im provements in Stoves." 1st October, 1370.

No. 641—D. A. JOHNSTON, Florence, Ont., "Improvements in machines for holding Saws." 10th October, 1870.

No. 642—B. ARMSTRONG, Sheffield, Ont., " Metallic Spring Dash Churn." 10th October, 1870.

No. 643—E. W. GOFF, Magog, Que., "Improvement in the art of Dyeing textile Fabrics and Wools." 10th October, 1870.

No. 644—T. FORHAN, Wallaceburgh, Ont., "Improvement on Neck-Yoks." 10th October, 1870.

No. 645—D. P. CROSBY, Waterdown, Ont., " Improvement in Hoisting machines." 10th October, 1870.

No. 646—H. JEFFERSON, Toronto, Ont., "Composition of matter for making Stone, &c." 10th October, 1870.

No. 647—C. G. C. SIMPSON, Montreal, Que., "Improvements on self-acting Lubricators for Journals of Railway Car Axles." 10th October, 1870.

No. 648 - J. HOMAN, Thurlow, Ont., "Improvement on Fifth-Wheels of Carriages." 10th October, 1870.

No. 649—C. F. BELL, of St. George, Ont., "Improvement on Field Cultivators." 10th October, 1870.

No. 650—F. SPIERS, Galt, Ont., "Improvement on Nails, Spikes, and Bolts." 10th October, 1870.

No. 651—J. WATKINS, Montreal, Que., "Improvement on Brick Kilns." 11th October, 1870.

No. 652—J, ATKINSON, Lambton, Ont., "Improvement on certain machines for Cooking and other purposes." 11th October, 1870.

No. 653 - D. J. WAGGONER, Kingston, Ont., (assignee of Andrew Johnson, Searborough, Ont.,) "Quilting Frame Holder " 11th October, 1870.

No. 654—J. BENNETT, Beverley, Ont., "Improvement on Fences." 11th October, 1870.

No. 655—D. W. PULSIFER, Hantsford, N.S., "Washing Machine." 17th October, 1870.

No. 656—G. COOKE, Napier, Ont., "Improvements on machines for cutting Scrolls in wood." 17th October, 1870.

No. 657—G. MANNING, of Montreal, Que., "Improvement in Land Fertilizers." 17th October, 1870.

No. 658—T ATKINSON, Newmarket, Ont., "Improvement on Sleigh Brakes." 17th October, 1870.

No 659—J. F. LASH, Toronto, Ont., "Improvement on Railway Carriage Windows." 17th October, 1870.

No. 660—T. YOUNG, Montreal, Que., "Improvements on Smoke and Gas consuming Stoves." 17th October, 1870.

No. 661—E. W. ZEIGLER and G. SCHATZ, Berlin, Ont., "Improvements on machines for Washing Clothes " 17th October, 1870.

No. 662—G. DAVIS, Nichol, Ont, "Improvement on Hay Rakes." 17th October, 1870.

No 663—V. PEARSON, wife of John E. Pearson, Toronto, Ont., "Abdominal Supporter," 21st October, 1870.

No. 664—H. WOOD, Lindsay, Ont., "Machinery for reducing Wood to a fine Pulp for the manufacture of Paper." 21st October, 1870.

No. 665—W. D. MISENER, West Flamboro', Ont., "Improvements on combined Root Cultivators and Heaping Ploughs." 21st October, 1870.

No. 666—J. ABELL and G. LANGLAND, Woodbridge, Ont., "Improvements on Furrow Ploughs." 21st October, 1870.

No. 667 - H J. RUTTAN, Cobourg, Ont., "Improvement in the construction of Buildings for Drying by hot air." 22nd October, 870.

No. 668—R. H. SARVIS, Hibberi, Ont., "Improvement on Farm Fences." 22nd October, 1870.

No. 669 - J. LEYDEN, Winchester, Ont., "Improvements in Expansion Drills." 22nd October, 1870.

No. 670—W. R. BAKER, Wellington Square, Ont., "Improvements on Car Couplers." 22nd October, 1870.

No. 671—E. W. HOWELL, Halifax, N.S., "Rotary Engine." 22nd October, 1870.

No. 672—H. R. IVES, Montreal, Que., "Improvements on Sad Irons and Heaters." 24th October, 1870.

No. 673—J. NELSON, Belleville, Ont., "Improvement on Tuyère Irons." 24th October, 1870.

No. 674—G. CAMPBELL, Toronto, Ont., "Improvement on Churns." 26th October, 1870.

No. 675—J. WOODRUFF, Pickering, Ont., "Improvement on Harvest Knife Guards." 26th October, 1870.

No. 676—A. PAUL, Reach, Ont., "Improvement on machines for cleaning and hulling Grain." 26th October, 1870.

No.077—T. F. McLEAN, Goderich, Ont., "Improvements in Brine Evaporators." 26th October, 1870.

No. 678—H. BERRY, Guelph, Ont., "Improvement on Bottle Stoppers." 27th October, 1870.

No. 679—C. G. C. SIMPSON, Montreal, Que., "Improvements on Knitting Machines." 31st October, 1870.

No. 680—H. WOOD, Lindsay, Ont., "Improvements in the art of Manufacturing Fibre from Wood for Paper making." 31st October, 1870.

No. 681—C. S. MOORE, Guelph, Ont., "Improvement in the art of Manufacturing Light Colored Lubricating Oil." 31st October, 1870.

No. 682—T. MURGATROYD, Smithville, Ont., "Improvement on Patent Fold Springs." 31st October, 1870.

No. 683—W. A. LEGGO, Montreal, Que , "Electro Metallic Printing." 31st October, 1870.

No. 684—C. S. MOORE, Guelph, Ont. "Improvement in the art of Manufacturing Parafine Wax." 31st October, 1870.

No. 685—M. HOWLES, Hamilton, Ont., "Improvement on Dampers for Stoves, Ovens and Furnaces." Re-issue of No. 146. 5th November, 1870.

No. 686—H. WOOD, Ont., "Improvement in Electro Magnetic machines and Magnets." 5th November, 1870.

No 687—J. M. MEHARG, Montreal, Que , "Improvement on self-closing Spindle Cocks." 5th November, 1870.

No. 688 - J. W. FRAIR, Picton, Ont., "Extension Ladder." 5th November, 1870.

No. 689—W. MILNER, Strathroy, Ont., "Improved Snow Gate." 5th November, 1870.

No. 690—T. J. CALBARRY, Darlington, Ont., ' Improvements in machines for Churning.' 5th November, 1870.

No. 691—J. J. WARNER, Otterville, Ont , " Improvement in Whiffletree-Hooks." 10th November, 1870.

No. 692—S. WASHBURN, St. George, Ont., "Improvement on Clothes Pegs." 10th November, 1870.

No. 693—W. TAYLOR, Montreal, Que. "Improvement on Expansive Inserted Saw Teeth." 10th November, 1870.

No. 694—R. S. BAILEY, Leeds, Que., "Horse Shoes." 11th November, 1870.

No. 695—C. H. GUSTIN, Toronto, Ont., "Improvement on Gates." 11th November, 1870.

No. 696—W. H. HANNAM, Whitby, Ont., "Improvement on Sewing Machines." 11th November, 1870.

No. 697—A. GROAT, Brooklin, Ont., "Improvement on Butchers' Knives." 11th November, 1870.

No. 698—S. S. McMULLEN, Belleville, Ont., "Improvement on Horse Shoes." 11th November, 1870.

No. 699—J. D. LAWLOR, Montreal, Que., "Improvements on Sewing Machines." 14th November, 1870.

No. 700—G. H. MEAKINS, Hamilton, Ont., "Improved Compression Cock and Check Valve." 14th November, 1870.

No. 701—W. R. BAKER, Wellington Square, Ont., "Door Fastener." 14th November, 1870.

No. 702—J. P. LONG, Peterborough, Ont., "Improvements on Edging Lumber." 14th November, 1870.

No. 703—A. H. BALCH and W. D. E. NELSON, Montreal, Que., "Improvements on Electro-Magnetic Iron Separating Machines. ' 14th October, 1870.

No. 704—J. N. BEARS, Malahide, Ont., "Improvements on Gates for opening and closing the same." 15th November, 1870.

No. 705—H. A. PARR, Yarmouth, N.S., "Composition of matter for the cure of Pains." 15th November, 1870.

No. 706—C. MEE, Kingston, Ont., "Improvement in Stove Pipe Shelves." 15th November, 1870.

No. 707—W. CHURCHILL, Blenheim, Ont., "Portable Fence." 15th November, 1870.

No. 708—S. E. PERKISS, Hamilton, Ont., "Improved art of tinning Iron and Metals." 15th November, 1870.

No. 709—A. McKAY, Montreal, Que., "Improvements on self-acting Flush Safety Bolts." 16th November, 1870.

No. 710—R. SCARLETT, Mooretown, Ont., "Improvement on Clothes Horses or Racks." 16th November, 1870.

No. 711—J. DEWE, Toronto, Ont., "Improvement in the art of closing or fastening Bags." 16th November, 1870.

No. 712—S. CATUDAL, Farnham, Que., "Improvements in Match Safes." 16th Novembe · 1870.

No. 713—E. W. SECORD, Bracebridge, Ont., "Machine for picking Berries, &c." 17th November, 1870.

No. 714—S. FELL, Brockville, Ont., "Improvements in Lanterns for indicating Railway trains." 24th November, 1870.

No. 715—A. PALMER, Pickering, Ont., "Improvements on Ditching Machines." 24th November, 1870.

No. 716—S. G. BUSH, Coaticook, Que., "Improvements in Horse Hay Rakes." 24th November, 1870.

No. 717—P. S. Van Wagner, Saltfleet, Ont., "Improvements on Holdback Hooks." 24th November, 1870.

No. 718—J. YOCOM, Danville, Ont., "Improvement in Ploughs." 24th November, 1870.

No. 719 J. FOSTER, St. Simon, Que., "Improvements on Churns." 24th November, 1870.

No. 720—J. T. MOREY, Montreal, Que., "Improvements on Hatchet-hammers, Nail-Pullers and Scrapers." 29th November, 1870.

No. 721—A. M. JOHNSON, Guysborough, Ont., and J. WILEY, of the same place, "Improvements on Stump Machines." 29th November, 1870.

No. 722—J. RICE, Whitby, Ont., "A new and useful improvement in Bob Sleighs." 29th November, 1870.

No. 723—W. BUCK, Brantford, Ont., "Improvement on Drum Stoves." 29th November, 1870.

No. 724—T. S. DETLOR, Prescott, Ont., "Drum Heater." 29th November, 1870.

No 725—A. MOYER, Beamsville, Ont., "Machine for coupling Railway Cars." 29th December, 1870.

No. 726—J. B. HULBERT, Quebec, Que., "Improvement on Wooden Railways." 6th December, 1870.

No. 727—J. DUVAL, Laprarie, Que., "Improvements on Breech-loading Rifles." 6th December, 1870.

No. 728—E. McMULLIN, Montreal, Que., "Improvement on Paving Streets." 6th December, 1870.

No. 729—T. SNAREY, Tilsonburgh, Ont., "Improvements in Pans for Baking Bread." 6th December, 1870.

No. 730—C. G. C. SIMPSON, Montreal, Que., "Improvements on self-acting Lubricators." 6th December, 1870.

No. 731—J. B. HULBERT, Quebec, Que., "Self-loading and Dumping Cart." 10th December, 1870.

No. 732 J. B. HULBERT, Quebec, Que., "Tie or Sleeper Framer." 10th December, 1870.

No. 733—I. W. FORBES, Windsor, Ont., "Improved Valve Gear." 10th December, 1870

No. 734—I. W. FORBES, Windsor, Ont., "Improvements on Steam Engines." 10th December, 1870.

No. 735—I. W. FORBES, Windsor, Ont., "Improved Mortar for Stamp Batteries." 10th December, 1870.

No. 736—I. W. FORBES, Windsor, Ont., "Improvements on those parts of steam engines called and known as the Steam Chest Valve and Valve Seat." 10th December, 1870.

No. 737—I. W. FORBES, Windsor, Ont., "Improvements on those parts of steam engines called and known as the Steam Chest Valve and Valve Seat." 10th December, 1870.

No 738—I. W. FORBES, Windsor, Ont, "Improvements on those parts of steam engines called or known as the steam Chest Valve and Valve Seat." 10th December, 1870.

No. 739—I. W FORBES, Windsor, Ont , "Improvements on those parts parts of steam engines called and known as the Steam Chest Valve and Valve Seat." 10th December, 1870.

No. 740—I. W. FORBES, Windsor, Ont., "Improvement in that portion now in ordinary use of the steam engine, called or known as "The Valve Gearing." 10th December, 1870.

No. 741—R. P. MITCHELL, Truro, N. S., "Improvement in the method of passing Streams of water through or under the road bed or embankment of a Railway." 10th December, 1870.

No. 742—J. HOOVER, Warwick, Ont., "Improvements in Field Gates " 10th December, 1870.

No. 743—S. W. HOOD, Windsor, N. S., "Potato Digger." 10th December, 1870.

No. 744—W. THOMPSON, Woodstock, Ont., "Improved Sewing Machine Top." 10th December, 1870.

No. 745—Hon. H. AYLMER, Melbourne, Que., "Art and Apparatus for Manufacturing Bark Extract." 10th December, 1870.

No. 746—W. R. BAKER, Wellington Square, Ont., "Improvements on Hold-back Hooks." 17th December, 1870.

No. 747—T. F. McLEAN, Goderich, Ont., "Scraper for removing salt from pans or dirt on roads." 17th December, 1870.

No. 748—H. L. CARR, Coaticook, Que., "Improvements in Stovepipe Drums." 17th December, 1870.

No. 749—J. HOOVER, Warwick, Ont., "Improvements in Field Fences." 17th December, 1870.

No. 750—H. HOWARD, St. Johns Que., "Improvements in the art of expelling Foul Air from Buildings." 17th December, 1870.

No. 751—R. A. GRIFFIN, Montreal, Que., "Improvements in the art of manufacturing Peat Fuel." 21st December, 1870.

No. 752—G. SMITH, Stratford, Ont., "Improvements on Bedsteads." 21st December, 1870.

No. 753—F. A. GARDENER, Hamilton, Ont., "Improvements on Sewing Machines." 21st December, 1870.

No. 754—J. STANSFORD and J. W. HENRY, Quebec, Que., "Improvement in the construction of Composite Ships." 23rd December, 1870.

No. 755—N. BELHUMEUR, Montreal, Que., "Improvement in the manufacture of Soles." 23rd December, 1870.

No. 756—D. O. PARKER, Liverpool, N. S., "Improvements on Cradles." 23rd December, 1870.

No. 757—A. TICHBOURNE, Goderich, Ont., "Manufacture of Butter." 23rd December, 1870.

No. 758—D. GHENT, Peel, Ont., and A. WEIR, Wellesley, Ont , "Improvements in Field Fences." 23rd December, 1870.

No. 759—G. B. PATTEE, Ottawa, Ont., "Improvements in machines for Swaging the Teeth of Saws." 29th December, 1870.

No. 760—A. McCANNEL, Caledon, Ont., "Improvements on certain machines for covering Hay, Straw, &c." 31st December, 1870.

No. 761—D. O. PARKER, Liverpool, N. S., " Bed Clothes Holder." 6th January, 1871.

No. 762—G. DUNCAN, York, Ont., "Improvements on Horse Powers." 6th January, 1871.

No. 763—D. AIKMAN, Montreal, Que., "Improvements in the art of Curing Peat Pulp for Fuel and Apparatus used therefor." 6th January, 1871.

No. 764—C. W. WOODFORD, Montreal, Que., " Improvements in the manufacture of Horse Shoe Nails." 6th January, 1871.

No 765—R. SMITH, Sherbrooke, Que., "A new and useful art for the manufacture of Seamless Boxes from Paper Pulp." 6th January, 1871.

No. 766—R. SMITH, Sherbrooke, Que., "A new and useful art for the manufacture of Seamless Boxes or other hollow articles from Paper Pulp." 6th January, 1871.

No. 767—G. F. BLAICHER, Windsor, Ont., "Improvement in Wooden Pavement." 6th January, 1871.

No. 768—A. McCANNEL, Caledon, Ont , "Improvements on Barns." 6th January, 1871.

No. 769—J. MITCHELL, Lansdown, Ont., "Improvements in Horse Hay Forks." 13th January, 1870.

No. 770—I. KINNEY, Toronto, Ont., " Improvements on certain machines now in ordinary use for Cooking." 13th January, 1871.

No. 771—J. A. BAZIN, Montreal, Que., " Improvements in the manufacture of mouth or Base Plates for artificial Teeth." 13th January, 1871.

No. 772—A. OWEN, Charlotteville, Ont., (assignee of T. A. Fisk, Walsingham, Ont.,) " Animal Trap." 13th January, 1871.

No. 773—G. SCOULLAR, Saint John, N B., " Improvement in the art of Tanning Skins." 13th January, 1871.

. No. 774—A. BROWN, Toronto, Ont . "Improvements on a certain machine now in ordinary use for Sweeping." 13th January, 1871.

No. 775—T. BARNES, Fairfield, Ont., and H. HUDGIN, of the same place, "Improvements in carriage Gates." 13th January, 1871.

No. 776—G. SEGER,' Humberstone, Ont.. " Machine for making Cider and Wine." 13th January, 1871.

No. 777—J. WAGGONER, Portsmouth, Ont., "Improvements on Hay and Barley Forks." 13th January, 1871.

No. 778—T. G. RICE, Montreal, Que., "Improvements on Swing Cots." 13th January, 1871.

No. 779—C. HARTLEIB, Normanby, Ont., " Improvement in Separator Thrashing Machines." 13th January, 1871.

No. 780—J. COMBS, Barton, Ont., " Manufacture of Agricultural Implements for a new and useful steel tine barley Fork." 13th January, 1871.

No. 781—I. W. FORBES, Windsor, Ont , "Art of cutting, grinding, cleaning and scouring crushed or pulverized Ores or Metals." 13th January, 1871.

No. 782—R. STANDING, Chinguacousy, Ont., " Improvement on certain machines now in ordinary use for raising Hay, Straw or other weights." 13th January, 1871.

No. 783—W. T. COREY, Hillsborough, N.B., " Improvement on a farm or truck waggon Box and Gearing." 13th January. 1871

No. 784—I. MILLS, Hamilton, Ont., " Improvement in the manufacture of Door Bell and other similar Knobs." 13th January, 1871.

No. 785—C. CARPENTER, Hamilton, Ont.. " Improvement in the manufacture of Knobs for locks, bell-pulls or other articles." 13th January, 1871.

No. 786—C. G. C. SIMPSON, Montreal, Que., " Improvements on Axles and Boxes of wheeled vehicles." 13th January, 1871.

No. 787—J. D. SMITH, Sandford, Ont., " Machine for holding Bags to be filled" 13th January. 1871.

No. 788—W. LAYNG, Delta, Ont., " Improvement on machines usually called a ' Tuyère' for the blast pipe of Forges." 16th January, 1871.

No. 789—B. M. BRISBIN and J. W. BRISBIN, Enniskillen, Ont., (assignees of C. Hastings, Hampton, Ont.,) "Improvement in the construction of Gates." 16th January, 1871.

No. 790—W. A. ROBINSON, Hamilton, Ont., " Useful improvement on Locomotive Engines." 16th January, 1871.

No. 791 - J. HOWARD, Hamilton, Ont., " Improvement on machines for splitting Wood." 7th February, 1871.

No. 792—J. LOUGH, Buckingham, Que., " Improvements on Lough's self-acting Saw-tooth Press." 7th February, 1871.

No 793—E. P. WHITNEY, Bolton, Que., "Improvements in the art of making Paper and Parchment impervious to water." 7th February, 1871.

No. 794—J. CAMPBELL and J. FRAZER, Windsor, Ont., "Improvements in the art of building Houses." 7th October, 1871.

No. 795—W. H. RODDEN, Toronto, Ont., "Improvement in the Prongs or Tines of hay, straw, barley or manure Forks." 7th February, 1871.

No. 796—J. FOOTH and J. CROUEN, London, Ont., "Improvements on certain machines now in ordinary use for replacing Rolling Stock." 7th February, 1871.

No. 797—S. H. BOONE, Douglas, N.B., " Churn." 7th February, 1871.

No. 708—S. A. DUNBAR, Mount Forest, Ont., "Improvements in Harness for horses." 7th February, 1871.

No. 799—J. J. WARNER, Ottersville, Ont., " Harness Hook and Buckle." 7th February 1871.

No. 800—C. MALCOLM. Oakland, Ont., " Machine for Sawing Shingles." 8th February, 1871.

No. 801—C. H. WATEROUS, Brantford, Ont., "Improvement on Fire Protection and Water Supply." 8th February, 1871.

No. 802—W. JOHNSON, Toronto, Ont., " Improvements on Self-rocking Cradles." 8th February, 1871.

No. 803—J. HOOPER and R. HADDEN, Picton, Ont., "'Improvement in the Back Strap and Hip Strap of Harness." 18th February, 1871.

No. 804—J. MILNE, Hamilton, Ont., " Improved Holdback Hook for Carriage Shafts." 18th February, 1871.

No. 805—M. BARLOW, Peel, Ont., " Improvement in Farm Fences." 21st February, 1871.

No. 806—A. BOYDEN, Hamilton, Ont., " Improvement in Waggon Tongue Supporters." 21st February, 1871.

No. 807—J. N. PITTS, Drummondville, Ont., and J. E. RUSSELL, of the same place, " Fire Alarm." 23th February, 1871.

No. 808—P. HAY, Galt, Ont., " Improvement upon Solid Shaft Coupling." 2nd March, 1871.

No. 809—J. MULHOLLAND, Blenheim, Ont., " Improvement in Bed Springs." 2nd March, 1871.

No. 810 - J. S. RANDALL, Grimsby, Ont., " Improved process of Seasoning Lumber by Steam Pressure." 2nd March, 1871.

No. 811—R. W. ELLIOTT, Toronto, Ont., " Useful art or process for removing the Incrustations of gypsum or lime from Salt Evaporating Pans." 2nd March, 1871.

No. 812—J. A. WOOD, Harwich, Ont., " Machine for Washing Clothes." 2nd March, 1871.

No. 813—R. MITCHELL, Arthur, Ont., " Trough and Hay Rack." 2nd March, 1871.

No. 814—H. WESTLAKE and R. BLATCHFORD, Usborne, Ont., " Improvements on Horse Hoe Cultivator and Drill Plough." 2nd March, 1871.

No. 815—L. WISMER, Preston, Ont., " Improvements on Fences." 2nd March, 1871.

No. 816—W. A. LEGGO, Montreal, Que., " Improvements on Spectacles." 2nd March, 1871.

No. 817—A. P. VON POEHRNHOFF, St. Catharines, Ont., "Manufacturing Illuminating Oil from Petroleum and Tar." 2nd March, 1871.

No. 818—W. H. BARKER, Windsor, N. S., "Improvements in Pot Covers." 2nd March, 1871.

No. 819—T. RAY, Pelham, Ont., "Machine for Coupling Cars on Railways." 2nd March, 1871.

No. 820—V. BEAUDET, Ste. Emélie, Que., "Improvement on the mode now in ordinary use for driving Water Wheels with pressed water." 2nd March, 1871.

No. 821—W. TOWNEND, Hamilton, Ont., "Machine for cleaning Boiler Tubes." 2nd March, 1871.

No. 822—F. SANDHAM, Ottawa, Ont., "Improvements in Coupling Carriage Thills." 2nd March, 1871.

No. 823—H. MATHESON, Toronto, Ont., "Machine for Drafting Coats and other Garments." 2nd March, 1871.

No. 824—S. CATUDAL, Farnham, Que., "Improvements in Tools for Boring and Counter-sinking." 2nd March, 1871.

No. 825—J. L. SMITH, Toronto, Ont., "Improvement in a certain art now in ordinary use for Road making." 2nd March, 1871.

No. 826—J. FLETT, Almonte, Ont., "Improvements in Dining and other Tables." 2nd March, 1871.

No. 827—J. A. CROSSMAN, Hamilton, Ont., "Machine for Sawing Wood." 2nd March, 1871.

No. 828—H. W. SMALLPIECE, Toronto, Ont., "Machine for Cleansing the Streets." 2nd March, 1871.

No. 829—J. WARREN, Montreal, Que., "Improvements on Stoves and Furnaces." 8th March, 1871.

No. 830—J. FINDLAY, Toronto, Ont., "Improvements on machines for holding the Tools of Lathes." 8th March, 1871.

No. 831—J. W. ABBOTT, St. Catharines, Ont , "Improvement in the plate of Sewing Machines." 8th March, 1871.

No. 832—R. POSTANS, Ancaster, Ont., "Machine for the purpose of applying more conveniently the dry earth system of Sewage." 8th March, 1871.

No. 833—H. B VINES, Toronto, Ont., "Improved Rolling Mill for repairing or reducing the sections of old Railway Rails." 8th March, 1871.

No. 834—H. COLLARD, Gananoque, Ont., "Improvement in the construction of Harrows." 8th March, 1871.

No. 835—M. WOOD, Yarmouth, Ont., "Improvement on Churns." 8th March, 1871.

No. 836—J. TEETZEL, Howard, Ont., "Ditching Machine." 8th March, 1871.

No. 837—C. F. MUELLER, Hamilton, Ont., "Improvement in the art of ornamenting Sewing machines and other articles of manufacture of Wood, Metal, Glass, &c., with gold, silver, or metal leaf." 8th March, 1871.

No. 838—E. W. COLLEY, St. Mary's, Ont., and W. JACKSON, of the same place, "Improvements in machines for Roasting Coffee and Malt. 8th March, 1871.

No. 839 C. G. C. SIMPSON, Montreal, Que., "Improvements on Hair and Wool Clipping machines." 8th March, 1871.

No. 840 —H. WORKMAN, Clark, Ont., and J. A. QUACKENBUSH, of the same place, "Improvements in Washers for securing nuts on screw bolts." 8th March, 1871.

No. 841—J. E. ATWOOD, Richmond, Que., "Improvement in the art of refining Iron and Steel." 8th March, 1871.

No. 842—B. F. DORSEY, Brantford, Ont., "Cider Mill." 8th March, 1871.

No. 843—J. B STONE, Hamilton, Ont., "Improved Air-tight Screw Cap, for coal oil and other Cans and fruit Jars." 8th March, 1871.

No. 844—A. BISSELL, Mount Forest, Ont., "Improvements in Churns." 8th March 1871.

No. 845—W. MILNER, Strathroy, Ont., "Improvement in Bill and Paper Files." 8th March, 1871.

No. 846—J. JONES, Sidney, Ont., "Improvements on Washing machines." 9th March, 1871.

No. 847—W. T. COREY, Hillsborough, N. B., "Improvement on Sled Brakes." 9th March, 1871.

No. 848—W. E. HUGHES, Aylmer, Ont., "Improvement on machines for Pruning." 9th March, 1871.

No. 849—J. W. ELLIOTT, Toronto, Ont., "Improvements on vulcanizing and preparing Artificial Teeth." 9th March, 1871.

No. 850—C. THAIN, Guelph, Ont., "Improvement on the machine for Sowing Turnip, Mango or Carrot Seed." 9th March, 1871.

No. 851—C. W. COY, Sherbrooke, Que., "Improvements on Sewing machines." 9th March, 1871.

No. 852—E. and C. GURNEY, Hamilton, Ont., "Improvements in Heating Stoves." 10th March, 1871.

No. 853—D. M. LAMB, Strathroy, Ont., "Improvement in Ploughs." 10th March, 1871.

No. 854—D. M. LAMB, Strathroy, Ont., "Method of producing Fruit Trees and causing them to grow from the cuttings or the severed twigs of other fruit trees without usual process of grafting." 10th March, 1871.

No. 855—J. STEINMILLER, Waterloo, Ont., "Improvements in machinery for Feeding Grain and Middlings to Millstones." 13th March, 1871.

No. 856—J. R. CARLE, Scotch Town, N. B., "Improvement in Jacks and machines for lifting the wheels of carriages and waggons, and for stowing cargoes in vessels." 13th March, 1871.

No. 557—T. POTTS, Brantford, Ont., "Improvement on Drums or Heaters." 13th March, 1871.

No. 858—E. R. McCALL, Simcoe, Ont., "Machine for grinding the Knives of Reapers and Mowers." 13th March, 1871.

No. 859—J. WESTLICK, Hope, Ont., "Improvement on Seed Sowers and Cultivators." 13th March, 1871.

No. 860—C. BLYTHE, Petrolea, Ont., "Machine for making Compressed Wooden Bungs." 13th March, 1871.

No. 861—S. H. PALMER, Tilsonbury, Ont., "Improvement on Churns." 13th March, 1871.

No. 862—P. ROBICHAUD, St. Hyacinthe, Que., "Improvement in the art of constructing Railways and in the apparatus and proper means of keeping in place the Rails, and to protect their butt ends or extremities against the unevenness or crushing produced by the passing of car wheels over the joints." 9th March, 1871.

No. 863—G. DAVIS, Nichol, Ont., "Improvement on machines for Sowing Seed." 13th March, 1871.

No. 864—A. KEELER, Prescott, Ont., "Machine for strengthening and holding Corn Brooms in Shape. 13th March, 1871.

No. 865—E. STONEY, Walkerton, Ont., "Improvement on Chairs," 13th March, 1871.

No. 866—J. HUBBS, Cramahe, Ont., "Improved Window Blind." 16th March, 1871.

No. 867 -C. H. GUARD, Toronto, Ont., "Improvement on machines for making Wheels." 16th March, 1871.

No. 868—M. REEVES, Hamilton, Ont., "Balance Churn." 16th March, 1871.

No. 869—J. FORBES, Halifax, N.S., "Improvements in machines for making Clips or Scabbards for the joints of railway rails, and for bending metal bars and plates to a required shape." 16th March, 1871.

No. 870—G. ARMSTRONG, Woodstock, Ont., "Improvement in the manufacture of King Bolts for Vehicles." 16th March, 1871.

No. 871—J. EDE and JOHN and JOSEPH SHORT, Woodstock, Ont., "Improvement on Whiffletree Hooks." 16th March, 1871.

No. 872—H. SELLS, Vienna, Ont., "Improvements on machines for shelling Corn in the ear." 16th March, 1870.

No. 873—R. G. LECKIE, Acton Vale, Que., "Improvements on the art, process and apparatus for evaporating and concentrating Brine and other liquids." 16th March, 1871.

No. 874—E. ROBLIN, Sophiasburgh, Ont., "Improvements in the form of Cutter or section Bars for machines now in ordinary use for Reaping or Mowing." 16th March, 1871.

No. 875—J. C. BOND, Vincent, Ont., " Machine for pulling Roots." 16th March, 1871.

No. 876—J. BUCKLEY, Cobourg, Ont , "Improvement in Pipe Wrenches." 16th March, 1871.

No. 877—R. WALKER, Toronto, Ont., "Improvements on Drilling and Boring Machines." 16th March, 1871.

No. 878—G. GIRVIN, Toronto, Ont., "Machine for levelling Billiard and Bagatelle Tables." 16th March, 1871.

No. 879—E. R. CARPENTER, Collingwood, Ont., "Machine for measuring Liquid." 16th March, 1871.

No. 880—H. FRASER, Clarkesburgh, Ont., " Machine for planking Vessels." 16th March 1871.

No. 881—J. N. TARBOX, Hamilton, Ont., "Improvements on Frillers for Sewing machines." 16th March, 1871.

No. 882—G. W. and A. B. PERKINS, Ottawa, Ont., "Improvements in machines for Swaging and gumming the Teeth of Saws." 16th March, 1871.

No. 883—A. FLETCHER, Harwick, Ont., "Machine for cleaning the Coulters of Ploughs. 16th March, 1871.

No. 884—J. RAPSON, Woodstock, Ont., "Improvements on King bolts." 16th March, 1871.

No. 885—Patent of Extension No. 1843.—W. C. NUNN, Whitby, Ont., "Improved railway-Signal." 21st March, 1871.

No. 886—J. CLOSE, Woodstock, Ont., " Improvements in the manufacture of Brick machines." 21st March, 1871.

No. 887—R. BENTLEY, Arran, Ont., "Coupling for Harness and Whiffletrees.' 21st March, 1871.

No. 888 —J. DEWE, Ottawa, Ont., "Improvement in the art of sealing with metal Rivets and Plyers." 21st March, 1871.

No. 889—P. C. VANBROCKLIN, Paris, Ont , " Improvement on Ploughs." 21st March,1871.

No. 890—S. C. HALL, Blenheim, Ont., " Improvement in Plough Shares." 23rd March, 1871.

No. 891—B. BLACKSTONE, Barton, Ont., "Saw Set, Clamp and Vise." 23rd March, 1871.

No. 892—A. H. BALCH and W. D. E. NELSON, Montreal, Que., "Improvement on Clasp Fasteners for bags and sacks, &c." 23rd March, 1871.

No. 893—D. M. R. PETERS, Haldimand, Ont., "Improvement on Horse Hay Rakes." 23rd March, 1871.

No. 894—J. V. SCHAAFF, Bowmanville, Ont., "Machine for sawing Wood." 23rd March, 1871.

No. 895—A. CULVER, Townsend, Ont., "Improvements on Gates." 24th March, 1871

No. 896—S. DAVIS, Clinton, Ont., "Improvements in heating Stoves." 24th March, 1871.

No. 897—A. McDIARMID, Howard, Ont., " Improvements on Ploughs." 24th March, 1871.

No. 898—J. PENMAN, Paris, Ont., "Machine for conveying Wool, Cotton or other light material from one part of a building to another, or from one building to another." 24th March, 1871.

No. 899—D. CAMERON and M. McCLEAN, Kincardine, Ont., " Composition of matter for making Fire Brick, and in the art of burning the same." 24th March, 1871.

No. 900—J. GRANT, Carleton Place, Ont., "Improvements in Covers for Pots, and other like culinary utensils." 30th March, 1871.

No. 901—E. J. BANFIELD, Quebec, Que., "Improvements in machines or devices for attachment to Bottles for securing the Corks." 30th March, 1871.

No. 902—M. A. HILL, St. Catharines, Ont., "Machine for regulating the speed and power of Wind Wheels." 30th March, 1871.

No. 903—F. LANE, Perth, Ont., "Composition of matter for Medicine for children." 30th March, 1871.

No. 904—W. F. GARDINER, Manvers, Ont., "Improvements in Burglar-Alarms." 30th March, 1871.

No. 905—R. P. COREY, Hillier, Ont., "Machine for pulling or extracting Stumps, &c." 30th March, 1871.

No. 906—T. CREVIER, Montreal, Que., "Improvements on Air Furnaces." 4th April, 1871.

No. 907—J. SHERMAN, Houghton, Ont., "Machine for feeding and watering Swine." 4th April, 1871.

No. 908—I. MILLS, Hamilton, Ont., "Machine for measuring and reeling Cloth, &c." 4th April, 1871.

No. 909—W. H. BARWICK, Montreal, Que., "Improvements on Wrenches." 4th April, 1871.

No. 910—A. FLETCHER, Harwick, Ont., "Improvement on Window Stoppers." 5th April, 1871.

No. 912—J. GALBRAITH, St. John, N.B , "Improvement on the appliances now in use to hold and keep in position House and railway Car window Sashes and Blinds when raised." 5th April, 1871.

No. 911—J. C. DRADER and C. S. FRETZE, Tamworth, Ont , "Improvements on machines for turning Barley, &c." 5th April, 1871.

No. 913—J. JONES, Hamilton, Ont., "Improvement on Railroad rail Chairs." 5th April, 1871.

No. 914—P. LAJOIE, St. Hyacinthe, Que., "Improvement in heating Furnaces," 5th April, 1871.

No. 915—B. E. CHARLTON and H. E. HARRISON, Hamilton, Ont., "Improvement in the art or process of manufacturing Vinegar." 5th April, 1871.

No. 916—P. W. STRONG, Farmersville, Ont., "Improvements on machines for making Cheese." 5th April, 1871.

No. 917—T. BEAUDRY, Quebec, Que., "Joint for joining the ends of Straps or Bands used for moving machines, Mills and Manufactures." 11th April, 1871.

No. 918—J. BAXTER, Yarmouth, N.S., "Improvements in Shaft Tug and Back Straps." 11th April, 1871.

No. 919—A. ROSS and M. H. UTLEY, Montreal, Que., "Improvements on electro-magnetic Motors." 11th April, 1871.

No. 920—G. H. KENDALL, Montreal, Que., "Improvements in the manufacture of Steel and Iron." 11th April, 1871.

No. 921—J. T. EGAN, Montreal, Que., "Improvements on Water Conductors." 11th April, 1871.

No. 922—R. McMILLIN, Storrington, Ont., "Machine for coupling Cars on railways." 13th April, 1871.

No. 923—I. McNAUGHTON, Egerton, N.S., "Improvements in Churns." 13th April, 1871.

No. 924—J. B. EDWARDS, Montreal, Que., "Method of Ventilating Houses and public buildings, and apparatus for that purpose." 13th April, 1871.

No. 925—D. Edward, Montreal, Que., "Improvements on combined Cloth, Brush and Mop holders." 13th April, 1871.

No. 926—W. D. BROATCH, Hamilton, Ont., "Improvements in Churns." 13th April, 1871.

No. 927—W. HICKEY, Addison, Ont , " Improvements in Stove-pipe Elbows." 13th April, 1871.

No. 928—E. STONEY, Walkerton, Ont., "Improvement on Chairs." 13th April, 1871.

No. 929—W. REYNOLDS, Tecumseth, Ont., assignee of T. CRANNEY, Schomberg. Ont., " Improvements on a certain machine now in ordinary use for transmitting motion to the cylinder of Thrashing machines." 15th April, 1871.

No. 930—J. GROSS, Pelham, Ont , " Apparatus for the purpose of economising the heat in Rooms and Buildings." 15th April, 1871.

No. 931—W. REYNOLDS, Tecumseth, (assignee of T. CRANNEY, Schomberg), Ont., " Improvement on Pumps." 15th April, 1871.

No. 932—W. DEPEW, Brantford, Ont., " Fire Escape." 15th April, 1871.

No. 933—J. MOYER, Waterloo, Ont., " Washing Machine." 15th April, 1871.

No. 934—J. L. DEWOLF, Windsor, N. S., " Improvement on apparatus for concentrating the Extract of Hemlock and other Bark, &c." 15th April, 1871.

No 935—J. E. WATEROUS, Brantford, Ont., "Machine for regulating the pressure of Water in Street Mains and Water Pipes." 18th April, 1871.

No. 936—J, LINTON, Orono, Clarke, Ont., " Improvements in Cultivators." 18th April, 1871.

No. 937—C. S. BELL, Morpeth, Out., " Improvement on Sewing machines." 18th April, 1871.

No. 938—W. J. MORRIS, Perth, Ont., " Improvements in machinery or apparatus for Evaporating Brine in the manufacture of Salt." 18th April, 1871.

No. 939—C. BOSS, Bathurst, N. B., " Improvements in Washing Boilers." 18th April, 1871.

No. 940—T. SULLIVAN, Belleville, Ont., ," Machine for Turning Scythes, Snaith or other crooked Sticks." 20th April, 1871.

No. 941—J. MAHON, Adelaide, Ont., and J. ACHES, Lobo, Ont., " Improvements on Bee Hives." 20th April, 1871.

No. 942—J. BROUGHTON, Hamilton, Ont., "Machine for Pruning." 20th April, 1871.

No. 943—F. BLAIKIE, Sarnia, Ont., " Machine for the purpose of Pumping and Blowing or Agitating Oil or other Liquids." 20th April, 1871.

No. 944—J. BASTED , Port Elgin, Ont., " Machine for Cutting or Pulling Peas." 20th April, 1871.

No. 945—E. EVANS, London, Ont , (assignee of W. T. LUNDY, Brampton, Ont.,) "Composition of matter to prevent potatoes from rotting." 21st April, 1871.

No. 946—A. CORNELL, Sheffield, Ont., " Improvements on Fence Gates. 21st April, 1871.

No. 947—A. GRAVEL, Ottawa, Ont., " Improvements in Boat Oars and the Apparatus to attach and work them on boats." 21st April, 1871.

No. 948—T. DRAPER, Petrolea, Ont., " Improvements in the construction of Pump Valves." 29th April, 1871.

No. 949—I. COLE, Conestogo, Ont., " Improvements in Field Fences." 29th April, 1871.

No. 950—B. FEE, Durham, Que., " Improvements on Metallic Planes. 29th April, 1871.

No. 951—T. LITTLE, Galt, Ont., " Machine for Drying Clothes." 29th April, 1871.

No. 952—H. SPENCE, Stamford, Ont., " Stove for the purpose of heating rooms or apartments. 29th April, 1871.

No. 953—W. J. BOYLE, Dresden, Ont., " Improvements in Sash, Door and Blind Stays." 29th April, 1871.

No. 954—H. D. COWLES, and G. STACY, Montreal, Que., " Improvements in the manufacture of Steel Horse Shoe Nails." 29th April, 1871.

No. 955—J. CONNELL, Jun., Collingwood, Ont , " Composition of matter for preserving Wood from decay and from the effects of fire." 29th April, 1871.

No. 956—W. S. HUNTER, Stanstead, Que., " Improvements in Clothes Lines." 29th April, 1871.

No. 957—G. WOODLAND, Mount Forest, Ont., "Improvements in Churn Power Machines and Dashers. 29th April, 1871.

No. 958—D. MAXWELL and A. WHITELAW, Paris, Ont., "Machine for Cutting Straw and for Chopping or Bruising Grain." 29th April, 1871.

No. 959—H. HUETHER, Normanby, Ont. "Improvements in Beer Coolers." 29th April, 1871.

No. 960—F. DUMORTIER, Guelph, Ont., "Improvements on a certain machine for Heating Houses." 29th April, 1871.

No. 961—J. THOMAS, Toronto, Ont , "Machine for Stopping Railroad Cars." 29th April, 1871.

No. 962—J. K. HOME, Almonte, Ont., " Improvements in Stovepipe Drums and Heaters." 29th April, 1871.

No. 963—A. BISSELL, Mount Forest, Ont., " Improvements in Churns." 29th April, 1871.

No. 964—R. BROCK, Metcalfe, Ont., " Improvements on Harrows." 9th May, 1871.

No. 965—J. BOYD, Halifax, N.S., "Improvements in machines for Washing and Wringing Clothes." 9th May, 1871.

No. 966 - T. J GRAFFE, Mount Forest, Ont., "Composition of matter for a Cement for Walks, Pavements and Roadways." 9th May, 1871.

No. 967—E. CHAMBERS, Wainfleet, Ont., " Improvement in Shovel-Ploughs and Potato-Diggers." 9th May, 1871.

No. 968—D. E. COOK, Brantford, Ont., "Churns." 9th May, 1871

No. 969 -W. B. SIMPSON, Sarnia, Ont., "Improvements in Churns." 9th May, 1871.

No 970—A. H. FOE, Strathroy, Ont., "Improvements in Suckers of pumps." 9th May, 1871.

No. 971 -F. CULHAM, Widder Station, Bosanquet, Ont., " Improvements on Gates." 9th May, 1871.

No. 972—J. HAGGERT, Brampton, Ont., "Improvement on a machine for Reaping and Mowing." 9th May, 1879.

No. 973—F. CULHAM, Widder Station, Bosanquet, Ont., "Improvements on Thrashing machines." 9th May, 1871.

No. 974—A. ROSS, Montreal, Que., "Improvements on machinery for separating Iron particles from foreign substances." 9th May, 1871.

No. 975—L. COTÉ, St. Hyacinthe, Que., " Improvements in manufacturing the Soles of Boots and Shoes." 9th May, 1871.

No. 976—J. COCHRAN, Cornwallis, N.S.," Improvements on Hand-spinning Wheels and Wheel-heads." 9th May, 1871.

No. 977—A. CORNELL, Sheffields, Ont., "Improvements in Fence Gates." 11th May, 1871.

No. 978—H. SELLS, Vienna, Ont., " Improvement on Straw Cutters." 11th May, 1871.

No. 979—J. BROKENSHIRE, Kingston, Ont., " Improvement on the Ship Pump, for which he obtained a Patent on the 15th day of June, 1867." 11th May, 1871.

No. 980- S. I. FIELD, Toronto, Ont., No. 146, N.B., "Improvements in the manufacture of Wooden Eaves Troughs and Conductors." 11th May, 1871. Extended for the second period of five years, 3rd October, 1871.

No. 981—J. P. PRÉFONTAINE, Beloeil, Que., " Machine for placing, tightening and hooking Wires around Bales of Hay." 11th May, 1871.

No. 982—C. G. C. SIMPSON, Montreal, Que., "Improvements on Hay Presses." 11th May, 1871.

No. 983—J. MILLER, Perth, Ont., " Improvements in Sewing machines." 11th May, 1871.

No. 984—J. W. ELLIOT, Toronto, Ont., "Machine for condensing Gold used when filling Teeth, also to assist in extracting the roots of badly decayed or broken Teeth." 11th May, 1871.

No. 985—J. DEAN, Orillia, Ont . "Improvements in the construction of Wooden Buildings." 17th May, 1871.

No. 986—E. BOLMAN and G. S. W. CLARKE, Halifax, N.S., " Improvements on Couplings for railway Cars." 25th May, 1871.

No. 987—A. CUMBERWORTH, Quebec, Que., " Improvements in: Monkey Wrenches." 25th May, 1871.

No. 988—D. B. GARTON, Barrie, Ont., " Machine for the easy and expeditious replacing railway Cars and Locomotives upon their railway track." 25th May, 1871.

No. 989—S. M. WHITMORE, St. François du Lac, Que., " Improvements on apparatus for forming Square Holes." 25th May, 1871.

No. 990—E. R. McCALL, Simcoe, Ont., " Improvements on his patented machine for grinding the Knives of Mowers and Reapers." 25th May, 1871.

No. 991—A. HORNE, Reach, Ont., " Machine to attach to a Plough for digging potatoes and destroying weeds." 25th May, 1871.

No. 992—B GALLAGHER, Portland, N.B., "Improvements in Skate Fastenings." 25th May, 1871.

No. 993—R. PETERS, Hamilton, Ont., "Improvements on Sewing machines." 25th May 1871.

No. 994—G. HUNTER, Tiverton, Ont., " Improvement in Steam condensers." 19th May, 1871.

No. 995—E. F. PRENTISS, Montreal, Que., "Composition of matter for use as a Fertilizer, and a new and useful art or process for the manufacture of the same." 23rd May, 1871.

No. 996—S. VIVIAN, London, Ont., "Improvements in the manufacture of Machine Oil or Grease from crude petroleum or from petroleum tar, and the finishing of Parafine Oil." 23rd May, 1871.

No. 997—F. McMANUS, Havelock, Que., " Improvement in Waggon Axles." 23rd May, 1871.

No. 998—E. F. PRENTISS, Montreal, Que., " Improvement in the apparatuses for Rectifying and Refining Alcoholic Spirits and other volatile products." 23rd May, 1871.

No. 999 - F. McMANUS, Havelock, Que., " Improvement in double Stoves." 23rd May, 1871.

No 1000—G. S. LONG, Montreal, Que., " Improvements on Smoke and Gas Consuming Furnaces, &c., &c." 26th May, 1871.

No. 1001—R RANSFORD, Clinton, O., " Apparatus for the manufacture of Salt. 26th May, 1871.

No. 1002 - S. E. McCULLY and G. F. BANER, of Windsor Mills, Q., " Improvements in Fanning Mills." 26th May, 1871.

No. 1003—J. B. SMITH, Galt, Ont., " Improvement on the machine for manufacturing Bent Stuff for Carriage work." 31st May, 1871.

No. 1004—C. GUIBAULT, Joliette, Que., " Improvement in Mowing and Reaping machines." 1st June, 1871.

No. 1005 - E. McMULLEN, Montreal, Que., " Improvement in sectional Wooden Pavements." 5th June, 1871.

No. 1006—W. LAYNG, Delta, O., " Improvement on Shafts for Vehicles." 5th June, 1871.

No. 1007—N. KIMBALL, London, Ont., "Improvement on Portable Fences." 5th June, 1871.

No. 1008—R. SMART, Charlottenberg, Ont., " Improvements in Churns." 5th June, 1871.

No. 1009—M. E. PERRIN, Montreal, Que., " Remedy for the chest and affections arising from disorders of digestion." 7th June, 1871.

No. 1010—E. PIPER, St. John, N. B., " Method of Preserving animal and vegetable substances." 7th June, 1871.

No. 10011—G. BEER, Erin, O., " Improvement on Thrashing machines." 7th June, 1871.

No. 1012—F. G. COVEY, St. John, N. B., " Improvements in machines for Cooking Food. 7th June, 1871.

No. 1013—I. WALLIS, Huntingdon, Que., "Sawing machines." 7th June, 1871.

No. 1011—W. MILNER, Strathroy, Ont., " Improvement in Tube Wells." 7th June, 1871.

No. 1015—G. ROBERTS, Montreal, Que., "Improvements on Stoves." 9th Jan , 1871.

No. 1016—E. MILNER, Strathroy, Ont , " Whip Holder for carriages." 9th Ju ie, 1871.

No. 1017 -JOHN WALMSLEY, London, Ont., " Improvements or Reaping and Mowing machines." 9th June, 1871.

No. 1018—J. CALDER, Hamilton, Ont., " Improvement in the manufacture of Shoes." 13th June, 1871.

No. 1019—F. PATERSON, Montreal, Quo., " Improvements on apparatus for loading Ships and other vessels. 13th June, 1871.

No. 1020—J. SHIELS, Kingston, O., " Improvements in Dairy Cans for carrying Milk." 13th June, 1871.

No. 1021—F. BORDUA, St. Charles, Que., " Improvements on Hay Rakes." 13th June, 1871.

No. 1022—C. MOODY, Toronto, Ont., " Improvement in Mortise Locks." 13th June, 1871.

No. 1023—W. A. BOYD, Strathroy, Ont., " Improvements in Churns." 14th June, 1871.

No. 1024—M. SWEENEY, Tyendinaga, Ont., " Improvement in Hay Rakes." 14th June, 1871.

No. 1025—C. STORER, Montreal, Q., " Improvements on Boot and Shoe Heels." 14th June, 1871.

No. 1026—J. T. LARKIN, Halifax, N. S., " Improvements on Skates." 14th June, 1871.

No. 1027—E. HUGHES, Howick, Ont., " Machine for Splitting Blocks of Wood into Bolts." 13th June, 1871.

No. 1028—W. J. SIMPSON, Northport, Ont., " Improvement on Barley Forks." 15th June, 1871.

No. 1029—W. MILNER, Strathroy, Ont., " Anti-friction Journal Box." 16th June, 1871.

No. 1030—M. P. HAYES, Seaforth, O , " Improvement on machines for the manufacture of Salt from Brine. 16th June, 1871.

No. 1031—J. P. OLIVER, Moscow, Ont., " Improvement on that part of Carriage known as Draw Clip." 16th June, 1871.

No. 1032—H R. IVES, Montreal, Que., " Improvement in Burning Soft Coal and Consuming Smoke." 16th June, 1871.

No. 1033—J. DICK, Oshawa, Ont., " Improvements on Combined Reaping and Mowing machines." 17th June, 1871.

No. 1034—A. T. COLLYER, Hamilton, Ont., " Improvement on machines for Blocking Hats." 20th June, 1771.

No. 1035—F. C. ZAVITY, Warwick, Ont., " Improvements in Milk Coolers." 20th June, 1871.

No. 1036—H. P BELL, Folly Lake, N. S., " Improvement in Rock Drills and in the machine for making the same." 2 th June, 1871.

No. 1837—H. COLLARD, Gananoque, Ont , " Cultivator." 24th June, 1871.

No. 1038—J. HAGGART, assignee of R. AITKIN, Brompton, Ont., " Improvements on Reaping and Mowing machines." 30th June, 1871.

No. 1839—S. DOWNIE, Exeter, Ont., " Improvement on Thrashing machines." 30th June, 1871.

No. 1040—M. MOODY and W. ROBERTSON, Terrebonne, Que., " Rake for Mowers and Reapers." 30th June, 1871.

No. 1041—S. P. GRAHAM, London, Ont., " Improvements on Buggies and Waggons." 30th June, 1871.

No. 1042 -P. S. VAN WAGNER, Saltfleet, Ont., " Machine for discharging powdered Hellebore, Sulphur, &c., on currant and gooseberry bushes, vines, &c. 30th June, 1871.

No. 1043—H. FRYATT, Aurora, O., " Combined Bag Holder and Cart." 30th June, 1871.

No. 1044—S. B. AYRE, Hamilton, Ont., " Improvements in Washing machines." 30th June, 1871.

No. 1045—C. SKINNER, Waterloo, Que., "Improvements on machines or instruments for the Cutting of Glass." 30th June, 1871.

No. 1046—J. G. COVEY, St. John, N. B., "Improvements in Gas Stoves for cooking purpose" 30th June, 1871.

No. 1047—D. B. McKAY, Brantford, Ont., "Improvement in Halter Mounting." 30th June, 1871.

No. 1048—I. McNAUGHTON, Egerton, N. S., "Improvements on Cart and Waggon Axles and Boxes." 30th June, 1871.

No. 1049—N. BIGAOUETTE, Montreal, Que., "Carriage propelled by hand and foot." 3rd July, 1871.

No. 1050—A. DESFOSSES, Montreal, Que., "Improvement in the manufacture of Beer." 3rd July, 1871.

No. 1051—D. CHABOT, St. Charles, Que., "Harpoon Gun." 7th July, 1871.

No. 1052—D. M. LAMB, Strathroy, Ont., "Process for propagating Fruit and other Trees." 10th July, 1871.

No. 1053—J. and F. BOLE, St. Vincent, Ont., "Hay Elevator and Conveyer." 10th July, 1871.

No. 1054—C. H. MACKINTOSH, Strathroy, Ont., "Composition of matter for Painting." 10th July, 1871.

No. 1055—J. DUVAL, Laprairie, Que., "Improvements on Breech-loading Rifles." 12th July, 1871.

No. 1056—A. MILLOY, Vinto, Ont., "Machine for separating cockle from wheat." 12th July, 1871.

No. 1057—C. LEVEY, Toronto, Ont., "Improvement on Steam Engines." 12th July, 1871.

No. 1058—C. VENN, Kastnerville, Ont , "Machine for Bathing." 15th July, 1871.

No. 1059—D. PLEWS, Toronto, Ont., "Improvements in wooden Pumps." 15th July, 1871.

No. 1060—A. ROSE, Marysburgh, Ont., 'Improvement in Burglar-Alarms." 15th July, 1871.

No. 1061—O. A. BRYHN and W. T. FANE, Montreal, Que., "Improvement in Corn Shellers." 15th July, 1871.

No. 1062—J. G. COUL and A. WHITE, Carleton place, Ont., "Railway Signal for the prevention of collisions." 15th July, 1871.

No. 1063—R. BEATTY, Hamilton, Ont., "Improvements in Funnels for filling bottles." 15th July, 1871.

No. 1064—W. DUFFIELD, London, Ont., "Steam portable cross-cut Sawing machines." 15th July, 1871.

No. 1065—A. KIRKWOOD, Toronto, Ont., "Soup Biscuit." 19th July, 1871.

No. 1066—D. MONASTESSE, Verchères, Que., "Improvements in Churns." 19th July, 1871.

No. 1067—H. D. COWLES and G. STACEY, Montreal, Que., "Improvements in the manufacture of cut Nails." 19th July, 1871.

No. 1068—W. H. SPENCER, South Gower, Ont., "Composition of matter for Roofing." 29th July, 1871.

No. 1069—H. BULMER and C. SHEPARD, Montreal, Que., "Automatic machine for the making of Bricks." 20th July, 1871.

No. 1070—T. S. TYSON, Pittsburg, Ont., "Improvement in Fanning Mills." 20th July, 1871.

No. 1071—J. W. ELLIOT, Toronto, Ont., "Compound Plugger and Root Extractor for Dentists." 24th July, 1871.

No. 1072—J. and E. S. DAVIS, Barton, Ont., "Improvements in Boats for fishing and searching." 24th July, 1871.

No. 1073—R. HALES, Matilda, Ont., "Improvements in Churn Dashers." 24th July, 1871.

No. 1074—E. G. SCOVIL, Portland, N.S., "Improvement in the art of Box piling fron preparatory to Rolling." 24th July, 1871.

No. 1075—J. K. BUTLER, Yarmouth, N.S., "Improvement in Window Sashes." 24th July, 1871.

No. 1076—J. R. HANNAH, Brampton, Ont., "Improvement on Hay Forks." 24th July, 1871.

No. 1077—R. H. LITTLE, Darlington, Ont., "Combined Bag Holder and Filler." 26th July, 1871.

No. 1078—A. P. Von POEHRNHOFF, St. Catharines, Ont., "Improvements in the manufacture of Illuminating Oil from petroleum or crude oil " 26th July, 1870.

No. 1079—G. SCHATZ, Berlin, Ont., " Improvement in Washing machines." 26th July, 1871.

No 1080—J S. SNOW, Danville, Que., "Improvements on Tidal machines." 26th July, 1871.

No. 1081—L. ARCHAMBAULT, Montreal, Que., " Improvement in Door Knobs." 26th July, 1871.

No 1082—W. McKAY, Ottawa, Ont., " Composition for drying all kinds of Oil Paints." 31st July, 1871.

No 1083—J. COWAN, (assignee of W. Cowan,) Ottawa, Ont., "Improvement on machines for sinking Wells." 31st July, 1871.

No. 1084—T. FORFAR, Watertown, Ont., "Improvement in Churns " 31st July, 1871.

No. 1085—R. S. HYKE, St. John, N.B., " Chain Cable holding mechanism for Vessels." 31st July, 1871.

No. 1086—G. F. DE VINE, Hamilton, Ont., " Improvement in Harness Hold'gs." 31st July, 1871.

No. 1087—J. F. W. EBEL, Mornington, Ont., "Improvements in Churn Powers." 31st July, 1871.

No. 1088—L. EUSTIS, St. John, N.B., " Improvements in Calks for Horse Shoes." 31st July, 1871.

No. 1089—G. JAMES, Montreal, Que., "Improvements in the cutting of Soles for Boots and Shoes." 1st August, 1871.

No. 1090—C. PLUMB, Montreal, Que., "Improvements on apparatus for consuming Smoke." 1st August, 1871.

No. 1091—A. CAMERON, Colborne, Ont., "Improvement in Harrow Teeth." 7th August, 1871.

No. 1092—J. D. LAWLOR, Montreal, Que., "Improvements on Sewing machines." 7th August, 1871.

No. 1093—E. BOWMAN and J. L. LANCASTER, of Bobcaygeon, Ont , "Self acting Car-Coupler." 7th August, 1871.

No. 1094—J. H. SWARTWOUT, Toronto, Ont., " Fluting or Crimping Roller." 7th August, 1871.

No. 1095—The Johnston's Patent Weather Protector and Dominion Sash Door and Frame Manufacturing Company, (assignee of J. JOHNSTON,) Lindsay, Ont., "Improvements on Weather Strips for windows, doors, &c." 7th August, 1871.

No 1096—T. BARNES and R. H. HUDSON, Harwich, Ont., " Improvements in Gates." 10th August, 1871.

No. 1097—S. WOODS, Montreal, Que., "Improvements in the manufacture of Felt for Boots." 11th August, 1871.

No. 1098—L. CROSBY, Markham, Ont., " Improvements in Gates." 14th August, 1871.

No. 1099—L. CROSBY, Markham, Ont., " Improvement in Portable Fences." 14th August, 1871.

No. 1100—J. TAUDVIN, Smith's Falls, Ont., " Improvements in Dog Power machines for Churns." 18th August, 1871.

No. 1101—L. COTÉ, St. Hyacinthe, Que., " Improvements in the art of cutting Soles and on the Dies used therefor." 18th August, 1871.

26

No. 1102–J. B. SMITH, Amabel, Ont., "Improvements on Water Wheels." 18th August, 1871.

No. 1103–W. S. TORRIE, Moncton, N.B , " Improvements on machines for the manufacture of Soap." 18th August, 1871·

No. 1104–C. G. C. SIMPSON, Montreal, Que., "Improvements on Sewing machines." 18th August, 1871.

No. 1105–R. PURSER, Windsor. Ont., "New Churn Dash." 18th August, 1871.

No. 1106–E. R. WHITNEY, Bolton, Que.. "Composition of matter for lubricating purposes." 21st August, 1871.

No. 1107 · W. S. HUNTER, Stanstead, Que , " Fastener for securing Clothes to lines." 21st August, 1871.

No. 1108–J. MORRISON, Elma, Ont., "Improvements in Drag Harrows." 21st August, 1871.

No. 1109–G. JAMES, Montreal, Que., "Improvements on Wooden Shanks for Boots and Shoes." 21st August, 1871.

N°. 1110–H. BAINES, Toronto, Ont., "Improvements in Power Hammers." 21st August, 1871.

No. 1111–J. FENSOM, Toronto, Ont.. "Machine for the making of Bricks and artificial Stone." 25th August, 1871.

No. 1112–J. SCOTT, Strathroy, Ont., "Composition of matter for lubricating Wool." 25th August, 1871.

No. 1113–G. S. BRUSH, Montreal, Que., "Improvements in Furnaces of steam Boilers." 25th March, 1871.

No. 1114–C. ETHIER, St. Eustache, Que., "Improvements in Sifting and Winnowing machines." 5th August, 1871.

No. 1115–J. McFARLANE, Otterville, Ont., "New carriage Spring." 25th August, 1871. (Extension of Patent No. 2878, Province of Canada.)

No. 1116–A. EYER, Richmond Hill, Ont., "Chaffing Sieve for thrashing machines or fanning mills." 29th August, 1871.

No. 1117–A EYER, Richmond Hill, Ont., "Improved Harrow Teeth." 25th August, 1871.

No. 1118–H. DIPROSE, London, Ont , "Machine to'keep Flies off dining tables." 29th August, 1871.

No. 1119 J. F. LEITCH, Prescott, Ont., "Improvements in cultivating Hooks." 29th August, 1871.

No. 1120–W. A LEGGO, Montreal, Que., " Art of propelling Vessels and driving machinery by gas explosion as a motor." 29th August, 1871.

No. 1121–M. QUIRK, Chatham, Ont., "Composition of matter to be used as remedy in pulmonary affections." 29th August, 1871.

No. 1122–D H. WARREN, Montreal, Que., "Improvements on Soap and the art of manufacturing the same." 30th August, 1871.

No. 1123–S. OLIVER, Toronto, Ont., " Improvements on Nail making machines." 30th August, 1871.

No. 1124–N. H. GOSLIN, Ottawa, Ont., "Improvements in Washing machines." 9th September, 1871.

No. 1125–F. VEZINA, Verchères. Que., " Improvements in Washing machines." 9th September, 1871.

No. 1126–H. COLLARD, Gananoque, Ont., "Improvements in Horse Hoes." 9th September, 1871.

No. 1127 J. R. McGUIRE, Almonte, Ont., "Improvemen's in Churns." 9th September, 1871.

No. 1128–J. H. KILLEY and W. J. KILLEY, Hamilton, Ont., "Steam boiler Detector Gauge." 9th September, 1871.

No. 1129—N. REYNOLDS, Scott, Ont., "Improvements in Suction and Force Pumps." 9th September, 1871.

No. 1130—J. ROSE, Richmond, Ont., "Improvement on Grain Sieves." 9th September, 1871.

No. 1131—W. E. HUGHES, Aylmer, Ont., "Improvements on machines for pruning and trimming Trees and garden Bushes." 9th September, 1871.

No. 1132—S. REESOR, Markham, Ont., "Preparation of Barley forming an article of diet for Invalids and children." 9th September, 1871.

No. 1133—W. L. THOMPSON, Stanstead Plain, Que., "Improvements in Dish Washers." 9th September, 1871.

No. 1134—J. J. LANCASTER, London, Ont, "Improvement on Wells." 9th September, 1871.

No. 1135—J. F. CASS, L'Original, Ont., "Improvement in Wrenches." 9th September, 1871.

No. 1136—J. MORIN and N. LEGROS, of Montreal, Que., "Improvement on the mode of fixing Sheets of metal for Roofing purposes." 9th September, 1871.

No. 1137—W A. SHOENAN, Carrick, Ont., "Improvements in Bee Hives." 9th September, 1871.

No. 1138—G. MILLER, Sheffield, Ont., "Machine for cutting Thin Boards." 9th September, 1871.

No. 1139—R. GAGE, Kingston, Ont., "Machine for mangling Clothes." 12th September, 1871.

No. 1140—W. YOUNG, Hamilton, Ont., "Machine for travelling on Water." 12th September, 1871.

No. 1141—D BATEMAN, Scugog, Ont., "Machine for sowing Grass and Clover Seeds." 12th September, 1871.

No. 1142 J. WOODLEY, Quebec, Que., "Improvements on the Art and Die, &c. for cutting Boot and Shoe Soles " 20th September, 1871.

No. 1143—D. H WINTER, Athol, Ont., "Improvements in Cultivators." 20th September, 1871.

No. 1144—H. M. FARR, Hespeler, Ont., "Machine for producing Gas." 20th September, 1871.

No. 1145—R. S. WATSON, Belleville, Ont., "Improvements in Hot Air Furnaces." 20th September, 1871.

No. 1146—R. EATON, Montreal, Que., "Improvements on the art or process of manufacturing Iron and Steel." 20th September, 1871.

No. 1147—P. MUTTER, Hamilton, Ont., "New art of imitating polished Marble, Granite, &c." 20th September, 1871.

No. 1148—G. PEDLER, Exeter, Ont., "Improvements in the construction of Reed Instruments." 20th September, 1871.

No. 1149—E. SOUTHERN, Boston, Ont., "Improvements in Gates." 20th September, 1871.

No. 1150—H. BAINES, Toronto, Ont., "Improvements in the art of constructing Railroads." 20th September, 1871.

No. 1151—R. S. LITTLE, Chatham, Ont., "Automatic Lubricator for Steam Engines." 20th September, 1871.

No. 1152—G. H. PIERCE, Cleveland, Que., "Improvement in the manufacture of Brooms." 22nd September, 1871.

No. 1153—J. ARCHER, Quebec, Que., "Improvement in Water Conductors." 22nd September, 1871.

No. 1154—J. BAKER, Trenton, Ont., "Improvement on Baker's combined Hand Flour Scoop and Sifter." 22nd September, 1871.

No. 1155—V. H. TISDALE, Toronto, Ont., "Improvement in Churn Powers." 22nd September, 1871.

No. 1156—H. C. FARNHAM, Sherbrooke, Que., " Improvements in draft scale Rules and Sweeps for cutting and fitting Dresses for women." 22nd September, 1871.

No. 1157—L. WISMER, Preston, Ont., "New self-closing Wire Gate." 22nd September, 1871.

No. 1158—E. SARGEANT, Westwood, Ont., "Improvement in Hay Gatherers." 2nd October, 187 .

No. 1159—W. M. SHAW, Georgetown, Ont., and R. W. ELLIOTT, Toronto, Ont., "Improvements in the manufacture of Paper Window Shades, &c." 2nd October, 1871.

No. 1160—G. HUDDLESTON, Brockville, Ont., " New Elbow and T-Stove Pipe." 2nd October, 1871.

No. 1161—A. MERRILL, Haughton, Ont., " Improvements in Cultivators." 2nd October, 1871.

No. 1162—H. SELLS, Vienna, Ont., 'improvements in Feed-Cutters." 3rd October, 1871.

No. 1163—D. D. TUPPER, Canning N.S., "Machine for jointing Barrel, Cask, or other Stav s." 4th October, 1871.

N 1164—D. DAVIS, Beamsville, Ont., "Improvements in Horse Hay Rakes and Packers." 4th Oc ober, 871.

No 1165—C. POWELL, Newton Brook, Ont , " Improvements in Gearing for Pumps." 4th October, 1871.

No. 1166—R HARPER, Oakville, Ont., "Improvements on Tail Boards of Waggons and Carts." 4th October, 1871.

No. 1167—G. H. PEDLAR, Oshawa, Ont., "Improvements in hot air Drums." 7th October, 1871.

No. 1168—G. SINGER, Waterloo, Ont., "Machine for regulating the Draft and Blast in smiths' Forges." 7th October, 1871.

No. 1169 J B. BLAIR, Trenton, Ont., "Arrangement for coupling railroad Rail Joints and for protecting the same." 7th October, 1871.

No. 1170—H. REDDING, Kentville, N.S., " New Water Wheel." 7th October, 1871.

No. 1171—W. MOIR, Nichol, Ont., "New Rail Fence." 7th October, 1871.

No. 1172—T. HODGSON, River Philip, N.S., "Improved Saw Gummer." 11th October, 1871. (Extension of Patent No. 197, Nova Scotia.)

No. 1173—J. ABELL, Woodbridge, Ont., "Improvement in the construction of Portable Engines." 11th October, 1871.

No. 1174—C. B. GEROW, Port Perry, Ont., "Improvements in Rufflers and Plaiters for Sewing Machines." 11th October, 1871.

No. 1175—A. J. STEWART, St. John, N.B., "Improvement in the manufacture of Soap." 11th October, 1871.

No. 1176—G. WOODS, St. Catharines, Ont., " Improvement on Harness Saddles." 11th October, 1871.

No. 1177—J. McMILLAN, Nepean, Ont , "Improvement on machines for Digging Potatoes." 14th October, 1871.

No. 1178—J. WALKER, Whitby, Ont., "Improvement in Ploughs." 18th October, 1871.

No. 1179—J. F. ROSS, Hamilton, Ont., "Improvement in Railway Signals." 18th October, 1871.

No. 1180 G. H. KEND LI Montreal, Que., "Improvement in the method of casting Edge Tools." 19th October, 1871.

No. 1181—E. ANGERS and C. FALARDEAU, Montreal, Que., "Improvements in the manufacture of Boots and Shoes." 19th October, 1871.

No. 1182—J. A. ROBERTSON, Montreal, Que., "Improvements on combined Beds and Chairs." 19th October, 1871

No. 1183—D. J. KNAPP, Wolfe Island, Ont., " Improvements in Washing machines." 19th October, 1871.

No. 1184—J. B. BLAIR, Trenton, Ont., "Improvement in Bag-Holders." 19th October, 1871.

No. 1185—J. H. SWARTWOUT, Toronto, Ont., "Machine for Turning Logs." 19th October, 1871.

No. 1186—R. NOBLE, Toronto, Ont., "Composition for making Artificial Stone." 19th October, 1871.

No. 1187—W. C. HOLT, Brantford, Ont., "Improvement on Heat Economizers." 19th October, 1871.

No. 1188—J. ABELL, Woodbridge, Ont., "Improvements in Thrashing machines." 19th October, 1871.

No. 1189—W. R. SMITH, Seaforth, Ont., "Improvement in Window Curtain Rollers." 19th October, 1871.

No. 1190—W. R. BAKER, Wellington, Ont., "New Holdback Hook for Carriage shafts." 19th October, 1871.

No. 1191—M. O. BRIGGS, wife of E. E. Briggs, St. John, N.B., "Improvements in Spring Bed Bottoms." 27th October, 1871.

No. 1192—M. G. BRIGGS, wife of E. E. Briggs, St. John, N.B., "Improvements on Abdominal supporters." 27th October, 1871.

No. 1193—T. J. GRAFFE, Mount Forest, Ont., "Stone Cement and Roadway." 24th October, 1871. Re-issue of Patent No. 966.

No. 1194—H. G. TAYLOR, Port Hope, Ont., "Improvement in the manner of attaching Drawheads to railroad cars." 24th October, 1871.

No. 1195—J. S. SHARPE, Sussex, N.B., and S. H. WEYMAN, Studeholm, N.B., "Improvements in Snow Ploughs for railway tracks." 24th October, 1871.

No. 1196—S. S. HALL, Montreal, Que., "Improvement on the Insoles of Boots." 24th October, 1871.

No. 1197—J. GAND, Hillsburg, Ont., "Improvements in Leather Dressing machines." 25th October, 1871.

No. 1198—J. FENSOM, Toronto, Ont., "Improvements in Hoists or Elevators." 25th October, 1871.

No. 1199—L. COTÉ, St. Hyacinthe, Que., "Improvement on Dies for cutting the Soles of boots and shoes." 25th October, 1871.

No. 1200—O. DUHAMEL, St. Roch, Que, and M. BEAUCHEMIN, Sorel, Que, "Improvement in the manufacture of Mowing machines." 25th October, 1871.

No. 1201—M. POURTIER, Quebec, Q., "Composition for the cure of Asthma, Consumption and Bronchitis." 25th October, 1871.

No. 1202—J. McARTHUR, Fenelon Falls, Ont, "Combined water and liquid Refrigerator." 25th October, 1871.

No. 1203—A. ANDERSON, London, Ont., "Improvements on machines for Harvesting Peas." 7th November, 1871.

No. 1204—J. CHALMERS, Montreal, Que., "Improvements on Composition for covering steam Boilers, steam Pipes and all highly heated surfaces." 7th November, 1871.

No. 1205—H. COBLY, Toronto, Ont., "New Shoe Clasp." 7th November, 1871.

No. 1206—H. J. EVANS, Iberville, Que., "Machine for use as a Wheel Barrow or Step Ladder." 7th November, 1871.

No. 1207—J. FORSYTH, Dundas, Ont., "Improvement in Drag Bars for Reaping and Mowing machines." 7th November, 1871.

No. 1208—J. FENSOM, Toronto, Ont., "Improvements in Tools for turning Shafting." 7th November, 1871.

No. 1209—R. BEATTY, Hamilton, Ont, "New Washing machine." 7th November, 1871.

No. 1210—A. D. COLE, Toronto, Ont., "Step for Turbine wheels." 7th November, 1871.

No. 1211—B. SEERY, Fort Eric, Ont., " Improvements in Caisson Coffer Dams." 7th November, 1871.

No. 1212—C. J. SWIFT, Toronto, Ont., "Improvements in ash Shovels." 7th November, 1871.

No. 1213—J. GIRODAT, Hawksville, Ont., " Improvements in implements for digging Fence Post Holes." 7th November, 1871.

No. 1214—W. R. SMITH, (assignee of J. Kidd,) Seaforth, Ont., " Improvements in Valves for pumps and water pipes." 8th November, 1871.

No. 1215—J. REECE, Stanstead, Que., " Improvement in Sewing machines." 18th November, 1871.

No. 1216—E. B. WASHBURN, Waterloo, Ont., " Improvements on Fences." 17th November, 1871.

No. 1217—O. M. GOULD, Montreal, Que., " Improvement on Grain Carriers." 17th November, 1871.

No. 1218—D. McGAVIGAN, Toronto, Ont., " Improvements in Venetian Blinds." 17th November, 1871.

No. 1219—W. HAMILTON, Peterborough, Ont., " Improvement on machines for Edging Lumber." 17th November, 1871.

No. 1220—THE CANADA BOLT COMPANY, (assignee of A. B. Simonds), Perth, Ont., " Improvements in machines for cutting Screws on bolts." 17th November, 1871.

No. 1221—THE CANADA BOLT COMPANY, (assignee of A. B. SIMOND·), Perth, Ont., " Improvements in machines for cutting Screw threads in blank nuts." 17th November. 1871.

No. 1222—T. NORTHEY, Hamilton, Ont., " Improvements in Steam Cranes." 17th November, 1871.

No. 1223—A. FOLSAM, Grand Manan, N.B., "Improvements on Water and Wind Wheels." 17th November, 1871.

No. 1224—J. J. WEBSTER, Magog, Ont., " Improvements on Pulverizing and Grinding machines." 17th November, 1871.

No. 1225—C. FARLARDEAU, jun., Montreal, Que., " Improvement in Metallic Heels for Boots." 17th November, 1871.

No. 1226 - J. B. THORNTON, Guelph, Ont., " Book Cover." 24th November, 1871.

No. 1227—R. HORNING, Grimsby, Ont., " Improvements in Spring Bed Bottoms." 24th November, 1871.

No. 1228—W. McLEAN, Peterborough, Ont., " Station Indicator for Railway Cars, Street Cars and Steamboats." 24th November, 1871.

No. 1229—L. R. COMSTOCK, Toronto, Ont., " A revolving Flue Radiator." 24th November 1871. Extension of Patent No. 2064, Province of Canada.

No. 1230—G. JACKSON and M. A. SNOWDON, of Guelph, Ont., "Improvements on Traveling Trunks." 24th November, 1871.

No. 1231—W. BAIN, Sandwich, Ont., "Improvement in Brick Making machines." 24th November, 1871.

No. 1232—G. C. FOOTE, Sherbrooke, Que., " Improvements in the manufacture of Gloves and Mittens." 24th November, 1871.

No. 1233—C. J. APPLETON, Hamilton, Ont., "Improvements in the Feed attachment of Sewing machines." 24th November, 1871.

No. 1234—A. ANDERSON, London, Ont., " Improvement on Cooking and Stove Furniture." 1st December, 1871.

No. 1235—N. MERCIER, Montreal, Que., "Composition of matter for the cure of cuts, burns, bruises, frost bites, &c., &c." 1st December, 1871.

No. 1236—D. P. DUNN, Walnfleet, Ont., " Improvement in Door Springs." 1st December, 1871.

No. 1237—W. S. HUNTER, Stanstead, Que , " Improvements in Clothes Washing Rubbers" 2nd December, 1871.

No. 1238—A. KEELER, Prescott, Ont , " Improvements in the manufacture of Milk Pans." 2nd December, 1871.

No 1239—D. M. LAMB, Strathroy, Ont., " Improvement in Ploughs and subsoil attachment combined." 2nd December, 1871.

No. 1240 J. FEE, Montreal, Que , " Improvements on Jig Saws." 4th December, 1871.

No. 1241—C. J. APPLETON, Hamilton, Ont., " Improvements in Knitting machines." 4th December, 1871.

No. 1242—C. J. APPLETON, Hamilton, Ont., " Improvements on the Shuttle Motion of Sewing machines." 4th December, 1871.

No. 1243—J. RADFORD, Belleville, Ont., " Machine for renovating Feathers." 4th December, 1871.

No. 1244—A. ARMSTRONG, Milton, Ont., " Improvements in machines for Scrubbing and Drying Floors." 15th December, 1871.

No. 1245—J. N. TARBOX, Hamilton, Ont., " Improvements in Frillers for Sewing machines." 15th December, 1871.

No. 1246—J. FLEURY, Aurora, Ont., " Improvements on Totman's Horse Power." 15th December, 1871.

No. 1247—C. McCARTER, Welland, Ont., "Improvement on machines for drying Clothes." 15th December, 1871.

No. 1248—W. H. McELHERAN, Hamilton, Ont., "Improvement in the art of Ornamenting and Lettering Sewing machines, Cars, &c." 15th December, 1871.

No. 1249—W. WEST, Otonabee, Ont., " Improvement on machines for sawing Lumber." 15th December, 1871.

No. 1250—J. MACMASTER, Brantford, Ont., " Process or method for making green sand Cores for columns, &c." 15th December, 1871.

No. 1251—S. B. WOOD, Bridgetown, Ont., "Improvements on Washing machines." 15th December, 1871.

No. 1252—D. HERALD, Gore's Landing, Ont., " Machine for turning the points of Nails." 15th December, 1871.

No. 1253—P. N. RUGG, Compton, Que., " Improvement on Washing machines." 15th December, 1871.

No. 1254—A. M. FORSTER, Hamilton, Ont., " Improvements on self-acting steam Heater Regulators." 15th December, 1871.

No. 1255—R. CUTHBERT, Montreal, Que , " Improvements on Gauge Cocks." 15th December, 1871.

No. 1256—J. UNSWORTH, Sherbrooke, Que., "Improvement in Whiffletrees." 15th December, 1871.

No. 1257—N. R. ALLEN, Montreal, Que., "Improvement on Treadles of Sewing machines." 15th December, 1871.

No. 1258—J. CLAYTON, Whitby, Ont., " Improvement to revolving horse Rakes. 16th December, 1871.

No. 1259—W. B. LANDON, Princeton, Ont., " Improvement in Stoves." 23rd December, 1871.

No. 1260—E. M. AUREY, Smithville, Ont., "Improvements in adjusting the Cutter Bars of Mowing machines." 23rd December, 1871.

No. 1261—R. E. STEPHEN, Owen Sound, Ont., " Improvement in Fences." 23rd December, 1871.

No. 1262—H. H. DATE and F. H. DATE, St. Catharines, Ont., " Process for converting Iron into Steel. 23rd December, 1871.

No. 1263—J. O. TODD, Waterloo, Que., "Composition of matter for cleaning Teeth." 23rd December, 1871.

No. 1264—F. H. REYNOLDS, Montreal, Que., "Improvements on Barrels." 23rd December, 1871.

No. 1265—T. FORWAR, Waterdown, Ont., "Improvement in Root Cutting machines." 23rd December, 1871.

No. 1266—J. PARSONS, Toronto, Ont." "New Clasp for joining leather Belting." 23rd December, 1871.

No. 1297 - W. W. McCLELLAN, Sarnia, Ont., "Composition for roofing and paving Sidewalks." 23rd December, 1871.

No. 1268—P. BEAL, Townsend, Ont., "Improvement in Waggon and Sleigh Stake." 23rd December. 1871.

No. 1269—L. MARTIN, St. Catharines, Ont., "A tanning Vat." 23rd December, 1871.

No. 1270—J. McNAB, junior, Owen Sound, Ont., "A horizontal Car-Coupler." 4th January, 1872. [Extension of Patent No. 787 for second period, 5 years.]

No. 1271—R. TYSON, Toronto, Ont., "Improvement in Fanning Mills." 11th January, 1872. [Re-issue of Patent No. 1070.]

No. 1272—N. WILSON, Woodstock, N.B., 'Improvement in the art or process for currying, tanning, soaking and finishing Skins and Hides, with or without the hair on, and a composition for the same." 11th January, 1872.

No. 1273—J P. RICHARDSON, (assignee of C. G. C. Simpson,) Montreal, Que., "Improvement on Flour disintegrating machinery." 11th January, 1872.

No. 1 74 - A. F. RIGBY, Stratford, Ont., "Improvements in snow Plows for Railroads." 11th January, 1872.

No. 1275—R. HENDERY, Montreal, Que., "Improvements on the art of Electro Plating with Nickel." 11th January, 1872.

No. 1276—T. TURNER, Clifton, Ont., "A Railway Switch." 11th January, 1872.

No. 1277—A. KAY, Hamilton, Ont., "Improvement in Steam Engines." 11th January, 1872.

No. 1278—J. ENNIS. Newmarket, Ont., "Method of constructing Tenons and fastening them in joints." 11th January, 1872.

No. 1279—J. H. DUNSTAN, Belleville, Ont., "A cylinder Furnace." 11th January, 1872.

No. 1280—W. FARQUHAR, Ottawa, Ont., "Improvement in the manufacture of artificial Fuel." 11th January, 1872.

No. 1281—J. W. MURRAY, Hamilton, Ont., "Improvement in the Governor Valve of steam Engines. 11th January, 1872.

No. 1282—G. W. PITMAN, Dartmouth, N.S., "Improvements on machines for heckling and drawing Hemp, Flax and other fibre." 11th January, 1872.

No. 1283—S. NOXON, the younger, Ingersoll, Ont., "Improvements on Horse-powers." 11th January, 1872.

No. 1284—S. NOXON, the younger, Ingersoll, Ont., "Improvements in Horse powers. 11th January, 1872.

No. 1285—W SMITH, London, Ont., "Improvements in the manufacture of artificial Fuel." 11th January, 1872.

No. 1286—J. S. FOX, Port Hope, Ont., "Improvement on Washing machines." 11th January, 1872.

No. 1287—W. MILNER, Strathroy, Ont., "Improvements on Waggon Axles." 11th January, 1872.

No. 1288—A. DICK, Hamilton, Ont., "Improvements on Signal Lights and Head Lamps for Railways." 15th January, 1872.

No. 1289—S. CRAWFORD, London, Ont., "Improvements on Reaping machines." 16th January, 1872.

No. 1290—C. D. MEIGS, Merreville Mills, Que., "Improvements on machinery for feeding Logs to Saws." 16th January, 1872.

No. 1291—H. J. LIVERGOOD, Brantford, Ont., "Improvement on Rakes of Reapers." 16th January, 1872.

No. 1292—J. E. MITCHEL, Paris, Ont., "A Churn." 16th January, 1872.

No. 1293—H. A. SHARP, Hopewell, N.B., "Improvements in Cabinets for holding oil or other liquids." 16th January, 1872.

No. 1294—H. J. HOWELL, St. Catharines, Ont., "Improvements in Stills for petroleum." 16th January, 1872.

No. 1295—W. McKAY, Ottawa, Ont., "Composition for Building and Architectural purposes." 19th January, 1872.

No. 1296—B. GREENING, Hamilton, Ont., "Improvement in Boiler tube Cleaners." 19th January, 1872.

No. 1297—R. LARARD, Oshawa, Ont., "Improvement in Hot Air Drums." 19th January, 1872.

No. 1298—J. H. STONE, Hamilton, Ont., "Improvements on Tubular Kerosene Lanterns." 19th January, 1872.

No. 1299—H. R. IVES, Montreal, Que,, "Improvement in the art of burning Soft Coal and consuming Smoke and apparatus used therefor." 19th January, 1872.

No. 1300—A. B. COLEMAN, Brighton, Ont., "A Sack-Holder." 19th January, 1872.

No. 1301—S. KINDER, Amherst, N.S., "Improvements in Washing machines." 19th January, 1872.

No. 1302—E. F. PRENTISS Montreal, Que., "Improvements in the construction of Iron Telegraph Poles." 19th January, 1872.

No. 1303—C. STORER, Montreal, Que., "Improvements on Boot and Shoe Heels." 19th January, 1872.

No. 1304—J. H. SNYDER, St Anns, Ont., "Improved Clothes Drier." 19th January, 1872.

No. 1305—H. DOTY, St. John, N.B., "Improvements in machines for the manufacture of Rope and Small Cords." 20th January, 1872.

No. 1306—C. STORER, Montreal, Que., "Improvements on Boot and Shoe Heels." 22nd January, 1872.

No. 1307—J. J. MURPHY, Montreal, Que., "Improvements on portable Gas apparatus." 22nd January, 1872.

No. 1308—E. P. HANNAFORD, Montreal, Que., "A railway Rail Joint." 22nd January, 1872. (Extension of Patent No. 1197, Province of Canada.)

No. 1309—A. J. DOTY, Oakville, Ont., "Improvement in self-oiling Carriage Axles." 26th January, 1872.

No. 1310—F. C. NOXON and S. NOXON, Ingersoll, Ont., "Improvement on Totman's Horse-power Sawing machine." 26th January, 1872.

No. 1311—R. PETERS, Hamilton, Ont., "Improvement in Sewing machines." 26th January, 1872.

No. 1312—W. FORSTER, Markham, Ont., "Improved Stove-pipe Shelf." 26th January, 1872.

No. 1313—J. H. GROUT, Grimsby, Ont., "Improvement on Reaping machines." 26th January, 1872.

No. 1314—J. WARREN, Montreal, Que., "Improvements on Stoves for burning soft coal." 26th January, 1872.

No. 1315—F. S. GRECE, North Dorchester, Ont., "A rotating Harrow." 26th January, 1872.

No. 1316—J. P. CLEVELAND, Barnston, Out., "Improvements in Boilers for heating sap and other liquids." 20th January, 1872.

No. 1317—O. B. HEATH, St. Stephens, N.B., "A Blind Fastener." 26th January, 1872.

27

No. 1318—J. STILES, Pointe Cameron, Ont., "Improvement in Sleighs." 29th January, 1872.

No. 1319—J. F. CASS, L'Orignal, Ont., "Improvement in Wheeled Vehicles." 29th January 1872.

No. 1320—F. A. HUMPIDGE, Strathroy, Ont., "Improvement in Sawing machines." 28th January, 1871. (Re-issue of PatentꞋNo. 188.)

No. 1321—S. L. PURDY, Brighton, Ont., " A Bag-Holder." 29th January, 1872.

No. 1322—P. R. DYER. Markham, Ont., "Improvement on Birdsell's Combined Thrasher and Huller." 2nd February, 1872.

No. 1323—W. JACKSON, Bathurst, Ont., "Improvement in Churns." 2nd February, 1872.

No 1324—R. E. STEPHENS, Owen Sound, Ont., " Improved art of manufacturing pressure formed Slabs for Pavements, Floors, Roofs, &c." 2nd February, 1872.

No. 1325—G. JAMES, Montreal, Que., "Improvements in the art of cutting Leather for the Heels of Boots and Shoes with combined Die therefor." 2nd February, 1872.

No. 1326—C. M. TAYLOR, (Assignee of P. H. Sims,) Waterloo, Ont., "Improvements in Liquid Heating devices for attachment to Lamps." 7th February, 1872.

No. 1327—J. GRANT, Gananoque, Ont., " A machine for securing Covers to Pots, Pails, and other Vessels." 7th Febuary, 1872.

No. 1328—B. L. BRADLEY, Woodstock, Ont., " A Stove Drum." 7th February, 1872.

No. 1329- T. BARNES and R. H. HUDGIN, Harwich, Ont., "Improvement on Barnes and Hudgin's Improved Centre Suspension Gate." 7th February, 1872.

No. 1330—G. McLEOD and R. MILLS, Rodgerville, Ont., " A machine for harvesting Peas." 7th February, 1872.

No. 1331—G. McKAY, Woodstock, Ont., "A machine for Measuring Ribbon, Cloth, &c." 7th February, 1872.

No. 1332—W. ORR, Madoc, Ont., "Machine for securing the Wheels of Vehicles." 7th February, 1872.

No. 1333—J. E. WATEROUS, Brantford, Ont., "Improvement in Steam Boilers." 7th February, 1872.

No. 1334—J. JOHNSTON, Cramahe, Ont., "Improvements in Fanning Mills." 7th February, 1872.

No. 1335—G. W. GOODWIN, Tamworth, Ont., " Improvement in Stitching Benches for Harness Makers." 9th February, 1872.

No. 1336—L. COHN, Montreal, Que., " Improvement in Paper Files." 13th February, 1872.

No. 1337—J. B. LAZIER, Reach, Ont., " Art or mode of making Carriage Seats." 13th February, 1872.

No. 1338—J. B. LAZIER, Reach, Ont., " Improvement in the art of manufacturing bent Stuff." 13th February, 1872.

No. 1339—J. B. LAZIER, Port Perry, Ont., " Improvements in the manufacture of Bee Hives." 13th February, 1872.

No. 1340—A. ANDERSON and J. ROBINSON, London, Ont., "Improvement in Reaping machines." 13th February, 1872.

No. 1341—T. PARTRIDGE, Hamilton, Ont., " A steam boiler Indicator." 17th February, 1872.

No. 1342—J. M. RYDER, Granville, N.S., " Improvements in Spring Bottoms." 17th February, 1872.

No. 1343—J. FORBES, Halifax, N.S., "Improvements in Metallic Handles for Tools and Utensils." 17th February, 1872.

No. 1344—J. FORBES, Halifax, N.S., " Improvement in Skates." 17th February, 1872.

No. 1345—A. ARMSTRONG, Milton, Ont., "Improvements in stove-pipe Shelves." 17th February, 1872.

No. 1346—W. TRUMFIELD, Stratford, Ont., "Composition to be added to, and mixed with Paint." 17th February, 1872.

No. 1347-J. McKENNA, Brantford, Ont., "Improvements in Dampers for Stove pipes." 17th February, 1872.

No. 1348—J. FORBES, Halifax, N.S., "A new Skate." 17th February, 1872. [Extension of Patent No. 116, Nova Scotia.]

No. 1349—J. W. VAUGHAN, Robinson, Que., "A Chimney-box and Cleaner." 21st February, 1872.

No. 1350—J. B. HULBERT and J. ANDERSON, Quebec, Que., "A railway Snow-Plough." 21st February, 1872.

No. 1351—E. BONHAM, Brantford, Ont., "Improvement on Washing machines." 21st February, 1872.

No. 1352—T. MOORE, Brantford, Ont., "Improvement on Mowing and Reaping machines." 21st February, 1872.

No. 1353—G. B. BURLAND and G. LAFRICAIN, Montreal, Que., (assignee of G. MATTHEWS,) "A Printing Ink." 4th March, 1872. [Extension of Patent No. 715, Province of Canada.]

No. 1354—D. O. PARKER, Liverpool, N.S., "Excursion Chair." 4th March, 1872."

No. 1355—D. O. PARKER, Liverpool, N.S., "A combined Child's High Chair and Work Stand." 4th March, 1872.

No. 1356—D. O. PARKER, Liverpool, N.S., "A combined Chair and Cane. 4th March, 1872.

No. 1357—D. O. PARKER, Liverpool, N.S., "A folding Washstand." 4th March, 1872.

No. 1358—D. O. PARKER, Liverpool, N.S., "A combined folding Cot, Settee and Invalid's Table." 4th March, 1872.

No. 1359—D. O. PARKER, Liverpool, N.S., "A folding Nursery Chair." 4th March, 1872.

No. 1360—J. S. KEMP, Magog, Que., "Improvements in Potato-diggers." 4th March, 1872.

No. 1361—W. MILNER, Strathroy, Ont., "Improvements in machines for Cleansing and Scouring Wheat." 4th March, 1872.

No. 1362—W MILNER, Strathroy, Ont., "Improvement in Door Springs." 4th March, 1872.

No. 1363—F. OAKLEY, Toronto, Ont., "Improvement in Fish Plates for Railway Rails." 4th March, 1872.

No. 1364—E. CLINE, Napanee, Ont., "Improvements in Cheese Presses." 4th March, 1872.

No. 1365.—E. FARR, Vaughan, Ont., "Improvement in the construction of Fences." 4th March, 1872.

No. 1366—J. B. BLAIR, Trenton, Ont., "A hot air Stove." 7th March, 1872.

No. 1367—E. CLINE, Napanee, Ont., "Improvements in the art or method of bandaging Cheese." 7th March, 1872.

No. 1368—J. MILLER, Upton, Que., "Improvement in manufacturing and preparing the concentrated extract of Tan-Bark." 7th March, 1872.

No. 1369—C. A. GREGORY, Quebec, Que., "A machine for bottling Ales, Wines, &c." 13th March, 1872.

No. 1370—J. MILNE, Hamilton, Ont., "Improvement in Buckles for Horse Traces." 13th March, 1872.

No. 1371—D. P. DUNN, Walnfleet, Ont., "Improvements in Power Hammers." 13th March, 1872.

No. 1372—D. O. PARKER, Liverpool, N.S., "A combination of Rocking Horse, Carriage, Sled, High Chair and Step-Ladder." 13th March, 1872.

No. 1373—A. CAMPAIGNE, Goderich, Ont., "Improvements on railway Car-Couplers." 13th March, 1872.

No. 1374—W. M. CLARK, Artemesia, Ont., "Improvement in Fence Gates." 13th March, 1872.

No. 1375—W. C. MACEY, Barrie, Ont., "Composition for Stove-pipe Blocks." 13th March 1872.

No. 1376—S. W. ;FRANCE, Hamilton, Ont., "Improvement in street gas Lamp Posts." 13th March, 1872.

No. 1377—A. YOUNG, Crowland, Ont., "Improvement on horse Hay Rakes." 13th March, 1872.

No. 1378—R. A. ALLOWAY, Montreal, Que., "Stopper for Bottles, &c." 13th March, 1872.

No. 1379—A. O'MALLEY, London, Ont., "Improvements in the manufacture of Horse Collars." 13th March, 1872.

No. 1380—W. SMITH, London, Ont., "Machine to carry off Steam and Noxious Gases during the process of cooking." 13th March, 1872.

No. 1381—E. GREGG, Toronto, Ont., "Composition for anti-friction Metal." 13th March, 1872.

No. 1382—C. MACNAB, Fraserville, Que., "Improvements in machines for catching Porpoises, Seals and Fish." 15th March, 1872.

No. 1383—G. WELLINGTON, Toronto, Ont., "Machine for fastening and holding Ropes." 15th March, 1872.

No. 1384—M. P. HAYES, Seaforth, Ont., "Improvements in Furnaces for heating Liquids." 15th March, 1872.

No. 1385—S. H. TURNER, Hatley, Que., "Improvements on gas lamp and other Lighters." 15th March, 1872.

No. 1386—C. G. C. SIMPSON, Montreal, Que., "Improvements in Stills, Vacuum Pans and Concentrators." 15th March, 1872.

No. 1387—M. A. HAWLEY, Napanee, Ont., and W. E. HAZARD, Richmond, Ont., "Improvements in horse hay Forks." 15th March, 1872.

No. 1388—A. SLUMAN, Wolfe Island, Ont., "A blacking Box." 15th March, 1872.

No. 1389—G. E. DALLYN, Hamilton, Ont., "Improvement in Trusses for the cure of Hernia." 15th March, 1872.

No. 1390—L. GODDU, Montreal, Que., "Improvements or apparatus for Nailing the Soles of Boots and Shoes." 25th March, 1872.

No. 1391—L. GODDU, Montreal, Que., "Improvements on the apparatus used for Driving Nails into the Soles of Boots and Shoes." 15th March, 1872.

No. 1392—W. WILSON, Ramsay, Ont., "Improvements in Churns" 25th March, 1872.

No. 1393—H. WHITE, Hamilton, Ont., "Improved Barrel Head." 25th March, 1872.

No. 1394—H. WHITE, Hamilton, Ont., "Improvement in Springs for Railway Cars and Wheeled Vehicles." 25th March, 1872.

No 1395—L. GODDU, Montreal, Que., "Improvements on the apparatus for Tacking the Soles of Boots and Shoes to Uppers." 25th March, 1872.

No. 1396—L. FORREST, Belleville, Ont., "Machine for Stretching Carpets." 25th March, 1872.

No. 1397—D. HAWKINS, Hamilton, Ont., "Improvements in Coal Stoves." 25th March, 1872.

No. 1398—J. DEWE, Ottawa, Ont., "Strap for Fastening Letters or Papers in bundles." 25th March, 1872.

No. 1399—J. MOUNCE, Darlington, Ont., "Improvements on Cultivators." 25th March, 1872

No. 1400—G. A. DRUMMOND and T. S HUNT, Montreal, Que., "Improvements in the manufacture of Sugar." 25th March, 1872.

No. 1401—J. LAWRENCE, Palermo, Ont., "Improvements on Reaping machines." 25th March, 1872.

No. 1402—A. YOUNG, Crowland, Ont., "Improvements on Washing machines." 25th March, 1872.

No. 1403—A. WHITE, Galt, Ont., "Improvement on 'White's Clasp and Hook Hay Lifter.'" 25th March, 1872.

No. 1404—J. B. DREWRY, Belleville, Ont., "Combination Saw and Plane." 25th March, 1872.

No. 1405—W. J DAWSON, Clear Creek, Ont., "Combined Grain Sower, Cultivator, Drag and Roller." 25th March, 1872.

No. 1406—O. C. HERBERT, Halifax, N.S., "Improvements on Gas Generators." 30th March, 1872.

No. 1407—E. H. THURSTON, Montreal, Que., "Improvements in the manufacture of Boots and Shoes." 2nd April, 1872.

No. 1408—B. COLLINS, (assignee of J. WAGSTAFF,) Dundas, Ont., "Bag-holder." 5th April, 1872.

No. 1409—W. McDONALD, St. Martin's, N.B., "Improvements on Gates." 5th April. 1872.

No. 1410—W. G. C. MASTERSUM, Hinchinbrooke, Que., "Improvements on Turbine Water Wheels." 5th April, 1872.

No. 1411—T. MIDDAUGH, Brougham, Ont., "Improvement in Tire upsetting machines." 5th April, 1872.

No. 1412—W. G. VON STADEN, Strathroy, Ont., "Improvements in Railway Cars." 5th April, 1872.

No. 1413—THE CANADA BOLT COMPANY, (assignee of A. B. SIMONDS,) Perth, Ont., "Improvements in machines for Cutting and Punching Nuts." 5th April, 1872.

No. 1414—H. BENJAMIN, Montreal, Que., "Improvements in the art of generating Heat." 9th April, 1872.

No. 1415—M. L. SMITH, Springfield, Ont., "Improvements in Platform Ladders." 9th April, 1872. (Extension of Patent No. 3,008, Ontario and Quebec.)

No. 1416—S. K. SHIPMAN, Almonte, Ont., "Improvements on machines operated by Animal Power." 13th April, 1871.

No. 1417—J. BRIGGS, Toronto, Ont., "A Cast-iron Chimney, fire-place and ventilating shaft combined." 13th April, 1872.

No. 1418—W. HARVEY, Woodstock, Ont., "Composition for Artificial Stone." 13th April, 1872.

No. 1419—R. M. ROY, Belleville, Ont., "Machine for Cutting Wood or Metal." 13th April, 1872.

No. 1420—F. W. BECKWITH, Merrickville, Ont., "Improvements in Wrenches." 22nd April, 1872.

No. 1421—W. DENNIS, Ottawa, Ont., "A combined supplementary Door and Damper for Cooking Stoves." 18th April, 1872.

No. 1422—J. W. SCOTT, Yarmouth, N.S., "Improvements in Carriage Shafts." 18th April, 1872.

No. 1423—J. FORBES, Halifax, N.S , "Mode of attaching Skates" 18th April, 1872. (Extension of Patent No. 116, Nova Scotia.)

No. 1424—S. H. SHAW, St. Thomas, Ont., "Improvements in Rotary Harrows." 18th April, 1872.

No. 1425—G. F. DEVINE, Hamilton, Ont., "Improvement in a Whip and Rein Holder." 18th April, 1872.

No. 1426—H. R. IVES, Montreal, Que., "Improvements in Screw Posts." 18th April, 1872.

No. 1427—A. PERRON, Chambly Basin, Que., "Wash for the protection of Animals against Flies," 18th April, 1872.

No. 1428—G. YOUNG, Trenton, Ont., "Improvements in Sewing machines." 18th April, 1872.

No. 1429—G. JONES, Montreal, Que., "Improvements on Car couplers" 18th April, 1872.

No. 1430—J. BATES, Thornbury, Ont., "Improvements in Churns." 18th April, 1872.

No. 1431—W. L. CHITTICK, Hantsport, N.S., "Improvements on Thimbles for the clews of ship's sails." 18th April, 1872.

No. 1432—J. WILSON, Portland, N.B., "A Liquid Measure and Tap." 18th April, 1872.

No. 1433—C. RAYMOND, Guelph, Ont., " Improvements in Sewing machines." 18th April, 1872.

No. 1434—B. BOURRET, St. Nicholas, Que., "Improvements in Mill Saw Gates." 18th April, 1872.

No 1435- N. JOHNSON, Newmarket, Ont., " A Grain Sower." 18th April, 1872.

No. 1436—R. SMITH, Sherbrooke, Que., "A Shingle machine." 24th April, 1872.

No. 1437—E. M 'SELEY, Dartmouth, N. S., "Paint for Ships' Bottoms and process for the same." 24th April, 1872.

No. 1438—O. THIBAUDEAU, Montreal, Que., "Pattern for uppers of Boots." 24th April, 1872.

No. 1439—J. B. ARMSTRONG, Sherbrooke, Que., "Improvement in Fences." 24th April, 1872.

No. 1440—J. E TRENHOLM, Point do Bute, N.B., " Improvement in Mowing and Reaping machines." 24th April, 1872.

No. 1441—A. M. RING, St. John, N.B., " Improvements in machines for distilling Salt Water." 1st May, 1872.

No. 1442—J. FOLEY, Lindsay, Ont., "Improvements in the manufacture of Paper." 4th May, 1872.

No. 1443—J. R. STEARNS, Toronto, Ont., "Machine for raising Water from Wells." 4th May, 1872.

No. 1444—A. WHITE, Yarmouth, Ont., " Improvement on Cranes." 4th May, 1872.

No. 1445—B. NELLIS, Dearham, Ont., "Improvement in Churns." 4th May, 1872.

No. 1446—I. FRECHETTE, St. Hyacinthe, Que., " Improvement in Shingle sawing machines." 4th May, 1872.

No. 1447—J. C. WISWELL, Lennoxville, Que., " Improvement on Railway Cars." 4th May, 1872.

No. 1448—J. DEAN, Orillia, Ont., " Improvement in the art of Plastering Walls." 4th May, 1872.

No. 1449—W. E. GARDNER, Yarmouth, N.S., "Improvement in Tables in use on board of ships." 4th May, 1872.

No. 1450—W. McKAY, Ottawa, Ont., "Composition of Matter for Paint." 4th May, 1872.

No. 1451—I. McNAUGHTON, Egerton, N.S., "Improvement in Pulleys." 4th May, 1872.

No. 1452—G. D. ARMSTRONG, Belleville, Ont., " Improvement in Washing Machines." 4th May 1872.

No. 1453—J. LAW, London, Ont., "Improvement on Tar and Petroleum Burners." 4th May, 1872.

No. 1454—D. D. TUPPER, Canning, N.S., "Improvement in Car Couplers." 4th May, 1872.

No. 1455—J. S. ARMSTRONG, St. John, N.B., "Improvement on Screws and Screw-Drivers." 4th May, 1872.

No. 1456—S. HODGINS, St. Mary's, Ont., "Improvement in Thrashing machines." 4th May, 1872.

No. 1457—J. BOLE and F. BOLE, St. Vincent, Ont.. " Improvement in Hay Elevators." 17th May, 1872.

No. 1458—W. MUSGROVE, Studholm, N.B., and J. S. SHARP, Sussex, N.B., "Improvements in Car-Couplers." 17th May, 1872.

No. 1459—P. N. RUGG, Compton, Que., " Improvement in Washing machines." 17th May, 1872.

No. 1460—M. O'REILLEY, Montreal, Que., "Improvements on Railway Switches." 17th May, 1872.

No. 1461—J. MACKAY, Dundas, Ont., " Improvement in Barley Mills." 17th May, 1872.

No. 1462—W. MUIR, Montreal, Que., " Improvements in Sewing machines." 18th May, 1872.

No. 1463—W. MUIR, Montreal, Que., "Improvements in Sewing machines." 18th May, 1872.

No. 1464—J. CRISPIN, Owen Sound, Ont., "Improvements in Apparatus for heating water for tan bark Leaches." 18th May, 1872.

No. 1465—J. M. TAYLOR, Fredericton, N.B., (assignee of the Hon. L. A. WILMOT,) " Improvement in Railway Snow-plough." 18th May, 1872.

No. 1166- S. DELL, Strathroy, Ont., ', Improvement in Hand Drills." 18th May, 1872.

No. 1167—J. C. JOHNSON, Palmerston, Ont., " Improvement in Churns." 18th May, 1872.

No. 1168- H. BERNIER, Lotbinière, Que., "Improvement in Stoves." 18th May, 1872.

No. 1469—F. L. NORTON, Ottawa, Ont., "Machine for Tightening the Tires of Wheels." 27th May, 187'.

No. 1470—A. N. COLE, Brockville, Ont., "Process and apparatus for extracting Oil from Cotton and renovating the same." 27th May, 1872.

No. 1471—D. S. AIKMAN, Colchester, Ont., " Improvement in Ploughs." 27th May, 1872.

No. 1472—J. PANTON and E. PANTON, London, Ont., "Improvement of Harvesting machines." 27th May, 1872.

No 1173—J. SULLIVAN, Thornton, Ont., "Improvement in a device for Administering Pills." 27th May, 1872.

No. 1474—W. POWELL, Belleville, Ont., "Improvement on Harrows." 27th May, 1872.

No. 1475 - J. PALM' R, St.Catharines, Ont., "Improved Bush of a Block Sheave." 27th May, 1872.

No. 1476- A. M. WILKINSON, Minto, Ont., "A vehicle Spring Seat." 27th May, 1872.

No. 1477—C. MURDOCK, Sarnia, Ont., "Improvement in Stave machines." 27th May, 1872.

No. 1478—C. MURDOCK, Sarnia, Ont., " Improvement in Cylindrical Saws for Staves." 27th May, 1872.

No. 1479—S. CROTHERS, St. John, N.B., "Improved carriage Clip Body Loop or Hanging Iron." 27th May, 1872.

No. 1480—J. W. SMITH, St. Marys, N.B , " A Shoe Creeper." 28th May, 1872.

No. 1481—L. LEES and S. BUSCHLEN, Port Elgin, Ont., " Improvements in Car-Couplers." 28th May, 1872.

No. 1482—A. E. SHERWOOD, Brockville, Ont., "Post and Bunk for Fences." 28th May, 1872.

No. 1483—H. SELLS, Vienna, Ont., "Improvement in Wheeled Vehicles." 28th May, 1872.

No. 1484—W. WILSON, Montreal, Que., "Improvements in the manufacture of Composition Drain Pipes and Artificial Stone. 28th May, 1872.

No. 1485—S. SMITH, Woodstock, N.B., "Machine for planting Roots and distributing Liquid Manure." 28th May, 1872.

No. 1486—R. EATON, Montreal, Que., "Improvements on Railway Wheels." 28th May, 1872.

No. 1487—A. LeMOYNE DE MARTIGNY, St. Romuald, Que., "Improvement in Lamp Snuffers." 28th May, 1872.

No. 1488—P. R. HIGLEY, Oshawa, Ont., " " Improvements in Bottle Stoppers." 1st June, 1872.

No. 1489—J. FISHER, Portsmouth, Ont., "Application of Friction Rollers to screw propelling shafts." 1st June, 1872.

No. 1490—J. MORRISON, Moore, Ont., " Improvements in the manufacture of Caps." 1st June, 1872.

No. 1491—G. H. KENDALL, Montreal, Que., " Art of Lighting Gas by electricity and Apparatus used therefor." 1st June, 1872.

No. 1492—W. G. NUTSON, Windsor, Ont., "Spring for Window Sashes." 1st June, 1872.

No. 1493—L. COTÉ St. Hyacinthe, Que., " Improvements in the manufacture of Toe Boxes for Boots and Shoes." 1st June, 1872.

No. 1494—L. C. THOMAS, Brooklin, Ont., " A Baking Repository." 1st June, 1872.

No. 1495—J. H. KILLEY and W J. KILLEY, Hamilton, Ont., " Steam Boiler Detector Guage." 1st June, 1872.

No. 1496—S. R. WARREN, Montreal, Que., " Improvements in the construction of Organs." 1st June, 1872.

No. 1497—S. NOXON, jun , Ingersoll, Ont., " Improvements in Reaping machines." 5th June, 1872

No. 1498—S. NOXON, jun , Ingersoll, Ont., " Improvements in Reaping machines." 5th June, 1872.

No. 1499—W. DUNLOP, Fullarton, Ont., " Improvement on Tools for trimming bolts." 5th June, 1872.

No. 1500—M. KENNY, Chippewa, Ont., " Improvement in the Art of Distilling." 5th June, 1872

No. 1501—A. O'MALLEY, London, Ont., " A Milk Cooler." 5th June, 1872.

No 1502—J. BOYD, Halifax, N.S , " Apparatus for Condensing Smoke and Steam, for steaming and baking food and heating apartments." 5th June, 1872.

No 1503—P. BRASS and T. IRWIN, Hamilton, Ont., " Improvement in the Art of Heating and Ventilating Buildings." 10th June, 1872.

No. 1504—J. J. MASON, Drummondville, Ont., " Machine for Cleaning and Sharpening Table Cutlery." 10th June, 1872.

No. 1505—R. HAWLEY, jun., Goderich, Ont., " Improvement in Apparatus for manufacturing Salt." 10th June, 1872.

No. 1506—J. E. STRONG, Newton-Brook, Ont., " Improvements in Gates." 10th June, 1872.

No. 1507—J. C. WISWELL, Lennoxville, Que., " Improvements in Railroad Rails and Chairs." 10th June, 1872.

No. 1508—D. DARVILL, London, Ont., " Improvement on Brick machines." 10th June, 1872.

No. 1509—J. LOUGH, Buckingham, Que., " Machine for Dressing the Teeth of Circular Saws." 19th June, 1872.

No. 1510—J. S. ARMSTRONG, St. John, N.B , " Improvement on Skates." 19th June, 1872.

No. 1511—L. RICHARD, Wilmot, Ont., " Improved Plow Coulter." 19th June, 1872.

No. 1512 - O. CHABOT, Sherbrooke, Que., " Oiler and Torch combined." 19th June, 1872.

No. 1513—W. HUMBERSTONE, Newton-Brook, Ont., " Improvements in Traction Engines." 19th June, 1872.

No. 1514—J. O. TODD, Montreal, Que., and E. R. WHITNEY, Bolton, Que., " Manufacture of Rope Textile Fabrics and Paper Pulp." 19th June, 1872.

No. 1515—F. H. REYNOLDS, Montreal, Que., " A Shingle making machine." 19th June, 1872.

No. 1516—J. ROBITAILLE, St. Célestin, Que., " Improvement in Washing machines." 19th June, 1872.

No. 1517—O. H MERRIMAN, (assignee of J. MERRIMAN,) Magog, Que., " Improvements Horse Power machines." 12th June, 1872.

No. 1518—J. W. CLAIR, Sackville, N.B., " Improvement on Handles for Forks, Hoes, &c." 19th June, 1872.

No. 1519—A. McLEOD, J. E. NUTE and J. H. NUTE, New Glasgow, N.S., " Improvements in Churns." 19th June, 1872.

No. 1520—T. COCHRANE, Petrolia, Ont., " Improvement in Stills for petroleum and other oil." 19th June, 1872.

No. 1521—E. BOLMAN, Halifax, N.S., " A combined Bed and Bureau." 19th June, 1872.

No. 1522—D. R. SHAW, Toronto, Ont., "Improvements in Corking machines." 19th June, 1872.

No. 1523—J. HARRIS, Montreal, Que., " Improvements on Pumps and Engines." 29th June, 1872.

No. 1524—J. CHART, New Hamburg, Ont., "Improvement in Flour Mills." 29th June, 1871.

No. 1525—H. CARTER, Aylmer, Ont., "Improvement in Ditching machines." 29th June, 1872.

No. 1526—J. EDE, Woodstock, Ont., "Improvements on Thrashing machines." 29th June, 1872.

No. 1527—G. GRAY, London, Ont., "Improvements in Gang Plows." 29th June, 1872.

No. 1528—J. FORBES, Halifax, N S., "Improvements in Wheel Tires." 29th June, 1872.

No. 1529—A. RACICOT, St. Césaire, Que., "Composition of matter for treating certain Diseases." 29th June, 1872.

No. 1530—J. SPEIGHT, Markham, Ont., "Machine for setting Tires." 29th June, 1872.

No. 1531—G. WEBSTER, jun., and J. F. WEBSTER, Hamilton, Ont., " Improvements in Sewing machines." 29th June, 1872.

No. 1532—T. SPARHAM, Brockville, Ont., "Composition of matter for lubricating Axles." 29th June, 1872..

No. 1533—J. MILNE, Belle-Ewart, Ont., "Improvements in Saw Mills." 29th June, 1872.

No. 1534—E. FISHER and W. CLARK, Kincardine, Ont., " Machine for chipping Boiler Plate." 29th June, 1872.

No. 1535—W. MILNER and D. B. CAMPBELL, Strathroy, Ont., "Composition of matter for making Sand Stone." 15th July, 1872.

No. 1536—R. MEIKLEJOHN, Rawdon, Ont., " Machine for Separating and Cleaning Grain." 15th July, 1872

No. 1537—G. O. FREEMAN, Chatham, Ont., " Machine for setting up Tents." 15th July, 1872.

No. 1538—A. MILES, Dundas, Ont., " A portable Fire Pump." 15th July, 1872.

No. 1539—P. M. THOMPSON, Kingston, Ont., "Improvement on the Coupling of Railway Cars." 15th July, 1872.

No. 1540—J. H. OSBORN, Guelph, Ont , " Improvement on Sewing machines." 15th July, 1872.

No. 1541—N. MALO, Varennes, Que., " Improvements in Pumps." 15th July, 1872.

No. 1542-J. FISHER, Clinton, Ont., "Mode of building Fences." 15th July, 1872.

No. 1543—P. B. CLINE, Thornton, Ont., "Improvement in Sawing machines." 15th July, 1872.

No. 1544—G. H. COMER, Indiana, Ont., " Machine for Staffing Millstones." 15th July, 1872.

No. 1545—J. WALMSLEY, Waterloo, Ont., " Improvements on Reaping and Mowing machines." 15th July, 1872.

No. 1546—H. LAFERRIERE, St. Félix, Que., " Improvement in Ploughs." 15th July, 1872.

No. 1547—G. CORMACK. Beechville, Ont., " An Improved Window shutter Hinge." 15th July, 1872.

No. 1548—E. FAKINS, Streetsville, Ont., " An Improved Harrow." 15th July, 1872.

No. 1549 - J. DEAN, Orillia, Ont , " A machine for Grooving boards." 15th July, 1872.

No. 1550—A. R. KOEBER, Berlin, Ont., "Improvement on Musical Reed Instruments." 15th July, 1872.

No. 1551—J. CRAWSHAW, Cobourg, Ont., " A Loom." 15th July, 1872.

No. 1552—D. M. LAMB, Strathroy, Ont., " A machine for Pulverizing Earth and Digging Potatoes." 15th July, 1872.

No. 1553 - C. F. MUELLER, Hamilton, Ont., "A Railway Station Indicator." 15th July, 1872.

No. 1554—W. BULMER, St. John, N.B., "A Harrow." 15th July, 1872.

No. 1555—H. MACKINNON, Guelph, Ont., "A Heater." 15th July, 1872.

No. 1556—J. REGAN, Brantford, Ont., "An improved Horse Collar." 15th July, 1872.

No. 1557—J. BOSTWICK, St. Catharines, Ont., " A Clothes Line Holder." 17th July, 1872.

No. 1558—D. MAXWELL, Paris, Ont., "An improved Straw Cutter." 17th July, 1872.

No. 1559—D. A. JOHNSTON, Ainsleyville, Ont., (assignee of M. SMITH, Grey, Ont.,) "Improvement in Sawing machines." 17th July, 1872.

No. 1560—L. BUTTERFIELD, Bradford, Ont., "Improvement in machines for Thrashing and Separating Grain." 17th July, 1872.

No. 1561—W. STODDARD, Three Rivers, Que., "Improvements in Saw Mills." 17th July, 1872.

No. 1562—J. SULLIVAN, Thornton, Ont., "Improvement in Chamber Pots." 17th July, 1872.

No. 1563—C. POWELL, Newton-Brook, Ont., "Improvements in Pumps." 17th July, 1872.

No. 1564—J. WEBB, Portneuf, Que., "Improvements on the art of manufacturing Paper Wood Pulp and on the apparatus used therefor." 17th July, 1872.

No. 1565—W. H. COLLINS, Colombus, Ont., "A Carriage Wheel." 17th July, 1872.

No. 1566—W. HAMILTON, St. John, N.B., "Machine for Washing Clothes." 17th July, 1871.

No. 1567—W. L. KINMOND, Montreal, Que., "Machine for Coiling Spiral Springs." 17th July, 1872.

No. 1568—J. H. SWARTWOUT, Toronto, Ont., "Improvements in Saw Mills." 19th July, 1872.

No. 1569—P. BEAUREGARD, St. Pie, Que., "An Improved Borer for Artesian Wells." 22nd July, 1872.

No. 1570--H. BOLTON, Elizabethtown, Ont., " Improvement in Churns." 22nd July, 1772. (Re-issue of Patent No. 258. Canada.)

No. 1571—A. A. WOOD, Whitby, Ont., "Improvements on Reapers." 22nd July, 1872.

No. 1572 - T. NORTHEY, Hamilton, Ont., "Improvement on Shaft Couplings." 22nd July, 1872.

No. 1573—W. CLARK, South Dumfries, Ont., "A Composition for Cattle Wash." 3rd August, 1872.

No. 1574—H. WHITE, Hamilton, Ont., "Improvements in Lamps." 3rd August, 1872.

No. 1575—J. M. WILLIAMS, East Camden, Ont., and J. BETTES, Cramahe, Ont., "A machine for Dressing Mill-Stones." 3rd August, 1872.

No. 1576—H. T. SARGE and H. C. IRELAND, Toronto, Ont., "Improvements in Boots and Shoes." 3rd August, 1872.

No. 1577—W. C. EVANS, Kingston, Ont., "Improvement in Bedsteads." 3rd August, 1872.

No. 1578—T. KATER, Hamilton, Ont., "Improvements in Pianos." 3rd August, 1872.

No. 1579—E. L. FENERTY, Halifax, N.S., "Improvement in Skates." 3rd August, 1872.

No. 1580—J. ROUÉ, St. John, N.B., "An apparatus for Cleaning Bottles." 3rd August, 1872.

No. 1581—E. M. COVENTRY, Hamilton, Ont., "An Improved Turbine." 12th August, 1872.

No. 1582—T. F. GOULETTE, Montreal, Que., "Improvements on Railway Ploughs." 12th August, 1872.

No. 1583—J. FISHER, jun., Woodstock, N.B., "Improvement in Ploughs." 12th August, 1872.

No. 1584—W. FISH, Ellers House, N.S., "Art or process of Converting Iron into Steel." 12th August, 1872.

No. 1585—J. MASSIE, Colborne, Ont., "Machine for Locking Window Sashes." 23rd August, 1872.

No. 1586—W. K. REYNOLDS, St. John, N.B., "Improvements in the Construction of Railways." 23rd August, 1872.

No. 1587—W. MILNER, Strathroy, Ont., "Improvements in Carriage Seats." 23rd August, 1872.

No. 1588—G. DIXON, Toronto, Ont., "Improvements in Railway Car Trucks." 23rd August, 1872.

No. 1589—J. J. WEBSTER, Magog, Que., "Improvements in Flour Mills." 23rd August, 1872.

No. 1590—J. F. CASS, L'Orignal, Ont., "Improvements in Hay Racks." 23rd August, 1872.

No. 1591—D. DAVIS, London, Ont., "Improvement on Brick Machines." 23rd August, 1872.

No. 1592—C. POWELL, Newton-Brook, Ont., "Improvement in Wooden Pipes." 23rd August, 1872.

No. 1593—G. L. BEEMER, Brantford, Ont., "Improvement in Fences." 23rd August, 1872.

No. 1594—J. HALLY, Valleyfield, Que., "Improvements in the manufacture of Peat and on the apparatus used therefor." 23rd August, 1872.

No. 1595—G. A. SAVARY, Plympton, N.S., "Improvements in Locks and Keys." 23rd August, 1872.

No. 1596—J. SCALES, Toronto, Ont., "Improvements in Tobacco Lamp machines." 23rd August, 1872.

No 1597—W. McKAY, Ottawa, Ont., "A Hydraulic and Plastic Cement." 23rd August, 1872.

No. 1598—C. M. TAYLOR, (assignee of F. H. SIMS,) Waterloo, Ont., "Improvement in Lamp Heaters." 31st August, 1872.

No. 1599—O. C. HERBERT, Halifax, N.S., "Improvements in the art of manufacturing Gas." 31st August, 1872.

No. 1600—R. FREELAND, Montreal, Que., "Improvements on the manufacture of Soap." 31st August, 1872.

No. 1601—B. F. STEWART, Frankville, Ont., "Machine for Sharpening the Calks of Horse Shoes." 31st August, 1872.

No. 1602—H. SMITH, East Zorra, Ont., "Improvements in Wind Wheels." 31st August, 1872.

No. 1603—A. SQUIRES, Miramichi, Ont., "Improvements in Cans." 31st August, 1872.

No. 1604—L. L. SJOSTROM, Sherbrooke, Q., "Machine for making Shingles." 31st August, 1872.

No. 1605—W. RICHARDSON, Amaranth, Ont., "A Fence." 31st August, 1872.

No. 1606—J. B. LAMB, Ottawa, Ont., "Improvement in Binding Rollers." 31st August, 1872.

No. 1607—L. C. SNYDER, Plantagenet, Ont., "A Clothes Pin" 31st August, 1872

No. 1608—W. HAMILTON, Peterborough, Ont., (assignee of M. BOYD, Bobcaygeon, Ont., and J. P. LONG, Smith, Ont.,) "Machine for Marking Lumber." 31st August, 1872.

No. 1609—A. SIMPSON, Hilton, Ont., "Improvement in Railways." 31st August, 1872.

No. 1610—J. H. STONE, Hamilton, Ont., "An improved Tubular Lantern. (Re-issue of Patent No. 1198, Canada.) 31st August, 1872.

No. 1611—J. TOMLINSON, St. Mary's, Ont., "Machine for Quilting." 31st August, 1871.

No. 1612—M. PETET, Hallowell, Ont., "A Spinning Wheel." 31st August, 1872.

No. 1613—L. BLUMBERGH, Toronto, Ont., "An Oil Can." 31st August, 1872.

No. 1614—C. LAPOINTE, Acton Vale, Que., "A Boot and Shoe Last." 31st August, 1872.

No. 1615—R. NOBLE, Toronto, Ont., "A composition for artificial Stone. (Re-issue of Patent No. 1186, Canada.) 31st August, 1872.

No. 1616—P. HOHMEYER, Waterloo, Ont., "Improvement on C. M. Taylor's Lamp Boiler." 31st August, 1872.

No. 1617—F. STRANGE and W. ATKINSON, (assignees of W. J. Killey,) Hamilton, Ont., "A Steam Boiler Indicator." 31st August, 1872.

No. 1618—M. L. SMITH, Arkona, Ont., "Improvements in Extension Ladders." 31st August, 1872.

No. 1619—W. LONSDALE, King, Ont., "Improvement in Wheel Tires." 31st August, 1872.

No. 1620—H. D. COWLES, Montreal, Que., "Improvement on machine for Pointing Nails." 31st August, 1872.

No. 1621—J. WATSON, Ayr, Ont., "Improvement on Grain and Grass Seed Sowers." 31st August, 1872.

No. 1622—J. A. CULL, Toronto, Ont., "Art or process for extracting Gold from Ores." 31st August, 1872.

No. 1623—N. R. ALLAN, Montreal, Que., "Improvements on Chiming and Crozing machines." 31st August, 1872.

No. 1624—J. HUNTER, Lancaster, N.B., "Improvement in Boiler Furnaces." 31st August, 1872.

No. 1625—D. BRADFORD, Hamilton, Ont., "Improvements in Car-couplings." 31st August, 1872.

No. 1626—J. ABELL, Woodbridge, Ont., "An adjustable Chute for the Samson and Jouville Turbine Water-wheel." 31st August, 1872.

No. 1627—C. STORER, Montreal, Que., "Improvements on Boots and Shoes." 31st August, 1872.

No. 1628—G ELMSLIE, Toronto, Ont., "Improvements in Car Wheels." 31st August, 1872.

No. 1629—G. S. LONG, Montreal, Que., "Improvements on Axles." 31st August, 1872.

No 1630—C. H. GUARD, London, Ont., "Improvements on Clothes Pins." 31st August, 1872.

No. 1631—S HICK, Columbus, Ont., "A Hay and Grain Fork." 31st August, 1872.

No. 1632—C. STORER, Montreal, Que., "Improvements in the manufacture of Boxes." 31st August, 1872.

No. 1633—W. DRUM, Quebec, "Improvement in Saw Mills." 31st August, 1872.

No. 1634—G. SCOTT, Montreal, Que., "Improvements on machine for Fitting Stove-pipes." 31st August, 1872.

No. 1635—W. CHAMBERLAIN, Brantford, Ont., "Machine for Digging Potatoes." 31st August, 1872.

No. 1636—J. W. KING, Ottawa, Ont., "Improvements in Railway Snow-ploughs." 31st August, 1872.

No. 1637—J. J. PEARCE, Robinson, Que., "Machine for Gumming and Sharpening Saws." 31st August, 1872.

No. 1638—L. A. WILMOT and J. M. TAYLOR, Fredericton, N.B., "Improvement on Railway Snow-plows." 31st August, 1872.

No. 1639—L. SOMERS, Moncton, N.B., "Device for Connecting the Thills to the axles of Carriages." 31st August, 1872.

No. 1640—D. D. WRIGHT, Oakville, Ont., "A Car-coupler." 31st August, 1872.

No. 1641—T. WILSON, Richmond Hill, Ont., "An Improved Fanning Mill." 31st August, 1872.

No. 1642—R. F. FAIRLIE, Montreal, Que., "Improvements in Railway Cars." 31st August, 1872. (Extension of Patent No. 2860, O. & Q.)

No. 1643—R. F. FAIRLIE, Montreal, Que., "Improvements in Railway Cars." 31st August, 1872. (Extension of Patent No. 2868, O. & Q.)

No. 1644—C. LAFLAMME, widow of L. LABRÈCHE-VIGER, Montreal, Que., "Cementation of Tools and other Articles of Wrought Iron." 31st August, 1872.

www.ingramcontent.com/pod-product-compliance
Lightning Source LLC
Chambersburg PA
CBHW030321270326
41926CB00010B/1449